THE LETTERS OF *Thomas Hood*

NOTE TO THE FRONTISPIECE

This drawing is in the possession of Professor I.R.C. Batchelor, Broughty Ferry, Dundee, Scotland. He very kindly had it photographed and allowed me to make use of it in the edition. The existence of the drawing was brought to my attention by my colleague Professor Gerald E. Bentley jr. Mr Richard Ormond, Assistant Keeper, National Portrait Gallery, is sure that the drawing is by Maclise, though he is less certain about the likeness to Hood. I feel that there are similarities with other known portraits, and that Hood's signature is authentic. Though the drawing seems idealized and flattering, I would like to date it 1842, since this is the only time that Hood refers to Maclise in his letters (513).

THE LETTERS OF *Thomas Hood*

EDITED BY
PETER F. MORGAN

University of Toronto Press

UNIVERSITY OF TORONTO
DEPARTMENT OF ENGLISH STUDIES AND TEXTS
18

printed in Britain for
University of Toronto Press
Toronto and Buffalo
Reprinted in 2018
ISBN 0-8020-5222-3
ISBN 978-1-4875-7887-9 (paper)
ISBN microfiche 0-8020-0089-4
LC 76-185726

For My Family

ACKNOWLEDGMENTS

I am personally very grateful to Lady Hermione Cobbold, R.E. Cameron, Professor John Clubbe, L. Handley-Derry, the late Professor E.L. McAdam jr, and George Milne for permission to print letters in their possession. I am also grateful for transcripts provided by J.M. Cohen and R.W. King. Professor Alvin Whitley has kindly allowed me to make use of valuable material from his 1950 Harvard University doctoral thesis on Thomas Hood.

I am similarly grateful to the following institutions and authorities: the Bodleian Library, the Trustees of the Boston Public Library, the Bristol Public Library, the University of Bristol Library, the British Museum, the Library of the University of California at Los Angeles, the Columbia University Libraries, Cornell University Library, the Dundee Public Libraries, the Edinburgh University Library, the Syndics of the Fitzwilliam Museum, the Folger Library, the Library of Harvard University, the Huntington Library, the University of Illinois Library, Indiana University Library, the University of Iowa Library, the Keats House, Hampstead, the Charles Lamb Society, the Liverpool Public Library, the University of Liverpool Library, the Maine Historical Society, the Manchester Libraries Committee, the Massachusetts Historical Society, the Pierpont Morgan Library, the New York Public Library (Astor, Lenox and Tilden Foundations), the New York University Libraries, the Historical Society of Pennsylvania, the Princeton University Library, the Carl and Lily Pforzheimer Foundation, Inc., the Public Record Office, the publishers of *Punch* magazine, the Royal Literary Fund, the University of Rochester Library, the John Rylands Library, the Trustees of the National Library of Scotland, Massey College Library, University of Toronto, the University of Texas, the Wisbech and Fenland Museum, and the Yale University Library, together with its Osborn Collection.

The University of Toronto and the Canada Council generously granted me financial support in preparing this work. Publication of the edition is made possible by grants from the Humanities Research Council, using funds supplied by the Canada Council, and the Publications Fund of the University of Toronto Press.

I would like to thank Dr J.M.S. Tompkins, Professor Kathleen Tillotson, and the late Professor A.S.P. Woodhouse for encouragement in the course of the preparation of this edition, and Professor Clifford Leech and Principal John M. Robson for helpful suggestions made when the work was in its later stages. I am finally grateful for the advice of the editors of the University of Toronto Press, especially Prudence Tracy.

P.F.M.

CONTENTS

INTRODUCTION

Thomas Hood's place in English literary history is secure. It depends upon his originality in romantic, comic, and humanitarian verse, and also upon his place in the traditions of such writings. In his twenties Hood writes in the romantic, lyrical mood of his period. In particular in his volume entitled *The Plea of the Midsummer Fairies* (1827) he reflects with uncanny skill the romanticism of Keats; he stands in the line between Keats and Tennyson, here as well as in such limpid lyrics as 'I remember,' 'The Death-Bed,' and 'Farewell, Life!' As a prolific comic writer Hood takes his place in a tradition that goes back to Shakespeare, but burgeons in the eighteenth century with Pope and Swift, Smollett, Sterne, and Fielding. From the more recent past he shares in the verse exuberance of Christopher Anstey, John Wolcott, and the brothers Smith, and looks forward to that of W.S. Gilbert. He belongs to the generation of comic prose writers, Theodore Hook amongst them, which nourished the early work of Dickens. He also looks forward to the achievement of Lewis Carroll. In his humanitarian writing – grotesque as in 'The Last Man,' serious as in 'The Dream of Eugene Aram,' 'The Song of the Shirt,' and 'The Bridge of Sighs' – Hood does not, as Wordsworth does, identify himself with the poor and outcast for the sake of the human spirit only (if one dare say only), but for the sake of social protest. Here he appeals most strongly to those modern readers who sympathize with the writer's attempt to combine his art with the expression of social conscience. The attempt was eagerly made in the years of crisis after the accession of Queen Victoria; it was made in the poems of Elizabeth Barrett Browning, Caroline Norton, Barry Cornwall, and Hood himself, and led to the didactically inclined prose fiction of Dickens, Charles Kingsley, and Elizabeth Gaskell.

The originality of Hood's comic contribution lies in his crackling puns, at which he is uniquely adept – see for example 'Faithless Nelly Gray' – and the teeming extravagance of his fancy which finds full and formal expression in a characteristic early Victorian work like 'Miss Kilmannsegg and her Precious Leg.' In his romantic writing Hood sets out on a mythological exploration of his own but, owing to personal limitations, economic necessities, and an unfavourable social climate, the exploration remained uncompleted. However, what is unique to Hood is the way in which the horrific elements of his romantic verse pass through his comic writing and are taken over in the later humanitarian work. The grotesque images of the perfervid youthful romantic imagination reappear to the maturer artist in the actual world of the early 1840s.

It is worth collecting the letters of a man whose work is of fascinating interest on these three levels, different but united through his personality. Yet the interest of the letters is not confined to Hood's personality. He participated in the commercialized movement which produced the literary annuals of the second quarter of the nineteenth century. This phenomenon has not received a great deal of attention, though many of the literary men of the time were involved in it, and one wonders whether it is not a particularly characteristic creation of an age of cultural uncertainty yet growing wealth. Secondly, Hood participated in tentative movements again characteristic of the age, to achieve professional status for literature. His involvement in the movement to change the terms of copyright in favour of the author is documented in the letters, together with his share in attempts to organize authors to ensure their economic security.

This edition of Hood's letters should enlarge and clarify the view provided by his children's *Memorials* (1860) and by his later biographers Walter Jerrold (1907), J.C. Reid (1963), and John Clubbe (1968). The new view presented in this edition is one of the age, the writer, and the man. Admittedly the age is seen very quietly, with few of its political, economic, intellectual, and aesthetic highlights in the foreground. The picture is primarily a quiet but fascinating personal one, with an interest not only for the close student who must have the information here presented, but also for the general reader who sees a human life running its course across many obstacles, with humour and heroic determination.

My main purpose in this introductory essay is to evaluate Hood's character as it appears and develops in his correspondence, and to indicate the range of this correspondence. In the first place, however, notice should be taken of his immediate background, which was bourgeois and professional. His mother was the daughter of an engraver, and his father was a largely self-made and successful publisher. His father and brother died when he was twelve years of age, and his mother when he was twenty-two. These deaths left a family comprising himself and four sisters. There seems to have been a strange coolness between him and them. His sister Betsy was a religious zealot and on this account antipathetic to him; Jessie was confined because of mental unbalance brought on, in his view, by similar enthusiasm. The death of his father probably deprived Hood of a decent education, and the early atmosphere of death is reflected in his own sickly life and morbid humour.

At the age of sixteen Hood was sent off to relatives at Dundee, his father's home, and from there his first family letters were sent. They show him at this tender age already a humorist, the admirer of Hogarth, Smollett, and Christopher Anstey. Hood remained the duteous nephew until the end of his life, as the late letters to his uncle and aunt, Mr and Mrs Keay, show (650, 684). In Dundee he made several youthful friendships, and their extent is indicated in the letters written on his return to London. Here some hints are given concerning his activities as a busy engraver, learning something of the harsh business world, and as an amateur of letters, facile but not dedicated. In his literary attempts Hood was encouraged by John Taylor, the publisher of Keats. Taylor saw him not only as a bright young writer but also as a potentially useful lad about the office. His letter to Taylor on the death of his mother (25) shows real gratitude formally expressed and a strength of feeling which is evident elsewhere in the letters.

Work for Taylor on his *London Magazine* introduced Hood to two groups of acquaintances, and hence to two sets of correspondents: the contributors to the magazine, and the family of one of these contributors, John Hamilton Reynolds, who had been Keats's friend. The *London Magazine* provided Hood with a perfect introduction to the world of letters. The drudgery of sub-editing was more than compensated for by the amiabilities of literary intercourse. The character of Hood's life work was fixed, and friendships made. These are not immediately documented, but their strong hold is indicated by letters written much later. In particular, the friendship between Hood and Charles Lamb leaves behind few epistolary relics, partly because the two men lived so close together that they did not need to correspond with each other. However, Hood gives a revealing account of the relationship in a letter to T.C. Grattan in 1837 (327), and there is a pleasant glimpse of Mary Lamb in her old age in a letter to J.T.J. Hewlett (473). Hood probably met Charles Wentworth Dilke, another friend of Keats, as a fellow contributor to the *London Magazine*, but their correspondence does not begin until the early 1830s, when Dilke was editor of the weekly *Athenaeum*. Thomas Noon Talfourd was another contributor to the *London Magazine*; Hood corresponded with him about 1841 on the subject of literary copyright, reform of which they both favoured. H.F. Cary, another contributor and the translator of Dante, is a correspondent of 1844 (594); so is Mary Russell Mitford, author of *Our Village.* B.W. Procter, the poet 'Barry Cornwall,' is the object of a pathetic appeal made in Hood's last months (683).

Hood's early letters to Reynolds' mother and to his sisters Charlotte and Marianne show a warmth which seems to have been but newly released, the playfulness and even passion which are his best characteristics as a letter writer, and a loquacity which shows his delight in writing for the delight of friends. (They contrast with the cool letters to his sister Betsy.) The one surviving letter to John Reynolds leaves us to regret the loss of the rest of this part of the correspondence. The letter to Jane Reynolds before their marriage shows Hood, already a sick man, amazingly easy in his wit, and restrained in his courtship. The floodgates of passion are only released in the earnest solicitude of the letters written during their later separations. At this earlier period, whatever the later developments, it was doubtless the Reynolds circle which fed that flame of romanticism in Hood which led to the production of the Keatsian *Plea of the Midsummer Fairies* volume and the melodramatic *National Tales.*

Once Hood had settled on making his living by writing, much of his correspondence took on a professional character. He writes, generally without enthusiasm, to publishers and editors. Amongst general publishers, he writes to Blackwood, Constable, Murray, Bentley, Bradbury, and Smith and Elder. He also writes to the unfortunately less well-known publishers who were mainly responsible for issuing his own work, Charles Tilt and A.H. Baily, as well as Lupton Relfe. He writes to the agents of publishers: Hurst acting for Colburn, and Edward Moxon acting for Longman. Hood also knew Moxon as a young friend of Lamb. In particular, Hood corresponds with the publishers of the literary annuals, the celebrated Ackermann and the forgotten James Fraser. These annuals illuminated with their superficial glitter the drawing-room tables of polite England and America from the early 1820s, and Hood contributed freely to them in these early years. He corresponded not only with their publishers but also with their editors, for example, Watts of *The Literary Souvenir*, Frederic Shoberl of *The Forget Me Not*, and Hall of *The Amulet.* At the end of 1829 Hood brought out his own annual, *The Gem*, and as importunate editor widened the range of his correspondents still further, appealing *inter alia* for the contributions of John Clare and John Poole, former contributors to the *London Magazine*; he also wrote to James Hogg, William Howitt, C.B. Tayler, Thomas Gent, Thomas Moore, and Sir Walter Scott. Hood's tones of appeal range from the playful towards Gent, through the slightly patronizing towards the Northamptonshire peasant, to the deferential towards Moore and Scott. He deferred to these last not only on account of their literary prestige but also because of their social standing.

Hood corresponded not only with the editors of annuals, but also with those of more frequent periodicals. This group included William Hone, editor of the *Every Day Book* and a friend of Lamb. It also included William Jerdan, editor of the long-lived weekly *Literary Gazette*, whose friendship Hood needed on account of his puffing reviews, with whom he quarrelled, yet whom we can finally name amongst his 'distant friends.' Hood also corresponded with Charles Ollier, sub-editor of the *New Monthly Magazine* and another friend of Lamb, and later with R.S. Surtees, creator of Jorrocks; Hood wrote to Surtees in his capacity as editor of the *New Sporting Magazine*, in which concern his brother-in-law Reynolds played an important part. He also corresponded with W.H. Ainsworth, editing *Ainsworth's Magazine*, and with Mark Lemon, editor of *Punch*.

Hood's editorship of *The Gem* brought him into contact with the artistic world as well as the literary for, in the annuals, plate illustrated text and vice versa. On this principle Hood's literary direction of *The Gem* was paired with the artistic direction of Abraham Cooper RA, who thus became a correspondent. One of the plates in *The Gem* was from a typically grandiose painting by John Martin, whom one unexpectedly finds as a friend of Hood. A peripheral member of the artistic world of those days was Robert Balmanno, who receives several pleasant, witty, and conversational letters from Hood. In league with Balmanno, Hood writes a lavishly witty letter to Sir Thomas Lawrence in order to gain access to the Royal Pavilion at Brighton. The aim of this visit, which did not take place, was to gain material to provide a text to match the engravings of W.B. Cooke, another artistic collaborator and friend, and the recipient of one particularly sympathetic letter (142). There is also a letter to the printseller and publisher F.G. Moon. Later, Hood corresponds with the engravers Wright and Folkard. John Wright did most of the illustrative work on the *Comic Annuals* and acted as Hood's business representative in London during his long absence abroad, and so receives from Hood letters anxious and friendly and exuberant by turns. In later years Hood corresponds with other artists: William Harvey, a pupil of Bewick, John Leech, a fellow-contributor to *Punch*, and Clarkson Stanfield, friend of Dickens.

In 1829, as well as editing *The Gem*, Hood attempted a connection with the theatre. One or two indifferent pieces by him were indifferently performed. And we have the impatient letters to R.W. Elliston, formerly manager of Drury Lane and now of the Surrey Theatre, and to Frederick Yates, part-owner, with the inimitable mimic

Mathews, of the Adelphi Theatre. There is also an earlier letter to Stephen Price, the American who was, for a time, manager of Drury Lane.

Mention has already been made of Hood's bourgeois origin and background. His own awareness of this is shown in the tone of deference which his correspondence takes on when it is addressed to social superiors. We have seen this in the letters to Sir Walter Scott, and it is apparent, though less markedly, in the pyrotechnic letter to Sir Thomas Lawrence (113). It reappears in letters to Sir Francis Freeling, the Duke of Devonshire, and the Prince Consort. Hood dedicates to Freeling, Secretary of the Post Office, the first volume of the *Comic Annual* (124), and he forwards to the Prince Consort a German translation of 'The Dream of Eugene Aram' (453). Hood is grateful for the patronage of the Duke of Devonshire, to whom the second volume of the *Comic Annual* is dedicated. In later years, Hood's spirit of deference is evident in a letter to Sir Edward Bulwer Lytton, expressing gratitude for his condescending to contribute to *Hood's Magazine* and for his help in obtaining Hood a pension, and in letters to Sir Robert Peel, the Prime Minister, acknowledging the granting of the pension.

During his stay abroad (1835–40), which was enforced by financial embarrassment, Hood had seven chief correspondents: his wife, Jane, when he was separated from her; his English friends, Mr and Mrs Dilke and Dr and Mrs Elliot; his new Anglo-German friend, Philip de Franck; and his collaborator and friend, John Wright. Hood's letters to Jane show the strength of his love for her. When he quits her to visit Berlin in the company of Franck and his regiment, he delights in every aspect of the trip and in his own unaccustomed role as attentively remarked camp follower, but his deepest thoughts are always unwaveringly with her. The same is true of the later letters from Scotland. Hood's long impassioned letter to Dilke before leaving for Germany shows the independent and stalwart Dilke's role as his trusted and confidential adviser. The expansiveness and the compulsive anti-German grumblings of Hood's later letters to the Dilkes from Germany show his loneliness there. These letters make one wonder what could have caused the sad break between the two men which occurred after Hood's return to England. Though Hood's friendship with Dilke came to an end, the friendship with his physician Dr Elliot and his wife grew more and more strong. He writes to them loquaciously and facetiously; he writes of them in terms of deep gratitude and even love. To their young children, as to his own dear daughter, he pens playful letters which show a delightful fancy and the ability to enter into the mind and spirit of the child. Hood's loneliness in Germany was happily relieved by the genial friendship with Philip de Franck, who, like Jane most of the time, was the good-humoured object of Hood's sometimes elaborate practical jokes and waggery. The business letters to Wright from abroad show how harassed Hood was by the distance separating them, particularly under the stress imposed by the monthly publication of *Hood's Own*, in 1838. (*Hood's Own* was largely a reissue of materials published in the *Comic Annuals* of the preceding years.)

In 1840 Hood returned to England alone, glad to be back in his homeland, saddened by memories, stricken by illness, but solaced by the attention of his friends. Jane followed him, and a financial crisis ensued. It was with difficulty that the children left behind in Ostend were extricated from the grasp of Hood's Belgian creditors. Hood proudly refused help offered by the Literary Fund but then had to swallow his pride and apply for what he had rejected. A tentative publishing arrangement with Bentley was only partially successful, but then Hood entered on a regular engagement as contributor to Colburn's *New Monthly Magazine*, of which he later became editor.

Hood's life as an editor provided him, at least at first, with a degree of economic security. It exposed his delicate health to a damaging strain, recurrent with the preparation of each issue of the magazine. However, in spite of his sickness, this life brought him to play a more public and active role in literary society, to which his correspondence attests.

Hood had a special sympathy for his fellow men of letters as members of a hard-working and unappreciated fraternity. In Ostend this feeling probably led him to seek, though without great success, the acquaintance of T.C. Grattan. In England there is no warmth, but neither is there coolness, in letters to Shirley Brooks of the *Punch* circle and to Captain Marryat. The thesis of 'fellow author, therefore dear to me' is stated in letters to Douglas Jerrold and Bulwer Lytton, and one is sure that this principle made these men Hood's friends even though their social life was different and apart from his. The principle is exemplified in a letter to Thomas Noon Talfourd, to whom Hood wrote forcefully on the topic of literary copyright. Hood valued the brotherhood of literature, and he felt the need for this brotherhood to take some tangible form and achieve some legal recognition. This is shown also in his letters to Dickens. At the same time, Hood was obliged to appeal pathetically to the brotherhood in his letters to Octavius Blewitt and the Committee of the Literary Fund.

To the broad category of authors and friends more or less distant belong John Britton, the antiquary, an acquaintance of Hood's father, and Manley Hopkins, the father of the great poet. To this category also belong Thackeray and Dickens. To the latter Hood writes at first with generous encouragement and always openheartedly. However, that such literary *bonhomie* is not always as deep as one could wish is shown in Hood's relation with Laman Blanchard. They exchange fulsome letters, but elsewhere Hood refers to Blanchard, less soupily, as 'one of the Marlboro' street gang' (570).

A large group of literary correspondents is made up of would-be and actual contributors to the magazines of which Hood was editor: the *New Monthly* and then his own. Would-be contributors included William Gaspey, Sheridan Knowles, and William Hazlitt the younger. Actual contributors included Charles Mackay, Cyrus Redding, and Sir Charles Morgan, husband of the volatile Lady Morgan, slightly beyond Hood's social range. Contributors who were also friends more or less distant included Hannah Lawrance whom Hood had known as a youthful dilettante of literature, H.F. Cary, an old *London Magazine* contributor, Mrs S.C. Hall and David Moir whom he had known in the atmosphere of the annuals, and the humorists Horace Smith and the Reverend R.H. Barham, the latter of whom exerted his influence to help Hood obtain financial assistance through the Literary Fund. Other correspondents in this last category of contributors and friends are W.J. Broderip, magistrate, naturalist, and man of letters, J.T.J. Hewlett, clergyman and humorist, to whom Hood writes encouragingly, whimsically, and often, and Samuel Phillips, who in Hood's last days became something more than a contributor, that is, a friend and collaborator. F.O. Ward was also a collaborator, stepping in to help when *Hood's Magazine* and its editor were teetering on the verge of collapse.

A final group of correspondents of Hood's later years is more amorphous in character. Hood writes to autograph hunters, particularly genially to W.F. Watson who later bequeathed his large collection to the National Library of Scotland, and he writes to dozens of poetical 'ladies, old and young; and prosaic gentlemen' (549) anxious to blossom in print. He writes business letters to officials, not only those of the Literary Fund, but also, in his role as important contemporary man of letters, to the secretaries of the Manchester Athenaeum, and to the secretary of the Liverpool Anti-Monopoly Association.

So much for Hood's correspondents. What of his character as shown in the letters which he wrote to them? In brief, he felt deep love, at times passionately expressed, for his wife, children, and intimate friends. He felt dutifully to his more distant relatives and to those men to whom he felt himself to be fairly indebted. He had every honourable intention of paying back his debts. He was sympathetic to his friends in their sickness and bereavement. He was hospitable to them when he had a chance to entertain them. It was his love of his family rather than his ill health which made his life domestic in character. He was buoyed up by a simple, undogmatic, optimistic, and firm faith, expressed rarely, though more frequently towards the end of his life. He was predominantly a humorist, his humour expressing itself in an outpouring of puns, a love of practical jokes and of teasing those closest to him. Humour was predominant in him: with it as his staff he met sickness and death itself.

Hood's misfortunes were not entirely inflicted from without. Though he would not admit to dilatoriness in himself, this characteristic was remarked in him by H.F. Chorley, an assistant on Dilke's *Athenaeum*, in his *Autobiography* (1873, I, 109–10), and by John Wright in a letter to Hood (in the Bristol Public Library). Furthermore, Hood seems to have suffered from a more than ordinary inability to get along with publishers. He writes of them with a harshness which he applies elsewhere only to religious bigots. He snarlingly compares the apparently innocent Hessey, of Taylor and Hessey, to a snake, and writes with similar vituperation but perhaps more justification of Henry Colburn.

Hood's interest in politics as well as his editorship will be considered more closely, because they present an unusually complicated situation which has not before been unravelled and which shows itself effectively in the letters. Hood's political attitude has three aspects. On the one hand, he holds himself aloof and apart from party politics. When someone publishes a weak political satire in his name he is horrified and pens an indignant letter of protest to *The Times*. As editor of the *New Monthly Magazine* and *Hood's Magazine* he abjures the intrusion of political controversy. At the same time, Hood is not indifferent to politics. He is upset about the satire just mentioned, not merely as a satire, but because it represents him as a partisan of the right rather than of the left. Indeed, he is hopeful of moderate social improvement. Chorley calls him a liberal, and he accepts the label. In one epistolary outburst he goes so far as to call himself a republican. In later poetical effusions he expresses sympathy for the poor, particularly the outcast harlot, the downtrodden sempstress, and the unemployed agricultural labourer. In the last instance his protest is aimed directly against the government. He tentatively associates himself with the leaders of the Anti-Corn Law League, which he is led to denominate their 'great cause' (595). At the end of his life, another attitude towards politics is apparent: Hood is influenced, firstly, subconsciously by the generosity of Sir Robert Peel in the matter of his pension and, secondly, by his acute awareness of the proximity of his own death. He writes finally with full seriousness of the folly of party divisions and the need of a united national spirit to face the problems of the age.

As a political man, Hood thought that right feeling could do much to solve social problems; this is what he admired so much in Dickens. As a man of letters, Hood's attitude was more practical. He felt that the status of his own profession could be improved by association and legislation. He suffered from piracy and plagiarism and the inadequate copyright law, and against them he wrote wittily, sensitively, fully, and with a sense of the importance of the position of the man of letters in society.

As editor, Hood felt that it was his duty to maintain the respectability of his profession. This was one reason for his rupture with Colburn in 1843, for the latter did not allow him the full control over the *New Monthly Magazine* which he felt a self-respecting man of letters should have had. Colburn bought serials which he decided to publish in the magazine; he inserted laudatory reviews by his own staff of books published by himself; and there is little doubt that he knowingly victimized his own editor by publishing and having reviewed in the *New Monthly* a novel con-containing plagiarisms of Hood and others.

Hood freed himself from Colburn and took the audacious step of inaugurating a magazine untrammelled by association with a large publishing house. Unfortunately he was injudicious in his choice of financier. Flight's support proved to be fraudulent. Hood himself succumbed to illness. He and the magazine were rescued by F.O. Ward, who secured the safe financial backing of Spottiswoode, the Queen's printer. During the summer of 1844 Hood recovered his health very slowly; Ward sent him to recuperate at Blackheath. However, serious differences in editorial policy arose between the two men, as the correspondence shows. Hood's scruples were not merely artistic – concerning, for example, the hard-won contributions from Browning – but also political. Ward sought to enliven with an infusion from Young England what Hood conceived of as a politically neutral entertainment. As his vitality returned Hood objected more strongly. Now he disagreed with Ward not only on artistic and political, but also on religious and moral grounds. Ward's policy was to arouse and stimulate; Hood's, less courageous, more delicate and difficult, was what we tend to think of as the typically early Victorian one of entertaining without giving offence to any section of his readers. At the same time Ward was working hard to obtain a pension for Hood. When he succeeded, Hood complained about the meagreness of the award. When Ward made a move to have the amount increased, Hood objected to his interference. When Ward sought to publish Peel's letter offering the pension to Hood, Hood refused. He struggled almost as against death itself to retain control over the magazine and over his own affairs against a young, energetic man who was both greatly helpful and tiresomely interfering. Ward's impassioned assistance continued to the end, as did Hood's petulant reaction to it, inevitable because of his mortal sickness. However, Ward described Hood's last days in convincing and calm terms which indicate their final reconciliation:

> He saw the on-coming of death with great cheerfulness, though without anything approaching to levity; and last night, when his friends, Harvey and another, came, he bade them come up, had wine brought, and made us all drink a glass with him, 'that he might know us for friends, as of old, and not undertakers.' He conversed for about an hour in his old playful way, with now and then a word or two full of deep and tender feeling. When I left he bade me good-bye, and kissed me, shedding tears, and saying that perhaps we should never meet again.[1]

1/Quoted in Samuel Carter Hall *A Book of Memories* (1871), 144

EDITORIAL PROCEDURES

My aim has been to present Hood's letters as authentically as possible, at the same time avoiding obstacles which can stand in the way of the reader's apprehension of the writer's intention. For the latter reason, I have imposed a uniform order on heading, salutation, signature, date, and address. I have not numbered the letters, but I have identified them with a title which indicates the recipient. When I am uncertain of the identity of a recipient, I have indicated this with a question mark; a few have had to be labelled 'unknown.' The date indicated, when not given by Hood himself, is provided by the postmark, the recipient, or, occasionally, another person in an annotation of the letter itself, a printed source, or my own conjecture. The source of the dating is indicated in the note following the letter. Where possible, I have provided the address and postmark or marks from the letter in the same note.

Hood's punctuation and spelling are, to a certain extent, mildly idiosyncratic, but they pose no problem to the reader. A little silent correction has been done where there is an obvious slip of the pen or omission of punctuation. Where my reading is conjectural I have indicated the original in the note. When Hood corrects himself, as he occasionally does, I reproduce his correction or second thoughts, and not the original form. Hood frequently underlines for emphasis; where necessary, I have extended the corresponding italics over the relevant sense group or word. When a word was underlined three or more times, I have indicated this in the note. I have not attempted to reproduce the flourishes and strokes which may follow the signature. Hiatuses and unintelligible words and phrases have been indicated through the use of square brackets.

I have followed manuscripts wherever possible, and otherwise the most reliable printed texts. The standardizations of earlier editors (for example, capitalized salutations), I have replaced with my own.

Immediately following each letter I give its source, in either manuscript or published version. When both exist, I follow the manuscript, but give a reference to the first or most authoritative published version. In referring to a book I give the place of publication only if it is not London. Some frequently used sources are represented by abbreviations, listed in the table on pages xxv–xxvi. In referring to a periodical, I give only the author's name, title of periodical, full date of publication, and page references.

I have intended to make the edition as complete as possible in its inclusion of Hood's private letters. To this end, I have included not only whole letters but also fragments, though not fragments of less than a sentence in length. I have omitted letters certainly intended for publication, such as the letters to the editor of *The Athenaeum* entitled 'Copyright and Copywrong,' published there in 1837 and 1842, the letters published in *The Athenaeum* (1840) as advertisements contributing to Hood's controversy with his erstwhile publisher A.H. Baily, and the letter to the Manchester Athenaeum of 1843 which was printed in order to be sold there. I have also omitted 'My Tract,' written in epistolary form in 1841. On the other hand, I have included a letter to the Manchester Athenaeum of 1844, not then published, together with a short letter of 1843 to the editor of *The Sun* newspaper, which I am not sure was intended for publication.

A few of Hood's engravings have been included; they are reproduced from *Memorials of Thomas Hood.*

The letters are divided chronologically by year, and also into three major sections: 'At Home' from 1815 to February 1835, 'Abroad,' in Belgium and Germany, from 1835 to March 1840, and 'At Home Again' from 1840 until the end.

ABBREVIATIONS

BM	British Museum
Bodleian	Bodleian Library
Cameron	Mr R.E. Cameron
Clubbe	John Clubbe *Victorian Forerunner* (Durham NC 1968)
Columbia	Columbia University Library
Dilke	Charles Wentworth Dilke *Papers of a Critic* (1875)
DNB	*Dictionary of National Biography*
Dundee	Dundee Public Library
Elliot	Alexander Elliot *Hood in Scotland* (Dundee 1885)
Harvard	Harvard College Library
HLQ	*Huntington Library Quarterly*
HM	*Hood's Magazine*
Huntington	Huntington Library
Jerrold	Walter Jerrold *Thomas Hood: His Life and Times* (1907)
Lane KSJ	William G. Lane 'A Chord in Melancholy: Hood's Last Years' *Keats–Shelley Journal* winter 1964, 43–60
Lawrance	Hannah Lawrance 'Recollections of Thomas Hood' *British Quarterly Review* October 1867, 323–54
Marchand	*Letters of Thomas Hood from the Dilke Papers in the British Museum, edited with an Introduction and Notes by Leslie A. Marchand* (New Brunswick NJ 1945)
Memorials	Frances Freeling Broderip and Tom Hood *Memorials of Thomas Hood, collected, arranged, and edited by his daughter, with a preface and notes by his son* (1860)
Morgan KSJ	Peter F. Morgan 'John Hamilton Reynolds and Thomas Hood' *Keats–Shelley Journal* winter 1962, 83–95

Morgan Library	Pierpont Morgan Library
NED	*New English Dictionary*
NMM	*New Monthly Magazine*
New York	New York Public Library
NLS	National Library of Scotland
Osborn	Osborn Collection, Yale University Library
Pennsylvania	Historical Society of Pennsylvania Library
Poetical Works	Thomas Hood *Poetical Works* ed. Walter Jerrold (1920)
Princeton	Princeton University Library
Reid	J.C. Reid *Thomas Hood* (1963)
Rochester	University of Rochester Library
Rylands	John Rylands Library
Shelley	Henry C. Shelley *Literary Bypaths in Old England* (1906)
Texas	University of Texas Library
UCLA	University of California Library, Los Angeles
Whitley	Alvin Whitley 'Thomas Hood' unpublished doctoral thesis of Harvard University 1950
Whitley HLQ	Alvin Whitley 'Hood and Dickens: Some New Letters' *Huntington Library Quarterly* August 1951, 385–413
Works	*The Works of Thomas Hood ... edited, with notes, by his son and daughter* (1869–73)
Yale	Yale University Library

THE MAIN EVENTS OF HOOD'S LIFE

1799 Thomas Hood born 23 May, in the City of London
1811 His father dies, 20 August
1815 A summer visit to Dundee extends to about 1817
1821 Contributes to the *London Magazine*, from July of this year to June 1823. Mother dies in July
1825 With J.H. Reynolds publishes *Odes and Addresses* in February. Marries Jane Reynolds 5 May. Publishes a satirical engraving, 'The Progress of Cant,' in December
1826 Publishes *Whims and Oddities* in November
1827 Publishes *National Tales* in February, and his only volume of serious poetry, *The Plea of the Midsummer Fairies*, in August. Publishes *Whims and Oddities, Second Series* in November
1828 Publishes an annual, *The Gem*, in December
1829 Publishes *The Comic Annual* at the end of the year, at the end of succeeding years until 1838, and again at the end of 1841
1830 His daughter, Frances Freeling Hood, born 11 September
1834 Publishes his only completed full-length novel, *Tylney Hall*, in October
1835 His son, Tom Hood, born 19 January. Settles in Koblenz in March
1836 Journeys to Berlin and back in October and November
1837 Removes to Ostend in June
1838 Publishes *Hood's Own* in monthly parts from January to May 1839
1839 Publishes his travel book, *Up the Rhine*, in December
1840 Returns to London in April. Contributes to the *New Monthly Magazine* from August this year to September 1843
1841 Edits the *New Monthly* for two years from September

1843 Visits Scotland in September. Publishes 'The Song of the Shirt' in *Punch*, 16 December. Publishes *Whimsicalities* in December

1844 Begins *Hood's Magazine* in January. Receives a government pension in November

1845 Makes his last contribution to *Hood's Magazine* in March. Dies, 3 May

THE LETTERS OF *Thomas Hood*

AT HOME September 1815–February 1835

1815

TO
HIS AUNT

Dear Aunt
I again take the pen for a double purpose – to endeavour to amuse both you & myself by a description of whatever attracts my notice. –
I am principally diverted here with the singular characters that come to lodge here in succession. When I first came we had a kind of itinerant minister who loved his bottle

– And oft would rehearse
In defence of his custom this scriptural verse
'Take a little wine for thy stomack's sake'[1] –
But in practice the little but jolly divine
Would oft substitute whisky instead of the wine

Since then we have been enlivened by a French Captain who possest in an eminent degree the gaiety & politeness peculiar to that nation and I have been particularly amused with a pedantic Perth Schoolmaster who went up to London during the vacation and resided a fortnight in *Wapping* in order to improve himself in English! & said he was 'vary sure he wadna be takken for a 'Scotsman'. – At present we have a Swiss who appears to be an agreeable man, but I do not know how he may be on further acquaintance.[2] –
The study of Characters (I mean of amusing ones) I enjoy exceedingly & have here an ample field for speculations, for independent of originality of character their ideas are also frequently of the same stamp as in the case of our hostess who thinks that fresh beef will keep better than that which is salted – but you will perhaps think this notion took its rise in – oeconomy – & not in originality of idea. –
About a week ago we had a company of Tumblers here who established a kind of lottery here at 1/– p ticket & the chief prize a Cow & Calf valued at 7 guineas – Now it agreed very well with the Scotch notion of oeconomy to get 7 Guineas for a shilling, but on the other hand they considered the chance they had of perhaps losing their bawbees & no doubt it cost a struggle before they determined on buying their tickets – but when the drawing began it was ludicrous to observe the whimsical effects of disappointment in the faces of some of the multitude. It was a scene indeed worthy the pencil of Hogarth. –
In the evenings it is a beautiful promenade before the barracks where part of the

79*th* are at present quartered & as they have a fine band which plays every evening I am there almost every night – This with walking, swimming, drawing &c constitute my principal amusements during my banishment. –
When you can spare time enough to write a few lines I shall be happy to hear from you & am with love to Cousin & all our other friends,

Your Affectionate Nephew,

Thomas Hood

The smack I intended to send this by is detained so that I have yet time to add more. –
As I am to remain & take my Christmas in the Land of cakes you will perhaps expect me to return a complete Scot – but to tell you the truth I approach as yet in but a small degree – I sicken with disgust at the sight of a singed sheeps head & notwithstanding the arguments of Lesmahago & the preference of the mouse, which he advances in support of them,[3] I cannot bring myself to endure oatmeal which I think harsh, dry, & insipid. – The only time I ever took it with any kind of relish was one day on a trouting party when I was hungry enough to eat anything. – As to their dialect I have acquired rather more than I could wish thro the broad brogue of our landlady – whose blunders would do credit to an Hibernian – Among the best of these are – A Chapel built in the *Bothy* style – and[4]

Dundee, September 1815. –

MS Dundee. Published in *Works* x 6–8. Hood, born in 1799, spent his early years in London. For reasons of health, he visited his father's home city of Dundee from the summer of 1815 to about 1817. This is a letter home, but the name of Hood's aunt is not known.

1/1 Timothy 5:23
2/Hood's Swiss acquaintance, Samuel Messieux (d 1859), later taught French at St Andrews University and achieved a certain fame in the history of golf.
3/Lieutenant Obadiah Lismahago, a character in Smollett's *Humphry Clinker*, letter of 20 September
4/The remainder of the letter is missing from the Dundee Library.

TO
HIS AUNTS

My dear aunts,
I duly received your agreeable letter, which had it been an 'Evening Lecture' would have come very *à propos*, as I received it on Sunday night. I received at the same time your handsome present, for which I beg leave to return you my best

thanks. I am sorry to learn that my aunts, Ruth and Cunlee,[1] have been so ill, but rejoice to hear of their recovery, and hope that your roast beef and pudding will restore them to a perfect state of convalescence. As you seem to have some fears of submitting your letters to my criticism, I must assure you that you need be under no apprehensions on that head, my own epistolary style being very indifferent, and I should fear by criticising to lose the pleasure of receiving your letters. Instead of giving you any regular description of this irregular town, I shall give you some extracts from my note-book, wherein I am endeavouring to describe it after the manner of Anstey's Bath Guide,[2] in letters from a family (Mr. Blunderhead's) to their friends in London.

The town is ill-built, and is dirty beside
For with water it's scantily, badly supplied
By wells, where the servants, in filling their pails,
Stand for hours, spreading scandal, and falsehood and tales.
And abounds so in smells that a stranger supposes
The people are very deficient in noses.
Their buildings, as though they'd been scanty of ground,
Are crammed into corners that cannot be found.
Or as though so ill built and contrived they had been,
That the town were ashamed they should ever be seen.
And their rooted dislike and aversion to waste
Is suffer'd sometimes to encroach on their taste,
For beneath a Theatre or Chapel they'll pop
A sale room, a warehouse, or mean little shop,
Whose windows, or rather no windows at all,
Are more like to so many holes in the wall.
And four churches together, with only one steeple,
Is an emblem quite apt of the thrift of the people.

In walking one morning I came to the green,
Where the manner of washing in Scotland is seen;
And I thought that it perhaps would amuse, should I write,
A description of what seemed a singular sight.
Here great bare-legged women were striding around,
And watering clothes that were laid on the ground.
While, on t'other hand, you the lasses might spy
In tubs, with their petticoats up to the thigh,

And, instead of their hands, washing thus with their feet,
Which they often will do in the midst of the street,
Which appears quite indelicate, – shocking, indeed,
To those ladies who come from the south of the Tweed!

Like a fish out of water, you'll think me, my dear,
When our manner of living at present you hear;
Here, by ten in the morning our breakfast is done,
When in town I ne'er think about rising till one:
And at three, oh how vulgar, we sit down and dine,
And at six we take tea, and our supper at nine,
And then soberly go to our beds by eleven,
And as soberly rise the next morning by seven.
How unlike our great city of London, you'll say,
Where day's turned into night, and the night into day.
But indeed to these hours I'm obliged to attend,
There's so very few ways any leisure to spend,
For they ne'er play at cards, Commerce, Ombre, or Loo,
Though they often are carding of wool, it is true.
And instead of 'piany's,' Italian, sonatas,
At their spinning wheels sitting, they whistle like carters.

A poor man who'd been reading the public events,
Amidst prices of stock, and consols, and per cents,
Observed Omnium, and anxious to know what it meant
With the news in his hand to a Bailie he went,
For he thought the best way to obtain information,
Was by asking at one of the wise corporation.
Mr. Bailie hum'd, ha'd, looked exceedingly wise,
And considered a while, taken thus by surprise,
Till at length the poor man, who impatient stood by,
Got this truly sagacious, laconic reply, –
'Omnium's just Omnium.'[3]
Then returning at least just as wise as before,
He resolved to apply to a Bailie no more!

I have seen the Asylum they lately have made,
And approve of the plan, but indeed I'm afraid

If they send all the people of reason bereft,
To this Bedlam, but few in the town will be left.
For their passions and drink are so terribly strong
That but few here retain all their faculties long.
And with shame I must own, that the females, I think,
Are in general somewhat addicted to drink!

Now I speak of divines, in the churches I've been,
Of which four are together, and walls but between,
So as you sit in one, you may hear in the next,
When the clerk gives the psalm, or the priest gives the text.
With respect to their worship, with joy I must say
Their strict bigoted tenets are wearing away,
And each day moderation still stronger appears,
Nor should I much wonder, if in a few years,
The loud notes of the organ the burthen should raise
Midst the chorus of voices, the homage, and praise.
For I cannot conceive for what cause they deny
The assistance of music, in raising on high
Our thanksgiving and psalms, as King David of old,
Upon numberless instruments played, we are told;[4]
Nor to music can theme more sublime be e'er given,
Than of wafting the strains of the righteous to heaven.
They've a custom, a little surprising, I own,
And in practice I think found in Scotland alone.
For in England for penance, in churchyards they stand
In a sheet, while a taper they hold in their hand;
But here in the Church, if the parties think fit,
On a stool called the 'Cuttie,' for penance they sit,
And, as though absolution they thus did obtain,
Go and sin, then appear the next Sunday again!
Superstition as yet, though it's dying away,
On the minds of the vulgar holds powerful sway,
And on doors or on masts you may frequently view,
As defence against witchcraft, some horse's old shoe.
And the mariner's wife sees her child with alarm
Comb her hair in the glass, and predicts him some harm.

Tales of goblins and ghosts that alarmed such a one
By tradition are handed from father to son.
And they oft will describe o'er their twopenny ale
Some poor ghost with no head, or grey mare without tail,[5]
Or lean corpse in night-cap, all bloody and pale!

Some large markets for cattle or fairs are held here,
On a moor near the town, about thrice in a year.
So I went to the last, found it full, to my thinking,
Of whisky and porter, of smoking and drinking.
But to picture the scene there presented, indeed,
The bold pencil and touches of Hogarth would need.
Here you'd perhaps see a man upon quarrelling bent
In short serpentine curves, wheeling out of a tent,
(For at least so they call blankets raised upon poles,
Well enlightened and aired by the numerous holes,)
Or some hobbling old wife, just as drunk as a sow,
Having spent all the money she got for her cow.
Perhaps some yet unsold, when the market has ceased,
You may then see a novelty, beast leading beast![6]

Dundee, December 1815

From *Works* x 8–12. The name of Hood's aunts is not known.

1/Jerrold, 12, identifies these as Ruth Sands and Jane Cunlee, noting the misspelling of 'Cundee' in *Memorials*, followed by *Works*.

2/Christopher Anstey *New Bath Guide* (1766)

3/'All the articles included in the Contract between Government and the original subscribers to a loan, which of late years has consisted generally of different proportions of three, and four per cent. stock with a certain quantity of terminable annuities:' authority (1819) quoted in NED

4/1 Chronicles 15:16

5/Like the mare in Burns' 'Tam O'Shanter'

6/The letter breaks off here.

1818

TO
ROBERT SANDS

Dear Uncle,

Having heard from my aunts of the measles having attacked your family, we are anxious to hear how you all are, and I seize upon this opportunity to thank you for sending my box, and for the kind expressions contained in your last letter, but have been so variously engaged, besides being unwell, that I have not had time to write till now. I have the pleasure of informing you that my voyage to Scotland has done wonders for me, as, since my return, my neck has altogether healed, and my leg has gained so much strength that I have been enabled to walk several times to the West End and back, without any injury, and I certainly feel and look better than I have done for years. I now hope to be able to look after business a little, and to do well, both in that and in health. I did some things for Mr. Harris[1] before I went to Scotland with which he was very well pleased, but have had no proofs, as I did them while H. was busy on the Battle of Waterloo, and could not prove for me. I desired him to send you a proof I did in Spring, which I suppose you have had. We had the pleasure of Mrs. LeKeux's[2] company to dinner while she was in town, and I was happy to see that she looked much better than when I left the country. I have seen some of your last works, which I have greatly admired, and was much gratified by a sight of the printed papers you sent to my aunt's, containing eulogiums, which, allow me to say, I think you justly merit, and believe me, gave me great and unfeigned pleasure. We beg that you will drop us a line or two by the first convenient opportunity to let us know how you all are. As for ourselves we are all well, and desire you will accept our love to you all. I am, in haste, dear uncle,

Your affectionate nephew,

Thomas Hood.

I hope to hear also that your farming is in a thriving condition.

[*Islington, 1818*]

From *Works* x 12–13. On his return to Islington from Scotland about 1817 Hood began work as an engraver. His uncle, Robert Sands, was engaged in that occupation in London.

1/Harris, the engraver

2/According to Jerrold, 62, 'Mrs. Le Keux was probably the wife of John, the elder of the two celebrated brothers.' The LeKeux brothers were celebrated as engravers. John (1783–1846) was the engraver particularly of architectural work; he was born in Bishopsgate, London, and baptized at St Botolph's Church, where Hood was later married. Henry (1787–1868) was associated with his brother and, like Hood but in a different capacity, with the fashionable annuals of the 1820s and 30s.

1819

TO
GEORGE ROLLO

Dear George
I have to apologize to you, for my delay in writing to you, which may seem inconsistent with the friendship I certainly feel towards you, but indeed I feel so much pleasure in writing to you in the expectation of hearing from you in return, that I trust you will believe, no slight cause could have prevented my writing to you before. –
I had a most agreable passage hither[1] of 5 days, with a jovial crew of shipmates, amounting in all to 20 persons – among whom I made an acquaintance quite to my taste, with a Mr Harding, an artist, who had been sketching in the Highlands. – A certain Dr Blair who resides in your parts, proved a most amusing companion and I felt myself so well supplied with spirits (animal ones) that I contributed my full share to the general fund of gaiety and Mirth. –[2]
Since my return, a slight illness, and a deal of unprofitable business, have kept me fully employed, and which you may easily imagine, when you consider, the task before me – to establish myself in a difficult profession, after little more than two years experience, in the art, in such unfavourable times, and in an age, so much improved in Taste, as to render it more difficult for the Artist to give satisfaction. – I have at this moment a very arduous task before me, an ordeal of the difficulty of which I am fully aware, but resolved upon. – I have been offered a drawing to engrave for a beautiful little work, for which MY MASTER has engraved plates.[3] – and what a struggle it must cost me to dress mine fine enough to appear in such company! – If not rejected but approved of – it will ensure to me a years employment from one source alone – if not, a years fagging – But the stake is worth playing for – is it not? – These things harrass me not a little, but happily with all its difficulties and disagreables my business supplies me with a certain enthusiasm which carries me thro' them all. – I am now looking forward to a winter of close, very close, application in order to atone for certain past times of illness & idleness – when I have not the point in my hand I have the pencil. – by day I engrave – by night I draw and am almost become a Hermit in London –[4]
I must confess, that these cares and anxieties have somewhat impaired that gaiety, which once was mine, and to borrow a technical term, I find I get the *graver* – but in the mean time I am very happy in finding that my health has improved

considerably, so as to seem, indeed, like a renewal of my lease – Latterly the improvement has been very rapid and I must with gratitude own myself indebted to your own dear Scotland. –

It did me good, to visit old haunts, and to see old friends, which by awakening pleasant thoughts in my memory, and giving fresh ones to dwell upon, both amused & relieved my mind and benefited my body. –

I often regret the High Street,[5] and the agreable chats we have had there – but most of all, those agreable Chess Parties, those desperate, but amusing combats! – I wish I had you here, and a chess board between us! but alas! distance says Check! George – and perhaps saves you a beating, unless you will begin by a Move – as far as to London. – I do not think that I have played within these three years. – To tell you the truth, I am more of a Hermit here than you would easily imagine – and will scarce credit me when I tell you I have not a single *male*/friend: – / *acquaintance*[6] in the neighbourhood, tho' I am occasionally blest with the Society of many young ladies. – I have some in the city (2 miles off –) but who are so engaged that I seldom see them, except when I go to town on business & I dislike so much all noise & bustle that I never go there but from necessity. – This makes me think of you much oftener than you would be led to infer from my silence, & whenever I do so, I cannot help regretting that fate so frequently allows people to be with each other just long enough to like each other and then separates them – perhaps for ever – I do not despair however of seeing you again & of some day reaching where I very much wished – Lochee[7] – My friendship then might have reach'd farther – –

The above was written about a month since, but I was unable to conclude for want of time – and I have since rec^{d} the favour of yours for Mr Wyllie, who took tea with us a night or two since –

It will be a great convenience to me if he will forward my letters, since the wharf is 3 miles hence and my business lies quite at the other end of the city. – but I frequently call within a few doors of his counting House.

I have delayed writing to Mr Miln[8] from not having been able yet to get the Dundee Guide from which I promised him extracts. – It has been so long out of my possession that I doubt whether I may obtain it again but that will not prevent my writing to him p first occasion which have the goodness to communicate to him with my Compliments. –

I did not learn from Mr Wyllie, any particular news relating to your place – and have as little to communicate as the London papers can inform you of all relating to politics if you ever trouble your head with such matters – We have from time to time a fresh subject – & at present it is the transactions at Manchester.[9] – As far as my judgment extends I think however that business in general revives. – If I might judge by myself I would say that people were smothered in business – but the worst is it is not always attended by any profit. – I have a restless head that will never be at repose for a moment – for when I have done with engraving I sit down to compose lectures upon trifles which I deliver to some young ladies[10] – I get out of bed & breakfast by 9 – & sit down to my plate with 2 of my Sisters beside me whom I teach to etch – We are undisturbed & busy till 2 when I go down to dine & sometimes meet the rest of the family for the first time – in that day – I leave them all at table & run up again to my plate – my 2 Sisters come soon after and we remain till dusk – when we shake off our business with a general romp or bit of fun – After tea I bring down my plate to the Parlour and contrive some job that will allow me to converse while I work. – & this is sometimes resumed after Supper till 11 Oclock when I go to bed – My day does not end here – for if I cannot sleep I amuse myself by writing like Bonaparte in Bed. – till 12 or 1 oclock – Sometimes this comprises the history of a week – during which I have never quitted our own territories – the House & garden –

Such is my life what do you think of it – yours truly T. Hood.

PS. – Have the goodness to remember me kindly to your Brother – & tell him I wish you both success in that *harmony* which Mr W. tells me you are endeavouring to promote at Lochee – I have a flute which I squeak upon occasionally and does very well to put my Sister out – when she plays on the piano.–

[*Islington, summer 1819*]

MS New York. Address: 'Mr Geo^e^ Rollo. / Messrs Sterling & Martins / Baine's Square. / Dundee.' Rollo was a young lawyer of Dundee who had shared lodgings with Hood there.

1/Back to London from Scotland

2/I have not identified Harding and Blair.

3/Hood's engraving was probably that of 'St. Cleons, Galway,' published 1 April 1821, and later appearing in J.P. Neale's *Views of the Seats of Noblemen* (1818–23), VI. The engravings for this volume were supervised by Messrs LeKeux.

4/Title of a series by Felix M'Donough published in *Literary Gazette*, 11 July 1818 to 23 October 1819. A selection from the articles was published in the latter year.

5/In Dundee Hood had lodged with Rollo, Robert Miln, and Andrew Wyllie, 'within a few yards of the High Street:' Elliot, 44, 48. Wyllie died in autumn 1828. Miln became a prominent Dundee lawyer, and died at the age of forty-four, during Hood's visit in September 1843.

6/In the MS 'friend: – ' is written above the line.

7/Rollo's home in Dundee

8/MS reads 'Mill.'
9/Centring upon the clash at St Peter's Field, 16 August 1819 – 'Peterloo'
10/This phase of Hood's life is discussed by Lawrance, 323.

1820

TO
GEORGE ROLLO

Dear George, – I received your obliging letter per Mr Wyllie, and am grateful to you for the great pleasure which it afforded me.

I promised Mr W. to call on him and try his strength at chess, which I have yet been unable to do, for Christmas brought me no vacation, and this, I trust, will excuse and account with you for my delay in answering your letter.

I have the pleasure in being able to tell you that the improvement in my health leaves me now little to wish for on that head, added to which my business and connection gradually extend. In short, that I succeed as well as I can reasonably expect in these days of universal depression. The little crosses and vexations, and the chicaneries of business in general, are now less new to me, and I can meet them with comparative calmness, so that in another year I hope to be tolerably settled.

I have made an alteration in the nature of my amusements, and flatter myself that they have now a more useful tendency, and may in the end be of benefit both to myself and others. I sometimes devote an hour to little mechanical inventions connected with my pursuits, and sometime ago completed a little instrument which I deem would be serviceable in copying drawings, etc. I sent it to the Society of Arts, and had the honour of explaining it before the Society's Committee on Mechanics, but found they were in possession of a similar one for the same purpose I had never seen. This was rather unlucky, but I have another one in progress which may succeed better. At anyrate I lose nothing.

I am at present trying to perfect an instrument for drawing lines to meet in a point at any distance, as used in perspective, in order to be able to draw them without going beyond the margin of your drawing, and thus obviating the inconvenience of having to rule so far.[1]

Since writing the above I have had the pleasure of seeing Mr Wyllie, who called to inquire the reason of my not seeing him, and I have returned his visit, and have, moreover, engaged him at chess, gaining five battles out of six. But one trial, of course, is not sufficient to determine the mastery. I must confess that I was afraid my want of practice would have served me worse, but, after leaving your country *unconquered*, I was resolved not to be beaten by your countryman on my own ground if I could help it. I shall now provide myself with a set, which I have hitherto been without for mere want of somebody of play with. It is true that a young lady within a few doors of us desires me to teach her to play at chess, but to learn it requires so much patience that I am not anxious to attempt the task, recollecting that Job was not a woman.

I should much like to know if Messieux has returned, and to have his address at St. Andrews, if you could procure it for me. He called here when I was with you, but I have not heard of or from him since. If ever you see him in Dundee I wish you would tell him to send it himself, or come with it himself, – whichever may be most convenient.

With respect to what you are pleased to call my poem,[2] you may delay it till any convenient time, as it is of no other use to me but to show of what has been the nature of my amusements. I cannot now find time for anything of the kind, except a few short bagatelles as New Year compliments, etc. etc. And, let me here, in adverting to those compliments, present you with my sincere wishes for that happiness which one friend should wish to another, and which it is customary to offer rather earlier; but, I assure you, they have not lost in strength like some things by long keeping, and therefore still are fit for me to present to you for yours and your brother's acceptance – only, that I regret to be thus obliged to send them wrapped up in paper!

I have said that I cannot find time to write such things now – and, indeed, after the study and close application necessary in engraving, it would cease to be any relaxation. But, independent of this employment, I have to keep my books (not my *ledger*, for that is kept too easily), but my rote and plate books, in which I keep account of any hints, occurrences, discoveries, instructions, etc. etc., relative to the art, together with a journal of my own operations and transactions – history of my plates, my own comments and those of others, difficulties, failures, successes, etc. etc. etc. etc., so that I have enough to do in that way. Altogether, these compose rather a medlied history, and one perhaps that will afford me more pleasure to peruse hereafter than it does at present.

In fact, I am now obliged to turn the amusing, if I can, into the *profitable*, not that I am ambitious or of a very money-loving disposition, but I am obliged to be so. Otherwise, I believe, if left to myself, I should be content with a very moderate station, for, like you, I believe I am of a 'domestic indolent turn.' But this is all speculative reasoning, perhaps; and I might find – that summit attained – that the content was as far off as ever, increasing by a kind of arithmetical progression. Thus, when seen from the valley, the summit of the mountain appears to touch the skies; but when we have ascended and reached its top, we seem, and no doubt are, as far from heaven as ever![3]

The most provoking part of my profession is that the fame and the profit are so connected that those who wish to decrease the price can only do it by depreciating the merit and withholding that fame which is, in fact, part of the price. This is all so much the worse for me, now that I have grown so wise, that if they took away the former I could philosophically console myself with the latter, I find that I am not yet quite *sharp* enough to cope with veteran men of business, but suppose every rub they give me will make my wit much keener. I am now tolerably content with what I pay for my experience, considering I have just concluded my first year's apprenticeship to the world.

I hope you will decipher this, for I see it is vilely scrawled; but deeming it more friendly to meet you *en déshabillé* than to deny myself to you, I send it with this one request that you will put those stops which I cannot stop to put.

Remember me kindly to your brother and all friends, and believe me, dear George, yours very truly,

Thos. Hood.

P.S. – I do not know anybody through whom you may send anything except Wyllie, unless Captain Lyon[4] would bring it here.

Somewhere near Islington Church, Sometime about 7th February. [*1820*]

From Elliot 109–13. Though Elliot suggests the date of 1819, it was on 26 January 1820 that Hood gave the explanation of his mechanical invention, to which he refers in the letter. The letter must therefore have been written after this date.

1/Nothing is known of the second invention.
2/'The Bandit,' a Byronic poem, first published by Elliot 73–102
3/The image occurs in Pope *Essay on Criticism* 225–32.
4/Charles Lyon was captain of the trading smack aboard which Hood had travelled to Dundee.

TO
ROBERT MILN

Dear Rob, – I have sent to my friend Rollo, – who will hand you this letter, – the book which you have requested me to send to you – the *Dundee Guide* – and which I have been unable to procure till lately.

Upon looking it over I think that many of the subjects to which it refers will now be out of date, and particularly that part of it beginning –

'And the French jockey hat is now worn in this town,' and ending at –

'He without her consent would not steal e'en a kiss,' which I have marked for you to omit in case you should make that use of it which was proposed.[1] It would be better, I presume, to send a few of the letters together instead of a single one at first, in order that the editor might see the design of them; and I shall endeavour to send a preface addressed to that gentleman, in case you should think proper, on conference with Mr R.,[2] to make use of them.

I have numbered the letters in the order in which I should wish them to follow, and marked some omissions in pencil.

I fear they are not worth the trouble of your writing out, and I cannot forget that *lawyers* are not over fond of writing for nothing.

I have now no news, but, hoping for at least as many lines in return, I am, dear Bob, yours truly,

Thos. Hood.

P.S. – I write, as you will perceive, in great haste.

Preface.[3]

Sir, – Although it is well known that Bath and Cheltenham have been visited by the celebrated Blunderhead Family, it has hitherto been unknown that some of their descendants have visited the town of Dundee in strict incognito.

This fact is, however, confirmed by some letters which have fallen into my hands, which I have arranged, and with the permission of the author, now send to be inserted, if you think fit, in your weekly paper.

Some subjects to which they refer may now be partially out of date, as they were written in 1815, but some remarks may still be applicable, – I am, Sir, yours, etc.

Thos. Hood.

Lower Street, Islington, May 1820.

From Elliott 118–20

1/All the 'Dundee Guide,' apart from the section quoted in Hood's early letter to his aunts (7–10), subsequently disappeared.

2/Perhaps Rollo, or Robert Stephen Rintoul (1787–1858), editor of the *Dundee Advertiser* (1811–25), later of *The Spectator* (1828–58). Neither of these men appears to have used the letters.

3/Elliot notes: 'Hood did not wait to write the preface separately to the editor, but indites it on the fly-leaf of the same letter he sent to Miln.'

1821

TO

GEORGE ROLLO

Dear George, – Mr Wyllie, in bringing me your welcome letter, found me very busy upon a plate from a drawing of a gentleman's seat which I told you, I think, nearly a year ago, I was endeavouring to obtain. I have just got it, and, as it is for a very fine work, I am obliged to pay very close attention to it, working from ten morning till ten or eleven o'clock at night for these last three weeks, so that this Christmas season has brought me no holidays.[1] But as I had been more idle before, and hunting for business rather than doing it (a general case now), I sit down to it cheerfully, and especially, as it shall open to me, if I succeed, a new and wider path. I have done so far as to form some idea of how it will be, and am induced to hope favourably.

From the midst of all this I write in order to ease your mind on the subject of a disaster, which in vexing you one hour has vexed you more than it has me, for I assure you your description of it had no other effect than that of making me laugh. The sudden and mysterious disappearance of the *Dundee Guide* has in it something so romantic as to make a very fine sequel to its history, by leading one to imagine that Apollo – or one of the Nine Muses, perhaps – had taken possession of it. I will tell you, too, a secret for your comfort, that the loss, even if great, would not be irreparable, for I could, if necessary, write afresh from memory, and nearly verbatim. It is the same with nearly all the rest of my effusions, some of which I shall hereafter send for your perusal, to show you that I do not consider you the 'careless friend' you represent yourself to be. I continue to receive much pleasure from our literary society, and from my own pursuits in that way – in which, considering my little time, I am very industrious – that is to say, I spoil a deal of paper. My last is a mock heroic love tale of 600 lines, with notes critical and explanatory, which I lately finished after many intervals, independent of two poetical addresses to the society on closing and opening a fresh session, with various pieces, chiefly amatory. The society only costs me a page or two once in three months or so, but I join in their discussions every fortnight, if able.[2] I receive few visits, and I pay still fewer, and thus my time wears away.

I am very happy, however, when I have time, to pay my visits on paper, as I now do, because I am sure of a greater pleasure in its being returned, not that I mean to stand on ceremonies with you more than Wyllie, for as we do not regularly balance visit against visit, so if it comes into my head to send you two letters for one, I shall not stick at it, and if you do the same, I shall not feel offended by such a breach of punctilio.

I have had no letter from Messieux, and feel obliged to you for your offer to him that you would forward any letter to me. I shall write to him ere long, and, as I know not where to find him, I shall perhaps give you the trouble of directing it and forwarding it to him. I learned from the newspaper the dreadful accident to which you have carried my attention in your letter, and have no doubt of its being an inexpressible shock to Mrs Brown. If you recollect, there was a pistol with which Messieux and I used to amuse ourselves, and is, I daresay, the one which has proved fatal to poor Henry.[3]

I am the more anxious to open or rather renew a correspondence with M., because – and I am sorry to say it – I see no prospect of seeing you or him next summer, not that I could make any trip more agreeable, but that I shall be able to make no trips at all. I find that I shall have so much to do to establish myself in business properly, and to attain to proficiency in an art which has made so great a progress towards excellence, that I shall have no time at my command, unless I should be able to get a long plate, and do it down with you; and, indeed, if I were engraving there you would have so little of my company as to make it of little or no consequence whether I were there or in London. I shall therefore defer my visit till I can make a thorough holiday of it, and enjoy the company of my friends without interruption.

I should like very much to make with you the tour you propose to make next summer. I could there find first-rate subjects for my pencil; and I wonder that so many persons who can or will travel do not first visit those places in their own country and neighbourhood which could afford them so fine scenery and so great hospitality as the Highlands of Scotland. These, and the western lakes in Cumberland and Westmoreland, I would rather visit, and next to these the romantic and wild scenery of Switzerland.

I hope that Sylvester's[4] translation to Glasgow will be a step towards advancement and happiness. You will, no doubt, regret that he should have to go there while you are stationary; but I hope that, nevertheless, they will not be prevented from coming to you where you are, lest when I go to Dundee I should have to look in vain for you, who are amongst my last friends there.

Grey[5] called on me here some months ago. He came only *en passant*, and was not long enough for me to learn what brought him to London. I was not very desirous of inviting him to an intimacy, for reasons you will readily guess, and I have not seen him again. But with Wyllie I am very thick, as you call it, and we have a duo at flutes and a duel at chess with great pleasure. He told you, no doubt, of his success at the latter, and I begin to doubt if I shall ever regain those laurels I once wore. But I am not cowed, and in a few days I hope to open a fresh campaign with greater success. He drank tea here together with Bailie Thoms' son,[6] who is also a player at chess, but as yet untried by me. I would not advise him to attack me now, for Wyllie has worked me up so, that like an urchin that has been thumped, I am ready to wreak my revenge upon anyone I meet – even though it should be yourself.

Since writing the preceding I have been waiting for a call from Wyllie to send it, but he has stayed away longer than usual, and I have been unable to call on him, as his business is on the other side of the city to where my business lies. I have also had more business on my hands these last six weeks than I ever had before; for, besides the plate I mentioned, I have three others all in hand at once, which I am obliged to superintend. I have been successful in the plate which has cost me so much anxiety; and the result of four years' learning and experience in the art will appear in a work along with those of my former master,[7] and of others who have generally served apprenticeships of seven years. I was but two years old in engraving when I set up for myself, and have been two more on my own fingers; and, as some of my friends seemed doubtful as to the success of such an experiment, I am very happy and somewhat proud of this result, in which I have obtained one object of my ambition.

I shall send with this or hereafter an impression of my plate for your acceptance, as a thing of no value, but as a token of my regard and esteem. I find that I shall not be able to send my poems to you for sometime, as they are in the hands of an intelligent bookseller, a friend of mine, who wishes to look them over.[8] He says that they are worth publishing, but I doubt very much if he would give me any proof of his opinion, or I should indulge in the hope of sending them to you in a more durable shape.

Wyllie has called, but I have been so busy – sometimes till two or three in the morning – that I could not really finish this. Besides the four plates, I have had two others as soon as I could finish two of the first, so that I am just where I was. I have not been able, therefore, to call on Wyllie till the date of this. I send, however, the engraving, and something for Messieux, which I will trouble you and thank you to forward at your convenience. I do not know his address, but, if you take charge of it, I have no doubt of its reaching him. I hope to write more at leisure next time, and am, dear George, yours truly,

Thos. Hood.

Lower Street [*Islington*], *Feb. 20, 1821.*

From Elliot 121–6. Elliot heads the letter 'sometime 1820,' and in view of the concluding date, 'Feb. 20, 1821,' comments that its contents 'extend over fully a year.' I prefer the dating 'sometime January 1820–20 February 1821.'

1/See 14 n3 above.
2/Hood's quiet activity in this society from the spring of 1820 is dealt with by Lawrance, 323. One of the addresses, dated July 1820, is printed in *Works* x 15–20.
3/The accident was reported in *Dundee Perth and Cupar Advertiser* 20 October 1820. Henry Brown, son of Mrs Lawrence Brown, was accidentally killed by a pistol he and his playmates found at the home of Captain Mason in St Andrews.
4/Unidentified
5/An acquaintance of Miln and Wyllie, Grey belonged to a firm of timber merchants in Dundee.
6/Unidentified
7/Probably Robert Sands
8/John Taylor (1781–1864), the publisher of Keats and editor and publisher of the *London Magazine*. He wrote on 23 August 1820 concerning Hood: 'His Talents are very good, & he has written several clever things in Prose & Verse. It occurred to me that his Assistance would relieve me from a good deal of the Drudgery of revising MSS etc,' MS Keats House, Hampstead. Nothing immediately came of this plan.

TO GEORGE ROLLO

Dear George, – You are a pretty fellow to send me such a short letter, and, if it were not for fear of falling short myself, I should scold you. But I heartily forgive you for hastening it, even in its infant state, or half grown, that I might sooner have the benefit of the enclosures.

That must, indeed, be your excuse for me, for I would have heard of no other. Your town, I know, is barren of news, and ours is all sent you by the papers, but I can feed upon very slight food, and the description of even a fishing excursion or anything of that kind would be very agreeable; or, if you were to sketch me any odd character who may fall in your way, or any odd sayings or stories. I know that you once dealt in such things, and I have not lost my relish for them.

As for me, I am just scribbling a Cockney's sentimental journey from Islington to Waterloo Bridge[1] – about three miles – so what a letter you ought to be able to give me by and by about your excursion to the Highlands, with kilts and Ben-Somethings and Loch-Somethings, and I know not what!

I wish I could go with you, and so do you, and so does R. Miln – but I have told the latter why I cannot. I have a literary engagement which will occupy my leisure time (that is to say, what I have heretofore devoted to scribbling), so that I shall not only write now for Pleasure but for Profit; and I begin to have hopes that what I have scribbled in verse will make its appearance in a little volume, and, should that be decided on, I shall necessarily have a great addition to my occupation in arranging, correcting, etc. etc., but I expect that they will, in that case, be out by Christmas.[2]

I do not think my health will suffer, for I shall be obliged to go out rather more than I perhaps should do voluntarily, and you may mention this to R.M. for his comfort. He says he supposes I am making my fortune, but he is out there, and, consequently, as I could not leave him anything if I were to die to-morrow, he may wish for my long life most sincerely.

I have written to him that I would rather the *Dundee Guide* should remain unknown, *for I think I can do better things*; and as for the other things (this 'Bandit,' I believe), it is yours if you like it.

I see our friend Wyllie as often as possible. We went together to an exhibition of paintings, some time since, and last Thursday he went with me to our Society, where I gave an essay on Poetry to close the session. But chess I must resign, my head is now so much occupied. Methinks I hear you say, what an altered being I must be to give up chess, and that, too, when I have been beaten! But, from the cause just mentioned, I have ceased to find any amusement in it, and therefore there is no hope of retrieving my laurels. Even my flute I must use but sparingly, although it delights me with my own music when I can get no better. But Health! health! – (show this to R. Miln) – I sacrifice them both to health! And as for my paper concerns, I can take them into a garden (and luckily we have one), so that I shall not want for fresh air.

I received very great joy from M. Messieux's letter, being only the second since our separation, and have answered it, as you will perceive. I do not know whether I may not be giving you great trouble to forward them to him; but, if not, I shall feel obliged by your becoming the medium of communication. There is never anything in my letters that will cool by waiting, so that you can take any opportunity of himself or his friend being in Dundee to forward them; but pray let me know how the matter stands.

I know not how it is that I find more time to write, now that I have more to do;

but it may be that I am more settled, and have got into more of a routine; and, perhaps, above all, I am oftener in the mood for writing. At any rate, I am happy, on looking back, to find that I can keep it up so well, all things considered.
I confess that I want subject more than inclination generally, for I am sick, and you will be too, of eternally writing about Self. But we may sometime start some interesting subject of controversy and inquiry, and then we shall go on better. And as those who challenge give the choice of weapons, so I, who propose, give you the choice of subjects; and I hope in your next you will give me some such things as I have mentioned in the beginning to comment upon. What think you of a discussing of Angling, which I know you are fond of? Pray give me some description of its pleasures, etc. etc. etc., and I will reply all that I can, *pro* and *con.*
Having paved the way, as I imagine, for long letters, I shall end this; and, though I have only occupied a page more than yours, yet, taking my dwarf hand into account, I think that I have really given you '*two for one.*' – I am, dear George, yours very truly,

Thos. Hood.

P.S. – It has been said that an angling rod and line hath a fool at one end and a worm at the other. I do not believe this, and want your vindication.

[*Islington*] *June 17, 1821.*

From Elliott 129–32
1/In *London Magazine* November 1821, 508–15
2/John Taylor wrote in the same month concerning Hood: 'he can give me assistance in correcting proofs, etc., for the Mag., and can look over some of the immense load of communications which are poured down before me ... I can return to him by this way some of the kindnesses I received from his good father': quoted by Olive M. Taylor, 'John Taylor' *London Mercury* 1925, 262. The volume to which Hood refers did not appear.

TO
JOHN TAYLOR

My dear Friend,
I have long promised in my heart that I would thus convey to you upon paper what I have not dared to entrust to my tongue; but if I have delayed the expression of my deep sense of your kindness and my thanks for the manner in which it has been displayed, it resulted only from the unsettled state of my mind, and a fear of my inability to do justice to my feelings.

Had I been ever inclined to underrate acts of Friendship, the loss of my dear Father and the consequent tenour of my life would have taught me their full value; and indeed I have learned to feel the full force & worth of the least expressions and even looks of kindness. But in justice to my heart I must declare that without this experience and ever since the death of my brother,[1] I have held you in affectionate remembrance – Your kind attentions to him in his last days would have insured my eternal gratitude even had there been no happiness in loving one who was his Friend, nor any in the hope that I might inherit those mutual feelings which must have been as delightful to him as they are now to myself. With this hope I have always had a firm reliance upon your Friendship, would tell you if I could, how much joy I have felt in finding that I was not deceived; but I have received so many proofs of it in words, looks, and deeds that I am quite unable to make you a sufficient acknowledgement. I would thank you in particular for its' late exertion in a way which is not only useful to me but highly agreable and in nothing more so than in bringing me so frequently to your company and conversation.
In the [future?] I wish that my abilities may be equal to your kindness and then I shall have no fear of not assisting you more effectually & more to my own satisfaction than in my first essays. –
In the mean time I am impelled to give you without delay what I know will be more grateful to you than any expressions or feelings of my own – and more proportioned to the extent of your Friendship than any thing else which I am able to offer. When I tell you that your kindness contributed to soothe the last days of my dear Mother – that she mentioned your name amongst her last thoughts and desired me to make to you her acknowledgements, I feel that I can add but a request that you will speak her sincere thanks in the language most grateful to your own heart, for I am assured that they were so intended. –
I have seen the end of the best of Mothers. She expired with her head upon my arm. – her eyes burning towards me with their wonted fondness, till the Spirit which looked thro them was called away and dragging my arm from the lifeless weight which it supported, I resigned my dear Mother for ever. It was a shock which in spite of long preparation was almost too much for me, & had it not been a release from a state of great suffering and agony at times; would have been quite overwhelming. But I have now no sorrow but for the loss of so much goodness & affection, & the regret that I may not nurse her & comfort her in a grey haired age. I have had the consolation of being with her & performing all the little offices in my power, for her comfort, and I have received from her the last marks of an affection which I can only deserve by the most affectionate regard to her

memory and a warm and unceasing kindness to her orphan children –
My mind is recovering its composure, but I am rather unwell from the fatigue & agitation which I have undergone of late, and I think a cold which I have caught in sleeping in the next room to my dear Mother, with the windows open. I have never felt such violent transitions from pain to pleasure as at the alternate, delirious, & sensible intervals with my dear Mother. In the first she could always recognize me but it was only in the last that with a feebler & calmer voice she resumed all her affection.
But at the last she was perfectly sensible and I had a late opportunity of learning that she had no further wishes upon earth & that in her mind at least she was perfectly comfortable & happy.
I request that you will show this letter to my friend Mr Hessey,[2] and assure him for me that I have the same feelings towards him as to yourself – for I am sure that he has been your partner in all kindness & good deeds toward me –

I am with sincere respect
My dear friend –
Yours very truly

Thos Hood

Lower Street, Islington/Thursday Morning [*July 1821*]

MS UCLA. Address: 'Mr Taylor.' The letter treats of the recent death of Hood's mother, in July 1821.
1/In December 1811
2/Taylor's business partner (1785–1870)

TO
GEORGE ROLLO

Dear George.
I write to you for several reasons viz 1st because my Sister is going to Dundee[1] – 2d Because I have not heard from you for a long time and 3rd to give you a troublesome commission. My youngest Sister is going on a Visit to her aunt Mrs Keay and will forward this to you, in order that you may provide me with a Plaid against my Winter campaign. There are such things to be got here – but I apprehend not so good – and I shall be sure to fancy it more for coming bona fide from Scotland as it is such a national article and moreover when I shall be wrapped in it I may fancy that I am in Dundee. – therefore, – you will oblige me by chusing me one &

ordering it to be made as follows. To tell you the truth I have fallen in love with our friend Wyllie's and should like one of the same family (a twin) that is to say a Stuart – and if that should be troublesome to get, I will put up with a Kyd or a (I have forgot this name but I will ask Wyllie and write it outside)[2] – but I should prefer the Royal Stuart on account of the romantic & practical associations connected with it. – The collar red shag (or green if there be green, if not, red) – the body without sleeves like Andrew's but not lined (and a large loose cape lined with green) I must write this outside too.) – and – and – and – that is all except have the goodness to pay for it for which purpose I enclose £2. which Andrew tells me was about the price of his – but at all events we will settle that – and now about the size – I am about 5ft 9inches high, and as thick as a rushlight, and I hope that will be measure sufficient. I think Wyllie calls his a Rachan (or some such name which I cannot pronounce upon paper)[3] but I hope you will know what I want and how large it ought to be – I think as I have described it, that it covers about a page of paper so enough of it. I trust it will not be a very troublesome commission, in which hope I send it but if it is at all likely to be so I beg that you will not take it upon you but let me give up my idea of Scottish fancies & associations – Bless me Geordie what's come owre ye, Man, that ye canna wwrite?[4]
I hope your hand is not rheumatised. I do nothing but write write day & night but I cannot resist a letter now and then and if my present fit continues this is likely to be a long letter. I was told or else I dreamt that a large trout (as muckle as a saumont) had put both your wrists out, and that you were past scribing, and consequently could not write to me a letter upon the Pleasures of Fishing as I had proposed to you to do. If it be true then write upon some other subject & you will forget your disaster – if you cannot use your fingers – tak your taes til't and I shall not mind the handwriting. Write at all events – whether you can or not – If you have nothing to say – say so. Perhaps if the truth must be told you are waiting for Messieux, but if the horses were to wait for the coach to move the mail would stand still – I shall perchance enclose a letter for that Gentleman to be forwarded at your leisure. –

Perhaps you will ask what I am doing. Why truly I am T. Hood Scripsit et sculpsit. – I am engraving and writing prose & Poetry by turns – I have some papers coming forth in next Months London Magazine signed Incog.[5] and in the meantime I am busy extending & correcting my long Poem and other pieces – perhaps for Publication –

I have a great deal to do now – more than ever but I have got my affairs into more regularity and therefore go on smoothly to what I did – but I have sustained a very severe and irreparable loss in the death of my dear Mother about three months since – by which event a very serious charge has devolved upon me and I have all the concern of a Household & a Family of 4 Sisters – a charge which can never be a light one – I have suffered an inexpressible anguish of mind in parting with my only Parent and but for the consolations which I have had I should have sunk under it. I have now recovered a great degree of my cheerfulness and though an event will be a cloud upon all my happiness my other prospects are brighter, – and enable me to look forward with a pleasure which I cannot have however without a sigh whilst I look behind. – The writing for the London – is a very agreable employment for my mind & prevents my thoughts from pressing upon me as they otherwise would do.

There appears now a prospect of my seeing you for should my Sister stay thro the Winter I shall most probably fetch her. In this I anticipate much pleasure as I shall be able to reach Lochee – yea & much further & perhaps see more of Scotland than I have ever done – but I must hush upon that subject as it is too long for any prudent man to look forward.

After a long interval I have attacked our friend again at Chess and with better success for our meetings stand thus –

H. W
1.. — —
2 —
1 drawn –

But I had a balance against me in our last campaign of 40 or 30. – which I do not expect to pay off –

Last Sunday we (Andrew & I) went to a very fine garden &c. & if you are at all a Botanist I shall regret that you were not with us – There were a green house 500 feet long, full of camelias and a hot house 40 feet high – the whole warmed by steam carried in two miles of pipe. The latter house was the great wonder being full of African & other plants – of the gigantic kind – Palm trees 30 feet high extremely beautiful – screw palm – fan palm – bread fruit – [word illegible] – teak – cinnamon – clove – all spice – and specimens of very rare and beautiful plants – there was also a contrivance by which they were watered by an artificial rain in small drops or rather a dew produced by turning a few cocks. There was a very beautiful passiflora and the wonderful pitcher plant each leaf containing about a table spoonfull of clear water – Mimosa and other curiosities.[6] I just mention this subject because if I recollect right you are a Gardener, or a Botanist neither of which am I. – but say you why go on Sunday? – Truly because we could not on any other day – but W.

and I went to Chapel in the evening & heard rather a ridiculous Sermon. W. has twice taken me to Chapel when otherwise I should not have gone & this was the second.

And now the end of my paper gives me warning to end – I am writing to you with my head in my night-cap & my legs & lower half in bed – my watch says ½ past 12 – and I am very dozy or I would take a fresh sheet. I shall be writing another against yours arrives with a packet for Messieux. I am Dear George Yours very truly

Thos Hood

Lower Street, Islington/October 11th 1821

MS Osborn. Published by Elliot 133-7

1/Elizabeth Hood, 'Betsy,' visited her Dundee aunt Mrs Jean Keay, but only for a short time; the exact dates are not known.

2/The name is not given.

3/Alex. Warrack, *A Scots Dialect Dictionary* (1911), gives 'Rachan, *n*, a plaid worn by men.'

4/The double 'w' in this last word is perhaps to indicate the Scottish burr.

5/'The Departure of Summer' and 'A Sentimental Journey' *London Magazine* November 1821, 493–5, 508–15

6/Hood may have visited 'Loddiges' garden at Hackney,' to which he refers in 'Literary Reminiscences,' *Works* II 382.

1822

TO
MRS CHARLOTTE REYNOLDS

My Dear Mother, for so I may now call you, with how deep affection do I redeem all that I owe to that blessed name, feeling that I am indeed your son in perfect respect and duty. Only in this can I have deserved to be so dear to you, that you would bestow on me thus willingly an object of so much of your love as our excellent Jane. She is beside me while I pen this, and as I look at her, I know that what I write is a record of one eternal and unchangeable feeling which is to become more and more intense as I approach her great worth. So much the likeness of my wishes, – so worthy of all admiration and affection that I should indeed exceed all others in the measure of my love as she in her virtues is excellent above all. Therefore I have singled her from the world, to be to me its grace and ornament, and its treasure above price, being proud above all things of her favour, and for this once, of my wisdom in this choice. And I desire that you should believe, that it is only for herself that I have loved, and will constantly while this life endures, which she has so blessed, and that in this only I can hold myself at all worthy of her invaluable heart. For I know that there is nothing like it in this world for excellence, and that its affection must of itself be my perfect happiness, whether I live or die, and in this knowledge I look forward with hopeful impatience to the time when I may claim her as mine for ever. And in the meantime I will always remember your exceeding kindness, and rest my everlasting love upon you and yours. Indeed, I have desired – but could not hope – that my happiness should be nothing but welcome to you, and perfect content, – but you have adopted me into your family in a manner that has made me twice grateful, and before I can forget it – and after – I must be as entirely miserable as I am now otherwise. I could not dream that so many would take me at once to their warm hearts, making me both exult and wonder, but hoped only that I might win such affection hereafter by becoming what you now believe me, and such as your welcome praise will most surely make me. I may thus prove a gratitude, which otherwise will not be expressed but to my own heart, making me distrust all words, and I pray God thus to bless you through me, that I may only be a addition to that happiness which through John has lately visited us.[1] I would not cost a sigh or a tear to any of you, nor a painful thought, so entirely is my love among you, that I would rather die than bring a grief to interfere with your affectionate union with one another. Our good Lizzy,[2] as I have learned to call her, has touched me deeply by her kind words, for I have seen quite enough of her to make me anxious to win her regard, and for this reason I have ever since been most earnest in wishes, – and now drink her birthday health with a brother's affection. I wish Upwell[3] were near Mrs. Butler's,[4] or near anywhere, that I might tell her audibly of this. Do not let her think that Jane, our dear Jane, can make me forget her, for we often mention her among other pleasant matters, such as Lotty,[5] for instance, to whom I am the dear Brother Theodore, that she has so baptized. I will never be otherwise, and would be if I could only a second edition (with alterations) of John, but this is to wish very much indeed, and I know my dear Lotty will so take it. I love Marianne,[6] too, though she is not at Upwell, – indeed, I think I like her rather better because she is not at Kennington. I ought to say much about our other dear Lizzy and John but I write in the midst of distractions.

Pray forgive me that I have not said this much even at an earlier time – I have longed to write but could not, and feel now how little in this haste I have done justice to my feelings, but I now know that you regard me as what I truly am. God bless you, my dear mother, my dear Lizzy, my dear Lotty, and all that are dear to yo[u], and believe me, one and all, your most affectionate

Theodo[re]

[*Islington, September 1822*]

From Jerrold 125–7. Mrs Charlotte Reynolds (1761–1848) was the wife of George (1764/5–1853). Mrs Reynolds later wrote her own novel, in the publication of which she was helped by Hood. Her husband had been a pupil at Christ's Hospital school. He taught at Shrewsbury and then became writing master at Christ's Hospital (1817–35). They lived in Little Britain, London. They had five children, all of whom are mentioned in the following letters: Jane (1791–1846), John Hamilton (1794–1852), Marianne (1797–1874), Eliza (b 1799), and Charlotte (1802–84). Jane married Hood in 1825. John, himself a poet and miscellaneous writer, later a lawyer, married Eliza Drewe at the end of August 1822. Marianne married H.G. Green sometime before 1833. Eliza married Dr George Longmore of Upwell, Norfolk, in February 1822. Charlotte remained a spinster. The family had been friends of Keats before his death in February 1821. Hood probably came to know them through John, as a fellow contributor to the *London Magazine*, from mid-1821. He is here writing to Mrs Reynolds, who was staying at Upwell, the new home of her daughter Eliza.

1/Through his marriage
2/Eliza Reynolds Longmore
3/The Longmores' home
4/Perhaps John Reynolds's wife's aunt, who lived at Kennington Common
5/Charlotte Reynolds, presumably also at Upwell
6/The fourth Reynolds daughter

TO
MISS CHARLOTTE REYNOLDS

My Dear Lotty, – How often have you turned your spiritual eye this way and aimed at us with your mental telescope? How often has fancy worked us into a piece like a schoolgirl's with double refined cobwebs, till memory came like a great buzzing blue-bottle and tore it into nothings? How often have you painted Mrs. John Reynolds as faint as water-colours thrice drowned and tease your wits to death for the finishing? Surely you must sometimes have felt your mind's eye at work this way in the middle of your forehead like a Cyclops, or as if you had a camera obscura where your brain ought to be. You must have been here, there, and everywhere. Sometimes seeming – in the body – to be playing at draughts with Mr. Longmore or breaking in a grey pony – or tickling the strings of music till it bursts into merry song – or mingling a part of your voice with Eliza's – but in spirit fluttering about like a midge in the sunshine of Little Britain and stealing a tiny taster into the ripe of our happiness. Indeed, your thoughts have been a part of our atmosphere and I have not been unconscious of your presence – using your familiar name with all affectionate reverence, and handling the peculiar china with a proper five-fingered fear. For – (I only repeat the family supersition) – the piano has played to me of itself – Jane and Marianne, poor dears, have heard noises – and, above all, Mrs. John R. is said to have felt the kisses she knew not wherefrom – but I say, Upwell. I saw her put her hand to her cheek the other evening, and the flies have been long gone. Oh, Lotty, is not she a sweet, kind, unaffected – and didn't John look well! – so merry, and so happy, and so like a fly in a honey-pot, as Rice[1] says – and I'm sure he loves the taste of his wings. And we have been so joyous round him as if he were a common centre of sweets like a sugar cask with all the little loves round it –

'So many and so many and such glee!'[2]

You must have been there sometimes. Nor has your good Mother turned the back of her mind upon us altogether. Jane has met her at the cupboard and the carving-knife, and I have seen her in her seat – and doubtless she has been here, not indeed by coach, but drawn by a 'team of little atomies'[3] – to watch our visible enjoyment with invisible eyes. Well Heaven give her some day a good safety coach and horses not given to drink, and we shall see her again – I have such a shake in my hand for her.

I was quite overjoyed to hear of your safe arrival after the adventurous journey which it proved to be – I shall quite love you if it be only for the perils you have passed,[4] as if of all days in all years you must needs go at the very hour of the opening of the fifty arch bridge at St. Ives, and do for it what the Duke of Wellington did here at Waterloo.[5] I could see that your Mother enjoyed it, putting her so much in mind of the Procession – with that train of people behind her holding themselves up instead of cupids – and then St. Hives and the honeycomb – and that simple Maid of the Inn[6] with her simple congratulation as if you had never opened a bridge before in your lives! It was very pleasant to be sure, and the very affectionate greeting of your head against mine at that sudden jolt when the traces broke, – what a mercy it was not the wheel – and our diverting search after your Mother's glasses among the tangled perplexities of the straw, will long endure in my remembrance, and the more pleasantly as our progress was unattended by any accident to the crowd. That man putting his silly wooden leg like a spoke in our wheel, and that pieman jamming his tarts through the window, made incidents more married to mirth than to misery and if your Mother had been a little less alarmed, the whole would have been extremely amusing. – But what is the use of telling you of what you know, and saw, and heard? I might as well describe Eliza to you or Mr. Longmore and draw a ground plan of Upwell with the water before the house, or repeat your own conversation with the gipsies, telling the story twice over – so stay – and I will draw you a little picture – as I saw it on Monday evening in that Blue Beard room of Little Britain, and so 'tease you out of thought'[7] about us and ours. You know the place – the folding doors – the tables, the two windows – the fire-place – the antique china teapots which if they were hearts, would break themselves for your absence – the sofa – and on it with her eyes like compressed stars, and her eloquent brows – but your father will tell you about those – and her mouth like somebody's you have never seen, and with her easy grace of manner which Jane will tell you of – and her smile which herself will show you – sits the unimaginable reality – the tantalizing mystery – the still-undiscovered Mrs. Reynolds – Mrs. John – John's wife – with a great thick misty veil between her and Upwell – which Jane is trying to fan away with a very circumstantial piece of paper – but it won't do – you must still wish to see her, and then see her to your wish – as I have done.[8] – Only look at John – what a talk he makes! With the horns of his mouth upwards like a fair moon – laughing like a fugleman[9] to let off our laughters – and lo! that farce brown with the steel but – and then that – like a footman with – did you ever see such a – it is impossible to describe it. There – between me and the teapot – her cheek the very colour of content, and her eyes how earnest, sits Jane, the kindly Jane – hugging her own hands for very happiness – she one side of me – I beside myself – and on the other hand gentle maid Marianne, making go[od] tea as if for Robin Hood and smiling

as if her heart drank cream and sugar. How the tea dimples in the cup and the urn sings for joy! Now if you look through the urn you will see your father smiling towards the sofa, and there is Rice smiling towards nine o'clock. How slily the under half of his visage sneers at the upper gravity, as if his nose were Garrick between Tragedy and Comedy,[10] and how his jests come stealing seriously out as if from his sleeve. There is Mrs. Butler with a face that Good Nature might borrow for a year's wear – and there are John Lincoln and William[11] – 'my friend,' as it hath been said. – And there in the distance, looking blue as is usual with such objects, is Lotty in the background of Upwell; – peeping perhaps thro' a little opera glass that diminishes us to nothing. This is the picture that I saw on Monday at Little Britain, – with all the drawing-room for its frame – but it will not leave the country and when you come to town therefore you may chance to see it, or one quite as good. So in the meantime comfort yourself at Upwell with your own Eliza, – and remember that happiness hath a home everywhere giving this to that and that to this[12] – we have no poney.
I ought to tell you that I have been to Kennington where Mrs. Butler grows a great deal of pleasure for the use of her friends, as I found – and indeed I brought mine home with me to keep as a dried flower through the Winter. To-night we all meet at Rice's, and I shall see Mrs. R. for the second time; for which I reserve my intended letter for your good Mother. Pray remember me to her as kindly as you can – and do not let me lose ground in her good graces. – Do say something kind for me to Eliza, that may win her esteem at a jump, and as much elsewhere as may be left to your own generosity. I will redeem it all. And lastly think of me sometimes rather than 'whistle for want of thought'[13] and believe me ever, my dear Lotty, your affectionate Friend,

Theodore.

P.S. – My pencil desires to be remembered to you and so I have let it speak for itself.[14]

[*Islington, October 1822*]

From Jerrold 127–31. The picture here is twofold: on the one hand, Hood at the Reynolds's home in Little Britain with Jane, Marianne, and John and his wife; on the other, his correspondent with Mrs Reynolds and the Longmores at Upwell.

1/This may have been either James Rice, Reynolds's law partner and later a witness at Hood's wedding, or, less likely, Edward Rice, who officiated at the wedding.

2/Keats *Endymion* IV 218: 'Whence came ye, merry Damsels! whence came ye! / So many, and so many, and such glee? / ... We follow Bacchus!'

3/*Romeo and Juliet* I iv 57

4/*Othello* I iii 167
5/Waterloo Bridge was opened on 18 June 1817 by the Prince Regent accompanied by the Duke of Wellington and others.
6/Recalling the title of Southey's ballad, 'Mary, the Maid of the Inn'
7/Adapting Keats, 'Ode on a Grecian Urn' 44
8/Since John Reynolds had married at Exeter, Mrs Reynolds and Charlotte at Upwell had not seen his wife.
9/A soldier who acted as a model for a line of untrained men in their exercises; 'farce' should perhaps be 'face,' but the phrase is unintelligible.
10/The subject of a well-known painting by Sir Joshua Reynolds
11/Both unidentified
12/Dryden, 'Cymon and Iphigenia' 85
13/The same, 84
14/Jerrold notes of this postscript, 'written in pencil.'

TO UNKNOWN CORRESPONDENT

Sir.

I have sent the accompanying sonnet to you in hopes that it may be considered not unworthy of a place in the Magazine. I am aware that it is not usual (or indeed possible) to answer all communications nor have I the right to hope for an answer on so slight a subject as a sonnet yet still should you have time to spare for a few words as to the fate of my poem you will confer a great favour upon

Yours very truly

Thos Hood

Sonnet.

'Tenuis fugiens per gramina rivus.'
Virg. Georg. IV.[1]

Look how a slender rivulet steals along,
In windings devious, through a meadow's grass;
Its waters all too scant to yield a song
Of murmur'd pleasure unto those that pass;
Therefore, with lowly aim, it does but seek
The thirsty herbage to refresh unseen;
Whereat each tiny leaf, and flow'ret meak
Doth clothe itself with sweets, and livelier green.

So the True Heart, who has not store of wealth
His poorer brethren to endow withal,
Doeth his gentle acts of good by stealth,[2]
That so the World may not perceive at all:
Nor should we know that virtue which he hath
Save for the brightening looks that mark his humble path.

Thomas Hood.

Louth, / Lincolnshire [*1822*]

MS NLS. I have not traced Hood's connection with Louth, or the magazine to which he refers in his letter. The sonnet has not before been published.

1/Virgil *Georgics* IV 19; the phrase is translated in the first two lines of the poem.
2/Pope, 'Epilogue to the Satires' Dialogue I 136

1823

TO

MRS CHARLOTTE REYNOLDS

My dearest mother, – I was to have written to you yesterday evening, but my hand was so tired with transcribing all the morning that I was obliged unwillingly to let it rest. I do not know how I am to put *interest* enough in these lines to repay you for the long time I have been indebted for your kind ones; I know they were written designedly to put me in heart and hope, and indeed they were more than a pleasure to me in the midst of pain. They were not only kind, but enlivened with such smart and humorous conceits as might account for some part of my difficulty in finding a reply. You know I am not used to flatter; and if I were to begin now, Heaven help me, but you should be the last woman for my experiment. I know you have a 'smashing blow' for such butter-moulds.

I am a great deal better. My hands are now returned to their natural size. From their plumpness before with the little nourishment I took, and their afterwards falling away, you would have thought I sustained myself like the bears, by sucking my paws.[1] I am now on a stouter diet, a Beef-eater, and devour my ox by instalments; so provide yourself against I come. I have nursed a hope of seeing you on Sunday. It has been one of the greatest privations of my illness to be debarred from a presence so kind as yours; but I trust, weak as I am, to make my bow at your next drawing-room. You know there is a hope for everything; your old rose-tree has a bud on it.

I wish you could patronise my garden, you should walk about it like Aurora, and bedew the young plants. It is quite green, and the flowers that were sown, are now *seed* coming up from the ground. I am just going there as soon as I have achieved this letter. The fresh air feeds me like a chameleon, and makes me change the colour of my skin too.[2] I shall need all my strength if you expect me to come and romp with your grandchild. My dear Jane writes that owing to Mr. Acland's[3] delay, it is likely that they may not come up till the week after next. Pray make use of the interval in double-bracing your nerves against the tumults of 'the little sensible Longmore.' She will put you to your Hop-Tea. I expect she will quite revolutionise Little Britain. The awful brow[4] of Mariane, the muscular powers of Lottie, the serious remonstrances of Aunt Jane, the maternal and grand-maternal authorities will be set at nought with impunity. As for Green[5] and I, we shall come up empty about dinner-time, and in the hubbub, be sent empty away. The old china will be cracked like mad; the tour-terelles, finger-blotted and spoiled; the chintz, – now *couleur de rose* – all rumpled and unflounced! You will get some rest never!

I had a note from that unfortunate youth Haley,[6] on Sunday. It commenced: 'Saturated with rain,' as if to show me the use he had made of my dictionary; and ended by begging a trifle to help him into the 99th. I played the sergeant's part and gave him a shilling, not from any bounty of my own, but because all the girls cried out upon me for their parts. 'They could not resist such entreaties.' However, do not blame me, for I mean to cut him off with it, and be deaf to his letters in the future.

I have been obliged to avail myself of the sunshine, and wish I could send you some by this letter, to sit in your thoughts. I hope you dwell only on the pleasant ones; for, with all your cares, you must have many such. Think of your good and clever daughters, who paint sea nymphs, and sing, and play on the piano; and of your son John, dear to the Muses. I think few families have been dealt with so well, if, indeed, any. There's Jane, and Eliza, Mariane, and Lottie, – four Queens; and John, – you must count 'two for his nob.' I was glad to hear that he came to you, and in such excellent tune and highly pleased with his praise of my Poem. It was worth the commendations of all a 'London Magazine' to me; with its Editor at the head, or, if you please, at the tail. Pray tell Mariane that I have written a long, serious, Spanish story, trying not to be more idle than I can help, which, as soon as it is transcribed, I shall send to her.[7] I have almost written some songs for Lottie, but want rhymes to them. I have never been allowed yet to sigh to your 'Willow Song' for the Album. Lambkins and Willows were indispensable to the old songs, but I thought such *fleecy-osiery* poetry went out with Pope. I almost think it a shame amongst all my rhyming that I have never yet mused upon you; but please God, you and I mend, you shall adorn a sonnet yet, and if it be worthy of you, I shall think myself some 'Boet,' as Handel used to call it. I might have a much worse subject and inspiration than the recollection of your goodness, and with that happy remembrance I will leave off. God bless you, my dearest Mother! You say you wonder how it is I respect and esteem you as such, as if I had not read in you a kindness towards me, which in such a heart as yours must always outrun its means; nay, as if in thinking me worthy of one of your excellent daughters, you have not in all the love and duty of a son made me bounden to you for ever. Perhaps after this you will bear with my earnest looks in knowing that they are attracted to you by a gratitude and affection which could never enough thank and bless you, if they do not do so sometimes silently and in secret.

Pray distribute my kindest love amongst all, and believe it my greatest happiness to join with your own in all duty, honour, and affection as your son.

T. Hood.

Lower Street / Islington [*Spring 1823*].

From Shelley 327–32

1/This 'vulgar error' is reported by Goldsmith, *An History of the Earth, and Animated Nature* (1774) IV 322.
2/Goldsmith VII 155
3/Unidentified. The baby is probably Eliza Longmore, see 60 below.
4/Milton, *Paradise Lost* IX 537, applies the phrase to Eve.
5/Probably H.G. Green, later the husband of Marianne Reynolds
6/Unidentified
7/Probably one of Hood's *National Tales* (1827)

TO ELIZABETH HOOD

My dear Betsy,
You did right to let me hear from you, as it was a pleasure in addition to my being here – where I am picking up a month's health in a fortnight, so as to make me regret that my stay here must be necessarily so short as it will be. My purpose is, to return on Tuesday, on which night I expect you will see me, if nothing occurs to prevent my departure from here, which is not likely. I did not write to let you know of my safe arrival, but took it for granted that you would not suppose I was killed by the way unless you heard from me to the contrary. I have found the place much pleasanter and prettier than I expected, certainly much more so than Sandhurst,[1] perhaps on account of my company. It is low and flat; but there are trees enough to make it agreeable to one who has lived two years in Dundee, and then for a change I have a little nursing! The baby comes to me very cheerfully, and I can make shift to carry her up and down the garden, without cramping her, or breaking her limbs. Indeed I could pass a month of my life in my present way very willingly, and I think it would make my life a month longer, I eat, drink, and sleep so well. By the way of this last particular, it will surprise you to know that I rise amongst the first of the family, the maids excepted, so that I can almost fancy myself, *vide* Humphrey Clinker, the cock at Brambleton Hall.[2] You will not have heard of my trip to Norwich with Mr. L., who was summoned there to the assizes.[3] It is about 50 miles hence, and we drove it in a gig, through

a most pleasant country. I was exceedingly amused for the four days we staid there. We went to the Cathedral by chance, one morning, when by good luck there was a grand Charity Musical Festival, as fine as an Oratorio.[4] Then we went to the theatre, (where Miss Holdaway now is, and was, instead of playing Safie,[5] as F.[6] erroneously reports), and last of all to Finch's Gardens, a sort of twopenny Vauxhall, where I laughed heartily at the ridiculous attempt to rival Bish, &c.[7] Finally, I am here again, so you see I have been in luck in coming just when I did, in all but one thing. The account of Frankenstein[8] is not mine, but F.'s. *I* should have spoken more favourably of it, and Mr. Peake will take it ill till the matter is explained, that it is not more kindly treated, for I understand it deserves no less. I sent him[9] a plot made up from Reynolds' account and the newspapers, but for some reason he did not make use of it.[10] I tried very much at Norwich to find out E.G., alias Mrs. R.,[11] but after a long hunt from street to street on the scent, I came at last to a wrong old Mr. R., who looked very ill-pleased at being called from his breakfast to a perfect stranger. I thought it must be his son I wanted, and told him so. He said he *had* no son, being an old bachelor! Dispirited by this unlucky result, I gave up the pursuit; otherwise I should have been happy to have brought to Mrs. R. an account of E. and her little girl, but she must take the will for the deed. Norwich is a very large place, and E. does not sit on a steeple, so there was little chance of finding her without her address.

I am glad to hear Kate [12] is going back, for I was afraid she would lose all her acquirements if she stayed much longer at home, I should have been glad if the girls' holiday had happened when I was at home.

Your hopes about weather have had no effect, at least within our neighbourhood. It has been anything but summer with us; and heaven knows how the fruit is to ripen, or the harvest, if the sun continues to bear this wet countenance. I have taken a sketch or two – the church for Mr. L., the rectory for – –, and the house here for Mrs. Reynolds; but if you should be in Little Britain before I return, be 'mum budget'[13] as usual on this subject. I have no news, of course you cannot expect any from a county only famous for its turkeys. Jane is very well, the baby improves very much and will soon toddle – besides having four teeth, which is a great comfort to her victuals.

Pray give my kindest love to the girls at Brompton; ask them to come home on the Sunday after I come home, if you be sending. Jane and Eliza desire their kind love, which with my own 'I wrap under one kiver,'[14] and am, dear Betsy,

Your affectionate brother,

Thos. Hood.

[*Upwell*] *8th August 1823.*

From *Works* x 20–3

1/The home of Robert Sands, Hood's uncle

2/In Smollett's *Humphry Clinker*, letter of 30 April

3/On 30 July George Longmore gave evidence in a trial for murder.

4/This festival took place on 31 July.

5/Reynolds had published *Safie, An Eastern Tale* in 1814. There is no record of a performance.

6/Unidentified, nor have I been able to locate his report

7/Miss Holloway of the Theatre Royal, English Opera, was performing at Finch's Ranelagh Gardens in Norwich. Thomas Bish, the lottery office keeper, had purchased Vauxhall Gardens, London, in 1821.

8/Richard Brinsley Peake's *Presumption; or, The Fate of Frankenstein* was first performed at the English Opera House on 26 July 1823. Peake (1792–1847), like Hood, was born in London and like him did some early work as an engraver. He began to write for the stage in 1818, and his later contributions included many of the pieces performed by Charles Mathews, for whom Hood briefly worked. It is odd that in a letter dated 10 December 1824, over a year after this present letter, Peake refers to Hood as though having recently met him for the first time: Mrs Anne Mathews, *Memoirs of Charles Mathews* (1838) III 462f.

9/Presumably 'F'

10/Reynolds's enthusiastic account of the play did not appear until September, in the *London Magazine* 322–3. Reynolds initialled the account as his in his copy of the magazine, now in the Keats House, Hampstead.

11/Unidentified. This should probably read 'Mr.'

12/Hood's sister (died 1828), presumably with his other sisters Anne and Jessie at Brompton

13/*Merry Wives of Windsor* 5 ii 6

14/Winifred Jenkins's phrase in *Humphry Clinker*, letter of 18 July

For letter to James Montgomery of 27 September 1823, see 686.

TO

ARCHIBALD ? CONSTABLE

Sir

When I had the pleasure of meeting you in town, – you were kind enough to express a desire to serve me, and accepting your offer as frankly as it was made, I will tell you where I think it lies in your power to do me a kindness. – My friends Mess[rs] Taylor & Hessey & myself are partners in a work which I am to edit, – it is intended to consist of Poems by Living Authors,[1] – and it is important to our undertaking that we should have something by Sir Walter Scott.[2] – I have written to himself to request this favour & judging that you possess some interest with him, I shall feel much obliged by any thing you will do in aid of my application. – I have already obtained the assistance of many of my friends here Mr Procter, – Mr Allan Cunningham, – Mr Lamb. – Mr Reynolds – John Clare[3] etc. & if you can help me to obtain such a name as Sir Walter Scott's it will go far towards my success.– Perhaps at the same time you might be able to render me a like assistance with Mr Wilson[4] or others of your Northern Poets – but I will not trespass too much upon your kindness.

I propose to publish, in the ensuing year – a Collection of my own Poems etc. – & if I should not print them on my own account I may trouble you to look at them.[5] – I owe you many thanks for the friendly interest you have expressed towards me, & which I beg you to accept.

I am Sir   Your moobed^{t} S^{t}

Thos Hood

Lower Street Islington / Octr 2^{d} 1823

MS NLS. Address: 'Mr J. Constable / Bookseller / Edinbro'.' Published by Morgan KSJ 86. Archibald Constable (1774–1827), the distinguished Edinburgh publisher, was closely connected with Sir Walter Scott. He could have met Hood during his visit to London in April–June 1823.

1/The volume to which Hood refers remained unpublished, though the Quaker poet Bernard Barton (1789–1849) had written to Taylor and Hessey concerning it on 11 February this year.

2/Sir Walter Scott (1771–1832), celebrated as poet and novelist, later contributed to Hood's annual *The Gem.*

3/These writers all contributed to the *London Magazine*: Bryan Waller Procter (1787–1874), London poet; Allan Cunningham (1784–1842), Scottish poet; Charles Lamb (1775–1834), Londoner, whose *Essays* were written for the *London Magazine* and published by Taylor and Hessey this year; John Clare (1793–1864), the Northamptonshire peasant poet, whose volumes were published by Taylor and Hessey. Five days before this present letter, on 27 September 1823, Hood had written to another poet James Montgomery (1771–1854), asking for a contribution to his *Muse's Almanack*, adding to the names above that of the Reverend Henry Francis Cary (1772–1844), another *London Magazine* writer and the translator of Dante.

4/John Wilson (1785–1854), poet and leading contributor to *Blackwood's Edinburgh Magazine*, a rival to Constable's publications.

5/Hood did not publish a collection of his own serious poems until 1827.

TO
MISS CHARLOTTE REYNOLDS

My dear Lotte, – You say a letter from me will be a charity, and you see I begin it at home. God knows I can sympathise with the dearth of news which must be commonly felt in such a place, and how by this time you must have emptied yourself of talk, and be ready to listen to anyone's letters. The Murder of Mr. Weare must have been a godsend to you; – it kept us a week in conversation, and a hungry person might have lived a day upon our crumbs, – but with you I doubt not it hath been chewed twice over like the Abyssinian sweetmeats. By-the-by, is it thought in your parts that Hunt was personally assistant and abetting in the murder? It is current here, that he stood on the left hand side of the Horse, – with his right hand holding the bridle, within two inches of the bitt that he might not start, – and humming the second part of Hummel's Fanchon, with Cramer's Variations. He was a public singer, you know, – and fond of *humming* as appears in his evidence.[1]

Talking of murder – we have been much amused by hearing of Mr. Rawngely's[2] falling in love, – and long to know the assassin. He has long looked 'pale with passion'[3] – or bleached white with bleedings, like the animal you wot of, to make his flesh delicate. Oh the she-Shylock! I have seen Mr. Green[4] but once, – it was a cold day, – and made him look blue and numb; but you must miss him at Upwell, – for I should think that you would miss the buzz of a fly if it left your Parish. – When I was there I heard the flowers grow – there was so little stirring. If it was not for the noise of Cambridge, half-way, I should think you could listen to us in Little Britain. – But you will have Taylor & Hessey's Magazine to speak for all London, and I envy you, for in your dull parts it must read lively!

How you must have envied us the debut of Mr. Daniel![5] – or indeed the first appearance of Mr. Any-one with a new face. Change, in your neighbourhood must be scarce and at a premium – only nineteen shillings and sixpence to the sovereign. You must tire of Mr. Terry's[6] eternal white hat, – and the muddy sluggishness of the river – A barge must be an incident in your lives, – and a fired chimney like a comet in your Calendar. Pray, – last Sunday, exactly at 5 P.M., did you observe a cloud – 52″ 20° North and very like a Whale.[7] – It passed directly over my house and disappeared in the horizon. – You must have seen it for it was in broad day-light. – I really wonder what you do (when the Child is asleep) for by this time you must have dissected us all, your friends here, into atoms. – Do you read? – I have been skimming Boxiana[8] and think you would like it for there are three thick volumes with plates. – Or do you sleep after dinner? or walk? I will send you a herbal to help you in your botany. You will find the study very amusing as well as endless; – and by help of a magnifier – taking care to have one strong enough, – may discover eternal new wonders. – I have heard that the Mosses are more than a man's life would suffice to reckon – and then when they are severally examined, that they will take as much longer to describe. – I am sure I shall be obliged to you for the account of them: – or of any other studies by which you may think proper to fill up your leisure. I doubt not you bestow much time and attention on that sweet child your sister's, – and I hope she will prettily show the fruits of such vigilant and indefatigable instruction. – Her Grandma has favoured me with many interesting particulars of her bearing and conduct; – and I feel much pleasure in sending her a little present, whilst she is so unconscious as she must be of the giver to show that my love is quite disinterested, and looks for no return. Pray teach her to carry it in a genteel and ladylike manner, – like her mother – or it may not be amiss to remind her of the carriage of her aunt in London, – Miss Marianne Reynolds, mind and call her Miss Marianne, so it will give the little dear a feeling of her own importance, and say that she – her Aunt Marianne – never soils the pretty pink lining by thrusting into it mutton bones or whatever else she may happen to hold in her ivory fingers. – Pray also give her a kiss for me – but wipe her mouth first – though her mother will call me over nice for it – and then give her the muff – calling it pitty-pitty, or puss-puss, or some other such words adapted to her comprehension, or tickling her little nose with it or bopeeping her eyes, – or creep-mouse,[9] creeping it as your own judgment shall think most expedient. – But I am growing Nurselike! – besides instructing you in your own business. – So, farewell, do not forget my love to Eliza, – and a thousand kind things which I would sooner write to her myself than by commission if my time were not so short. She shall say what she likes for me to G[eorge] and I shall still have to spare for yourself. – Accept then, my dear Lot, my most brotherly love, and believe me in serious and sincere earnest, Your affectionate,

T.H.

P.S. – Marianne and Jane have new Bonnets, but I do not know how they fit.

[*Islington, November 1823*]

From Jerrold 135–7

1/Weare was murdered on 24 October 1823; the investigation began four days later, and in the course of it Hunt confessed to his complicity. The inquest took place on 31 October and the following day. As a result of the trial which took place on 6–7 January 1824 Hunt was transported for life. 'Humming' means 'cheating.' Johan Nepomuka Hummel (1778–1837) and Johann Baptist Cramer (1771–1858) were celebrated musicians, but I have not found Hummel's 'Fanchon'.

2/Unidentified

3/Compare *Much Ado About Nothing* 1 i 214: 'pale with love ... With anger, with sickness, or with hunger.'

4/Probably H.G. Green

5/Unidentified

6/Unidentified

7/*Hamlet* 3 ii 372

8/By Pierce Egan, sporting writer

9/A nursery game

TO
MISS CHARLOTTE REYNOLDS

My dear Lotte

Once more I write to you out of pity – for I know that the very sight of a letter must make you – move your ears, – like Baby's rabbit or as Mr Darley[1] doth, I have observed, – in little twitches before he speaks. – But those who listen to him feel as if theirs were turning inside out with impatience – which I hope is not your case, with me, for I could never hope to fill the double drums of your female curiosity: – You must gaze your fill therefore upon Jane's or Marianne's letters before you venture upon mine; – tho I do suppose that in your parts, – the least scrap is a godsend, – that you lick every word off the butter-papers. – It must be a comfort to you then to know that here we have Marianne Longmore,[2] & have seen Brides and Bride's Groom, by pairs,[3] – but I will not meddle with these matters. – Jane and Marianne will describe their dresses & trimmings to a nicety, – with endless quotations as it were of Mr Harvey's[4] shopbills, – and I do not expect till you have read these letters twice over that you will turn your blue eyes upon mine. – Heaven however, has kindly blown up something like an incident for your amusement, – and according to your desire to draw all the particulars of so extraordinary an occurrence – (as Browne the novelist would begin)[5] tho indeed you have expressed no such desire, – I commence my Narrative. – It was on Wednesday, the 16 Ins$^{\text{t.}}$[6] – at ½ past 6.PM. – squally with rain, – that I set off for a dance at Hackney with my Sister & two others – (your Sisters were no party to my party so I have this slice of news to myself.) – but the wind was so high, that whether we *sailed* or rode thither I have some doubts. – It it had been a boat I should have thought we rowed; – but it was in a Coach, – Number 1776. – There was a large party when we arrived – I think it was said there were 16 or 18 ladies arrived; – and the entertainment was given by the *single* unmarried daughter of Mr & Mrs Gouldsmith, – late our Neighbours of Islington. She is a young girl of a very solemn aspect, – giving the lie to the proverb about old heads & young shoulders, – and of a very *pious* turn, – & when she complains of the most winding & melancholy voice possible. – Then we all had tea & coffee in the back parlour – I could send you a cut of the House & grounds like Probert's[7] but for want of time; – yet suffice it that there are two large rooms communicating by folding doors; – and both entered from a large Hall on the left. – I sat in the back room close to the garden window, – with my feet in the fourth position – talking of I know not what to a young lady with very lobster like eyes. –

I only remember that she said, – with a flirt of her fan that she liked 'the simplicity of the country & I thought of you when she said it. – In the mean time the gale roared without, & the Gentlemen came dropping in like windfalls. – & I remember remarking – the only remark I made aloud – that the hurricane without made a most pleasant contrast to the comforts within, – for the wind was making a sort of pan's pipes of our stack of chimneys, & played such an air in a little ante chamber behind the hall, – where all the fruit & custards &c were laid out, – that the grate would hold no fire within its bars. – And now a game of bagatelle was proposed, before dancing, – & all the company adjourned to the front room, – except myself who took that opportunity of examining a picture which hung in the extreme corner. – It represented a group in a hayfield, during a storm, – watching the sky, as it seemed in awful expectation of a thunderbolt, – when – just then, at that very moment, – in the silent pause, just on the eve of the bagatelle, – I heard a most tremendous fall overhead – right on the ceiling, – as if a lady, in practising her steps upstairs, – some dowager, – only as loud as twenty dowagers, had tripped & fallen. – But it was not as I thought a lady, but a whole stack of chimneys that had tumbled – beating thro the roof & stamping on the first floor, like the very giant of the castle of Otranto.[8] The explosion was tremendous; – & might aptly be compared, – yes most aptly for this *was* to have been a Ball – to the first awful cannon-shot at Brussells! –

– *Hackney* had gather'd then
Her beauty & her chivalry all bright
And there were well dressed women & brave men[9] –

but now – at a blow – the glory of the Ball was demolished for ever! – I looked thro the folding doors, – and it was like a glimpse of L fill'd with smoke, and darkness palpable,[10] – and in the midst moved shapes of Men & Ladies; – demons, & soil'd angels, – whilst the huge grate continually spit forth its flames in fiery tongues towards the infernal centre. – And the soot whirled round & round with the wind, – & the smoke, like black bandalores,[11] – so that some fled into the wide gusty Hall;[12] – & others stopped not till they had reached the forecourt or garden, – wherein they stood shaking & blowing out of all shape. – Amongst these, – I found my Sister, – planted in the mid walk, – with a white pocket handkerchief pulled round her black face! – 'each lent to each a double charm,'[13] – and waiting as if for a tile from above. – Then I pulled her into the Hall, – & looked round me on the grimly company. – O how Beauty (– if any beauty *was* there,) – was soil'd & dimmed! – What lustres were quenched! What silks were tarnishd, what fair faces were *rawnsely'd*[14] by filthy smoke & soot! – It was like a May day in high life! – The rich Sweep's Jubilee! – or a Revel amongst the blacks! – Only there was no 'white lass' for Blackman to kiss; – they were all Wowskis[15] – I looked for the lady with lobster-eyes, whom I had conversed with but she was run away out of the House, & like De Quincey's Ann – with all my search I could never find her again.[16] – I spoke to another, – but she only stared, & could make no answer, – & then the Lady of the Mansion came to me, with her hands flapping up & down with wonder & fright, & asked me which way the wind blew. – Then came a little old Lady from over the way, to offer beds for the family but in reality to slack the quicklime of her own curiosity, – & then came an old Gentleman, hastily fetched over by one of the daughters who thought he was a Surveyor, – but he turned out to be an old Stockbroker. – This is he, who would not come, – tho the young woman said that her ma was dying of terror, – till he had put on his best gaiters. – Of course he was of no service, so he went off with as many of us as lived near, but some were forced to wait for their coaches. – Thus we stood all about, & for some of the ladies we wiped chairs, – in that little back room you wot of, – behind which perchance we stood, like Pompey, – or Mungo [17]– & served them with wine & tarts; – I only, – owing to my fortunate station at the time of the fall – showed off amongst these grimed Othello's like – forgive the comparison – like a Swan amongst ravens. – I believe they would have been glad to smut me out of envy & spite. – I asked one a Frenchman how long he had been from Africa, – but he mistook my drift & replied he was not from Africa, – but the United States. – Another, unmannerly, had stood between the ladies & the fire, – & the spurting flame had singed his blue pantaloons to a nice crisp brown; – but the object of all objects was the young lady – our invitress, – who with mingled soot & disappointment, looked blacker than black, & in a crow's voice croaked a thousand regrets, for this uncomfortable entertainment. – Then she rated her brother for stuffing at the tarts & custards when he might be dusting the chairs, or blowing the soot off the pictures. – As for the relics of us – the guests, – we were invited to the next house – a Mad house – till our coaches came for us, & thither we went, – & were formally introduced,[18] – to the Family. – We were quite strangers to each other – but to be sure had we *been* Friends they could scarcely have known us, – and here we were provided with houseroom coal & candle and young ladies till ½ past 11. – They did not offer us any refreshment however, – thinking perhaps that we brought our own *grub* – & might sup off each other's faces – but for the rest we were very comfortable, and I met with amusement enough for another chapter.–

II.

Of the People at the Madhouse: their appearance and Behaviour.

On entering the Madhouse, we were ushered into a very handsome large room, with a fine blazing fire, that seemed to crackle & enjoy its safe & sound Chimney. – Indeed the fall of ours seemed to have cleared up the weather, which had settled into a fine moonlight; – nevertheless we all sat at a respectful distance from the fireplace, – protesting we were not cold, – and the corners were occupied by the family. – The Lady of the House was a goodly well grown dame, I guess Welsh, – and opposite to her sat two daughters who took after their mother, in size, – & might have visited the great Cattle show, at Sadler's without any very humiliating sense of their own insignificance. – They kept all their conversation – in the family – so that I cannot speak of them beyond their looks, – but I should take them to be young & good tempered – the first because they had very girlish faces, – with sleek combed braided hair, & altogether rather a bread & butter look, – & the last, because they seemed to thrive so well on their victuals. – The Father was a very respectable sort of man but rather homely betwixt his nose & chin, – and there were three Brothers – one tall, – nothing uncommon in appearance except that he wore spectacles, – the other ditto except the spectacles and the third – but of him more anon. – We, – the Accidentals, – were five in number, – myself – two ladies, – their Brother, the gentleman of the scorched pantaloons – & the Frenchman. – The latter – I should tell you, had suffered most in complexion, – and sat with his grim black face, in most agreable relief, – between the *white* busts of Paris, & Canova's Venus,[19] which stood upon two chiffonières. – He addressed most of his animated discourse to the Mother, – and she received it with a most polite & inflexible gravity, in spite of all the smoky workings of his face & fingers, by which he illustrated his meaning. But the consciousness of her stiff crisp immaculate double & triple frills & smooth white kid like face, by the side of his dingy flesh & cravat might account for some part of her complacency – I sat silently watching them, till I believe the Father, – thinking that I wanted amusement, sent his youngest son, who anchor'd himself in a seat beside me & began to pour in a regular volley of talk great & small – He had been a Sailor, – & the climate had tanned his face into a mahogany brown, which advantageously set off his curly flax coloured hair. – He had too a strange crooked upper lip to his mouth that twisted & worked whenever he spoke enough to turn all his letters to an S. – Of his discourse as well as I can, I will give you a sample. – He began with his last voyage to Jamaica. – The Captain was a Scotchman & *pinched* his crew very much, – hoped I was not a Scotchman he was a Welshman – That Gentleman opposite (the Frenchman) was talking of Deal Boats – so he described the Deal Boats – He had been in the Downs in a storm – very bad anchorage in a storm – and the ship ran down another with a cargo of ivory on board, – but they had a freight of timber, – but the crew of the ivory ship were all ashore but two – what a providence it was. – How should I climb up a mast? – Really I could not tell. – Why when he tried, he endeavoured to get up the pole but it was greased & he slipped down again, – you should lay hold of the two backstays & *warp* yourself up hand over hand. – Begged I would excuse his nautical phrases & then explained what a hobby de hoy was. – Really *those* black girls (not our ladies) but the negresses in Jamaica – were very humane, – he had a deep cut once in his ankle & they healed it. – Did I ever wake at a thunderstorm – No; or very seldom. – No more should he if it was not for that fellow (pointing to the man servant who came in with coals) – who waked him always & said 'See sir what beautiful lightnings!' – Did I ever eat a dolphin? – but he forgot, – they were not allowed by law to be brought into England; – What did I think Bill would do for (pointing to his Brother) – I guessed a Dr – from the spectacles, – No he was to be a Parson. – Dick, – pointing to the other was a painter & Poet, & played on the flute & keyed bugle, – and in this very candid ingenuous way he ran on till we parted when he shook my hand & bid God bless me, and I parted from one of the most amusing frank open hearted little Boy-men[20] that ever twaddled about Ships & canvas. – There! – feast upon him in your fancy. – I am sure such a mere shadow of a young Tar as I have given you must be a comfort in your country. – I wish I could have packed him up & sent him to you per Canal. He would outtalk Mrs H.![21] – & make you quite enjoy the Barges. – We have had Mr Green here with three of your ribbons in his hat, beating up for recruits to go abroad with him to Upwell – but he can get no one to take your shilling. – I have however volunteered some riddles for Mr Hardwicke which you shall receive per first opportunity, – & my next letter will be to Eliza; – provided she will from this sample condescend to take it in. – If she pleases I will pay the postage. – I could write a deal of nursy-pursy to Baby but I will not take it out of your mouth. I am quite delighted with the accounts I hear of her mimicry, – & count her already as clever as Clara Fisher,[22] – but as she imitates, – it behoves you who are so much with her to be very guarded in your own conduct, – that she may profit by her pattern. – I own I should be sorry to see her, on being paid a compliment by a young Gentleman, – sidle off, & hold down her head & shake it, – like a poney about to *shy* – or when she begins to talk, to hear her fumbling & poking out her explanations, like broken corks picked piecemeal out of the necks of bottles; – a comparison, which to be candid, I have known to be inspired by yourself. – I know you will not be offended, at my telling you of all your little faults, since I do it only for that dear child's benefit; – and I shall not have room in this letter or I would tell you of all the rest which I have observed in you with the affectionate vigilance of a Friend. – I would also favour you with a few of her Mother's, – if I could just now remember what they were, – but I abstain, lest they should seem easier invented than recalled. – I merely suspect in the meantime, that that dirty little trick which Miss has, of poking her mutton bones into other people's eyes, must have been learnt of her Mother, for I do not recollect that you had any such practice, when I have sat with you at dinner. – If such be the case, however much it may divert & entertain you for the present, & tend to her Father's amusement yet I cannot but consider her talent for imitation rather as a *bane* (the Scotch for *bone*) than as a blessing to her, if it is to lead to such consequences. – But I will not school you in your own duty & province – only I must send a kiss through you to your little charge, – and I wish it were a bullet for your sake. – Do give a little hug to her then for my sake, & kiss her mouth, – so pretty & little as Rowland Prince[23] says of *his* child 'that it might be cover'd with a sixpence.' – But give her a shilling kiss! – Her Aunts have sent her some toys – I did not think she would take to the rabbit; – but perhaps by rubbing it over with a little parsley & butter at the beginning she may be tempted to like it.[24] – Do – do take care that she does not get the ninepins under her little feet, & so fall, – in which caution I have got the start of her Grandmother. – I went with Jane for the toys – and our purchases were oddly enough as follows; viz. – *Pins* for Baby – *Pegs* for Ma, – and *stumps* for Marianne! – Can you club together such another set of commissions? – I have no news but that I am learning quad –

A parcel-knock at the door and a general skuttle! – Your letter is come, and I have got thus far, – so you must give me credit for writing all in advance of this without being *coaxed*. – But I am grieved to hear that our good Eliza is unwell; – if any thing I could wish would cure her, it is entirely hers. – I believe I like her better & better, as Baby grows, – & you may tell her so for me, and very sincerely. – I hope I do not need Jane's & Marianne's affidavits to confirm this assurance; – & so venture to offer my simple love to her, and pray present it in your kindest manner. – I need but to mention George – for I know she will box your ears or mine for forgetting him, – but as I am out of reach of her gent[le hands] he will receive my remembrances as from reg[ard] more than fear. –And now, dear Lotte, accept [my] own love, & this long letter in token of my des[ire to] please you, – but do not presume upon it, or [presume] upon me, by sending up all Mrs Hardwicke's notes [...] for you. – Such a wish is not expressed, – but [I have] guessed it. – God bless you. –

I had nigh forgot to wish a Merrie Christmas to you all my dear good Masters & Mistresses and also the Young Lady from London. – So, in the name of the Bellman, God bless your House and all the wery worthy people as is in it. – Have you heard the Bellman yet, – & what time do your Waits play at Upwell. – I do suppose by this, that little Miss has ate all the plumbs from your pudding. – A little dear, – to seem to know so naturally what Xmas means!
So you have been to hear the new Bells for the sake of their tongues! – Did you make any conquests among the Triple Bob Majors![25] –

*Islington, Lower Street / Sunday Morni^g^* [*December 1823*]

MS Osborn. Address: 'Single Miss Lotte Reynolds. / In the care of G. Longmore Esqre / Upwell / Norfolk.' Published by Jerrold 138–48

1/George Darley (1795–1846), poet and contributor to the *London Magazine*
2/George Longmore's sister (d 1838)
3/Unidentified
4/Unidentified
5/Charles Brockden Brown, whose *Wieland*, for example, begins: 'I feel little reluctance in complying with your request.'
6/This should be the 17th.
7/Probert was an accomplice in the notorious murder of Weare which took place near his cottage. The *Morning Chronicle*, 8 November, contained a plate showing 'Probert's Cottage and Garden.'
8/Walpole *Castle of Otranto* ch. I
9/Byron *Childe Harold's Pilgrimage* III 182–4
10/Milton *Paradise Lost* XII 188
11/'A toy containing a coiled spring, which caused it, when thrown down, to rise again to the hand by the winding up of the string by which it was held,' NED
12/Keats, 'Eve of St Agnes' 360–1
13/Quotation unidentified
14/This may be a play on the name 'Rawngely,' mentioned in the previous letter to Charlotte.
15/In George Colman the younger's popular play *Inkle and Yarico* (1787), the West Indian girl Wowski marries an English serving-man. During their courtship (I iii), she sings:

> White man, never go away –
> Tell me why need you?
> Stay, with your *Wowski*, stay:
> *Wowski* will feed you.

In Hood's friends' embarrassing situation, they were all made black, that is, 'Wowskis,' so there was no 'white lass' – substituting for 'white man' in the song – for 'Blackman' – reversing roles – to kiss!
16/'Confessions of an English Opium-Eater' *London Magazine* September 1821, 304, 312
17/Conventional names for coloured servants

18/A phrase is illegible here. It seems to end with the words 'of our faces.'
19/The original is in the Pitti Palace, Florence.
20/Lamb's word, used by him in *London Magazine* January 1823, 21
21/Probably Mrs Hardwicke, who, with her husband, is named later
22/Unidentified
23/Unidentified
24/In the MS 'lick' is crossed through, and 'like' inserted above the line.
25/In bell-ringing, changes with a dodging course rung upon eight bells

1824

TO
MARIANNE REYNOLDS

My very dear Marianne ...
I have thought – before you went to Chelmsford, – that there was a comfort for every evil, and I can think so still. You must give me credit for philosophy when I can indifferently bear your absence, – but I am not stone – I am not marble – and if it were not for a longer period, – and not for your pleasure and good I might repine.

[*Islington, 13 January 1824*]

From Maggs Bros *Autograph Letters* no. 473 (1926) 112. The complete letter came to hand after this book was in pages; it can be found on page 687.

TO
MARIANNE REYNOLDS

My very dear Marianne
Such kind Messages as yours are irresistible – and I must write again if only to show you that I feel more than repaid for my last letter. – I know that you do not like to correspond, yourself, – but it shall be enough for me, dear, if I may believe that I am not quite the last person you would write to. – Indeed I know that I should not, if you could imagine how very much I am pleased with whatever you say or do; – which is far too much to let me become the graceless & ungrateful Critic. – But I know that you do not wrong me, by any such fear, and therefore, till you write to others, & not to me, – I shall consider that my letters are answered by the pleasure they may give you. – I am sure they are not without their delight to myself, and still more when I learn that you are to keep them, – for I know whatever kindnesses they may contain, that they will never be belied by Time. I might even crowd them with more affection, and still be justified, for I have a thousand reasons for loving you, – if you were not my dear Jane's sister, which is a thousand reasons in one. – But I can afford to wave that, – for your own sake, tho' when I remember that I might have had a Drewe[1] instead, – I cannot feel too happy, too proud, or too fond

of you in that relation. – I wish I could but give you a tenth part of such causes to make me dear to you: – however it is some merit to love you, and you must give me the benefit of that consideration. – Therefore dear, do store up these letters, and if hereafter you lack a true wight to do you suit or service, let them remind you of the hand and heart of a Brother. – Would he were as potent as proud of this title, – for yours & other's dear sake – but it is not the fault of my wish that I cannot make you Queen of the Amaranths – or pluck a bough of green leaves & turn them into emeralds for your casket. – There is a tale of a little prince, who had a ruby heart, and whatever he wished on it was instantly granted – but it is not so with mine. Neither have I Aladdin's lamp: – or it should have been scrubbed bright ere the Chelmsford Ball. – But now, it is a dark lanthorn, – & the glory of Fairy land is bedimmed for ever. – Only the fiery dragons remain, which be cares, many & fearful, – & the black cats, – & the demons & imps, – and the ogres, – who are the Booksellers, – except that they have no eye in their foreheads. – But I am not writing King Oberon's Elegy: – so away with this lament for the little people, and let's think of the living! – the interesting little Miss Kindred has enquired after you & you have been missed at the Le Mercier's.[2] We met the former at Mrs Butler's last night; – and she seemed what the world would call a sweet girl, full of sensibility & commerce. – Her sister I should think has a smack of Prudence Morton.[3] – I like her best for she was absent. – Jane has made a very pleasant addition to her friendships, by her introduction at another party (Le Merciers) – to a Mrs Simpson, – & a Mrs Cockle, – I quite wish you had the former at Chelmsford. – There was a Mr Capper[4] too, – with a fac simile of Woodhouse's[5] profile, – as if such a one was worthy of two editions; – & I wish you could have seen him too. – You should have him in, for nothing, in exchange, with all the others, against Green,[6] when it shall please you to export him. – The ladies of Chelmsford might grow their own – they have had time enough to shred him like Angelica.[7] – No doubt he hath often gone, purposely to the Coach, when it was too late, – like dear Miss Longmore: –

'Farewell so often goes before 'tis gone! –'[8]

He has been so long expected here that we are afraid he is coming by a Hearse. – Tell him, – the House at Blackheath has been robbed, & his little Nephews Wielanded.[9] – only think that Butler likes St Ronan's well & does not dote on old Im(—) no, – old Mortality ! ! – Have you any blue Stocking at Chelmsford – Tell them that you know a Gentleman that knows a friend of Barry Cornwall.[10] We are plotting here to go to the play when it shall be worth seeing: – but do not let that hasten you. If you stay a week longer you shall have another letter: & a better. Now I am rather hurried, & must put in an appearance before Mr Hessey: – so God bless you, dear, tho, I say that deliberately, – Accept my sincere love & kind wishes & believe me, for ever Your affectionate Brother

T. Hood

A P.S. for Miss Longmore.
London is very dull & foggy – & the baked codlins very dear. – Pray wear list shoes, this nasty slidy weather & keep your feet warm, – there's nothing like that. – I have got a sprain'd ankle, – but do not let that grieve you: some people like a well turn'd one; – but I don't. – It gives me a great deal of pain, but I must say good bye good bye, – good bye – go – goo – good – by – by – bye –

Lower Street Islington / Tuesday Morn^g^ [January 1824]

MS BM. Published by Shelley 333–7. Hood refers in the letter to Scott's *St Ronan's Well*, published at the end of 1823. His postscript indicates a wintry time of writing.
1/John Reynolds's wife's family name
2/Names unidentified
3/Unidentified
4/Names unidentified
5/Presumably Richard Woodhouse (1788–1834), lawyer and Keats's friend, who was associated with the Taylor and Hessey circle
6/H.G. Green
7/'Cultivated for the large ribs of its leaves, cut ... to make a candied preserve:' authority quoted in NED
8/ Quotation unidentified
9/Wieland, hero of Charles Brockden Brown's novel of that name (1798), was the victim of diabolical ventriloquism.
10/*Nom de plume* of B.W. Procter, who expressed admiration for Hood's serious poetry in *London Magazine* January 1823, 38

TO
JANE REYNOLDS

[...] matters on the face [...] the riddles on the outside of this – our [...] now here ½ past 3 it quite annoys me. – I always fancy [...] when I think you will be reading my letters, & shall look over you on Sunday – How delightful is it to please you dear, – I am quite happy to think that I shall fulfil your wish, and would exceed it if I could. – It is enough to pay me, that you take delight in my letters it makes me so proud & so happy, that I can never write enough. There is nothing in the world to me so dear as your pleasure, and that you look for it, & acknowledge it at my hands.

My Doctor[1] is just gone and as usual we have had a long literary chat. He says I must expect to feel such days as this – & not to gain much strength till I get out of this room, – and he has given me leave to go down the first fine day – I have hopes, after so much rain, that it will happen tomorrow – He says part of what I feel, is from the confinement, and want of exercise, – and indeed I seem to ache & get cramped with so much sitting. – Well is it said: – I translate from the Latin – of the poor Statue

He sits, & eternally will sit, – *unhappy* Theseus. –[2]

My Doctor's call has been quite a comfort to me, – a little chat is a windfall! – You will share in this I know dear, – and wish that you could multiply my visitors. I keep an eye fixed on May – & remember my promise.[3] Think of me then dear cheerfully, – & let us dream away the interval of each other. I know when that hour comes, with the delight of clasping you again to my heart, I shall [find] the pain of separation is all atoned for – and that you will [ma]ke me all possible amends by an increased affection if greater can be –

I must now put my riddles here – & will find other snug little corners for my kindnesses – Some of them are new. – Mr Hardwicke must really give you another bunch of vilets when you give them to him –

Why is a Farmer like a fowl? – Because he likes a full crop. Spell a large bird in two letters. – P.N – Why is a man who hangs himself like a porter? – Because he finds life a burthen & takes a knot to it. – Why is the wind like fashion – because it regulates the *vane*. Why is a cow a finer animal than a horse – because a horse is a courser. Why is a towel like a snake – Because it's a *wiper*. – Why are horses like Sentimentalists – Because they like to indulge in *wo*. – Why does good wine resemble the game of draughts – Because an extra draught makes a common man a king. – What is the rudest kind of diction. Contradiction. Why are icicles like listeners – because they are eavesdroppers. – Why is a hatter the most respectable of tradesmen. Because he serves the heads of the nation. What Judges are all of a bigness – the Judges of *Assize* – Why are rabbits like Electors – Because they live in *burrows* – Why are fish-women like Dr Faustus. Because they sell their soles. – Why is a Bow Street officer when heated, like a bean. Because he's a scarlet runner. Why should secret drops of sorrow be shed in the sea. – Because that's the place for private-tears. – Why are the children of the Chinese capital like sickly children? Because they are all Pekin ones. – Why is the sky when the sun's coming out, like the King on his road to the Pavillion. Because it's going to *brighten* – There, – this fold just embraces them all. –

[*Islington, March 1824*]

MS Osborn. Published by Jerrold 148–50, who suggests the date. This is the first surviving letter to Hood's future wife.

1/Perhaps N. Clifton, to whom Hood later writes (76, 127)

2/Virgil *Aeneid* VI 617. Hazlitt applied this passage to the Theseus amongst the Elgin Marbles, *London Magazine* May 1822, 449n.

3/The reference here is obscure. Hood and Jane were not married until May 1825.

TO

MISS CHARLOTTE REYNOLDS

My dear Lotte, – I have been obliged to make a long pause in our correspondence and that, too, when I was your debtor for a very kind and sister-like letter – but I have the good bad excuse of having been ill and you know one cannot write from the inspiration of slops and gruel. – You must look upon this letter then as a bulletin of my recovery, – and it is a pleasure after the restlessness and delirium of a fever to turn my thoughts to you and Upwell, – your fresh budding trees, and cool clear air, – and your crystal canal. – I have had a little relish of such enjoyments to-day – for I have just come out of my garden, and have watched for a change a few tiny clusters of crocus, and my lilies just pushing forth from the mould, tender and red, like vegetable chilblains. Mr. Hardwicke's seeds make quite a show – or at least the labels, – promising in some instances I know not what for the coming summer, – and the Upwell roses, I am glad to say, are all alive and growing – I hope you will perceive something of the fresh air I have been breathing in this letter, – for it gives a spring to the heart, and makes one twice pleased with everything, which, as I am reading your letter over again, makes it a great enjoyment indeed. – How little cause had you to fear writing to me when you could do justice by your expression, to so much kindness as just then prompted you to overcome that fear of my criticism. Indeed it was a very pretty letter, earnestly affectionate and unaffected as a country born epistle ought to be – there – I think now you will write to me again; at least once! before you come hither, and sadden all the echoes of Upwell.

Talking of talking – I have indeed been very much delighted with the accounts you have given of the little tricks of Lizzie (Jane says you are her Boswell) and above all with that which described her as coming by your desire to have 'a little chat.'

It was so characteristic. We all cried 'That is so like Lot!' – Look here's a *cut* for you. I call it 'Bid me discourse!'[1]
Pray observe how the rabbit pricks up its ears! I am afraid Eliza will not acknowledge her own as I have drawn her – but it is impossible to satisfy a Mother's eye – or even a grandmother's – I leave likenesses to Marianne.
And now, what next –
'You have not the book of riddles about you, have you?' No, but reading this enquiry of Slender's in the 'Merry Wives of Windsor' I remembered Mr. Hardwicke, and have given Jane a list of such riddles as I could muster[2] – and if you keep the answers to yourself you may retaliate upon him the puzzlings he has cost you. If any others should occur to me I will send them, but just now I feel very little inclination to tease my brains with such entanglements. – I have found out I believe most of his conundrums on the flow'rs, but there are some still obstinate against solutions. – I am afraid the Sphinx had a hand in them. Perhaps I am dull, – indeed, in one sense I am, – for the time that I spend at home I wish I could spend like a dormouse by sleeping it over. I have so little change and the worst of company – my own. I am almost too impatient and fidgetty to write or read, and have learnt to know all the hours of the day by the street cries. – Those evening bells,[3] the muffin bells are just beginning to ring – and remind me that I have not been able to hear Mr. James Green.[4] I verily believe that my dear Jane's kind visits have kept me alive – by rescuing me from those most tedious letters of the alphabet N U E – (that will make a pozer for Mr. Hardwicke) – Marianne too has been to see me and your mother! – and your father several times, – and both of the Greens – but then the dismal intervals – but I forget – you can no doubt get 'The Diary of an Invalid'[5] at the Wisbeach Circulating Library. I ought not to complain now, for I can get out – by coach – and spent yesterday in Little Britain – I should tell you that in spite of the wearisome sense of restraint and confinement I have read through the Simple Story[6] with an unimpaired interest, and it was the only real pleasure of reading I have enjoyed. – Don't you think Miss Woodley is very like Miss Good? I thought so all the while I was reading it. Miss Fenton is Miss Butler – and the Mistress Hortons are as 'plenty as blackberries' [7] – when they are sour. Don't you respect Mr. Sandford, he is such a monitor? I wish you knew him. Do you think Donif [...] most like [Mr T]erry or Mr. Townley?[8]
What does [Mrs. Hard]wicke think of the last [volume of] St. Ronan's W[ell?] We call it very dry – but in your country that may s[eem] no fault. Do you think she has ever read Herwald de Wake?[9] It is very sleepy. Your good mother, by the way, has turned authoress, and has written a long poem in Miss Acton's[10] album.

Her Advice to a Mother by a Grandmother, has reached a fourth edition, and Longmans are in treaty for the copyright. You know I always thought she wrote it. She asked your father some weeks ago for some blank copy books, and it turns out that she has just completed the Child's First Book, – of course with a reference to little Eliza. – I have mustered, for Eliza, as many as I could of the *Lady's Museum*,[11] to amuse her, when you leave her, – but I am afraid that you have talked at the rate of more than a number a month. Why, it would kill you to publish only twelve times a year. She should have kept G.'s Encyclopaedia to go through when you are gone. Poor thing. The moss will grow in her ears! I will write to her out of pity. However, I am almost glad I shall not have to write to you again, which I cannot help doing. I shall be glad to see you; – I understand you are to come the end of March, – or the beginning of Wisbeach – but do not make it late. We cannot do without you on the 1st of April. – We shall have much to say to each other on that day. Wish I *could* fetch you, for it were worth two Jews' eyes[12] to see our good Eliza – large and small – or if you please the diamond edition – and I should like to tell G. how J. Green abused Norwich. I wonder if Mr. Lemon[13] is alive yet. Pray kiss Baby for me again and again; I wish she were here; can't you steal her, with your black hair and eyes and berry face you might pass for a gipsey, or why can't her mother pawn her and send us the Duplicate, or why wasn't she a Twin for her grandmother to cry halves! – but as she is one and indivisible, I suppose it would ossify G.'s pericardium to part with her. Pray tell Eliza to tell her not to spoil her father, – and pray – for I feel like getting up into a corner like Randall[14] against the ropes – pray give my love to them right and left, as hard as you can put it, and believe me, dear Lotte, in very haste, – Your most affectionate brother,

Thos. Hood.

[*Lower Street, Islington, 30 March 1824*].

From Jerrold 150–4. Jerrold provides the address and date.

1/Jerrold notes: 'Here comes a rough pen and ink sketch of a lady and a child seated, with a toy rabbit behind the child's chair.' The caption is from Shakespeare *Venus and Adonis* 145.

2/These occur in the previous letter.

3/The title of one of Thomas Moore's *National Airs*

4/Unidentified

5/By Henry Matthews (1820)

6/By Elizabeth Inchbald (1791)

7/*1 Henry IV* 2 iv 231, 'plentiful as blackberries'

8/The names of the characters in Mrs Inchbald's novel (1791) are Miss Woodley, Miss Fenton, Mrs Horton, Mr Sandford, and Dorriforth. Mrs Inchbald herself calls Sandford a monitor, 1 v. Of Hood's

acquaintances, Miss Good I have not traced; Miss Butler is probably the daughter of the Mrs Butler mentioned elsewhere; '[ ] erry' may be a reference to 'Mr. Terry,' mentioned above; Townley remains unknown, though Towneley was the Christian name of Marianne Reynolds Green's second son.
9/Novel by Hewson Clarke(1823)
10/Unidentified
11/*Ladies' Monthly Museum* (1798–1828), at one time published by Hood's father
12/Slang expression meaning something very precious
13/Unidentified
14/Jack Randall, the Nonpareil, pugilist

TO
MRS CHARLOTTE REYNOLDS

My dear Mother, – If I had not another line in the world I must write to congratulate you upon so interesting an event as your being made a Grandmother. Indeed, I feel Uncle already for if I do not I have not another sister in the world who is married enough to make me one, and besides my dear Jane, looks already as if a sluggard might go to her, as Solomon says, 'and consider her ways and be wise'[1] – not but that in this respect she seems to have had a nephew for [y]ears. I wish I were within fourteen lines of him, and he should have a sonnet for certain, – but if I were now to begin,

'Thy father's eyes, thy mother's lips'

and it should not be like him, I fear he would never grow into his Portrait. I once sowed Marry Golds in my garden and they came up Larkspurs.
Nevertheless if 'our good Lizzy' desire it, I will strive to label the sweet son-flower – but at present his god-Father Apollo – (which is only another name for the sun) – will not inspire me, and moreover, somebody is so pressing for her package that, without haste I shall not parcel of it. – Good-bye, – and the hearty blessings of the Gods 'be with you, over you, and round about you,'[2] making your lives longer than this letter, and far happier than the wit of it; or as a better blessing, Heaven make you all Grand Mothers – but not now – so that I may often wish you joy of nephews or nieces, as it may happen to be.
Pray accept my love, which is large enough for a longer letter if time allowed me, and believe me how truly, my dear Mother, I am yours, and dear Lizzy's and dear Lotty's, affectionate Son and Brother,

Theodore.[3]

P.S. – We desire our kind thanks to Lotty for her Flour, which were very sweet Smeling and odious; as if she had picked the Best of them if not all with her one

hand. The Roses came safe and went to bits for Joy of it, but we have kept the remains of them to make Essence of Lavender with to wash one's lining in – but I must shut up, for the Porter has got the Box on his ear and we have only time to call after him, our loves to the little boy, – for he won't stop for the kiss as he has not brought his knot with him. – If I had thought of it – hollo! – Here! we shall divide all your Honourses healths, upon mine, that we shall – to the House of Longmore, root and branch, and there's half-a-pint of small Beer for little Master's Health, till he gets stronger.
Pray do not forget to express my love to Mr. Longmore and Lizzy and – but I have done it before.[4]

[*Islington, August 1824*]

From Jerrold 156–8. Hood writes after the birth of George Moody Longmore, the second son of George Longmore and Eliza Reynolds, at Upwell, 22 August 1824.

1/Proverbs 6:6, 'Go to the ant, thou sluggard; consider her ways and be wise.'
2/John Banim *Damon and Pythias* (1821) 17: 'The blessing and the bounty of the gods / Be with you, over you, and all around you.' This passage was quoted in *London Magazine* July 1821, 83.
3/Hood had been nicknamed 'Theodore' by Charlotte Reynolds.
4/Jerrold notes: 'At the foot this letter has the following jumbled up direction, "G. Upwell, Esqre, care of Mrs. Reynolds, Longmore, Norfolk." '

TO
JOHN HAMILTON REYNOLDS

My dear Reynolds, – I send you the Ode on Martin, which, with those on Graham and Kitchener, makes three completed.
These are the names I have thought of to choose from, – Elliston you would make a rich one, – and then there's Pierce Egan or Tom Cribb – ditto – Mr. Bodkin – Mr. McAdam – Mrs. Fry – Hy. Hunt – Sir R. Birnie – Joseph Grimaldi, sen. – The Great Unknown – Mr. Malthus – Mr. Irving – Mr. Wilberforce – Prince Hohenlohe – Capt. Parry – Dr. Combe – Mr. Accum – The Washing Company – Sir W. Congreve – Bish – Cubitt on the Treadmill – Tattersall – Owen of Lanark – – Bridgman, on the Iron Coffins – W. Savage Landor, on the use of cork armour and bows and arrows – Fitzgerald on Literature – Dymoke. I think the thing is likely to be a hit – but if *you* do some, I shall expect it to run like wildfire. Let's

keep it snug. – Pray, remembrances to Rice – and in the kindliest at Home. – I am, dear Reynolds, yours very truly,

T. Hood.

[*Islington, autumn 1824*]

From Jerrold 163–4. In February 1825 Hood published with his future brother-in-law, Reynolds, *Odes and Addresses to Great People*. This letter concerns subjects for that volume. The people mentioned are identified in the following list: Richard 'Humanity' Martin, founder of the RSPCA, 1824; Graham, the aeronaut; William Kitchiner, author of *Apicius Redivivus, or the Cook's Oracle* (1817); R.W. Elliston, actor and manager of Drury Lane Theatre; Pierce Egan, sporting writer; Tom Cribb, pugilist; W.H. Bodkin, secretary to the Society for the Suppression of Mendicity; J.L. McAdam, improver of the surface of roads; Elizabeth Fry, prison reformer; Henry Hunt, radical politician; Sir Richard Byrnie, police magistrate at Bow Street; Joseph Grimaldi, clown; The Great Unknown, the popular name for Sir Walter Scott; T.R. Malthus, political economist; Edward Irving, divine; William Wilberforce, philanthropist; Prince Hohenlohe, performer of supposedly miraculous cures; W.E. Parry, Arctic explorer: he returned to England in October 1823 and left again in May 1824; George Combe, phrenologist; F.C. Accum, chemist, advocate of gas light, who left England after having been charged with embezzlement in 1822; Sir William Congreve, inventor of the Congreve rocket: a 'tremendous explosion' occurred at his factory on 10 June 1824, *Annual Register*, 'Chronicle,' 68; Thomas Bish, lottery promoter; Sir William Cubitt, inventor of the tread-mill: according to *Annual Register*, 1824, 53, 'The merits of the tread-wheel, as an instrument of prison-labour, have, during the past year, excited considerable interest'; Richard Tattersall, head of the centre for betting on horses; Robert Owen, socialist; W.S. Landor, poet: his *Imaginary Conversations* was published by Taylor and Hessey early in 1824: Hood is referring to that work, II 365–71; W.T. Fitzgerald, poet: 'On all public occasions Mr Fitz-Gerald's pen was ever ready,' *Annual Register* 1829 'Appendix to Chronicle' 239; Henry Dymoke, the King's Champion. I have not discovered who Bridgman was.

1825

TO

MARIANNE and CHARLOTTE REYNOLDS

My dear Marianne: my dear Lot

I shall leave Jane to explain to you why we have not written sooner, – & betake myself at once to fill up my share of the letter. – Jane, meanwhile resting her two sprained ankles, – worn out with walking, – or rolling rather upon the pebbly beach: – for she is not, as she says the *shingle* woman that she used to be. – This morning I took her up to the Castle, – & it would have amused you, after I had hauled her up, with great labour one of its giddy steps, – to see her contemplating her re-descent. Behind her, an unkindly wall, in which there was no door to admit us from the level ridge to which we had attained – before her, nothing but the inevitable steep: – At the first glance downwards she seemed to comprehend that she must stay there all the day – and as I generally do I thought with her. – We are neither of us, a chamois. – but after a good deal of joint scuffling & scrambling & kicking I got her down again – upon the *Downs*. – I am almost afraid to tell you that we wished for our dear Marianne to share with us in the prospect, from above. I had the pleasure besides of groping with her up a little corkscrew staircase, – in a ruined turret, – & seeing her poke her head like a sweep, – out at the top. The place was so small, – methought, it was like exploring a marrow-bone. –

This is the last of our excursions. – We have tried but in vain to find out the Baker & his Wife, recommended to us by Lamb as the very Lions[1] of green Hastings – There is no such street as he has named throughout the town, – and the ovens are singularly numerous. We have given up the search therefore but we have discovered the little church in the wood, – & it is such a church![2] It ought to have been our St Botolph's.[3] (Pray tell Ma by the way that we read our marriage in the morning papers, – at the Library & it read very well.) – Such a verdant covert would Stothard paint for the haunting of Dioneus, – Pamphilus – & Flametta – as they walk in the novel of Boccacce.[4] The ground shadowed with bluebells, even to the formation of a plumlike bloom upon its little knolls, & ridges – & ever thro the dell windeth a little path chequerd with the shades of aspens & ashes – & the most verdant, & lively of all the family of trees. Here a broad, rude stone steppeth over a lazy spring, – oozing its way into grass & weeds, – anon a fresh pathway divergeth you know not whither Meanwhile the wild blackbird startles across the way & singeth anew in some other shade. To have seen Flammetta there, stepping in silk attire, – like a flower, – and the sunlight looking upon her betwixt the branches! I had not walked (in the body) with Romance before. – Then suppose so much of a space cleared, as maketh a small church *lawn* – to be sprinkled with old gravestones, – & in the midst the church itself a small Xtian dovecot – such as Lamb has truly described it like a little Temple of Juan Fernandez. – I could have been sentimental & wished to lie some day in that place, – its calm tenants seeming to come thro such quiet ways, – thro those verdant alleys – to their graves. –[5]

In coming home, I killed a viper in our serpentine path, – & Mrs Fernor says, I am, by that token to overcome an enemy. Is Taylor or is Hessey dead? – The reptile was dark, & dull, – his blood being yet sluggish from the cold; – howbeit he tried to bite, – till I cut him in two with a stone. I thought of Hesseys long back bone when I did it. –[6]

They are called *Adders*, – tell your Father, – because two & two of them together make four. – [7]

Tomorrow we go to Lovers Seat,[8] as it is called, – to hallow it by our presence. Oh how I wish we had you upon Lover's Seat, which took its name from the appointments of a fair maiden with a gallant Lieutenant! – He was in the preventive service – but his love was contraband – & there in a romantic bay, they used to elude the parental excise – Goodbye. God bless you, my dears till we meet again. – I long to meet you again as your Brother – most proud & happy in your affection. My love & duty to our Good Mother & to our father, – your own affectionate Friend & Brother. T. Hood. –

Mrs Fernor's – The Priory – Hastings / Tuesday Morning [*11 May 1825*]

MS Harvard. Published by Shelley 338–42. Hood and Jane Reynolds were married on Wednesday, 5 May, so the letter was probably written on the following Tuesday.

1/Sights worth seeing

2/Lamb begins the letter to which Hood here refers: 'And what dost thou at the Priory? *Cucullus non facit Monachum*,' *Letters* II 434. His editor mistakenly gives the postmark of the letter as 10 August. 1824. Hood's friendship with Lamb, a fellow contributor to the *London Magazine*, began after Lamb became his neighbour at Colebrooke Cottage, Islington, in August 1823.

3/Hood and Jane were married at St Botolph's Church, Aldersgate, London.

4/According to the *English Catalogue*, an edition of *The Decameron*, with plates after Stothard, appeared in August 1825.

5/In a letter to Bernard Barton, Lamb had written of Hastings in general: 'There are spots, inland bays, etc., which realise the notions of Juan Fernandez;' the church at Hollington stands alone with 'only passages diverging from it thro' beautiful woods to so many farm houses,' as though it had 'nothing but birds for its congregation,' *Letters* II 392. Fernandez, the Spanish explorer, flourished about 1570.

6/This is the last reference in the letters to Hood's connection with Taylor and Hessey. He had

helped on their *London Magazine* as editorial assistant, and his last contribution appeared there in June 1823.
7/George Reynolds was writing master at Christ's Hospital. A section of the letter, omitted here but published by Shelley 341–2, was written by Jane. Hood himself concludes the letter in the margin.
8/A spot also recommended by Lamb. No doubt the Hoods stopped at the 'capital farm house two thirds of the way to the Lover's Seat, with incomparable plum cake, ginger beer, etc.,' which Lamb later recommended to J.B. Dibdin, *Letters* III 50.

TO
RUDOLPH ACKERMANN

T. Hood presents his Comp[ts] to M[r] Ackermann –
He would have been glad to have seemed more ready with his contribution for the forget-me-not, – but his Marriage must be accountable for the delay. – His best wishes attend on the accompaniment, – for the success of M[r] Ackermann's elegant little Work –

[*Islington, summer 1825*]

MS UCLA. Rudolph Ackermann (1764–1834), the art publisher, had brought out his first literary annual, the *Forget Me Not* at the end of 1822. These illustrated anthologies were popular in the eighteen twenties and thirties, though their literary merit is held to be slight. Hood contributed to several of them and edited *The Gem*. To the *Forget Me Not* for 1826 he contributed 'The Water Lady.'

TO
MRS CHARLOTTE REYNOLDS

My dear Mother
It has been my fault that this did not go into the post yesterday – but the time went by whilst I was over my picture. – You, who are an Artist know [how] difficult it is to leave off whilst you have all your subject in your mind's eye. – The drawing (as they say of the lottery) will be over today, – and I am very well satisfied, – such is my vanity with its effect. –[1]
We have imagined you in a rare bustle, as tho a babe had been dropped from the clouds.[2] I wish the new one may be as gentle & fair a boy as the other, whom I was disappointed not to see. I always look upon him as half a godchild. Does he seem to feel his being made a ward of? – Has it hurt his appetite, – or encreased his relish for Books – Liz & I are the best of friends, – and perhaps the best children in the world, – for our years I am quite a father to her, – so let her parents be easy

on her account. I never saw any child so sensible beyond her years, & yet so childish, as she is: – to which you would add bless her heart I have taken pains with her indeed. – However out of so many grandchildren as you have now you must expect a bad one, – to turn out, – which I hope will not be the Watford[3] cadet, – in spite of all our congratulations. – I think I hear you in your rash way pronouncing that he is like Eliza, without your spectacles: – & refusing to entrust him, with your accustomed vigilance, even to the experienced arms of Mrs. Dyson.[4] – But I shall drop this subject (as gently as I can without hurting him) lest you should think me more of a Gossip than I wish to be thought – only let me suggest that if the parents have not thought of a name, & are not particular that Aminadab[5] is soft & well sounding & he might be called Dab for shortness.
It was Jane's Birthday on Sunday which of course you did not forget, – we remembered yours on the 5th. & burnt you in effigy to the infinite amusement of your granddaughter, who could hardly be restrained from playing with the fire. It is fine today – for the Lord Mayors Show – but Jane & I have agreed not to take Liz to see it for fear it should give her a taste for gaudy & vulgar fripperies.
Lamb called the other day & brought us a delicious hen-pheasant which is reckoned the genteelest of presents, – not excepting *epergnes*. His sister is no better. Marianne still mends, – but Mr R.[6] like a lonely turtle is pining in proportion Mr & Mrs. H. are quite well & united afresh, in love for each other & to you. – My best Congratulations to Eliza & Longmore, on the advent of their little Unknown – & believe me my dear Mother, – very truly your Affectionate son

T. Hood

[*Islington, 9 November 1825*]

MS Osborn. Address: 'Mrs Reynolds / G. Longmore's Esqre / Surgeon / Watford / Herts.' PM: 'F NO 1825 /9,' '7 NIGHT 7 1825 / NO.9.' Published by Jerrold 203–4.
1/Hood's satirical etching *The Progress of Cant* was published at the end of the year. It led Lamb to dub the artist 'that half Hogarth,' *Letters* III 32. Though the work was generally admired, Hood found engraving too laborious, and did not repeat this sustained attempt. The etching is reproduced in Clubbe, facing p. 18.
2/Jerrold notes: 'William A. Longmore, born November 7, 1825.'
3/George Longmore must have removed to Watford from Upwell after August 1824.
4/The nurse?
5/Popular name for a Quaker
6/Presumably George Reynolds

TO
LUPTON RELFE

Sir

As I have occasion to send into your neighbourhood I have desired the Bearer to call that if you have a 'Friendship's Offering' ready for me, it may save you the trouble of sending so far as here.

I shall be glad to see it, – besides, – for I have not chanced yet to glimpse it any where – but understand that it is out.–

With my best wishes for the Book, I am
Sir Yours truly

Thos Hood

Lower Street / Islington [November 1825]

MS Morgan Library. Lupton Relfe published *Friendship's Offering*, like Ackermann's *Forget Me Not*, one of the illustrated literary annuals popular in the eighteen twenties and thirties. To *Friendship's Offering*, which appeared at the beginning of November 1825, Hood contributed two pieces, one of them being the well-known 'I remember.' Relfe later published Hood's *Whims and Oddities.*

TO
THOMAS ALLSOP

I have seen Mr. Lamb again today, when he appeared much the same as yesterday, but I have just received a message, that he is much better since the morning, & has been well enough to play a game of cards.

[*Islington, 1825*]

From Maggs Bros *Autograph Letters* no. 801 (1951) 35. Allsop (1795–1880), was a friend of Lamb and Coleridge.

1826

TO
WILLIAM HONE

Lamb has just called with the enclosed. He bade me say it was not to prevent any account of other parts of the picture or the Beadle you might like to give. – This, contains the Extract from the London Magazine.

[*Islington, January 1826*]

MS Osborn. Address: 'Mr Hone.' William Hone (1780–1842), bookseller and writer, engaged in political controversy, but in this year commenced the weekly miscellany, the *Every Day Book*. The work was dedicated to Lamb. The issue for 28 January 1826 contains 'An Appearance of the Season,' illustrated by a picture of 'The Beadle' from Hood's engraving *The Progress of Cant*, and containing a quotation from the *London Magazine*, December 1822. This article is followed by an account of Hood's engraving.

TO
JOHN MURRAY

Sir
You were pleased to say some time since that you should like to see any thing new by the Authors of 'Odes & Addresses to Great People.' As I wrote the greater part of that work, you will perhaps be disposed to treat with me for a book of 'Whims & Oddities' In Prose & Verse. With Forty Original designs, – by the Author.' – One of the Authors of Odes & Addresses to Great People & the Designer of the Progress of Cant.'
As I am going out of town, I should feel obliged; if you would appoint an early day for an interview, & am

Sir Your mos obedt

Thos Hood

Lower St. Islington[1] [*June 1826*]

The above address will find me.

MS Fitzwilliam Museum. The letter is endorsed with the date here given. John Murray (1778–1843), the distinguished publisher of both Byron and the *Quarterly Review*. He did not take advantage of Hood's offer.

1/The upper part of this address is cut off.

TO
ALARIC ALEXANDER WATTS

My dear Sir.

I expected to hear from you on Saturday – but am not sorry that you did not write, – because you will perhaps come instead, & take a plain dinner with me, – any of the ensuing days, and at whatever hour, late or early, it may suit you to appoint.

If you should not be at home, on the arrival of my messenger, – let me know by a Twopenny,[1] when I am to look for you. –

Yours very Truly

Thos Hood

A.A. Watts Esqr –

Lower Street / Islington [*autumn 1826*]

MS E. McAdam jr and George Milne. Alaric Alexander Watts (1797–1864), poet and periodical writer, worked for NMM and *Literary Gazette*, before editing the *Literary Souvenir* (1824–38). Hood was amongst the contributors to this annual. This letter sounds as though it were written before the following and more intimate one.

1/'The twopenny delivery was restricted to an area including the Cities of London and Westminster ... comprising, on the whole, the thickly built-up area. The threepenny district lay beyond this area ... By 1829 the distinction between the two areas was having less meaning ... the deliveries were made six times a day:' Howard Robinson *The British Post Office* (Princeton 1948) 196, 198.

TO
ALARIC ALEXANDER WATTS

My dear Sir, – My best thanks for the 'Souvenir.' We, I and my wife, have read together your poem of the 'First-Born' and admire it exceedingly.[1] I hope this will please you, as I have been pleased and gratified by the praises of Mrs. Watts. I return the proof of 'A Retrospective Review,' with additions, which you will please return or not as you please. I am glad you like the thing so much, for I was really anxious to do something worthy of your book. The other thing I wrote, and rejected, for you will help me through a sheet of the 'Whims and Oddities.'[2] I saw M — for a moment yesterday, which sufficed for his telling me in so many words, that the book will not suit him. As I had a handsome letter of introduction to him,[3] I think he might have treated me with a little more courtesy than poor FitzAdam.[4] But I am obliged to him for a hint, that there is a capital subject which I had not set down in my list, for the next of my 'Odes and Addresses to Great People.'

I observed, in a certain last Sunday's paper, a malicious attack on your *Literary Magnet*.[5] The editor of this Sunday news-waggon is a Scotchman, heretofore Editor of a Dundee newspaper. To my mind it shows no signs of editorship, and is but a hulking lubber of a paper; but it serves to wrap up twice as many parcels as any other. It plumes itself chiefly on its size, as though the mere superficial extent of paper and print ensured the *spread* of intelligence. A large sheet quotha, – a patchwork quilt rather! Twice as big as a daily without being any better, like a spread-eagle to an eagle *au naturel!* A little intelligence going a great way, like a puddle overflowing a Lincolnshire level. Poor in matter but prodigious, like Bankruptcy enlarged! A Gog among newspapers, – and as wooden.

Pray give my respects and remembrances to Mrs. Watts, and believe me, very truly yours,

T. Hood.

[*Lower Street, Islington, 10 October 1826*]

From Jerrold 211–12. Jerrold provides the information in square brackets at the end of the letter.

1/Watts' sonnet 'The First-Born' appeared in his *Poetical Sketches* (1824).

2/'A Retrospective Review,' together with 'Sonnet written in a volume of Shakspeare' and 'Ballad,' appeared in Watts's annual the *Literary Souvenir* (1827).

3/'M—' is John Murray, to whom Barron Field had written 'a handsomish letter' on Hood's behalf and at Lamb's request: Lamb's *Letters* III 63, and Samuel Smiles, *A Publisher and His Friends* (1891) II 244–5. Barron Field (1786–1846), lawyer and miscellaneous writer, friend of Lamb and his friends, abroad 1816–24, contributor to the *London Magazine*.

4/A slang expression meaning a nobody

5/In *The Atlas*, edited by Richard S. Rintoul. In the issue of 8 October 1826, 333, a reviewer says that Charles Knight, publisher of *The Magnet*, has there 'fixed upon the popular device of vending personalities, tittle tattle, and false reports, under the disguise of literature.' Furthermore, 'If *Literary Magnets* did not exist, there are many young ladies who would never see their compositions in print.' Hood himself had written dramatic criticisms for *The Atlas* between 21 May and 13 August 1826.

TO
LUPTON RELFE?

I forgot to beg of you to desire the woodcutters to take care of the Original Sketches as they belong to Mrs Reynolds's Scrapbook.

My dear Sir
I send you four more – 'As it fell upon a day' – is a new one. – It is to be accompanied by a Wordsworth-like Sonnet, – To a Child that had broken her Pitcher. – I have found in my portfolio, – two or three sketches in prose & verse that will be available: – so that the design gets on. –
Next week I expect I shall get up something for the paper – the English Gentleman: – but I shall perhaps look in upon you tomorrow. – In haste, Yours very truly

T. Hood

P.S. Whilst I was writing this, – a whim has occurred to me, – which has a reference to the Banker's Mishaps. – P.T.O.

The other three I have sent are
Come oer the sea / Maiden with me
My Eldest Son, Sir., –
Take O take those lips away. –

[*Islington, October 1826*]

MS State University of Iowa. The sketches referred to in the letter appeared in Hood's *Whims and Oddities*, published by Lupton Relfe at the end of the year. 'As it fell upon a day' faces 52 and accompanies a mock-Wordsworthian ballad rather than sonnet. I have not traced 'the English Gentleman.' Perhaps the whim with 'a reference to the Banker's Mishaps' found expression in the sketch facing 88, 'My banks they are furnished.' 'Come o'er the sea' faces 76, 'My son, Sir' faces 50, and 'Take, O take those lips away!' faces 106.

TO
LUPTON RELFE?

Dear Sir.
I enclose the 8th sheet in which you will see that an error has been made in the arrangement of the 'Dreams.' The Irish Schoolmaster will make ¼ in the 9th sheet. I am writing the preface therefore, that I may see how much I shall have open for other matters.
There are yet to come 'Authors from their Works,' & the Ballad – to match Sally Brown, which will perhaps make it necessary to have 9½ sheets.

Will you enclose me by tonights post, – a copy of the particulars you have given to Knight, as I shall have to see him tomorrow. –

Yours very truly

T Hood

Lower Street [*Islington*] / *Monday morning* [*October 1826*]

MS Editor. Hood is here referring again to the contents of his *Whims and Oddities*, published by Relfe at the end of the year. The reference to Knight may be to Charles Knight.

TO

UNKNOWN CORRESPONDENT

Dear Sir.
Will you send me the address of Mr Steele, – that I may write to him. As he is quite a stranger to me, & you stated it was a mere matter of business I shall feel no hesitation in writing to him.

Yours very truly

Thos Hood

I am no further with copy – I have been necessarily abroad all days since I saw you.

Lower Street [*Islington, before March 1827*]

MS Princeton. This letter must have been written before March 1827, because Hood then moved to a new address. I have not identified the 'Mr Steele' referred to in the letter.

TO

EDWARD MOXON

Dear Moxon,
Lest you should come out of your way this evg – we shall be at Islington tonight where perhaps you'll join us. –

In haste

Yours very truly

Thos Hood

[*Islington, 1826*]

MS Edinburgh University Library. Edward Moxon (1801–58), publisher and poet. From 1821–8 he was employed by the firm of Longmans which published Hood's *Plea of the Midsummer Fairies* in August 1827. Moxon became a friend of Lamb and Hood about the time of this letter. He moved from Longmans to the firm of Hurst, where he was befriended by Frederick Mullett Evans (1803/4–70), later of the printing firm of Bradbury and Evans, connected with Hood and the comic weekly *Punch*. In 1833 Moxon set up his own business, and married Lamb's protégée Emma Isola (1809–82). He published both Lamb and Wordsworth, as well as Shelley, Tennyson, and Browning.

TO
WILLIAM BLACKWOOD

Mr. Hood's Complts. to Mr Blackwood, – with a volume of his Whims & Oddities. If such a contributor as he might be occasionally would be useful to Maga he is ready to receive Mr B's propositions. –
Mr. H has besides a Volume of 20 Short Tales (original) – somewhat in the manner of Boccaccio – (one of them, 'The Owl' is printed in Friendship's Offering' of the present year, which it strikes him might suit the Mag. to be published afterwards in a Volume, or in 2 Vols, – one of which could be written (materials being ready) whilst the first one went thro the Magazine: or Mr B would be willing to treat perhaps for the Volume now written as a single one.
If so they shall be forwarded per Messrs. Cadell.[1]
The favor of an early answer will oblige – addressed 'Lower Street' Islington near London.

[*Islington, November 1826*]

MS NLS. William Blackwood (1776–1834) was the successful publisher of many works, including *Blackwood's Edinburgh Magazine*, 'Maga.' *Blackwood's*, January 1827, 45–60, lavished praise on Hood's *Whims and Oddities*. His *National Tales*, to which he also refers in the letter, was published by W.H. Ainsworth in February 1827. The plates were drawn by T. Dighton and engraved by Charles J. Hullmandel.

1/Probably the firm of Thomas Cadell (1773–1836)

1827

TO
WILLIAM BLACKWOOD

My dear Sir.
I have found it impossible to make up a packet for you as I hoped – remaining up to this hour in horrible confusion, – My publisher besides has just thought proper to let me know that he has no prints remaining, – so that I fear the progress of Cant has not been forwarded. I shall make up for both these deficiencies the next parcel.
In the mean time I send you a little Poem, just to show that I mean [to be] a contributor – I hope it will rea[ch you] in time, – though I have a doubt, as [this] letter has been lying here some days, instead of finding its way into the post office. Chaos I hope will subside ere the 6th when you shall certainly hear from me –[1]

2 Robert Street Adelphi [*March 1827*]

MS NLS. Hood moved to 2 Robert Street on 9 February. His 'Ode to the Moon,' dated 1 March, appeared in *Blackwood's Magazine* April 1827, 407–8. The publisher he refers to is Lupton Relfe.

1/The letter breaks off here. A letter to Blackwood which precedes this one is found on 690.

TO
R. SEATON

Sir.
I am much obliged by your friendly communication – & honoured by the confidence you have reposed in me, which be assured shall never be violated.
The information, you have been so kind as to convey to me, was not unexpected, – and I feel bound to tell you, that whatever can happen to Mr. L R will affect me in a very trifling degree, as I have disposed of the interest I had in the work of mine, which he publishes. The obligation, I owe to you on that account is not diminished, & I beg of you therefore to accept of my thanks, as from one friend to another.

I have the pleasure of remembering your name, & shall be happy, to return your civility by any means in my power.

I am Sir
Your moobedt

Thos Hood

R. Seaton Esqre

2 Robert St Adelphi. [*March 1827*]

MS Harvard. I have not identified Seaton, nor his connection with Lupton Relfe, mentioned in the letter.

TO
N. CLIFTON

My dear Sir.
I have the pleasure of sending the last of my publications for your acceptance. They are the first portion of a proposed Hundred of Tales.
The Second Series of 'Whims & Oddities' will come next,[1] – & I hope before long to make an arrangement with a Publisher, which will enable me to send some money to you, which with the remembrance of your constant kindness & attention towards me, is continually in my remembrance. –
I hope, whenever you come to this neighbourhood & have leisure, you will favour me with a call, – I need not say that I shall be as happy to see you, now that I am well, as I need to be when ill.
Mrs Hood begs of me to express to you her gratification, in the prospect of your attendance upon her in her confinement, which she expects to occur, the end of the present month or the beginning of April.[2] In the meantime she is very well indeed. –

I am
My dear sir
Yours very truly

Thos Hood

N. Clifton Esqre

2 Robert St Adelphi [*March 1827*]

MS Editor. Clifton was Hood's physician at this time.

1/Published by Charles Tilt at the beginning of November 1827. Tilt also published Hood's *Comic Annual* (1831–4), as well as *The Gem*, *The Epping Hunt*, and *The Dream of Eugene Aram*.

2/See the following letter.

TO
CHARLES OLLIER

My dear Sir.

I send you an ode which you should have come some days ago – but that I have been knocked up. Mrs Hood has been confined – but our poor little girl was obliged to be sacrificed to the mother's safety.[1]

I wrote to Mr Colburn some time back touching the Whims & Oddities accordg to our conversation – but I have not heard from him & am about to give up any expectation of it I am my dear Sir –

Yours very truly

T Hood

Let me see you soon.

2 Robert Street / Adelphi [*April 1827*]

MS Harvard. Published by Lane KSJ 45. The May number of Henry Colburn's NMM, of which Ollier was sub-editor, contained Hood's 'Ode to the late Lord Mayor.' Colburn (d 1855), publisher, started NMM in 1814, with the help of Frederic Shoberl; Thomas Campbell became the editor of this successful periodical in 1820, to be followed by Bulwer Lytton, Theodore Hook, Hood (1841–3), and William Harrison Ainsworth. Colburn also started the weekly *Literary Gazette* (1817–62). He published Evelyn and Pepys and many contemporary novelists. Charles Ollier (1788–1859) himself published Leigh Hunt, Shelley, and Keats, as well as Lamb, before working for Colburn and his partner from 1830–2, Richard Bentley.

1/On 12 April Lamb wrote to his friend the actress Fanny Kelly: 'My sister has been ... much affected this morning with a letter from Hood, saying that Mrs. Hood after intense suffering for two days, almost to the despair of her life, has lost her first little Baby,' *Letters* III 84.

TO
ROBERT BALMANNO

Sir
I have delay'd answering your polite note till I could be sure of health enough to enjoy your Festival. – I have now the pleasure of saying that I intend to be present. Be so kind therefore as to enclose a ticket. –

I am Sir

Yours truly

Thos Hood

2 Robert Street Adelphi [*11 May 1827*]

MS Rochester. Address: 'R. Balmanno, Esqre / 23. Mornington Place. / Hampstead Road.' PM: '18. PAID. 27+8. MORN. 8+ / 11. MY.' '10. F. NOO N. 10. 1827./ MY. 11.' Robert Balmanno (1780–1861), born near Aberdeen. Professor Richard Haven of the University of Massachusetts describes Balmanno in a letter to the editor as 'a bibliophile and art collector, for a time secretary of the Artists' Benevolent Fund in London, who emigrated to the United States in 1830–1, and was for many years an employee of the Brooklyn Customs House. He was one of the original subscribers to Blake's plates for Job, and he brought with him to this country a copy of Blake's Songs. He was the friend and executor of Henry Fuseli.' Jerrold notes, 226, that Balmanno was 'a neighbour of the Hoods, living as he did in Craven Street, Strand.' Balmanno's wife Mary was also an artist and writer; she published her reminiscences in *Pen and Pencil* (New York 1858).

TO
WILLIAM BLACKWOOD

My dear Sir
Between indisposition, & other engagements I have been quite unable to get any thing done in time for your parcel – but shall send some thing *direct* in time for your next No.
That May day article in your last is a delightful one. It seems to have improved our weather. 'Le revenant' in the No. before is talked of by every body I know, – Pray bid him (the author) roar again: – Beheading is yet undescribed.
I see on referring to one of your letters that you give me to expect a review of my switch [?] Tales in Maga. I shall be much gratified by such a Notice from Maga, whose Criticisms *are* influential.[1]

2 Robert Street – Adelphi [*May 1827*]

MS NLS. The articles to which Hood refers in the second paragraph of the letter are in the April and May numbers of *Blackwood's Magazine* 409–16, 501–19. There had been a slight reference to Hood's *National Tales* in the April number, 487. Hood's own next and final contribution appeared in the June number, 706–8.

1/The letter breaks off here.

TO
MRS CHARLOTTE REYNOLDS

Madam,
I have the pleasure of enclosing to you £15 on acct of Mrs Hamerton on whose behalf I have this day signed an agreement.
Mr Tilt requests that the Lady aforesaid will provide a new title for the work without delay as the presses are standing idle.

I am Madam
Your moobedt St

Thos Hood

Mrs Reynolds
Little Britain.

2 Robert Street / – Adelphi [May 1827]

MS New York. Address: 'Mrs Hamerton / Care of Mrs Reynolds / Little Britain.' Published by Jerrold, 213. 'Mrs Hamerton' was the pseudonym under which Mrs Reynolds wrote *Mrs Leslie and Her Grandchildren*, published by Charles Tilt, probably early in June 1827.

TO
WILLIAM JERDAN

Dear Jerdan. I send the enclosed per first post. I know you would have chosen it of the two, & therefore don't send you the other. Don't mention that the Demon ship will come into the next Whims & Oddities.

Yours very truly

T. Hood

P.S. – Mrs Leslie *& her Grandchildren* Longmans took 50 of them.

[Adelphi, 25 June 1827]

MS Harvard. PM: 'EVEN / 25. JU / 1827.' William Jerdan (1782–1869), Scottish journalist, came to London in the first decade of the century. He part-owned and edited the *Literary Gazette* (1817–50). Hood made several contributions to the *Gazette* (1827–8), including 'The Demon-Ship,' 30 June 1827. In the same periodical a week later appeared a notice of Mrs Reynolds's *Mrs Leslie and her Grand-children.*

TO
EDWARD MOXON

The printer's have blundered by going on with the minor poems instead of Hero & Leander. I sent the latter to Mr. Rees – a small book in boards, of a purple-marbled paper ... The accompanying dedication to Mr. Coleridge is to precede the Hero & Leander ... I suppose you were at Nfield yesterday – spending your Sunday – but no 'day of rest – for the soul of the foot at least. I wonder the country people thereabouts do not take L— for the Wandering Jew.

[*Adelphi, summer 1827*]

From Myers and Co. *Catalogue of Autograph Letters* no. 371 (spring 1952) 17–18. Moxon was employed by the publishing firm of Longman, Rees, Orme, Brown and Green until 1828. They published Hood's *Plea of the Midsummer Fairies* at the beginning of August 1827. This volume included the poem 'Hero and Leander,' here referred to. Lamb, to whom Hood refers at the end of the letter, removed to Enfield about the end of May 1827.

TO
ALARIC ALEXANDER WATTS

Dear Watts.
We have been at Enfield for some days on a visit to Lamb, – or I should have replied sooner. I shall quote the Souvenir as you wish, – & moreover will write something (good I hope) certainly, for your next volume. Only give me as much time as you can, for both our sakes. –[1]
I have made an arrangemt for the next Series of Whims & Oddities, – & Longmans are to bring out my Serious Poems. You shall have one of the first sets of sheets I can get. I expect it will be out in about a month – & any notice you can get for it will oblige me. Poetry I suspect is nowadays of somewhat suspended animation & will require artificial inflation alias puffing. I do not mean this of your critiques.[2] Why don't you look in here sometimes without ceremony & balancing of visits? I think it may be oftener in your way than T. Souare in mine – but I shall some day

get there on purpose. This is only a business note – but pray give my respects to Mrs Watts. I hope to hear good account of her; & am very truly

Yours

Thos Hood

A.A. Watts Esqre

2 Robert Street – / Adelphi [*18 July 1827*]

MS Rylands. Address: 'A.A. Watts Esqre 58, Torrington Square.' PM: '12 noon 18 Ju.' Watermark: '1826.' Lamb appears to refer to Hood's visit in a letter to Hone of about 17 July 1827, *Letters* III 100. George L. Barnett corrects the date of Lamb's letter, HLQ February 1955, 147.

1/Hood contributed 'Stanzas to Tom Woodgate' to the *Literary Souvenir* for 1828.
2/Four years later Watts defended 'The Plea of the Midsummer Fairies' in the *Literary Souvenir* for 1832, 245n.

TO
EDWARD MOXON

... I have 'not' heard from Mr. Rees, & think that people 'noted' for dilatoriness ought to be protested. I am anxious about the thing, because I merely stay in town to see the book thro the coach, & then we start for the seaside ... The fact is, the later the worse the season will be. I rely on capital notices in Blackwood, Jerdan, the N. Monthly, besides a host of the Minors.

[*Adelphi, July 1827*]

From Maggs Bros *Autograph Letters* no. 522 (summer 1929) 114. Owen Rees (1770–1837) was the second partner in the firm which published Hood's *Plea of the Midsummer Fairies*. The volume was appreciatively reviewed in William Jerdan's *Literary Gazette*, 11 August 1827. NMM, September, did not approve of Hood's 'poetical mania,' 'Historical Register' 372–3; and *Blackwood's Magazine* did not mention the work. Jerdan allowed Hood space to defend himself in verse against 'a host of the Minors' in the *Literary Gazette* 25 August, 558–9.

TO
STEPHEN PRICE

I send you at last the Comedy so long promised ... I could not get it into two acts ... will call upon you at the Theatre at 2 o'clock.

[*Robert Street, Adelphi, July 1827*]

From *The Collector* LXXXI 1968, 14, where the address is given. Stephen Price (1782–1840), American theatre manager, was at this time lessee of Drury Lane Theatre. The letter is annotated: 'The Comedy would not do.' It seems to belong to the period of the previous letter, before the visit to Brighton indicated in the address of the next.

TO
WILLIAM BRADBURY

Dear Sir.
Please to send a Boy to Drury Lane Theatre, with this letter, which will be his authority for receiving from Mr Price the M.S of 'York and Lancaster'.[1] If Mr Price should not be there let it be left sealed & it will remind him to send it to Robert Street

Yours very truly

Thos Hood

13 King's Road Brighton.[2] [*July 1827*]

MS Yale. Address: 'Mr Bradbury / Oxford Arms Passage / Warwick Lane.' This is crossed through, no doubt by the recipient, in favour of '– Price, Esq. / Drury Lane Theatre.' Hood's correspondent is probably William Bradbury the printer (d 1869), who, with Dent, printed the first *Comic Annual*, and, with Frederick Mullet Evans, the remainder until 1839. They also printed *Up the Rhine* (1840). Bradbury and Evans later published *Punch.*

1/Hood sent the play to which he here refers to the actor Frederick Henry Yates in November 1828. It was first performed on 5 October the next year. Yates (1797–1842) was born in London and educated at Winchmore Hill and the Charterhouse. With Charles Mathews he managed the Adelphi Theatre from 1825 to 1835.

2/The King's Road was opened in 1822. The author of *Brighton and its Environs* (6th ed. Brighton, n.d.), 58, writes that 'The houses on the King's Road generally consist of elegant residences and excellently constructed lodging houses.'

TO
W. FRASER

My dear Fraser
I return you the tableau – Shakspeare hath forestalled me. I will get a subject of my own. Genius hates shackles. The Man that loves liberty loves freedom. (I defy Joseph Surface[1] to make a better sentiment). I will write you something tender

something pastoral – something whimsical. – all in one, or in parts three. – I'll do my best & worst. Pigmalion liked pettitoes – the Irish spell the last word differently: – Aristotle is no authority. You may gather from these hints what will be the subjects [of my] Contributions. My remembrances

Yours irrevocably

T Hood

2 Robert Street / Friday – Adelphi [*summer 1827*]

MS BM. Fraser, first name unknown, edited *The Bijou* for 1828. The illustrations for this annual were in part selected by Hood's friend Balmanno. Perhaps the 'tableau' which Fraser had sent Hood was R. Westall's 'Dreams of the Youthful Shakespeare.' Hood eventually contributed 'A Lament for the Decline of Chivalry.' The annual appeared in October.

1/Character in Sheridan's *School for Scandal*

TO
CHARLES TILT

My dear Tilt. –
Have the goodness, the first time you send in this direction to let me have some more paper of this kind – I am happy to say I have used all the last: – for I am getting on rapidly with the Whims: –
There are exactly 20 cuts CUT, – so that I think Willis may get through after all. – Let's see you, some day, or night, shortly – I don't go out at all, – but write and draw, quite domestically. –

Yours very truly

T. Hood

2: Robert Street. [*Adelphi, autumn 1827*]

MS Huntington. Tilt published Hood's *Whims and Oddities*, second series, in November 1827. According to the title page it contains 'FORTY ORIGINAL DESIGNS.' The engraving is the work of Edward Willis, of whom Hood wrote in the Preface: 'I have been seconded by Mr. Edward Willis, who, like the humane Walter, has befriended my offspring in the Wood.'

TO

FREDERIC SHOBERL

Dr Sir

I was so ill all yesterday & the night before that tho I have my Poems written I could not correct & polish 'em to my mind if you could give me till as early as you like on Monday you may rely upon them at that time.

Yours very truly

Thos Hood

[*Adelphi, August 1827*]

MS Pennsylvania. Address: 'Mr Shoberl.' Frederic Shoberl (1775–1853) was editor of the *Forget Me Not* for 1828, published by Rudolph Ackermann, to which Hood contributed two poems, 'The Logicians' and 'Death in the Kitchen,' the latter to go with a plate illustrating an episode in Sterne's *Tristram Shandy*. The annual was published at the end of October 1827. Shoberl with Henry Colburn originated NMM. He was associated with Ackermann, editing his *Repository of Arts*, *Forget Me Not*, and *Juvenile Forget Me Not*. His son William worked for Colburn.

TO

RUDOLPH ACKERMANN

My dear Sir,

I have the pleasure of sending you 'The Logicians.' It being rather a crabbed subject, and myself not over well, I have been longer about it than I promised. The other subject is in progress, and you shall have it in proper *trim*, I hope, in two days.

Yours very truly,

T. Hood.

R. Ackermann, Esq.

Robert Street. [*Adelphi, August 1827*]

From *Works* v 310. Hood refers to contributions to the *Forget Me Not* for 1828, published by Ackermann.

TO
WILLIAM JERDAN

My dear Jerdan.
An't I good? – you have herewith the block and the article. The motto under the Cut is to be –
'A GLASS OF HALF-AND-HALF.'
which must be printed below it. Let the block be taken good care of for me.
I am a sort of half-&-half myself – partly Author partly artist. Which moiety prevails?
The dft was duly honoured.

Yours very truly

T Hood

2. Robert Street / Adelphi [*August 1827*]

MS UCLA. The cut and the article referred to appeared in the *Literary Gazette*, edited by Jerdan, 1 September, 572.

TO
ALARIC ALEXANDER WATTS

My dear Watts
I had the agreable receipt of your packet at Enfield – where we have been spending the last fortnight with the Lambs – & only got back last night. – I take your early notice of the book very kindly indeed – that is to say in the very same spirit with the deed on your part – which must have been one of no little trouble. Pray accept of my best thanks – – your aid must be very serviceable to the book – which is of a kind too, that in these times requires all helps.
I am very glad you liked the Fairies so much – for in spite of all, I am most vain of these *grave* things – in spite of Thalia.[1] I have not forgotten your claim upon me for the Souvenir – but the truth is, others who possessed not my better will, but were more importunate, have worried me into action; merely to get rid of the things.
I am obliged, really by your better kindness – & hope not to put you to any inconvenience by waiting for me – for I certainly will do my best as soon as I can hit on a subject – which is sometimes half the deed done. – You know I don't care at

at all about place – & if I come next to 'Finis' am as well content, as next to the title.[2]

We were truly sorry to hear of Mrs. Watts' tedious illness – & hope speedily to have better accts. – If I should not see you, my intention being to call at the office, pray convey our best wishes & regards to her.

Do you never come into my neighbourhood – we cannot chat well on paper. I am My dear Watts,

Yours very truly

T Hood

[*Adelphi, 1827*]

MS New York. It is hard to tell when in 1827 the visit to Lamb mentioned in the letter could have taken place. However, the later references seem to be rather to *The Plea of the Midsummer Fairies*, published in August 1827, than to Hood's annual *The Gem*, published in October 1828.

1/Muse of pastoral and comic poetry

2/To Watts's *Literary Souvenir* for 1828 Hood contributed 'Stanzas to Tom Woodgate.'

TO

ALARIC ALEXANDER WATTS

Dear Watts

I am waiting for your answer to my last, that I may know how to proceed, – for time now is precious. At all events send me back the paper.

In haste

Yours very truly

T. Hood

I've heard from Lamb – who says if he can get any thing out of his head for you he will.

2 Robert Street Adelphi [*18 September 1827*]

MS Bodleian. Address: 'To A.A. Watts Esqre, 58 Torrington Square.' PM: '4 Even 4. Sp. 22, 1827.' The letter is dated in another hand, four days earlier. Lamb, to whom Hood refers, wrote to him about his contribution to Watts's *Literary Souvenir* on this day, *Letters* III 131. Hood himself contributed 'Stanzas to Tom Woodgate.'

TO
WILLIAM JERDAN?

Dear Sir
I shall be obliged by your forwarding the packet to Mr Elton. I am just in the hurry of preparation for setting off on Monday for Hastings, – or the Poem should have been sent more immediately: – but yesterday, I was not at home till night.

I am
Dr Sir
Yours truly

Thos Hood

[*Adelphi, October 1827*]

MS Wisbech and Fenland Museum. This note accompanies a MS of Hood's verses 'The Kangaroos,' first published in the *Literary Gazette*, 13 October 1827, 667, and a version of the first verse of 'Stanzas to T. Woodgate,' first published in the *Literary Souvenir* for 1828. The MS bears a note signed 'WJ'. For this reason Mr W.L. Hanchant, Curator of the Wisbech and Fenland Museum, who kindly informed me of the letter and poetic MS, suggests that the letter is to William Jerdan, editor of the *Literary Gazette*. This is credible, except that Hood's other letters to the editor about this time are introduced with 'Dear Jerdan,' the reference to Elton is unexplained, and there is no other indication of a visit by Hood to Hastings at this time: it seems an odd time of year to visit that resort. The Elton referred to is perhaps Charles Abraham Elton (1778–1853), formerly a contributor to the *London Magazine*, or even Edward William Elton (1794–1843), the actor, who, according to the DNB, 'contributed a little to periodical literature.' When the latter died at sea in 1843, Hood wrote an address for the benefit of his orphaned family.

TO
WILLIAM JERDAN

Dear Jerdan
I have a friend or two coming to dine with me on Thursday next the 25th Ins^tt at 6. Will you give me the pleasure of seeing you amongst them? – An answer will oblige

Yours very truly

Thos Hood

[*Adelphi, October 1827*]

MS Pennsylvania. The 25th fell on Thursday in both October and January 1827. By October Hood seems to have been on terms of slightly greater familiarity with Jerdan, so I have preferred this date.

TO
SIR WALTER SCOTT

Mr Hood has done himself the honour of associating Sir Walter Scott with his new Volume: – partly because 'great names ennoble' books, as well as song[1] – but still more in acknowledgment of Sir Walter's kindness, and high claim to such tokens of literary respect.[2] He begs leave to say that he offers it most heartily & sincerely, & with a fervent wish that the Chronicles of the Canongate,[3] may be but as the Waverly of a New & a very numerous Series. –
Sir Walter Scott etc.

2 Robert Street / Adelphi Novr 5th / 1827.

MS NLS
1/Quotation unidentified
2/Hood dedicated to Scott his *Whims and Oddities*, second series.
3/Published 1 November 1827

TO
WILLIAM JERDAN

Dear Jerdan.
I wrote to you on Friday week, & have waited daily for your answer, – expecting a cheque on Longman's[1] – which just now would be acceptable.
Pray tell L.E.L. that she shall hear from me soon,[2] – you shall have an article yourself this week.[3]
I was pleased with your review of the Whims, – it was judicious & not overdone.

Yours very truly

T Hood

W Jerdan Esqre

You shall have something this week[4]

2 Robert Street, Adelphi. / Monday – [*November 1827*]

MS UCLA. Address: 'W. Jerdan Esq[re]/ Grove House / Brompton.' In his third paragraph Hood refers to *Whims and Oddities*, 2nd series, reviewed in *Literary Gazette*, 3 November 1827.

1/Partners with William Jerdan and Henry Colburn in the publication of the *Literary Gazette*
2/Letitia Elizabeth Landon (1802–38), poet, was Jerdan's 'effective colleague' on the *Literary Gazette*: Jerdan *Autobiography* (1852–3) III 173.
3/Hood's known contributions to the *Literary Gazette* extend only from 9 June to 27 October 1827.
4/This sentence is written on the outside of the letter.

TO
WILLIAM JERDAN

I should never have dreamt of asking for money in advance.

[*Adelphi, November 1827*]

From *Athenaeum*, 23 July 1892, 132, where the rest of the letter is paraphrased: 'Hood has asked Jerdan for an order on Longmans' house for payment for three articles. In sending the order Jerdan has assumed that it was "an advance." Hood replies that it was nothing of the kind, the articles having been sent in ... Jerdan endorses the letter, "... Pettish!!" ' Perhaps there is a hidden continuity between this letter and the last sentence of the preceding.

Brighton. March 23. 18[illegible].

The Wreck.

TO
CHARLES TILT

My dear Tilt.
I am really sorry to trouble you so – but if you can enclose me £5 more – by the bearer you shall have the whole in a few days.
I am bored to death by the delay of the Annual Editors – & Jerdan as well.

Yours very truly

T. Hood

2 Robert Street / Adelphi [*January 1828*]

MS Yale. Address: 'Mr Tilt.' The letter is dated in another hand.

TO
CHARLES TILT

Dear Tilt, If the enclosed is convenient I shall be obliged by having it by bearer.

[*Adelphi, early 1828*]

From Anderson Galleries, *Library of the late Adrian H. Joline* pt. VII, to be sold 19–22 October 1915, 46. The phrasing suggests contiguity with the preceding letter.

TO
CHARLES TILT

Dear Tilt
I don't know whether it will influence you in your design of the juvenile illustrations – but I think I could help you, mayhap, either by pen or pencil, – and if I could be useful to you in any of those ways or by any hints you may reckon on my best assistance: – In haste, –

Yours very truly

T. Hood

2 Robert Street [*Adelphi, date unknown*]

MS Rylands. I have been unable to date this letter, but simply put it next to other letters to Tilt.

TO
ROBERT BALMANNO

Is the *Fellow* within?
If he will be so good as to send on a slip Sir W. Scott's address, for Mr Hood, who is dunce enough not to know whereabouts Abbotsford really is.[1] N.B. A – great – deal – better – and going to attack Mrs Balmanno's Grayling. – Hers and Yours very truly

T. Hood

P.S. Better still – & the Grayling demolished.

[*Adelphi*] *7 February 1828*

MS New York. Address: 'R. Balmanno Esqre F.A.S. / Craven Street.' The letter is dated in another hand. Balmanno comments: 'This note was sent the day after I was elected a Fellow of the Society of Antiquaries.'

1/Hood was writing to Scott concerning verses which the latter was to contribute to *The Gem*, an annual published by William Marshall and edited by Hood. Abraham Cooper RA (1787–1868), battle and animal painter, an acquaintance of Scott, was in charge of the illustrations for *The Gem*, and Hood was in charge of the text. Cooper later contributed, like Hood, to the *New Sporting Magazine*.

TO
UNKNOWN CORRESPONDENT

Your note has found me almost in the coach for Brighton ... having been most miserably shattered by rheumatism ...

[*Adelphi, March 1828*]

From Sotheby *Catalogue*, 5 December 1921, 58. Perhaps this note precedes the recuperative visit to Brighton depicted in the following letters to Balmanno.

TO
ROBERT BALMANNO

Pray write soon.

My dear Friend.
We got down here safe, but heartily tired – I think Jane most fatigued of the two – and took up our quarters for the night at the Norfolk.[1] The next morning to my own astonishment & my wife's I got out & walked about a mile, on the shingles partly & against a strong wind, which now & then had the best of me. Here we are now settled in a nice lively lodging – the sea fretting about 20 yards in front, & our *side* window looking down the road westward – & along the beach, where at about 100 yards lies the wreck of a poor sloop that came ashore the night we arrived. Nobody lost. She looks somewhat like the 'atomies in Surgeons Hall,'[2] with her bare ribs & back-bone, & the waves come & spit at her, with incurable spite. We have had one warm beautiful day quite like summer, with the *flies* (the hack flies)[3] all about too; but today is cold – squally with rain. – The effect of the sea upon me is almost incredible, I have found some strength & much appetite already tho I have but sniffed the brine a single time. – The warm bath[4] has removed all my stiffness – an effect I anticipated from something that occurred in the coach. The approach to the Coast, – even at halfway had such an effect on the claret jelly that it took away all *its stiffness*, & let it loose in Mrs Hood's bag. The 'regal purple stream' has caused some odd results. – Made my watch a *stop*watch by gumming up the works – glued Jane's pocket book together & fuddled a letter to Dr Yates in such a style that I'm ashamed to deliver it. Pray don't let Mrs Balmanno take

any reproach to herself for the misconduct of her jelly – I suspect it was so glad to set off it didn't know whether it stood on its head or its heels – I rather think it was placed for safety Bottom uppermost. I forgot to say that the jelly got into her purse & made all the money stick to it, an effect I shan't object to if it prove permanent.

Jane is delighted with Brighton & wishes we could live there, – regretting almost that I am not a boat man instead of an Author. Perhaps when my pen breaks down I may retire here & set up a circulating library like Horace Smith.[5] I shall deliver my credentials to that Gentleman tomorrow.

So far was written yesterday. I got up today – ate a monstrous breakfast & took a walk, but could not fetch Horace Smith's – for I set out along the beach which being *shingle* the fatigue was *double*. As yet I don't think I have any ankles. I don't bore myself yet with writing (don't tell Yates this)[6] but amuse myself with watching the waves individually – or a seagull or the progress of a fishing boat, matters trifling enough, but they afford speculation seemingly to a score of old smocked glazed-hatted bluebreech'd boatmen or fishermen before my window & why not to me? There is great pleasure in letting a busy restless mind lie fallow a little – & mine takes to its idleness very complacently. Jane murmurs & wants books – (Scandal). *Her* mind is so used to be idle it requires a change. She takes to her victuals as well as I do & has *such* a colour, particularly on her chin! – Here is a look out of our window raging main and all – Jane made me draw it in my best style for your satisfaction. I leave to her the scraps to write upon – & subscribe myself with best regards to Mrs Balmanno & yourself, my dear Friend, Yours very truly,

Thos Hood

P.S. Mind & put on your hat when reading near the open window.[7]

25 King's Road, Brighton, / Begun on / Thursday / – finished on Friday 21 March 28

MS New York. Published by Jerrold 226–8. Address: 'Robt Balmanno Esqre/ 7- Craven Street / Strand / London.' PM: 'BRIGHTON-55- / MA 21 / 1828,' 'A/22 MR 22 / 1828.'

1/'The Norfolk Arms Inn, on the West Cliff,' *Brighton and its Environs* (6th ed., Brighton, 1825?), 23–4

2/'The surgeons have their own hall ... in Lincoln's Inn Fields ... The *Museum* within [contains the anatomical] collections of the great John Hunter ... among the curious objects is the embalmed *wife* of the celebrated Martin Van Butchell,' *The Original Picture of London*, 26th ed., ed. John Britton (1826), 303–4.

3/'Fly' is 'The name of a light vehicle, introduced at Brighton in 1816,' NED

4/Explained in n 3 to the following letter to Balmanno

5/Horace Smith (1779–1849), poet and author, contributed to Thomas Hill's *Monthly Mirror*, published by Hood's father, and achieved fame with *Rejected Addresses* (1812), written in collaboration

with his brother James. Smith retired from business in 1820, and settled at 10 Hanover Crescent, Brighton, in 1826. He wrote for the *London Magazine* and the NMM. Between 1825 and 1828 Smith published five volumes, which may account for the 'circulating library' of the text. Smith was the friend of many authors, including Shelley, Thackeray, and Hood.
6/Hood is probably here referring to Frederick Yates, the actor. Pieces called *Yates's faces under a Hood* and *Harlequin House*, reported to be the work of Hood, were to be performed on 14 April at the Adelphi Theatre, owned by Yates and Daniel Terry. However, the performance did not take place for reasons which appear to have been financial.
7/A reference to Hood's drawing below

TO
WILLIAM BERNARD COOKE

My dear Sir
I have just received yours & am pleased that the lines suited your purpose.[1] Mrs Hood desires me to present her best thanks to you for the Views in Rome, which I know well, having admired the free and spirited style of the etching. They will be a great addition to her collection and she is delighted with them from my description.[2] I cannot help regretting that your descriptive part of the work on Brighton is engaged – I am so fond of the coast, that any writing of that sort would be quite to my taste. I only mean by saying this – to place myself in your way in the event of any similar undertaking being proposed hereafter. If any verses should occur to me you shall have them – & perhaps when I come to town you'll show me the work. – I shall return on Thursday – in fact I must be back on that day so that my stay here will be very short – but it has done all for me that I could expect. – The Sea is always a great Physician to me – and Apothecary too.
As for my initials, you may use them or not as you think best, – Hoping to have the pleasure of seeing you speedily I am

My dear Sir,
Yours very truly

Thomas Hood

25 Kings Road – Brighton. [*23 March 1828*]

MS UCLA. Address: 'W.B. Cooke Esqre / 9. Soho Square / London.' PM: 'BRIGHTON / MA 23 / 1828,' 'A / 24 MA 24 / 1828.' William Bernard Cooke (1778–1855), engraver, especially of marine views, did much work for Turner.

1/Cooke's engraving of Smart's 'The Embarkation of the Doge of Venice,' in *The Gem*, facing 217, was illustrated by a prose passage by 'Thurma.' Presumably Cooke is checking the appropriateness of the prose to accompany his illustration. 'Thurma' was a pseudonym of Charles Wentworth Dilke (1789–1864), civil servant and critic, who had been a friend of Keats and a contributor to the *London Magazine*. He became a friend of Hood and the editor of *The Athenaeum*, 1830–46.
2/The *English Catalogue* dates Cooke's *Views in Rome* 1834.

TO ROBERT BALMANNO

Many thanks my dear Balmanno, for your very welcome letter – a treat, even where *letters* are numerous for almost every house has a little bill on the window. Along with yours came a lot of others, like an Archangel mail, just *thawed* – & they served very much to relish my breakfast. The Literary Gazette too was a godsend particularly as we afterwards exchanged it, or a reading of it, for the perusal of the Times, with our fellow lodger. I had amongst the rest an epistle from W. Cooke & one from Ackermann, recommending me to try Mahomet's vapour baths here[1] – that damn'd C. Croker[2] certainly put him up to it. – But I trust I know better than to trust my carcass to the Infidel, – I might get into his hot well & come out a *Muscleman*. The hot brine of the *Artillery* Baths[3] – (so called I suppose because they heat water for Perkins[4] & his steamguns) – has done more good for me – taken the stiffness out of my limbs – but my ancles still suffer from a very *strong weakness*. Thank God that I have found out that I have a stomach, – from the former state of my appetite I seem now to have *three* like a camel,[5] – & when the loaf comes up, I take off a very large impression. For example I have eaten today for dinner a turbot – a tart – & a tough old fowl that nothing but a coast appetite would venture on. But on the Beach you may munch anything – even an old superannuated fisherman –

I called on Horace Smith yesterday but he was out – today I have had better luck tho he was out still – for we met at his door, & I gave him your letter on the steps. I was delighted with him – & with *her*. – He was all that is kind & gentlemanly & I shall break thro my resolution & take a family dinner with them – tho I had vowed to accept no such invitations. I hope that he & I are to be quite thick ere I leave – if such a stick as I, may be thick with any one. Mrs Smith is an invalid on the sofa, & she & I regarded each other I believe with fellow interest on that account – I was taken with her very much, – & with the little girl too, who seems destined to make hearts ache hereafter. She has all the blossom of a beauty about her.[6] There were some grown up misses making a call so that we had not our visit to ourselves, but Smith & I contrived to gossip – he calls here tomorrow.

I should like to have made one at Green's – Your account of it is very amusing. Your meeting with Reynolds pleases me much & your liking of him, which I find is reciprocated on his part. – I trust you will sometimes meet in Robert Street – if there still be such a place. I can fancy Zillah Madonna's[7] pallor & her voracity – her '*blanc*' and her '*Manger*'. I can fancy Allaric A too – but after all *What*'s *Watts*? *We* are to be up to the Golden Square[8] party – or rather I am to be up to every

thing on Thursday & we shall meet in the evening of that day. Dont you think a crowded assembly *may* have all the effect of a *hot air Bath*? –
But the real thing is Brighton. C.C. didn't give it a fair trial – he was only shampooed, & dived, not into the bath, but the bathos – The fact is, he mistakes his Complaint – he keeps his *room* & calls it *room*atism. No man who pretends to such an affliction should lay claim to Fairy *Leg Ends*.
I am much amused with a squad of mer-men before the window – I observe they never walk more than eight paces on end – & then back again – 'all things by *turns* – & nothing long.[9]
They seem like old duellists so accustomed to that measure of ground that they can't help it. Today has been beautifully fine, sunshine & a fresh breeze, – luckily all the winds have been from S & west – great *points* in my favour – & quite 'equal to bespoke' – I watch over the expanses & Jane over the expenses, – so that I am more careless than cureless, & enjoy myself as tho there were no Tilts in being. I hear the waves constantly like woodpeckers 'tapping the hollow *beach*' Jane says there is something solemn & religious in its music & to be sure the sea is the *Psalter* element. – Besides my warm baths in hobbling along the beach, a great surge gave me an extempore *foam*entation of the feet & ankles so that I have tried the cold bath also. – But we have not had any Elizabethan sea – that is in the *ruff* state, tho we have violently desired to see a storm, and a wreck, – a pleasure admirably described by Lucretious. – 'Tis sweet to stand by good dry land surrounded – And see a dozen of poor seamen drownded'.[10] In the meanwhile Jane has picked up three oystershells, & a drowned nettle as marine curiosities – also a jelly fish, but she fears it will melt in her bag & spoil more watches. She enjoys every thing akin to the sea – even our little *moreen* curtains – & swears that Ossian's poems are nothing to *Ocean's*. She is only astonished to find *sheep* in our *Downs* instead of *ships*. With great labour I have taught her to know a sloop from a frigate – but she still calls masts *masks*. – Pray tell Mrs B. that Mrs H. will write tomorrow to her if the tide comes in – it is at present low water with her ideas. The fact is she gets fast & *idle* – but she was always *idol*ized. – The Fairy Legends she has perused (borrowed of Moxon) but don't send her any books here – as it will be but more kindness thrown away. I have offered to get Whims & Oddities for her at the Library but she says she wishes for something lighter & newer. She has overfed herself like the bullfinch & I am persuaded can't read. – Pray give my kind regards to Mrs Balmanno with my best thanks for all her good wishes, though she may suffer by the fulfilment – as I am regaining my impertinence. The Sea is coming in & the post going out – so I must shorten sail – It is lucky for you we stay but a week, or

you would find our *post* quite an im*post*. – Thanks for the *frank*ness of yours – We don't hold them *cheap*ly notwithstanding.

I am, My dear Balmanno
Yours very sincerely,

Thomas Hood

I expect there will be a letter for me from Lamb in Robert Street – if so will you have the goodness to put this address on it & commit it to the post.[11]

25 King's Road. [*Brighton, 23 March 1828*]

MS Yale. Published by Jerrold 229–32. Address: 'Robt Balmanno Esqre / 7- Craven Street / Strand / London.' PM: 'BRIGHTON / MA 23 / 1828,' 'A / 24 MR 24 / 1828.' The letter is dated in another hand, 24 March 1828.

1/'On the East-cliff there are ... steam and vapour sea-water baths, upon the Indian construction. Mr. Mahomed, the proprietor of the larger establishment of the kind, is a native of India, and well skilled in the art, termed by the Indians, *Shampooing*, a practice found peculiarly useful in the cure of chronic diseases, especially rheumatic and paralytic affections,' R. Sickelmore *The History of Brighton* (Brighton 1823) 44–5.

2/Thomas Crofton Croker (1798–1854), author of *The Fairy Legends and Traditions of the South of Ireland* (1825), to which Hood refers at the end of his third paragraph. Like Balmanno, Hood's correspondent, Croker was, from 1827, a member of the Society of Antiquaries. He was Registrar of the Royal Literary Fund from 1837 until his death.

3/'There is a ... suite of complete hot, cold, vapour, etc., public baths, in Artillery-Place,' Sickelmore, 44. Artillery Place was situated next to the West Battery House.

4/Angier March Perkins (1799?–1881), engineer and inventor.

5/According to Oliver Goldsmith *History of the Earth* (1774) III 307, the camel 'besides the four stomachs, which all animals have, that chew the cud ... has a fifth stomach.'

6/Probably Smith's second daughter Rosalind, b 1821: 'the beautiful, overburdened with eligible offers of marriage, though dying unmarried in 1893,' A. H. Beavan *Jas and Horace Smith* (1899) 289

7/Mrs Watts' maiden name was Priscilla Maden Wiffen. According to Alaric Alfred Watts, *Alaric Watts* (1884) 185–6, she had 'almost a Madonna-like expression ... It was, perhaps, that circumstance, rather than mere affectation, which led her young husband ... to transform her second name of Maden to Madonna, an euphemism whereat ... the profane made mock.' Zillah was the name of the wife of Lamech in Genesis 4: 19, and of Abel's virtuous wife in Byron's *Cain* 1821. Watts bestowed it on his wife, and it later became the name of their daughter. Mrs Watts died in 1873.

8/Reynolds' address

9/Dryden, 'Absalom and Achitophel' 548

10/Lucretius *De Rerum Natura*, beginning of Book II

11/Lamb had received a 'melancholy epistle' from Hood on 18 March 1828, *Letters* III 156.

TO
RUDOLPH ACKERMANN

... I should be happy to be a Contributor as usual to the Forget-me-not – but this year it will not depend upon myself. I have an Annual under my own Editorship, and am bound not to write for the others, a stipulation I regret certainly for your sake, as the connexion has been attended only with pleasure ... If I can procure absolution from my Publisher, I will place myself at your command.

[*Adelphi, 25 March 1828*]

From Maggs Bros *Autograph Letters* no. 234 (November 1907) 37. The date is given in the catalogue.

TO
JAMES HOGG

Sir
It is my pleasant duty to address you on behalf of a New Annual which has been placed under my care – to obtain, if I may, your valuable name & assistance for its pages. – In the absence of all claim upon you for such a service, I can only make this request as for a personal favour & obligation which I shall be most happy in any way to acknowledge. It is my *earnest* wish to see you numbered with the Contributors who grace my list – already a goodly company – & the very respect & value I attach to their names make me the more desirous of your own in the association. –

Pray believe in the respect with which I am Sir
Your most obed[t] S[t]

Tho[s] Hood

Ja[s] Hogg. Esq[re]

2 Robert Street/ Adelphi April 22nd 1828.

MS NLS. Published in *Notes and Queries*, 27 December 1941, 355. James Hogg (1770–1835), the Scottish poet, was a friend of Scott and contributed to *Blackwood's Magazine*. He did not contribute to Hood's *Gem*.

TO
JOHN CLARE

My dear Clare.
I have heard of your call upon Mr Marshall[1] & have been in expectation of a visit from you which I should have been glad of, for the sake of old acquaintance. – Perhaps I shall see you the next time you come to London: – and in the mean time I very much wish to hear from you in the way of all Editors of Annuals, – for you have heard of course that I am numbered with those yearlings. I hope to gather all those known to us of old in *the* '*London*' – so pray let me have some of your best verses, *and I will take care that they shall be properly acknowledged.*

Wishing you all happiness & comfort, I am My dear Clare, Yours very truly

Thomas Hood

Please turn over.
If Mr Van Dyk, be with you, as I heard some time since, will you say something kindly to him in my name – & that I sincerely hope he is better. I need not say that I should be glad of a communication from his pen – but pray do not trouble him if he be not well enough.[2]

2 Robert Street – Adelphi [*26 April 1828*]

MS BM. Address: 'For / Mr J. Clare / Helpstone. / Northamptonshire.' PM: 'STAMFORD / AP.28 / 1828,' 'PAID 1828 / 26 AP 26,' 'MISSENT TO NORTHAMPTON.' John Clare (1793–1864), peasant poet. Clare's *Poems* (1820), *Village Minstrel* (1821) and *Shepherd's Calendar* (1827), were published by Taylor and Hessey, and he contributed to their *London Magazine*. As a contributor he met Hood. Clare also wrote for the fashionable annuals. He published *The Rural Muse* (1835), but was confined to an asylum from 1837.

1/Publisher of *The Gem*

2/Harry Stoe Van Dyk, periodical writer, contributor to the *London Magazine*, and friend of Clare, died 5 June 1828.

TO
ROBERT WILLIAM ELLISTON

I am still a prisoner, but I shall be happy to talk over the Don Juan with you.

[*Adelphi, April 1828*]

From Myers & Co., *Autograph Letters* no. 348 (1947) 33. Robert William Elliston (1774–1831), actor and manager. He leased Drury Lane Theatre 1819–26, but became bankrupt at the end of the last year. From 1827 he leased the Surrey Theatre. Lamb and Leigh Hunt lauded his merits as an actor. A sequence of letters to Elliston follows, with the postmark on 102 providing the key date.
I doubt that the 'Don Juan' was ever written.

TO

ROBERT WILLIAM ELLISTON

My dear Sir.
If you continue of the same mind as to a Burlesque, will you favour me with an appointment to call upon me at your earliest convenience; as I should like to decide speedily to what other engagements I shall next direct myself. I have at present so many subjects on my hands that it is an object with me to settle without delay whether or not the Don Juan is to be one of them. I am My dear Sir

Yours very truly

Thos Hood

R. W Elliston Esqre.

2 Robert Street, Adelphi / Monday [*28 April 1828*]

MS E.L. McAdam jr

TO

WILLIAM ELLISTON?

My dear Sir
Will you put your Father in mind of me? I have expected to hear from him before this, and as my stay in town is uncertain I hope it will be early. – I have a project in my head I wish to submit to him, but *that* I must defer till I come to town again or till I see him at Winchmore.

I am Yours very truly

Thos. Hood

2 Robert Street / Adelphi [*end April 1828*]

MS Osborn. The addressee would appear to be Elliston's son, see next letter. Hood may refer to his visit in May 1828 to Lamb at Enfield near Winchmore.

TO
ROBERT WILLIAM ELLISTON

My dear Sir
I have waited at home for your Son yesterday & today, & I beg leave to remind you that my time is precious, & that I must come to an *immediate* conclusion on the subject of our Burlesque. Since I had the pleasure of seeing you I have had two fresh applications, & as I am about to leave town, I am anxious for a decision before I leave. Pray let me know therefore your resolution in the course of tomorrow.

I am My dear Sir Yours very truly,

Thos Hood

R.W. Elliston Esqre

2 Robert Street, Adelphi / Friday Evg [*2 May 1828*]

MS UCLA. Address: 'R.W. Elliston Esqre / Surrey Theatre.' PM: '8.MORN.8.1828 / 3.MY.' Friday was the 2nd. Published by Alvin Whitley *University of Texas Studies in English* 1951, 198.

TO
ROBERT WILLIAM ELLISTON

My dear Sir.
I am in possession of yours containing your Son's acceptance of the terms I proposed for writing the 'Juan Burlesque,' – & am glad that we have reached this point; as on the rest I expect we shall find no difficulty.
You will I trust absolve me of meaning any thing personal towards yourself or Son, when I state that it will be necessary for the Sum in question to be paid to me before I begin upon the work,[1] – an arrangement merely intended to meet my convenience – as it would be provided for by other engagements. I shall be ready in return to sign any agreements you may think proper for the production of the piece in one Month from its date.
I propose to leave town on Wednesday morng to commence instanter on the work, – but I should occasionally take care to see you in its progress: – If you will favour

me with a note tomorrow & an appointment for Monday, I will meet you either here or at your own house, that there may be no loss of time. I am

My dear Sir Most truly Yours

Thos Hood.

2 Robert Street / Adelphi Saturday [*3 May 1828*]

MS Fitzwilliam Museum. The letter was perhaps written the day after the last.
1/Elliston had been declared bankrupt in 1826 and had only received his certificate of release in June 1828.

TO
ROBERT WILLIAM ELLISTON?

My dear Sir
Business has detained me in town longer than I intended, but I have not yet received your promised communication as to the result of your interview with the other parties. I presume it has been unfavourable to your wishes, – but I was the more anxious to see you, because by an arrangement I have made I could in some degree meet you, for I should be sorry if we departed on so trivial a point. If you can therefore manage to give me a certain portion of the amount in cash, & the remainder by a Bill at a Month I could make it answer my purpose, – & I would remain at home till 3 tomorrow to settle every thing with you – but if on the contrary this mode should be unlikely to suit your convenience pray favour me with an immediate notification to that effect, by the Bearer, who is instructed to await your answer.

I am My dear Sir
Yours very truly

Thos Hood

Will you oblige me by taking charge of the note for Mr Blewitt, – whose address I have mislaid.[1]

2 Robert Street – Adelphi [*early May 1828*]

MS Cameron. This letter probably follows the preceding. Hood visited Lamb at Enfield in May. It may have been this visit from which he says he had been detained.

1/Jonathan Blewitt (1782–1853), prolific composer, was at this time musical director of the Surrey Theatre. He later collaborated with Hood in *Comic Melodies* (1830), and he set to music three of Hood's comic songs in the *Ballad Singer*.

TO
THOMAS GENT

Dr. Sir
On behalf of an Annual, for which I am literary A*gent*, I apply to T. *Gent*, for the favour of a contribution. Be pathetic, if you like, as on the Daughter of the Re*gent*, or jest, if you please, & be Pun-*Gent*, – but, pray be dili*gent*, and for this co*gent* reason, that time is ur-*gent*.

I am Dr. Sir
Yours truly

Thos Hood

For T. Gent Esqr –

2 Robert Street, / Adelphi / 2nd June, 1828

Transcript at UCLA. Thomas Gent was the author of 'Lines suggested by the Death of the Princess Charlotte' (1817) and of *Poems* (1828). The latter volume, 185–6, contains a tribute to Hood. There is no signed contribution by Gent in *The Gem*.

TO
ROBERT BALMANNO

My dear Balmanno
My Wife sent to Golden Square yesterday & Mrs Reynolds is at Egham & expected back today or tomorrow.[1] Mrs H— will be happy to go if you will take her & wishes to know the hour. I am sorry that I shall not be able to join you myself – being bespoke by business another way.
I am my dear Balmanno

Yours very truly

Thomas Hood

2 Robert Street / Adelphi / Friday 6 June / 1828

MS Rochester. Address: 'R. Balmanno Esqre/ 7. Craven Street / Strand.'

1/Golden Square was the address of John Reynolds, so the Mrs Reynolds referred to is presumably his wife.

TO

JOHN POOLE

Sir

Some years since it was my fortune to be the sub editor of the London Magazine, – when you were its contributor; – & I believe nobody could relish your very pleasant writings in that work more than I did. Pray let the vividness of that remembrance excuse the liberty I am now taking – as it will account for the earnestness of the request which I have to make to you: on my own behalf, and on that [of] a new Annual of which I am Editor. The great pleasure I derived from a 'Cockney's day in / France / *Paris*'[1] & similar papers from your pen, makes me extremely desirous of some little article from the same source for my collection: – and if you will so far oblige me, I shall consider myself your debtor for a personal favour. The annual I have charge of is yet unchristened but I am happy to say that Sir Walter Scott has entered himself on my list, & I expect to have the assistance of most of the old Contributors to the London.

Hoping for the favour of your early reply
I am Sir Your most obed^t S^t

Thomas Hood

J Poole Esqre

2 Robert Street Adelphi / 12th June 1828

MS Maine Historical Society. John Poole (1786?–1872), miscellaneous writer and dramatist, author of the popular play *Paul Pry* (1825). He contributed to the *New Monthly Magazine.*

1/In MS 'France' is written above 'Paris.' Perhaps Hood is here referring to Poole's 'New Year's Day in Paris,' *London Magazine,* January 1823. Though Poole did not contribute to *The Gem,* he wrote a polite reply to this letter, which is preserved at NLS.

TO
FELICIA HEMANS

Madam.
I had the pleasure of addressing you some time since, but the letter, I fear, never reached its destination. The purport was to bespeak your valuable assistance, for a new Annual which has been placed under my Editorship: – for I am very anxious to place you amongst my poetical contributors. Sir Walter Scott I am proud to say, heads the list, – & if you will so far oblige me, as I request, it will be a personal favour which I shall be most happy to acknowledge.

In the hope of your early answer
I am Madame Your Most obed^{t} Servt

Thos Hood

Mrs Hemans.

2 Robert Street Adelphi / 21st June 1828

MS Osborn. Felicia Dorothea Hemans (1793–1835), poet, dramatist, and contributor to magazines. There is no contribution from her in *The Gem.*

TO
THOMAS MOORE

Sir.
Will you oblige & honour me by your acceptance of a brace of books, without any reference to the request I shall have to make hereafter? – Having occasion to address you, I could not resist the opportunity for making this acknowledgment of the infinite gratification I have derived from your Works.
The request I have to prefer – and it is an earnest one, – is in behalf of a new Annual under my Editorship, – which I am extremely anxious to make illustrious by your name & aid. I need not say how proud I should be of any contribution in poetry or prose from your pen, – if your kindness may stretch so far to favour one who has the

misfortune to be quite a stranger to yourself. I beg leave to say that Your own conditions, in such a case, would be gratefully accepted.

I am Sir
Yours very respectfully

Thos Hood

Thos Moore Esqre

2 Robert Street / Adelphi [June 1828]

MS Cameron. Moore (1779–1852), Irish poet, published *Irish Melodies* (1807–34), *Lalla Rookh* (1817), and the *Life of Byron* (1830). Moore did not contribute to *The Gem,* though he replied pleasantly to Hood's letter: this reply is quoted in a cutting from a sale catalogue inserted in a collection of Hood's letters to Dickens from the library of Frederick Locker, now in the Huntington Library.

TO
MISS CHARLOTTE REYNOLDS

My dear Lot,
There's a blot! –
This is to write
That Sunday night
By the late
Coach at eight,
We shall get in
To Little Britain, –
So have handy
Gin, rum, Brandy,
A lobster, – may be –
Cucumbers, they be
Also in season
And within reason –
Porter, by Gum!
Against we come –[1]
In lieu of Friday
Then we keep high day
And holy, as long as
We can. I get strong as

A horse – *i.e.* pony
Jane tho keeps boney.
How is your mother,
Still with your brother,
And Marian too –
And that good man too
Call'd your papa, Miss
After these ah Miss
Don't say I never
Made an endeavour
To write you verses
Tho this lay worse is
Than any I've written –
The truth is I've sitten
So long over letters
Addressed to your betters
That – that – that
Somehow –
My pen,
Amen,

T. Hood.

[*Enfield, 11 July 1828*]

From Jerrold 246, who gives the above date as that of the postmark. The Hoods were on a visit to Lamb.

1/MS reads 'Egainst.'

TO

JOHN CLARE

Dear Clare,

Your poem came safely to hand, and I wish that in return I had only to send back a proof of it, – but the truth is that is is not exactly the kind of thing I should like to have of yours in my Book. You tell me it was intended to precede another work, – & it has so much the air of an Introduction, that it will not stand well, I fear, by itself. Now if you would write one of your Songs to Mary – or suchlike, it would be just the thing. I hope you will believe that I intend this only kindly, and that I am

Yours very sincerely

Thos Hood

Will you let me know if I shall return it to you or send it any where else?

2 Robert Street Adelphi / Friday [18 July 1828]

MS BM. Address: 'To / Mr John Clare / Helpstone / Northamptonshire.' PM: 'PAID 1828 / 18 JY 18,' 'MISSENT TO NORTHAMPTON.' The poem by Clare which Hood rejects in this letter was 'To the Rural Muse'; it was replaced by 'Thou art gone.' Clare was puzzled by such comment as Hood's, for he wrote on 3 January 1829: 'these Annuals are rather teazing to write for as what one often thinks good the Editors return back as good for nothing while another gives them the preference & what one thinks nothing of they often condescend to praise,' *Letters* 222.

TO
ROBERT BALMANNO

Dear Balmanno
Will it put you out of the way if I bring a brace of Friends, Mr Dilke & son,[1] to Craven Street, this Evening, to look at some of your Prints – at Eight o clock or so. Pray dont hesitate to give a *positive negative* if it be not quite convenient.

Yours very truly

Thos Hood

2 Robert Street Adelphi [29 July 1828]

MS Pennsylvania. Address: 'R. Balmanno Esqu / 7 Craven Street / Strand.' The letter is dated in another hand.

1/Dilke's son, Charles Wentworth (1810–69)

TO
HORACE SMITH

My dear Sir
The opportunity of a gig – the whim as it were of a moment – allows me the sudden opportunity of sending the accompaniments to this, – which were promised to Miss Smith long since: – They were to have been done sooner – Mrs Hood has added a

couple of views of Abbotsford – to make Scott & Lot. – She unites with me in kindest regards to yourself – & Mrs Smith, & family down to the Infanta[1] – I have only time to say that we number the seeing you all amongst our Pleasures of Hopes, & the remembrance of you amongst our Pleasures of Memory. –

I am Dear Sir
Very truly yours

T. Hood

2 Robert Street Adelphi [*summer 1828*]

MS Osborn. Hood met Smith for the first time in March this year, see 96.
1/Surely Laura (1828–64)

TO
WILLIAM HOWITT

I have received a packet from Mr. Marshall from you, for his Annual, and have with much pleasure availed myself of 'The Lost One,' 'The Three Pilgrims,' and the 'Nabobs.' I have printed besides some little Poems, with which I was favoured some time ago, under the Signature of R. Howitt; I presume a member of your family ...

[*Adelphi, summer 1828*]

From Maggs Bros *Autograph Letters* no. 234 (November 1917) 31. William Howitt (1792–1879), a Quaker, belonged to a family of writers. He and his wife Mary (1799–1888) published *The Desolation of Eyam and other Poems* (1827). *The Gem* contains 'Sonnet' and 'Song' by Richard Howitt (1799–1869) William's brother; 'The Nabob's Curse' by William; and 'The Lost One' by Mary. 'The Three Pilgrims' does not appear.

TO
CHARLES BENJAMIN TAYLER

Sir.
I have the pleasure of enclosing to you a plate for illustration, according to the desire of Mr. Marshall. The Painting is by Howard – & the subject I believe

Spanish Peasants. As the season is somewhat advanced, I have to request that you will favour me with the illustration at your earliest convenience.

I am Sir Your mo obed[t] Serv[t]

Tho[s] Hood

2 Robert Street – Adelphi / Saturday Morn[g] [*summer 1828*]

MS UCLA. In *The Gem* H. Howard's picture 'Nina' is accompanied by a text by the author of *May You Like It*, that is, the Rev. Charles Benjamin Tayler (1797–1875).

TO

UNKNOWN CORRESPONDENT

I am sorry to hear you have been annoyed in head or heart. My own head troubles me at times, & I am hardly reconciled to it, by flattering myself that it is 'an enlarged idea' – or that, 'tis one of the wise achers. –

Yours very truly

Tho[s] Hood

[*Adelphi*] *Augt 13. 1828.*

From Lawrence B. Phillips *Autographic Album* (1866) 209

TO

EDWARD MOXON

Dear Moxon
C.L. & Emma come up tomorrow evening & she goes off on Monday Morning. Will you come & dine with him here at 4 on Sunday? – They sleep here. –

Yours very truly

Thos Hood

[*Adelphi, August ? 1828*]

MS Osborn. Published by Peter F. Morgan *Tennessee Studies in Literature* 1964, 76. Address: 'Mr Moxon / Messrs Hurst & Co / 65 St Paul's ChurchYd.' Moxon worked for this publishing firm between 1828 and 1830. In July 1833 he married Lamb's protégée Emma Isola. This note shows Hood furthering the romance.

TO
EDWARD MOXON

Dear Moxon
Can you procure for us your Ticket for Friday Night to Vauxhall – If you can manage it let me know as early as you can as it is for a party.

Yours very truly

Thos Hood

2 Robert Street, / Adelphi [*August? 1828*]

MS New York University Libraries. Address: 'Mr Moxon / at Messrs Hurst & Chance / 65-St Paul's Church Yard.' Endorsed: 'If you like to have one for Wednesday evening let us know –.'

TO
ABRAHAM COOPER

My dear Sir.
I understood – (perhaps misunderstood you) – that you would let me know on Monday whether Mr Marshall complied with our arrangement. – viz that I should draw for £50 on Mr Marshall – say from 18th Septr – to come due on the 21st October. 50 from 18th October to come due on 21 November 50 from 18 November to fall due 21 December – the Bills to be given to me on the whole of the M.SS. for the first Sheet being in the printer's hands.
Pray let me know at your earliest convenience that I may proceed to complete the work, & believe me

My dear Sir
Yours very truly

Tho Hood

2 Robert Street Adelphi [*August 1828*]

MS BM. Address: 'A. Cooper Esqre R.A. / New Milman Street.' Cooper was in charge of the artistic arrangements for Hood's annual *The Gem*, which was published at the beginning of November 1828. The *Monthly Repository*, December 1829, 872, referred to 'its extraordinary sale, 5000 copies of the first edition, and 2500 of the second.' In spite of this success, Hood did not edit *The Gem* for the following year. His brother-in-law John Hamilton Reynolds wrote in 1829 to Hartley Coleridge, calling the publisher Marshall 'a very mean, impracticable, disagreeable sort of personage:' Hartley Coleridge *Letters* ed. G.E. and E.L. Griggs (1936) 100. Hood himself in 1843 called him 'an old Pirate – & hypocrite:' see 545. Several of the contributors to *The Gem* went unpaid.

TO
ROBERT BALMANNO

My dear Balmanno.
Jane & I were sent for at 3 o clock this morning to see my Sister Kate who was dead before we arrived. – I have not therefore been able to send to Reynolds as I intended, about Sir T. Lawrence. Will you, therefore have the kindness to do what you think best, –

Yours very truly

Thos Hood

[*Adelphi*] *10 Sep 1828*

MS Morgan Library. Sir Thomas Lawrence (1769–1830), portrait painter, President of the Royal Academy since 1820. Balmanno had been acquainted with Lawrence since 1824. The reference to him in the text is explained in the following letter.

TO
SIR THOMAS LAWRENCE

My Dear Sir
There are some sketches of Brighton – (in Cookes copper) & I have undertaken to scribble some notes on the margin of the sea.[1] To this end, I am here enjoying the breezes – which I in*hale* like a sea *sider* looking over a prospect that in its calm reminds me of a sea *peace* by Vandervelde & in its shingles of *Beechey*.[2] It is now like royal Bess – in its rough – and the wind, that great *raiser* of waives, is accompanied with a suitable *lather* on Neptunes face. It is besides high water – or more properly high *waiter*, for the tide *serves at the bar*: – & there is a great influx of the weeds that grow in 'the Gardens of the Gull'[3] ie Sea Gull. Afar off a lonely vessell is tumbling about – and observe here the goodness of providence that the rougher the storm the better the boat is *pitched* – while here and there in the foreground may be seen what Moliere with his French inversion would call a *Tartough*. The skeleton of a lost brig, like the bones of a sea monster lies at the extreme left; I am told by the

Brighton people that ship disasters are not uncommon here – they have often had Georgus Rex. You will understand, Sir, from this sample that my Guide will be unserious chiefly – but I contemplate a graver description of the Pavilion provided I can gain entrance to the interior which I understand is more difficult than aforetime. In a conversation with Mr Balmanno it occurred to me however, that you could put me in the way; for I do not even know the proper quarter to apply to – amongst the *Chain Piers*, but of course not Captain Brown's.[4] I have spent some time in making up my mind to trouble you on this subject – or head – considering how many better ones engage you – but pray *frame* some excuse for my freedom, which originates in my reliance on your kind feeling towards me. I have no doubt but that you can at any rate direct me how to get access, and even that will accessively oblige

My Dear Sir
Yours very respectfully

Thos Hood:

Sir Thomas Lawrence P R.A.
etc etc etc

31 King's Road Brighton, Sunday morning 16 Novr 1828

Transcript made by Robert Balmanno, in the editor's possession. Published by Mary Balmanno, *Pen and Pencil* (New York 1858), 146–7.

1/'Brighton, by Thomas Hood, with Engravings by W.B. Cooke, from original drawings by Samuel Prout,' was advertised at the back of the *Comic Annual* for 1830, but remained unpublished.
2/Van de Velde (1633–1707), Dutch marine painter; Sir Wm. Beechey (1753–1839), portrait painter
3/Byron, 'The Bride of Abydos,' 8
4/Sir Samuel Brown (1776–1852), engineer, devised an improved method of making chain-link structures and constructed the Chain Pier at Brighton in 1823. Hood's word-play here is not clear.

TO
ROBERT BALMANNO

My dear Balmanno
Many thanks for your kind attention. Your last arrived this morning (Sunday). I shall send what Bradbury[1] requires: – & I enclose Sir Thomas's letter.[2] – We shall return on Tuesday Week, – but if I get the Pavilion order, I shall perhaps remain a week longer. –

Your account of the Gem* was very gratifying, – not that I must reckon on my contingencies, – they are more likely to prove *dead* certainties. If Booksellers have a main sale they will pretend it was only a mizzen. –
I go on Tuesday to Smiths to meet a Mr Ricardo who wants to see me. Perhaps I may have seen him already but Non me ricardo.
We have been wishing for rough weather & it is come – blowing hard from the Sow Sow West – a pig gale of wind.
All our Compliments to all your Complement, – & all our regards in every regard. I am obliged to close hasily to save the post: but am deliberately My dear Balmanno

Yours very truly

Thos Hood

31 King's Road – Brighton. / 16 Nov: 1828

*Note
By the way our females here have taken to gather gems ie pebbles on the Beach & are cracking stones like so many ninny hammers. I expect they will be taken up by the Coast Blockade[3] for striking lights on the Beach – as they look for diamonds in flints. Editor –[4]

MS editor. Address: 'Robt Balmanno Esqre/ 7:- Craven Street / Strand / London.' A partly erased line after the recipient's name reads, 'Society for [illegible] of little Debtors.' PM: 'BRIGHTON-55-/ NO 16 / 1828,' 'A / 17 NO 17 / 1828.'

1/William Bradbury printed the *Comic Annual* for 1830.
2/The preceding letter
3/Coastguard
4/Here Hood playfully presents himself as the editor of his own letter.

1829

TO
ROBERT BALMANNO

My Dear Balmanno.
Can you give me the address of Sir John Phillipart. – You have a Blue Book I guess.

Yours very truly

Thos Hood

[*Adelphi*] *12 Jan 1829*

MS Morgan Library. John Philippart (1784?–1875), military writer. He is not listed in the *Royal Blue Book Fashionable Directory* for 1829.

TO
FREDERICK HENRY YATES

Dr Yates
You are quite correct as to the sums – I have received – £230 for the Entertainment & £195 being three quarter's salary according to our last arrangement.[1]
The only presentable matter to the Public you say you have received against this money is the One Act Piece – an assertion I wonder you could venture to make.[2]
That without one presentable act you could rehearse & announce an Entertainment with *particulars* in the Bills within three days of opening would stagger Faith itself. – The first Table Act was complete.[3] –
The Monopologue – 'Harlequin House' – was complete & to your entire satisfaction I remember, whatever you may now choose to say of it.[4]
The Second Table Act was complete except one Ballad Fishmonger's Hall, which when the stoppage took place you desired me not to go on with as a better subject might this year occur. The whole of the papers were left with you at Epsom. I am positive on this point.
On the new Engagement I have done a one act piece – & the completion of a 3 act nautical piece was postponed at your own particular desire:[5] I presume in favour of Mr Weaver's or Mr Ball's Red Rover.[6] It was however to be ready next year,

with a new Entertainment – which would complete the two years work. – When I spoke therefore of the alterations and re-writing in your last Entertainment as gratuitous I spoke correctly. In the same spirit which led me to bestow so much pains on York & Lancaster, I was willing to revise & work up the Entertainment as well as I could – but after what took place I naturally felt averse to any extra trouble, especially when the writing would have been rendered difficult & irksome by dissatisfaction if not disgust.

And now for what you state to be my only grievance – the postponement of York & Lancaster. You ought to remember that my connexion with you *began with a similar annoyance to the present: – but of much greater vexation.* I allude to this because the Gentleman in partnership with you, not allowing for such a remembrance, may think I feel too strongly on the subject. You had York & Lancaster in November but you speak of it as if it had only been in your possession just previous to the appearance of the Rover, for you attribute its' being deferred to the success of that Piece & Mallet.[7] I presume the Rover was not accepted & got up in a week & yet within that period of its coming out, you positively assured me that mine would be played. I had received the same *promise* weekly for some 4 or 5 Thursdays before: – besides being made to go thro the farce, for I must call it so, of a reading. Had you treated me with common candour & courtesy – putting friendship out of the case – I might have borne with the mischief and discomfort of the rest: – but in addition to an injury to my interests you have thought proper to trifle with my feelings in a manner I must & do resent. –

As to the future you tell me it will be time enough to talk of other arrangements when I have completed this year's engagement. The deferred Nautical Piece would have completed it, – & I can only say that if my 4th quarterly paymt should be duly made, the piece in question shall be ready for your opening next season – & there our connexion will terminate.

I shall forward a copy of this to Highgate that Mr Mathews[8] may be in possession of my views of the case, – & in the mean time I must defer calling on you, – as I have two days been kept at home to no purpose, by your appointments.

I am Yours truly

Thos Hood

Robert Street [*Adelphi*] *26 Feby 1829.*

MS Bodleian. Published by Alvin Whitley *University of Texas Studies in English* (1951) 192–3.

1/The complications of Hood's theatrical contributions are discussed by Whitley 'Thomas Hood as a Dramatist,' *University of Texas Studies in English* (1951) 184–201. The 'Entertainment' here referred

to is possibly *Yates's faces under a Hood!*, intended to be performed at the Adelphi Theatre on 14 April 1828, but postponed because of the financial troubles of the joint managers, Yates and Daniel Terry. Terry (1780?–1829) was an actor and friend of Walter Scott.
2/Possibly *York and Lancaster*, referred to in the text below. Though this piece was registered with the Lord Chamberlain on 24 December 1828, it was not performed until 5 October the following year. Six days later it was termed by *The News* 'a laughable one-act burletta.'
3/Unidentified
4/Probably *Harlequin and Mr. Jenkins; or, Pantomime in the Parlour*, according to Whitley 197, 'a vehicle for Yates, who played all its eight divergent characters, both male and female.' *Harlequin House* was intended to be performed on 14 April 1828 as part of *Yates's faces under a Hood!* After the failure of his partnership with Terry, Yates undertook an association with Charles Mathews (see below). The *Harlequin* piece was thus first performed as part of Mathews and Yates's *At Home*, 30 April 1829. The *Court Journal*, 9 May, 27, commented: 'This entertainment was originally written by Oddity Hood, for Yates, and *not* for Mathews; and was to have been given by the former, last year, but was deferred in consequence of Terry's embarrassments. Since then, however, some of the papers have been lost – (*said to have been* – is the malicious interpretation that we have heard), and the gaps have been filled up by Moncrieff, who has also adapted the whole to Mathews's talents and taste.' The writer sympathizes with Hood 'in the predicament in which he seems to have been placed by this sinister accident,' and identifies 'the whole of the piece at the end' as Hood's. This, according to the playbill, was 'a new grand pantomimical monopolylogue, etc., called "Harlequin and Mr. Jenkins." ' The entertainment received its fortieth and last performance in July. In 1832 a manuscript of this work was urgently sought after on Yates's behalf from Hood.
5/The actor Thomas Potter Cooke (1786–1864), who performed at the Adelphi in 1828–9, wrote to Hood's friend John Wright in December 1834: 'I wish you would ask Mr. Hood if he finished a nautical piece he promised for me *six years ago*!', Hood *Works* VI 194. The piece has not survived.
6/Edward Fitzball's *Red Rover* was first performed at the Adelphi, 9 February. R.T. Weaver's version was first performed at Sadler's Wells, 2 March 1829.
7/William Thomas Moncrieff's *Monsieur Mallet*, first performed 22 January 1829. *Mallet* and *Red Rover* were successful. On 29 September the Adelphi reopened with what *The Spectator* called 'those favourite performances,' 3 October, 631.
8/Charles Mathews (1776–1835), actor. In 1803 he married the half-sister of Lamb's and Hood's friend Fanny Kelly. From 1819 Mathews's *At Homes*, showing off his mimetic talents, were regularly performed; from this present year, 1829, often in partnership with Yates.

TO
WILLIAM JERDAN

My dear Jordan
... There is a little musical piece of mine come out at Surrey. My very first attempt done years since. Will you do me & Elliston a service by a mention (a paragraph merely) in the Gazette.

[*Adelphi, March 1829*]

From Maggs Bros *Autograph Letters* no. 451 (summer 1924) 202. Hood's *Mr. Sims* was first performed at the Surrey Theatre, 25 February 1829. It was mentioned in the *Literary Gazette* 28 March, 213.

TO
JOHN WRIGHT

My dear Sir,

I will accept your kind invitation for Monday.[1] I have never seen a deer, & therefore have never seen one hunted. What offence are they *carted* for? – I like the idea of the Wells.[2] *Rounding Squaring* reckonings must seem like a solution of the famous problem of the *Quadrature* of the *Circle*. – Am I to bring a dog with me or not – that is to say is it a Pic Nic? – The hour is very early – but I suppose I must be 'got up' for the occasion. At all events in the spirit of the Work – if Mr Cruickshank[3] *designs* to go, I suppose I ought to go in company. Perhaps it may turn out well – as well as the stag. – But how can one hunt in a Barouche? A single horse can leap a single gate but can 4 horses clear four gates at once. Has a Stag any brush that I can bring home & make a hearth brush whilst relating the exploits beside a winter fire.[4] –

I shall come in red with a cap & an umbrella which I trust is the Costume – Are pumps & silks indispensible? I have no top boots –

Yours very truly

Thos Hood.

2 Bob : Street. Adelphi [April 1829]

MS UCLA. Address: 'J. Wright Esqre / 4 New London Street / Fenchurch Street.' Wright, with his partner Robert Branston, engraved George Cruikshank's drawing of Thomas Rounding, referred to in the letter, for Hood's poem *The Epping Hunt*, an imitation of Cowper's *John Gilpin*; *The Epping Hunt* was published in September this year. Branston and Wright also engraved William Harvey's illustrations to Hood's *Dream of Eugene Aram*, published separately in 1831, and they were responsible for Hood's own illustrations to the early *Comic Annuals*. According to Jane Hood, the firm of Branston and Wright became bankrupt in 1833. Branston occupied Lake House, Wanstead, after Hood left it to escape his own creditors in March 1835. In this month, a partnership between Wright and William Armstrong Folkard, Branston's successor, was dissolved. Wright continued to engrave Hood's illustrations to the *Comic Annuals*, and to assist in their publication. This invaluable help, not always appreciated, continued until Wright's sudden death in December 1839. Folkard and his partner Orrin Smith engraved the illustrations to the *Comic Annual* for 1842.

1/Easter Monday, this year falling on 20 April, was the occasion for the annual Epping Hunt, at which deer were carted to Epping Forest, let free and hunted, for the amusement of Cockney

sportsmen like Hood and his friends. The event is described by William Hone, *Every-Day Book* II 27 (March 1830) cols 460–3.
2/At Woodford Wells Thomas Rounding was the popular landlord of the Coach and Horses, one of the hostelries at which the Epping Hunt began and ended.
3/George Cruikshank (1792–1878), artist and caricaturist, born in London, illustrated William Cowper's *John Gilpin* (1828), in an edition published by Charles Tilt, with engravings by Branston, Wright, and Slader. Hood's *Epping Hunt* followed the next year. Cruikshank also contributed to Hood's first *Comic Annual*. The very titles of many of the other works which Cruikshank illustrated show a temperament which must have been congenial to that of Hood.
4/*Macbeth* 3 iv 65

TO
WILLIAM BERNARD COOKE

Dear Cooke
Many thanks for your past present. – We are such Cannibals as to contemplate eating your little deer, if we can find how to Cooke it. It is pleasant to find a Friend who can *fawn* without flattery – I wish I could send you its mother, in return, – for we should '*Doe* as we are' done by[1] – according to the old orthography. –
My acknowledgments come late, but the servant said you meant to call some time today – as I would this evening, on yourself, but that I have been Doctoring myself without a Diploma –

With kindest regards male & female from us to your self & Mrs Cooke I am
My dear fallow
or Fallow Deer
Yours very truly

Thos Hood

2 Robert Street. Adelphi [*summer 1829*]

MS Huntington
1/*Book of Common Prayer*, 'Catechism'

TO
WILLIAM BERNARD COOKE

Dear Cooke
The following is a recipe for making a cheesemonger
Take
A single glo'ster cheese for the face – a piece cut out will form the mouth
Take a roll of ninepin butter for a chin
A cheesecutter for brows & nose
Two eggs for closed eyes
A scrap of butter paper for a collar or cravat
Two Dutch cheeses for shoulders
A Cloth
And the result will be a bust such as I have rudely sketched & which you can draw better if of any use. There's a sketch of an owl besides
You shall have the inscriptions on Monday
When do you mean to bring Mrs C to c us

Yours very truly

T. Hood

A cheesemonger

[*Adelphi, summer 1829*]

MS Cameron. The letter concludes with a sketch. Hood seems to be referring to '*Comic Composites for the Scrap-Book*. With humorous Lines by Thomas Hood, Esq. W.B. Cooke,' which was noticed in *Literary Gazette*, 25 July 1829. Similar *Implemental Characters* were advertised at the back of the *Comic Annual* for 1830.

TO
WILLIAM BERNARD COOKE

My dear Cooke
I think the best would be perhaps 'Comic Composites.' – in allusion to the composite order: – each figure being a medley. – Our kind regards wait on you both

Yours very truly

Thos Hood

[*Adelphi, summer 1829*]

MS Yale. Address: 'W.B. Cooke Esqre / Soho Square.' This letter is related in subject to the preceding one.

TO
FRANCIS GRAHAM MOON

My dear Sir.
I have seen Mr Mann & understand from him that your objection to the mode of payment, I proposed, is the disbursement of so large a portion of the expences on the 1st No. –
I have told you why such an arrangement was necessary, to suit my accommodation, – however, as I wish to meet you, as far as I can have this proposition to make – which will at all events equalize your payments – viz – that you shall pay me, now 30 Guineas, instead of sixty – for the first – & so on in advance of each no of 6 subjects. –
If this should not accord with your views – it will not be in my power to make any other alteration. – otherwise I am ready instantly to proceed, & therefore beg an immediate answer. Mr M. informs me that you have no objection to a clause engaging to complete the 4 Nos – which I should like inserted provided the above shd meet your assent.

I am Dear Sir
Yours very truly

Thos Hood

2. Robert Street, Adelphi [*1829*]

MS Cameron. A note says that this letter was addressed to 'Mr. Moon. Threadneedle Street.' Francis Graham Moon (1796–1871), printseller and publisher, became Sheriff of London in 1843, Lord Mayor in 1854, and was knighted in the following year. The work with which Hood deals in the letter seems to have remained unpublished. It might possibly be connected with the previous letter. The 'Mann' referred to might be G. Mann, bookseller and stationer, 59 Cornhill. According to the *City Press*, 28 October 1871, 2, Hood wrote a quizzing verse on Moon:

'Mid graphic gems,
At F.G.M.'s,
Whose taste no man impugns,
I spent an hour!
Would that were all
I spent at F.G. Moon's.

TO

SIR WALTER SCOTT

Dear Sir

Not having had the honour of hearing from you I have indulged in the hope that you meant to favour me with some little humorous anecdote for the Comic Annual, according to my late request.

I need not say that having been able to pride myself on your poem in the Gem, I am very anxious to have some such token of your kindness in an annual of my own. I do not desire a quantity, or – to speak it reverently – *Scott & lot* – a few lines only would suffice to make me as proud as the lady of Tilliebudlem,[1] – and I should be happy to acknowledge the obligation by note of hand – as well as heart.

I hope I have not been poaching on your New Editions of the Novels by the Illustration I enclose.[2] It is one of the cuts of my New Work – which is now printing in *fools*cap – but with *post* haste – pray therefore oblige me My dear Sir, with a line at your earliest convenience, & think me ever

Most respectfully & truly yours

Thos Hood

Sir Walter Scott Bart

2 Robert Street Adelphi. 3rd Septr. [*1829*]

MS NLS. Published in part by Reid 114–15. Hood dates the letter 1828, but it was written after the publication of *The Gem* at the end of that year, and before the appearance of the *Comic Annual* at the end of 1829, so it must belong to 1829. In spite of Hood's appeal, Scott did not contribute to the *Comic*.

1/In *Old Mortality*

2/Perhaps Hood sent Scott 'Enjoying the "Tails of my Landlord,"' which faces 105 in the *Comic*.

TO

SIR FRANCIS FREELING

Sir,

Having been desired by Sir Walter Scott last year to apply to you for a frank, I take the liberty of doing so again for the enclosed letter, & by your giving it a pass to Scotland, I shall be much obliged.

A similar desire for franking a book – by putting your name to it, has made me draw up the enclosed dedication of a comic annual, to which I was as much induced by your known regard for literature as by the joke – but lest there should be any thing in it in the least degree contrary to your inclination or feelings, I have thought best to submit it to you beforehand, with the assurance that if you prefer an undedication to you, the wish shall immediately be complied with.

I have the honour of being
Sir Your most obed[t] Serv[t]

Tho[s] Hood

Sir F. Freeling Bar[t]

2 Robert Street – Adelphi / Wednesday Morng. 3rd Sept[r] / 29.

MS Massey College Library, University of Toronto. Sir Francis Freeling (1764–1836) was Secretary of the Post Office and a book collector. The dedication which Hood encloses was included, with minor changes, in the *Comic Annual* for 1830. Hood was so impressed by Freeling's kindness that he named his daughter after him. She was born 11 September 1830.

TO

JOHN WRIGHT

Dear Wright

The cut is capital – & in good time. I will look after the printing. – The Zoolog. Catalog is the very thing. I shall do the ode on Sunday. – I took the Hunt to Jerdan but did not catch him and have written. – He will view it I have no doubt on Saturday. – I am going out of town on Saturday for a few days – but shall see you before I go – so no more at present from

Yours very truly

Tho[s] Hood.

M^rs. H. desires her particular thanks for the annuals.[1] – I am just finishing my last cut.[2]

[*Adelphi, September 1829*]

MS Harvard. Hood's *Epping Hunt* was reviewed in Jerdan's *Literary Gazette*, 19 September 1829. The first two monthly parts of N.A. Vigors' *Gardens and Menagerie of the Zoological Society*, with engravings by Branston and Wright, had been reviewed in *Literary Gazette* a week before. Hood's ode to Vigors on this publication was published in the *Comic Annual* for 1831.

1/Wright had presumably sent Jane a number of the annuals which had recently appeared.
2/The *Comic Annual* for 1830 was published at the end of November.

TO
WILLIAM BERNARD COOKE

Dear Cooke.
I have only the liberty of giving orders tonight for my New piece at the Adelphi. So I send the enclosed

In great haste
Yours very truly

Thos. Hood

[*Adelphi, 5 October 1829*]

MS UCLA. Hood's *York and Lancaster* was first performed at the Adelphi Theatre, 5 October 1829. This 'one-act burletta' was reviewed sensibly in *The News*, 11 October, p. 324: 'The story has no object but to give Mr. MATHEWS, Mr. YATES, and Mr. WILKINSON, an opportunity of displaying their peculiar powers; which they do much to the amusement of their auditors. / The author ... seems to have rested his hopes of success principally on a large assortment of puns, and some of them told well.' The play received its last performance on 2 December. 'Orders' were free passes to the theatre.

TO
WILLIAM BRADBURY

Dear Sir.
You must not proceed any further with the woodcuts – those I have seen are far from what I wish. – I regret that you did not send me a proof of them before going to press – the last 150 of the 'Single Blessedness,' according to the condition, will be

quite useless. I have sent the block to the Engraver & he fears it is spoiled; – which is a great vexation to me as I was particular about it, & requested you would let me know how it worked.
I have looked over the others – 'the Dutch Steamer' above all does not justice to the Cutter's proof, & I fear has got a similar injury to the other's. – It does not appear to me, on the whole, that the defect lies with the paper – & I beg therefore, that at all events you will stop where you are for the present.

Yours very truly

Thos Hood

2 Robert Street Adelphi. / Monday Eveng. [*autumn 1829*]

MS UCLA. Address: 'Mr Bradbury/ Warwick Lane.' Hood is here writing to the printer about his first *Comic Annual*, published at the end of November 1829. It was printed by Bradbury and Dent, Warwick Arms Passage. 'Single Blessedness' was cut by Branston and Wright, and 'A Dutch Steamer' by Slader.

TO
MISS KNIGHT

Mr Hood presents his Compts to Miss Knight & informs her that the copy of the Comic Annual which comes with this is meant merely that she may have an early one, – a better copy being in preparation – & Miss K's books of drawings will be returned to her with the latter, in a week or ten days.

2 Robert Street / Adelphi [*November 1829*]

MS Osborn. The *Comic Annual* to which Hood refers was published at the end of November 1829. In the Preface, viii–ix, he writes: 'I am indebted ... to one highly talented young Lady, who has liberally allowed me to draw upon her drawings, and with an unusual zeal for my woodcuts, has, I may say, devoted her head to the block. It is difficult to return thanks for such deeds, but I feel deeply indebted to the kindness by which her pencil was led.' Miss Knight designed the frontispiece and three other plates. Nothing more is known of her.

TO
N. CLIFTON

My dear Sir.
I did myself the pleasure of calling – having come here this evening. –
I only received your kind note within the last few days having been obliged to take Mrs Hood to Brighton immediately I got rid of the Comic. She has been dangerously ill with a liver complaint, – her Brother in law[1] said it was. – The hurry & anxiety prevented me from fulfilling many intentions – amongst the rest the presentation of a book to you, – which I have the pleasure of sending with this.
I have to acknowledge your kindness & patience with respect to the account which I hope very shortly to liquidate or greatly reduce. With a good deal of difficulty, belonging to these times – I have got uphill & acquired some little reputation: – but the effects in profit follow at some distance. The Comic, at least, will bring me a handsome income which you will be happy to hear, but the profits of the first will not be receivable, till about the birth of the second – thanks to the System of Book selling & Bills at 9 months which with me are most difficult of discount. I am accordingly prest at present, – but after the publishing acct in February shall be in possession of my Bills, – which I hope will be in part convertible, – & you may rely upon it, the very first consideration with me will be your claim on me. – I am

My dear Sir
Yours very truly

Thos: Hood

N. Clifton Esqre

4 Upper Street. [*Islington*] *Friday evening* [*December 1829*]

MS Huntington. Hood formerly lived in Lower Street, Islington, but I do not know his connection with the address given above. The letter was written after the publication of the *Comic Annual* for 1830.

1/Dr George Longmore

1830

TO
JOHN MARTIN

My dear Martin
I hope you will excuse my delay in answering your kind invitation which Mrs Hood & I were unwilling to decline if we could see a possibility of meeting you. – I had to take her for her health to Brighton whence we have recently returned & ever since I have been cottage hunting my lease here being at death's door & we are going I believe about the 8th Feby. to remove a few miles from town. The shortness of the time makes us in great confusion and I fear it will be quite impossible to have the pleasure we hoped on the First. – We intend to do ourselves the pleasure of calling on you before we go – Pray accept our kind regards to yourself Mrs Martin & family and believe me

My dear Martin
Yours very truly

Thos Hood

2 Robert Street Adelphi [*January 1830*]

MS UCLA. John Martin (1789–1854), painter of the sublime. His friendship with Hood is referred to in Mary L. Pendered *John Martin* (1923), 118. Hood is writing prior to his removal to Winchmore Hill, near Lamb at Enfield. He stayed there from February 1830 until February 1832.

TO
SAMUEL CARTER HALL

Dear Sir.
I should have much pleasure in complying with Mrs Halls request and your own, – but whatever comic pieces I may write will certainly be engrossed by my own comic annuals, – & having been a loser hitherto by annuals I have been compelled to make up my mind not to lend my pen or name again in that way without a retainer of fifteen guineas. – If this should seem a serious price for serious pieces – I can only say that the urgent demands upon my time, will not allow of any thing else: – Under these circumstances if you should still wish for any thing from me,

pray let me know at once, as I shall shortly be too much occupied to undertake any thing of the kind in question. – With best Comp[ts] to M[rs] H. & good wishes for your mutual success,

I am Dear Sir Yours very truly

Tho[s] Hood

2 Robert Street Adelphi. / Thursday Morng [January 1830]

MS editor. Address: 'S.C. Hall Esq[re] / 10. Stationer's Court.' Watermark, 1828. Samuel Carter Hall (1800–89), journalist and editor. From 1826 to 1837 he edited *The Amulet* annual, to which Hood this year did not contribute. Hall was associated editorially with the *New Monthly Magazine* from 1830; he edited the *Art Union Monthly Journal* from 1839. He married Anna Maria Fielding (1800–81) in 1824. Mrs Hall was herself an author and editor.

TO UNKNOWN CORRESPONDENT

Madam.
I addressed a Note to your Brother some days ago requesting to know whether it would be inconvenient for me to retain the chambers here a few weeks beyond the term (which expires on Monday) – at the same rent. – I am anxious to be informed on this point that I may make my arrangements accordingly – & if Mr. Bocquet should be still absent it will perhaps be in your power to give me an answer.

I am Madam
Your most obed[t] Serv[t]

Tho[s] Hood

2 Robert Street Adelphi / Saturday 6th [February 1830]

MS Cameron, where the date is given as '1829.' 'However, the only 'Saturday 6th' in 1829 was in June, while 6 February 1830 was a Saturday, and this seems a more appropriate date for the letter, which sounds as though it is written to Hood's landlady at Robert Street two days before he is due to quit that address: see 128. There is no evidence as to Hood's exact movements, nor as to the identity of his correspondent or the Mr Bocquet to whom he refers in the letter.

TO
UNKNOWN CORRESPONDENT

My Dear Sir.
I send you the key of the chambers, & on Friday will leave the Balance of rent due, at Mr Rogers's – my receipts & tax-papers got packed up by mistake & are gone down to Winchmore Hill, so that I must go down after them. – I will leave the list of the fixtures at the same time.
With all good wishes, in which Mrs Hood unites, I am

My dear Sir
Very truly yours

Thos Hood

I have made the above arrangement in case I should not have the pleasure of calling on you – I am so much pressed by business at present but if I find it possible will call, instead, in Royal Row.

2 Robert Street Adelphi [*February 1830*]

MS Yale. A draft reply appended to this letter seems to be signed 'E B,' perhaps the Bocquet referred to in the previous letter. Mr Rogers in the letter is unidentified.

TO
JOHN MARTIN

My dear Martin
I am to have a few friends to dine with me on Sunday next, – & on Monday Morning they go in a coach with me to the Epping Hunt, where we shall dine – & thence return to my cottage. *If you wish it* you can be in town on Tuesday by ½ past 10.
Now I think, – (with Mrs Martin whom I had the pleasure of meeting today) – that such a couple of days will do you good & I'm sure it will afford me very great pleasure if you will come. There is a stage goes at ¼ to 10 on Sunday Morng. from the Pastry Cook's within a door or two of the Saracen's Head Snow Hill, – which will set you down at my door at Winchmore Hill – & *unless I hear to the*

contrary I shall retain a place for you. I can manage your sleeping here. So pray come if you can which is all I can say for

Dear Martin
Yours very truly

Thos Hood

P.S. Winchmore is within the threepenny post district[1] – but I hope not to hear from you but to *see* you. –

[*Winchmore Hall, early April 1830*]

MS Huntington. Hood seems to be writing in the first flush of his enthusiasm for his country residence at Winchmore Hill. The Epping Hunt as usual took place on Easter Monday: in 1830 this was 12 April.

1/The threepenny district extended about twelve miles from the General Post Office.

TO
CHARLES TILT

Dear Tilt
I was sorry you could not get to the Hunt – as we had a pleasant day of it. Wright has promised to dine with me here on Sunday at 5. – & I shall be very glad to see you by the early coach on same day – there is one goes from the confectioner's Snow Hill close to the Saracen's Head *at* 10 in the Morng which will bring you here about 1 – If you miss that there are ½ hourly Edmonton stages which bring you within 1½ miles. – the other sets down at the door – which I would have you come by, & later the whole of a fine day before you. I don't expect any one else except *perhaps* Andrews[1] Drop me a line in answer – I am Dear Tilt Yours very truly

Thos Hood

Winchmore Hill – near Enfield [*14 April 1830*]

MS Cameron. Address: 'Mr. C. Tilt / Bookseller / 88 Fleet Street / London.' PM: '7 – NIGHT – 1/AP 14/1830.'

1/Unidentified

TO
CHARLES TILT

My dear Tilt
You shall have the announcement of the Epsom in the course of tomorrow – Tuesday – *without fail* – I got your letter & will write its answer at same time I am in haste.

Dear Tilt
Very truly yours

Thos Hood

[*Winchmore Hill, June 1830*]

MS Liverpool Public Library. Address: 'Mr C. Tilt / 86 Fleet Street.' The work to which Hood refers in this letter, *Epsom Races*, was announced in the second edition of his *Epping Hunt*, 1830, the announcement being reprinted in the *Literary Gazette*, 17 July 1830, 465. However, the work was not published.

TO
P. HURST

I fully meant to call on you on monday but the weather kept me too long a prisoner at Pimlico.

[*Winchmore Hill, June 1830*]

From Anderson Galleries *Library of the late Adrian H. Joline* pt VII, to be sold 19–22 October 1915, 45. Perhaps P. Hurst was partner in the firm of Hurst and Chance which published the *Comic Annual* for 1830. Pimlico was the address of Hood's friend Charles Wentworth Dilke, whom he was presumably visiting. The date and address are given in the catalogue.

TO
CHARLES LAMB

Dear L, –
I am afraid you have had but little comfort yet of your change – pray let us know when your Sister is better.[1] – Jane is as usual, hitherto, – but I expect now will lay up in a week or two.[2] –
I suppose it's a sin to tempt you or ask you again to these pastoral parts but I need

not say we should be glad to see you. –
I send you the 'Hercules,' which I shall be glad to see again in Blackwood[3] & am

Dear L Very truly yours

Thos Hood

Winchmore Hill / near Enfield [*6 August 1830*]

MS Cameron. Address: 'C. Lamb Esqur / 34 Southampton Buildings / Holborn.' PM: '7. NIGHT.7 / AU.6 / 1830.'

1/Mary Lamb (1764–1847), after fatally stabbing her mother in a fit of insanity in 1796, had been put in the care of her brother. Together they wrote *Tales from Shakespeare* (1807). The Lambs had removed to 34 Southampton Buildings at the beginning of July 1830. Mary had immediately fallen ill and remained so until the end of the year. They returned to Enfield probably at the beginning of November.

2/Jane was expecting a baby.

3/Hood had perhaps seen the MS of Lamb's 'Hercules Pacificatus,' first published in Moxon's *Englishman's Magazine*, August 1831, 606–8.

TO CHARLES WENTWORTH DILKE

Every day I am a step-father to being a parent.

[*Winchmore Hill, August 1830*]

From Dilke I 27. Jane Hood gave birth to a daughter on 11 September 1830.

TO WILLIAM BERNARD COOKE

My dear Cooke –
You will be very glad to hear that I am at last a Father. Jane was taken ill on Friday evening, & on Saturday Morning at 6 presented me with a little daughter – tho it was *sun*rise.[1] They are both doing very well indeed, – The Mother wished for a Girl; & to make her the more happy, it is a striking likeness of the infant she lost, so that I am very glad it was a girl too; for my own sake as well as hers, for the last was a great regret to us.
My pretty babe seems to improve hourly, & is quite a pet with me already, – I have had a very anxious time, – but now my head & heart seem so light, I am going to

settle to work with cheerfulness & conclude the comic con amore.
I have had another addition besides to my establishment a bay pony, lately. Britton's which I have bought of him, chaise & all,[2] – I shall soon hope to drive you down in it to see Miss, & Missis, – the last of whom joins with me in kind regards to you; Jane & Child are almost 'better than can be expected,' may be your account to any of our friends you may see, –

I am My dear Cooke
Very truly yours

Thos Hood

Winchmore Hill – / Sunday. [*12 September 1830*]

MS New York. Address: 'W.B. Cooke Esqre / 27 Charlotte Street / Bloomsbury.' PM: '12. NOON.12. 1830 / SP.13.'

1/Hood's daughter Frances Freeling was born on 11 September 1830. She was named after Sir Francis Freeling, Secretary of the Post Office. 'Fanny' Hood in 1849 married the Reverend John Somerville Broderip; four daughters were born of the marriage. Fanny collaborated with her brother Tom (1835–74) in compiling the *Memorials* of her father and in editing his works. She also produced many volumes for children, which have been overlooked by historians in that field. She died in 1878. Tom Hood studied at Pembroke College, Oxford, but went down without getting his degree. He wrote and illustrated several books, including *Rules of Rhyme* (1869); he edited *Fun*, the rival of *Punch*. Though married twice, he left no children.

2/Probably John Britton (1771–1857), antiquary and topographer. With Edward Brayley Britton had worked on *The Beauties of England and Wales*, published until his death by Hood's father. In his *Auto-Biography* (1850) I 118n, Britton calls Hood his friend.

TO
EDWARD MOXON

I have not left Winchmore, but am father than I was by the length of a little girl. She and mother are doing quite well.

[*Winchmore Hill, 16 September 1830*]

From Sotheby *Catalogue* 30 November 1892, 6. The date is given there.

TO
MRS MARIA DILKE

My dear Mrs Dilke
If it be a fine tomorrow – Wednesday – which it seems likely to be, I shall come for you, – I guess about one or two o'clock I reckon; – Jane is very well & down stairs. – Baby ditto ditto. – The latter has enquired after you several times. I intend to drive Dilke down on Saturday – lest he should pine after you – & I dare say I shall see him tomorrow in going thro the city – I beg pardon the West End. Janes desires her love, in the meantime, & I really am

My dear Mrs Dilke
Very truly yours

Thos. Hood

P.S. I find since writing the above that I must be in the city on business – would you therefore take one of your stages to St Pauls & meet me at Little Britain – before 3 or 4.

Winchmore Hill. Tuesday. [*September 1830*]

MS UCLA. Maria Dilke was the wife of Charles Wentworth Dilke and the friend of both Hood and Jane. According to Reid 117, she was Fanny's godmother.

TO
JOHN WRIGHT

Here follows a learned letter

Chère (French for dear) Wright
Ego (I in Latin) – agree with you & feel the cover need not be so very braw (Celtic for fine.) – If the song of the Bulbul Persian for Philomel cannot recommend itself – a fine plumage will be all gumberry jah! –(Australian for I know not what)[1] I agree also about giving the Defence & the introduction of it is as easy as Alpha Beta Gamma – (the Greek ABC) I have done it slick right away (American for off hand)[2] I trust the title will suit to a Pekoe – (the Chinese for a tea) – If we can sell 3000 it will bring in the mopusses (the Spanish). You say you liked the preface & my announcement & I am glad of it by Gum (Arabic). When I am quit of the Comic you must come & be merry at my Bungalow (Hindoo for cottage) – & in

the meantime my cara sposa (Jane Hood in Italian) joins in kind regards to your self & frow (Dutch – Wife) & Ich Bin (German)

Your semper eadem

Thos Hood

Let me see a revise of the whole.

[*Winchmore Hill, October 1830*]

MS Bodleian. Perhaps the defence to which Hood refers in the letter is that against his newly sprung-up rivals which appears in the Preface to the *Comic Annual* for 1831, vi–ix.

1/The phrase 'gumbery jah' is quoted by Barron Field from an 'Australian National Melody' in his 'Journal of an Excursion across the Blue Mountains of New South Wales,' *London Magazine*, November 1823, 465.

2/According to Craigie and Hulbert *Dictionary of American English* (Chicago 1938–44), the phrase first appeared in print in 1818. The first English usage given in NED occurs in a letter of Macaulay of 1832.

TO JOHN WRIGHT

Dear Right, – All right and thanks. Saddle my horse by all means – the 'Harriers' will do as it is – the sound is sufficient to indicate the meaning[1] ...
Have you got the Vigors Ode – I have just made the following addition to it after the line –

'Like real creatures natural and true
Ready to prowl, to growl, to pounce, to fight,
I've lauded Harvey who their portraits drew
But to the Cutlass, no mean praise is due
To Branston always and to Always Wright.'[2]

I am getting on well, and very much to my mind.[3]

[*Winchmore Hill, 20 November 1830*]

From Maggs Bros *Autograph Letters* no. 270 (October 1911) 47. The date is given in the catalogue.

1/The frontispiece to the *Comic Annual* for 1831 is labelled 'Engraved in the OLD SCRATCHY Style by T. Hood,' and is entitled 'A DAY AT THE DEVIL'S DYKE. WITH THE OLD HARRIERS.' It is dated 1 November.

2/'Ode to N.A. Vigors, Esq. on the publication of "The Gardens and Menagerie of the Zoological Society" ' is published in the *Comic Annual* for 1831. Branston and Wright engraved William Harvey's illustrations in the first volume of the work referred to in the title of the ode; it was published on

9 October 1830. In the *Comic Annual*, 70, the fourth line of the addition runs more sensibly, 'And to the cutters praise is justly due.'
3/Hood needed to be 'getting on well,' for three rival comic annuals had already appeared, W.H. Harrison's *The Humourist*, the *New Comic Annual*, audaciously put out by Hood's former publishers Hurst and Chance, and Louisa M. Sheridan's *Comic Offering*.

TO
WILLIAM JERDAN

My dear Jerdan
I send you the first set of sheets I can get, & will send the blocks of the Step Father & one or two others to Moyes's in the course of this day.[1]
Wife Self & Babe are in town for a week & intend to have the pleasure some morning of calling in at Grove House.

I am Dear Jerdan
Very truly yours

Thos Hood.

27 Golden Square. [*December 1830*]

MS Pennsylvania. Address: 'W. Jerdan Esqre / Grove House / Brompton.' The letter was written from the home of J.H. Reynolds. Moyes, referred to in it, was the printer of the *Literary Gazette* which, 18 December 1830, included a review of the *Comic Annual*, illustrated by three cuts. The review welcomed 'the true Amphitryon of wit and pun at last.'

TO
SIR FRANCIS FREELING

My dear Sir.

Many thanks for your kind present & still kinder remembrances. The last give me great pleasure & the first will do me great good. As food, *two* birds must be of a bracing quality.

I am just at the fag end of my Annual, but hope in a few days to endorse myself 'Free,' & to soon appear accordingly at your office.

I am My dear Sir
Very sincerely & gratefully yours

Thos Hood

Sir F. Freeling Bart

Winchmore Hill / Wednesday Night [*December 1830*]

MS editor. I guess that the letter belongs to the end of this year. In the previous year Hood had dedicated the *Comic Annual* to Freeling, and this year he had named his daughter after him.

Chubb's Locks. O what a Goose!

1831

TO
ROBERT SANDS

Dear Uncle – For certain reasons I do not think Tilt would like to interfere between you & Le Keux in the matter you mention ... I propose calling on Bess & Jess on Friday morning ... rides & roads permitting, which, with the present weather, 'seems dubbious.'

[*Winchmore Hill, 2 February 1831*]

From Maggs Bros *Autograph Letters* no. 343 (spring 1916) 66. The date is that of the catalogue. I do not know what the matter referred to in the letter was. Bess and Jess are Hood's sisters Elizabeth and Jessie.

TO
THE DUKE OF DEVONSHIRE

My Lord Duke,
On learning that Your Grace is at Chatsworth, I send off as many titles as have occurred to me; promising myself the honour and pleasure of waiting upon Your Grace with some others on the 14th, and am,

My Lord Duke,
Your Grace's most obliged and obedient servant,

Thos. Hood.

Winchmore Hill. [*April 1831*]

From *Memorials* 1 31, where the date is given. William George Cavendish, sixth Duke of Devonshire (1790–1858), possessed marked literary taste. The titles for a door faced with sham books, which Hood adds to his letter, have been here omitted, though the first might stand for the rest: 'On the Lung Arno in Consumption. By D. Cline.' Hood had dedicated to Devonshire the *Comic Annual* for 1831.

TO
SAMUEL CHAPPELL

Sir
I am likely to leave here for Ramsgate on Wednesday morning. If you can make it convenient therefore to call upon me on Tuesday, I shall be happy to see you, – & in the mean time have only to say that my last letter to you precisely states the case as it stands between Mr Blewitt &

Sir Your moobedt Servt

Thos Hood.

Chappell Esqre

Winchmore Hill / Monday Morng. [*summer 1831*]

MS Indiana University. Hood and Blewitt collaborated in *Comic Melodies* (1830), and Blewitt set to music three of Hood's comic songs in the *Ballad Singer*. The 'case' between Hood and Blewitt probably involved these publications. Chappell is probably the music publisher, Samuel Chappell (d 1834) who started business in 1811 and published songs by Hood and Blewitt.

TO
ALARIC ALEXANDER WATTS

Many thanks, my dear Watts, for your kind attempt to rescue my 'Plea' from the 'Common Pleas.'

[*Winchmore Hill, November 1831*]

From Alaric Alfred Watts *Alaric Watts* (1884) II 153. Watts praised Hood's *Plea of the Midsummer Fairies* in the *Literary Souvenir* for 1832, 245n. The *Souvenir* appeared at the end of October 1831. Presumably Hood is here thanking Watts for saving him from the adverse judgment of complete oblivion at the bar of public opinion.

TO
WILLIAM JERDAN

My dear Jerdan,
Many thanks for your kind note. You will, of course, receive one of the earliest Comics. It is at present riding on my back, like a centipede spurred on each foot, to be out by 1st December. This must be my excuse for haste. As it is all but a

monopolylogue, it takes all my moments at present.

You will receive one of these days a reprint of 'Eugene Aram's Dream,' with designs by Harvey. It was coming out with the 'Comic,' but will precede it. It has already been indebted to your good word, without plates, and I dare say you will find something very praiseable in those. With reciprocation of kind regards, I was, is, and shall be,

Dear Jerdan, yours ever truly,

Thos. Hood.

W. Jerdan, Esq.

Winchmore. [*November 1831*]

From Jerdan *Autobiography* (1852–3) IV 201. *The Dream of Eugene Aram,* to which Hood refers in the letter, was noticed in the *Literary Gazette,* 26 November 1831. The *Gazette* had noticed the poem among the contents of *The Gem* three years before, 18 October 1828: 'Were it not that the end is rather feeble ... we would say that this is one of the most remarkable poems of modern literature.' Hood needed to hurry with the publication of the *Comic Annual* this year, 1831, because *The Humourist* and the *Comic Offering* had already appeared in October. The *Comic Annual* itself received a front-page review in the *Literary Gazette,* 10 December.

TO
WILLIAM JERDAN

Dear Jerdan

I send you the Copy – you might well think it was not coming – printer & binder made so long a job of it.

A pretty stand my friend made yesterday against Campbell & Co.

Yours very truly

Thos Hood

In the midst
of moving or at least packing.

[*Winchmore Hill, November 1831*]

MS editor. Water-mark '29.' The first sentence seems to refer to *The Dream of Eugene Aram,* published in November. The second sentence I cannot explain.

1832

TO
ROBERT SMITH SURTEES

With regard to becoming a contributor, I send a ballad to break the ice, and have no doubt we shall fall in – I mean as regards terms.

[*Winchmore Hill, February 1832*]

From *R.S. Surtees by Himself and E.D. Cuming* (Edinburgh 1924) 125. Robert Smith Surtees (1803–64), creator of Jorrocks, was the editor of the *New Sporting Magazine* (1831–6), which reviewed the *Comic Annual* in February 1832, 230. To the following issue Hood contributed his ballad 'Jarvis and Mrs Cope,' but he did not contribute again until November 1839.

TO
WILLIAM BERNARD COOKE

My dear Cooke
Your letter & the enclosure came safe – if you should want such a thing again, have the goodness to remember me. – I shall have much pleasure in doing it. I saw Jennings[1] the other day & he told me what you have written. I came back in the full intention of writing to you but I had a doubt afterwards whether you were now in the Square[2] & deferred it as I expected to be soon up in town.
I am truly concerned to hear of so many troubles coming upon you at once. Your affairs I hoped were in better train – but you must not despond. – I think if you would contrive to spend a day or two here with me in quiet, it would refresh you in both mind & body & you have need of it in both. If you can any how manage to [get] away – there is a bed here, & we shall be by ourselves, – which I know you would like best, so let me know at once when you will come. It has done me a world of good. I am quite in love with the place & so are all who have seen it. I think you know me well enough to have no doubt of the sincerity of the welcome that would meet you. Let me hear from you on this.[3]
Mrs. Hood was very much concerned to hear of poor Mrs. Jackson's death, &

desires to write[5] with me in all kindness to you & particularly in the request that you will come down here. – Believe me

My dear Cooke
Ever yours sincerely

Thos Hood

P.S. I have just arranged to be at Mr Reynolds in Little Britain on Saturday with Jane. See us there if you can or at all events leave word there.
God bless you.

[*Wanstead, early 1832*]

Transcript at UCLA. Hood is probably writing from Lake House, Wanstead, whither he moved in February 1832.

1/Unidentified
2/Cooke's address was 9 Soho Square.
3/Charles Macfarlane, who does not appear to have been an intimate friend, comments on Hood at Wanstead: he 'was invaded by the insane fancy that he could save expenses and even make money by farming ... [so he] took a large house on the edge of Epping Forest ... As the house was so roomy, he could give his friends beds, and as a general rule those who went to dine stayed all night ... The house was seldom devoid of guests ... and Tommy's cockney friends ... took up quite a romantic passion for the scenery of the Forest': *Reminiscences of a Literary Life* (1917) 106. Macfarlane (d 1858) settled in London in 1829 and supported himself by miscellaneous literary work.
4/Unidentified
5/This should perhaps be 'unite.'

TO
JOHN WRIGHT

Dear Wright
I send three more blocks, the articles for which are making up. Verbum Sat.
I shall be all done I hope to morrow – I wish the books were as done up as feels

Yours very truly

T Hood.

Pray don't forget to stir Harvey with the gravy spoon.[1]
Air – 'Time – Time – time'!

[*Wanstead, autumn 1832*]

MS Harvard

1/William Harvey (1796–1866), engraver, was apprenticed to Thomas Bewick, before moving to London in 1817 and studying under Benjamin Robert Haydon. A popular artist, he designed illustrations for the *Comic Annuals* for 1831, 1833, and 1835. Hood's only rival in 1832, apart from the upstart *Comic Magazine*, begun in April, was the *Comic Offering*, which appeared early in October.

TO CHARLES TILT

Dear Tilt

I send you the placing of cuts for all the rest of the sheets, – Harvey has made a *beautiful* frontispiece. If you think best to subscribe before, do – but you can have a proof of it on Tuesday –

I have asked Wright to explain all he can to you about Jerdan &c.[1] & am Dear Tilt Yours very truly

Thos Hood

[*Wanstead, autumn 1832*]

MS New York. Hood discusses William Harvey's frontispiece for the *Comic Annual* for 1833.

1/Jerdan's *Literary Gazette*, 15 December 1832, reviewed the *Comic Annual*, which had been received late in the week. The following letter suggests that Hood's friend and artistic collaborator Wright needed to explain the fact that the *Comic* had been reviewed in advance of publication.

TO CHARLES TILT

Dear Tilt.

I think you are right – but the stopping of it in the Athaeneum is I know too late, – & the other must therefore stand. But I am all but done – shall be by Saturday & Bradburys must push on *night* & day if necessary – & we have nothing for it but to get out as soon as possible after the notices.

Please send me p. Bearer three sets of the Sheet Cuts. – of former Comics I mean.

Yours very truly

Thos Hood.

[*Wanstead, December 1832*]

MS Cameron. The *Comic Annual* for 1833 was reviewed in *The Athenaeum* 15 December 1832. It was printed by Bradbury and Evans.

TO
WILLIAM JERDAN

My dear Jerdan,

I have often had to thank you for kindly mention of my works, and I will not omit my acknowledgments when I find in the 'Gazette' all that man ought to wish for. 'Man wants but little here below, nor wants that little long.'[1]

There are other arguments in favour of brevity besides its being the soul of wit – 'short accounts make long friends' – and I cannot but be flattered by a Lilliput account of the Comic from a friend of Brobdignag Standing.

I write this, dipping by turns into a glass of ink and a glass of sherry, poured out to your health, and I shall never take 'something short,' without dedicating it to the same toast.

Friends ought to be friends, whether in Long Island or the Inch of Perth, and as even semibreves conduce to harmony, your little 'taste,' or rather sip 'of my quality,' still leaves me,

My dear Jerdan, yours very truly,

Thos. Hood.

Lake House, Wanstead. / December. [*1832*]

From Jerdan *Autobiography* IV 202. Jerdan reviewed the *Comic Annual* for 1833 in the *Literary Gazette* 15 December 1832.

1/Goldsmith, 'The Hermit'

TO
THE DUKE OF DEVONSHIRE

My Lord Duke.

I am extremely obliged to your Grace for the kind and early answer to my request concerning Lady Granville.[1] With my best thanks I have the honour of presenting a copy of my annual, & sincerely hope to have the same pleasure for many years to come.

The enclosed titles were for a long time 'titles extinct' – being lost with other papers in my removal hither, – or as Othello says – thro' '*moving* accidents by flood & field'. Some memoranda subsequently turned up, but I feared too late for use, and besides I could not disentangle the new from the old. This has been matter of regret to me, but I have made up my mind to send them to your Grace on the chance of their becoming of use, & that some secret door may yet open to them like those in the old Romances.

I have the honour to be
My Lord Duke
etc etc

Lake House [*Wanstead*] / *22 Dec: 1832*

MS Bristol Central Library. Published in *Memorials* I 33–4, with, 32–3, a further list of sham books for Devonshire's library door. As an example: the first title reads, 'Boyle on Steam.' The MS is a copy, since it is written on the same sheet as the letter to Devonshire of August 1833.
1/Hood dedicated the *Comic Annual* for 1833 to Lady Harriet Elizabeth Granville (1785–1858), Devonshire's sister.

1833

TO
CHARLES TILT

My dear Tilt.
Everything is settled about the Novel, so that if you will draw out a memorandum and forward per post, I will sign and return it.
Have the goodness to let the Bearer have ten pounds for me.
I shall want to draw for about 50 more as soon as convenient to you ...

[*Wanstead, early 1833*]

From Maggs Bros *Autograph Letters* no. 266 (Easter 1911) 66. Hood refers to his novel *Tylney Hall*, published not by Tilt, but by Alfred Head Baily, in October 1834. Baily published not only *Tylney Hall*, but also the *Comic Annuals* from 1835 to 1839, *Hood's Own* (1839), and *Up the Rhine* (1840). However, Hood came to distrust Baily, quarrelled with him, and went to law against him. The reference to an advance and to Tilt's unwillingness to publish the novel in the next letter has led me to place this one just before it.

TO
CHARLES TILT

Dear Tilt
I have but just been able to find the Mids[r] account, & consequently to go thro the present one which appears to me to be correct.
Your alarm at my applications for money, must have originated in some peculiar nervousness at the time for I want but the usual advance on the next Comic altho from my Xmas receipt falling so short I shall require it earlier – say 200 now. With regard to the bal[ce] agt me of £187 – a hundred & fifty of that *was to have been* an advance on the Novel – but as you decline that work I must seek another publisher tho I much prefer my books going from the same House.
You may possibly be disinclined also to enter into the engagement for the Comic for 1834 – in which case I have only to request an early intimation, – for really

these delays uncertainties & annoyances become of serious injury to me in their interruption of my Writing.

I am Dear Tilt

Yours very truly

Thos Hood.

Lake House – Wanstead / Wednesday [*20 February 1833*]

MS Cameron. The letter is dated in another hand 21 February 1833, but Wednesday was the 20th. The last sheet carries Tilt's comment:

'In reply I said

that the balance as Mr Hood states was	187
reduced by subsequent sale of the Comic	77
	110
Since which Mr H by a dft has had	23
& by Wrights bill paid today	100
Say –	235 I am now in
advance	
I offer to advance in addition	115
	350 – ie 150 £ on
the novel & 200 £ on Comic 1834	
also after the novel is published	
and not before – in addition	100 and when
the Comic is hf printed	100 more –

I state that I will not go beyond these terms and request in the event of Mr Hs agreeing to my proposals that he should write a letter promising to sign an agreement to this effect.'

Although Tilt did not publish *Tylney Hall*, he continued with the *Comic Annual*.

TO

MRS MARIA DILKE

Mrs. Dilke,

Madam,

By having seen some Benevolent recummendations in the *Athenium* and supposing their by the Editor too be humain disposd and Having no other Means of Publishing my own case which is as follows I humbly Beg leav to say I am left with Eleven offspring the yungest off whom But a munth old none so much as taste Butchers Meat and nothing in the World to lay on xcept straw winter and summer owing to my Family am unabel to get or do ether nedle work or charing and there father am sorry to say not willing if he could get work but peple wont employ Him on account of caracter to be sure he was Born to very different Prospects in life my mane object being to get sum of the children of my hands am intending to send one up to you by the Saturdays carryer hoping you will excuse the offence and if approved of god willing may be the Means of getting him into such sittiation in London witch is verry scarse hearabouts and the Allmity Bless and prosper you for such and as the well noon gudness of Hart of you and Mr. Dilke will I trust exert in Behalf of our deploribible states and am begging your Humbel pardin for trubling with the distresses of a Stranger But not to your gudness your humbel servant LP.

[*Wanstead, April 1833*]

From Dilke I 39. Dilke notes: 'The next morning there came by carrier's cart a sucking pig from Hood, of which this had been the "envoi!" '

TO
MRS MARIA DILKE

I have had half a spill out of my gig & have hurt my hand but I shall be able to cut my own victuals. Can I bring any thing acceptable with me – a Small Porker that might pass for a roast, sucking-pig, if set before the bulk of Dilke Senr – ? – Or a deformed cucumber – or two new laid eggs. – or a couple of chickens as big as blackbirds or a few young ducks?

Hood

[*Wanstead, spring 1833*]

MS BM. Published by Marchand 93–4. There is no clue as to the date of this fragment, but the 'small Porker' recalls that of the previous letter. The accident perhaps led to the new shay, see 156.

TO
FANNY HOOD

My dear good little Fanny.
I know you will like to have a letter from your Pa, though you are such a little girl that you cannot read it yourself – but your Grandma' or your friend Liz will tell

you what the writing says. – Ever since Pa and Ma have been at Ramsgate they have wished all day long for their own little Bobe, – for the little children run about the sands & ride upon donkeys & seem as happy & merry as larks. There are a great many ships & boats sailing about & splashing through the waves & great smoking steamers paddling along, – when Toby is a little older & bigger she shall go to Ramsgate in a steamer too & we will have fine fun with the waves & the donkeys & the boats. – Every morning Pa & Ma go down to the sands to pick up shells for our Fanny & we have got some very pretty ones which we will bring home in a little basket. There are some like cups which Toby will like very much. Pa will bring her too some of the curious leaves & flowers that grow in the sea under the water but the waves come jumping one after another & throw the shells & seaweeds onto the ground for little Bobe. As today is Sunday all the ships & boats have got their flags flying of all manner of colours – & they are very pretty indeed. I wish Fanny could see them, but I will draw a picture of them when I come home to Lake House. The little children here of a morning go in a covered cart into the sea & the old woman takes off their clothes & gives the boys & girls such souses into the water – & dips them under like the ducks in our pond. Some of them like the fun of paddle daddleing – but some of them are afraid & squall & squeak like the pigs when Moot[1] is killing them. – & while they are squalling the sea goes dab into their gaping wide mouths, & the water is so salt it makes them spit & splutter like frogs in a gutter. Bless the children, how they niddle noddle[2] their heads when they are trotting on the donzeys. I expect to see their noses shake off, & their eyes drop out like green gooseberries! – One little fellow was kicked off splash dash into a wave, with his best blue breeches on, & had a pocket full of water instead of money. All the rest of the boys & girls laughed at him & grinned till I thought their wide mouths would swallow their ears. Tom Thumb is down here. He creeps into the shells & eats the little fishes that live in them. I expect some day an oyster will pinch his fingers, – for he is always at his tricks & troubles. When I have done this letter I am going to sail in a boat. I hope the sea will not splash in my face, for the waves are very frisky & are jumping about like winking. So God bless you my own dear little Fanny. I know you will be as good as gold till I come home, when I shall be quite delighted to see you – & so will Ma. I wish I had a horse with wings to fly over the hills & the tops of the houses to Toby – but we must come home again in the steamer. Ma sends her love along with Pa's to their dear little pet – Bobe knows who that is. We shall almost kiss her head off I expect when we get back to the flower of Wanstead. God bless you darling says your own dear old Parby-barby. Give my love to Grandma' & your friend Liz-biz – & Rose-pose – & Di-pie.

Ramsgate. Sunday morning. [*26 May 1833*]

MS UCLA. Address: 'Miss Fanny F. Hood / Care of Mrs Reynolds / Lake House / Wanstead / Essex.' PM: 'RAMSGATE / MY 26 / 1828.'

1/Probably a servant at Wanstead

2/The first example given in NED of the use of this verbal phrase is taken from Hood's 'Miss Kilmansegg.'

TO
JOHN WRIGHT

Ramsgate, May 26, Wind E.N.E. weather moderate. Remain in the harbour, the Isis, snow – Rose-pink – Daisy, cutters. Boyle, steamer. John – Ketch – Powerful lugger. In the Roads, the McAdam, with Purbeck stone. The Jane, on putting out to sea was quite upset, & obliged to discharge.

My dear Wright.
It was like your landlubberly taste to prefer the Epsom Salts to the ocean brine but I am glad to hear you do mean after all to trust your precious body, as you have sometimes committed your voice, to the 'deep deep sea'.[1] Should its power overwhelm you, it will only be a new illustration of the saying that might overcomes Wright.
(Jack enters to say the wind & tide serve, so I am off to a sail, – which I hope with respect to my health will prove a 'sail of effects.')
(3 p.m. Reenter the Ann[2] with T.H. his face well washed, his cloak dripping, – collar like two wet dogs ears, – & his old hat as glossy as a new un. He eats a Biscuit as soft as sopped granite, a dram of whisky – & then resumes the pen.)
I have had my sail, my first since I have been here, – delightfully brisk. What some would call awfully rough; and am come in all in a glow. – The land Gods & Satyrs may be *your*-thology – but Neptune & the sea deities are *my*thology. Bless them & their little pickles!
Altho they are prose I defy a Poet to write better descriptive lines of the sea than the three last.[3]
The Derby seems to have been highly creditable to Glaucus & the rest of the favorites, as well as exceedingly flattering to the judges in general. Outsiders – (and seasiders) for ever![4]
There come over here boats from France laden with boxes of white things, of an oval shape, the size of eggs; – I rather think they *are* eggs – and I was much

amused with an energetic question which one of our local marines put to one of the French ones. 'Where *do* you get all your eggs'? As if they had some way of making them by machinery. For certain the quantity is great, & the French hens must lay longer odds than mine. Please to copy the following verbatim & send it to Dilke per post.

Pencilled annotation, on Prince Puckler Muskau – from Sackett's Library, Ramsgate, p 212 vol 1.[5]

'What a lie. You *frog-eating* rascal what do you mean by telling such a twister.'

The weather is so fine you will be a great Pump,[6] if you do not come here sooner than you propose. When you talk of the *middle* of the week you may as well embrace the *waste* of the week & come down here at once by Tuesday's Margate steamer.[7] Every hour will do you good – so don't stick Thursday, obstinately, on your back like an ass ridden by *Day*.[8] Seriously I shall look for you – & my Doctor says all disappointments will throw me back. Mind, – while you are on board have a crust & good cheshire and bottled porter for a lunch. The last is capital! – no entire[9] can match that which hath been ripened & mellowed by voyaging. – Even Annie Porter[10] is improved by crossing the channel. – Don't forget the pigtail – that is the porter – & sit, not with your back to the bulwark, on acct of the *tremor* of the engine. The sound is as of a perpetual *gallopade*, performed by *sea-horses*. – just go to the chimney & listen. – There was no illness whatever when I came down, at least human sickness. The only symptom I saw was the *heaving* of the lead. –

I remain

My dear Wright Yours distantly,

Thos Hood R.N.

P.S. Wind has veered half a point. Forgot to say we forgot my birthday on the 23rd so are keeping it to-day ex post facto, but not completely as usual for I had no artillery to discharge at one o'clock

[*Ramsgate, 26 May 1833*]

MS Osborn. Published in *Memorials* I 44–7.

1/A quotation from Hood's sonnet 'Silence'

2/Ann Porter, 'a young lady-friend of Hood's,' *Memorials* I 45

3/The paragraph 'I have had my sail ... little pickles' is written in wave formation.

4/The Derby, run on 23 May 1833, was won by Dangerous at 25 to 1. Glaucus, the favourite, was unplaced.

5/*A Tour in England, Ireland, and France, in the Years 1828 & 1829* (1832)

6/'A solemn noodle': J.S. Farmer *Slang and its Analogues* (1890–1904)

7/Hood is writing on the Sunday.

8/The name of two of the jockeys in the Derby
9/Beer similar to porter
10/Pun on the name of Hood's and Wright's mutual friend

TO
THE DUKE OF DEVONSHIRE

My Lord Duke, It will doubtless appear to Your Grace that one request brings on a second as certainly as one Scotchman is said to introduce another, when I entreat for my new novel of Tylney Hall the same honour that was formerly conferred on the Comic Annual.[1]
If a reason be sought why I desire to address a second dedication to the same personage I can only refer to the 'on revient toujours' principle of the French song:[2] and no one could have better cause so to try back than myself. I hesitate to intrude with details but I know the goodness which originated one obligation will be gratified to learn that the assistance referred to has been, and is, of the greatest service in a temporary struggle – though arduous enough for one of a profession, never overburthened with wealth from Homer downwards. Indeed the Nine Muses seem all to have lived in one house for cheapness. I await, hopefully anxious, Your Grace's pleasure as to the new honour I solicit, fully prepared in case of acquiescence to exclaim like the Tinker to the 'Good Duke of Burgundy' in the old ballad,

'Well I thank your good Grace,
And your love I embrace,
I was never before in so happy a case!'

With my humble but fervent wishes for the health & happiness of your Grace, and one not quite so favorable to the long life of the Grouse

I have the honor to be,
My Lord Duke
Your Grace's most obliged & devoted servant

Thos Hood

Lake House, [*Wanstead*] / *August*, / *1833*

MS Bristol Central Library. Published in *Memorials* I 35–6. The MS is a copy, written on the same sheet as the letter to Devonshire of 22 December 1832.

1/*Tylney Hall*, like the *Comic Annual* for 1831, was dedicated to Devonshire.
2/In Charles-Guillaume Etienne *Joconde* 3 i, first performed in 1814

TO
CHARLES TILT?

Dear Sir.
Mrs Hood is in town if you have any thing to send down – she will be at L. Britain till the Evening.
More M.S. shortly.

Yours very truly

Thos Hood

[*Wanstead, autumn 1833*]

MS Osborn. Perhaps the addressee is Charles Tilt and the letter concerns the *Comic Annual* 1834.

TO
CHARLES TILT?

Dear Sir.
I ought to have had two sheets of letter press by this. You will keep my leaves till they get as brown as Autumn's. Pray get on. Of course you have the cuts for the 6th sheet of plates by this time. The M.S. with this to be made up at once to follow Over the Way. –

Yrs very truly

Thos Hood

[*Wanstead*] *Wednesday / Night.* [*autumn 1833*]

MS UCLA. Since this letter concerns the *Comic Annual* for 1834, published by Charles Tilt, I assume that it is addressed to him. The *Comic* appeared in November.

1834

TO

WILLIAM DILKE

My dear Dilke, – You will surely suppose that we have some insurmountable old grudge against some one, some where in Chichester or its neighbourhood – or that we are unusually timid on the subject of earthquakes,[1] when so many kind invitations fail to bring us under your roof – for we must again regretfully give up the pleasure of seeing you this year. I did hope last year to visit you this season at your race time, but with us 'The course of *Goodwood* never did run smooth.'[2] The change of a publisher, and the delay and difficulty of finding another, honest and responsible, delayed me so this spring, with my novel, that as soon as that is launched I must put my annual on the stocks.[3] So your other friends must enjoy the bed, and your hospitality, which we must take for *granted.*
I will not dilate on the enjoyment we thus lose. Jane and I are equally disappointed: – for she does not like my racing against time in lieu of yours for a cup. She unites with me in kindest regards to yourself and Mrs. Dilke, with which my inexorable printer warns me to conclude and write myself, my dear Dilke, Yours very truly,

Thos. Hood.

[*Wanstead, 21 July 1834*]

From Jerrold 270–1. Jerrold supplies the date. William Dilke (1796–1885) was the brother of Hood's friend Charles Wentworth Dilke.

1/Chichester suffered three earthquake shocks between September and November 1833, and yet another on 23 January 1834.

2/An adaptation of *Midsummer Night's Dream* I i 134

3/In March 1834 Hood made an agreement with A.H. Baily for the publication of the *Comic Annual* for 1835, as well as *Tylney Hall.*

TO

ALFRED HEAD BAILY

My dear Baily.
I have drawn two rabbits for your acceptance, please to duly honour the same. One killed yesterday, before I went to bed, & one killed today, before I went to

bed; for I was performing in 'Up All Night.'[1]
It depends on an answer from Reynolds whether I may not come to town tomorrow in which case you will see me or not
Vol. 2 of Tylney is done every word. Part of Vol 3 is ditto. So we shall soon be out at last.
I will bring all papers wanted if I come

Yrs very truly

T Hood

Lake House. / Wanstead [*1834*]

MS UCLA. *Tylney Hall* was published by Baily in October 1834.
1/The title of a play by Samuel James Arnold, first performed in 1809

TO
UNKNOWN CORRESPONDENT

Dear—
If you should feel disposed for a day or two to relax here, Wright will drive down my new shay (your old friend Bob is out of office, and a bay mare is premier) Saturday evening, or Sunday morning, which you like, and let him know where to meet you.

Yours very truly. T. Hood.

P.S. The novel is printing, and christened Tylney Hall.

[*Wanstead, 1834*]

From *The Corsair*, ed. N.P. Willis and T.O. Porter (New York) 27 April 1839, 105, and Jerrold 270

TO
MRS GEORGIANA ELLIOT

My dear Madam
I have to acknowledge the receipt of your Lock on the Human Understanding, which, like one of Bramah's, effectually defied my picking. Like Tony Lumpkin I felt persuaded there was something in the letter, but I could not make it out.[1] It seemed a Chinese puzzle done into English.

I thought at first that I had obtained some new incomprehensible Contributor to the Comic Annual – then that it was a communication from one of Irvings female mystics – and then that I had heard from Horace Walpole's 'Mysterious Mother.' Your signature at last upset these conjectures, but it did not help me to read the riddle: & in my ignorance I imagined the most out of the way commands or requests, for instance, that having received a little rare turnip seed, you begged a little leg-of-mutton seed to sow with it –

Finally I sighed 'Poor Lady'! and was meditating a hint to Governor Elliot, – I don't mean the Gibraltar man,[2] but your own Defender – to keep your fingers from pen, ink, & paper at the full of the moon, when a key was placed in my hand which converted the bewildered Sphynx into a rational sensible daughter of Eve; with whose request, as soon as decyphered, I hastened to comply.

The enigmatical epistle, however, I shall carefully preserve,[3] for in case my Correspondence should be published hereafter (and a one-sided Correspondence it will be, for I do not always answer so punctually as the Irish echo) the mysterious billet signed Georgiana may suggest to an imaginative Biographer some little romantic episode to introduce into the even tenor of the Life of one who is & will be

Yours dear Madam very Sincerely

Thos Hood

Lake House / Wanstead [*22 September 1834*]

MS Pennsylvania. Address: 'Mrs Elliot / Stratford Green.' The letter is dated in another hand, '22 Septr 1834.' Published in *Catalogue of the Collection of Autographs formed by F.J. Dreer* (Philadelphia 1890) I 298–9. Georgiana Elliot was the wife of Hood's physician and lasting friend, Dr William Elliot.

1/Goldsmith *She Stoops to Conquer* act 4

2/George Augustus Eliot (1717–90), general and defender of Gibraltar

3/The letter, to which Hood so teasingly responds, has not been preserved.

TO

ALFRED HEAD BAILY

Please to let the Bearer have two copies of Tylney Hall for me. I hope you sent an early one instanter to the Duke ...

[*Wanstead, October 1834*]

From Maggs Bros *Autograph Letters* no. 396 (autumn 1920) 115. *Tylney Hall* appeared in October, dedicated to the Duke of Devonshire.

TO

CHARLES WENTWORTH DILKE

You have revived in me the delights of young authorship, and I *am* young in the path I am treading ... Raby and Grace[1] are failures; I can't write love scenes; as a fellow said at my piece at the Surrey, 'I can act the part, but I forget the words' ... I am fagging hard at the comic.[2] It's an ill fire that bakes nobody's bread,[3] and the Great Conflagration will make an excellent subject.[4] I was up all last night, bright moonlight, drawing cuts and writing, and watching a gang of gipsies encamped just out of my bounds. I saved my fowls, and geese, and pigs, but they took my faggots. However, I shot two cats, that were poaching. As Scott says, 'My life is a mingled yarn.'[5] To-day, the man's missing. I'm afraid he's scragged.[6]

[*Wanstead, October 1834*]

From Dilke I 55, 56. The first two volumes of Hood's novel *Tylney Hall* were favourably reviewed in Dilke's *Athenaeum*, 4 October 1834, and the review was completed two weeks later.

1/The hero and heroine of the novel

2/Though the *Comic Offering* appeared this month, the *Comic Annual* did not come out until January 1835.

3/Hood's own version of the proverb

4/The Houses of Parliament were destroyed by fire on 16 October.

5/I have not traced the quotation in Scott, but compare *All's Well that Ends Well* 4 iii 67.

6/Hanged

TO

WILLIAM JERDAN

Sir.

For the sake of my Publishers I feel bound to correct the statement contained in your note to the Review of Tylney Hall.

The first two volumes were sent to you, on the same day as to the Athenaeum, namely Thursday the 2nd October. It is impossible therefore that the Publishers should have stated in writing, that the third volume would be ready 'ten days before the date of your Gazette of the 11th October.' In other words that the third volume would be ready before the first & second.

I am Sir
Yours etc

Thos Hood

Lake House – / Wanstead / Tuesday [*4 November 1834*]

MS UCLA. *Tylney Hall* was noticed unfavourably in the *Literary Gazette*, 11 October and 1 November 1834. In a note it was added that the *Gazette* had been charged in regard to *Tylney Hall* with breaking its rule not to criticize unfavourably a work sent to it before publication. They could only excuse themselves in the terms which Hood repeats in his letter. On the 8th, p. 758, the *Gazette* replied to Hood's letter without publishing it. They supposed that the delay had been due to 'the author's procrastination.'

1835

TO

CHARLES WENTWORTH DILKE

Lake House, Monday Night.
7. o'clock.

My Dear Dilke.

Here I sit, solus, in that large drawing-room, with a sick wife upstairs,[1] – a sick child in the next room to this – (Fanny has sickened with the measles) – & a fly-load of company has just departed, containing Mr & Mrs Green & Miss Charlotte Reynolds the two children[2] & nursemaid. As a true Philosopher I have found comforts in the three predicaments – Jane is better, enough to atone for all the rest – but then poor Fanny is ill, – yet hath her illness this relief in it, that it hath hastened away the aforesaid fly with its living lumber, – The Greens the Charlotte, – the 2 young Greens, – & their nursemaid; no slight relief to the larder of a man whose poulterer hath today refused a pair of fowls – & those were people who would eat fowls if fowls were to be had. But that is a trifle to the load off my head. I have had misgivings whether my anxiety for Jane might not make me somewhat rough in my remonstrances, but in a case of such vital interest, a little hardness on my part might have been forgiven – but the manner of their departure reconciles me perfectly to all I have done, so as only to leave a doubt whether I went far enough. Only the old lady remains & if sometimes wrong headed she is always right-hearted, & I am sure forgives me for sometimes opposing the first characteristic. I tried to make all smooth, with Marian, with whom I had gone most smoothly, – before they went – but as she chose to consider herself insulted (ie that Green had insulted me, – I let them go, without seeking or finding a farewell, feeling that such treatment of a man who has devoted himself life, soul & body to their sister's welfare, deserved something better than they could bestow, & had it already, in the recovery of his better self. My last words were, that as they had *given Jane over*, they would forgive me, any offence on my part if I should restore her whole to them – a contemptuous reply sealed my feeling towards them for ever, – & I have whistled them down the wind.[3]

No one of them has worked the tithe of what I have – twice have I pitched headlong from my chair with extreme watching, – but still I am in heart & alert for the dear object of my efforts is I hope accomplished, yet what was done to oppress me in my sore time of trouble I cannot forgive or forget – it must be as endurable in memory as 'The Most Terrible Ten Days of My Life.' How should I relish the comfort of true friends if I am not to feel & taste the baseness and bitterness of false ones? Green in defending Lotte against me chose to tell me that I had been guilty of 'disgraceful caballing'. I, who stood *alone* – caballing with myself – or with the Doctors – or with my poor Wife – for I had no other confederates! My indignation has settled into a deep deep disgust & and we shall never be well again whilst I retain my nature. I can forgive their oblivion of me, the little credit I have obtained for efforts, superhuman, in proportion to my own exhausted strength, having just got thro my two books, – tho on this *personal* acct I could never condescend to admit such on my list of friends – but I cannot forget that thro them or some or all of them my poor girl went thro all but the torments of hell. A curse I say on such selfish ones! Jane never saw *me* shed a tear, or heard a misgiving word till given over, – that true tenderness will be called callousness, – my love to her will be called hate to them, – I know what I am to expect from the style of their departure. My comfort is I have real friends (as yourself) who know me better – & I can appeal to a very domestic life, in proof of my sincere love for Jane, & to unbiassed testimony, in favour of my exertions 'not to be a widower before my time.' It relieves my jaded heart to throw itself thus upon yours, – to requite me for such unworthy treatment. – There – I am better – & they are worse. What a world we live in! – I am quite convinced all my theories of laughter & tears, &c – are gospel. What think you of a rat hunt in a sick Chamber? Yet was it enacted today at Lake House, & Rose[4] killed her rat in style having hunted it under the bed to the fire-place. I believe I shall be an altered man – more of a philosopher – scorning the hollow & enjoying the real in joy or grief. I feel something of the spirit of Lamb when he wrote to me –

'We have had all the world (ie Green) & his wife here in the last week or two – they seem to have come I know not whence, but they have all gone & have left room for a quiet couple. We are quiet as death, & lonely as his dark chambers, But parting wears off as we shall wear off – the great remedy is to be as merry as we can, & the great secret is how to be so.'[5]

Even so with myself, – emerging from the Valley of the Shadow of Death[6] – wherein I have made a progress beset by the fair but false fiends. My dear Dilke love me, as I love you, – or I could not write thus, with a free outpouring of spirit – you must be my ventilator – for I have lately been choked with cursed moral fogs vapours & stinking ignes fatui, bright but rottenness. An hour with you would do me good – but next to that, is this letter, wherein I do most cordially grasp your hand & grapple you unto mine heart with hooks of steel.[7] But I am rambling as wildly almost as Jane has lately wandered, – you must allow for the revulsion of feeling that seeks this vent. Times of intense stealthy agony – hours of forced cheerfulness – long nights of earnest watching, of breath & pulse, – myself a very spider as it were on the fine spun web of life – lovings, sorrowings hopings despairings – hope sometimes a comet, sometimes a fixed star – sometimes a shooting one, dropping suddenly from the seventh heaven – add every energy of mind concentrated to observe, understand, & discriminate the phoenomena of a very nice case, – the internal conflicts, the external skirmishes, – all these & more might be my excuses for a more than usual excitement, now that a favourable result has been obtained, after a storm, during which I had seen every hope but my own driven from its anchor – Oh my God Dilke if ever I fought the good fight of faith,[8] or had any pretensions to a mind it was during this frightful struggle! There was a hope – but it was like a Romeo awaiting the revival of his Juliet in a dank charnel, of bones hideous, chokefull,[9] – musicked by a Choir of Ravens. Love, only, love, could have stood the ordeal & it did. *That* will be the blessing of my life. Come what may Jane & I henceforth must be dear above dear to each other! It will be as we had passed the tomb *together* & were walking hand in hand in Elysium! Out of the fulness of the heart & of the head I write – but I am dreadfully mistaken, if you do not understand me in every word – have no fear of my firmness of mind or self command – this is only a *relief*, which, if you have had as kind a friend as I write to, you have sometime or other, I guess, had reason to appreciate. Moreover, I may be depreciated, misrepresented & in the tenderest point – & these my feelings will remain upon record in your hands – you will know, little as I have paraded it elsewhere that my heart soul & strength have been engaged in the struggle that has just passed, & that whatever I may have seemed to the senseless & shallow, my dear Jane was an object that I have been diving deep after, nigh unto drowning, in the river of Life. As I sat serene & silent in the darkest hour, & cheerful in the dreariest, so even now, with people round me in common converse, my heart is singing paeans of joy for *my* Eurydice. It only grieves me that I cannot yet get her out of the accursed Cavern, of her Fears – to use her own words she 'still smells of earth' – a shovel-full of earth's dirtiest in the dismal faces that first planted that cruel terror! She must have suffered terribly – I read most unutterable things in her face, – & curst the spell that was laid upon her spirit. Think me not mad, my dear Dilke, but I am writing of things words cannot reach. Horrors, horrible, most horrible, must have been her portion. Still, I beg, let this not pass beyond ourselves, but when we meet I can circumstantially prove to you what I say – namely she was half-killed by fear, & her friends, if so to be called. You may suppose therefore that amongst the other Demons that beset & tormented me, Scorn, Indignation, Anger, & I was going to say Hatred were not missing.

I have not written myself calmer for I began calmly – but it is time to talk of calmer things. My best, & dearest, has been composed all day, no rambling, but a doubt how to decide between me (Hope personified, – but a unit) & 'her family' – as many Despairs as Members, *here*. I have as it were to clear the mire from her eyes, to take the dust out of her mouth – to restore her from among that marble multitude, in the Arabian Nights. But the sweet end is this – *all other* troubles disappear, – & come poverty, age, [word illegible], & all other ills, with my wife & honour & poverty & my two babes, I still will love the world & thank its ruler. And now you know more of T. Hood than you could gather from a Comic Annual, or the whole series, or the Whims, or any thing I have ever written, – saving this letter, – & you will believe I am happy – tho much moved. This is one of the few outbreaks I have indulged in, thro a trying & variable storm, – & you will excuse it, perhaps thank me, for addressing it to yourself, always kindest to me in trouble, & I have therefore the less remorse in troubling you with my joy. I have not written such a Gog of a letter for years, – nor have I gone thro such gigantic feelings. But it has cost me no pains – my pen ran away with me – or rather my heart with my pen. The light of my hearth is not extinguished – and I delight in the fresh blaze up of the old fuel of love. May my domestic agonies avert yours – a little while since I scarcely thought again to enjoy your fire side or my own. I am perhaps writing weakly, foolishly, – but it is because I have nothing to do. When called upon I was not wanting – but a heavenly rest has arrived – a calm after a storm, & thro the clearing up rack I see *Home*! – still *Home*! A word that had almost slipped out of the dictionary of my life. I have still a Wife – a comfort I would have poor J.H.R. hug to his heart as I do – poor fellow, I pitied him in the midst of my own seeming calamity, – for I thought of my next Star of Magnitude, my own Fanny.[10] Curse Halley's Comet! – it is high unpropitious.[11] I have not a friend whose star shines as it ought.

It will gratify you both to know that Jane mentioned you both repeatedly in her delirium even, – for the heart looks after the head in its wanderings, like a mother after a stray child. In hot days men open their windows, – in the warmth of passion & feeling so we open our hearts to give the soul a breathing – thus you see into mine. I am becoming Coleridgean Kantean, high Metaphysical, – but commonplace suits not my present mood. There is much of positive & negative moral electricity to work off & I make you one of my conductors. God bless you, – I feel tonight a

Rothschild[12] who might have been a beggar, supposing ones purse of wealth carried somewhere about the left breast pocket. But I have learned to know the true metal from the base, – no Marian flash notes, no Lotte smashing, none of Green's flimsies for me. As they have voluntarily left my house, without *farewell*, they must not look for Welcome, which is its Irish Echo, – they are gone with Bad Taste & Bad Feeling for their companions & black & bad be the day, that sees them over my threshold. If I love *her* – if I respect myself so it must be. *Locke* says know thyself, – and unto you my dear Dilke I entrust the *key* to what may be the future conduct of

Yours in confidence & in true
& everlasting friendship

Thos Hood.

I do not say burn this letter, but preserve it. Have no fears for me, – for till we meet, herein I bury my feelings. I ought to give you some news however, if only for the sake of Mrs Dilke, whose kindness, like yours, I know by intuition. My views in life are changed – & would have been whether Jane lived or died, as you know, & I shall want your advice & will draw upon it at once, without scruple. But I am changed. In some things my eyes are opened & my heart is shut. I disdain hypocrisy. Towards Jane I must feel more devoutly loving than on that dear day that made me her husband, – she has given me proofs of her love, from the tomb, & beyond the tomb, – I am sure of her heart as if I now held her in heaven. But the same dreadful security that sealed that bond, hath shown me where I *am not* loved & no hollow professions in this world shall make me prostitute a holy passion of benevolence & goodwill, by bestowing my friendship even on the hollow and heartless. I have accompanied my Jane to the brink of the grave, & some stood there to see her into it – & when she was rescued from it, they did not joy as I do. I will not curse them – but the veriest *stranger who never knew her* hath more share in my regard than they have. Selah, as the Psalm says – for it is getting like a Psalm. My eyes have been widely opened – to the present, the past & the future. My beloved seemed to see visions & so did I in reality. I know my position. Should it ever be said, – as it may, & I think will be said – that I was no devoted husband, these pages will be in proof. My life will be in better proof, – with the best opportunities, if cultivated, of moving in the best society, I have sought my domestic joys. My friends in general will do me justice, tho I should be in disfavour with a few. I do not mean to submit to Little Britain Leading Strings, – my Jane is tenfold dearer to me for this trial, but some others have blotted themselves even from my Black Book, – they will be to me, as they had never been.

I take fright at the length of this letter, but my feelings write twenty such a day. It is a comfort to me. It is a scorn, a loathing, to me to see petty spites, & passions, congregating around death beds, which are but the stepping-blocks to heaven. Good God that the presence of Death himself cannot control our most paltry passions! They pretend to love my wife, & yet but for me, & the very measures they hate me for, she would have been a victim! The next wife I have next to deaths door the next relation that comes next her, with a hope next to nothing & a face to match, shall enjoy the next common.[13]

This is a *great big* letter already – so I need not bid you *make much of it* I have never before written such an one, & may never again. But I can never again have such cause. So treasure it. It is a record of the present feelings at least of one you know & may prove an illustration of permanent opinions. I will not go further, – Jane, tonight, (Monday 12 a/m is better and improving, – would we could all say as much.

Believe me
Dear Dilke
Yours very truly

Thos Hood.

I mean what I write. The *realities* of life have come so home to me that I will not put up with its *humbugs*. This is henceforth the motto of yours ever
T.H./ –

Another morning – and Jane is better. She may now be thought out of danger. I took a whole sleep last night for the first time, – & did not dream. If I had it would have been of Jane trying to swim in the River of Life with sisterly Millstones round her neck, – or to fly in the vital air, with a deep-sea lead to each leg, like those encumbered pigeons of St Mark, – I mean those turned out from the Basilica on Palm Sunday at Venice, with weights tied to their legs. I shall love Clark's fly for ever – the man who drove & the horses that drew it. Sweetly did it diminish in distance, & lose itself thro that gate at Can Hall Lane. Then did I feel with Shandy – 'Go poor fly – there is room in the world for thee & me.'[14] There is no magic nowadays – or had I known a formula for transforming that onehorse vehicle into the Andromeda, or the Amphitrite, bound any where, – say New South Wales, – God forgive me, but I fear I should have pronounced it on the spot! What *could* be their sports when children? – Did they dramatize De Foe's History of the plague & go about with a tiny go cart & a bell & a cry of bring out your dead![15] I shall never believe in hearts, – they have but two of those stone urns in their bosoms, as funereal & unfeeling. In strict justice & consistency, ought[16] not such death-doing thoughts & feelings to turn homeward, – making them suicidal, – felo de se – ought not one to take laudanum, or deadly nightshade & hellebore, & the other to drown herself in the blackest pool that can be found search England thorough – some pond in a cut-throat lane, with water as still as death & as black as a coffin, from running thro the sable mud of the Slough of Despond. Or is the despairing feeling only a show – an affectation, – born of a damnd pride – disdaining to have been mistaken, – & resenting the idea of being outgone in firmness, common sense, age & good feeling for the sufferer, – by such a thing as a Sister's husband – a brother-in-law? – The male sex stand not on a high pedestal in L.B. Fathers – Brothers – & so forth are but hewers of wood & drawers of water,[17] – domestic spaniels to fetch & carry – & verily that Green is the pet lapdog of the house, with an ignoble collar round his neck to show to whom he belongs. He looks tame and fat. You are right about fools – give me the Knaves, with crooked heads, – they have sometimes hearts. But who can bear a fellow with a head like a cocoa-nut & a heart like a walnut's. As my gate closed behind them, I felt a corresponding slam in my bosom – they are shut out & for ever. This is not written in anger, under the fever of irritation; but after rest and sleep, – with a steady hand & a cool head, – between them & me there is henceforth a great gulph fixed,[18] – impassable whilst memory endures – even that dreary Inferno of Dante into which they would have dragged my Beatrice – bless her! This is bitter writing but treacled words cannot flow from a pen that dips in a cup of gall, forced upon me. I have had a Revelation of Saint John's, by the light of the star Wormwood, when 'the third part of the waters became wormwood & many men died of the waters because they were made bitter.'[19]

I am not mad most noble Dilke but speak the words of truth & soberness. – It is no splenetic misanthropic mood against all the world. Warmly I feel to you or I could not write thus – & sweet intensely sweet is my little Goshen, as it were widened by this narrowing. Sweet it is to have been able to pay off a dividend of that tender care, nursing & devotion I owe of old to my most excellent Jane. There are harsh chords which will jar if touched upon, but there are others that discourse most excellent music,[20] & those mute melodies are now singing in my soul, lulling many worldly cares to sleep. Have no care for me. My mind which has stood firm throughout will not fail me *now*. But there are times in a man's life when his thoughts become intensified, so as to review a past life & project a future in a few short hours. Such has been my case. Jane's illness will be a marked aera to me, – & will have much influence on what is to come. The exigency of the time has called forth a decision I knew not belonged to me, and I mean to cherish it. It has been a great comfort to me to think & know that I have true friends who will feel with & for me, – who will appreciate my motives & give me credit for right feeling, & consequent right conduct, in the most critical & trying crisis of my life. I know that J.H.R. was told otherwise, but I sent him yesterday a copy of the following; which I send for your satisfaction – it is from Dr. Elliot. I merely asked him to certify as to Jane, in order to contradict the sinister reports they persisted in spreading.

My dear Sir.

I am quite delighted to observe so much amendment in Mrs. Hood even since last evening. There is now fair prospect of her complaint going off smoothly. And you have kept up your courage surprisingly under the severe & tedious trial. Your health seems not to have suffered at all.

Yours mo truly

W Elliot

9th. Feby.

My health did suffer tho for awhile from incessant watching, which if I remitted, every good was undone again. But I kept that to myself – & fought myself well again – on Sunday I was threatened with a fit – my mouth was convulsed – & no wonder. I cannot describe my torments I will say atrociously inflicted. *The cup was full enough before.* I have just heard that Lotte (the worst) was to return here today. If so my mind is made up to tell her she shall not stay – I will not have my all endangered at the 11th hour. What think you of such infernal sentiments as follow. When the Dr. had said Jane was in a good sleep, – the best thing for her – Lotte said *to me* 'I hope she will wake sensible, & then pass away quietly.' – And Wright heard her say, 'What gave her horror was, that if Jane had been let alone she would have died days ago!' Damn such pestilential sensibility – Does she want a dead sister to cry over, let her give her good wishes to Marian.

The Dr. has arrived & I will give you his report ere I close. He says she is as well as yesterday the head &c, well, – but some disorder of the bowels has supervened which requires care. I have just seen her – she is quite collected, & conscious of the past, that there has been a struggle between me & the rest. I have had it from her own lips. And now haven't I been well beset – to say nothing of annoyances, signed sealed, & delivered, – but which I do not feel *now.* God bless you & yours & keep your roof from all such visitations.

[*Wanstead, 9–10 February 1835*]

MS BM. Published by Marchand 15–28. The date, '9th Feby,' is written in another hand at the head of the letter, but the letter was written over two days, Monday and Tuesday, 9 and 10 February. The initials on 165 are underlined three times.

1/Jane had given birth to their son Tom on 19 January 1835.
2/Reference is to Mr and Mrs H.G. Green, she being the former Marianne Reynolds, and their young children Charles and Townley.
3/*Othello* 3 iii 262
4/Possibly the maid, or the cat
5/*Letters* III 160 (spring 1828)
6/Psalm 23:4
7/*Hamlet* I iii 63
8/I Timothy 6:12
9/*Romeo and Juliet* 4 i 81–2
10/Reynolds' only child, a daughter, ten years of age, had recently died.
11/The periodic return of Halley's comet was expected in 1835; it duly appeared in August.
12/Hood no doubt had in mind especially Nathan Mayer Rothschild, who lived in London (d 1836).
13/That is, shall be ejected from the house onto the nearest piece of waste ground
14/Sterne *Tristram Shandy* ii 12
15/Defoe *Journal of the Plague Year* (ed. 1950) 58
16/'out' in MS
17/Joshua 9:21
18/Luke 16:26
19/Revelations 8:11
20/*Hamlet* 3 ii 374

TO
CHARLES WENTWORTH DILKE

My dear Dilke

I shall be later than 6. – ½ past say, – I have got my passport & have left it at the Prussian to get backed,[1] – if the secy should be there before 6. if not I must take it as it is. Not to be idle I wrote to my neighbour the Duke,[2] & he has sent me a very handsome note, with a billet in french to show in a difficulty, giving me a good character & as enjoying his 'connoissance' & estime

Yours ever truly

TH

[*Wanstead, February 1835*]

MS BM. Published by Marchand 89, who gives the address: 'C.W. Dilke, Esqre / Clarence Club / 12 Waterloo Place.' Hood is preparing to go abroad to avoid his creditors, to live more economically, and thus to be able to pay off his debts.

1/Endorsed
2/Probably the Duke of Devonshire

ABROAD March 1835 – April 1840

1835

TO

JANE HOOD

Keep this to refer to.
address me – poste restante à Coblentz.
At last my own dearest & best I sit down to write to you and I fear you have been looking anxiously for news of me – In truth I wrote a long letter at Nimegen which I suppressed having nothing certain to say. I will now tell you first that I am *safe* & *well*, – which is the very *truth*, – & then I may relate how I got on. I had a dreadful passage to Rotterdam. Wednesday night was an awful storm & Thursday morng. I was *seasick* & *frightened* at sea for the first time so you will suppose it was no trifle – in fact it was unusually severe. I went up at midnight & found *four* men at the helm, hint enough for me, so I went down again & in the morning a terrific sea tore the whole four from the helm, threw the captain as far as the funnel, (20 paces) & the three men after him. Had it not come *direct aft* it would have swept them into the sea, – boat, skylights & every thing, in short have left us a complete wreck. Eleven others miscarried that night near at hand, so you may thank the cherub I told you of[1] – but such a storm has seldom been known. It was quite a squeak for the Comic for 1836. But when you come the weather will be settled, & such a sea comes but once in 7 years. When you see 4 at the helm you may be frightened – but mind, – not till then. Steam I think saved us – you ought to offer up a golden kettle, somewhere. You were given over & I was given under, – but we have both been saved, I trust for each other, & heaven does not mean to part us yet. But it made me very ill, for it was like being shaken up in a dice-box, and I have had a sort of bilious fever, with something of the complaint Elliot cured me of – and could not eat, – with pains in my side etc. – which I nursed myself for as well as I could. I made two acquaintances on board – one gave me a letter of introducn. to a Dr. at Coblentz whom I have not seen – the other gave me an introduction to his father here, where I took tea tonight – their name is Vertue[2] so you see my morals are in good hands. I got to Rotterdm. only on Thursday night, & I supped there very merrily with the young Vertue and two of his friends. On Friday night I stopped at Nimegen which is in a state of war[3] & could proceed no further till Saturday, which night I passed aboard & on Sunday arrived & slept at Cologne. Here I was detained on Monday by the steamer having broken a paddle,

but made myself agreable to an old general Sir Parker Carrol[4] who took me with him to see the lions. I gave him a bulletin to carry to Dilke – strange to say the genl. once lived at their house. Also made acquaintance with a Revd. Mr. Clarke,[5] a gentlemanly young man, & we started on Tuesday for Coblenz, where we slept, – again on Wednesday to Mayence, slept there, – & today he set off for Frankfort & I returned here. At all these starts I have had to rise at 5 – & was too worn out & weak to undertake the walking plan I had concerted with Dilke – so I went up & down by the boat instead. Luckily I got better on Tuesday & that day & Wednesday, & today being fine, I enjoyed it very much. From Cologne to Mayence is all beautiful or magnificent – I am sure you will enjoy it – especially if, as I will try, I meet you at Cologne. I want you to see the Cathedral. I am going to-morrow on foot to look among the villages, – but my impression is, from what Mr. Vertue says there will be some difficulty in finding any thing there, – but at all events there are lodgings to be had in Coblentz which is a place I admire much. I therefore think you might start for Coblenz at once, without hearing further from me, when you feel able, letting me know of course – your day of sailing for in case of my getting any thing at Bingen or such, you would have to stop *here* – and unless I meet with something to my taste, above, I shall make this our fixture. Consult Dilke. For my part, if well enough, I think you may safely come on the chance, as it would take you 5 days – 1 to Rotterd*m* 1 to Nimegen – 2 to Cologne & 1 to Coblentz. I am writing but a business letter & you must give me credit, own dearest, for everything else, as I wish to devote all the space I can to describing what will be for your comfort. You must come to Rotterdam by Der Batavier, which has female accomodns. & a stewardess. You may tell the steward I was nearly swamped with him in the Lord Melville, for he was with us & will remember it. I should advise your place in the *back* cabin, not the steerage in front which is not well protected, – & I am afraid about Fanny – besides the engine is in front. – pray keep her from it. In rough weather – setting out or getting in any where – keep below till the bustle is over & go up & down stairs as seldom as possible as generally slippery & unsteady & you might get a fall. You can dine at the ordinary[6] on board – or have anything you wish. Put your name to all your luggage – Mrs. Hood, to Coblentz, via Rotterdam – & have as *few* packages as you can. At Rott*m* it will be examined. They will perhaps take your passport, & tell them you are going to the Hotel des Pays Bas (Hotel day pay bar) repeat that to the men on the quay who will take you there & from thence they will send to the Customs for your luggage. I advise that hotel because there are 2 English ladies living there, known to the Vertues, who may be of help to you. Snd for your passport if taken –

mine was given back to me on the spot, & when you write in the book they bring at the hotel, always fill it up in the same way, – Keep Fanny close & don't get separated on the quay:– & do every thing coolly, & take time. Change no more money than you can help there – as Dutch money is puzzling. Have *sovereigns* with you. Your best hotels generally will be those *nearest* the spot the steamers come to, – as they start again early – & the children would cumber you to go any distance. They will ask for your passport when wanted, – but never start without it – the people at the inn will send for it, *overnight.* Mention each stage you are going to next, as at Rott^{m} – say Nimegen, – then to Cologne, – then to Coblentz. You will have to pass a night in the steamer, & there are no beds – but you can make shift for the children on the seats. Have plenty of wraps, cloaks etc. – & be sure to get into the right boat up, not, down. The boats to Cologne are dangerous in front for children – the great cabin will cost a little more, but so active & curious as Fanny is, we must not risk. Tell her I do hope she will mind every word you say & never leave your side, & if she is good I will come to meet her & give her a treat such as she never had. You may meet with English – but the stewards & conductors mostly speak French & on the other side I will write a few words as pronounced, copy them out on a card & keep them at hand. You will find them useful at a pinch. The watercloset in the boats *on the Rhine* is one of the doors at the foot of the great cabin stairs. You must expect some nuisances & inconveniences but they will do to laugh at when we meet. Above all keep up your heart & do not give way to fear – I assure you it takes a deal to sink them – & Der Batavier is a splendid & powerful steamer. My own spirits have kept up wonderfully considering I did not start strong, & have been so tried since. Do you follow my example – I rely on your firm fondness & fond firmness. Like my storm, – this is the one heavy sea we must go thro to reach the haven. I should like you to bring out 6 months money, at least to place one above the *thought* of want in a strange land. I have no doubt of being able to earn our current expenses & do the Comic besides, but I should like to feel a *hedge* at my back against possible contingencies. Let the plate in Skinner Street[7] & every thing be turned into money – I much regret my watch, but it can't be helped. With my dear ones by my side will gambol thro the Comic like the monkey who had seen the world. We are not transported even for 7 years & the Rhine is a deal better than Swan River.[8] I have not been able to economize personally as I wished, from being ill, but still every thing is cheap here. I have made a great many notes. My mind was never so free, & meaning what is right & just to all, I feel cheerful at our prospects, & in spite of illness have kept up. I must yearn for you till you come – but be strong enough first, or you spoil all. This will not reach you for 4 or 5 days & then it would take you as much more to come, during which I should be sure to get a place, so do not wait to hear from me again if you felt able. It is best on shore to do without sheets, & sleep in the blankets they don't know warming pans. Here you have a little feather bed or bag to pull over you. Bring me some *socks*. I find I have the key of the wine cellar – but there is another in the plate-chest. Ask the Conducteur or steward on board to recommend you a hotel at Nimegen or Nimvagen – and at Cologne, if I should not come, ask for the Hotel du Rhin (Dew Rang) or Monsieur Yops. Let them know at each that you are going on – that you may be called.

Rest yourself on the cabin seats by day with your feet up, like a sofa – Fanny can look thro the window. There will be plenty to amuse her. By the by bring some soap in your pocket or bag you will find *none* at the hotels – & if you dine at the table d'hote,[9] expect to have something solid *after* the pudding. I have done my best to prepare the people for your coming after me. – Remember the stages are Rotterdam – Nimegen (or Nimvāgen) – Cologne – Coblentz – & enforce that your aim is Coblentz. Don't lose your passport, but keep it in your pocket, or at hand. – & when they are long in returning it ask for it. But ladies are not much hindered. You may reckon I think on settling at Coblentz – it is a capital & clean town, & does justice to Dilke's recommendation. And now, own only, dearest best & sweetest wife, a part must be give up to love & let me beg you to believe [with what][10] gushing gratitude of heart I contemplate your self devotion for [...] better, if better can be, I must love you hereafter. That you [...] made me amends for all, & kept me up in heart & hope under [...] even absence, illness, & suffering, – it has made me well & will [sustain me] till you come, – & let me own wife seek & find the same co[mfort] in me. Think that every wave but brings us nearer, – that every [...] by the way will have an end – be cool – be firm – be cheerful [...] that ere long we shall put up our joint thanks in the Cat[hedral at] Cologne, tho' catholic, which did not prevent my breathing a pray[er for] you dearest, before its altars. I will meet you there to lighten the latte[r] end of your travel, though I should have to write an extra article to atone for my ext[ravag]ance. I have already begun some 'Rhymes of the Rhine, of which [the] first is justly dedicated to your own self.[11] But tonight is my first leisure, – I have been like the Wandering Jew. How my thoughts & wishes fly over these vine covered hills to meet yours! I feel *certain* that at this very moment I am in your mind too, – & that reflection is as a kiss for every mile between us. For the first time we are separated by hundreds: – but come to me dearest, & in life, we will part no more. Some happy day next year, we will revisit our old England & renew all ties, – free from those cares which were robbing our children of their parents. – Hug my dear little Fanny for me – I will trust her word to be good & then she may come over the sea to me & have me again. Kiss my boy – he will grow big enough for me to nurse. I leave for you to speak for me all what is kind – I cannot bear at the end of my paper to rob *you* for any messages – my love sets towards you like the mighty current of the great Rhine itself, & will brook no impediments. I grudge the commonplace I have been obliged to write, & wish every line were filled only with such words as make me thrill whilst I set them down. Every sentence should claim you as my own dear wife, the pride of my youth, the joy of my manhood – the hope of all my after days. Twice has the shadow of death come between us, – but our hearts are preserved to throb against each other. I am content for your sake to wait the good time – when you may safely undertake the voyage & do not let your heart run away with your head. Be strong before you attempt it. Bring out with you a copy of Tylney Hall, which I shall want to refer to – I want no others, but the *last* Comic. Perhaps you had better bring a few shirts ready made – or they may be as cheap here – ask Dilke. M^rs^ D's coming must have been a comfort to you[12] – if only in *her* ignorance of French. Pick out my instructions about hotels etc & make memorandums of them. If you are likely to be some time, treat me with one letter – addressed to M. Thomas Hood poste restante à Coblentz. Dilke will tell you how to send it. I long to be settled & at work. I owe *him* much & wish to do C. Lamb, while it is fresh.[13] I hope Reynolds's spasms are gone. *They* could not do better than come up the Rhine this summer – it would not cost so much as Brighton, & such a change of scene! I have had some adventures I must tell you when I meet. I bought this paper all by telegraph of a girl at Cologne. We could not speak a word to each other, & the whole ended in a regular laugh throughout the shop, when she picked the price out of the money in my hand. Was not I in luck to meet the only two or three English that were out, & make such friends with them. But I really am getting a traveller, & am getting *brass* & push my way with them. I forgot to say at Coblentz the men frequent the Casinos & the women make evening parties of their own, but I do not mean to give up my old domestic habits. We shall set an example of fireside felicity – if that can be said of a stove for there are no grates here – the more's the pity. God bless you ever.

Your own TH.

I long to hear from England – I am now all alone again & no English[14]

Coblentz. Thursday Evening. [*12 March 1835*]

MS Bristol Central Library. Published in part in *Memorials* I 52–7. Address: 'Mrs Hood / care of J.H. Reynolds Esqre/ 27 Golden Square / London.' PM: 'COBLENZ 5–6 /13/3,' 'FPO/MR 19/1835.' Hood had gone abroad ahead of Jane in order to find a home for her, their daughter, and recently born son. This is his first letter from Germany.

1/'There's a sweet little cherub that sits aloft, / To keep watch for the life of poor Jack,' Charles Dibdin, 'Poor Jack,' *Songs* (1848) I 192.
2/Unidentified
3/Belgium and Holland were in dispute with one another at this time.
4/Lt-General Sir William Parker Carrol (1776–1842), KCH, CB, served with distinction in the Peninsular War. His home was in Tipperary, Ireland.
5/Unidentified
6/Dining room, where a public meal was provided at a fixed price.
7/Name of a street in Somerstown and Clerkenwell
8/Western Australia, centring on the Swan River, became a struggling colony in 1829. Convicts were excluded until twenty years later. Hood had made fun of the emigrant's lot in 'A Letter from an Emigrant' and 'A Letter from a Settler' in the *Comic Annuals* for 1830 and 1833, *Works* I 23–7, 160–4.
9/Ordinary: see note 6 above
10/The MS is torn at the places marked by square brackets here and below.
11/Perhaps 'To –. Composed at Rotterdam,' published in *Athenaeum* 4 July 1835, 512, and *Works* VI 319–21.
12/A reference to Mrs Dilke having called on Jane
13/Hood did not contribute an article about Lamb to Dilke's *Athenaeum*, but he later wrote of him in his 'Literary Reminiscences.'
14/The last sentence is written across the first page of the letter. The letter also contains 'a list of words – Pronounce as spelt.' This is followed by the phrase, 'Your own ever & evermore T Hood.'

TO
JANE HOOD

My own dearest & best love

The pen I write with – the ink it holds – the paper it scrawls upon – the wax that will seal it were all bought by me à la telegraph, – except that I had the assurance – (ignorance & impudence go together) to look a pretty young German lady in the face & ask her for the use of her lips, not to kiss but to translate for me, but she couldn't. The purport of this is to tell you what I hope will give you ease & comfort, that I am fixed here in a snug, cheap, airy lodging, thanks to the kindness of the Virtues who have taken great trouble for me. Lodgings *furnished* are scarcely to be had here at all & when the Vertues came they had to stay at an inn 7 weeks. They say, & I feel I am fortunate. There are three little rooms, one backward, my study as is to be with such a lovely view over the Moselle! My heart jumped when I saw it, and I thought – 'There I shall write volumes!' My opposite neighbour is the

Commandant, so it's a genteel neighbourhood – & today I visited the Church of St. Castor who is to be our patron Saint (vide address) & saw a bit of his bone. Seriously, it is quite a snuggery, where I should want but you & my dear boy & girl to be very happy & very loving, – I went up a mountain opposite yesterday evening, commanding a magnificent expanse of view, – but the thought would come that you were not in all that vast horizon. But it is splendid, and I'm sure what you would enjoy. The Virtues have been very kind, – I have just taken tea with them & they will call tomorrow to see me set in. Widow Seil is a woman of property & always aboard her own barges travelling up & down the Rhine, – & her daughter is here keeping house. She seemed wonderstruck this morng. & so was I, to reflect how we are to get on, for she knows nothing but German, – but tonight I have delighted her by telling her in German (which I poked out) to send to the hotel for my bag & cloak. She said over & over again 'das is gude,' – I hope we shan't end in Eloisa & Abelard & in the fullness of her approbation the maid fairly gave me a slap on the back. You must know servants here are great familiars, – the waiters at the inns are hail fellow with the guests and in truth but for them, I must have foregone discourse, for they generally speak French. I find my French reviving very fast – & get on well enough. I dine at a table d'hote, & sleep here, and breakfast – then coffee at the inn & no supper. You can have your dinner sent in here, – I mean for us all, – very reasonable & without trouble; & on the first of May, I can have Virtue's servant, as they are going to England. She understands English wants, & has a high character – so I think I have provided for you tolerably well. Tell Dilke I am highly pleased with Coblentz & quite confirm his choice: – it is by far the best thing I have seen. I do hope you will soon be able to come, & in in the mean time I do every thing I can think of to facilitate your progress. Shirting will be cheaper here so do not bring any – but I should like a set of Comic for Virtue, & bring with you the bound up Athen^ms. – & your own bound books. Get the steward of the Batavier to see you ashore at Rotterdam, to the Hotel des Pays Bas, & in case of any difficulty about Customs, which is very unlikely – send from the Hotel for Mr. Virtue Junr. there – the English ladies will explain for you – & he will lend his help, I feel sure. Let me know exactly when you sail from London & I will meet you at Cologne, some how. Tell Fanny she may see soldiers here if she likes, all day long. They are always exercising; it seems like – 'A month he lived & that was *March*.' If she behaves well on the voyage & minds what you say I will show her wonders here. To-day has been beautiful quite warm – & the weather looks well set in for fine. My little room has the reputation of being very cool in summer – I saw a vision of you dearest, today, & felt you leaning on me and looking over the Moselle at the blue mountains & vineyards. I long but to get to work with you & the pigeon pair by my side, and then I shall not sigh for the past. Only cast aside sea fears & you will find your voyage a pleasant one. Your longest spell will be from Nimegen to Cologne when you must pass a night aboard, – but then I shall meet you to take care of the pair & you will have a good night's rest. Get yourself strong – fret not a moment for the past – there is still a happy future, – fix your eyes *forward* on our meeting, my best & dearest. I forgot to tell you – but drink up Fanny's 4 bottles of good port to do you good. Our little home, tho homely[1] will be happy for us, & we do not bid England a very long goodnight.[2] Good night too – my own best, dearest kindest, loveliest wife, my joy, pride, hope, & comfort –

'And from these mountains where I now respire
Fain would I waft such blessing unto thee
As with a sigh I deem thou now might'st do to me.'

Sunday Morning. The hens *do* lay in Coblentz – they are cackling rarely under my window. I am located thus[3] – Dilke will understand how good the look out is – just at the junction of the Rhine & the Moselle, it is almost the corner house of Coblentz. It is sixteen pounds a year, to comfort you at leaving Lake House. No taxes – no Barkers. I am charged extra because I eat two rolls at breakfast so you see I improve in my habits. The Germans eat great suppers, & little breakfast. I also sleep well, for except on your acct. I feel relieved of a load of care – I have long been struggling against the stream with a millstone round my neck, which is now removed and I am free to strike out with all my might, with a fair prospect of keeping above water, where I must have sunk. I know by what I feel now that the struggle was killing me – & you too. I fear you will meet with the annoyances I have left behind, or at least some of them – but keep up your good heart & shake them off like dewdrops from a lioness's mane,[4] – the present disgrace & dishonour time will amply remove, if I exert myself, – and it is for this reason that I banish every thought of the past which might interfere with the present or the future. For the sake of every one I keep myself in fighting condition, & have brought myself to look *forward* with a firm nay cheerful composure of mind I hope you will share in. The less treasure I have elsewhere the more I feel the value of those I have within my heart,– & never could your dear presence be more delightful & blessed in its influence than it will be to me now. Our grapes though sourish now will ripen into sweetness by the end of the year – and I shall work like the industrious Germans whom you will see labouring like pismires,[5] on the face of their mountains. Tell the Reynolds's they could not do better than take a trip here in the summer, when it must be delightful –

it cost me, illness included, but about ten pounds & I lost something by *change* in Holland to get here, including Mayence, – & the hotels, barring the first rates, professing to be English ones, are moderate & comfortable. My dear Fanny will enjoy herself here – there is so much bustle, barges steamers, & soldiering, – & children like dwarf men & women. Bless her good heart, I long to see her. Tell her I expect she will take great care of you & her brother on the voyage & not give you trouble. The first thing I shall ask when I see you will be if she has been good, & if so, I will take her with you to see the Cathedral at Cologne which with its painted glass &c will be to her like Fairy Land. To Rotterdam will be 24 hours. I should see you in 4 days, – from your leaving London. Do not change much money in Holland, – after Nimegen, ask for dollars – (spelt thalers, pronounced tarlers) – and groschen. 30 little pieces marked silber groschen make 1 Thaler, value three shillings. You will probably have also some pieces about as big as a shilling, marked 6 / Ein Thaler / meaning that 6 of them make a dollar – each being worth 5 grochen, – 30 of which make a dollar – consequently the silver groschen is worth rather more than a penny – not quite 5 farthings. Thus you may reckon how to remunerate any little service such as porterage &c – the groschen 5 farthings – the 6 ein thalers, 5^{d} each & the thalers (like our 5 shilling pieces but smaller) 3 shillings each. – There is a premium in favour of gold – thus if you have pieces marked X / Thaler / or ten thalers – they are worth *eleven* silver thalers / dollars / and ten groschen. The english sovereign is worth six thalers and 24 groschen. You can pay your fares in the steamboat in English money, by that standard. Get your father to draw you out a table of it on a card. You must bring blocks enough with you for the whole comic – or more than that will be better as I may do the Epsom[6] or something else – bring a good stock. I hope Reynolds may be able to beat the receivers about the house – it is hard to pay up after giving the 100 for a lease I can't get. If you can – let me have my watch. – it is indispensible here for table d'hote &c. Also have my little gun kept for me – Wright has the lock of it. Let all the rest be sold or returned – one is Skelton's & one is Holt's,[7] & one stick gun is John's. Give Wright the Bittern for Branston[8] – but not his gun. Woodin[9] would stare to see calves here going to slaughter 7 days old attended by dogs bigger than themselves. I hear that the Ostend steamers got well knocked about in our storm & had some men washed overboard; – my head still reels occasionally & the stairs seem to rock – so you may judge what it was – the very worst for many years. The Batavier is an excellent boat. Have *porter* in her, – you will get none after Rotterdam. Up the Rhine take Cogniac & water – not the sour wine. Children pay halfprice. Wrap yourself well up & when the bustle of departure is over, you may be very comfortable but up to Cologne there is little worth seeing – except the towns. Dusseldorf for instance. From Cologne to Coblentz is superb & I shall enjoy it with you – but mind be sure to come when you appoint, as I cannot stay long at Cologne. Write to me (poste restante à Coblentz) as I go to the post office every day to enquire like Monsieur Mallet.[10] Bring me out a stock of steel pens. Tell Baily to chose stout ones. – not thin & weak. Also plenty of pencils. I have bought some collars here – cheap. You would be quite in the fashion here with a silk bonnet, & one of those cloaks with a deep cape to the elbows of plain or *figured* silk or stuff such as I saw about the streets in London ere I left. Bring all my clothes that are worth any thing – as they are as dear here – my green coat to boot – as a pattern for one I shall have made to travel in – or get *that* done up & put to rights, bring a few knives forks & spoons – sheets & table linen. It is very quiet here except when *Mrs* Commandant gives a party opposite, when there are carriages. You get a glimpse of the Rhine in front. You must not expect *carpets* here & you will have stoves instead of grates – those are universals. By the by Mrs Dilke told me to have my linen well aired – I suspect only her ignorance, – & that she had taken what is up in all the packets – *Dampschiffe* – for damp shirts. It signifies steam boats. Not an unnatural mistake. Pray let a Comic be sent from me, to Hardwicke. Bring me a set for my own use (your bound ones will do) & a copy (or two) of the N[...] Flanders brick[11] of course – & my desk with all my papers in it. That box that was the tool chest, with handles, would be very useful for sending over all the Comic blocks in, – ditto the small oak one I used to use for the purpose – put your name on each package perhaps you had better say, Mrs Hood, – à Coblentz. – & then they will not go the wrong way: – or put the whole address 372 Caster Hof, Coblentz. My young landlady has paid me a smiling visit this morning, & we have had a little conversation in German & English, – neither of us understood. St Castor has just dismissed his congregation in various grotesque gaieties – the most distinguished feature was a violet & pink shot silk umbrella. I have also had a visit this morng. from a strange young gentleman, but for want of the gift of tongues he took nothing by his motion. I am in fact a sort of new Irving, – with the girl here for a proselyte. She *will* hold forth, understood or not. Yesterday I gave 2 groschen to two little girls, like Fanny, on the top of the mountain. They went apart & after a consultation one dispatched the other to present to me I guess an address of thanks – or to ask for more, I don't know which but I think the former. I found on the same eminence a good honest fellow, very civil for nothing, & a good Christian no doubt – altho, like Satan he thence pointed out to me all the kingdoms of the earth. Whenever my eyes leave the paper they see the Moselle still gliding on & my own verses occur to me – (in the novel) – with a powerful application of them to *you.*[12] They are true, best & dearest – one figure flits & hovers about me wherever I go – & my little Fanny too – & my boy – all beyond the bluest of the blue hills! I shall give you good measure & cross this letter, writing only what is of no moment on the flaps, which may be seen. I do not pretend yet to write letters worth reading for as yet my head is confused & I am but just settled down – otherwise I have made many notes & mems which I need not write either to you who will I hope see the things they refer to. Keep up your heart & health & shorten our separation, my own beloved Jane. You will regain here health & peace of mind. Remember how happy we were at Islington.

The Vertues have called & kept me beyond my time. They have begged me to make their house my Home and are very obliging. Today being Sunday we dined in state, with a band playing, & I indulged in a glass of Wine in which I drank your health dearest, as tho my heart's blood had been in the glass. I have just bought with much trouble an instantaneous light [13] to seal this with. Pray keep up your heart & get well & come out here – we shall be very happy. The first shock over, it will be a relief to us both. I cannot say how I love you & long to be with you on your passage hither – I know I should be a great comfort to you, but the Fates forbid. Bless you ever & ever my own Girl, My dear Wife the only being that ever loved me for my own sake – My little loving Fanny excepted who takes after her Mother. Think what I must feel for *You* – Away as I am from every body and every thing and contented to be so for I shall never consider myself unhappy till my misfortune parts me from you. Only come to me and I shall regret nothing – I am still amongst the richest of men. Bless you ever & ever my dearest only to think of you is a blessing to me – I know that one – nay two in the world love me, – & will whatever I may become. A thousand kisses on your good heart, my dearest & may they do you good as they do me only in wishing. It is *now* I want a Wife and feel that I have one. I cannot find words fond enough for what I have to say – nor shall I find deeds enough to repay you for what I shall owe to you when you come here. I feel happy – very happy in that prospect, and I almost fancy you will lay this letter beneath your pillow – sleep sweetly – & wake next Morning almost well enough to start. I could write much but I will only say, if I ever said any thing kind or tender, if I was ever fortunate in expressing what cannot well be expressed I *feel* it now – beyond all words. My dearest Jane, My own kind best Wife, God bless you ever & ever, – If I have not shed a tear, it is because they were all shed when I thought of losing *you* – Nothing else can hurt me that concerns only 'world's gear' so hug me in fancy to your heart, & live in the hope of soon resting on the bosom of your own, true, loving & loved husband here & beyond the grave or there is no heaven for

Yours, dearest, in heart & soul
Thos Hood.

Give my dear boy – & my good Fanny plenty of kisses for me – Fanny was a great comfort to me when I saw her – I'm sure she loves me dearly, as I love her, & will be all that is good to please me, – and then I shall try to please her. My heart yearns at every child in the street. There are some little Vertues she would like – such as Liz & Minny. I say nothing about Elliot or any one as it would lead me into too much & I have no thoughts to spare. Keep an acct how the Cow &c sold, as I should like to know but reserve all your detail till you see me. I am sure the plan is right from what I feel & know – tell Dilke so – & my only care now is about you & to have you here. I am become quite a citizen of the world, I talk to everyone in English, broken French & bad German & have the vanity to think I make friends wherever I go. Tell Dilke this – it will please him. Say to John I shall write him a long letter as soon as I hear from London, – & also to Dilke. I have seen today the whole troops on the parade – governors demi governors &c. – Their bands do not equal ours – some of our drums would *beat them hollow*. And they have no good horses – Bob would be a Prince here & the black horse a King. Our set out at Wanstead would eclipse the Commandant's – but I have done with those vanities. May God have all those I love, or who love me, in his holy keeping, is the prayer of the subscribed,

Thos Hood[14]
[*Koblenz, 19 March 1835*]

MS Bristol Central Library. Address: 'Mrs Hood / care of J.H. Reynolds Esqre / 27 Golden Square / London.' PM: 'COBLENZ 7-8A,' 'FPO/MR 19/1835.' Published in part in *Memorials* I 58–65.

1/John Howard Payne, 'Home, Sweet Home!' *Clari* (1823)
2/Byron *Childe Harold's Pilgrimage* I xiii
3/The text is illustrated at this point.
4/*Troilus and Cressida* 3 iii 224
5/Ants
6/*Epsom Races* was announced in Hood's publications in 1830 and 1831, but the work did not appear.
7/Names unidentified
8/Wright's partner in engraving at this time. He seems to have moved into Lake House.
9/Unidentified
10/In the play of the same name by W.T. Moncrieff, first performed in 1829
11/Preparation used for cleaning polished metal
12/'Still glides the gentle streamlet on,' *Poetical Works* 213
13/Name for a kind of match in use at the time
14/Jane and the family set out two weeks after the date of this letter, and were met by Hood at Cologne, as he had promised.

TO
CHARLES WENTWORTH DILKE

My Dear Dilke,

You ought to have heard from me before, but I was loth to inflict upon you bad news in return for your very kind letter, for every syllable of which I thank you, and instead of quarrelling with what you have said, I thank you for the meaning beyond. The truth is I have been unchanged from the hour I left you, my mind has not faltered for an instant, but though the spirit is willing, the body is weak. My health broke down under me at last, after a series of physical, as well as mental trials, and I am not a-Gog corporeally, witness my experiments in your night-gowns. 'Tylney Hall,' the 'Comic,' Jane's illness, and the extreme exhaustion consequent thereon, disappointment, storm and travel, came a pick-a-back, and I am not a Belzoni[1] to carry a dozen on each calf, two on my head, &c. I broke down – not but that I fought the good fight, like a Widdrington,[2] with a good heart, but I was shorn of my physical powers. The storm was a severe one. What pitched over, literally, stout mahogany tables, where eight or ten may dine, might derange anyone; and the change of climate, which is really considerable (we had hotter suns in March than in England during May), had its effect. The safe arrival of Jane with my darlings all better than I had hoped for, did me a world of good. * * * I assure you sincerely as to my personal feelings, with a decent state of health I could be very happy and contented; the presence of a very few friends would make my comfort complete. But I now suffer mentally, because my health will not keep pace with me. I have at last reluctantly called in medical aid; the whole system here seems based on Sangrado's practice, bleeding, blistering and drastics.[3] I had the prudence to mitigate his prescriptions, which in the proportion of two-thirds almost made me faint away. They do not recognise our practice here, or I could doctor myself. But according to Sir F. Head in 'The Brunnens,' Germans require horse medicines.[4] I think I never in my life felt such a prostration of physical power, I can hardly get up a laugh, and am quite out of humour with myself. If I were Dick Curtis[5] I could give myself a good licking, I mean my body, for not being more true to me. The 'Athenaeum' has been a great delight to me – it costs me here only two groschen, about two pence. Is it not singular that a fortnight ago, as the *only* exception to the rule, it cost me four or five groschen. I understand that throughout the Rhine, everything within the last two years has risen nearly fifty per cent. from the great influx of English. Notwithstanding this, many of the necessaries are very good and cheap, butter, bread, &c. I am going to make a calculation whether

home cookery will not be the cheapest, though we have hitherto dined at the hôtel, *pour voir le monde*. I have bought some brandy here very good, though it is rather scarce, bottles included 2*s*.6*d*. each, and some Oberwesel wine, something between Hock and Moselle, 1*s*. a bottle. I have got Jane some bottled Bavarian beer, which is very good. Butter is 8*d*. per pound, three rolls 1*d*., and eggs about 2½*d*. a dozen. I was going to resume this, but was prevented by what soldiers call a night-attack. On going to bed I was seized with violent spasms in the chest, which after some time compelled me to send for the Dr. at midnight. I could only breathe when bolt upright, and rarely then at the expense of intense pain; I thought every breath would be the last. My Dr. certainly does me good, and, though a Jew, does not repeat his visits unnecessarily, but 'waits till called for;' he talks a little English, and as Pope says I feel assured, 'a little learning is a dangerous thing.'[6]
Jane said to him, 'I wish you could give to Mr. Hood some *strengthening medicine;*' to which he replied, 'Who is that physician you speak of?' But a more whimsical mistake arose out of my lay-up, which I must give you dramatically. Our servant knows a few words of English, too, her name is *Gradle*, the short for Margaret. Jane wanted a fowl to boil for me. Now she has a theory that the more she makes her English un-English, the more it must be like German. Jane begins by showing Gradle a word in the dictionary.

GRADLE. 'Ja! yees – hühn – henne – ja! yees.'

JANE (a little through her nose). 'Hmn – hum – hem – yes – yaw, ken you geet a fowl – fool – foal, to boil – bile – bole for dinner?'

GRADLE. 'Hot wasser?'

JANE. 'Yaw in pit – pat – pot – hmn – hum – eh!'

GRADLE (a little off the scent again) 'Ja, nein – wasser, pot – hot – nein.'

JANE. 'Yes – no – goodtoeeat – chicken – cheeken – checking – choking – bird – bard – beard – lays eggs – eeggs – hune, heine – hin – make cheekin broth – soup – poultry – peltry – paltry!'

GRADLE (quite at fault). 'Pfeltrighchtch![7] – nein.'

JANE (in despair). 'What shall I do! and Hood won't help me, he only laughs. This comes of leaving England!' (She casts her eyes across the street at the Governor's poultry-yard, and a bright thought strikes her.) 'Here, Gradle – come here – comb hair – hmn – hum – look there – dare – you see things walking – hmn, hum, wacking about – things with feathers – fathers – feethers.'

GRADLE (hitting it off again.) 'Feethers – faders – ah hah! fedders – ja, ja, yees, sie bringen – fedders, ja, ja!'

JANE echoes 'Fedders – yes – yaw, yaw!'

Exit Gradle, and after three-quarters of an hour, returns triumphantly with two bundles of stationer's quills!!! This is a fact, and will do for Twig.[8]

* * * * I will now write as well as I can a description, which may serve to extract for the 'Athenaeum.' The bound volumes were, though only a Dilke-send, like a God-send. You cannot think how well they read here, where there is nothing else to read. There's a compliment for you, worthy of our Irishman. On the first of May here, when I was wondering what would replace the *round*elays of the London sweeps, the deficiency was kindly supplied by a whirlwind, which made a great many sundries dance in its vortex. I was gazing from the window of the Belle Vue Hôtel opposite the bridge, when my attention was excited by a great cloud of German dust, waltzing after the German fashion, to the great embarrassment of some untaught crows or rooks, who were flapping about quite bewildered in its mazes. It came from the direction where the Moselle mingles with the Rhine. The dust cleared off in about a minute, and the whirlwind itself became distinctly visible, travelling diagonally across the Rhine, at a leisurely pace, and showing to great advantage against the rock of Ehrenbreitstein, at that time bright with a gleam of sun, and strongly brought out by a mass of ink-black clouds; of a grey colour – slender, of equal width throughout – bellying before the wind, with a curve equal to that of the longest kite-string, and moreover towards the top, serpentining in three or four undulations, as if from various currents of air. The phenomenon presented the appearance of a narrow but long ribbon let down from the clouds. It apparently rose to a great height – I should guess a mile – and terminated above in a sort of ragged funnel of scarcely twice the diameter of the tube. I could not detect any circular motion; in fact, I repeat, it looked like a ribbon. On reaching the opposite side of the river it raised a surge on the bank, as well as a wash of linen which lay there, and which, after a few pirouettes, disappeared – of course it got a good wringing. I have since learned that it also made free with some skins from the leather manufactory situated near the Moselle, and carried them almost to Ems – I suppose to be *cured*. The whirlwind itself disappeared between Ehrenbreitstein and its neighbouring height, following apparently the road to the baths, as if to get rid of its dust.

But mark the truth of the proverb 'one good turn deserves another,' the first had scarcely vanished, when looking upwards, I discerned overhead a second, but *parallel with* the earth, in the shape of a long black cloud, slowly revolving, and pointing in the direction which its predecessor had travelled over. It had the wind, as the sailors say, right fore and aft, and was somewhat shorter and lustier than the vertical one, ending obtusely towards the wind; but at the other, terminating in a long fine point! I could not help exclaiming as I saw it, 'there's a *screw loose* in the sky!' for which even the Germans who knew English were little the wiser.

In expectation of seeing you this summer I have made a rough sketch of the thing, however incompetent, for a whirlwind especially demands a *Turner*.

My illness has been a sad hindrance to me in the 'Comic,' as to the executive, but I have collected some materials. I think I can hit off a few sketches like Head's as to the Germans. I have seen many funny things here.

Jane is evidently much better, and has walked up the hill to Ehrenbreitstein; and the children, thank God, thrive apace. The baby, Tom junior, has been vaccinated according to law here; he gets on well and is very good, giving as little trouble as a baby can. Fanny seldom walks out but with some little Germans walking parallel before and after, and wondering at her to her great amusement. She is quite a model here, for 'strange yet true it is,'[9] *all* the children here are bandy-legged! You never saw such a set of legs as go to school daily down our street. But the people here are very stupid; mere animals; they take no interest in Science, Literature, Politics, or anything I can find, but eating and drinking.

The 'Athenaeum' which I one day read at the table d'hôte before dinner, has I fear stamped me a *pedant*. Pray did you ever taste '*Mai Drank*' or May Drink; if not, you have a pleasure to come. I look forward to your advent with great joy, and hope some of you at least may come. For my own part, if God would but grant me a stomach, I have heart enough to stay here a couple of years. I only want health and strength. But those will come and the rest with them.

Thanks to Dr. B—,[10] who acted as dragoman or interpreter, Jane has got her fowls at last! Only an old woman brought them alive and crowing! It so happened that to-day two hens have appeared for the first time, and the moment Jane saw them she thought we were still at fault and that we were supposed to want to keep fowls. But the real ones have come home at last, dead and plucked, and we *have* hopes of one to-morrow, having been three days in getting it.

Oh! how I wish I wrote for A.K. Newman, and lived near Leadenhall Market![11] *Mon perruque!* how we are to get it boiled is a mystery yet unsolved. I guess Jane or I must just parboil ourselves by way of making signs. I only wonder, in my illness, when Jane sent for a doctor, Gradle did not bring me a bootmaker! But as Jane says, 'there is a cherub up aloft for us.'

I dined to-day on bread and Swiss cheese. I have no appetite, and German cookery is 'rank – it smells to heaven!'[12] Salt fish they wash till it is fresh, and what is fresh they just make sour enough for you to think it is *turned*. What ought to be sour – pickled walnuts – are *sweet*, tasting of cloves, – you never know where to have 'em![13]

There are but few roofs in England under which my thoughts find a pleasant resting-place. So Coblenz would be a sort of Noah's Ark to me, but for the olive branch at 9, Lower Grosvenor Place.[14] Jane sends her love to Mrs. Dilke and will write by the next post. News is scarce here both ways. A raft the other day carried away part of the bridge about half a mile; and though the Rhine is not so rapid now, they were about forty hours getting it back again! No great credit to their mechanical powers. God bless you all, if the benediction from an *Anti-Agnewite* be worth having.[15] Kind regards to all friends. Rogers's Reminiscences[16] to everyone who cares to remember,

My dear Dilke,
Yours ever faithfully,

T. Hood.

Coblentz, May 6th, 1835.

From *Memorials* 181–9

1/Giovanni Baptista Belzoni (1778–1823), actor, engineer, and traveller, came to England in 1803 and exhibited feats of strength in the streets and fairs.
2/In the ballad 'Chevy Chase'
3/In LeSage's *Gil Blas*
4/Francis Bond Head *Bubbles from the Brunnens of Nassau* (1834) 364. This book would appeal to Hood both for its local subject matter and for its lively, whimsical style.
5/Celebrated pugilist
6/Pope *Essay on Criticism* 215. Hood's doctor is probably Beerman, recommended by the Vertues.
7/Nonsense word
8/Character in Hood's *Tylney Hall*, though I do not understand the point of the allusion to him
9/Byron *Don Juan* XIV 101
10/Beerman
11/A.K. Newman, publisher of popular fiction, 32 Leadenhall St. Leadenhall Market was the big London centre for country-killed meat.
12/*Hamlet* 3 iii 36
13/Compare *1 Henry IV* 3 iii 127: 'she's neither fish nor flesh: a man knows not where to have her.'
14/Dilke's address
15/The *Comic Annual* for 1834 contained an ode attacking Sir Andrew Agnew, an ardent Sabbatarian.
16/Samuel Rogers was the author of *Pleasures of Memory* (1792).

TO
CHARLES WENTWORTH DILKE

My Dear Dilke,
I did not expect to write to you again so soon, but having to send the above, I do so.

I have had a fresh attack of the spasms, – scarcely so severe as the first, but longer; they have left me so weak I can hardly walk. But the weather is favourable, and I try to get out, and take exercise and fight it off. The worst is over I think now, but it has been a sad hindrance to me. Next month we are going to alter our arrangements, and dine at home; with our own kitchen, &c., it will be much better and cheaper, and these one o'clock table d'hôte dinners cut up my mornings terribly. Thank God! Jane appears to get on in her health, as well as her fatigues will let her, and Fanny is hearty and happy. But the babe is necessarily poorly from vaccination – he thrives otherwise famously. The air here seems very good and pure, and the country is beautiful now with the spring greens. We have heard the nightingale once, singing beautifully. Neither the Rhine nor Moselle, however, is very blue yet, – mud-colour rather, we have had so much wind and wet; but the 'arrowy river'[1] is fine anyway; what a rush it makes, as if there were something very good at the end of its course: here I could moralise, but I won't. I am washy and spiritless, and should degenerate into twaddle.
The 'Athenaeum,' by special request, when I have done with it, goes to the Hotel, for the benefit of the English who come there. They are not numerous yet, but must be coming, when they do come, in shoals. I was diverted with one young fellow who came up to go to some clerkship at Mayence, a true Cockney. He thought his 'dampschiffe' billet was a passport, so left the latter at Cologne, and came on here. He got me to explain the money to him, and after all was done, exclaimed in a real Bow-bell voice: 'Well, arter all, there's no place like Lonnon!'
I also met at a shop here with a Parisian cockney – of whom I shall make a sketch à la Sterne – a cobbler's boy! He told me he came from Paris several times; asked me whence I came, – 'from London.' 'Ah, Monsieur, est-il près de Paris?'
Pray tell Mrs. Dilke one of the last little table displays I have seen here. At the table d'hôte, the English are fond of copying foreign customs and manners. First pull out the crumb of your roll, about half of which roll up, and work between your fingers (if snuffy the better) into little balls as big as marbles. They will not look exactly like Wordsworth's 'White Dough,'[2] but rather dirty putty. When you have

used your quill toothpick, stick it up, bolt upright, in one of these dirty balls, a little flattened beneath, as you may have seen candles stuck in extempore clay candlesticks at an illumination. Should it (the toothpick) want cleaning, furbish it up with one of the other dirty bread balls; then it will be ready for further use! This I should think a very polite piece of manners, for I had it from a gentleman who wears a black velvet great coat and a ribbon at his button-hole, and who evidently does not think small beer of himself, or vin ordinaire, as I ought to say here. Mind, don't extract this in the 'Athenaeum' or 'twill be recognised. It is dangerous writing to the editor of a paper, so in want of original extracts! Shall I write you weekly a foreign letter here, as your correspondent from Munich? There are no fine arts, or literature, or scientifics or politics here, but I can make them. Have you heard of our young sculptor, Hoche? his group of Goethe supported in the arms of Charlotte and Werther is just put up, but the pedestal is too low. Professor Swaltz's 'Essay on the Architecture of the Catti' has made a great sensation here, and has quite filled all mouths, which a week ago were occupied with the project for having a new pump in the Rhein Strasse, and enclosing the parade with posts and rails. *Nous verrons*. In my next, I shall give you an account of the grand party at Prince Pfaffi's,[3] &c., &c., &c. I could make you a *double number* of *very Foreign* intelligence. Or shall I send you some *free* translations from the German? They translate from me,[4] and I ought to show my gratitude. If I may choose, I should like to make my first experiment on Kant's Transcendentalism. I have been to the Hotel of an evening, and got a good notion of German philosophy, – perhaps you are not aware that it is laid on with *pipes*, like the gas in London! I have tried to draw some of them, but a real smoker beats the pencil. It is a mistake, by the way, to say 'he is smoking,' he is not *active* but *passive*, – 'being smoked!' How they suck their pipes, like great emblems of second childhood, so placid, so innocent, so unmeaning! 'Mild as the Moonbeam!'[5]

My kindest regards to Mrs. Dilke and Wentworth, and believe me ever, my dear Dilke,
Yours very truly,

Thos. Hood.

[*Koblenz*] *19th May, 1835*.

From *Memorials* I 90–3. I have not been able to identify the enclosure mentioned in the first sentence.

1/In *Childe Harold's Pilgrimage* III 71, Byron writes of 'the blue rushing of the arrowy Rhone.'

2/A quipping reference to Wordsworth *The White Doe of Rylstone* 1815

3/Hoche, Swaltz, and Pfaffi are imaginary names; Pfaffi may be linked with the Countess Pfaffenheim, 216.

4/I do not know to what translations Hood is here referring.
5/Quotation unidentified

TO
PHILIP DE FRANCK

Sir,
I regret that I had not a card about me to offer to you in acknowledgment of a *rencontre* so agreeable. I beg leave to enclose one, lest you should suppose me infected with that national shyness, which makes foreigners so apt to consider us as a grand *corps de réserve.*

I have the honour to be, Sir,
Yours obediently,

Thomas Hood.

Lieutenant de Franck,
19th Polish Regiment, Ehrenbreitstein.

[*Koblenz, summer 1835*]

From *Memorials* 1 80. Philip De Franck, an Anglo-German officer, became Hood's only close friend in Germany.

TO
MRS MARIA DILKE

My dear Mrs. Dilke,
I write to you instead of *the D*— because I am sick of him as a correspondent: as a countryman of Taylor's[1] said, 'who would go out with a fellow, that when you fire at him with a blunderbuss only returns it with a pocket-pistol?' even so have I sent Dilke huge letters full and crossed, enough to drive him blind and stupid, and give him a chronic headache; and what does he send in answer but a little letteret that cannot do anybody any harm? I suppose some day I shall come to, 'T.H. is received' at the fag end of the Athenaeum, amidst the mis-called Answers to Correspondents.
In short, I resent, as people resent who know the world, – that is, cut him when he is making advances. *You* shall have this, who will put it amongst the *haughty*graphs

you are most proud of, instead of telling me coolly that my 'account of the whirlwind at Ehrenbreitstein, and the story of the tooth-pick you had mislaid, and had never been able to lay your hand on it since.' It is long since he wrote so; but I can *harbour* malice quite as well as Margate pier. I scorn his paltry excuses for brevity without wit, and am astonished that he could have the face to plead 'the disturbance of the gentleman overhead,' whose noise he confessedly slept through. As for his cock and a bull about 'Mr. Pap,[2] who was burnt at Nottingham,' I am of Jane's nursery opinion, that '*pap* oughtn't to be burnt,' and that is a sufficient notice.

Regarding his whole 'pistle, in reality but a pocket 'pistle, candour compels me to say, I cannot conceive how any man alive could write a duller, 'with Liston[3] on one side of him, and Miss Kelly on the other.' You see I do not spare him; but I have heard that in England it is a sort of genteel flirtation with the wife to abuse her husband to her face, so I mean to go my lengths. Poor dear wretched woman! I can well conceive your perplexity with him at those Kentish cliffs, for as you say 'change of air *will* bring out any *complaint* that is hanging about.' I can fancy him complaining that all the *chalk* was not *cheese*, and then the cheese not all *rhine*, in his megrims. Editors, as you say, are but bad travelling companions, and as Taylor would say, they are but bad visiting companions, or before this he would have left his card at least at our door; but he preferred Margate, and I can only say, *de disgustibus*, &c.

I don't wonder you 'prefer *divines*,' as I do, especially if they are not attached to any particular church or chapel; in token of which I last week gave a trifle to two Catholic priests towards building a new St. Castor's; being perfectly persuaded that the money would never be applied to its ostensible use. I hope all stiff and back-bone Protestants will be satisfied with this my apology.

They were very modest, and would take anything they could get, even copper, so I gave them a very small feather for the tail of the weather-cock.

If I recollect rightly your style of singing, you were also in favour of 'tollol'eration; besides one of the priests allowed too that '*tous les hommes sont des hommes*,' and I felt obliged to pay him for being converted so far into a Protestant. If Mr. Dilke exerted himself, he might get me a missionary stipend. The man's a brute, and I'll prove it by his own contrarieties; for if, as you state, his only wish on the coast was to 'avoid the sea,' why on the same principle of logic did he take you with him, but to get rid of you? Jane feels for you, and so do I, and indeed so do Fanny and Tom when you describe taking him by the fin, and hauling him up 'all along shore there' to the fish-market, only to hear him complain like a porpoise on land that he couldn't 'get enough fish.' As to lugging him up to the Fort, you ought to have recollected how little your own piano*forte* used to interest him.

By your leave what you did with him was an error of judgment; you should have stuck him on a high stool at the parlour window, and made him pay every man in a blue jacket and trousers, one and threepence ha'penny. Besides, you forget his travels. Was it likely that a man who had crossed the Simplon, would care to cross a donkey? or that he who had seen St. Peter's at Rome, would give one of St. Peter's pence to see St. Peter's in Thanet?[4]

You must have forgotten that he had been at Venice, when you took him to 'Snobs' watering-place.'[5]

To get him into plain 'yellow shoes and a pepper-and-salt dressing gown', must have been a mere Margate miracle after the outlandish nightcaps with no hole to 'em, but like tasselled rainbows I used to find on the pillow of the spare bed at number nine. Even at Coblenz, here, – and he recommended Coblenz, – a plum-coloured coat, sky-blue pantaloons, and a waistcoat of patchwork in silk is the costume. When he does make a holiday in future, pray make him look more like an Editor, that is to say, clothe him in all the 'miscellaneous articles' you can muster. Judging by this costume, I suspect a good many of the Germans here are editors, and that accounts for Dilke wandering in this direction. But you will do well to egg him on in this fancy, for then, next year I may see you, and in the interim I will look out for German J.C—, S— and Mrs. C— to meet you, – not forgetting a Mrs. Pap, who (Dilke says in his confidential letter to me) is 'a very sociable, good-tempered woman.'[6]

I am sure he means *her*, though he cunningly lays it on Mr. P. He says 'Mrs. Pap, whose husband was burnt at Nottingham – *the latter* is a very sociable,' &c., &c. But don't be blinded so grossly.

Thank God you will have left ere this; a little longer and you would perhaps have been left, like Ariadne, on the shingles, looking at your husband gone off in a Pap-boat.

But 'henuff hov'im,' as of course you used to say at Margate. * * Tom, Junior, who came to Cologne a little 'shabby, flabby, dabby babby,' has grown a young Kentuck, who can lick his father – as hard as nails, and as brown as rusty ones. – For his temper, only fancy mine 'with sugar.' So unlike Jane's 'warm without.' Then he is already so good on his legs. I wonder he ever required D. 'to stand for him,' and as to talking he can say papa when he likes. I have no doubt he only don't cut his teeth because he don't *choose*. In bulk, he is really a double number, but a good deal more amusing.[7]

His love for Gradle is more beautiful than its object, for she is like a plain Chinese; but he will know better as he grows up.

Your Godchild is well and very good, but from seeing processions, &c., is half a Catholic, so if you please, you will come next year, and, according to your vows, teach her High Church.

I think we could make you very comfortable, – at least you would not need to lie in bed, and eat split peas as you did in Paris. Jane can cook a little. She had the honour of making the first pie ever seen in Coblenz, and the baker so admired it that he abstracted half of the contents – greengages. Gradle can cook in the English style too, but she will not eat what she has so cooked, and yet I imagine it must be a good style, for a poor woman comes for 'the broth the ham was boiled in,' but Jane suspects that it is for a night-light, – being nothing but water and oil. You shall try it when you come. If you liked Tivoli, we have dozens of such tea-garden places. Mozelweis, Schönbornlust, the Salmiac hut, &c., &c. I took the Elliots to the first by moonlight, and gave them punch, but nothing to eat was to be had save some cold plum-tart.[8] We are not too refined here to go to German White Conduits and Bagnigge Wellses.[9] In the garden of Schönbornlust (which reminded me, by the way, of some of the shrubberies of Lake House), we saw the lady of our opposite neighbour, the general commander-in-chief of the Rhenish Provinces, or as Fanny calls her, Mrs. Generous (pro general).

His Excellency is much taken with our brats, and often, as he rides by, gives Fanny what she calls a 'laughish smile.' But the admiration of the Castor Hof is Tom, or as Fanny says, 'all the boys that *traverse* the street call him *Timmus*,' (she got the fine word out of the lesson-book). He quite takes after his godfather Dilke, in eating everything he can get, and plenty of it, and he is as stout accordingly – not fat but solid. This has been a great blessing, and altogether we are as comfortable as need be. Our lodgings are very commodious and pleasant. A sketch I send Dilke will show our look out at the back: and we have a tiny kitchen – but it does – it does. We shall be able to give the Elliots a dinner on their way back.

I am writing in a little study with a bookcase and a sofa in it, so you see I am not without *my* luxuries; Fanny has a little bed-room next ours; Tom has regularly outgrown his cradle.

Thank God, Jane and I have stopped growing, for as it is I cannot stretch as full length in the bed, except diagonally, because of the head and foot boards. The Prussians are universally shortish and the beds are in proportion, I ought to call them cribs. Ours is like a 'coffin for two.' So you may suppose we shall have no difficulty in finding *spare beds* for *you* when you come. Dilke must sleep upright in a cupboard. Mind you must not expect to be saluted when you arrive, it is not the fashion here, we have had many greater personages, and they did not get a single gun. Queen of Naples, Princess of Beira, Prince Frederick of Prussia – not a pop – at last came the King of Würtemberg, and as nobody else did, he saluted himself with some tiny guns from his own steamer.

But you may get kissed a few; Lieutenant Franck told us that when the third battalion of his regiment came here, he had to be kissed by about thirty officers of it. It has a very droll effect to see these moustached veterans embracing each other, like boarding-school misses.

Franck, who is an Englishman, cannot bear it, and unluckily he is rather short. Allan Cunningham might escape it. I saw a young couple, lovers or newly married, kiss on separating in the steamboat, and, after going a few paces, the *lady* turned back and had another! The gent by this time had got amongst a party of English, for whom the scene was too funny to withstand, and as the lady's 'second thought' took effect in the midst of us, we all burst into a general roar. The King of Prussia will not allow his officers to marry unless, independent of pay, the couple have between them about 80 per annum.[10] I have some thoughts of writing a pretty little romance on the subject, – only fancy the distress of a pair of such turtle-doves £5 short!

Imagine them getting up to 79, and then the captain obliged to shell[11] out 10*s*. a year for a new uniform. Sitting in the *stocks* can be but a flea-bite to it. I should not like to be a father with money, for fear Wilhelmina or Charlotta should take it into her head to imitate Miss Blandy.[12]

To be sure the king has some right to look after the officers' matches, for he pays their debts, (I wish I was in his service,) and altogether he seems to be very kind and considerate towards them. What I hear of his Majesty I like, and am therefore *pro tempore* his loyal subject, and drank his health on his birthday.[13] Yesterday we toasted 'the Snobs' in Hocheim wine, it only costs 4*d*. a bottle, and was quite good enough for such a pledge. I cannot help thinking your Margate trip has a little let you down, and you will want a jaunt up the Rhine to restore you to gentility. But pray cast off your Margatory manners and costume ere you come. One night there was *such* an English party at the gardens of the Weissen Ross, that Franck in horror told his brother officers that they were French people.

'It warn't hus,' we are among the respectables at present, and one comfort is, that when Jane has worn out her bonnet and all her caps, if we can't afford new ones, it's very fashionable for ladies to go bare-headed in the street.

Then for me a blue smock frock is a sort of sporting or pedestrian dress for gentlemen, (and though I can't walk much, or shoot, I can make believe), when I have worn out my best brown and my old black.

I bought a cap to save my hat, and when I wear it, I am so thin withal, you would take me for a jockey who had been overtrained. But I hope to fill up again, for I am going to dinner with an appetite far sharper than our knives, which you may set your heart upon without hurting it. I feel quite a gourmand now, after going for months without dining, indeed it appears to have been a joke against me at the hotel, that I went to the table-d'hôte *not* to eat.

Now, I scold so, if the dinner is not ready at two! Jane likes nothing less than to hear me exclaim, 'slow coach!' which means that our household affairs are not going on at the proper pace.

That will sometimes happen, for plain as she is, our Gradle has a lovyer (perhaps more), and goes out gallivanting. I wonder she has not lost him, for the departure of some five thousand troops to the reviews, must have left many of the Coblenz servants at a loss what to do with their hearts. Comparatively we are as a city of the plague, and the streets appear deserted; the officers and men off duty were always lounging about them. Dinner and turn-out is as common here as tea and ditto in England.

We often see a party of a dozen officers in full twig, go to dinner at two, and hop the twig[14] at five or sooner, over the way. I cannot quite get out of my habit of sitting up to write at night, and when I am going to bed at eleven or twelve, and look out of the window, all Coblenzers are in bed; the only living thing is the sentinel at the general's. At noon the whole town literally smells of dinner; the shops are all locked up; and great is the consumption of grease and garlic. Dilke, who is anything but peaking and delicate, will laugh, and say he never met with anything *he* couldn't eat; but, upon my 'davit,' I saw a starved-looking dog in the steamboat refuse to touch a plate of scraps set before him by the steward. On looking over Jane's letter, for fear we should jostle on the same subject (you know we don't agree very well), I see she has given you a description of Gradle's dinner; so I refrain from mentioning it, and will only say that a knife, not without reason in Germany, is called a *messer*.

As for Dilke (to recur to him), you know his infatuation about everything outlandish. Doesn't he send to (the further end of the Edgeware Road or where is it?) for German mustard – only because it looks dirtier than the English! I'll be bound, if it would give him time, he would give an elaborate panegyric on *Prussic* acid, because it is Prussian. Only try him! We would give a trifle here for a good Margate whiting for all his skits on that very delicate flavoured fish, at this distance almost *too delicate*.

I should like to have all the skate and flounders he refused; and if I possessed but a brill (that 'workhouse turbot'), I almost think I should venture to ask his excellency to dinner; at a pinch we could enjoy sprats. I hear we *can* have oysters here in the season, rather stale-ish, that is to say they come like all other travellers, all 'open-mouthed,' as if they were looking at our lions. They eat them with vinegar and lemon, and Franck says you cannot eat them without; for though you have them in their *shells*, they taste a little *too* corpse-like; I think I could even eat the great big horse oysters *with their beards on*, that we used to leave to the coal porters and draymen about Lonnon. We have had those lobsters of Lilliput – small crayfish – we thought we must have bargained well when we got 25 a penny, but when Franck supped upon them with us in the evening, he said we ought to have got a hundred; perhaps we ought to have had a dozen for nothing. But the poor rich English are very much imposed upon! A *maitre d'hôtel* (a very good authority), told me candidly on coming up, that there were three tariffs for the English/French /Dutch.

He stood in the middle predicament, and I have found his statement perfectly true. The good honest Germans are as great cheats as any, though I confess they look honest, they are so stupid-like, and perhaps honesty is stupidity. I had some shirts made here, and they not only changed the cloth I had bought of them, but sent me home some shirts so laughably short, I could only make shift with them; this was a respectable shop. Franck says he interfered once (he has a good national spirit about him), when he found some English deplorably fleeced at an Inn. The fact is, though we pay three times as much as the natives, it is still so cheap in comparison with England, 'dear, dear' England, that one is blinded to imposition. In my last letter to Wright, I ventured to conjecture that there would be a revolution in England, if it were from so many English coming up the Rhine, and finding what a deal they can get for their money; not that they would wish to remove their *king*, but that they would wish their sovereign to go farther.

Only think how you may be charitable on next to nothing by giving a pfenning, the third part of a farthing; and in this blessed country there is something to be bought even for that low denomination. I wonder what you can get in England for a farthing, for the 'little farthing rushlight' is only a fiction. Only fancy Fanny coming to me when Gradle is going to market, for a shilling to dine the whole household.

We have not tried, but I really believe you might have a snug little evening party for half a guinea! I suspect you never enjoy the sensation of fulness in the only place where repletion is a pleasure, in the pocket!

You might here go out of an evening with your bag *full* of money; and such is the nature of the coin, it would only suffice to pay for a lost game or two at shilling shorts.[15] For example, fancy youself the mother of a dozen strapping Wentworths (father or son they are both of a bigness),[16] and even so does a little dumpy shirt-button-mould of a groschen (a penny), expand by changing into twelve goodly pfennings – each almost a ha'penny – whilst for a dollar (3 shillings), you get 6 pieces, each as big as the old eighteenpenny tokens.[17] You might fell an ox with a long purse that had a pound translated into Prussian at the other end of it; I wonder Mrs. Fry never came here, one might do such a deal of good ostentatiously for a shilling a week.[18] For my own part, I have not gone further in contemplation than a little feast to the poor children in Coblenz, as I used to see the orphan school regaled in the avenue at the back of dear One-Tree Hill[19] at Wanstead. It would be a pretty sight in the Castor Hof; and fruits being cheap, only think that, buying wholesale, I could for three shillings give a hundred little ones nine greengages a-piece.

This would be as good as dining them; for you may read in the 'Bubbles' of a tailor and his son who lived in the season on plums.[20] If you would like to join in the entertainment, you might make all the parents drunk for about fourpence a head, with music *ad libitum* for eighteenpence. I assure you I was in doubt at the hotel at a *table d'hôte* whether I could offer a penny farthing to a nice lady-like young woman, who had been so obliging as to sing, accompanied by her harp, all dinner-time. However, as the coin was neither silver nor copper, I managed not to be vulgar altogether, nor yet extravagant. You will be surprised to hear that *nothing* at all seemed to be very genteel, and some of the gentlemen gave it with a smirk and look as if they expected a salute in return. Never mind Dilke, *I* say Germans are not liberal (of course only speaking from the sample here), and yet we have an instance of liberality under our eyes enough to redeem a nation. How munificent are the poor to the poor, casting into shade the most splendid benefactions of princes! Next door to us (a tavern) there lives a poor maniac: the house is her own property, and therefore the charitable lunatic asylums are closed against her. Her brother, and *heir*, ill-treats her, and is supposed to starve her, for the sake of the freehold; and the poor wretches at the back tenements, weavers and other famished human weazels (the woman who begs our ham-broth amongst the rest), thrust up to the poor mad creature, on the points of sticks, fragments of bread and food, of which, God knows, to look at them, they are scant enough themselves. This I call charity; and it makes me so pleased with the givers, that I wish I were but that King of Hams, the King of Westphalia, to allow them ham-broth to swim in if they so pleased.

And now, having given you this pretty episode to sweeten my asperities in my letter, I will leave you with an agreeable impression of human nature and myself. I have written a long letter, because I thought your kindness would be pleased with it, being a cheerful one, after some anxiety on my account. Besides, I write to you (I hope Dilke won't be jealous) *con amore*, seeing that we have been always very good friends, and have never disagreed but at secondhand. I mean when I could not put up with your pickled oysters, and you could not endure my preserved sprats. So I heartily reciprocate your 'God bless' – which, I remember, when only females were in the case, used to be followed by a sort of smack that might have been heard from No. 9 to Pimlico palace.[21] I do not know whether I ought – but the Germans do – and I'd rather *you* than Dilke; and besides, I recollect how you sobbed and cried when Doctor S—[22] went away without offering –. So here goes – consider it enclosed! On second thoughts I have judged it better to keep up appearances with your husband by writing to him. So that while I get you to remember me kindly to William and Wentworth and Taylor and Chorley and Holmes,[23] and all other friends, I can get Dilke to forget me kindly to all the rest, which, I feel sure, he will punctually fulfil. He must have forgot *himself* when he went to Margate. I only wish when he goes to the coast again 'may I be there to sea.'[24] Of course you did not dip him, for he is more than a mould already. Fanny asked, in her innocent way, 'Did Mr. Dilke go about with a basket and pick up shells?' I told her 'No; but he used to take a ride out on a donkey with you behind him on a pillion.' I don't wonder at the child's wonder. In the name of Earl Goodwin (who rented the famous Sands), what did you do with his appetite? He is not a man to go about picking shrimps and teazing periwinkles out of their shells with crooked pins. As the sea air is sharpening, I wonder he did not eat you, who are as plump as a partridge, with Mrs. Pap by way of bread-sauce. Then the hot weather you both talk of must have made him open his coat wider than usual, that the wind might get down the arms. I think I see him courting the sea-breeze. 'Upon my soul, Maria, this is a delightful place! So like Coblenz! So you call this Margate, do you, my beauty? Well –' (a grunt like a paviour's), 'and I suppose you call that the fort – humph! Considering we might have stood before Ehrenbreitstein instead of it – hah!' (a sigh like an alligator's). 'My God! – that we could be so insane! – how any Christian being could stay a month in it! – why I should hang myself in ten days, or drown myself in that stinking sea yonder! There is not one thing worth looking at – not one! I know what you are going to say, Beauty; but because the Crosbys and the Chatfields[25] are such donkeys, and the Lord knows who besides, is it any reason because they don't act like common rational beings – ? But come along!' (no offer to stir though) 'let's go up to the market and look at the fish, for I suppose you know there is none to be had here, because it is so near the coast. To be sure, says you, there is whiting – and so there is at Billingsgate! If ever I go again to a watering-place – I believe that's what you call it, Maria – it shall be Hungerford Market.[26] My God! it is a madness – a perfect madness – to leave home and come down here to see – what? a parcel of yellow slippers and pepper-and-salt dressing gowns.' Here he draws down his mouth, and hoists up his shoulders, till his coat-collar hides his ears. 'Well, it's too late now to listen to common sense. It serves me right for being such an ass. By the time my holidays are over, I shall know how to spend them! But perhaps *you* like it better than I do, for there's no disputing of tastes.

'There may be something to recommend even Margate, though an angel from heaven couldn't find out what it is. I know *I* can't, unless its having a drunken noisy vagabond overhead to keep you awake all night long. But I forget, my darling, you don't sleep so light as I do – so much the better for you! Then there's his sister that Mrs. — what d'ye call her, Tops-and-Bottoms, with her infernal bobbings and curtseyings and over-civility. Damme if I know how to answer the woman! I suppose according to Margate manners, we ought to ask her to Grosvenor Place. But mind, Maria, when she calls, I'm at Somerset House![27] Come along' (not a stump stirred yet). 'I suppose we must see what isn't to be seen in our salt-water Wapping. All *I* have seen is 'London butter,' – just think of that, Maria, – 'London butter may be had here.' Why so it may in London without going sixty miles by sea for it; and you, my darling, as sick as a dog! Spasms! I don't wonder you've had spasms; I've almost had them myself. It's the cursed negatives, and the place, rather than anything positive, – the utter bleakness and desolation of the country against the stinks of the sea-shore. Lord! that a man with a nose on his face should come here; and here too one has to remember that there are such places as Coblenz; and such a river as the Rhine. I'll tell you what, Maria!' Here he tells you nothing; but stooping over his base, like the leaning tower at Bologna, he takes a very long pinch of snuff, and then anathematising, shakes the dust off his fingers against all Margate and all its inhabitants, present and future.

There! isn't that a portrait of him to the life – a cabinet picture – a gem! Pray take care of it, to be a comfort to you when you are a widow. Perhaps I shall send him a sketch of you as a companion picture, for I can fancy you quite as vividly. If I recollect rightly, *you* were at Margate before and liked it amazingly. Between your raptures and his disgusts I suppose you got up a quarrel, for I observed you say in your letter that 'you are both getting a little more *reconciled*.' He must have been

awful – and I guess it was his splenetic attacks on the donkeys to vent his humane notions that originated the notice to visitors about 'wanton cruelty.' Take my advice *if ever you get him to Margate again* put him up to be raffled for. And now as the Germans say 'ah chied!' or as you would say, 'a do.'
'If these pages should be the happy means of exciting one virtuous impression, or confirming one moral or religious principle, or lightening one moment of human suffering, or eradicating one speculative error, or removing one ill-founded prejudice, the writer will have his reward, and will not have written in vain.'[28]

I am,
My dear Mrs. Dilke,
Yours ever very truly,

Thos. Hood.

P.S. I dined well to-day on such a haricot! that I'm persuaded Jane is the best cook in Coblenz. So I have done the handsome thing and *riz* her. She had nothing a-year before, and I have doubled it. We got a Westphalia ham against the Elliots' return, at five pence a pound. It is the finest I ever tasted; such a flavour, quite answerable to its odour, which is as unique in its kind as that of the best Eau de Cologne! They call it here the 'rauch,' answerable to the Scottish reek; but I will say no more about edibles or you will compare me to Matthews, who began with writing 'The Diary of an Invalid,'[29] and ended a Gourmand. I should like to send you a real Westphalian, but then the *duty!* You ought to take one with you here, as Miss M—[30] did her sweetmeats from India; she brought a large box of them – preserved Lord knows what – but the customs demanded so much that instead of bringing them ashore she went and ate them all up on board herself. I had this from Dr. E—,[31] who was called in to her after 'the *Gorge.*'

P.S. God bless.

372, Cast-him-off, God bless, [*Koblenz, late*] *1835.*

From *Memorials* I 107–27
1/William Cooke Taylor (1800–49), miscellaneous writer, was a contributor to *The Athenaeum.*
2/Unidentified
3/John Liston (1776?–1846), comic actor
4/'A pleasant place, and worth a walk to view. The church is an ancient Gothic edifice, and kept in good repair ... The church-yard is open to the public, and deserves investigation by the curious reader,' *The Picturesque Pocket Companion to Margate* (1831) 192.
5/Margate, though I have not identified the quotation
6/Names unidentified

7/At the end of 1835 Dilke boasted that in the past year he had issued 'no less than *nineteen* double numbers,' *Athenaeum* 969.
8/The Elliots were travelling in Europe.
9/*The Original Picture of London* 26th ed., ed. J. Britton (1826) 362, contains the entry: 'TEA GARDENS. The following are much frequented by the middling classes, on Sundays especially. White Conduit House, near Islington ... Bagnigge Wells, near Battle Bridge.'
10/*Memorials* reads '180,' but in view of '79' below, this is probably a mistake for '80,' so I have altered it accordingly.
11/*Memorials* reads 'sell.'
12/Hood is referring to Mary Blandy who murdered her father at the request of her lover and was executed for the crime in 1752. The episode is recorded in the *Newgate Calendar*.
13/Friedrich Wilhelm III (3 August 1770–1840)
14/Suddenly depart
15/Short whist
16/A reference to Charles Wentworth Dilke the younger
17/The circulation of tokens was suspended in 1797.
18/The philanthropist (1780–1845) had been criticized in *Odes and Addresses: Poetical Works* 5–8.
19/Unidentified
20/Francis Bond Head *Bubbles from the Bubbles of Nassau* 337
21/Presumably Buckingham Palace, situated in Pimlico. The palace was under construction from 1825 to 1836 and not occupied until the accession of Queen Victoria in the following year.
22/Perhaps Dr Mateo Seoane. Marchand 76 describes him as a Spanish medical man of repute, a close friend of Dilke, and a reviewer of Spanish books for *The Athenaeum*. He returned to Spain in 1834.
23/Henry Fothergill Chorley (1808–72), author and music critic, contributed to *The Athenaeum* from 1830. James Holmes was the printer of the periodical, as well as owner of a quarter of the property.
24/William Cowper *John Gilpin* last line
25/I have not been able to identify the Crosbys; Dilke's son married Mary Chatfield in 1840.
26/Fish market in the Strand, near Charing Cross
27/Where the Navy Pay Office, Dilke's official place of work, was situated
28/Quotation unidentified
29/Henry Matthews *Diary of an Invalid* (1820)
30/Unidentified
31/Probably Elliot

TO
JOHN WRIGHT

My dear Wright,
You will be glad to hear that I cannot write at great length to you, because I am busy, and able to be busy. You may imagine what a delight it was to us to see the Elliots, – they are so very kind and friendly. Besides, it was a comfort to have his opinion about me, though I am much better.[1] I almost growl at feeding-time if the dinner is not ready. We dine at a very genteel hour – two o'clock – which is also the Governor's time. The universal people take it at one. But I find the difference

more striking mentally than corporeally even; and ideas now come of themselves without being laboured for — and *in vain*. In fact, I know that I have a mind, or according to the famous form, '*Cogito, ergo sum*.' I believe that's something like the Latin for it, but I forget, for *I had a Latin prize at school!* As I find a positive pleasure in the power, its exercise must be equally pleasant, and I think I shall get on rapidly; indeed, some evenings I have been quite delighted with my comparative fertility of thought. I have got some good stories, or hints for stories, from De Franck, whose loss I fear I shall shortly have to regret, for I really like him. How odd his knowing C— and H.D — ;[2] there must have been some mysterious animal magnetism in his accosting me. A joke with him has led to my writing a poem of some 700 lines, which you will soon receive. My own impression is, if good enough for the 'Comic,' it had better be there to advance;[3] but consult with Dilke, who will judge better than I can. I have been so unwell, I am down, and diffident as to what I can do. I shall have some more Sketches on the Road, and some German stories,[4] so I have not been quite idle even in bed. I did hope to be earlier this year, but, as all philosophers must say when it comes to be impossible, 'it can't be helped.' I am only too happy to exclaim, like the poor scullion in 'Tristram Shandy,' 'I'm alive.' But some day I hope to make my account even with the storm; for there were some Eugene Aram-like verses rambled through my brain as I lay for the first night alone here – I believe a trifle delirious – but I remember something of their tenour, and I have a storm by me to work them up with. You see I am cutting out work for the winter. I went, the day the Elliots left, to Metternich, and in a wood at the top of a hill I found a large patch of wild purple crocuses in full bloom. I suppose they, too, had suffered a storm, and could not bud as they ought to have done in the spring. To-morrow I dine on game! – 'Think of that, Master Brooke!'[5] for it will make me think of you. I am sorry about Gilston Park. It would have turned all my hares white in one night, and then such a herd of *deers*. I have only three here, Jane, Fanny, and Tom; but they make a strong ring fence about me. What a lot of Tremaines he must write to get it back again.[6] *We* authors are an unlucky set – freehold, copyhold, or copyright!
Kind regards to all. God bless you, and send you bright days, that we may meet in 1855 like two Rothschildren just come of age and into our fortunes.

Yours ever truly,

Thomas Hood.

P.S. – 'Vallnuts is in, and thrippins an underd, and will be lowerer!' Think of that!

372, Castor Hof, Coblenz, Sept. 12th, 1835.

From *Memorials* I 93–6

1/Jane wrote in the following January: 'Hood getting better, set to work – it was then "all work and no play," but I do not recollect seeing him get through it better – he finished with good spirits,' *Memorials* I 143. Wright was concerned about the progress of Hood's work because it was he who saw the *Comic Annual* through the press.

2/'H.D.' may be Harman Dilsoon, see 333.

3/'Love and Lunacy,' *Comic Annual* for 1836

4/'The Domestic Dilemma' and 'Sketches on the Road' appeared in the *Comic Annual.*

5/*Merry Wives of Windsor* 3 v 108

6/Jerrold 290 notes that Gilston Park was the seat of Robert Plumer Ward (1765–1846), the author of *Tremaine* (1825). Ward took up residence at Gilston Park when he married Mrs Plumer Lewin in 1828. I do not know what catastrophe befell him, though after his remarriage in 1833 he spent much time abroad.

TO PHILIP DE FRANCK

My dear Mr Wood

The departure of a friend for Coblentz affords me an opportunity of which I avail myself with much pleasure; and especially as it enables me to prove in spite of your facetious hints of my inconstancy, that I am not unmindful of my absent friends. On the contrary, I assure you, on our march hither, my thoughts often wandered back to Coblentz and rested on you and your amiable wife and interesting family. Nay although I am now quartered in a city of infinitely more bustle and gaiety and have besides more military duties, still I can honestly declare as this letter is a proof, that in spite of such numerous avocations and distractions, my memory has never failed to recur to the many pleasant evenings I passed at your apartment in the Rhein Strasse. Indeed I may almost say that I find Posen itself rather dull for want of such hours and companionship, and especially that of your lively little girl whose remarks used to please me so very much. I never hear the name of *Georgiana* Maria but I think of her, & her merry dark eyes, not forgetting her little brother *William* Peter. Sometimes I wonder whether Lina (you see I do not forget any one) gets more intelligible to her mistress; and I often wish my German could be again tasked to interpret between her and Mrs. Good. These are delightful reminiscences to me, and I shall cherish them to the last moment of my life. Let time rob me of what it may it cannot ever efface these traces of past friendship – even if I did not possess such a souvenir to remind me of you as the *Chemical Annals*, Comic Manual, which you were so kind as to present to me for a keepsake. I assure you, my dear Mr Woodthorpe, I value it much, and I did not forget it and leave it behind me at a little wine house, on the right-hand side of the road between Pfaffendorf and Hocheim. The landlord's name I think was steibel. Your story about 'Was the other dead man a beggar' runs in my head as much as ever[1] and often sets me thinking of you which always ends in the wish that I could say here to my servant as I used when I was quartered at Ehrenbreitstein – 'I am going to Mr. Blood's!' Even Juno seems to miss your indulgence; she looks melancholy, and, I dare say, longs in her heart to have another romp with your little boy, or a race with Miss Sarah round your garden. Poor Juno! I never take a walk with her of an evening without regrets at our separation. I assure you I have marked as a lucky day in my calendar the one on which I first met yourself, Mrs. Woodroffe, and little Margaret, on the banks of the Rhine. I can only comfort myself with the hope that I am allowed to live in your remembrances as you do in mine; in my mind's eye I see you all plainly at this moment, seated in that little room which looks on the Mosel bridge. As for little Caroline, I picture her, of course, surrounded with her dolls, or playing with her old favourite cart and horse. I suppose, by this time, through running about under a German sun, her little brother is as brown as she is; but there is no harm in that, for one is not very solicitous about having fair boys. If my memory serves me, the complexion of her other brother was very dark. It is very singular, but when I arrived at Posen, I did not find any old friends. You will say, of course, that I had *forgotten them;* but I will leave my defence to Mrs. Wedgwood, who used to stand my friend in such cases when you ran me so hard, and promised me a slice of bread and butter for a keepsake. The faithfulness and minuteness of my recollections in this letter ought also to speak for me. I can only say, if it should please Fortune, even twenty years hence, to throw us again together, you will find that neither your features not the name of Woodley have escaped my memory, which was always reckoned a very good one. But we shall meet, I trust, in a much shorter interval than a score of years. I am tantalised here sometimes with rumours of our returning to Coblenz early in next spring. Should we do so, I suppose I shall hardly know Miss Flora again, for by that time her pretty black hair will be long enough to tie into tails, as the German little girls dress their heads. Pray give my love to her, and ask her if she remembers Lieut. von F— and his dog Juno. There is a little girl here, thirteen or fourteen years old, just about her height of figure, and talking a little French also, who reminds me vividly of my little friend in Coblenz. She has the same black eyes and hair, and is equally fond of skipping-rope and swinging. If I remember rightly, those were little Katherine's favourite pastimes.

And now, my dear Mr. Goodenough, my time of duty warns me to conclude. It will give me sincere pleasure if you should think this letter worthy of a return in kind, in which case I beg you will be particular in giving me every information of yourselves and your family. Pray take care of your health, and do not neglect my advice about currents of air. I remember you had a discoloration under the eye as if from a severe blow through sitting in a thorough draught. You must not prosecute your medical [mathematical][2] studies too closely. By this time I trust Mrs. Woodbridge is quite well, and has no further occasion for the services of Dr. B— : I sincerely hope she will feel no more ill effects from the dreadful storm she encountered in coming from England. Have the kindness to present my respectful regards to her, with my best wishes for her health and welfare, and a happy and a safe return in due time to Northamptonshire [Scotland]. I think you told me you came from Edinburgh; indeed I remember you had the Northern accent, which no doubt enabled you to pronounce the German so correctly. Pray give my love to Miss Anne, and tell her I hope she does not neglect her pianoforte. I remember all the airs she used to play to me. Her brothers, I fear, will have forgotten me, otherwise I should desire to be named to them with kindness. I shall eagerly expect every post to hear from you; and let me again beg of you to mention every one belonging to you, even your dog. You could not afford me a greater gratification; and if little Charlotte would add a P.S. in her own hand, for I remember she wrote very well, my pleasure would be complete.

Accept my kindest regards to you and yours, and pray believe me,
My dear Mr. Woodgate,
Your very sincere friend and well-wisher,

Philip de Franck.

P.S. I shall watch the newspapers for announcements of your new works. I hope that some day you will publish another novel like your Tilbury House [Hall].

To James Wood, Esq., Coblenz.

Posen 30th October / 1835

MS as far as 'Ehrenbreitstein – I am' Bristol Central Library. Published in *Memorials* I 96–101. Hood's daughter notes that this 'letter was written by my father as if from M. de Franck to himself, as a quiz upon the bad memory of the latter. It is a curious jumble of wilful mistakes.'

1/Probably the story of 'The Last Man' *Poetical Works* 41–3

2/The square brackets here and below are in *Memorials*, and take the place of underlinings in Hood's MS.

TO
JOHN WRIGHT

My dear Wright,

I had yours with great delight, for I was *very* anxious about the fate of my box. I have made some inquiry, and suspect the cause of the delay was that they were *things never sent before;* and that when examined at the frontiers between Prussia and Holland, they did not know what to do or to charge. I think such a delay not likely to happen again, but shall take every precaution. I had declared here what they were, and will in future get them sealed by the *Douane* here if I can. The MS. I will send post after post as I write it. I am glad what I sent made so much. Before this you will have found out what was to be done. * * * I am glad you liked Doppeldick.[1] If I can only travel a bit in the spring here I will make 'sich a Comic as never vos.' I know nobody here now but R— ,[2] a teacher of languages, who drops in every Sunday. The last I had such a long palaver with him in French; and I really believe I must be to him as Horam the son of Asmar,[3] or one of the relaters of the Arabian Nights – though only in giving him an account of England – of which he asks me such questions as 'have we any oaks?' almost if 'we have any sun or moon!' I make him stare with truths sometimes. And though he is polite like all foreigners nearly, he almost constantly has an involuntary shake of the head.

A shopkeeper, who also spoke French, one of the few I am on speaking terms with, died the other day of 'nervous fever,' being swelled like a man with dropsy! Verily I have no faith in the doctors here – we are sure to see a funeral every day – the population being only 20,000, including troops. I heard the other day of a man having *fifty-five* leeches on his thigh! My wig! why they out-Sangrado Sangrado![4] One of their blisters would draw a waggon. If I should be ill again I will prescribe for myself.

I will conclude with a Coblenz picture. Jane in bed, smothered in pillows and blankets, suffering from a terribly inflamed eye. In rushes our maid, and without any warning, suddenly envelopes her head in a baker's meal-sack hot out of the oven! prescribed as a sudorific and the best thing in the world for an inflamed eye by the baker's wife (there's nothing like leather!). What between the suddenness of the attack and her strong sense of the fun of the thing, Jane lay helplessly laughing for awhile and heard Gradle coax off the children with 'Coom schön babie – coom schöne Fannische – mama kranke!' Encore! I sent a pair of light trousers which were spotted with ink to be dyed black; after six weeks they came

back like a jackdaw, part black, part grey. I put my hands in the pockets like an Englishman, and they came out like an African's. I think seriously of giving them to a chimney-sweep who goes by here! full grown, long nosed, and so like the devil I wonder Fanny has never dreamed of him. There were two; but the other was stoved to death the other day at our neighbour the general's. They lit a fire under him when he was up. Our Dr. B—, who was sent for, told me gravely, that he could not revive him, for when he came, 'the man was *black in the face!*'
I forgot to tell you that when Gradle first proposed the hot flour prescription of the baker's wife, Jane had flattered herself that it was only a little paper bag of hot flour; and it was only when she was tucked in that she began to feel what a *cake*[5] she was! I wonder what they do for rheumatism! God bless you!

Yours ever truly,

T. Hood.

P.S. Fanny sends her love, 'not forgetting Jemmy and Freddy,'[6] and how they would like to come to Coblenz and see all the soldiers, and the generals. There is a man of the general's who rides upon a horse with a helmet on his head. I can almost talk German, I shall be glad to come back to England. Tommy has grown and is very fat. He has two sharp teeth, and he bites my fingers when I put them in his mouth. I am very happy here, because I can see the band go into the general's. I can say how many months make a year, and how many weeks make a month. I can write upon my slate A.B.C. and figures. And oh! I have a great house for my dolls, and three rooms in it! and I can't say any more, for my head aches, and I have a great many teapots and mugs, and I have got a cold, and a kitchen! Good night and love to you and Jemmy and Freddy.

'All of this stuff is Fanny's, every line,
For God's sake, reader, take them not for mine.'[7]

372, Castor Hof, Coblenz, Nov. 3rd, 1835.

From *Memorials* I 101–4
1/'The Domestic Dilemma' in the *Comic Annual* for 1836
2/Referred to in the following letter as Ramponi
3/The narrator of James Ridley's *Tales of the Genii* (1764)
4/In LeSage's *Gil Blas*, noted for bleedings
5/Fool
6/Perhaps Wright's children
7/Variant on Byron *Don Juan* I 222

TO
JOHN WRIGHT

My dear Wright,

Your letter arrived yesterday evening to my great relief, for I began to get very anxious, supposing the book would be published on the 15th, and feel sure I shall be pleased with it, when I see it.[1] All parties appear to have done their best, and for your own share I can only say that I feel you have done for me, as I would for you – your very best; so accept my best thanks accordingly. And now, what will you think of those abominable three months' old letters? up to this very hour they have never come to hand.

It has been a great nuisance to us, for we have not written to any one, in the daily expectation of having something to answer, so that Dilke and I, for example, have not been on writing terms for three months, and I fear many things I had to tell him have escaped me.

To estimate our expectations and disappointments, you must remember we are here as in a sort of desert, with one friend, De Franck, and one acquaintance Ramponi, the language master, who jabbers French with me, and every now and then a fellow with an orange collar, *i.e.* a postman, comes to the very next door. And now you will laugh to be told that I am this evening going with De Franck to a grand ball at the Casino, where will be all the rank, beauty, and fashion of Coblenz, of course not to dance, but at De Franck's advice, who says that the German New Year ceremonies are worth seeing, and I mean to see all I can, and turn it to account. I expect to commit myself by laughing aloud, for when the clock strikes twelve I shall find myself all of a sudden the only unkissed, unembraced individual in the room; Franck dined with us on Christmas day, and by his help in the evening we had a pretty German celebration to the high delight of Fanny; but thereof no more, as we hope some day to introduce it in England.[2] Our weather is variable, generally frosty – we have a little while had cold enough in all reason, the oil froze in the night light and the pound of butter in the middle, and as Katchen made a pudding in the kitchen the crust froze. The Rhine and the Moselle are full of ice, and the bridge being taken away, Franck for a month to come cannot stay with us later than nine in the evening, for he is quartered at Ehrenbreitstein on the other side, and must boat it across. He is really a treasure to us, thoroughly English, unpresuming, gentlemanly, and full of good sense, fond of a joke withal. Between him and the children it is quite a mutual flame; on their side, sometimes, so as to be laughable.

One night after his long absence I hung him up in effigy as a deserter, and he came in and found Fanny crying at it as if breaking her heart.

I have no local news to tell you, but that recently a priest at Cologne was convicted of poisoning a man from whom he had purchased an estate without paying for it. He is supposed to have given one or two their viaticum before now.

N.B. My thunder and lightning waistcoat is come! so I must go and dress for the ball. To you who know my *habits* all this must seem very funny, as it does to myself. I expect to be highly amused.

Jane is going to curl my hair, and I am going to comb and brush it, more attention altogether than hair generally gets here. I drink, in a glass of holiday hock, to you and all friends, wishing many new years happier than the happiest you have ever known or unknown. 'Tis pure rich juice of the grape; would you could taste it! the worst here, at 3*d.* a bottle, we should think something of in England.

To-morrow I set in for a new year with many serious thoughts, a few sad ones, but some hopeful ones. I will make play and fight the good fight,[3] never fear me. Remember me kindly to –, but tell him I mean nothing short of payment in full – no composition![4] The example of De Foe is before me.[5] Somewhat widely is known, and honourably and honestly shall be known if I live the name of

Yours, dear Wright,
Ever sincerely,

Thomas Hood.

Coblenz, 31st Dec., 1835.

From *Memorials* I 104–6, with a slightly different version in *Works* X 107–8, illustrated with a Union Jack

1/The *Comic Annual* was advertised for publication on 10 December 1835.

2/Hood's daughter notes: 'This is in allusion to a Christmas tree, – those pretty things being then quite unknown in England.'

3/1 Timothy 6:12

4/I cannot identify the creditor whose name is here omitted.

5/Daniel Defoe (1660?–1731), author, went bankrupt about 1692, but 'honourably discharged in full debts for which composition had been accepted' DNB.

1836

TO

MRS MARIA DILKE

My dear Mrs Dilke. 'Prosit Neujahr!'

When a lady writes to a gentleman that she 'dotes on his hand' and 'adores his correspondence' he cannot do less than let her hear from him again at the first convenient or inconvenient opportunity. He ought to address her – even instead of being introduced to the beautiful Miss Doubt or Miss Hasebeck, or messing with the officers of the 19 . – dancing with Lina – scolding Gradle, – gallivanting abroad with De Franck – drinking Kissingen – ditto Rüdesheimer – waltzing – smoking, – & other pleasures of the kind – all of which I forego at the present writing for your sake. I only hesitate, – on account of the deep dip it must make in your private funds for postage – but you must write another Index or two, for which you are so handsomely paid & make up the loss. –[1]

Your 'long & delightful' letters came to my hand at the very fag end of the year which they helped to wear out: & perhaps at no other moment during 1835 could they have found me so out of myself. I was only dressing to go to a grand New Year's Eve Ball – (you know I don't dance any more than the Tenth)[2] to meet all the rank fashion & beauty of Coblentz. Here methinks Dilke to whom you have given this to read, lights a candle with it, & suddenly goes off either to bed or to sit in his old recess on the stairs. You know you could never get him to take a ball well – without a balling-iron[3] – any more than a horse. Imagine my plight. Altho only half beautified, & regardless of a bran new bright figured satin waistcoat, that cost me 4 dollars, – & as yet never tried on to see how it looked – I jumped up & read your respected favours in my shirt sleeves, but with my head well frizzed by Jane – meanwhile de Franck in full feather with a cocked hat to it, awaited my companionship. I really wished the new year put off for another day – & indeed for a moment, I feared my gaiety was at an end. Happening to look up I saw Jane, red as a turkey cock – her head thrown back against the wall, a letter on her knees, choking & chuckling as if going off into hysterics at some fatal news. Luckily it proved to be only Mr Lindo's[4] bell that wrung her so: and you may suppose I went off to the Ball in good humour & spirits, thinking every now & then of that unfortunate gentleman, intending to go to Cork but finding himself suddenly at *Belfast*. My ticket to meet all the rank beauty & fashion cost only twenty groschen,

& it was worth every shilling of the money.[5] His Excellency General de Bostle Commander of all the Rhenish Provinces, was there, – & so was my tailor – & the man of whom I bought my black stock. To be sure altho in one room, there was a West End. The rank particularly occupied the top corner to the right, & the left corner next the door seemed to be the favorite with the snips & snobs.[6] To do the latter justice however they behaved with much more decency & decorum, than would have prevailed in such a motley assemblage in London. How would you stare too in London to see at a Ball, a score or two in the uniform of common soldiers, offering their partnership to the ladies – but the fact is, as every body must be a soldier in Prussia & there is no purchasing commissions, some of these common soldiers are the sons of Barons. The dances were Waltzes – gallopades – & contredanses – the last like our quadrilles. They mostly danced well especially the Waltz – which is such a favorite that I saw girls stand up for it – steady looking, decidedly serious as my sister Betsy whom I should as soon have expected to see whirl off with a young man, round a room, after some sixty other couples. They made my head spin at last with looking at them: – but the music was beautiful & excellently played. I think I could at least have flounced about *in time* to it myself. The instruments were many & various. They seemed never to tire of the whirling: – & de Franck says they often waltz on those *polished* floors where we can hardly walk, without breaking a leg as the Duke of York[7] did. I was amused to see de F & a lady each pull out a card or little book & register something, much in the Tattersall style of betting – it was an engagement to each other, to dance together at some certain ball, perhaps a month to come. – From time to time the company refreshed in a suite of rooms, laid out with tables – each company paying for its own. For my part I got pleasantly enough amongst a party of Franks brother officers – one of whom instantly tendered to me a glass of *Cardinale* – ie *Bishop*[8] (only cold) with wine, sugar, & the rind of a small green orange they grow here as large as a cotton ball, – & which has the peculiar property that a little too much of the rind in the mixture will infallibly give you the headache. Oddly enough, – when I looked in his face I recognized a tall strange officer, to whom I have frequently bowed by mistake in the street, – which according to the etiquette here was returned by himself & all who happened to be along with him, so that I gradually got on bowing terms with half the officers in Coblentz. As he spoke French which I have picked up again, we had a little gossip – during which he informed me that Franck had let him taste some genuine English Plumb-pudding. – *but that it lay very heavy all night.* Whereby hangs a tale.[9] – We were all hail fellow & hobbed & nobbed – & I told through D.F. the story of the *bell* which *told* very well. Instead of lobster sallad I ate herring ditto & really it was very nice – much more so than you would have expected from the fish. Jane's health was drunk: – but of course all on *my* account. The officers of the 19th are very popular – the ladies dance with them & the brothers enlist in their corps. For one blue or red epaulet there were nine or ten yellow ones – & there is no little jealousy on these accounts amongst the other warriors. I wish I could say much for the beauty of Coblentz – but there were only, to my taste – three or four with any pretensions – one of those even with a complete english, devonshire, face, & another black haired, on a minor scale a Mrs Chatterly,[10] if you remember her – decidedly any thing but German. Her name translated is Miss *Doubt*. The great favorite is Miss Hasebeck, – the officers hardly reckon it a ball without her – yet she is not handsome – her nose is decidedly plain & nobby even – but she seems clever, – which is rare enough here I guess. I had also a little young wife of 16 pointed out to me as 'very interesting' – but she looked too like a school girl. As to dress – you know I always got scolded because after *your* parties I could never describe whether Miss A or B was in blonde or bombazine – so you must excuse the millinery – especially as being of all grades they wore all sorts of fashions. There was a Belgian officer present, who I hoped would dance, as they say he does it execrably – what a comfort for *me* – but he did not show himself up that night. Perhaps as our old friend Mrs Dilke used to say, 'he had had a nint.' At last came the dance I had come to see. Exactly at twelve – bang went a minor cannon in an adjoining room & the waltz instantly broke up, & the whole room was in motion – every body walking or running about to exchange salutations, & kisses & embraces with all friends & acquaintance male or female – Such *hearty smacks* – such hugs – & handshakings – to the chorus of Proast Ni Yar! Proast Ni Yar! Some of the maidens methought kissed each other most tantalizingly on the lips & neck, & languished into each others arms – I am afraid because so many nice young men & gay officers were by, to see it – but then their fathers & mothers were as busy too kissing & bekist. With some of the older codgers it was quite a ceremony & I should think the demand & consumption in the sentimentals was very great. And there, all the while stood your humble servant – the poor English creature – the disconsolate – the forsaken-*Dummy* – a looker on – what you will – with my lips made up & my arms empty – a lay figure – whilst the very fiddlers were hugging. Of course I could not embrace my tailor or kiss the man I bought the black stock of – but luckily I had recognized two young ladies I had *seen* at Vertue's – (you see I stuck to the *virtuous* tho Jane was *not* present) – we had never been on speaking terms – because they did not like to own to French *something like yours*. However I convinced them that mine was no better, & we complimented each other with a good deal of bad language. So I went and looked a salute at them, which made them smile – & then the tall officer came & shook hands with me, – & even this, which was my *all*, comforted me. De Franck told me his back ached with bowing. It was really a funny scene – & if you will give a New Years Eve Party – & have plenty of *beauty* rank & fashion I will try to introduce the custom when I return. I mean to try to draw or sketch the scene – so you will see something like it.[11] Dancing is much in vogue. Jane has a young girl to help whilst Tom Junior is weaned – not untimely, as the Bavarian beer, which was Jane's tap, has been stopped from coming by the ice. – Tis a fattish maiden, not with very 'light fantastic toes'[12] tho she always affects to walk on them, – & it turns out that on her early evenings when she leaves us precociously she goes to learn to dance of a Frenchman – whom she pays a dollar a month, her wages from us being about two dollars per ditto. But *hops*, or balls as they call them, at the taverns prevail during winter, & the young ladies of the lower class are not very steady or serious accordingly. By Franck's account who has officially to visit such places, they must be like the dignity balls in the West Indies – hot noisy dusty thirsty & *very hard work*. In Poland sometimes the soldiers sing the tune to which they dance in chorus, doing double duty. As for Lina our dancing maiden her head runs so on her legs, she is all but good for nothing as to memory. Even Tom took such a contempt for her she was obliged to be turned into the kitchen in lieu of nurse-maid – whereof came three lenten days running for us, seeing that, full of dancing, she could not keep the pot boiling or the meat broiling. Gradle in the meanwhile (like Leigh Hunt's pig) set off down all sorts of ways of her own[13] – as to child management – & you will read in mine to Dilke how Jane scolded her into the right road. I am afraid she too had been dancing & kissing & got *tippy*[14] too on New Year's Night – for instead of putting the boy to bed she was found lying on it with him in her arms & his cap off. However Tom is very fond of her – as far as regards her nursing – but as to her cooking he splutters her German broth out again without ceremony, & I do not wonder. It is toast & water, with a strong dash of onion, – nothing more. He follows his Father's good taste – and when *I* offer him any thing he gapes like a young blackbird. I only regret that I was not present at Jane's Anglo German flare-up. It must have been a good one as for some hours after Lina walked sedately with her *heels* to the ground – & Gradle looked astounded. To tell the truth we are all of us made up for scolding, & what is called showing fight. We have found out so much cheating & jewish dealing we mean to speak our minds 'bow wow skow wow anyhow'[15] – even Fanny who can't be kept out of the row *nags* sometimes in German in which she is actually fluent – nay having been tickled with the novelty of its *gutturals* she out-herods Herod,[16] & never parts with a rough word till she has *well gargled her throat* with it. Seriously, as Lord Liverpool said tis 'too bad' – for thanks to Franck we are let into all the mysteries of their extortion. We were beginning to find them out ourselves & I began to marvel how much longer one ten pounds lasted than its predecessors. – But on comparing notes, – our expences with those of certain Colonels & Majors with which Franck supplies us – we are grossly *done* – as he says his own family was at first, – so we mean to take care of our bawbees as well as our baby. – When Jane returns to London you will never like to go shopping with her she will haggle so. For my own part I get savage & am for 'beating them down' with a club. Then they are so pig-headed – we can hardly get what we like. Little Tom in spite of ourselves, if we had not been *very obstinate* too, would be flourishing about in a scarlet or skyblue embroidered cap, with a gold tassel – & I am not quite sure when out of sight of the house, whether he does not wear his cloak inside out – a showy tartan lining being more pretty to their fancy than the marone or claret cloth without. A pair of ink spotted fawn summer trowsers I sent to be dyed black – but I half expected to see them come home, pea green or skyblue. Purple was strongly recommended. Pink wouldn't have been objected to. Rampone the Italian who has married a German says obstinacy runs in their blood – which hints much as to his domestic felicity. But it is very true. Gradle, who gives us our dinner when she likes will argue with the clock staring in our faces that 3 is 2 – so we are obliged to turn pigs like the swinish multitude[17] & only after a good deal of grunting get our own way. To my comfort, all our tragics have a goodly proportion of farce along with them. Even the doctoring makes one laugh as well as cry. You heard of Jane's inflamed eye – & her having a hot baker's sack over her head as a sudorific specific. Also her blistering & leaching. As you I believe also have 'blood suckers at you'[18] sometimes I will give you a hint how to avoid the trouble & tediousness generally of getting them to bite. Put them into a bason of tepid water, & let them swim about for 5 minutes which makes them lively and eager & saves much time & trouble – for they are beasts apt to bite when not wanted to do so, & vice versa. The unprinted leech story, – which Wright has towards next Comic refers to what really happened to Franck in Prince Radzivils Park.[19] And now I will answer your question as to our Xmas dinner. We did not attempt a sirloin – which is not to be had, nor could we cook one with our apparatus. So Jane thought of a fillet of veal & never could you dream of such a noble festive display for the season. It came in, about *as big as a plate!* – a *dessert* plate! I saw it ordered, & all the while Jane pointed out how it was to be cut, I saw the butcher shaking his chuckle-head behind her back & I predicted that he meant to have *his own way*. So he split it in half, & Dilke will have a notion what ½ the fillet of a Coblentz calf would be. – indeed Jane thinks I have exaggerated the size – however, I feel sure, Dilke with only one of his ordinary appetites could have eaten it all up: – & then asked for a plate of the boiled salt beef we fortunately had in addition. Perhaps also he would have put his lips moreover to our pig's-face – Those were the three courses. Thanks to Jane we had a plum pudding & a very good one – which Franck 'took to heart' so that Jane afterwards made one for him. You will not suspect me of jealousy – but I did threaten to pop some tenpenny nails or bullets[20] into the composition, & Jane, who takes a joke as a pike takes a minnow, watched over her work with catlike vigilance. I could never get near the mixture, – & she stuck by it like a hen by her eggs till the pudding was fairly in the pot. Will you believe that after all, as she went to bed before me, she sent Gradle with it when done, to have it locked up in the drawing room where I was writing all alone. It was put down smoking under my very nose — & the spirit of mischief was irresistible. We had bought a groschen worth of new skewers that very morning – I cut them a little shorter than the puddings diameter & poked them in across & across in all directions so neatly that Jane never perceived any outward visible sign of the inward invisible wood,[21] altho she stood & admired it for five minutes next morning before she sealed it up in white paper and sent it to Ehrenbreitstein. The next time Franck came he praised it very highly – I asked him if it was not well trussed – & he answered 'Yes' so gravely, that I thought he meditated some joke in retaliation & kept on my guard. At the ball the truth came out – he actually thought it was only some new method of making plumpuddings & gave Jane credit for the wood-work. You may guess I caught a rare scolding – not only at home, but when we went out it lasted all the way up Nail Street – to the text of 'practical jokes are the lowest things in the world.' And to this day Jane believes *almost* that the long officer who partook & complained of such uneasiness afterwards, had swallowed a skewer. Lord help their peaking german stomachs – they think the English are perfect ostriches at digestion. Franck makes toast for his breakfast & tea, English fashion – & they complain that *that* 'lies heavy' – They ought to go to the Sandwich Islands where the cooks *chew* the victuals for the table. After dinner we had some good Hocheimer, for which at the Hotel they *would fain* have charged me 2½ dollars a bottle – at which price I could drink it I guess at the first Hotel in London – So we did pretty well for a Christmas dinner. But lent is coming – or rather *is* come. There is no mutton to be had – & no ham. We tried a bavarian one the other day & it was literally like a pickled leg of pork. And the salt haddock are stopped – & the Bavarian beer. I miss the mutton which is better than the beef – coz why? The oxen go jobbing about the fields & roads before they are made beef of – & the cows even go out charing. So the calves are killed at 9 or 10 days old poor things mere flabby dabby babbies. As to beer the Coblentz-made is not good & I do not wonder. You see written up 'Beer Brewery & Bath House' the mystery of which singular connexion I have only just dived into. For some complaints the Germans bathe in malt: – Good God! I should not wonder if they bathe in the beer. It certainly has an odd very odd flavour. What a new way of giving *a body* to it. Fancy – only fancy a fat dirty brown stout gentleman, stuffed with garlic & grease & sourkraut – & well smoked with tobacco, sitting stewing in a vat of Krug & Co's[22] entire! But you drink London porter. 'Tant *Meux*'[23] for you, to quote a bit of your own French. I think here I shall have a triumph over the Brunnens man – He has not mentioned *Swipes*[24] – Bad amongst his Baths! Now for the Lurley-hurly-burly.

The other day Franck told us all the Rhine ice after leaving Bingen had stuck fast at the Lurley[25] in a manner never seen within memory of man. Upon this hint we went Jane Fanny & I. Dilke knows the spot; – & can show you some view of it – there is one in Tombleson's book.[26] It was a beautiful day for us, & tho' the Germans who are apt to exaggerate had talked of icebergs not to be found the sight was well worth seeing. Imagine that narrow passage blocked up with a storm of ice – for the immense pressure had heaved it up in huge waves & furrows – eight or ten feet high: each ridge composed of massive slabs of ice tossed about in all Directions – at every bend of the river there had been a dreadful scuffle, & the fragments were thrust upwards endways. But the mighty river would not be dammed up – you saw it now & then in a narrow slip rushing like a mill race, – then it plunged under the ice & boiled up again 100 yards further. We followed it to Oberwesel part of which was under water. This was but last week – but a steady thaw set in since & tomorrow the bridge will be replaced to the great convenience of the Ehrenbreitsteiners, who have had to pass in boats to & from the many balls at this gay season. Franck could never stay beyond ¼ to 9 at night. The Moselle ice carried away one foolish lad who was tampering with it – & a more romantic incident occurred on the Rhine. On an island just above this resides a Countess Pfaffenheim, – unfortunately neither young nor pretty enough to complete the romance – heaven knows what foolish process brought her to it – perhaps she was pushing the bits of loose ice along at the edge as the children do – but she managed to plump in. However some german cherub that sits up aloft, brought a willow bough to her assistance & there she hung well preserved in ice – a good long spell –

till the genius of German romance brought to her rescue the son of a man, who has been long at law with her father. I know not the denouement: – whether the suitor prevailed:– but how well she can enter now into the fancy of that Arabian Tale wherein the people princesses & all had their lower half of cold marble. Jane was delighted with our jaunt – the scenery is so beautiful – & we dined at St Goar very well & reasonably. In the river by St Goar I saw some salmon. The Moselle & Rhine swarm with fish & as the Germans don't angle, rods & lines go free. Franck & I mean to try our skill. Perch so large as to be sold by the pound: & in the absence of all sea fish they are valuable to us. Jack & barbel abundant: & a large white fish peculiar to the water. So that fishing – a desirable item that Reynolds recommended – is here in perfection. Besides independent of the sport the perch are as dear as meat. I have just had some for dinner – & the Bavarian beer is come again – which I am glad of for Jane's sake. She works hard poor soul at times – should you know of any one who wants an excellent sick-nurse, or nurse from the month – a good occasional cook & willing to make herself generally useful besides – can curl gent's hair – take a hand at cribbage if required – act as amanuensis *over hours* – or reader – cut pencils – & other jobs in the fancy line – no objection to go abroad – & salary no object – so as she's in a small genteel not decidedly serious family – where no footman is kept – will undertake teaching the rudiments of reading & writing, in lieu of nursery governess – also music – where there's a piano – can have an undeniable character for honesty sobriety & industry from her first & last place – should you know of any one in want of such an invaluable creature – they shall have her when I *don't* want her. The invaluable creature by the way has just set me right about Countess Pfaffenheim. She is young – but not handsome. A chubby brick colour face thatched with tow coloured hair – & squabby figure – the very image of some of the plainer she peasantry. She ought to have been *darkly* interesting. If I may judge of German gratitude she gave her preserver a lock of tow, and advised her father to go on with his lawsuit. This sounds splenetic, but we have some right to be angry. But we are going to be politic too. I have played the part I promised in Dilke's letter as a *scold*. After a lecture on the very subject in the morning, I found that Gradle had walked off into the street or more probably on the cold banks of the Rhine (where Joseph her sweetheart works) with Tom, Junior, scarcely out of the measles, & nothing more on his back or head than he wears in the house. So I gave a good John Bull lecture, with a chorus of a word that rhymes with *lamb* but doesn't *reason* with it – & frightened her well. Thank God Tom's as well as ever – he does not seem to have got over the measles but to have jumped over them – he is a rare strong hearty fellow worthy of his Godfather. But I must tell you of Joseph, the Carpenter. He came innocently to see Gradle at the street door every night & as that is the custom here we couldn't object – but when the weather grew colder he got into the kitchen & we couldn't get him out again. Gradle *would not* understand he was unwelcome. So he was there morn noon & evening – of course 'not for nothing' & a *very large* hare we had one day *wouldn't* hash the next – I was thinking of translating my English into cuffing & kicking when Rampone came & we made him scold for us – & she promised & gave up Joseph in all appearance. But it is only in the house. The children go to meet him, & she makes errands – & wilfully forgets half her commissions that she may go out again – & what is worse we begin to doubt she *sells* us, in *buying* for us. 'Tis such a conspiracy against the English we could never have found it out but for Franck – 'tis like freemasonry. They have double lists, double bills of fares at the inns &c &c. – And then they never can mistake you however you may speak German. As an instance Franck got for us (as if for himself, & he passes for a German by name & speaks it perfectly & wears the uniform) a printed list of all articles with the prices, from one of the most respectable houses in Coblentz. They were so deep they asked him '*where they should send it*' – but he was not to be had & called again for it – & accordingly we find what we had paid 15 pence for is by rights only 10 & so on. But such is the system from the highest to the lowest we could not have found it out but for Franck. So we are meditating a domestic revolution or rather coup d'etat – to change lodging servant & all at once & begin de novo. I must do Rampone the justice to say he has helped fairly to undeceive us – & as he has married a German, & has to make shifts, he is au fait – It is really disgusting. We were told direct solemn lies, as to the rent our predecessors paid for our lodgings – & I feel sure had I applied to them to know (such is the system) they would have confirmed the falsehood. It is hardly possible to conceive it – & we are very indignant. I am making enquiries & collecting *documents* to establish facts, which I mean some day to treat them with. My Doctor for example in his bill has chosen to dub me *Sir* Thomas Hood – it is his own handwriting – he knows me well, what I am, has read Eugene Aram, – & only fancies a *Knight's* vanity may lead him to overlook an overcharge. He does not know that I would not give a dollar to be a Knight in reality – no offence to *Sir* Charles Dilke. I could almost forgive him for one thing – he knew our dear Doctor Seoane by *reputation.* It gave us sincere pleasure to be remembered by him – as Dilke elegantly says he is 'a good anti-emetic to take to heart against being sick of human nature.' I wish the Queen may fall in love with him.[27] Pray say every thing kind for us when you write – I do wish I could send him a book. Tis piteous to think we may not meet

again but in heaven – that is if Doctors & punsters go to heaven: – & yet tis not more unlikely that I *may* be [in] Spain than that Green *might* have been. Who knows after last year's whirl! We may all meet *done brown* in Mexico! – The Lindos are in fortune's round about too. She forgot part of her commission[28] so we had a postscript packet – containing the favour of your two packs of English cards – which Dr Beermann pulled a frightful face at, & informed us that the penalty was only £15 upon each! As we are on *very friendly* terms with De Franck we have given him, (handsomely) one of the packs & half the risk – so pray – (with our best thanks) – send no more – it is playing '*rayther eye*' As for the newspapers I was luxuriating in, he says the Germans must not have them 'at all, at all'
The said *Jew* Doctor informs me he is going to London in the summer – of course I shall *not* give him a letter of introduction to you – but I shall insidiously give him a recommendation to seek the Westminster Medical Conversazione where I hope they will give him a *physicker*. Jane who is writing to Mrs Elliot has just read to me a bit I must quote. – she says I am so on the high ropes as to the impositions on the English, I shall be 'seen at the arrival of every steam boat, like a Bow Street officer at a mob, calling out "Gentlemen take care of your pockets." ' It is not bad for *her* – is it? Being confined to my conversation she grows funny. In the mean time we get from the Library a 'Monthly Magazine' printed at Leipzic – extracted *wholly* from English Authors & what is worse not the best of them – (such people as write in the Keepsake)[29] – but from a memoir at the end, of R. Ackermann, I have found that the English people & government gave the distressed Germans 1.333.333/10 dollars.[30] – which same I do roll up into a monstrous great choke-pear, to put as a set off to the Anti-English tariff. However there are some *spots* as Wiesbaden,[31] & the Radzivil's & a few more where the English are the *rage* – & the Germans *rage* at it, they say, in proportion. Mind – poke it well into Dilke, about Bettine – when you want to plague him – whoever wrote that review had got up on a high german metaphysical horse – but I trust I have shown up *the lady on the pillion.*[32] Seriously I am dead sick of the people hereabout – & not without cause – but I love the *country* & cannot forgive them for not being in *keeping*. So you must think of us as very comfortable & happy & reconciled – with a wholesome vent for carrying off our spleen. After all the gospel & the epistle, & the collect & the litany gone before, my amen is God bless us all & huzza for the New Year! It's unlucky for *huz* as the Scotch say, that this present Lent there is for the first time doubt of a *Carnival* which would be a novelty for *hus*. Good & bad customs seem going equally out of use: besides it spoils a good joke. I thought of going, hung all over with 'good 4 groschen pieces' – as a representative of the Athenaeum –

Perhaps I *may* go, with Tom Junior pickaback, bare legged & bareheaded, – as a representative of 'the English disease,' alias rickets. In spite of the uncertainty – this affair occupies all heads at present. I will tell you all I know. Jane in a cottage bonnet with a slice of brown bread in one hand & a German sausage in the other is to go as *Content*. Gradle carrying Tom is to represent Peace nursing Innocence – & Innocence is to wear a tartan kilt to show that his legs are straight. Fanny in a pink frock orange handkerchief sky blue apron & lilac bonnet her two tails tied with pea green, & scarlet shoes, is to represent simplicity – But farewell to fancies – I have subjects in realities.

One blow is struck of our coup d'etat! It is the first ordonnance. Gradle has had warning! Prepare for a domestic revolution like that of Stoke Pogis![33] As usual there is plenty of farce in it. This morning (Sunday 31st) Gradle went to mass before breakfast – after which we received thro Fanny our Dragoman, a desire from the Priest that Gradle should come to church. This was evidently a fictitious message or else a very impertinent one from his reverence. We took no notice – the understanding being Gradle is to go every other Sunday, *if convenient*, & when we have been able we have sent her *out of turn*. Church time comes – & behold *Joseph* – not of Arimathea tho a carpenter. As a charity, as it was represented, I gave him *some two months ago* a black coat (No. 3) & wondered what he had done with it – when today out he comes, with a new velvet collar put to my old coat – instead of his prussian cap a new *round hat* (I wear an old one) minus his constant pipe, – in fact a perfect parody of 'the English gentleman' only, if any thing a little more stylish. This we only laughed at. – Having letters to write to England & the day being fine Gradle was told to take the children a walk & the route indicated. She made no objection but drest in her best, & set forth up Nail Street. However when she thought I was hard at work at easy writing & Jane boggling at sentimentals, she retraced her steps, & (passing the house, with her *brazen* censer of incense) marched the children off to St Castor's. I chanced to see it – but in spite of St Castor & the Priest, Fanny did not chuse to be diddled out of her walk & remonstrated with all her German might in the Vicar's presence. – whereupon Gradle brought my little Protestants home again under a pretence that it rained. Only think of this! To have Bunyan's Holy War in your own house – and I am of course Diabolus! Jane is Mrs Martin Luther! You know how I always stuck up for Church of England & only knew the Vicar of Wanstead, of all its people – the father of the Albigensian *Gilly* – not a Highland gilly.[34] Thereupon I – spit her spite. She told Fanny 'she didn't like Jane – she'd leave her – she was ill treated &c' – which Fanny reported not forgetting a guttural. Then in the bedroom, Fanny brought *indirect* messages that she needn't go out with G again – not to stay in the room &c – whereupon Jane went in & flared up English & German chopped up together like a lobster sallad. I'm sorry to say again I did not hear it. However Franck came & hearing the case, & taking Fanny's evidence, *in German*, – & moreover knowing we meant to give her warning, instead of any explanation he only said to her in his military style (tho it went against the Calendar) 'On the first of *February* – March!!!' I am afraid this abrupt word of command of Franck's will make Jane ill of a great deal of suppressed motley eloquence. Perhaps she will vent it on me. As for Gradle – this very instant the doorbell sounds – & as if it were a race Jane exclaims '*she's off!*' a moment, & Joseph will know it – & all the rest of the Holy Family – (Of course there is one). But do not grieve for us – we shall get a better & a cheaper by $\frac{1}{3}$. – The English, however, will be in worse odour. I hope she won't kill De Franck. Jane fears she will poison Fanny – & doubtless will look her over every night for blue spots as she would for flea-bites. I feel a little burning in my own throat. In case I should never be able to address you again, believe me my dear Mrs Dilke

Yours ever in the next world very truly

Thos Hood

I think Dilke does not care to read *crossed* letters[35] – and thus we may keep our correspondence to ourselves. You will *find* that I have written at very great length – indeed like a Boa Constrictor determined to swallow up all your leisure. But be comforted. It will be some time before you have from me even a little wiper again – I have other fish to fry if I may say so where there are frying pans but no fish – As to health Tom is a giant – I am as well as ever I was & Jane no worse – Fanny is delicate but we hope to mend her – Our spirits are good. – Yesterday Jane made some potted beef – & I almost choked her and De Franck by insisting that she had *chewed* it – and as she had a face ache & was holding her jaw at the time it seemed to be a certainty. – You see we can cook a little without much more apparatus than God has given us. Moreover she contrived to make a mince pie on a large scale – only as it was a novelty the Baker stole half its *inside*. So if you come out *you* need not live a fortnight on baked potatoes as you did at Paris – Save up your pin money & come – We shall make much of you & little of Dilke – & there you will both be of a size – There is doubt whether the review will be at Cologne or here but we shall have early intelligence –

The first steamboat from Rotterdam is expected here tonight – it feels very pleasant as repairing a broken link with England – I have no more *news* – I would not trust the Editor with my reminiscences – But pray give our kind regards to Chorley

Taylor Holmes & all who ask of us – As for yourselves we do hope to see you – but till then give us credit for all kind feelings & good wishes – Do not forget Wentworth, though he should be keeping term[36] or William tho he should be with you – Jane sends her love & will write when my letter has *evaporated* – She accuses me of forestalling her news – as Dilke complained of you. But more will turn up – Fanny desires her love & an everlasting German Kiss to her Godmama

Your agin

T H.

372 Castor Hof Coblentz. / 12[-31] January [1836]

BM MS. Address: 'Mrs Dilke / 9 Lower Grosvenor Place / Pimlico / London / Angleterre.' PM: 'COBLENZ/2/2,' 'FPO 1836/FE.' Published by Marchand 61–82.

1/Mrs Dilke compiled indexes for *The Athenaeum.*

2/Probably the number of a regiment stationed in Koblenz

3/Meaning undiscovered

4/Perhaps Louis Lindo, later Lindon (1812–72), who married Fanny Brawne (1800–65) in June 1833. According to Hyder E. Rollins, ed. *The Keats Circle*, 2nd ed. (Cambridge, Mass. 1965) I xlviii, they lived mostly in Germany, with occasional visits to London. The same authority states that Dilke supervised the financial affairs of the Brawnes as a trustee, while his wife took Fanny under her social wing, lxxxiii–iv.

5/Marchand 63 notes that Hood also describes the ball in *Up the Rhine: Works* VII 131–2. His Excellency Karl Heinrich Ludwig von Borstell (1773–1844) had been commander in Koblenz since 1825.

6/Tailors and shoemakers, ie, inferiors

7/Frederick Augustus, Duke of York (1763–1827). I do not know how the Duke broke his leg.

8/Sweet drink, variously compounded: NED

9/*As You Like It* 2 vii 28

10/Unidentified

11/See the engraving of 'The Omni-Buss' in *Up the Rhine* facing 160.

12/Milton, 'L'Allegro' 34

13/Marchand 57 refers to Leigh Hunt's essay 'On the Graces and Anxieties of Pig-driving,' in the *Indicator and the Companion* (1834) II 285.

14/This probably should be 'tipsy.'

15/Quotation unidentified

16/*Hamlet* 3 ii 14

17/Burke *Reflections on the Revolution in France* (1790) 117

18/*Richard III* 3 iii 5

19/*Comic Annual* for 1837, 9–21. Franck belonged to the large circle of the aristocratic Polish family of the Radziwills. They had a palace in Berlin and an estate at Antonin near Ostrovo in Posen.

20/Large in size

21/*Book of Common Prayer*, 'Catechism'

22/See the engraving of 'Beer with a Body' in *Up the Rhine* facing 197.

23/A pun on the French phrase and the name of a still well-known brand of beer

24/Poor weak beer

25/Lorelei, or Loreley, rocks rising above the Rhine between Koblenz and Bingen, celebrated in Heine's poem (1823)
26/*Tombleson's Views of the Rhine* ed. W.G. Fearnside (1832), plate facing 162
27/I do not understand the point of this allusion.
28/Apparently Mrs Lindo undertook to bring over parcels for the Hoods from England.
29/In fact, one of *The Keepsake's* contributors this year was Tennyson, who, however, wrote in December: 'Provoked by the incivility of editors, I swore an oath that I would never again have to do with their vapid books,' T.R. Lounsbury *Life and Times of Tennyson* (New Haven 1915) 269.
30/After the battle of Leipzig in 1813 Ackermann organised the distribution of over £200,000, of which more than half was contributed by public subscriptions. 'In 1815 he collected and distributed a large sum for the succour of wounded Prussian soldiers and their relatives,' DNB.
31/Spa, frequented by the English
32/See 240, n 22.
33/This fictional event was the theme of 'The Parish Revolution' in the *Comic Annual* for 1831: *Works* I 89–101. Stoke Poges is a village in Buckinghamshire, associated with Thomas Gray.
34/I have not identified the vicar or his heretical son.
35/This postscript is written across the first and second pages of the letter.
36/The younger Dilke graduated from Cambridge in 1834.

TO
CHARLES WENTWORTH DILKE

'Prosit Neujahr!'
My dear Dilke.
The letters came at last – on the last day of the year! Some of them dated October the fourteenth! It was an expressive silence enough but we did not muse your praise.[1] Sometimes we thought all England must have drowned itself – sometimes we doubted we were only at Coblentz & fancied ourselves like Elia's Distant Correspondents, on those shores where 'haunts the Kangaroo.'[2] There seemed a *spell* against those letters & with me I fear it occasionally spelt d-a-m-n. To be sure twas provoking to Christian patience to see that infernal orange band & orange collar go so often to the very next door. The *eil*wagen[3] seemed turned to winegar. First Jane fumed, – & then I did, – for which I got lectured, Madam being comparatively cool, from having fumed herself out. By way of climax, think of Mrs. L[4] being detained nearly a fortnight with our letters at Rotterdam, because somebody in England had neglected to ship her/our/luggage. In the meantime, as dumbness proceeds from deafness our not hearing prevented our writing, – Jane, particularly, who is here a strict protestant, fearing that our letters should turn catholics & cross each other on the road. However now we each having something

that will answer, – and accordingly I write to you, this time, lest by addressing Mrs. D. again, I should make you a green-spectacled monster,[5] though I have matters fitter to write to the she D– than to the He one. At all events I will write *at* her, in my description of such things as Balls & New Year's Eve festivities.

You were right in your prophesy about me, derived from my former letter. Excepting a little exhaustion, partly from anxiety in getting it off, after my last box of cuts, I have regularly progressed in health, from the epoch I marked of my strange malady. – Never indeed did I complete the Comic with such ease & satisfaction. Except that I am more in figure a Greyhound I came in like a Spaniel winning the Derby, fresh & full of running. Indeed I set to work directly on my Sketch Book[6] with some matters not so well fitted for the annual as a sort of Bubble book I contemplate. I could write a *monograph* on Coblentz. But the place is healthy – witness Jane whose legs have grown smaller, & Tom's whose ditto have grown larger – whilst my own promise to '*calve*' in the spring. At anyrate I have abundance of *hock*. Then we keep better if not the best & most regular of hours, – we do not take our mittag – exactly at midday but at 2 or 3. – & then I am away from evil company & bad example & too much wine, – in which particular I have brought in & carried a *reform-bill* which I paid at Xmas. And then, biggest of all the thens, I am away from that dreadful *personal* pressure which made the light work heavy & the short work long. I have not the knocks & rings at the heart, as well as the gate, which startled the Present – nor the long forecoming shadows of the future Days, coming each after each, like the old English warriors *bill* in hand. There were the menaces of the harsh & the requests of the gentle each equally urgent, nay where all were just, the demand backed with kindness & consideration gave me most pain & inquietude. There was the agony of the Potent will & the impotent power. I believe I may say I was never a *selfish* debtor for I paid away money when I had it & left myself penniless almost, exposed to mortifications & deep annoyance for trifles. My struggles have been great & my sufferings unknown. I do not indeed forget my responsibilities here because they are not so often called for, & that I am out of the reach of legal measures, but I do feel released from the overpowering cares of a heavy expenditure & the transition from a hopeless to a hopeful state. In spite of some sharp pangs in the process I am ready to confess that the crisis which sent me here was a wholesome one; – although to do myself justice, I must say that without the absolute necessity I should have adopted some other course than that I was upon. I have been blamed I think not deservedly about Lake House, by Judges from the event, – but the truth is my prospects & standing were latterly completely changed – & I should have acted accordingly. You may doubt but I can prove this fact in favour of my prudence. Some parts of your letter have set me feeling or thinking or rather have stirred up my feelings & thoughts, for they have been mine before – & lead me to speak thus. If not as a thoroughly independent man (I mean morally, for I am so here actually) I have felt at second hand the inestimable blessing of being *free;* which can hardly be said of any one in England in the circumstances you allude to, to which I am in *some* degree a martyr. The struggle to maintain caste is indeed a bitter one & after all I fear we must say 'le jeu ne vaut pas la chandelle'[7]. The aspiration for 'the peace the world cannot give'[8] is a really heavenly one; – though I doubt whether the world cannot give a very heavenly peace, if a man seek it the right way. At least I felt it could on my recovery for the first time in the balmy air of August taking a cheap ride to a cheap dinner along the banks of the beautiful Rhine to Capellen – & again further on in the harvest season, thro the cornfield – vineyard – orchards to Braubach with *all* my happy healthy family in the same vehicle. It is true I miss *home* – old friends – books *the communion of minds* – & I cannot I would not forget I am an Englishman. I love my country dearly and a sonnet I shall send you is one from the heart's core not the head.[9] Oh Dilke tis the pity of all the pity's of the world that 'that sweet little Isle of our own' should be what it is! Jane says in one of her letters what a pity there is not a cheap Coblentz in England – but why should not all England be a Coblentz? There never was a more senseless cry raised than that for taxing absentees, nor more unjust! But for our intolerable taxation there would not be those absentees – indeed some of our imports make me blush. For instance the other day Rampone the Italian took up a pocket-book & in the first page there was price $2^{s}/3^{d}$ – duty $1^{s}/3^{d}$ – I can hardly think but that many reformers *must* have been made amongst the thousands that come up the Rhine, by the direct contrast of cheap and dear. Indeed I said in a letter to Wright, that it was enough to cause a pocket-revolution, not that the people would wish to remove their *monarch* but that their Sovereign should go further. Perhaps the Police did not understand my *calembourg,*[10] for of all my letters this alone miscarried. Still, I *do* hope in the bottom of my heart to return honourably to England, – where I *do* believe a man may live comfortably, with some diminished feeling as to caste, if he preserve character. No matter how plainly he may live, should *he pay his way* he ought to be & I conceive would be, respectable. Still I shall be in no hurry to leave here – peace permitting – in duty to my children I ought to save all I can – but it is questionable when free to do so, whether for business sake I should not be amongst you. But of that hereafter. I am writing seriously because I trust my serious will give you as much comfort as my Comic, for I conceive myself now to be in the right path. I would give any thing for a day's talk or two – writing is so unsatisfactory but from what you have you must & perhaps can grasp the rest. I think there is no reason to be dissatisfied with the experiment. Coblentz is dearer than it was, – & will be cheaper. The English rush is falling off. But as it is we have done well, – In spite of illness inexperience & outfit – we have lived at but a trifle over 200 a year – I shall know better when the Doctor & Apothecary's bills come in. All the three extra items I have given have been heavier than you might suppose. Rent is very dear here contrary to what you supposed. The population is not great but the large military garrison brings a quantity of officers into lodgings – indeed fresh houses are building – & *furnished* lodgings are especially rare. When I came there were hardly *any* to be had. The best plan is to *buy* furniture & sell it by auction when you go away, often for as much as it cost – but then I had not spare money so to lay by. – Then till we got a kitchen the sending for portions to a Hotel cost us double to what we could cook at home – as to outfit we have had to buy glass, crockery, tinware &c, which does not come into their furnishing, & I had not a shirt in my bag that was wearable, – & we have bought children's clothes &c. – My illness will cost something considerable tho cheap by comparison – & in order to *discount* my recovery, for I was dreadfully low & languid, I felt justified in taking more wine than I should have done if well – & it answered the purpose. Lastly experience has had to be paid for – as for instance our washing is now done at half the cost for the first three or four months & almost every thing is down from 25 to 50 per cent. Indeed the *dead set* at the English is to an extent nobody but a resident can discover – & really disgusting considering the great benefactors they are to the place; and that it is accompanied with envy jealousy & detraction, utterly illiberal. I speak advisedly & from full knowledge. The Virtues who resided here before us were *done* thro thick & thin & yet he was a merchant a smart active little man of the world with all his eyes about him & somewhat mean & with a family of 12 that made him cut close. But *we* know they were cheated. In fact they the Coblentzers are Jews (if that be a term of *reproach*) stopping only short of giving you bad money or ledgerdemain in the giving the articles. 'Tis not cheating but next door to it. One day in joke I offered a fruit-girl ¼ of what she asked. Jane said I had affronted her & she would never come again – but she did – & we have had a bargain in something like that proportion. I could forgive this — but spite of all their sentimentality there is no *feeling*. I told you I gave a dollar to two begging catholic priests as a token of my wish for universal toleration & liberality of opinion. Ever since every German beggar is sent up to me, – some literally better dressed than myself – but I have laid down a rule not to give a pfenning the 12th of a penny to any but a countryman. And why? Of all the cases I have had here, not one Englishman has ever owned to asking or at least getting any thing of the Germans. The consequence is Mrs Ainsworth[11] & myself, are the he & she English *consuls* of the town – Her husband is almost always travelling & she is the only other English resident. We send our distressed Country people to each other & they get relief on both sides which is all they get. My blood boils & I hope I shall never hear again of Subscriptions in England for Distressed Germans. I will only mention one indisputable case. About three weeks ago Mrs Ainsworth sent me a poor Irishman his Wife & Child – on their way to England – He had been engaged in a small manufactory of his own at Jonsac in France[12] which caught fire & he lost a child in the fire as well as having his arm burnt to the bone as he showed me in the attempt at rescue – & was deaf from falling on a beam. It was attested by Lord & lady Granville whose hand I know[13] Louis Philippe & a French Bishop & sundry English names. – The poor fellow, Irish all over, – in search of a rich English benefactor who lived at Frankfort had set out for Frankfort on the Maine instead of Frankfort on the Oder, – his wife lay in by the road, – & incurring some trifling debt in consequence, even their *shoes* were sold & he was sent in irons to Frankfort. By the German law, necessaries cannot be sold for debt – chairs, table bed or working-tools (England might take a hint there) – and Cartwright, our Minister at Frankfort[14] was so indignant that he tore up Pat's passport (I suppose *branded with poverty*), & gave him another. In the list of donations he brought there was scarcely a German name – he said he had found it useless to ask them – & what had they done for him at Frankfort? Lest Cartwright should stir in it, the police took the mat out of his bed & never left him till the boat sailed with him hitherward. – Hence he was advised by a German (who only gave advice) to apply to a rich wine merchant who spends six months a year in England & has made a fortune out of that little island. He gave him nothing. We gave him a trifle, & I gave him all the use of my name – & Jane had Coffee made for the poor woman & her infant – they had to travel to Rotterdam on foot thro bitter weather – & what was the result? – The sneers of our servant – who could not disguise her spleen, & the refusal at the Hotel to admit him to see an Englishman to whom I sent him. This is too true & I assure you but a sample of the rest. Never may the English be such asses as to be liberal where they are only laughed at for it. I could allow for national prejudice, envy, & jealousy, but they are so amongst themselves. There was a woman drowned her child because she could not maintain it & herself tho she worked hard, on some very low earnings. There was no established or private charity in the town to save the life of an infant! – & here everybody almost knows the other & their means. Damn their sentimental tenderness – where is the practical? On the back of this English affair, as we had assisted a Countryman, (Pat is & shall be my countryman if only for Taylor's sake) came a modest request from a friend of our landlady's that we would *lend* her 10 dollars, – *because* none of her own neighbours or country people would lend her 10 groschen. She was honest enough in her confession, – & if I had had them to spare I would have read them a lecture by lending them. – Then we had a poor Polish woman a lodger over head who was starving literally for some money she had expected had not arrived *as might have happened to ourselves*. So we sent her some dinner daily in return for which she voluntarily knitted some stockings for Fanny, – but her penniless state was the laughing stock with the servants. They *are* a heartless race set on the bawbees – from high to low. Indeed, in a thousand things language & all, I could fancy myself again, as when a boy, in Dundee. They have *some* of the virtues all the vices & most of the peculiarities of the Scotch. Above all they are dreadfully beastly filthy horribly dirty & *nasty*. I have some stories on this head to tell you *orally* that will disgust but make you laugh. Then they are stupid & like all stupid people intensely obstinate. Franck says there is not a carpenter in the town can make a common guncase. They do not often show themselves drunk; but between wine & smoke their heads are in a continual *muddle* – There is a great sort of dog here which you see driving a calf not so big as himself – kept exclusively for that purpose that the butcher may walk behind with his pipe in his mouth.[15] – But I will give you a laughable instance of their dulness. The general opposite had ordered some great poplars in his yard to be cut down & we saw the whole operation. Each tree was nearly *cut thro* with the hatchet some ten yards from the ground by a fellow on a ladder which rested against the stem a dozen feet *above* the cut. I expected an accident every moment. The head gardener, pipe in mouth, looked on & superintended. The first tree all but lashed them in its fall – there were 12 men & 4 trees & twas a two days' job. At last came one of the biggest poplars in its turn. I saw even from my window, & predicted that the rope would break, there was a join in it, – a knot, with a streamer of loose tow hanging from it – that could not be mistaken. Down they all went accordingly on the rugged stones – pipes & all – from which they got up looking very foolish & rubbing their behinds. However they only tied another knot and tried again! – the head man, & one or two who had looked on lending a hand. Down again, – as a matter of course. Jane & I shrieked with laughter & they evidently heard us. Well, what does a foggy headed fellow do, but go into the house & bring out a coil of literal *cable* fit to pull down a church with, & what do they do with it, but tie it at the end of the old rotten rope, & then haul away again! Twas a miracle they had not a third summerset, – but the tree thought proper to give away – there was a dozen heads together, in spite of the proverb no better than one! This ignorance as usual is joined to its Siamese brother conceit. I ventured to praise their method of applying leeches here which is good, – when the operator turns round on me & says 'Now then Sir you can write to England & tell them how to put on a leech.' I could have retorted that they could not make a blister as poor Jane found to her cost – for nothing of it *drew* except a wall of cobler's wax round the edge – as round a copper plate when being bit in. You see I am writing with my bristles up – but not without cause. There is a daily *nay hourly* skirmishing with our great chinese looking servant, – from these national attributes – equally vexatious & ridiculous. But I find I *must* write to Mrs. Dilke I have so much in *her* line, – so she shall have particulars. We have twice well scolded Gradle thro Rampone & Franck, – but last night Jane's patience gave way & she got into a towering spluttering Anglo-German passion, of ludicrous eloquence, that astounded the two maids – for we have a second for a few days to assist in weaning. It was all about the English & German modes of that same – but Jane made use of an argument I had hinted & it was a floorer namely 'Vat can kennen, twey young Maidkins, *unmarried*, so as you, mair den me, a Mutter of a Family, of vaning de Bibi – Have du Bibi? Have Lina Bibi?' As Gradle has to my knowledge a bibi mind it is two years old before I came – & Lina most probably has – it was a settler. On the next occasion *I* am to try my powers of scolding, indeed I have my own grievances & as Gradles knowledge of English always deserts her when we scold, & she takes refuge in obtuse German, I mean to *act* a passion & be the English 'God Dam' personified. I am quite in the humour for a flare up. My Apotheke bill has come in whilst writing, with its 18 Groschen for emulsion – & *4 shillings for an elixir!* Then the Dr. in respectable practice here – what would you think in England of a medical man who took advantage of his patient being a foreigner to charge double fees? But it is fact. I *know* it. These things deserve exposure – & it shall come out if I live – I am no he Trollope,[16] but I am indignant at the bad feeling against the English. Franck, an excellent witness for he was bred from boyhood in Germany, & his father is a German (his mother English) corroborates me. He says they are inconceivably jealous & envious of us & malicious accordingly. The other day he commissioned me to get for him the Book of Beauty[17] – which I found out was to be used in repelling the taunts of his brother officers, who if they see an awkward queer ugly woman of any nation but their own say – 'there, – she is English.' So I sent for a portrait of Lady Blessington to help us. As you are a gallant & gay man, pray get Caunter to send me some beauties out of the Court Magazine to fight on our side.[18] Then comes that d-d

Rampone the Italian with whom I have fought over again the battle of Waterloo, where we were all to be écrasés – only but that Bonaparte 'had not time for it' – having vainly tried all day. But the forms this jealousy takes are so ludicrous it provokes as much laughter as spleen & I enjoy the conflict. He asked me seriously one day, when I set up our Navy against the Continental army, whether an English captain ought to run away from a French ship – I answered he would certainly be tried, if of equal force, & perhaps shot. Well, then he gave me an instance in point. A French frigate was building at Genoa – & an English captain sent in a polite message by a fishing boat, that when she was in fighting order, they need not stop to paint or decorate her, which the English understood best – but to send her out. Accordingly, when the two English frigates had sailed off, or *taken flight* in opposite directions, out came the frigate with 2 more to take care of her, when to the confessed horror of the whole place, the two fugitives retraced their course & a third appeared in the offing, – enclosing the three in a triangle, so as to *force* them to fight which ended as usual, in their capture & destruction. I have taken this engagement for my model, – & lead him forth into deep water & then give him a broadside of good hard facts. I venture no theories or assertions. Luckily the other day among some other papers came a *double* Times[19] – with which I astounded him, – as well as some of our statistical tables – &c – & as he had held a meanish opinion of London its size & population I sent him home with 14000 rabbits sold weekly by one salesman of Leadenhall, sticking in his Italian gizzard. Apropos of this Italian. With all our faults he is anxious to get some money out of us by teaching French Spanish & Italian at London – with the slight drawback, that, like Goldsmiths attempt[20] – he does not know the language of his proposed scholars. I told him moreover that we had such swarms of refugees of education & rank even I feared language masters must be drugs with us – but I undertook to get a better opinion than my own – *So pray in your next write me a sentence I can read to him.* Touching said Double Times – Dr Beerman who called with a New Year compliment saw it & I could get nothing said for it – but an insinuation that the English could not be industrious if they read such papers – with an excuse that the Germans had not such papers *only* because they had not time to read them. When be saw my woodcuts, he took great pains to impress on me that woodcutting was a German invention from Albert Durer, though I made him confess I could neither get wood here for love or money, nor if they had wood could they saw it & give it the surface. I am not writing thro spleen or prejudice but one has a right to retort on impudence & insolence. Nor do I mean to include others in one sweeping condemnation. I speak only of this place – what I have seen & heard. I know the

English are made the standing joke of the coffee-rooms. Nay I have heard the Zeitung publicly read aloud at the table dhote of the principal hotel, with shouts of laughter, at the expense I was informed afterwards of the English. This I take for gross ill manners, to say the least of it. But there is a vile spirit here against us – I believe elsewhere also. In the German dictionary Rickets is called expressly *The English complaint* – but what is the fact? Travellers too often look only at the same things – churches scenery &c one after another – nursing diet, & other matters of infinite importance being beneath their notice. Besides they pass too hastily to see into such things. It would really make your heart ache here to observe the immense proportion of deformity – not in the lower class merely but the middle one – the children of tradesmen for instance. – The number of literal dwarfs – the wretched crooked humped objects – the crippled children – the stunty bandy, bowlegged, huge headed manikins & womanikins that swarm the streets – not of Fannys stature, with 12 year old faces. For a bet I would produce 20 from the neighborhood of those years without her height. But their legs & feet – I am not exaggerating – tis a sight full of pity and pain, to see so many foredoomed almost to helplessness thro some great radical defects in management on the part of parents. I never saw so melancholy a sight in my life, as they present – but the *amount* of this misfortune is immense & incredible – they are blind to it from its being, like the dirty scabbed scalps of the infants, all but universal. It is literally shocking and disgraceful – & the result is seen in the numerous deformities & cripples – & a stunted ill made population. For one man above our average standard there are ten below it – 'squat, my lord, squat – & bad on his pins.'[21] Nb This without

THE GERMAN DWARFS.

reference to Jane's quarrels about Bibi – although with such results before our eyes we might well have a horror of the system. Let them look at home. I have taken some sketches – veritable portraits in illustration which would astound you. Some day you shall have them, by a private hand but remember these are all subjects in reserve for a volume à la Head – so do not let any body forestal my observations. Mind, not a volume of prejudices – there are many things here we might & ought to copy – & after all my view embraces only a certain circle with Coblentz for its centre. Whilst on the German theme, – I must tell you how delighted we were with Bettine on the 1st notice of her letters in the Athm & how disappointed & disgusted with her in the second.[22] Of her talents there can be no doubt – but like Patmore who apparently sacrificed Scott to the éclat of a duel,[23] so did Bettine sacrifice, or suffer the martyrdom, of Gunderode her friend, to the eclat of the suicide – the romance. Like Charlotte kissing the pistols & dusting them for Werter![24] De Franck knows all about her. She is quite notorious at Berlin. After the manner of L.E.L[25] she affects to be the girl – so young & innocent, that she lays her head on gentlemen's bosoms or sits on their laps, as my Fanny might!! But she met with a rebuff. In the public theatre, she actually laid her head on the shoulder of a strange Polish Officer, – who whispered to her, 'I hope you haven't lice.' She must lead her husband the poet[26] a rare life of it! Verily I am out of humour & confess it honestly, with all things German nearly but their country & their wine. There is Schlegel – Shakspeare Schlegel – in your last Athem but one, truckling & lecturing at Vienna *for place* – nothing else.[27] I wish to like em but I can't. Perhaps I have here a bad sample – I suspect so for one fact speaks volumes. At the military Casino you will see the officers of the 29*th* sitting separate each with his quantum of wine – those of the 19*th* which is Francks regiment make a common bowl, as 'banded brothers,'[28] – The 29th belongs to the neighbourhood, & yet, it has but about 1 in 4 of *volunteers* compared with the other. At the balls the Coblentzers are as decidedly in the background – but vide Mrs Dilkes letter on this head. However I am a very loyal subject of the King of Prussia whose health I have drunk sincerely – and I have a really high opinion of him from what I hear. There are many things too in the army we ought to copy – for instance corporeal punishment, rarely ordered by sentence, & then inflicted only by three taps with a stick – the degradation of it is considered sufficient. This is a fine spirited distinction, & what is more it *tells*. I am somewhat of Puckler Muskau's opinion as to the making every man a soldier here – it has civilized them, in manners, feeling every thing – at the very least mechanical gentlemen instead of 'practical' boors.[29] You will laugh at my opinion on such topics – but I could write much on the army – & in its praise. What I have seen &

know is admirable, as regards the infantry & artillery – of the cavalry I will say nothing – as they have no horses but what Reynolds or I or you could ride & 'tis saying a great deal. Head is quite right about their rational system of harnessing with the head & eyes free.[30] I have seen perhaps more than he, from the season of the year. Tis beautiful to see them exercising their own sagacity this frosty weather & picking out for themselves their way across a huge patch of ice before our window for which by the way in London his excellency our Governor would be fined every day of his life as it flows from his kitchen &c, but tho they have no spirit or skittishness the horses are hardy & enduring tho slow, & were I to return to England to travel, single horse, I would accustom him, as here, to eat a loaf of brown bread, which you might stow in a gig far better than a truss of hay. Now – methinks I hear you say – Hood is amiable – for the last 5 or 6 pages he has been vicious – & of course he is softened and warmed by a glass of brandy & water. True as to that. But I was always notoriously illnatured in my cups – so set down all that follows to the credit of candour. I am going to praise the gend'armerie. I had watched & inwardly applauded their behaviour, – before I was told by Franck that they were all veterans, preferred to it by their general good conduct. I firmly believe it. As to espionage I know nothing, for I am not obnoxious to it – but in every other respect they seem to me to be a most effective & inoffensive police. I would rather have such a body than our raw lobsters[31] &c – men who for the novelty of shedding blood make such massacres as at Peterloo & Spa Fields.[32] Two instances of police & law process here might put ours to shame. Virtue during his one year's residence was robbed of his plate & had the ill luck to receive & pass a forged note for 50 dollars – In the first instance the thief was discovered & the property restored *without expence* – in the second he did not lose the value of the note & had no trouble about it, but saying whence he had it & where he paid it. In such matters we are *barbarians*. What a contrast too is their Debtor law, leaving the Artisan his bed his seat his table & his tools of trade, attaching only superfluities & luxuries, to our White Cross Street atrocities & our Rich men living luxuriously in the Rules.[33] By the bye the Jerdan story – his application to you for character &c is astounding! – The rest is plain a plan to entrap some easy rich man into marriage with his daughter – but the application to you reads to me like a drunken audacious Garrick Club or Beefsteak Joke!!![34] Are you sure it is not one of your own on an innocent at Coblentz? After that, come any thing. – Is the day fixed when Wentworth & Agnes Jerdan are to be united? I will come to that wedding anyhow. I must believe you – but after that I think I can play the Boa with a whole rabbit. Bismallah! – (I ought to say Potztausend!) To proceed. There is another

paramount subject here we ought to get a wrinkle from on our blushing brows – I mean general education. It is I believe obligatory for all children however poor to know the rudiments & the means are provided. But this subject is in abler hands.[35] Yet I must tell you how De Franck & I compared notes, for he had been like myself (at great expense), sent to first rate Private Schools, – where we learnt *nothing*.
I hope you will some day meet that you may hear him on that head – & the figure he cut when he went into the Royal School at Berlin. He is really an acquisition to us & I like him much. Tho a young man & a soldier & gay – & fond of his joke, & mine – well principled, gentlemanly, an ardent lover of his country, unassuming, temperate – one I feel sure you would like & do hope you may meet. God grant you may come next year – I see an advertizement of the Batavier from London to Mayence only £4. 1. 0!! I feel sure the Moselle is as fine if not finer than the Rhine – & not to be selfish, or I should wish for you earlier, the royal review here will be worth seeing as a picture of war. It is still doubtful but should the King not come the Prince Royal may. I shall know in good time. Would it were tomorrow our mutual tasks accomplished!
That last phrase has set my thoughts in a serious mould – & so let us to business. All this is supposed to pass in that family circle *of your own* into which you have confidentially invited me, & wherein I find myself with such delight. So to business. I must first of all as to the past not only beg you to give me credit for the best intentions, but the best exertions under my extraordinary circumstances that you may enter into my plans for the future. In the first place as to the Comic I stand better than I did last year in means & comfort, & materials for an early publication – I will not say before 1st Septr[36] – which will be in time for American export & here let me say I have a notion of dedicating to Washington Irving whom I know personally[37] adopting Willis's principle that tis the duty of every writer to lessen the distance between the two countries.[38] It will be with me matter of policy as well as sincere feeling. And here as a corroboration of my notion of Tilts villainy let me just mention the following. I sold 500 of my *first* annual (with Hurst & Chance) to America. Of the second I sold some more having been applied to *myself*, for some. After that for 3 years I sold none Tilt telling me there was no demand or that the Americans reprinted it. For the 6th annual, in Baily's hands, I have a demand again for 500 – & amongst the letters sent out to me is one from Philadelphia, with an offer of money for *early sheets* to reprint in Knickerbocker's Magazine of New York. It says, 'you are every where admired in the best parts of America & your puns & sayings are extremely quoted. I think that the advent of your annual is a matter of as much moment in this country as that of the President's

message.' – Coupling this with the late order for 500 & knowing the Americans cannot well reprint *for want of woodcutters,* I think 'tis at least a suspicious case. However as I hope for an order for next book the Magazine forestalling will not do.[39] As to Baily you are right[40] – but I am in his power, – and I believe him in money matters to be safe – a most important point. He is latterly very civil in his letters – he seems to have found out I am worth something to him – & I guess has published nothing else to any purpose. I shall hint to him my *opinion* on what he has done. And now to one main point. I have directed him, – after I am provided with money for next year, that I may have my mind at ease to do its best – to pay over to YOU any balance due – *I have none else I can so well trust;* – and I fear attachments being laid at Baily's, – by which the worst behaved, & least needing might get paid before the better deserving. Would you take this trouble? – merely to hold it subject to my order to pay so & so. I conceive this might be better than a trifling dividend to all, & some I have heard from are both *able* & *willing* to wait. Others are necessitous – & one (not Martyr)[41] barely honest, deserves to be last. My harvest this year will be a short one to what I hoped – but I thank God 'tis not worse. I feel what I can get thro with a free mind. I believe my last book to be a good one – for I made the most of my time when well. I have often gone to bed in the morning with my hand quite cramped with drawing – but they are a better set of cuts than last year's. And now for your opinion – for you must be my guide. I should like not to run myself too close, in money for this ensuing year, – because a little *travelling*, leaving Jane &c here would not merely advantage the Comic, – but I think I could make it pay generally for the eventual benefit of all concerned. The little I have seen has been of great use to me – tho' I have not used all of it yet. I meditate some pedestrian expeditions hereabout – but I want to see cities – capitals – man & manners. I fancy I can make something out of them serious as well as comic – Am I right? Pray write without reserve – in the confidential tone of your letter & indeed of all your advice to me – I can, will, take nothing ill. For my own part, I own to a strong impression – & it makes me regret former money misspent. Some may grumble but I seriously believe such outlay would be for the benefit of *all*. Tis not 'a truant disposition, good my lord'[42] – that inclines me to this wandering. I hope too not vanity but methinks even in this well travelled continent there is much to glean. I wish I knew the language but I am bad at learning tongues & with my dulness of hearing do not catch the pronunciation. And now to the Club.[43] Am I not entitled to remain in it as a resident abroad without paying till I return – if not, – ought I to pay up this year? I was one of the original members – & it would be pleasant & useful to me, when I return. Apropos. Neither at the

Clarence nor elsewhere did I ever see a *red* wine from these parts tho some are excellent as the Ingelheimer. But there is one worth your attention & I think the Club's perhaps – but it is not very generally known here. Franck who goes to reviews in the Eifel & has been marched & quartered all round about told me of it – & I have tasted it. It comes from the banks of the river Aar, a small rapid trout stream that falls into the Rhine near Andernach. It is bright, beautiful in colour, – *quite rosy* – & excellent in flavour. I prefer it to any claret I ever tasted. So would any one I think, like yourself, who is fond of rhenish wines. It also bears transport better than other reds (which are somewhat ticklish in that particular) & cheaper. The price *here*, – best quality per dozen, bottles included, is five dollars – It seems to me so excellent that I have purchased a case of two dozen which when our steamers go again, sometime next month you will receive. If you will not accept it at my hands, you may repay me in the shape of a Cheshire Cheese some day: – but I would rather you would take it, & give me credit only for good taste. I have of course no purpose to serve – but as you dispense much wine hospitably I think it would be worth your notice as good & cheap & *a novelty*. I believe it ranks among the *Palatinate* wines. NB. I drank some extra Hocheim on Xmas day which *un*naturally enough sent my thoughts *from* the Rhine to Grosvenor Place (Lower)[44] where I first learned to like rhenish. As to my sketch I am glad you liked it – but your criticism is hardly criticism, as such, – but matter of fact. The two parts – the foreground & distance were separate parts, intentionally – the first is not literal – the second is, a portrait. – I intended to give *costume, uniform sentry-box barge* &c in front, – considered per se – without reference exactly to pictorial effect – & yet, let me say – I almost believe to better eyes than mine, those objects might appear with as much distinctness – the distance from our window to the other side of the Moselle is not very great – & in the *early summer*, the air is peculiarly pure & *clear*. The distant hills *then* appear with all their minutiae like an elaborate coloured map. Had I generalized more the colouring ought to have had a different tone, as autumnal, – but when it was taken, I was struck myself by the *actual appearance of the country*, from the purity of atmosphere – exactly, as you express it, as if you looked at it thro a telescope. In the autumn come the extremely heavy dews which ripen and give *such a bloom* to the grapes. How I have longed to be able to *paint* a group of them! They are quite a study for colour. Every mountain almost produces its separate tint of green, tawny, purple – & many shades on one identical sort of grape according as each has been scorched by the sun, on its peculiar soil. You might erect them into a sort of thermometer. Paintings of fruit are generally very insipid, – but one day when a plate full of Muscatels & Rieslings &c was set before me I could not help thinking the artist who could give them properly would be in a good school for colour. By the bye did you ever eat here a small peach – a skin very like a very dirty blanket enveloping it, but within of a rich crimson with a flavour rather bitter, but far to my taste preferable to some of our handsome potatoes called peaches? You see I find something to like here – where indeed as Byron says, 'all save the spirit of man is divine.'[45] And I like some of the people too – that is to say the peasants. I admire their industry, frugality, & content & cheerfulness – they are better *to the eye* too. But I detest the townspeople. Jane I really believe is reconciled – & to tell the truth we live very comfortable & I am very philosophical & thankful. We have many cheap luxuries – & comparative ease of mind. I sometimes feel again what is a spring of the spirits. Then the cheap fine scenery. One of my great delights at Lake House was that lookout behind – in my mind's eye I saw it in its *purple bloom*, nay its 'purple light of love'[46] last summer – it was worth *some* money that home view – with Temperance, divided from the wine cellar by a pond.[47]

I have said nothing yet of the Athm. or its notice.[48] The paper is a great treat to me – & latterly it has been more interesting than usual. You do not say but I hope indeed feel it must go on flourishingly. Wright says the reviews of the Comic are by J.H.R.[49] I own I cannot detect his hand. They read to me like your own. I predicted the Girls' Boarding School bit would be extracted, – & Miss Norman was my pet story[50] – so I could not have been better pleased had I *reviewed myself.* The Ocean was written con amore[51] – tho' rather contra amore, too, for I *do* love the sea in spite of its last spite to me. I miss its fish tho we get tolerable salt haddock & middling herrings & bad oysters. You cannot imagine how I adore shrimps even – now I cannot get 'em. And Miss Seil has ornamented our drawing room with a painting of a dutch fisherman at his stall, smoking his pipe, – over a magazine of all sorts of scaly finny & shelly eatables, – with a glimpse of the sea & a boat coming on with a fresh live cargo in the distance. Sometimes it makes me savage, – & I curse his soul. Especially now – when there is no *hammel* flesh to be had in Coblentz not *ham* but mutton. – Nothing but beef – fit to eat. The very huge pork & the very tiny veal is out of the question. Both are abominations. Especially to Farmer Hood who reared both calves & pigs of his own. The fun of it is, there is a great pig fair at Ehrenbreitstein in November, – after which all Coblentz eats pork & nothing but pork whilst the stock on hand lasts. I popped on a domestic party busy killing two hogs, for they are literally not porkers but bacon hogs, & Wanstead recollections came over me so as to make me laugh aloud, to the great disconcerting of the Master & Mistress. By the bye Franck tells me they have discovered a very active poison only second to *prussic* acid in *prussian* black puddings – several persons have died. Of course the pig blood was in a bad state. By the way, I suspect German pigs smoke actively as well as passively (in hams) they are so apathetic. I saw a whole barge load come over the Rhine, and expected on the boat touching the shore after struggling thro the ice, to see all the drove run away – but I was mistaken. They had no notion of running like Leigh Hunt's pig ['up all manner of] streets'[52] but each went quietly with its owner seemingly to their education under some such [Schwein-Ge]neral as Head describes.[53] We have had some sharp touches of [frost. The oil] of the night light froze. The middle of the lb of butter – & a piecrust Jane was making. It was once very intense – & as our back bedrooms look northwards over Rhine & Moselle, the stove there is not a good one & moreover that side of the house is slightly built, one night we actually decamped & all slept on a row with our beds on the ground in my little study. *Now* it is frost & thaw by turns, which is worse. The Moselle ice has given way & come down at a racing pace, but the Rhine is still frozen over at St Goar. The *variation* is great & trying. I have a regular sore throat at 9 P.M & Frank has one every morning. Every house almost has the measles in it & ours has not escaped. Poor Tom has got them – & weaning & cutting his eye teeth at same time. I am finishing this sitting up while Jane sleeps. I am almost ashamed of the length of it – for it will cost more than it is worth but I shall not be able to write often. I rejoice in your good account of the Doctor,[54] I wish we had only as good a mediciner here. Beerman tells me they call Sydenham[55] the second Hippocrates, – but I cannot edge in a word for the later professors. The Germans in Typhus give cold water – Franck says a little while back cold water was the cure for all complaints – as they clip all their dogs foxdogs, wolfdogs, poodles, all sorts into lions. Should *I* be ill again here I have made up my mind to doctor myself & trust to nature, & Providence. – I have had a letter from Moxon applying for letters of Lamb's which he wants to publish. If you say aye to this he shall have them. – But I meant them for your use.[56] It is too late now perhaps to write the article I proposed, but I think if you could collect for me & save all that has been written about him (C.L.) I could make a good review of it – corroborating, contradicting & giving my own view. Pray rem*ber* this in yr next. By the way, knowing all we do of the affair – Moxon's sonnets to Emma read 'sufficiently fulsome.' He sent them to Jane.[57]

The measles have been so prevalent even several ladies have been prevented going to the Balls – by having them.

Little Tom is well again after a three days bout of them. I have just recd the Athem of 1st Jany It is an excellent one – first rate. By the bye, I suppose I have learned to bow well here as you have borrowed my bow in the Comic for your Athm one at

the end of the year[58] I have not seen a Comic yet (the 17*th*) – & we are anxious for the fate of a parcel to have been sent out before Xmas. Mrs Dilke's letter will come by next post – after which I must write other guess matters than letters.[59] I wrote to JHR & he talked of writing to me but has not yet. – All good wishes to you *all* – not forgetting *Lord* Chichester[60] should he be in town – & with huzza for 1836 believe us Dear Dilke Yours ever very truly Thomas Hood & Co. Jane's love to M^rs^ D & will write soon.
Since writing the foregoing a little newyear's gift of a needle case very pretty has come from Maintz for Fanny from our grateful little Pole. Fanny alone was on *speaking terms* with her. It has given us great pleasure, liking to have human nature redeemed as much as we can from reproach. De Franck has also brought me a present a most useful one, an excellent case map of Germany & its adjacents – it is indorsed 'to Mr Hood from his friend P de Franck, as a reward for trussing puddings' – 'Thou shalt heap fiery coals on the head of those that betray thee.'[61] To understand which mystery you must read mine to Mrs D. Also the operative-surgeon's bill has come in in English for me thus, in one item. 'for his Lady. To put blood suckers at her eyes – 6 shillings.' 6 times the regular charge – I am going to dispute it – The ice on the Rhine today (12th) is coming down & de Franck is blockaded on the other side. We are looking for some huge masses when it breaks up at St Goar. All Bingen has been & is under water – We expect a flood 3 or 4 feet deep in Castor *Street* next to ours – & the engineers are contriving *rafts*. One day here was so suddenly warm nay hot, in the midst of the frost it was quite annoying & made us all ill.[62]

372 Castor Hof Coblentz. [*17 January 1836*]

MS BM. Address: 'C.W. Dilke Esqre / 9 Lower Grosvenor Place / Pimlico / London. / England.' PM: 'COBLENZ/17/1,' 'FPO 1836/JA 21.' Published by Marchand 28–61; illustration from *Memorials* II 247.

1/The last line of James Thomson's 'Hymn to the Seasons'
2/Lamb refers to his friend Barron Field 'where the Kangaroo haunts' in 'Mackery End' *Works* ed. E.V. Lucas (1903–5) II 78.
3/Mailcoach: 'eil' means haste.
4/Probably for 'Lindo.' It reads as though she took some of the Hoods' letters to England with her.
5/Variation on *Othello* 3 iii 170
6/To appear eventually as *Up the Rhine*
7/Montaigne *Essays* II 27
8/*Book of Common Prayer*, second collect at Evening Prayer
9/'Sonnet to Ocean,' *Poetical Works* 476; the next sentence adapts Moore's 'Oh! had we some bright little isle of our own.'
10/Marchand 33, notes: 'Hood meant to use the French word for pun – *calembour*.'
11/Unidentified
12/Jonzac, a town in Charente-Inférieure

13/Lord Granville Leveson-Gower, Earl Granville (1770–1846), was ambassador at Paris (1830–41). Hood doubtless knew Lady Granville's hand because he had dedicated the *Comic Annual* for 1833 to her. Louis-Philippe (1773–1850), king of France, 1830–48
14/Sir Thomas Cartwright (1795–1850), minister at Frankfurt 1830–8
15/See the illustration in *Up the Rhine* facing 232.
16/Mrs Frances Trollope (1780–1863), author, especially of *Belgium and Western Germany* (1834), to which Hood refers on 248. He is probably thinking of her disparaging *Domestic Manners of the Americans* (1832). *The Athenaeum*, 12 July 1834, 522, had anticipated that she would 'pass like a blight' over Belgium and Western Germany, but found her book a week later 'kindlier ... than we had anticipated,' 529.
17/The *Book of Beauty* was an annual edited after its first year by Lady Blessington, of whom Charles Greville wrote: 'she produces those gorgeous inanities, called Books of beauty ... to get up which all the fashion and beauty ... of London are laid under contribution. The most distinguished artists and the best engravers supply the portraits of the prettiest women in London; and these are illustrated with poetical effusions of the smallest possible merit,' *Memoirs*, ed. Lytton Strachey and Roger Fulford (1938) IV 130.
18/John Hobart Caunter (1794–1851), miscellaneous writer, obtained his BD at Cambridge in 1828. According to Marchand 41, he reviewed frequently for *The Athenaeum* in the 1830s, and 'must have had some connection with the *Court Magazine*, which occasionally "embellished" its pages with pictures of the fashionable ladies of the day.'
19/'Double' issues of *The Times* appeared in 1806 and 1817, and increasingly frequently after 1825. By 1831 such issues 'came out more than once a week, and by January, 1836, they averaged four a week,' *History of the Times* I (1935) 325.
20/Rather, George Primrose in *The Vicar of Wakefield*, ch. xx
21/Quotation unidentified
22/Elisabeth (Bettina) von Arnim (1785–1859), author of *Goethes Briefwechsel mit einem Kinde*. This work was reviewed in three notices in *The Athenaeum*, 1835, between pp. 754 and 816. In the third notice is given Bettina's account of the emotional circumstances leading to the suicide of her friend.
23/Peter George Patmore (1786–1855), author and journalist, friend of Hazlitt and Lamb, father of the poet Coventry Patmore. In February 1821 Patmore seconded John Scott, editor of the *London Magazine*, in a duel which originated in a quarrel with *Blackwood's*; Scott was fatally injured.
24/In fact Charlotte cleaned the pistols, Werther kissed them; Goethe *Sorrows of Werther*, translated J. Pratt, 2nd ed. (1809) 159.
25/Letitia Landon
26/Ludwig Joachim von Arnim (1781–1831), married Bettina in 1811
27/Marchand 46 notes that Hood confuses the two Schlegel brothers. August Wilhelm von Schlegel (1767–1845) translated Shakespeare (1797–1810), a work which was only completed, under the supervision of Ludwig Tieck, in 1833. Karl Wilhelm Friedrich von Schlegel (1772–1829), August's younger brother, lectured at Vienna on *Philosophie der Geschichte*, a work published in the year of his death. A translation of these lectures was reviewed in *Athenaeum* 12 December 1835, 925–7. Hood's misapprehension of names and dates indicates the irritability of his comment, which he himself admits.
28/Perhaps a reference to *Henry V* 4 iii 60, 'we band of brothers'
29/Herman Ludwig Heinrich Prince von Pückler-Muskau (1785–1871), author and traveller. His *Briefe eines Verstorbenen* (1830–1) was translated by Sarah Austin as *Tour in England, Ireland, and France*. His *Tutti Frutti: Aus den Papieren des Verstorbenen* appeared in both original German and English translation in 1834. Pückler-Muskau was the dedicatee of Bettina von Arnim's *Goethes Briefwechsel*.
30/In *Bubbles from the Brunnens of Nassau* 49, 255
31/A lobster was a soldier, in red; a raw lobster was a policeman, in blue.

32/On both of these occasions Henry Hunt, the radical orator, was implicated in the disturbances. The Spa Fields Riots of 1816 were handled by a few constables and the military. The Peterloo Massacre of 1819 was the work of yeomanry and military.
33/The Rules of the King's Bench prison were privileges, which had to be paid for, for prisoners to live in an area within three miles of the prison. A person incarcerated in White Cross Street prison lacked these privileges.
34/The Beef-Steak Society flourished from 1735 to 1867. It was restricted to twenty-four members. Among the founders was William Hogarth. Samuel Johnson was a member later in the eighteenth century. At the time of Hood's letter the membership included Lord Brougham, John Cam Hobhouse, Byron's friend, and the dramatist Richard Brinsley Peake. William Jerdan was a delighted visitor. The Garrick Club was founded in 1831 as a society 'in which actors and men of education and refinement might meet on equal terms,' Percy Fitzgerald *The Garrick Club* (1904) 1. The president of the Club was the Duke of Devonshire, and the large original membership included many names which occur in Hood's correspondence; one of them is that of Jerdan.
35/Marchand 50 notes: 'Hood probably refers to the work of Dilke's friend Mrs Sarah Austin, who in 1834 translated the report on the "State of Public Instruction in Prussia" ... She made a careful study of German institutions ... and sent considerable foreign correspondence to the *Athenaeum*.' Sarah Austin (1793–1867) settled in Germany in 1827. She published *Characteristics of Goethe* (1833) and translated Pückler-Muskau's *Tour in England* (1832) and Raumer's *England in 1835* (1836).
36/The *Comic Annual* did not appear until 20 December 1836.
37/Hood did not dedicate the *Comic Annual* to Washington Irving (1783–1859), American author of *The Sketch Book* (1820). Irving lived mostly in England from 1815 to 1824.
38/Nathaniel Parker Willis (1806–67), American journalist, described his European travels in *Pencillings by the Way*, published in England in November 1835.
39/The English annuals were popular in the United States. In 1829 over 40,000 copies were imported.
40/Dilke's distrust of Baily as Hood's publisher is indicated by a comment in *The Athenaeum*, 21 November 1835, 873, on a squib called *The Battle of the Annuals*: 'A fortnight since it was found out by a daily paper, that [Hood] was the writer of "The Comic Almanack", and last week a critical contemporary [*Spectator*, 1092] stated, that only [Hood] could have written this "Battle of the Annuals" ... he did not write a line of the former, for we were requested by his publisher to contradict the report; and ... we cannot find a trace of him in the latter, except indeed the announcement of the forthcoming Comic, and one of its woodcuts *on the cover* ... [We] are somewhat surprised that ... Mr Hood's publisher ... who was so alarmed at possible consequences in the one instance, should so incautiously risk them in the other.' Over a year later (on 20 April 1837), John Wright wrote to Hood: 'The advertisement of the Battle Baily is innocent of ... He is so angry at it that he is determined to cut it out of his catalogue & advertise it no more,' MS Bristol Central Library. *The Battle of the Annuals* was advertised in the *Comic Annuals* for 1836, 1837, and 1838.
41/Perhaps Charles Martyr, wholesale stationer, 32 Bouverie Street, Strand
42/*Hamlet* I ii 169
43/The Clarence Club, of which both Dilke and Hood were members
44/Dilke's address
45/Byron, 'Bride of Abydos' I 15
46/Gray, 'Progress of Poesy' 41
47/Hood seems to be here obscurely defending his abstemiousness at Wanstead.
48/Review of the *Comic Annual* for 1836 in *Athenaeum* 12, 19 December 1835
49/John Hamilton Reynolds
50/'The Sudden Death' *Comic Annual* for 1836

51/In the *Comic Annua*
52/See 222 n13.
53/Resort to Hunt's and Head's texts enables one to fill the gaps in Hood's MS. Hood refers to Head *Bubbles from the Brunnens of Nassau* (1834) 95.
54/Perhaps Seoane
55/Thomas Sydenham (1624–89), celebrated physician
56/Marchand 59 notes that Moxon published none of Lamb's letters to Hood in Talfourd's edition of 1837.
57/Moxon's *Sonnets: Part Second*, published November 1835
58/At the end of the volume for 1835 *The Athenaeum*, 26 December, 969, makes its farewell bow to the reader with the words of Hood in the preface to the current *Comic Annual*.
59/That is, matters of another kind: a slang expression
60/Dilke's brother William, who lived at Chichester
61/Proverbs 25:22
62/At the side of the first page of the letter there is following reference to 189 above: ' – dirty bread balls – toothpick stuck in them' etc – I took a great disgust at him originally. I have just learned he is a Russian spy.'

TO
JOHN WRIGHT

My dear Wright,
We have been anxiously waiting to see our promised parcel, and as it has not come at this present writing, I have made up my mind to let you know, fearing it may have stuck at some of the custom houses on its way through. Should it have been despatched, pray let us have all the particulars that I may try to recover it. You may, however, have heard of the ice; if so, and it has deterred you from sending, I am now able to tell you that the ice is all gone, our bridge will be up again, if it is not already, and the papers announce that the *Rhine* steamboats will start for the season to-morrow.
I have been very anxious – for except your last before Christmas, we have only had the *back* letters, and those by Mrs. L—[1], which came to us on New Year's Eve. I long to know what luck my book has had. It seems odd to me not to have seen the Comic yet; but judging from the fragments sent, which I had not time to look at before I last wrote, it is excellently got up on all hands, myself included. The cuts come very well indeed, and the text seems very correct: quite as much so as *I* could have made it. As this is only a business letter, I must refer to the Dilkes for particularities as to our domestic concerns, they have each had long epistles.
I think I told you De Franck is come back for good. He fishes, and means to fish more, in the Rhine and Moselle, as there are really good fish; both sport and profit may be looked for here (where we are very badly off for sea-fish, even *salted*). Perch, Barbel, Roach, Jack, and higher up, even Salmon, and a peculiar fish, not

English: rod and line fishing is free. De Franck wants a few things, and I want an outfit for bait fishing, I do not pretend to troll, or throw a fly; do as you judge best for me. Pray do not forget to send me plenty of blocks, as I shall have much use for them – I have, however, a present supply. I do much wish, and almost hope you may come this spring. You may pay in London, per the 'Batavier,' the whole fare here, which is the cheapest way; with liberty of staying at any place on the road a few days, as at Rotterdam, Nimeguen, or Cologne, and then on again. Should you come, I project some pedestrian rambles, inland – to see the people and country. –I know enough German now to 'get along like *ile*.'

I keep my health tolerably well, and hope to be better. The winter has tried us all with colds, coughs, face-aches, &c., and Tom has had the measles, but mildly. As Ollapod recommends, I am taking my 'spring physic'[2] – (N.B. I am my own M.D.) – and mean to go into mental and bodily training for a good campaign. It is a great thing for us, De Franck's return, in every sense, for he will save us from a great deal of imposition, of which the honest Germans hereabouts are too fond. And he is a very good fellow as a companion, without thinking that he is our only one. I must cut this short, for Franck is come, and we have to get him to scold Gradle, and give her warning. She gave us a message from her priest, and when we sent her out with the chicks this morning, she took them to church. So we mean to protest as good Protestants, and Jane is quite a Luther at it. My kind regards to Mrs. Wright, and all of your name, and all friends of other names. Kiss my Godson, and 'Prosit neu jahr!' from

Dear Wright, yours ever truly,

Thos. Hood.

P.S. Postage is not dear. Pray let us know how matters go on. We have not the thousand and one occupations and acquaintances, and so on, to divert our anxieties like those of your great city: and molehills seem mountains. Franck swears that potted-beef story kept him laughing all night. 'Ah Chied!'

372, Castor Hof, [Koblenz] 31st January, 1836.

From *Memorials* I 148–51

1/Probably Mrs Lindo

2/In George Colman's *Poor Gentleman* (1802) 2 i

TO
CHARLES WENTWORTH DILKE

My dear Dilke,
Many, many thanks for your letter, and the kind interest and trouble it evidences on my behalf. They are such as I might have expected from the best and last friend I saw in England, and the first I hope to meet again. * * * *
We are in much better lodgings, at the same cost, though our address, literally translated, is at 'Mr. Devil's, in the Old Grave.' We are now near the Moselle bridge, in a busy, amusing street, but out of the town in three minutes' walk.
We did not part with Miss Seil without some serio-comic originality in her struggles between extortion and civility. One moment she kissed Jane like a sister, and the next began a skirmish. First came Suspicion that, as we left a little before the time agreed on, we would not pay up to it. Satisfied on that point, Content fell to kissing. Then Memory suggested we had broken two or three old chairs and a glass, but finding we had replaced or sent them to be mended ourselves, she fired a fresh salute. Away we went, and then, Avarice prompting, she sent a volley of chairs, &c., we had *not* broken, to be repaired, and requested the use of the rooms. That promised so soon as we should have cleared out and cleaned up, she fell to compliments again; but sniffing that she meant to whitewash, repair, and brush up at our cost, we were obliged, in self-defence, to hold the keys. Thereupon she had the *locks picked*, and set to work, and hinted she would favour me with the bills. So I entered into the correspondence, and as she had sent Jane a quantity of notes in German, I thought it only fair to give her one in English, which I knew she must carry half over the town to get translated, and then, I fear, it will not be very flattering. I pointed out to her that she had no right to both rooms and rent, and as picking locks *is* a grave offence in Prussia, she must have, and had, presumed on a foreigner's ignorance of its laws. This has shut her mouth, and stopped the bills, and also the *billing*. Gradle marched on the 1st of March[1] (military again), and, I am sorry to say, made a bad end. First, as Tom didn't at all want physic, she showed, or let him find his way (whilst his mother was out) to the cupboard 'wot holds the honey-pot.' Secondly, having 'vained de Bibi,' she did her best to unvain him again, and set him roaring all at once after his 'Mutter.' Thirdly, as Fanny had the face-ache, she opened all the windows directly our backs were turned, and, having taken a fit of cleanliness, she was busy one day brushing down the dust from the ceiling and walls over Missis's gowns. She had warning for the 1st of March, but, as Jane is as unlucky as 'Joe,'[2] this of all years was leap year. It is too certain

the dear departed made a per-centage on everything she bought for us. I declined to sign a certificate of honesty Vertue had given her, so she cast her eyes on Joseph, the carpenter, whom she got to marry her, induced by the fortune of a 'bibi' two years old, and 150 dollars saved out of the 60 she had received from Vertue and us. Joseph's mother, whom he partly supported, dying opportunely the day before she left us, the wedding was fixed for the fortnight after the funeral; but, owing to some mysterious interdict of the priest, did not take place till a fortnight later.

We have now a servant with a seven years' character, and the consequence is everything is much cheaper, albeit she is not a good bargainer. Of course, though we do not quarrel, we have plenty of *misunderstandings*. We have changed our butcher, and gained a penny per pound; ditto laundress, and saved nearly a dollar a week. In short, Jane, whatever be her political principles, is a practical reformer; and I look on with a Conservative eye, lest the spirit of change should go on madly too far, and I be *Skeltoned*[3] like the rest.

By the bye, I do not wonder at the separation of that worthy couple, the —s.[4] I should rather think they never met – or, at least, only like the Rhine and Moselle, which show a very decided inclination to keep themselves to themselves from the first moment of union. Jane and I, however, take the warning, and shall be particularly careful of quarrelling, as she has not '*a piano*' to be the harmonious means of bringing us together again.

As for 'chimney ornaments' (except a very tall, long-nosed gentleman in black, remarkably like our English 'devil,' who sweeps for all Coblenz), we have not even a chimney-piece. The climbing boy here is really one of the finest men in the place. He sweeps the chimney, – the long iron pipes of the stoves are cleared by a live Friesland hen, a sort of fowl which has its feathers turned back the wrong way. When she is in the pipe a fire is made, and the heat forces her to make her way into the chimney with the soot among her ruffled feathers. She then cries 'grauchschlacht!' which is the German for 'all up!' and this is at least as true as some bits of Von Raumer.[5]

I am writing this gossip partly to amuse Mrs. Dilke. The barber-surgeon I settled with thus: He wrote that in consideration that I might not be able to afford it, he consented to take one dollar instead of two. To which I replied, that I merely resisted an imposition, and should hand over the difference to the poor. This I did to the poor of Arzheim, near Ehrenbreitstein, where 280 have suffered from scarlet fever; and a subscription was opened by public appeal from the over-burgomaster of Coblenz, and is now closed, after two months' collection, having raised twelve pounds! – a smallish amount for a city containing a governor-general, two commandants, over and under-presidents, ditto burgomasters, and about twenty-five to thirty carriage families, and many rich tradesmen: but these are anything but the honest, conscientious, liberal, orderly, warm-hearted, intellectual Germans we give the country just credit for. The Coblenzers have other attributes. To return to my *leech-gatherer.*[6] I do not intend to want again either physician or apothecary. I am no believer in astrological conjunctions, but I must insist on a sinister aspect in that case. A Jew doctor playing into the hands of his brother-in-law, the apothecary, who has been described beforehand by 'Gil Blas,' viz.: 'He goes strictly to mass, but at the bottom of his heart he is a Jew, like Pilate, for he has become Catholic through interest.'[7]

As Jews must not be apothecaries here, and Hebrews do not forgive apostacy in their own brothers even, I fear their good understanding must be allowed to be ominous. Now for a bit of farce in one of the same tribe. He came to me to draw up an advertisement for him in English, on the strength of which, I suppose, he has set up here as Professor of Philosophy and *English.* Franck knows an officer who has *learned*, and he cannot understand his English at all. The officer will have his revenge when he has to drill the Professor! We are now more *au fait* here, but we have to fight every inch. I am now in health and spirits and do not mind it; but I wish, for the sake of the lovely country I am now able to enjoy, I could come to other conclusions. I am not writing from spleen or prejudice, or resentment at the loss of money, but to give you my cool and deliberate impressions for your guidance; and a resident has peculiar opportunities for observation. Prejudice be hanged! and I will help to pull its legs. But I want fair play for my countrymen, against whom there is much illiberal feeling, which is the more annoying, because Germans from other parts, who think well of us, are surprised to find opinion against us on the Rhine where it would be presumed we are so well known. As a sample of what I mean, there is Schreiber's sketch of 'Die Engländer in Baden' referred to in your No. 431 of the 'Athenaeum,'[8] which I wish had fallen to my lot to review. I would have answered him with facts. The charge that the rectitude of many of the English is not to be uniformly depended upon is a grave one, on which I might retort fairly from my own experience as equivalent to his; and choose for my motto, in a new sense, 'Beware – for there are counterfeits *abroad.*' With few exceptions, judging from those I have had to do with, I should put them in two great classes – Jew Germans, and German Jews. It may seem a harsh verdict, but it is *forced* upon me. As for the English quarrelling about coachmen's fares, &c., it is hardly worthy a traveller to squabble about petty over-charges, but extortions may become too gross and palpable to put up with. There is all along shore here, now-a-days at least, a sharking, grasping appetite, which growing by what it feeds on,[9] has become ogre-like; and knowing the English to be rich, they have not known where, prudently, or with good policy, to stop. There was a colonel here, the other day only, crying out, naturally, at being charged in this *cheap* country five shillings for a bed; the landlord of the hotel in question chose at the Carnival to burlesque an English family travelling: he has told me, the English are by far his best customers, but the ridicule was congenial to the spirit of the inhabitants. The truth is, we are marked for plunder; and laughed at, for the facility with which we are plucked, as if it were a matter of difficulty to cheat those, who in some degree confide in you – for we do generally set forth with a strong prepossession in favour of German honesty. I believe in it myself, but not here, where the very peasantry (whom I like) seem to lose it. The other day a woman, who used to sell us a sort of curd cheese, taking advantage of Fanny, who carried the money, took six instead of three groschen, and has never since put in an appearance. Again, a man, who left a flower for Jane's approval, who declined it, called for it over night quite drunk, took it away, brought it back next morning, and made her pay for it because a bud was broken! these two are within ten days. Schreiber taunts residents like ourselves with 'a petty and ridiculous economy,' but it is mere resistance to extortion directed pointedly against the English. I never will concede that the rule, that we are to be robbed, only because we are, or are supposed to be, rich, is anything but a brigand feeling. Yet so it is. There is a separate tariff, well-understood, and tacitly acted upon, so that you shall see an English and German gentleman sitting at the same table d'hôte, eating the same dinner, and drinking the same wine, but at very different cost! It is quite a freemasonry, and the very figures in the *carte* stand for several amounts. One night we sent for a bill of fare for supper, and De Franck pointed out to me roast beef, (in English) four groschen, and directly under it, the same dish, (in German) three groschen. These things are somewhat repuslive to those who happen to be their guests, should they chance to find besides that their character is attacked as unfairly as their purse. I *know* that they retail stories about us, which have falsehood on the face of them, such as the Bible story in Schreiber, which is altogether out of keeping.[10] As to our getting into rows and trespassing,[11] I used to watch the steamer's arrival, and never saw a disturbance, but with a *German* lady, accused by the steward of secreting a spoon. But that Englishmen *might* get into rows I think very possible, and natural; I expect it myself. The lower class, not mere thieves and vagabonds like Londoners, but apprentices, workmen, and boys almost well-dressed, are blackguardly disposed.

Fishing has brought me in contact with them. I have *never* been without annoyance, and it is positively *unsafe* to stand within pelt of the Mosel bridge. Those officers, who have taken to it after our example at Ehrenbreitstein, have positively had to post men to defend them from *large* sticks and stones. I hope, as the clown says, here be *facts*. Good or bad politically, the making all men soldiers serves to lick these cubs into human shape; it makes them cut their hair, wash themselves, and behave decently; in fact as Puckler Muskau says, the men, who have served, and those who have not, are different animals indeed.[12] I wish I could with honesty write more in the tone of Mrs. Trollope, whose book, by the way, I have just read; but although so treacley, it does not please the natives. Heaven knows why, for she does not object to one thing in Prussia, but the smoking. She is however, wrong there in one point, as may be gathered from the pretty strong sentiments she puts into the mouths of the German girls against pipes. A likely matter when they have been used to sniff '*backy*' from the father who took them first on his knees, to the brother they played with.[13]

On the contrary, and quite the reverse, they embroider tobacco bags for presents to the young gentlemen as English girls knit purses. But so Anti-English a writer as Mrs. T., who never omits an opportunity of letting down her countrymen, might be expected to be blind to the Anti-English feeling abundant in these parts. There is no doubt of its existence, I manage to read their papers, and the tone is the same. Extracts for example headed, 'Distress in *Rich* England.' Like 'the haughty Isle of shopkeepers,' a phrase made use of by Schreiber. 'Tis the mark of the beast;[14] they covet our riches, they resent our political influence, and perhaps are jealous of the distinction shown to the English in *some* of the highest quarters. In spite of Raumer (a *jewel* by the way)[15] I think the spirit enters into our commerce.

The merchant here, I had your wine of, said he did not hope for any reduction of our duties on their wines, because the Prussian Tariff is so very unfavourable to us. Our goods are in request, so that even they simulate English labels, &c., &c., but I think their introduction is not coveted by the powers. My little package was detained some time at the frontier, on the frivolous pretext, that the weight of every article, a fish-hook for instance, was not specified. I believe the tariff is also adverse to French and Italians; all I know is, many of their products are bad and dear: say, oranges from two pence halfpenny to 3*d.* a piece; salad oil dear and execrable, &c., &c. And now to Schreiber again; I take his for my text-book, because he represents the mass. Their usual ridicule of our habits, &c., might fairly and with interest be retaliated. For instance an Englishman with coat-pockets 'big enough *to hold a couple of folios*,' is no more ridiculous a figure than a German with ditto capacious enough for a pipe and a bag of tobacco; but this far from unusual sneer at our literary and reading propensity is somewhat misplaced in Intellectual Germany *the country of Goethe*. A book here seems a bugbear. I think I told you of the remark of the Jew Doctor on seeing a 'Times' paper; in the same style my new Doctor took up the 'Athenaeum,' supposing it to be a monthly.

When I said, 'weekly,' he threw up his hands and eyes, and wondered how we found time for it. Time, however, is the thing least wanted here, for they do not live at *our rate*, and consequently have more leisure; but it is not 'learned leisure,'[16] from simple want of will.

They prefer the Virginian to other leaves, – and volumes of smoke.

The 'Rhein und Mosel Zeitung' supplies them with abundant reading, and its standing articles, probably therefore favourite ones, are on beet-root, sugar, and rail-roads.

Their talk is of thalers, thalers, thalers, except when they smoke in the hotels of a night, or at the Casino, and then the Quakers could not hold a more silent Conversazione.

Galignani[17] *is* prohibited, and the only English papers allowed are the 'Globe,' 'Courier,' and the 'Albion,' or some such name.[18] So much for the Intellectuals. Personally I cannot complain, for a Colonel has translated my Eugene Aram for his wife, having heard of it through Bulwer's novel:[19] Bulwer (who is a demi-god here) and the Pfennig Magazine,[20] and native works on medicine and mechanical arts, are the main bulk advertised here, but I guess not much sold. Another fact, and I quit the subject. The extorting spirit is known, and admitted by some of the better class – Jane, at request from the other side, has formed a very agreeable intimacy with a Miss von B—,[21] who was educated at Nieuwiëd, and speaks tolerable English. She *volunteered* to accompany Jane to buy anything, saying she knew the English were imposed on, and informed her, that her late father, a lieutenant-general, paid Dr— at the rate of ten silber groschen or a shilling a visit. He charged me forty-five, or four shillings and sixpence a visit, for being an Englishman. What follows is, I think, conclusive as to what I have said of a sort of freemasonry, &c.

I happened to doubt whether the majors and captains here, could afford to keep up such equipages on their pay, when F— referred me to another officer (of ancient Polish family), I have met, and he frankly told me that they could. But supposing a major with family, &c., to make a certain appearance, and live in a certain style on his pay 2000 dollars, I must at once *for the same things* set down 1000 more for being an Englishman.

It follows that tradesmen, inn-keepers, all who have to do with the English, exact a *profit* of 33 per cent. *extra*, and yet cannot be pleased with their customers. Suppose some English Schreiber, in inditing a sketch of the German watering-places, were to adopt the portentous text of 'take care of your pockets.'[22] Suppose he were to end his book with a sarcastic hint of Sir Peter Teazle's, 'I must go, but I leave my character behind me!'[23] I give you the facts, because in the Athenaeum you are sometimes called upon as a judge, between the natives of both countries, as in Schreiber's case. I do not want, like Jonathan in England, 'a war, and all on my own account,'[24] nor, Irish-like, to whiten the English by blackening the Germans. Above all, I speak only of what I have seen and know, or have heard from good witnesses, and my *locale* is Coblenz; though the same thing may prevail on the other routes of the English, *pro ex:* Baden. It is for you that I have set it down, and I beg you to believe, in no spite, or resentment, or prejudice; but to put you on your guard, and prepare you for perhaps a very altered state of things on the Rhine, not belonging more to the natives than to human nature, except in degree. But I wished justice for my countrymen, and disclaim personal vengeance, though I confess to have felt irritation. The tone of my book[25] will be quite otherwise, I know it is unwelcome to read as to write such passages, and especially to introduce such actors on such a stage, with the Rhine and its mountains for the scenery. And moreover there is good and beautiful and whimsical to discourse of pleasantly, so pray read the foregoing in the same spirit that its author writ, and then hand over the substance of my remarks to the censor to be used 'as occasion may require.' Fair play is a jewel,[26] and I like to see it set in the 'Athenaeum.' Besides I do not know your Editor[27] personally, but I suspect him of a little over-leaning towards the Germans. I picture him with 'an awful fell of hair,'[28] and a serio-comico-metaphysico-romantico visage, moulded in brown bread made rather heavy, a big body made dropsically corpulent by fattening on thin wine, and a pair of stout legs of no particular shape, on which he partly walks, partly marches, having been drilled when a student. Like Pope and Cowper, and others of the learned, he wears a cap; but with a conceited cock on one side, and hangs a tassel from its apex. On his forefinger, a huge ring with an engraved stone or glass, that might serve Mrs. von D— at a pinch for a jelly-mould; and he has chains enough on his bosom to hang him in. His waistcoat seems cut out of the train of Iris's court-dress, set off by a snuff-brown coat, and sad-green breeches – a sort of hybrid between a peacock and Minerva's fowl – grave and gaudy. When he eats, he prefers after soup the meat that was boiled in it – a mere residuum – like the patent ginless bread of Pimlico. He seasons it with mud-coloured mustard. He drinks a wine so sharp, that like the 'Accipe Hoc*k*' of the Templar, it pierces your very vitals. When he is awake he dreams, when he is asleep he snores music, that, as Zelter says, by its very noise 'reminds you of the universal silence!'[29] If he look pensive it is because he cannot fathom the immeasurable, grasp the infinite, or comprehend the incomprehensible. Should he be a little cracked he writes – when he gets purblind he paints, and you have the portrait of his mistress the Muse, as a little old woman with red toads dropping out of her mouth. Poet or Painter, he tries to be sublime, and makes a monster a 'most ridiculous monster,'[30] or rather a herd of monsters, and makes them act monstrously, like the fantastic shadows in Carpenter's microscope,[31] supposing you had mixed their drop of water with a ditto of brandy. If he smiles, it is with the idea of 'reading much, learning much, and dying young!' by a horse-pistol with a leaf out of Bettine for wadding.[32] Whilst he smokes he pastoralises; drunk, he moralises; sober, he romanticises; mad, he philosophises. There Wolfgang von Dilke there's a rally *à la* Randall,[33] in return for your fighting me up into a German corner. By the bye your notices made me long to read Von Raumer's England. It must be a capital book, but methinks he is apt to make azure of Prussian blue. Yet when I spoke of him here to our doctor, he seemed not to like him, and said he was considered a Jacobin. For example too much credit is taken as to their contented and tolerant clergy. For instance, *here*, this is a Catholic province; the magistrates and a few more Lutherans must tolerate perforce a whole population nearly of unreformed. Prussia is formed of many provinces, some oughts, and some crosses, like the old game on the slate, and to be intolerant would be only to set one province against another, 'hey dog – hey bull!' so that it would be dangerous for one party to tyrannise over the other.

A thing occurred here the other day, that made a great sensation: the priest or curé refused to bury a drawing-master, who professed, but had not attended, his church, for many years. He said he was forbidden by the rules of the Council of Trent. The Lutheran minister was applied to, who buried him at once, and as it is usual to preach a funeral sermon for each defunct, the following Sunday his church was crowded with Catholics, Jews, and all denominations, who were eager and curious to hear how he would treat the subject. He preached a good temperate sermon on the text 'Judge not, that ye be not judged,' which made a great impression. The plan here, which is good, is that of both religions the ministers are paid by the King or State, an arrangement I should like for England and Ireland, – or let every one pay their own, as in America. As to Education, I think our Government does wisely not to interfere too rashly. Something may be left to the sense of the people. The infamous boarding-schools of former times are dying or dead, and replaced by proprietary ones without Government interference.[34] If they meddle, let it be to reform Oxford, and the like; and, least of all, let us have the School a dependant on the Church, – with a Parson-Usher in each, preaching and teaching German philosophical 'spiritualism', and 'illumination and sanctification,' which 'reaches far beyond steam-engines and hydraulic presses.[35]

But even Von Raumer is not reliable. Come lay your Frankfort hand, just above your Heidelberg or Darmstadt stomach, on your Dresden heart, and tell us with your München mouth, do you really believe the story of the factory boy's lament for pigs and poetry?[36] Did you ever with your Ingelheimer eyes, on the Royal Birthday in London, see the innumerable children with flowers and flags, or hear with your Langen Schwalbach ears their chorus of 'God save the King'? Again did you never hear with your Berlin auriculars, that row of street blackguard boys notorious *throughout* Germany, and characteristic of the Prussian capital, which Von R. with his national taste for music calls 'the prattle of little children'?[37]

As for his quizzes on our cookery (Mrs. Dilke, I am appealing to you and your old cook, who went away and is come back again), *is* English soup so sloppy that it must hide its weakness by a covering of pepper and spice? Lord help the man! he has been souping with the Sick Poor! I never saw any soup or broth in England but when cold was a perfect jelly, 'as you might chuck over the house.' As for his pepperless rice soup, *chacun à son goût*, but was not Bedreddin Hassan capitally sentenced for not putting pepper in a cream-tart?[38] What does he mean by the 'monotony of our roast beef, roast mutton, roast veal'? Why should not roast beef be roast beef, and always roast beef, like 'the bill, the whole bill, and nothing but the bill?'[39] I like that decided style. Is it any better for being, as here, roast horse, or with rank oil, or turned butter, sometimes like roast 'sea horse'? Is Williams's boiled beef any the worse for being *only* boiled beef, is it better for being here like land stock-fish? Is our roast veal worse than theirs? – how they roast it is a culinary miracle, unless on a lark spit. Their seven-day calves, and seven-year porkers ought, according to Lamb's celebrated wish about his sister, to 'throw their joint existences into one common heap!' I defy you to eat their roast mutton here, without scriptural reminiscences of rams, and burnt offerings. And then for *his* sauce about *our one* sauce for fish, don't they make pickled salmon of everything with scales, fresh or salt, with vinegar, vinegar, vinegar? As for his twaddle about Phidias and Praxiteles being French cooks, and his comparison of our joints to 'an Egyptian divinity in simple dignified repose, *with arms and legs* closely pinioned in the same position!' (he has mistaken a trussed turkey for a round of beef or a fillet of veal) I will only say a village jobbing carpenter would be ashamed of such a *style!* Egyptian indeed! don't they poison everything with garlic, and consume

Egyptian wages (onions) enough to build a new set of pyramids? Now for his Linnaeus and Jussieu, if our vegetables *do* 'appear in puris naturalibus,' is it not better than if they were in '*im*puris naturalibus,' full of 'snips and snails,' and the huge red slugs that crawl about here, in size and shape looking like live German sausages![40] How do *they* dress vegetables? Why make salads of them first, and then boil them, or *vice versâ*. I do believe the 'Devil sends cooks,' and they are German ones. The French are *artists*, the Germans are *daubers* in cookery. They are (in all that is grub-berly) lubberly, blubberly, and in regard to cleanliness, not over scrubberly! Wasn't I nearly choked once by fishbones amongst a dish of fried potatoes? 'Tis fact; and didn't I see a starved dog refuse to take the place and portion of a German gentleman unexpectedly absent from his accustomed place at the table d'hôte? Von Dilke be hanged! Catch him having a German cook at the Clarence! Haven't their own doctors discovered that their sausages contain an active poison, and is not every one of their messes a slow one? I *will* stand up for our English kitchen, especially now Jane is a cook in it. Vive Dr. Kitchener![41] if he isn't dead: and an echo responds from Düsseldorf, very like Mrs. L—'s voice, 'Vive Dr. Kitchener!' When she last wrote to Jane she was watching a hash with one eye, according to his 'oracle.' Ask Head about German cookery, he says their sauces are always either sour or greasy, but I have gone a step beyond his experience, they can be sour and greasy too.[42] And now for a triumphant clincher as to the respective merits of German and English cookery. There is a sort of *mésalliance* that occurs in England sometimes; nay I know personally of an instance, for W.C.[43] married the woman, that dressed his dinner, but I have now before me 'Der Preussiche Staat, in allen seinen Veziehungun,' an authentic work,[44] and I cannot find one instance of a German, who married his cook. This is not prejudice but statistics! But don't let this frighten you, Mrs. Dilke, from coming here, lest you should have to feast on *pommes de terre frites*. Jane can stew, and boil, and roast, and bake. You should hear her battering her beef-steaks, as if they were the children, or see Tom walk in with his little wig powdered or floured, from his mother-sick fit having interfered with her fit of pigeon-piety. You should hear De Franck congratulating her on her high health, or Miss von B. on her rosy English complexion when the real secret is fried chops. So I speak not complainingly, but critically only, of the national cuisine.

You *must* come to the grand manoeuvres (end of August), which will be well worth seeing. Better to see than be *born to*, say you. De Franck amused us much with his description of drilling the Dominies. Every man here must be a soldier, and two years is the rule; but the school-masters have the *indulgence* of only six weeks of it.

But then in those six weeks they are expected to become as proficient as the 'two year olds,' and accordingly they are hard at it, soldiering 'from morn till dewy eve'[45] – the poor sedentaries! Franck described them drawn up with round shoulders, bent thighs, and other pedagogical attributes, so weak, and so bewildered! Sometimes an unlucky Dominie mounting guard, has even to put up with the gibes, nay missiles, of his quondam scholars, whom he cannot, for once, punish. Is it not laughable to picture to oneself? What a subject for me! I must make a new revolution at Stoke Pogis,[46] and let the mayor, having been up the Rhine, attempt to form a Landwehr. You know the place Dilke; just fancy Dominie Sampson, with a musket on his shoulder, standing *at ease* on Ehrenbreitstein.[47]
Pray tell Mr. Reynolds[48] what he has escaped by being born, as Dr. Watts says, in a Christian land.[49] He is an excellent *Blue*, but would not turn up well with *Red*. What a 'six weeks' vacation!' What a march of mind for the schoolmasters abroad![50] It must seem to them like a nightmare dream, till assured of the reality, by feeling instead of the long flowing locks, affected here by the student, the bald *regulation* nape. The situation must seem as bewildering as Dr. Pangloss' with a tulip-eared bull puppy between his knees.[51] Fancy Westminsterian Braine learning the 'brain-spattering art.'[52] Imagine Dr. G— mounting guard at the Mint, or Principal O—[53] standing sentinel by the Regent's bomb, whistling 'Lawk a'mercy on us, sure this be not I,' with a pantomime change, in the distance, of the London University into Sandhurst College. Our doctor's son is doing duty as a private in De Franck's regiment, so is the son of another M.D., and they are under no slight apprehension of having to carry a knapsack at the review. How should you like a taste of that same? Imagine yourself wanting to march in *three divisions*, in request by Lord Hill,[54] Holmes,[55] and Mr. Jack Junk,[56] at the same time. Fancy Wentworth dancing at one of his mother's genteelest parties in the uniform of a private of the Tower Hamlets. And what a review you would make; mind, not a criticism. Yourself, with your eye-glass, in the Rifles; A. Cunningham in the Grenadiers; Chorley in the band; H— in the Artillery; T— a Lancer; the stout C— in the 'Light Bobs;'[57] and John F— a 'worthy Pioneer.'[58] Alas! for the 'Athenaeum!' Mrs. Dilke would have to be a suttler! By the bye we got our present lodgings in spite of the captain of the —th, who would have given five dollars a year more; but his wife, a termagant, was well known as the 'suttler,' (her nickname amongst the military), and our landlord would not have her at no price. I hope Jane won't lower his rent still further. * * * *
There are some here, in appearance to the eye, anything but gentlemen, in the best sense of the word. You cannot mistake them.

Perhaps they have got the worst attributes of the French Revolution, a *nominal equality*, which puts the low, base, vulgar, and rich on a *false level* with 'God Almighty's gentleman,'[59] which rank I do seek with all my heart; and endeavour that the English character shall not suffer at my hands, and though I resent, on public grounds, what I meet with, I am content to be a dweller here, whose character is to be judged by its own merits. But I feel the question gravely, and recommend it to your consideration. *I* may be prejudiced, but *F*— is a good witness. Give me credit for honesty, when he tells you he as readily fights, what you may call my prejudices, as those of the Germans. After all, *cui bono*, what I write? Why, after all, I appeal to the 'Athenaeum,' because it is as free from party and prejudice as myself, *and no more*. There's a hit for you, Big Ben,[60] in answer to your 'write-hander.'

Besides, it has, and must have, an influence from its honesty, impartiality, and ability, and therefore, with all my humble three dittos, I endeavour to give it the benefit of my views.

W—,[61] the other officer, says the same thing of the Rhenishers.

He calls them 'méchant,' and says they are a much better sort of people elsewhere.

He says, moreover, that some Germans, lately returned from Switzerland, have made the observation, that the people there are corrupted and deteriorated, in the same way as I judge them to be partly here. There are two subjects which form handles against us, and are rather favourite topics here, – Ireland, – and the Duke of Wellington's remarks on the discipline of the Prussian army, – which have provoked much angry discussion.

As for Ireland, I am glad to see there is a chance of righting her at last, but what a sorry figure do some of the Peers cut![62]

I have just got the Athenaeum containing Raumer. He is very flattering to us in some things, but his true picture of Ireland gives one pain, abroad, – to think what foreigners *must* conceive of our wisdom or government.[63] I doubt, however, of the wisdom of returning for a remedy to the good old times when '*mendicant* monks imparted *their* goods to the poor.' He learnt to *bull* in Ireland, seemingly. Again, I do not clearly understand whether the 'unhappy nation that has been for four-and-forty years seeking for liberty in all directions,' refers to France or England.

But, in either case, I do not agree with his prescription of 'moderation, contentedness, and humility,' by which I understand a sort of waiters on Providence, gaping for 'a thrice happy Prussian's' condition, a 'free, proprietary peasantry, – a contented and tolerant clergy, and well educated youth,' at the hands of the Tories or their equivalents. But I, perhaps, misunderstand him, – the issue, being to be Murrayan, gave me the impression.[64] The two countries are widely different; what a *good, absolute* King can do here, cannot be done with us. If our peasantry were free and proprietary, I think they would work as hard, and be as contented as the Germans. But the English labourer, labour as he may, can but be a pauper; and it seems a little unreasonable to require him to sit at Hope's or Content's table, eating *nothing*, with the same cheerfulness and gaiety as the barber's brother at the Barmecide's.[65]

They have just carried by, in procession, with boys, two and two, a *dead schoolmaster!* Poor fellow; have they drilled him to death, or is he a deserter by anticipation? What a new translation they have of '*cedant arma togae!*'[66] How would Othello's pathetic farewell to arms read to a Prussian Pedagogue? Methinks he would have the black boy well horsed for it. Well! poor * * * – is gone, and, parodying Coleridge's apostrophe on the death of the Dominie, 'May he be wafted to heaven by disembodied spirits that are no *Corporals!*'[67]

I was very much amused the other day with R—'s[68] acount of his taking an emetic. He says he sat for an hour expecting naturally something would come of it, but nothing stirred.

It agreed with him just as well as if he had taken any other wine than antimonial. It was rather comfortable than otherwise. So he had recourse to warm water, of which he drank about a dozen large cups consecutively, but they made themselves quite at home with the wine. Then he tried tea, – in hopes of 'tea and turn out,' but it staid with the wine and water. So he had recourse to the warm water again, which staid still, and so did some soup which he took on the top of all: and then, despairing of the case, he went to bed with his corporation unreformed![69] Now, was not this a tenacious, retentive stomach, so determined never to give up anything it had acquired, good or bad; a lively type of a Tory! It would make a nice little fable done into verse like Peter Pindar's.[70]

We have had several little excursions. One to the Laacher Zee, amongst the volcanic mountains. We went on Whit-Monday, but it ought to have been *Ash*-Wednesday, considering the soil of the road we went through. Their proper scavengers would have been Cinderellas. The walls and houses thereabouts are built with lava, and the lake itself is supposed to occupy an extinct crater. What a lovely, little, secluded lake it is, embosomed in trees, and perched on the crest of a mountain, not like an eagle's nest, but a water 'Roc's.' It is said to be, in the middle, 200 yards deep,[71] and the water is supernaturally clear. We fished, but of course could catch nothing, though there be huge Jack and Perch; in truth, as I could see my line from the top, of course they could see it at the bottom. There is a decayed church and cloisters, and the monkery and gardens afford delightful residence. There is also a referendarius here who does not care for it; what a taste! He is seldom there. It is a delicious spot. I honour the olden monks for the taste with which they pitched their tents. Methought as I walked in their cloisters I could have been willingly a Benedictine myself, especially when I saw a pair of huge antlers, over one of the doors, – like a sign of 'good venison within.' We have booked this place for you to visit, when you come. Indeed, we thought of you, at our 'champêtre,' and drank your healths in our wine, for as the 'hospitallers' have quitted, we had to carry our cold baked meats with us. The return was through a country reminding me of some of the romantic parts of Scotland, but on a larger scale, and more diversely wooded. Through mountain-passes, and by rapid, winding, trout-streams, we suddenly came upon Tönnenstein;[72] a little Brunnen in a lovely glen. I asked the priestess (a buxom young damsel in a Cologne cap, which you know is somewhat like a muslin soup-plate) very gravely whether the water was good for a man 'with a wife and children,' and she replied as gravely in the affirmative, handing me a glass of *bubble* without *squeak*. With wine and sugar, it drinks like champagne, but it is good neat. But, Lord! what an effervescing, gunpowder plot of ground do we Germans live upon! I scarcely seem safer than your brother at Chichester.[73] Every spring beneath us seems boiling hot, or boiling cold. And if I was a freeholder, I should feel some quakings in reckoning all between the sky and the *earth's centre* as my own. I should certainly content myself with tilling the upper crust of the soil instead of being too curious in mining. Bless us all! should our Teutonic Terra be seized with active inflammation in her stomachic regions, instead of the evident chronic one she suffers under! If we have any living Saurians below, as the Rev. Kirby opines,[74] they must be salamanders. How little do the infant Germans, with an eruption on all their heads, dream of another that may happen under their feet. We have been once or twice to Lahnstein, a favourite resort here, on the river Lahn, where we have obtained the credit of fishing with 'a spell,' on account of our success; when the old native anglers had failed, simply because we fished at the top and they at the bottom. They have no notion of fly-fishing. The only attempt we ever saw was a Captain of Engineers gravely fishing in the Moselle with a hackle-*fly* and a *worm*, at once; but the *infancy* of his art may excuse the *tops* and *bottoms*. For the sake of Mrs. Dilke, I must relate two adventures at Lahnstein, the first almost as laughable as Mr. L—'.s[75] Whilst we were fishing, all of a sudden I missed De Franck, – but spied him at last up to his neck in the middle of two rocks between which he had slipped in jumping from one to another. He made a strange figure when he came out, – the best lay figure for a River-god imaginable, – for German sporting jackets have an infinity of pockets, and there was a separate jet of water from every one, as well as from his sleeves, trousers, and each spout of his drowned moustachios (N.B. they're very long.)[76] He did not seem much improved, when, having gone to the Inn, he returned in a suit of the landlord's, who, though twice as tall, was not half so stout. However, we did not care for appearances, for we thought nobody would notice him, as it was not a holiday, and there was no company. But we were mistaken. The landlord's dog sniffed a robbery, and knowing his master's clothes again, insisted on stripping the counterfeit, and was obliged to be pulled off *vi et armis*.[77] The landlord was very much distressed, and made a thousand apologies; and, to do him justice, was a very obliging, honest, reasonable fellow, and certainly deserved to be paid better than *with his own money, out of his own waistcoat pocket*, by De Franck, as we discovered afterwards. This was the comic part, now for the tragic. In the meanwhile, Jane, whose legs are not so elephantine as they were, you will readily suppose, made shift to scramble, with Miss Von B—, up to the ruined castle of Lahn-eck.

Having seen everything on its old ground-floor, female curiosity, prevailing even over female fear, tempted them up a dilapidated staircase to one of the mouldering attics; and then, how unfortunately fortunate! some half-dozen of the topmost stairs caught the contagion of curiosity, and paid a visit to the cellars. You may imagine the duet that ensued *in a very high key* – but as you know I am deaf and De Franck was more intent on the *perch below*, than on the *perch above*, it was, consequently, a long hour (Jane says six) before they were rescued, heartily sick, you may be sure, of the local and the vocal. They swear they will never *ascend* any old ruins again, so I suppose the next time we shall have to *hoist* them out of some old subterranean.

However, the event has supplied a new lay or legend of the Rhine – only in *my* version, after a lapse of half a century, two female skeletons were found on the battlements, with their mouths wide open.[78]

These excursions have done me good every way, and joined to a *rule* of going out every practicable evening to fish in the Rhine or Moselle by way of exercise, have restored me to some strength. I have prospered in health ever since the great effusion of blood – in fact, had I been well bled at first, all would have been saved. My friends may now be easy about me – and all the rest are well. Jane and Fanny mean to bathe at a bath-house on the Rhine bridge. It is very healthy and pleasant, only the tow-rope of a barge took off the whole roof, and so frightened the female dippers, that some of them ran out and fainted on the bridge.[79]

The bath man and bath woman, concerned for their subscribers, very wisely *restored* them by carrying them all *in* again – one by one.
I am glad you liked the wine, but you must come here for the next. You may drink my improvement in Art with all my heart – but as to my sketch, the distinctness you object to is characteristic, and peculiar in Spring.
I am as clear as to that, as the atmosphere. De Franck and I verified that you could see the smoke of a pipe *beyond* the Moselle. De Franck made the remark the other day, that it was like 'seeing through a glass.' In fact, I have once or twice neglected my spectacles from not feeling the *want* of them. You must see it to believe it, I grant. Why I almost fancy myself an eagle, or at least a Dollond,[80] as I look along the mountainous horizon with the minutest shrubbery defined on it. I recollect, especially last year, when I came up the Rhine, I felt almost that I had seen gnomes and fairies – the people at work on the face of the mountains, looked so *distinct* and yet so *small*, they appeared literal dwarfs – for want of that medium mistiness which ordinarily signifies distance. The only conviction you had, sensually, of their being so remote was from the silence: you saw, but you could not hear, the blows of their pickaxes, etc. The effect is really miraculous. My eyes seemed well washed with fairy euphrasy; methought, what a pure element it must be that we German fishes now swim in! as good for the lungs as the 'Lung Arno.' Some of us find it too pure if taken neat, and so mix it with smoke.
N.B. The defunct, lately carried by with 'dirges due,' was not a schoolmaster, but a butcher, whose widow had borrowed the boys to give éclat. The Spanish general, Spinola,[81] died 'of having nothing to do,' and I suppose Lent killed the Flesher. That same Lent was a horrid invention, at least for inland towns. I hope it is not the bad fish, but they are dying here on all hands, – two or three children a day. Thank God, we seem in a little Goshen, all well! But we have had an omen, at least equal to a raven on the chimney-pot. The children are just come in from a walk, and a *strange* doctor stopped Fanny, and talked to her in the street!

I have never had any of the vulgar insane dread of the Catholics. It appears to me too certain that they are decaying *at the core*, and by the following natural process:– men take a huge stride at first from Catholicism into Infidelity, like the French, and then by a short step backwards in a reaction, attain the *juste milieu*. You see I philosophise, but it is in the air of Germany; only I do not smoke with it.
I cannot help agreeing with Von Raumer about English music; I am deaf and have heard as little good as he; but why sneer at our buying *better?* If we purchased Italian, we paid lately the same compliment to the German. I believe in their 'real

music,' but as for their 'real song' I have a creed that the 'sickly sentimentality' is as much a characteristic of the best German as the worst English.[82] As for our painters, whom he despises, let him show me a German Turner (except of the stomach), a Stanfield, an Etty,[83] a Stump, a Gump. They are as unheard of as our musicians, except a notorious German, who daubed for George the Fourth.[84] But when were the German artists pictorially great with pen or pencil? Fuseli represented both classes.[85] In their sublimest they introduce the ridiculous, whereas a real genuine Kentuckian in his ridiculous approaches the sublime. I would rather, as to style prefer the last. Fair play's a jewel: if you want examples, I'll give them to you out of Goethe himself. We had a specimen of their fine arts yesterday, on a flag carried before a funeral: on one side was a Virgin and Child, both *dark*, mulatto, as if inclining to Lord Monboddo's theory that Adam was *black*, or half-and-half[86] – whereas, on the other side was a bishop, *in pontificalibus*, blessing three little children in a literal washing-tub, washed as fair as an English mother could desire[87] – as Jane, for instance. This is fact, and it is as fair to judge from it as from the drawings of lap-dogs and poodles at our Society of Arts, an imbecility long since marked down as a subject for the 'Comic' – with that void Aiken,[88] at its head or tail, whom Coleridge used to compare to an 'Aching void!' *Apropos* of Art, in the palace here; in the concert-room, there was to have been a series of frescos from the 'Last Judgment' of Rubens, very appropriate supposing the orchestra *all trumpets*. But as the laws of *acoustics* only had been neglected, the concert-room was abandoned, and it is now devoted to the sittings of assize when the frescos would be of some relevance, and accordingly they are *not* there. I have this on the authority of Schreiber, the guide-man, noticed shortly before Raumer, to whom I owe a grudge and will pay it. As the Americans say, if they *poke* their *fun* at me,[89] I will poke again.

I am hard at work at my 'Comic,' somewhat puzzled for subjects, as most of my foreign ones must go to the German book, which I want to make as good as possible.

I do get the 'Athenaeum,' though somewhat more tardily than formerly, and it is a great treat. It *ought* to be very successful. We admired much the articles on Talfourd's 'Ion,' and Taylor's political book: my mind misgives me they are yours.[90] Pray write as often as you can. Jane desires me to say she longs for Mrs. Dilke's promised letter. As for myself, you will not soon have some more last words. But I do live in hope of meeting you bodily this autumn, and would write a whole 'Athenaeum' (a double one) to *help you out*.

Methinks *fat* as most of the company would be, we should almost talk ourselves into

consumptions. Mind, no more Margate! If I chalk all along the dead wall in Grosvenor Place, it would be, 'Ask for Coblenz,' 'Try the Rhine,' 'Beware of Dublin,' 'Inquire for Alten Graben!'
We often fancy ourselves in your family circle, and wish you could take a stick to it, and trundle it over here. Pray remember us kindly to everybody, to William and Wentworth, and the rest of the family, 'by hook and by *Snook*.'[91] Desire Fanny Staunton to add moustachios to my portrait, and put a pipe in my mouth.[92]
Jane goes all lengths with me in her love, and so does Fanny, and so would Hood jun. if he could, as he should. The manoeuvres will begin the last week in August, and then the King will be here; so, dear Mrs. Dilke, mind you keep Dilke in marching order. I have only post time to add God bless you all in my more serious style, which some prefer to my comic, and Jane says Amen religiously, though she has fished of a Sunday. She denies it, and I believe it is an error – she only went to an equestrian play.

Mind the address – as the quacks say – of, Dear Dilke,
Yours every truly,

Thomas Hood.

I forgot to mention that the soldiers have an odd-sounding mode of suicide. As *ball* is hard to get at, they sometimes shoot themselves with *water*, – which blows the head to atoms worse than shot. Now for something in the grand style. One fellow, in the true spirit of the *German sublime*, did it with a forty-eight pounder, and went off with *éclat*. How proud some Charlotte must have been of such a Werter!

At Herr Deubel's, / 752, Alten Graben, Coblenz, June 20th, 1836.

From *Memorials* I 151–87. There is an hiatus in the text after the first paragraph.
1/The title of an illustration in *Up the Rhine* facing 303
2/'Unlucky Joe,' a character in Hood's novel *Tylney Hall*
3/The name unidentified
4/Names unknown
5/Friedrich von Raumer's *England in 1835* was reviewed before English publication and with copious extracts in *The Athenaeum* February 1836, between 97 and 145. Mrs Sarah Austin's translation was reviewed in *The Athenaeum*, 26 March.
6/Play on the name of Wordsworth's character
7/LeSage *Gil Blas* VI I
8/*Athenaeum* 30 January 1836, 81–2
9/*Hamlet* I ii 144
10/In this story Schreiber said that the only intercourse he had with an Englishman staying in the same hotel was when the Englishman presented him with a Bible.
11/The accusation not of Schreiber but of his *Athenaeum* reviewer

12/This observation occurs in *Tutti Frutti* 133.
13/Mrs Trollope *Belgium and Western Germany in 1833* I 183, 184 and II 182, 183
14/Revelations 13:17
15/See note 5 above
16/Cicero *Tusculanae disputationes* 5, xxxvi 105
17/*Galignani's Messenger*, published at Paris
18/Hood's uncertainty about the name of *The Albion* is understandable, since this newspaper was discontinued at the end of 1835.
19/*Eugene Aram* (1833)
20/A reference to the *Penny Magazine* (1832–45) published by Charles Knight for the Society for the Diffusion of Useful Knowledge
21/Unidentified
22/Hood's son notes that his father made use of this text in a song included in *Up the Rhine*, in *Works* VII 65–7.
23/Sheridan *School for Scandal* 2 ii
24/Unidentified
25/*Up the Rhine*
26/Scott *Redgauntlet* ch xx
27/Dilke himself
28/*Macbeth* 5 v 11
29/Karl Friedrich Zelter (1758–1832), musician, was a friend of Goethe. Their correspondence was published in 1833–4. I have not been able to trace his phrase.
30/*Tempest* 2 ii 155
31/Unidentified
32/See 240.
33/Pugilist
34/Brian Simon *Studies in the History of Education* (1960) 114, writes: 'Out of the chaos of competing private schools there had begun to emerge, in the late 1820s and early 30s, the new, specifically middle-class proprietary schools.'
35/Raumer's phrases were quoted in *Athenaeum* 1836, 127.
36/Raumer had put into the mouth of a factory boy a long speech which included the phrase: 'How much do I long to be back with my swine,' *Athenaeum* 125. By using the city names in this sentence Hood is making fun of his Germanophile friend.
37/*Athenaeum* 124, 123
38/In the *Arabian Nights' Entertainments*
39/The cry which had been raised especially in *The Times*, over the Reform Bill of 1832
40/Raumer discusses English cookery *Athenaeum* 1836, 142.
41/William Kitchiner (1775?–1827), miscellaneous writer, wrote (1817) *Apicius Redivivus, or the Cook's Oracle.*
42/Francis Bond Head *Bubbles from the Brunnens of Nassau* 70
43/Identified as W.B. Cooke in a MS version of this part of the letter in the Bristol Central Library
44/By Leopold von Zedlitz (Berlin 1836–7)
45/Milton *Paradise Lost* I 742–3
46/Hood refers to 'The Parish Revolution' in the *Comic Annual* for 1831, *Works* I 89–101.
47/A reference to Scott *Guy Mannering* ch. xxx
48/George Reynolds, Hood's father-in-law, writing master at Christ's Hospital. Blue is the Christ's Hospital colour.
49/Isaac Watts *Divine Songs* vi

50/'The schoolmaster is abroad, and I trust to him armed with his primer, against the soldier in full military array,' Brougham, speech at the opening of parliament, January 1828. 'The march of mind' and 'The schoolmaster is abroad' were phrases used in connection with Brougham's campaign for the wider diffusion of knowledge.
51/In Voltaire's *Candide* Pangloss was sentenced to the galleys where he 'received twenty lashes a day with a bull's pizzle,' ch. XXVIII (tr. 1759) 123.
52/Byron *Don Juan* ix 4. I have not identified Braine, or 'Dr G.' in the following sentence.
53/Possibly the Reverend William Otter (1768–1840), principal of King's College, London, from its inception in 1831 until 1836, when he became bishop of Chichester. He contributed a paper on the death of Malthus to *The Athenaeum* 10 January 1835, 32–4.
54/Perhaps General Sir Rowland Hill (1772–1842)
55/James Holmes, printer of *The Athenaeum*
56/A hero of Charles Dibdin *Songs* (1842) 147
57/I have not identified the names here.
58/*Hamlet* I v 163. Reference here is possibly to John Forster (1812–76), historian and biographer, friend of Hunt and Lamb, possibly contributor to *The Athenaeum*, certainly critic in *The Examiner*. Forster was called to the bar in 1843. He was also the friend of Dickens and Hood.
59/Dryden, 'Absalom and Achitophel,' i 645
60/Big Ben Brain (d. 1784), pugilist
61/Perhaps Wildegans named on 271
62/'On the 17th May, the House of Lords rejected the clauses of a ministerial bill which went to re-construct the Irish corporations' in favour of the Catholics, *Annual Register* (1836) 299.
63/*Athenaeum* 1836, 99
64/The meaning of this passage is obscure.
65/In *Arabian Nights' Entertainments*
66/Cicero *De Officiis* i 22
67/Coleridge's apostrophe is quoted in Lamb's 'Christ's Hospital Five and Thirty Years Ago.'
68/Probably Ramponi
69/The Municipal Corporation Act became law at the end of 1835.
70/John Wolcot (1738–1819), popular satirist and poet, wrote under this name.
71/About 175 feet, according to Karl Baedaker *The Rhine* (14th ed 1900) 103
72/This should be Tönnisstein.
73/A reference to the Chichester earthquakes, see 155.
74/William Kirby *On the Power Wisdom and Goodness of God as manifested in the Creation of Animals* (1835) I 32–3
75/Probably Mr Lindo although the nature of the adventure is not known
76/Illustrated as 'The Water Kelpy' in *Up the Rhine* facing 276
77/Cicero *Ad pontifices* xxiv
78/'The Tower of Lahneck,' published in NMM February 1842, and *Works* VIII 156–68
79/Used in *Up the Rhine*, *Works* VII 201–2
80/George Dollond (1774–1852), celebrated optician
81/Ambrogio de Spinola (1569–1630)
82/Hood is referring to *Athenaeum* 1836, 143
83/Joseph Mallord Turner (1775–1851). In 1834 he illustrated the works of Byron, Rogers, and Scott. Clarkson Stanfield (1793–1864), elected RA 1835, friend of Dickens. William Etty (1787–1849).
84/John Hoppner (1758–1810), the son of German parents, rumoured to be an illegitimate son of George III, in 1789 appointed portrait-painter to the Prince Regent, later George IV

85/Henry Fuseli (1741–1825), born in Switzerland, came to England in 1763.
86/The original theories of James Burnett, Lord Monboddo (1714–99), do not appear to take him so far.
87/Hood's son notes: 'This was a representation of St Nicholas restoring to life the "Three Young Men of Noble Family," ' *Memorials* I 184.
88/Arthur Aikin (1773–1854), scientific writer, secretary of the Society of Arts, 1817–40
89/For the first American use of this expression Craigie and Hulbert *Dictionary of American English*, give 1815. For the first English use NED gives Hood's *Up the Rhine*.
90/*Athenaeum*, 28 May, contained reviews of Talfourd's play and Henry Taylor's *Statesman*.
91/Dilke's sister's married name
92/Unidentified. The portrait to which Hood refers might be a copy of that probably painted at Wanstead by William Hilton RA.

TO
CHARLES WENTWORTH DILKE

My dear Dilke,
You will wonder at hearing from me so soon again, but it is a broken day, and an epistolary one, as I have other letters to write – and perhaps the French letter will be worth the postage;[1] and, above all, I have a positive pleasure in writing to, as well as receiving letters from you. You see I can make as many good excuses for writing, as others for their silence. But the truth is, I have not many correspondents, nor many conversables; so that I select you, both to write to and to talk to on paper – for fear I should die of that most distressing of complaints, a suppression of ideas. I do not, however, though I am in Germany, pretend to open a regular account of debtor and creditor, and expect you to liquidate every letter of mine, as if it were a foreign bill of exchange, by an equivalent on your own side. I know your time is too valuable to be so drawn upon, and so is mine too; but, then, for me to write to you is a matter of recreation. You have *too much* of that of which I have *too little* – society; so that if I choose to call on you, or leave my card, *i.e.* letter, I do not peremptorily expect your returning my visits. Now we understand each other; and *should* you ever tire of my billets, you can give me a genteel cut, by returning my last under cover, which ought to be equivalent to 'not at home;' or you can get Mrs. Dilke to make spills of them, for I hate my writings to be of no use to any one; a case, I believe, peculiar to my 'Plea of the Fairies.'[2] I had, I remember, to bid myself for the waste, for fear of their going to the book-stalls. So you can publish my letters if you do not like them, and trust to my buying up the remainders.

We are all well – as well as the heat, that is to say, will let us be. But we never had, as apparently all the world has had, a stranger season. First, a long, cold, wet spring; and then, all at once, out of the ice-pail into the frying-pan, like preserved fish. Our powers of contraction and expansion were well tried. I am, as you may guess, not strong, and wonder I did not become literally *friable*. At mental work I sat in a room (always in shade) with the glass at 80; and at bodily work at a true African heat.

We went one day to see the Royal Iron-works at Sayn,[3] and really, with all the great furnaces and the ladlefuls of glowing red liquid metal, the process going on under a *roof*, the sun seemed to heat the fire, without any great bellows.

One day, while fishing at Lahneck, De Franck and I pursued a trout stream till it ended in what I have several times observed about here, where there is water. There was a sort of earthy cauldron sloping down, almost a regular circle, till you came to a level surface of meadow and water, as the Laacher Zee. The whole country is volcanic – tremendously so, if you think of all the hot springs – a real Solfaterra.[4] Extinct crater, or not, I felt *boiled dry* in it, till I longed to plunge into the clear little stream before me, so cool, so clear; but probably it would have been my death; for, do you know, trout live here in rivers too *cold* for any other fish, and we caught nothing but trout, nor has anybody else. However, in this beautiful picturesque bottom I almost *devilled* myself, without curry or cayenne – in spite of a queer brown holland smock-frock, garnished (as the Germans cannot do even *simplicity* without a flourish) with a flowing brown holland frill! It was one of their sporting costumes, lent me by De Franck; and whilst wearing this, and he in another like thereunto, we had deposited our ordinary coats at a house in the village. And here note, for I wish to be just, that the conservators of our said coats would not, without the greatest difficulty, accept a doit – I ought to say a groschen – for their trouble, although Germans, and *Jews*. I had, perforce, to give it to a poor sick boy, as an excuse for leaving it, and whom I singled out with a sort of Irish philanthropy, to prove we are all Christians. I wish I could hope to give him another little piece of *bad* silver (you know, of course, the *washed*, or rather apparently *unwashed* face of Friedrich Wilhelm on our Prussian coinage), but he seemed destined to abstract a unit from the gross sum of the twelve tribes at present in existence. Set this off against my last picture of the people of these parts, and lament with me that you must go *from* the Rhine to meet with *natures* that correspond with its natural beauties. Perhaps I am wrong; I know you think I am prejudiced, but I think I am not. Every day fresh *facts*, not fancies, corroborate my views. You will find a new one in my notice of M.[5] The imposition, I know, was

made light of, and made a joke of even, as against the English.
I could quote political reasons for this jealousy, which certainly does obtain, besides more private ones. Namely, under the heads of free trade, probable union of France, Belgium, and England against the Holy Family, alias Holy Alliance, which I guess is a main head and front,[6] besides avarice and envy, and most exaggerated notions of our wealth. I am translating a *serious* tale, illustrative of England from the 'Zeitung,' where a lady of Euston Square offers £50,000 *per annum*, a mine in '*Cornwales*,' and £20,000 in 'East India Actions' (? shares),[7] as a reward for finding her lost child. The lady dies – the King's carriage and all the nobility go to the funeral; the will bequeaths *all her property* to the *finder*, and nothing to the child; and the said child is eventually found by a dog called 'Fog'! Imagine a *London fog* finding anything! And these are 'Sketches of our Manners,' gravely written and read on the Rhine – one of our thoroughfares!! It will make a good chapter in my book as a German exercise!

752, Alten Graben, 12th July, 1836.

From *Memorials* I 187–91
1/I do not understand Hood's reference.
2/Hood's volume *The Plea of the Midsummer Fairies* sold poorly. According to his daughter, Hood himself 'bought up the remainder of the edition,' *Memorials* I 22.
3/In *Memorials* the name is spelt with an *umlaut* over the 'a'.
4/Mass of sulphur, NED
5/Review untraced
6/*Othello* I iii 80
7/The meaning given in NED. The parenthetical query may be that of Hood's daughter, editing the letter.

TO
ALFRED HEAD BAILY

Dear Baily, I send you an Announcement, & a *correct* list of the Mottoes to the Cuts. You have of course received the box with the blocks, ere this will come to hand. I must write to Mr Scott[1] per next box, for Coblentz now pulls me different ways. It is all alive – & I *must* see the Camp, & yet finish the Comic. Your brother has not put in an appearance – & I want the two articles left over last year very sadly. I hope to heaven they be not lost – but I hate to prophesy for fear of turning out a

Profit – the same as a loss. Should any curiosity arise from the announcement, as to my politics, *you must play the mysterious, & refer to the Annual.*[2] And mind – do not let the cuts get abroad. You will soon have all – I am well, & busy

Yrs very truly Thos Hood.

[*Koblenz, 30 August 1836*]

MS editor. Address: 'Messrs Baily & Co / 83. Cornhill / London.' PM: 'COBLENZ 6–7/30/8,' 'LONDON/5/SEP/1836.'

1/J. Scott designed several of the plates for the *Comic Annual* for 1837.
2/The announcement is printed in *Athenaeum* 1 October 1836, 708, and *Works* VI 331–4.

TO
JANE HOOD

My own dearest & best love, my kind & good Jane,
I send you a packet for Baily – The Love Lane is longer by some verses, so send the present copy[1] – so much for business – now for the pleasant.
We parted manfully & womanfully – as we ought. I drank only a ½ bottle of wine, & only the ½ of that ere I fell asleep on the sofa, which lasted two hours. It was the reaction – for your going tired me more than I cared to show. Then I drank the rest – & as that did not do I went & retraced our walk in the park *& sat down on the same* seat, – & I felt happier & better. – Have you not a romantic old Husband?
Today I had some pain, – but I had written hard – and I resolved at dinner, out of prudence, & to set you at ease, to ask for advice – when good fortune engaged me in *english* conversation with a young German Physician – a capital fellow, & over a bottle of champagne, between us, I frankly asked his advice & stated my symptoms. He [jumped] at once on the cause, asked if I had travelled [long in] one position &c – I gave the history of our journey & said that it was nothing else than what I supposed a cold in the pectoral muscles, from *that* night ... I am to wear flannel on the chest & that is all – there is nothing to apprehend. As this coincides with my own views I hope it will set you *quite at rest* on the subject, – & that you will thank me for putting it out of doubt. He was a nice fellow & we are to meet again at Berlin: I go off tonight at 7 & have little time – but I refer you to my song for my feeling.[2] My spirits are *high* almost. I think you will like the Desert Born.[3] Kiss my darling Fanny & Tom for me, over & over. – my next will not be so hurried. – I hope you got home well & found all so – Kindest love to Dilkes if they remain – I

have a world to say to you & them – but must send my terrestrial globe of talk some other time. I am highly pleased – & no disgusts. God bless you ever & ever – Kiss my boy & my girl for me, & try to find some way to kiss yourself on the same account. Be cheerful my own as I am in the hope of again being, face to face

Your own body & soul, here & hereafter,

Thos Hood

Gotha. – [*18 October 1836*]

MS Bristol Central Library. Address: 'Madame Hood / 752 Alten Graben / Coblentz / Sur Rhein.' PM: 'GOTHA /18 OCT 1837,' 'COBLENZ 7–8M/20/10.' Published in Memorials I 202–3. The date is that of the postmark, though there the year is mistakenly given as 1837. Hood's friends the Dilkes came over at the end of September 1836, but on 11 October Hood and Jane left them. At Gotha, five days later, they separated; Jane returned home, and Hood joined with the regiment to which Franck belonged and marched with it to Berlin. Such a journey he had long purposed, in order to gather material for 'a work ... something like [Head's] "Brunnens," and yet not like it,' *Memorials* I 142.

1/In the *Comic Annual* for 1837

2/Perhaps 'A Toast,' in *Works* VI 330, though Hood's son thinks that this was written on his mother's birthday, 6 November.

3/Included in the *Comic Annual* for 1837

TO

JANE HOOD

Arrival at Halle.

My own dearest & best Jane.

I feel quite happy & more for your sake than my own, that I have nothing but good news to communicate. I got to Halle yesterday rather late, 4 or 5 in the afternoon – there was a short examination of passports at Erfurt & mine was refused a vizé or frizzé as Heilmann[1] calls it – I believe because it was in French – the Dumm Kopf! but I came boldly on, & found Franck domesticated, – I ought to say quarter'd, but it would sound like cutting up, in *Butcher* Street, – the very place for filling one's cavities. After some good beer & bread & cheese, by way of dinner, & a rest – we went in the evening, settled all the passport affair right, – & then went to headquarters. My reception was very gratifying indeed, they all seemed really glad to see me, – & Franck's Captain was particularly friendly: I quite regret my loss of German as he is very merry & likes to talk. There were some gentlemen from

Merseburg who had known some of the officers when the battallion was formerly quartered there, – & all was jollity. They too were very friendly – & I felt quite at home & more over supped on the famous Leipzig larks, – things Martin of [?] Street would lick the lips of his heart at.[2] Finally I packed up my trunk &c – went to bed & slept soundly – & dreamt don't be jealous, for we cannot command our dreams (I wish I could!) but it was of little Tom God bless him. I rose, with the larks – was well up to my time, – marched to the muster – mounted my nag – & here I am at ¼ past 1, writing to you, after completing not only my first march, but a hearty dinner. Luck turned at last, – for I rose without any pain, for the first time, & consequently in good spirits I am delighted with my nag, Franck has got him into such excellent order; I was only *off him* twice, but thank heaven without hurting myself, as it was merely dismounting according to the regular mode when we halted. Tell Tibby[3] he walks after Franck & knows him like a dog: – I expect to be equally friends with him – by feeding him with bread. Fanny herself could ride him – & I only fear I shall be sorry to part with him at last. I rode so well as to pass muster for a trooper – & *did* the turnpikes. At one village a man said 'there goes the Doctor!' The morning was beautiful – the road good & straight as a line over the immense plains / near / round Leipzig – where so many a battle has been fought. For some distance I rode between the Captain & a gentleman in plain clothes: – it turn'd out he had formerly been a soldier in the batallion & is now a Professor, – & there was I the author turn'd soldier! I did wish you could have gone with us – the first halt was very amusing – such miscellaneous breakfasting – & a boy with a large tin of hot sausages sold all off in a minute to his surprise, & regret that he had not brought a whole barrow full. The Colonel passed in a carriage: – I did not see him but he stopped Franck to ask if I was there, & sent his Compts. – Tell Fanny I was introduced to Minna's father[4] – Minna is not going to leave Coblentz yet so that she can have her with her sometimes, before she goes. I assure you I found myself getting better every mile – & when we got here, about 10 o'clock I felt so fresh, indeed not even stiff, that I could not believe the march was ended. I expected to feel stiff in the back – but not a bit of it.

From Gotha to Halle was somewhat tedious, in a byewaggon[5] – without any adventure save one. At supper, for we did not leave till 9, there were two gentlemen one of whom talked with me a good deal in my bad German – but to my surprise when we had gone some miles he addressed me in English. We sat together in the coupé & gossipped nearly the whole night on England, Bowring,[6] Campbell[7] &c &c &c. He told me he had been an emigré from Germany on account of his politics which had got him into great trouble – & had held an office, at the London

University, but having settled his differences with Government, is a Professor at some College in Prussia. Perhaps Dilke will know who he is.[8] I have had very good quarters as yet. Bill of fare today – roast pork ditto goose with apples – good soup – good beer – pickled cherries – celery roots – large & round sliced as turnips – lamb's milk cheese stuck full of carraways – I should like to see *your* face at the last article. I have no more to say in the victualling line – except that Franck caught Heilmann ramming matches into his cayenne by mistake for a fire: bottle.

And now dearest & best & own, for yourself. It delights me to hope & think that whilst I am writing you are at home, safe & well – & just now sitting down – it should be – to dinner with our pretty little pair – perhaps with the pretty big pair besides – you know who I mean. It was fine weather for you, & it was in favour of your impatience that you would travel quickest nearest home. I hope you enjoyed the Rhine from Mayence. I shall long eagerly to know about you all, whether Dilkes are gone & how he was &c – & you bore your solitary travel. I have thought of you continually with delight, & comfort, & heart's content, – and I enjoy by sympathy before hand the joy you will feel in reading this, a *true* & not *flattering* picture of my mind body & estate. I feel really as well as I say, & have now no doubt of getting very very much better if not quite restored by this trip – with other advantages to boot. So pluck up your dear affectionate heart – & let kind & pleasant thoughts make amends for this our beneficial separation. For me I am in such good humour withal I think I shall never be irritable again. – and I am very sober drinking only beer. (There is a bunch of comforts for you like the posies chucked in at a coach window!) Keep in mind, as I do, all our mutual promises!) We drank your health in the same: – excuse the liquor. – I must ramble on how I can having to take a sleep & then go at evening to meet the others – perhaps to play at whist, halfpenny points. We are in a prettyish village – & among people the reverse of Rhinelanders. The sudden change from marching soldiers &c is quite laughable – look out of window & there is not a trace of military – not even a cap – all are indoors, snoozing &c. – In the evening we shall swarm like bees. The weather seems set in fine. Franck talks of introducing me to the Radziwills – they are likely to be in Berlin from a marriage of one of the Princesses. He will write to you next – as I shall be busy – but I determined to show you today, by a long letter, how well I was after my march. I shall also write a few lines to Fanny who I hope loves you for me, & helps & pleases you all she can. Pray do not fail to write – but I am sure you will have written ere this comes to hand. If the Dilkes be not gone give my love to them – & say all that is kind – I left them in a sad hurry & had not even time to thank Mrs D without whom I should never have been launched. Tell her I shall be as grand over my March, as if I had cross'd the Simplon. I spend very little now for self & horse every thing is cheap & the extortionate spirit not awakened yet if it exist much in the style of the Bauer. If you write of your journey faithfully to your Mother, the break down in the field & all, I suspect it will be verdict 'sarve 'em right. Hood & Jane are both gone mad together.'[9] Do not forget to make the arrangement with Poltgeisser,[10] as I shall go on I expect as far as I can consistent with certainty of getting back. – The officers who were in love seemed reconciled to their fate. I have found 'my own Carlovicz' again – only time to shake hands – but expect him this evening. Wildegans[11] is well again – but gone forward two hours farther than us – he was with me all the way nearly. It will be our turn next I guess for a long spell – but I could have gone much further today than we did. I seriously think it will save me – for I was going into a bad low way irritable in body & mind – a plague to you & a curse to myself. But that is past:– & now you have nothing to make you uneasy about me. Pray enjoy yourself wherever you can & let me find you well and happy when I come back: I have promised the captain to get fat under his command – & think I shall make you happier, as you make much of me now, by making more of myself. God bless you again & again, as you deserve my own good & true wife – my heart is all your own, & would ache for you, if I did not, & could not have you so constantly & vividly before me. I envy your kisses from little Tom & my Fanny. I know my name is very often on all your lips. Hug them well for me the darlings, & bless them both. If you can think of any kind words & fondness for me to your self, fancy such words & deeds as would please you best, & give me credit for them all. Think that I send you a thousand kisses on the wings of wishes, – & call you all those many names you have borne in my love since we first met. I am glad I wrote that song for you for I know you will read it sometimes – and believe that I felt what I wrote.[12] I fear you will have no more long letters till comic is done – but am I not good for this one? I am quite repaid by the anticipation of your pleasure in it. – Franck sends his love – and I am sure all the others would send messages if they were here. And now dearest kindest, best, my paper grows short – but a long & fervent blessing is upon you – nor could any paper my own contain all I feel to you, beyond writing & beyond saying – the dear finger, with the ring at my lips could only explain it for

Your ever affectionate & faithful husband

Thos Hood.

I fear you will have to copy what I send you (of M.S.S) for fear of their miscarrying. I sent you a packet from Gotha.

My dear Fanny.
I hope you are as good still as when I went away – a comfort to your good Mother & a kind playfellow to your little brother. Mind you tell him my horse eats bread out of my hand, & walks up to the officers who are eating, & pokes his nose into the women's baskets. I wish I could give you both a ride. I hope you like your paints – pray keep them out of Tom's way as they are poisonous. I shall have rare stories to tell you when I come home: but mind you must be good till then or you will find me as mute as a stockfish. Your Ma' will show you on the map where I was when I wrote this – & when she writes will let you put in a word. You would have laughed to see your friend Wildegans running after the sausage boy to buy a würst – There was hardly an officer without one in his hand smoking hot. The men piled their guns on the grass & sat by the side of the road, all munching at once like ogres. I had a pocket full of bread & butter, which soon went into my cavities as Mrs Dilke calls them. I only hope I shall not get so hungry as to eat my horse. I know I need not say keep school & mind your book, as you love to learn. You can have Minna sometimes her Pa' says. Now God bless you my dear little girl, my pet, – and think of Your loving Father.

T. Hood

This letter will be a treat for you.

[*Halle, 20 October 1836*]

MS Bristol Central Library. Address: 'Madame Hood / 752 Alten Graben / Coblentz / Sur Rhein.' PM: 'BRENHA/20 10,' 'COBLENZ 8M/23/10.' Published in part in *Memorials* I 204–9. The date, excluding the year, is that of the postmark.

1/Probably a comrade of De Franck, whom the Hoods had known at Koblenz
2/Perhaps John Martin the painter, though his address was Allsop Terrace
3/Nickname for Fanny Hood
4/Unidentified
5/German, 'Beiwagen,' meaning extra coach
6/John Bowring (1792–1872), linguist, writer, politician and traveller, contributor to the *London Magazine* and *The Athenaeum,* editor of the *Westminster Review* from 1824 to 1836. In 1838 Bowring helped form the Anti-Corn Law League, and later tried to involve Hood in that undertaking. He was knighted for political services in China in 1854.
7/Thomas Campbell (1777–1844), Scottish poet, edited the NMM (1820–30). His idea concerning the University of London was discussed in the NMM circle, publicly proposed in 1825, and realised three years later.
8/Hood's travelling companion may have been Ludwig von Mühlenfels (1793–1861), a man who 'played a notable part in the history of German unification.' He was imprisoned from 1819 to 1821, when he escaped to Sweden. He was appointed to the chair of German, itself an innovation, at the University of London in 1827, being 'in personal touch with much of that which was most vital in

German thought.' He wrote for the *Foreign Review* and published two textbooks, before returning to Germany in 1831: H. Hale Bellot *University College London* (1929) 120–2.
9/Jane describes her journey, *Memorials* I 195–7.
10/Unidentified
11/Carlovicz and Wildegans were comrades of De Franck, with whom Hood had been friendly at Koblenz.
12/Probably the song which Hood wrote when he first came to Europe. See 176.

TO
JANE HOOD

From having gone through woods, full of old stumps and roots of trees, without a fall, I begin to pique myself on my horsemanship, but yesterday got into a bit of a caper. I was anxious to inquire at the post-office of Belitz, so had to get before the others, which I all but effected, when, just entering the town in a narrow street, I was obliged to wait with my horse's nose just against the big drum, which he objected to pass; but I contrived to keep him dancing between the band and the regiment. I was more lucky than a captain in Coblenz, whose horse ran away with him slap through the band, all of whom he upset, breaking their instruments to the tune of 300 dollars damages. I am glad I did not know this at the time.

We rise at four, and march about five or half past: it is moonlight earlier, but then becomes dark, so I march till I can see the road, and then mount; after about three quarters of an hour we halt for a quarter of an hour, and then on again to the general rendezvous, overtaking or passing other companies on the road, for we are quartered sometimes widely apart. At the rendezvous we halt and breakfast – a sort of picnic – each bringing what he can: if I had been searched yesterday they would have found on me two cold pigeons, and a loaf split and buttered. I have learned to forage, and always clear the table at my quarters into my pockets.

It is an amusing scene when we sit down by the roadside; some of the officers, who have had queer quarters, bring sketches of them; one the other day had such a ruinous house for his, that his dog stood and howled at it.[1] At the inn at Kremnitz,[2] I had dinner, supper, bed and breakfast for 7 good groschen, about 11 pence! Think of that, ye Jewish Rhinelanders. Many of them moreover returned the common soldiers the five groschen the king allows for their billeting, and gave them a glass of schnaps besides. They are a friendly, kind people, and meet you with the hand held out to shake, and say 'Welcome.' I like the Saxons much. Then we marched to Wittenberg, where a Lieut. J—, an old friend of Franck's, made us dine

with him at the military Casino.[3] He spoke French, and I found him very intelligent, and somewhat literary, so we got on well. He asked me if we English had not a prejudice against the Germans, and I assured him quite the reverse.
He seemed pleased, and said, 'To be sure we are of the same race' (Saxons). He took me over the town, famous as one of Luther's strongholds. His statue conveyed the very impression I had from a late paper in the 'Athenaeum,'[4] a sturdy friar, with a large thick-necked jowly[5] head, sensual exceedingly, – a real sort of bull-dog to pin the pope's bull. From thence we went to Pruhlitz to our quarters, which were queerish; Franck was put in a room used as the village church, and I in the ball-room; we were certainly transposed. Our second quarters were at Nichel near Truenbritzen.[6] We arrived after a march of eight hours and a half; think of that for me! and I came in all alive and kicking. We got at it over wide barren heaths, and plenty of deep sand. Our billet was on the Burgomaster, or schultze, and his civic robe was a sheepskin with the wool inward, the usual wintry dress in those bleak parts. The lady mayoress a stout, plump, short-faced *mutterkin*, with a vast number of petticoats to make amends for shortness. I told my host I was an English burgomaster, so we kept up a great respect and fellowship for each other. You would have laughed to see Bonkowski[7] hugging and kissing the Frau – it is reckoned an honour – and the husbands stand and look on; we shook hands all round, and then dined; I was not too curious about the cookery, and ate heartily. Every time I came to the window, a whole group in sheepskins, like baa lambs on their hind legs, pointed me out to each other, and took a good stare, so I suppose Englanders are rarities. At leaving, the Burgomaster inquired very anxiously about me, and being, as he thought, in the way to get information, he said he had heard of *Flanders*, and wanted to know if it was money like *florins*! There was a Worship for you!

We had but two beds, one for me, and one for Bonkowski, and Franck was on the straw.
Thence we went to Schlunkendorf (what a name!) near Belitz; quartered at a miller's, very clean and wholesome, but only two beds, so Franck was littered down again. I wanted the host to give him corn instead of straw by mistake, and then come and thrash them both out together. I forgot to say the little captain called on me at Pruhlitz to see how I was, and took tea with us. Last night I called on Bonkowski, who was opposite to us; I found him flirting with the Frau. I told her I had come 50,000 miles, was married at 14, and had 17 children; and as I was in yellow boots, and Mrs. D.'s present of a robe, and really looked a Grand Turk, she

believed me like Gospel. We made a Welch rabbit for supper, and then played loo till bed-time for pfennings; I had a young officer for our third instead of Bonkowski. This morning I rode over from Schlunkendorf to Belitz, Heilman taking back the mare, where I found your welcome letter, and started by diligence to Potsdam, where I am, having just eaten a capital dinner – chiefly a plate of good English-like roasted mutton – and a whole bottle of genuine English porter. I am to brush up here to see them parade before the king to-morrow morning.
Then a day's rest here, and then to Berlin. After the parade, a party of us are going to Sans Souci, and so forth, sight seeing. Franck hopes to introduce me to the Radziwills at Berlin; I have no pain, and really wonder how I *march*. But I had made up my heart and mind to it, and that is everything; it keeps me, I think, from falling off my horse, I am so determined to stick to him, and keep my wits always about me: in fact I quite enjoy it, and only wish I could return so, 'tis so much better than being jammed up in a diligence, and, says *you*, 'less dangerous!'[8]
Pray tell me dear *good* Fanny that at Schlunkendorf, there was a tame robin, that killed all the flies in the room, hopped on the table, and the edges of our plates, for some dinner. I am delighted with her keeping her promise to me.
My project is to go with the 10th Company to Custrin, and then home by Frankfort on the Oder, Breslau, Dresden, Frankfort on the Maine, Mayence, Coblenz, where God send I may find you all well.
I forgot to say I composed a song for the 19th, which made them all laugh. I send it for you.

Song for the Nineteenth.

The morning sky is hung with mist,
The rolling drum the street alarms,
The host is paid, his daughter kiss'd –
So now to arms! to arms! to arms!

Our evening bowl was strong and stiff,
And may we get such quarters oft,
I ne'er was better lodged, – for if
The straw was hard, the maid was soft.

So now to arms! to arms! to arms!
And fare thee well, my little dear;
And if they ask who won your charms,
Why say –' 'twas in your *nineteenth* year!'

Berlin, October 25th.

The country round Berlin, the Mark of Brandenberg, is bitter bad, deep sand almost a desert; I don't wonder the Great Frederick wanted something better. Some parts of our marches, through the forests, with the bugles ringing, were quite romantic, and the costume of the villagers, when they turned out to see us pass, really picturesque. I have now made five marches, and am not fatigued to speak of. I am sworn comrade with most of the officers; one rough-looking old captain told me when he got to Berlin, he should have his Polish cook, and then he should ask me to dinner, promising me an '*over-gay*' evening, which I shall take care to get out off. By-the-by, when we were at the burgomaster's, I saw said captain, striding up and down in a great fume before the house; it turned out he was to sleep in the same room with a man, his wife, and *seven* children! which he declined. Finally, I believe, he was put in the school-room in an extempore bed. We are often short of knives, spoons, and forks, but the poor creatures do their best and cheerfully, so that it quite relishes the victuals. I shake their hands heartily, when we part. Yesterday I had a nice dessert of grapes, sent over to me by Bonkowski, and they are scarce in these regions.

Carlovicz one night got no quarters at all: it is quite a lottery. You should have seen Wildegans riding on a baggage waggon between suttlers! Tell Tom that Franck comes to pat my horse, and she spits all over him sometimes, for she has rare yeasty jaws; and yesterday I had the prudence to take myself to leeward after spangling the captain's cloak all over! She eats rarely, and will sell well I dare say, but I shall be sorry to part with her. When I find myself on horseback, riding through a long wood with the regiment, it seems almost like a dream; your mother will no more believe it than your upset. You have subjects enough now for the Elliots with a vengeance, and so shall I have! I wish I *could* wish the Dilkes may be comfortably in Coblenz by my return. As they are not wanted, they would see the vintage; God bless them any way, and say everything kind for me. I really think they might stay longer in Coblenz, quiet and cheap enough, and recover thoroughly, against their winter campaign of company; I long to see them again ere they cross the sea.

I have rambled on to amuse you, and left little room to say all I could wish to yourself; but you will find in your own heart the echo of all I have to say (rather an Irish one, but a truth-teller).

I seem to have scarcely had an inconvenience, certainly not a hardship, and it will ever be a pleasant thing for me to remember. I like little troubles; I do not covet too flowery a path. By-the-by I have some dried flowers for my flower-loving

Fanny, gathered at odd out-of-the-way places; I will show her where on the map when I return.
It was singular in the sheepskin country, whilst the men were all so warmly pelissed, to see the women in their short petticoats, their legs looking so cold. I suspect I pass for very hardy, if not foolhardy, I slight the cold so; but it seems to me a German characteristic, that they can bear being sugar-bakers, but can hardly endure what I call a bracing air.

Bless you, bless you, again and again, my dear one, my only one, my one as good as a thousand to

Your old Unitarian in love,

T. H.

P.S. If Desdemona loved Othello 'for the danger he had passed,' how shall I love you?[9] With my utmost *diligence*, or rather so much more than my heart can hold, that it must get a *beiwagen*! And with that earnest joke, good bye.

Potsdam. [*22–5 October 1836*]

From *Memorials*, I 210–8. I have dated the letter to fit in with the surrounding letters, which have a postmark, 272, 282.

1/Illustrated in *Memorials* I 211; reproduced below, 294
2/This should be Kemnitz.
3/Unidentified
4/*Athenaeum*, 11–25 June 1836, 409ff. The statue was by Schadow, 1821.
5/The first use of this word given in NED is dated 1873.
6/This should be Treuenbrietzen.
7/A comrade of De Franck, with whom the Hoods had been acquainted at Koblenz
8/Jane discusses this episode in a letter to Mrs Elliot of 29 October, *Memorials* I 195–7.
9/*Othello* I iii 167

TO
JANE HOOD

My dearest love,
Here I am safe – but my march is over! The Prince Radziwill[1] has invited Franck to stay two or three weeks here, so he of course stays. As he was the pretext for my journey, I cannot well go without him, but had planned to return by Dresden and Leipsic. To-day, however, it snows; and for fear of bad roads, &c., I think I shall

come direct. Moreover, owing to the hurry, I have none of my papers or lists with me, so that I find it difficult to do anything with the 'Comic.' You may look for me, therefore, in a fortnight from the date of this. I hope the Dilkes will not be gone.
I shall not write again. I am very well, and busy going about. I saw the Cadet school here yesterday morning. I swig away at good London porter. Don't you envy me?
Last night I was at the opera – 'Undine'[2] – the whole royal family present; it was very well done, and I really longed for Tibbie, it was so full of fairy work. Nearly the whole of the 19th were there, and Wildegans says he regrets not to have heard the comments of the men. I have been with him to the exhibition of pictures this morning. Then we took leave, and it made me quite down to say Goodbye to so many, and probably for ever. He desired me to say everything that is kind to you, Fanny, and Tom. I was introduced to the Colonel last night, at the opera. We have a great joke amongst us: half the officers having a day or two's leave, stay here behind the regiment; they lunch with me sometimes, and we call it 'eating the horse.' I suppose I shall get rid both of him and his price before I leave.
I have met with no disagreeables here, which will please you, and shall reserve all stories for our *tête-a-têtes*. In a fortnight you may expect me.
Tell my dear Fanny I was very much pleased with her letter, and so was her friend Franck. I gave her love to Wildegans and Carlovicz. I parted with Wildegans yesterday, about two o'clock. I reckon I shall never see him again. He desired everything kind to be said to you, and said he should never forget us, and spoke of the children, '*kleine* Tom and Fannie *la petite*.'
If I have any public aim, to make my name distinguished – the private one must ever go along with it; that you were part and parcel of myself, I never was anything dearest, till I knew you, and I have been a better, happier and more prosperous man ever since. Lay by that truth in lavender sweetest, and remind me of it when I fail

God bless you all three, dear ones!

Berlin, October 29th. [*1836*]

From *Memorials* I 218–9. The final paragraph is reproduced from Christie, Manson and Woods Ltd *Catalogue* 5 April 1967, 28.

1/Wilhelm Radziwill (1797–1870), Prussian general and head of the Radziwill family. In 1832 he married a Princess Cläry (see 279).

2/Perhaps E.T.A. Hoffmann's opera, based on the story by La Motte Fouqué

TO
JANE HOOD

My own dearest & best love.
I do not know whether this will reach you on your birthday but I hope so, love, that it may bring my blessing to you, and every loving wish that heart can frame. You must give me credit for many many kisses & fond embraces besides to show you how dearly I prize the treasure this day prepared for me. I do love you fondly & dearly & think you will believe me, when I say, from our marriage day to this I have never thought on you as mine really, without blessing my happy fate that it was so ordained for me. – I know we shall be very very happy & comfortable when I return, indeed I shall try my best to make your comparative solitude as cheerful as possible – indeed I look forward to quite a new honey moon on my return. My mind is turning homeward & in 5 or 6 days from receipt of this you may begin to look for me. – The dear last long kiss you gave me is still living on my lips, – & I must get you to give me change for it then, in a hundred sweet short ones. Think of every thing kindest best & fondest, & fancy it best dear own and only love, for your birthday greeting. Pray kiss the ring for me, – above all things.
I have been very busy sight seeing – & very gay. The day before yesterday Franck brought me an invitation from Prince William Radziwill – the head of the family – to dine with him – at 3 o'clock. I was run for time having to buy dress boots &c &c – & to crown my bustle a coach ordered at ½ past 2 did not arrive till three – nor could I make them understand to get another. Thank heaven the dear Princesses were long in dressing – it would have been awful to have kept them waiting. They say no man is a prophet in his own country – & here literature certainly came in for its honours. The Prince introduced me himself to every one of his family – who all tried to talk to me, – most of them speaking English very well. Some spoke French – so I got on very well save a little deafness. The Prince placed me himself next him at dinner on his right hand, & talked with me continually all dinner time, – telling me stories & anecdotes, – and I tried to get out of his debt by some of mine. There were present, Prince William – Prince Boguslaw Radziwill.[2] Prince Adam Czartorinski[3] – Prince Edmund Cläry. Count Wildenbruch (I had met him before) Count Lubienski – Councillor Michalski – Hofrath Kupsach – a captain Crawford R.N. (english) – Princess Cläry Senior – Princess Felicia Cläry – Princess Euphemia Cläry – Princess Boguslaw Radziwill – Princess Wanda Czartonski – Miss von Lange lady of honour – Franck was obliged to dine at the Duke of Cumberland's.[4] I was quite delighted with the whole family – they are excellent. I staid till 7 – we

were very merry after dinner – Franck came in – & the Princes kept telling me sporting anecdotes about him & themselves. Prince William proposed to call on me, & see my sketches; – but I told him I had none & then begged his acceptance of my books, which I am to send – The Princesses asked to send them this year's Comic. Both the Radziwills shook hands with me at parting. They, the princes, have since spoken of visiting me, – but Franck declined it on the plea of my being so far off – for the place was so full, not a bed was to be had when I arrived at that end, – & I am in quite a thirdrate hotel, at the opposite quarter. I have more particulars to tell you when we meet but I knew you would be pleased to know of this. The Duke of Cumberland asked Franck who the gentn was who march'd with his reg^{n} & was surprised to hear it was me – he had been told it was an officer. Prince George[5] spoke in such very handsome terms of me, that I left my card for him – & shall probably be sent for. As he regretted not having / heard / *seen* the the last Comic, Franck presented one of his – but the Prince is quite blind – a fine young man and very amiable. I do not know whether I shall see any of the Radziwills again before I go, but I expect I must call to take leave. They had read Tylney Hall.

Since writing the above, I have been unwell, & could not meet Franck as I had promised, at 12, at the Exhibition. Swellings in the old place, & lassitude – I believe principally on account of a very sudden change in the weather from really severe frost to rain. – Only yesterday we were walking in the fish market, where the huge tubs of carp jack &c were almost frozen hard, – & today the streets are cover'd with genuine Londonlike mud. Moreover I ate too heartily perhaps last night, for thro my bad german they brought me a good sized roast chicken instead of a partridge, and *I ate it every morsel.* I have seen Franck however at the café where I dine – & he tells me that Prince William called on me yesterday, & the other princes today, – I have only got card of Count Wildenbruch – but I know they came as they talked of the stairs, (I am up two pair) till Franck said it was all I could get. This is really most flattering, & places one on a level, *equal to that occupied by singers & dancers in England.* I sent today to one of the Princes, a written account of Franck's tumble into the Lahn, which I expect will make them laugh; – as I had highly embellished it.[6] Franck is gone again tonight to the Duke of Cumberland's. We only meet by snatches. He and a young lieutt. von Heugel are all I see now of the 19th. The latter & I are very good friends – he is quite young, – & having a leave as long as Francks & more leisure, we go about a good deal together. You should hear the lamentations of Franck & myself that you are not here – it is really very amusing. Yesterday I was in the Musée & saw some wonderful pictures – the Titians daughter, for instance,[7] – I should like to be one of the attendants for a month. There were some curious antique pieces I will describe when we meet. Altogether I have had a most happy time of it & in health & every respect have had reason to be highly gratified. I am now all right – a little good port wine, which all the officers recommended me to take has tonight cured me – & here I am writing to you, with the spirits of a lark in the hope that after a couple or three days, every hour will bring me nearer to what is dearest to me on the face of the earth. We will love, fondly & dearly my pet, so as to make us look back on Coblence, as a part of paradise. I only hope I shall not cling too much to this world, when on looking at the map I remember in how many places widely apart, I have been blest with your sweet companionship, and then the Bauer's, at Nagelstadt, not to be found scarcely in any map! I shall have much to talk & act over with you when we meet, & hope to make dear amends to you for your solitary night travelling. I quite long for your head on my heart again, – & devote a great part of the night & morning, sweeter than sleep, to thinking of my best & dearest wife. Twelve years have scarcely seen us apart, and I hope the next twelve will never separate us, for I find it harder & harder, to be from you, & miss those tender & affectionate cares which keep me, I truly believe, alive, because my life is so dearly worth living. As we are always together, you have necessarily all my crossnesses as well as my kindnesses, for I am all yours, imperfections & every thing, – but I flatter myself that in your heart of hearts you reckon me the best of husbands, as I really ought to be to the best of wives. And now, dearest, sweetest, best, as I shall not write again keep your door, heart, & arms open for me, – I shall not be long in throwing myself into them. We shall be very happy to meet dearest, shall we not? I can fancy your cheek with a lovelier glow, your eyes brighter, your lips warmer, your hands stronger, – your bosom softer, – because I am near you. Do I not paint it aright? – I know what a hoarded treasure of love, sweetness, fondness, & enjoyment awaits me; – & I cannot help wishing with Imogen (– your own image) for 'a horse with wings.'[8] – My dear children seem to cling around me with a love they have derived from you; – my own little Tom, taking after his father in his doating on ittle Ma! – and my own Fanny, so well taught by her Mothers example to cling to her Pa – We ought to be happy my own dear Jane & we will be, by day & by night till the years seem months, & the months weeks. We have all the elements of blessedness within us, – & it will be our own fault, – nay my own fault, good one, if we throw them away. I am writing into the hours of sleep, & my paper gets scant, – so now farewell for a while, true sweet virgin wife of my bosom & bed; – I think of you ever and every where, & with nothing but thoughts of praise love & delight. Let me live, also, in your happiest contemplations, – & in the little sacred rites we have devoted to each other. I have blessed you, & addressed you, & loved, & prayed for you ever as we agreed – and a great deal more into the bargain, for as the marches have taught me, I wake very early, & cannot pass the time more happily than in thinking of you, my own, as past, present, & to come. Kiss my dear children for me, – my good clever Fanny, & good, funny little Tom. – I do hope you are well love, – but you know, I never shun nursing when you are the patient. So keep up your good heart till we meet, & whichever is well shall cure the other – but I trust there will be no occasion for this arrangement. God bless you again and again my dearest, sweetest, kindest best – heart's treasure & jewel of my love best of all *my own Jane*, & true wife to her

Ever Affectionate husband

Thos Hood

My kind regards to Mrs Lindo, & hope I shall have the pleasure of seeing her.

Berlin [*4 November 1836*]

MS Bristol Central Library. Address: 'Madame Hood / 752 Alten Graben / Coblentz.' PM: 'BERLIN 12/4/11,' 'COBLENZ/ 8/11.' Published in part in *Memorials* I 219–23. The date is that of the postmark.

1/6 November
2/Boguslaw Radziwill (1809–73), brother of William
3/Adam Czartoryski (1770–1861), Polish aristocrat, friend of Emperor Alexander I of Russia and Russian Foreign Minister (1804–6), in exile after 1831. The other persons mentioned are no doubt members of the Radziwill circle.
4/Ernest Augustus, Duke of Cumberland (1771–1851), fifth son of George III and Queen Charlotte, became King of Hanover in 1837.
5/George (1819–78), only son of the Duke of Cumberland, succeeded his father as King of Hanover in 1851. In 1834, when he became blind, the Duchess of Dino wrote of him: 'He is a fit object at once of pity and admiration; his resignation is angelic,' *Memoirs* (1909) 144–5.
6/Compare *Up the Rhine* 272–8.
7/The Königliches Museum contained Titian's portrait of his daughter Lavinia.
8/*Cymbeline* 3 ii 47

TO

UNKNOWN CORRESPONDENT

I hope to write to your Son by Monday, when a gentleman going to Heidelberg will take a small parcel for me.

I am Sir Yours very truly

Thos Hood.

[*Koblenz, 1836*]

MS Osborn

TO

ALFRED HEAD BAILY

I am all in the dark about the quantity I have sent – & must know as soon as possible.

T. H.

[*Koblenz, 1 December 1836*]

MS Morgan Library. Address: 'Messrs Baily & Co / 83 Cornhill / London / Angleterre.' PM: 'COBLENZ/1/12,' 'LONDON/8/DEC/1836.' These lines come at the end of the MS of 'Spanish Pride: a Yarn,' published in the *Comic Annual* for 1837.

TO

PHILIP DE FRANCK

Tim, says he,[1]

It was odd enough I should have my accident too as if to persuade me that German eilwagens are the most dangerous vehicles in the world – but about four o'clock on the third morning, after a great 'leap in the dark,' the coach turned short round, and brought up against the rails at the roadside; luckily they were strong, or we should have gone over a precipice. There we were on the top of a bleak hill, the pole having broken short off, till we were fetched by *beiwagens*, to the next station, where a new pole was made; but it delayed us six hours. Here I got the first of my cold, for the weather and wind were keen; the night journey from Frankfort to Mayence in an *open* coupé confirmed it. I could not help falling asleep in it from cold. So I came home looking well, and as ruddy as bacon;[2] but the very next day turned *white* with a dreadful cough, which ended in spitting blood; but I sent for the doctor, was bled, and it was stopped: but I am still weak. To make things better I had not sent enough for the 'Comic,' and was obliged to set to work again, willy-nilly, well or illy.[3] I have not been out of doors yet since I came home, but shall in a day or two. The Rhine and Moselle are very high – the Castor street is flooded – the weather being very mild – but I guess cold is coming, for I saw a fellow bring into the town to-day a very large wolf on his shoulders. He was as fat as a pig. I found all well at home. Tom stared his eyes out at me, almost, and for two days would scarcely quit my lap. He talks and sings like a parrot. I should have liked to see your Grand Hunt (a Battue),[4] but for sport I would rather take my dog and gun and pick up what I could find. The night procession must have looked well. Poor Dilke went away very unwell, but the last account of him was better. I did not get home soon enough to see him. I am going to give him a long account of my march. I think the horse sold very well, but cannot fancy what you will do with the saddle, unless you put it on a clothes-horse when you want to ride. Don't forget in your next to let me know the fate of the cheese. I guess it got 'high and mity' enough to deserve a title. Oh! I do miss the porter at Berlin! Schumacher's is to let again, and the beer we get is '*ex-crabble?*' I hope next winter to taste it in London, but can form no plans until my health clears up more. I must beg you in your next to give me the list of the officers. I was to have had it before we parted, as I begin my German book with the march.[5] How do you find your quarters? Are there any Miss A—s at Bromberg? By-the-by, I undertook a letter from Lieutenant B—[6] to deliver here, and sent it by Katchen, who says the mother came in and made a bit of a *row*. But I cannot well understand what she said in German. Perhaps there has been a cat let out of the bag, the young lady having left the letter lying on the table in view of the mamma.

How is Wildegans? and do you ever see him and Carlovicz? My kind regards to both, and most friendly remembrances to all you see, not forgetting *my* captain. How you will delight in settling down to your drill duties and parades after so much gaiety! I quite envy you: a few raw recruits would be quite a treat! You do not tell me whether you had any trolling with Prince Boguslaff: all our old fishing-stands by the Moselle are under water. I hope to get you out a 'Comic' early in the spring, and the books for Berlin; but I shall not know how to get anything over before, as I guess land-carriage cometh very dear, and they must come *via* Ostend till the Rhine-boats run again. Perhaps my painter will come out early;[7] as Jane has told you I am to be 'done in oil.' I have now no news – how should I have? for I have at least been *room*-ridden. I shall take to my rod again as soon as the season begins; but I shall miss you, Johnny,[8] and your 'wenting in.'[9] I must promise you a better letter next time. This is only a *brief* from,

Dear Johnny,
Yours ever truly,

Johnny.

Fanny and Tom send their little loves.

152, Alten Graben, Coblenz, Dec. 2nd, 1836.

From *Memorials* I 224–7

1/The opening phrase of a whimsical Irish dialogue in Jonah Barrington's *Personal Sketches* (1827–32) I 150
2/Hood's son comments: 'These were almost the last days of my father's health,' *Memorials* I 191.
3/Hood's daughter remembered the conclusion of work on *The Comic Annual*: *Memorials* I 243–4.
4/Hood probably used Franck's account in 'Shooting the Wild Stag in Poland,' in *the Comic Annual* for 1842, *Works* VIII 134–45.
5/*Up the Rhine* ends with the march: *Works* VII 245–54
6/Perhaps B— is Bonkowski, referred to on 274.
7/Thomas Lewis
8/A new nickname for Hood's friend
9/An example of Franck's broken English. Hood's son comments: 'Of course this gave my father an opportunity of *inwenting* endless fun,' *Memorials* I 227.

TO
JOHN WRIGHT

My dear Wright,
Now for a slight sketch of my march. Our start was a pretty one. We were to go at six, Jane and I, by the coach, and were to be called by four. Everything ready, but not all packed. I woke by *chance* at half-past five, our servant – hang her German phlegm! – being still in bed. Now, as all mails, &c., here are government concerns, you pay beforehand, at the post-office, fare, postilions, turnpikes, and all, which makes it very pleasant to lose your place.
By a miracle – I cannot imagine how – Mrs. Dilke helping, we somehow got Jane's bag and my portmanteau rammed full, and caught the coach just setting off. A fine day, and a fine view of the Rheingau, for we went round by the Baths to Frankfort-on-Maine, but 'dooms' slow, for it is hilly all the way, and they walked up, and *dragged* on slowly down.

Started in the evening-coach from Frankfort for Eisenach. Myself taken very ill in the night; but had some illness hanging about me brought to a crisis by being stived up, all windows shut, with four Germans stinking of the accumulated smoke and odour, stale, flat, and unprofitable,[1] of perhaps *two* years' reeking garlic and what not, besides heat insufferable. I was for some time insensible, unknown to Jane, and, coming-to again, let down the window, which let in a very cold wind, but delicious to me, for it seemed like a breeze through the branches and blossoms of the tree of life. But it was the cause of a severe cold on the chest. We slept at Eisenach; next morning posted to Langen Seltzers,[2] the head quarters. * * *

I shall soon begin on my German book with 'wigger.' I have material prepared. Minor adventures on the march I have not given, as you will see them there. I pique myself on the punctuality of my brief military career. I was never too late, and always had my baggage packed by my own hands ready for the waggon. It was almost always dark at setting out, and I had to lead my horse till I could see. After half an hour, or an hour, we took generally a quarter's rest, for a sort of after-breakfast; then made for the general rendezvous, where we piled arms, and all fell to work on our victuals, – a strange picnic, each bringing what he could; and we made reports, and some showed sketches of their last night's quarters. On the whole, I was very fortunate. Some were regularly hovelled, in pigeon-houses or anywhere. It was a lottery. On the march I rode by turns at the head or the tail of the companies, talking with such of the officers as could speak French. They were, one and all, very friendly, and glad of my company. I almost wondered at myself, to find that I could manage my horse so well, for we had queer ground sometimes, when we took short cuts.

I assure you sometimes I have almost asked myself the question, whether I was I, seeming to be so much out of my ordinary life, – for example, on horseback, following, or rather belonging to, a company of soldiers; the bugle ringing through a vast pine wood to keep us together, or the men perhaps singing Polish songs in chorus, for this is a Polish regiment chiefly.

About a year ago I had a military cloak, at the contractor's price, from Berlin, but without any idea of a march. Thanks to it, and my horse, having been a captain of engineers', with its saddle-cloth, &c., I cheated the king of all the road-money, for they let me pass all the toll-houses as an officer. I was taken alternately for the chaplain and doctor of the regiment. It did me a world of good, but the finish marred all again. I was disappointed at not going to the end with them, but as De Franck stays, I could not well proceed; and I have since heard he has been stopped three weeks more, to go on a grand hunting party into Austria. I am going to set to work to learn German during this winter, as I know I shall be able to turn it to account. I am reading the papers, but they are not worth reading.

I shall be very happy to see Mr. L— and show him all the *countenance* I can in Coblenz as a portrait-painter, by letting him take my own; but, for my part, I never got any good of my face yet, except that it once got me credit for eighteen pence at a shop, when I had gone out without my purse. If he has not yet seen the Rhine, he will find the 'face of nature,' very well worth his attentions, and I shall have much pleasure in offering him such hospitality as we have here, – for it is not quite English in its fare, this good town. But a change is sometimes agreeable. I had a change of it on the march, and I cooked our supper of Welsh-rabbits one night, but though it was good Stilton cheese, no less, the two German officers we invited express wouldn't eat it. It ran a near chance of being thrown away, *because it was turning blue.* I must tell you of a good joke. I sent De Franck's servant with my passport to a country Burgomaster to be *visé*, – he brought it back with a message that 'I could not be "*frizzé*," without coming in person!' Encore. They use little fire bottles very much here, – one morning at four o'clock we were an immense time getting a light, the bugle had sounded long ago, – at last we found him with a bundle of about fifty phosphoric matches, trying them all by turns in our little *phial of Cayenne*, very much bothered that they would not catch fire. And now, dear Wright, adieu, with kind regards,

Yours ever truly,

Thos. Hood.

Coblenz, December 15th, 1836.

From *Memorials* I 227–31
1/*Hamlet* I ii 133
2/Langensalza

TO
CHARLES WENTWORTH DILKE

My dear Dilke,

I intended to write to you long ago, but, as usual, I have been laid up in ordinary,[1] a phrase you must get some Navy Pay Officer to translate.[2] My marching in fact ended like Le Fèvre's (it ought to be Le Fever) in a sick bed[3] – my regiment came to a regimen! Oh, Dilke, what humbugs of travellers you and I be now, that we cannot compass a few hundred miles, but the leech must be called in at the end! I came home, looking ruddy as a ploughboy, and excepting some signs of my old local weakness, better apparently than since I have been here; but almost the next day after my return, I turned white, with a most unaccountable depression, which ended in a fit of spitting blood as before. Dr. S—[4] was immediately sent for – I was bled, and there was no return.

Now I cannot believe that such a poor crow as I can have too much blood. I suspect this time it was a touch on the lungs, which were never touched before, being indeed my strongest point. I attribute it to our unlucky accident of the coach – at four o'clock of a cold, windy morning. However, I am nearly right again, but weak and low – rather: your kind letter has just arrived with its good news, quite equal to three cheers, one for Dilke, one for the 'Comic,' and one for myself. I was afraid the first would be worse for his homeward journey. I must and will think you set off too soon, and as a prophet after the fact, you had plenty of mild fine weather before you, for it only snowed here for the first time yesterday, Christmas Day! I am heartily glad to hear of so much decided improvement, but it will be a weak point always and require great care; – even at the expense of having a fell of hair[5] like a German.

If he cannot get it *cut at home*, he deserves to have his head shaved for that last expedition. What would Dr. S— say, only I can't tell him. I hope *you*, *Mrs.* Dilke, preached a good sermon on it, and you will do well to read him daily a morning lesson out of the Bible, showing how Samson lost all his strength by going and having his hair cut.[6] What an epitaph must I have written, if he had died through *that* little outbreak of personal vanity: –

'Here lies Dilke, the victim to a whim,
Who went to have his hair cut, but the air cut him'.

I certainly do not agree any more than Dr. Johnson as to his being a *Cyst*-ercian; from the great tenderness, the evil did not seem to me to be so deeply seated as Dr. B.[7] supposed, but nearer the surface; I have now great hope of him – barring barbers – and especially that leaving Somerset House;[8] the change will perhaps add to his years, and let him live a *double number*, provided always he don't come up the Rhine again. I am always happy to see friends – but really I *do* wish you had not come, for now we have nothing so agreeable to look forward to, and not much at present to look back upon! I wonder if the visit will ever be returned – shall I ever go *down* the Rhine and drop in at Lower Grosvenor Place?

I live in hope of the first part at least; I try to fill up my own cavities instead of the sexton's by every care I can take; for instance, I am sailing on Temperance principles. I drank your health, and the compliments of the season to you yesterday, in a glass of Jane's ginger wine; and at night, being Christmas, indulged in a glass of – lemonade! As for you, Maria, having lost your sides, you must expect to be always middling, but no more spasms! So huzza for us all – who knows but our united ages may become worthy of a newspaper paragraph, some forty years hence.

I am glad you relish the 'Comic' so well: indeed I always try that it shall not fall off, whatever its sale may do – that the fault may be the public's, not the private's. But it seems doomed never to be early – thanks to that slug-a-bed, Katchen, and her German phlegm, it was some three weeks after it should have been out.

In the meantime, I will give you some particulars of my excursion. You have heard how well I got through my first day's ride – it was a fine morning, and we crossed part of that flat which surrounds Leipzic – what an immense flat it is! An ocean of sand literally stretching beyond the reach of the eye. It seems to have been intended for the grand armies of Europe to decide their differences on. That is to say, if Nature or Providence ever intended to form convenient plains for wholesale butcheries, of which I have some doubt.

However, it is classic ground to the soldier, as several great battles have taken place in the neighbourhood. The next morning, I packed up and started at four, and after rather a longer spell got to Brenha, where I found my quarters at a sort of country inn and butcher's shop rolled into one. I only breakfasted at Brenha – spending the rest of my time at a château of Baron B—'s,[9] with De Franck and the Captain – the old Major-domo, the image of a Scotchman, doing the honours. He sent down to invite me, and thenceforward I boarded at the château, and only slept and breakfasted at the inn. I had the prettiest girl in the place for my waitress – and told her I was a prisoner of state on parole with the regiment, which interested her in my favour, I suppose: anyhow it brought up the mother – dram bottle in hand – who sat herself down, *tête-à-tête* at the table, and seemed determined to hear all the rights of it: but I grew very English, and her curiosity could get nothing out of me. At the château we lived like fighting-cocks, and drank a very good wine, made on the estate, as good as much of the Rhenish.

We had a sort of under-steward for our host, and for our waiting-maid, an ugly, grisly female, with the addition of an outlandish head-dress, and a huge frill – stiff, and *fastened behind to her cap*, so that she was in a sort of pillory. The pretty girl at the inn, did not get half so much of my attention. The fare – poultry, jack, carp, beetroot, neat's tongue. I saw in the farm-yard some very fair pigs – one with a stiff neck – his head regularly fixed on one side; some excellent Polish fowls; and in a long stable a range of fine-ish cows, with a long solid bench before them, where each had a circular hollow scooped for it like a bason. I have seen tables for human beasts, in Berkshire, with the dishes and platters, scooped out in like fashion – not a bad plan for sea-faring furniture – not over cleanly, perhaps, but fast and not breakable. There was also a garden and a fish-pond in it.

The next day being a rest, we spent at the same place, and we went trolling, the steward giving us leave, in a mill-stream, where we only caught one little jack before dinner, who had tried to swallow the bait, a carp as broad as himself. We brought both into the house, as they were, by the way of a curiosity, but leaving tackle and all in the passage, during dinner, we hooked the favourite cat to boot, who had taken the bait too. Our bad sport in the morning procured us leave for the afternoon, in the *garden pond*, a sort of preserve, where we immediately hooked a good large jack. As soon as the line went off under the weeds, I pulled out my watch to give the fish eight or ten minutes to pouch the bait, while De Franck stood still as a statue with the rod; the captain up at his window wondering what solemn operation was going on. At last we got him, a good jack; then a second, a third, and a fourth, the face of the steward lengthening at each catch, in the most laughable manner. He evidently thought we should 'distress the water,' as it is technically termed. Jack are much esteemed, you must know, in inland Germany, and the old man was quite glad when we packed up our tackle. He was comforted at last to find three were so little hurt, that they might be thrown in again. But he told us, half in joke, half in earnest, when we came again he should set a watch over all his ponds.

Three years since there were four thousand trees blown down on the estate by a storm, they stopped all the roads in the neighbourhood, which took fourteen days in clearing; and some of the trees are not yet removed.

They must have had some such treats in Germany elsewhere, I guess, during the late hurricanes. At the inn I had one dinner, one supper, bed twice, and two breakfasts, for ten groschen, or one shilling. But these bye-places are poor, and a little money goes a great way. Here I not only found soap for the first time in Germany, but a place in the *bason* expressly for holding it. The Saxons seemed generally good sort of people. Our next march took us across the Elbe to Wittenberg. A Lieutenant J—, an old crony of De Franck's, met us on the bridge, and insisted on our dining with him, so we got leave, dined at the Casino, and J— showed me the lions of the place.

As to Luther's statue, I could not help thinking of Friar John, in Rabelais, as a brother of the same order. Thinks I to myself, so I am to thank that fellow up there for being a Protestant. I had remarked at Wittenberg the peculiar tall glasses, a full foot high, with a glass cover (no stems), and afterwards at Berlin I saw Luther's drinking-cup, or vessel, made after the same jolly fashion. J— showed me his residence, now a College, where he said, a good deal of mysticism prevails. J— drove with us, in a hired carriage, to our quarters, about an hour's ride through deep sand to Pruhlitz, a very tiny village. We passed, by the way, a well miraculously discovered by Luther when he was dry, by a scratch of his staff in the sand – he looked more like the tapper of ale barrels. In our quarters I had for a wonder, a *four-post bed* with the old feather beds below and above, and as the bed was made at an angle of thirty-five degrees, I slept little more than I should have done on a 'Russian mountain,'[10] always sliding down and getting up again. Hereabouts this slant was quite the fashion. Partridges are so plentiful about Leipsic and Wittenberg, as to be three groschen the brace. Next morning we got to the Mark of Brandenburg. We went over sands, and such desolate, bleak, bare heaths, I expected on every ascent to come in sight of some forlorn sea-coast (we took often short cuts across country, rendezvousing in the high roads). Our march lasted eight and a half hours, having a grand parade (as rehearsal) on the way, and were quartered at last at Nichel, near Treuenbritzen, so called as the only place that stood *true* to Frederick the Great.

When we arrived here, the whole population had turned out to see us, as military do not often appear in such parts. The females look very picturesque – for the single wear black head-dresses, the married red ones, quite a game of *rouge et noir*. I don't think Cook could have been more wondered at by the Sandwichers, than I was by the Nichelites. A party waited in front of the house, and pointed me out whenever I came to the window, and stared with only the glass between us, as heartily as if they had really been sheep and not merely skins. The Captain of the 11th company (mine was the 10th) called politely to see how I was lodged. * * * I was much amused in the evening to see the gaunt hogs trotting home of their own accord, from I know not where – each going into his own quarters as regularly as we did – and the geese the same, though some next door houses were infinitely to appearance more selectable than their neighbours.

I saw a goose wait for a long while at a house, where no door happened to be open, till at last she was admitted. I will give you a recipe for our dinner. First make some rice-milk rather watery, and strew in a few raisins. Then cut a fowl in pieces, six perhaps, and make a broth with it. Pour the first dish and the second together, and the mess is made. We had two beds for three; so De Franck slept on the straw. Next morning we got to Belitz; from here we rode across to Schlunkendorf, quartered with De Franck and another at a miller's. Millers', by the way, are the best quarters everywhere, though we got but two beds, and so De Franck was littered down. I went out after dinner, and could see nothing but a sandy waste with a windmill. In my yellow boots, and figured robe (Mrs. D.'s present), I was not at all out of costume, for such an Arabian-like scene. Next day being a rest, I took advantage of it to push on to Potsdam to see all I could. Here ended my actual marching with the regiment, for the next morning the King came to Potsdam to review it. He was much pleased; but as an instance of his love for military minutiae, and correct ear, when they were giving him cheers, the huzzas and the drums did not time exactly together, and he exclaimed 'What beating is that?'

Everything about Potsdam smacks of the Great little Frederic, but nothing is more striking than the superabundance of statues. They *swarm!* – there is a whole garrison turned into marble or stone, good, bad, and indifferent. They are as numerous in the garden as the promenaders; there is a Neptune group, for example, without even the apology of a pond. The same at Sans Souci – in fact, everywhere. The effect, to my taste, is execrable, or ridiculous. Solitude and stillness seem the proper attributes of a statue. We have no notion of marbles mobbing. I saw, of course, all the apartments and relics of Frederic. The chairs torn by his dogs, his writing-table, &c. The Watteaus on the walls, containing the recurring *belle* Barberini,[11] pleased me much; he seems to give a nature to courtliness, and a courtliness to nature, that make palace-gardens more like fairy-land, and their inhabitants more like Loves and Graces than I fear they be in reality. I was much interested by a portrait of Napoleon when consul (said to be very like), over a door in the palace. It had a look of melancholy as well as thought, with an expression that seemed to draw the heart towards him. There must have been something likeable about him, to judge by the attachment and devotion of some of his adherents; but I could not help believing before the picture, that when younger, he had been of a kinder and more benevolent disposition than is generally supposed.

One of the other curiosities was the present king's bed – a mere crib. I visited the Peacock Island, of which I thought little; and two of the country-seats, the Crown Prince's and Prince Charles's.[12] The first in the style of an Italian villa,[13] with frescoes, in the medallions of which are introduced portraits of personal friends, &c.; but the German physiognomy does not match well with the Italianesque. The public are admitted into the gardens – even when the Prince is enjoying himself in them with his parties: this is very, almost ultra, liberal; but it seems to me a German taste to enjoy nothing without this publicity. At Prince Charles's (he is attached to the sea, and wished to be a sailor) I saw some annuals on his table, and an English caricature; also English prints and pictures hung in the rooms. He

is partial to us, and I entered my name in a book he keeps to know of his visitors.
I saw some fine pictures in the gallery – Titians; a most miraculous *living* hand of flesh and blood, as it seemed to me to be, in one of them.
I entertained some of the officers here to luncheon; they dined by invitation with the Guards, who gave them a dinner, first for the king, and secondly for themselves.
I saw here the Russian colony, living in cottages *à la Suisse*. I saw, of course, the famous mill that beat Frederic in a battle, like Don Quixote;[14] and I sat down at Frederic's table where he worked, with a statue of Justice in sight through a window at the opposite end of the room – 'a conceit! a miserable conceit!' – that he might always keep justice in view. An acted pun! As his favourite dogs were all buried with a tombstone apiece, very near Justice's feet, there ought to have been some *meaning* there, too; but I could not find or invent it, unless that Justice had more to do with dead dogs than with living ones.
The garrison church, externally, looks like an arsenal, 'tis so be-stuck with helmets, flags, and military trophies, carved in stone; but in the interior it is worth one's while to go into a dark narrow tomb, just under the organ, only to reflect on the strange chances of finding Frederic and his father so near, and yet so peaceable, as they lie side by side – *not* 'lovely and pleasant in their lives, but in their deaths not divided.'[15]

And now, my dear D., with kind regards to Mrs. Dilke,
Believe me ever
Your faithful friend,

Thomas Hood.

752, Alten Graben, Coblenz, 26th Dec., 1836.

From *Memorials* I 231–42
1/Out of commission
2/Dilke retired from the Navy Pay Office when it was abolished in 1836.
3/In Sterne *Tristram Shandy* VI 6
4/Unidentified
5/*Macbeth* 5 V 11
6/Judges 6:19
7/ Probably Hood's first physician in Koblenz, Dr Beerman
8/Where the Navy Pay Office was situated
9/Unidentified
10/Hood's reference is unclear.
11/'Adjoining the royal palace is the *Barberini Palace*, erected by Frederic the Great in imitation of the palace of that name at Rome,' Karl Baedeker *Berlin* (Leipsic 1903) 184. Hood, or the person reading

his MS, is no doubt confusing this name with that of *la belle* Barberina, a dancer, whose relation with Friedrich is discussed by Carlyle, *History of Frederic the Great* (ed. 1897–8) IV 493–7.
12/Third son of Friedrich Wilhelm III of Prussia (1801–83)
13/Presumably the Charlottenhof
14/'The famous *Windmill*, the owner of which is said to have refused to sell it to Frederic the Great,' Baedeker 187
15/2 Samuel 1:23

1837

TO
JOHN WRIGHT

My dear Wright,

I have no doubt but the Count you are doing some cuts for, is the same that Prince Radziwill mentioned to me, as engaged on a work on modern German art. The Prince alluded to the excellence of our *wood-cutting*. You would do well to send the Count some of your *best specimens;* I saw some wretched German woodcuts in the Berlin exhibition. I think the name I recollect was something like Raczynski. I should not be surprised if seeing the Comic had suggested you to him as good wood-engravers.[1] The Germans cannot cut; and if they could make fine cuts, couldn't print them. And yet Albert Dürer, a German, was the founder of the art.

I am hard at work at my German book. You will soon have a box. Some of the subjects are larger than usual, and must be printed the long way of the page.

Have the goodness to make a polite message to Messrs. Saunders and Otley for me, saying, that till I return to England I cannot well undertake any such arrangement as they propose; but that when I come back I shall be open to offers of the kind. Indeed, for the next six months my hands are full.[2]

I have no time to write more, except to present all good wishes and seasonable compliments to yourself and Mrs. W. Pray remember me kindly to all friends, not forgetting poor Ned Smith.[3] Did I name a book for Harvey? But I trust to you, who know my wishes, to rectify all casual mistakes and omissions.

I am, my dear Wright,
Yours ever truly,

Thomas Hood.

I shall write a chapter on German Draughts (of Air), and their invention of cold-traps. I have a stiff neck, that goes all down my back, and then comes up the other side, thanks to their well-staircases and drying-lofts in the attics.

752, Alten Graben, Coblenz, 13th January, 1837.

From *Memorials* I 245–7

1/Many of the engravings in Court Athanasius Raczynski's *Histoire de l'art moderne en Allemagne* (Paris 1836–41) were executed by Wright and Folkard.

2/The publishers' offer concerned serious contributions to a proposed annual which ultimately fell through.
3/Unidentified

TO
PHILIP DE FRANCK

My dear Johnny,
Aren't you glad to hear now that I've only been ill and spitting blood three times since I left you, instead of being very dead indeed, as you must have thought from my very long silence. I began a letter, indeed, a long while ago; but, on hearing of the setting off of the box, I waited for its arrival, and a precious wait it was. Only a month and three days, and my box was still longer in going to London. Hurrah for German commerce! It must thrive famously with such a quick transit! One might almost as well be in America.
I had a sharp brush with the Customs' officers after all, for they wanted to unpack it at the office, which I would not stand. I think I scared Deubel, I was in such a rage; but I gained my point. You know last year they offered to send an officer to the house, and even declined to see it at all; so I told them. There was a full declaration of every article, and I was charged for '*plumbing*,' by which I understand the putting of *leaden seals* on, but there was no trace of anything of the kind. To make it worse I have since ascertained that the scoundrels had already opened it at Emmerich. This has been such a sickener to me that I have made up my mind to leave this place, with no very pleasant recollections of its courtesy towards strangers.
However, I shall have my revenge: the materials of my book are in London, and so let the Rhinelanders look out for squalls.[1] I hope you will like the tackle; it all came safe; and Wright assures me it is the very best made, and at the wholesale price. I send the Prince's and Wildenbruch's at the same time. The bad weather for fishing hitherto will make the delay of less consequence. Did you ever know such hot and cold, such snow and rain? It has been killing work; we were all well 'gripped;' and a nasty insidious disease it is, leaving always its marks behind it.
I have got all my books (save one, which is out of print) for the Prince, in the newest fashion of binding.

Tim, says he, I laughed heartily at your description of the fishing at Bromberg, for you seemed in a whimsical dilemma enough; and so, after wishing with all your heart, soul, and strength to be within reach of salmon, you were frightened at them when you had them at hand!

I should be rather nervous for my tackle myself. It would have been no use writing to R—,[2] who knows no more about it than I do: nor have I any practical salmon-fisher of my acquaintance – they are chiefly Scotch and Irish. But I am pretty certain of this point, that there is nothing peculiar in it from other fly-fishing, but that all use stronger tackle, larger bright flies, big as butterflies, and that you must play with the fish a wonderful deal more, – say half or three-quarters of an hour, – to wear them out. There is a famous winch and line coming with this. If I were you, I would get up some sort of a German rod extempore, put this winch on it, and make the experiment before risking your good rod. For myself, Johnny, I must give up all hope of ever wetting a line at Bromberg; not only are my marching days over, but I fear I shall never be able to travel again. I am now sure that this climate, so warm in summer and so cold in winter, does not suit my English blood. Inflammatory disorders are the besetting sin of the place. Witness poor Dilke. And at my last attack Dr.— told me he saw the same thing every day.[3] The man who bled me, and there are *several* bleeders here, told me he had attended eighty that month. Moreover, I had been not merely moderate, but abstemious; at one time only drank Jane's ginger-wine, and at my last attack was actually only taking two glasses of wine a day. We even get good English porter now at the Trèves Hotel, *and I dare not touch it!*

This low diet does not at all suit me. When I was a boy I was so knocked about by illness (and in particular by a scarlet fever so violent that it ended in a dropsy) that as I grew up I only got over it by living rather well. Besides, as all doctors know, studious pursuits exhaust the body extremely, and require stimulus at times, so I have made up my mind to decamp. My present idea is *per* Cologne and Aix to Ostend or Antwerp, when I shall be able to get over to England in a few hours at any time, if necessary; and should I get strength to travel, I can see something of Belgium and France. I rather incline to Ostend on account of the sea air, which always does me great good. I shall regret the children not completing their German here; but the difficulty of intercourse (which neutralises all my efforts to be early with my books) and the climate forbid it; and, in addition, I have quite a disgust to Coblenz, or rather its inhabitants. I have begun German myself, through L—,[4] but that must be at an end. I find him as a German Jew better than the Jew Germans of the place. I have not seen the General, 'cos why?' I have only

crossed the door three times, perhaps six, since I came from Berlin. But I shall call some day before I go. When my plan is once arranged I shall go at once. Towards the end of this month, I suppose, I shall trouble the chub again for the last time.
I have some famous large chub flies by the box – some like small cockchafers. I am not sure whether my chest will stand the casting. It is miserable work, Tim, to be such a shattered old fellow as I am; when you, who are in years my senior, are gallivanting about like a boy of nineteen! The artist who is coming out to take my portrait will have a nice elderly grizzled head to exhibit! What! that pale, thin, long face the Comic! Zounds! I must gammon him, and get some friend to sit for me. *Àpropos*, I sent up two months ago a box full of sketches of my Rhine book; and I had managed such a portrait of D—[5] in a Rhenish spare bed! I have drawn, too, the captain who gave me leave to make use of his jolly red nose, Mr. Schultz, Mrs. Schultz and all, not forgetting the maid in the pillory-ruff at Burg-Kremnitz.[6]
D'ye know, Johnny, I half suspect the Rhinelanders opened my box going down, and were not best pleased at my sketches of some of the dirty dandies hereabouts, which perhaps makes 'em so uncivil. Should all happen that I have wished to the Coblenzers in general, and the Douane in particular, during the last ten days, they will be far from comfortable. Only imagine that I blessed everything for them down to their pipes. They have the worst of the French character without the best of the German. I have no news to tell you about them; how should we pick up any, for we are not on speaking terms with any one in the place, save the two teachers. Nor have I been to the Military Casino, so that I cannot answer your inquiry how the young ladies take the loss of the 19th.
I have just asked L— if there is any local news. He knows nothing except that this last winter there have been *more* balls and parties than usual, so that the ladies have not kept their faith to the 19th.
As to the breaking off the *verlobbing*[7] with Von B. we have not heard one word about it. How should we? Perhaps it is not true, but has only been reported to quiz you, and make you fancy you have a chance again. But I will drop that subject, or I shall make you as savage as you were one night with me and Wildegans, and even with yourself, till I expected you would call yourself out. Oh, Tim, she enjoyed hitting you over the heart, like the man who had a donkey with 'a bit of raw.'
She is learning English, of course for your sake says you – but I forget! I see you in fancy twisting your moustaches and pouting. Mrs. N—,[8] through L—'s means, is reading some of my Comics.
I guess they will puzzle her pretty considerably. Also Mrs. A— has had them. She and Captain A—[9] have been living at the Weisser Ross for months, and he is a

member of my club; but we have not met, and they are now going. I am not sorry to have missed them, for I saw them pass, and they not only look queer people, but awfully Scotch! Besides, we have had our share of luck in picking up friends on that side the water.

Since writing the foregoing, Tim, I am a little better; but wasn't I in luck, after spitting blood and being bled, to catch the rheumatism in going down-stairs. I ordered leeches on my foot, and the wounds bled all night, so I was uncommonly low, as you may imagine. I suppose I shall get out some day. This morning I was going to have a ride for the first time, but it clouded over, and I gave it up. What a precious season we have had – eight months' winter. But now the ice will be broken up, and you will be blessing me for not sending your tackle. It has had to wait here almost a week for a frachwagen,[10] which only goes on Sundays. I had little or no news from London by the package, but I have heard that poor Dilke is in a very precarious state: he doesn't rally well, and the least illness flies to the old place. The last account, though, was a little better.

What do you think, Tim, of a black man, who, by dancing and singing *one* little song called 'Jim Crow,' has cleared, in London and America, 30,000*l*.![11] There's one string to your bow for you! I never heard of the history of the bit of Stilton that went on to Bromberg. The Cheshire we send makes Welsh rabbits well – don't forget to try it. Also you will find some ginger for ginger-beer. I send a box of lozenges for 'Ganserich,'[12] for the cold drill mornings. I shall always be glad that I saw you as far on your road as I could; but when I look back and think how very little I have stirred out of the house ever since I came from Berlin, that march seems to me a dream.

I do not think that the book about it will come out before the next Comic. I have been so delayed, the spring season for publishing is over. You'll be sure to have it. I have drawn you just as you came dripping out of the Lahn,[13] and I mean to try some way or other to commemorate Wildegans. Tom Junior does not forget any of you. The other day he pointed to that old fat major or colonel of the 29th, who walks about with a thick stick, and laughed, and said: 'There is Franck.'

He says 'Franck bought Bello – Bello is Tom's dog' – and he always toasts Vildidans and Tarlyvitz when he gets a drop of wine. He talks a strange jumble of English and German, and English according to the German Grammar. 'That is hims,' 'There is you's chair,' 'Will you lend it for me,' &c., &c. Fanny is very well again, and very good; Jane is as usual; she is now drinking porter, at which I look half savage. Only think, porter and Cheshire cheese, and I daren't take *both!* I mustn't even *sip*, and I long to *swig*. Nothing but water. I shall turn a fish soon, and have the pleasure of angling for myself. I am almost melancholy, for I never had any serious fears about my health before; my lungs were always good. But now I think they are touched too. I've had a sort of plaister on my chest, which will not heal; but I won't bother you with my symptoms. In spite of all this, I ordered this morning a new fishing-jacket – a green one: so you see I mean to show fight, and keep on my legs as long as I can. But one must reckon the fishing calendar a month later; those that used to spawn in May will do it in June, I expect. Of course they would not come out while there was snow. I meant to have got some gudgeons this month, which is the prime, or ought to be the best season – but this is all gone by. I have such difficulty in writing, I cannot send you so long a letter as I should wish: it is some exertion to me at present to think of anything: I am obliged to keep myself quiet.

Moreover there is so little news stirring that it is not easy to fill up a letter. Mind and give my remembrances most kindly to every one of my old comrades, and pray thank them for thinking of me. I only wish I could put myself under our Captain's orders again, and have to trouble your Quarter-master.

It will be a pleasant subject for life for me to think upon that same march – for though I was not on speaking terms with many of your officers, I was not the less friendly. Do not forget my best respects to the Colonel, whenever you see him, – nor my compliments to the Major: I suppose Carlovicz is not with you, but send our regards to him – and tell him Tom is an excellent master to Bello – indeed more attentive to him than to me even – for at the least scratch at the door, whatever play he is engaged in, he breaks off to go and let in his dog. Say everything kind to Wildegans – he and I ought to insure each other's lives. I hope he likes the Brombergian quarters.

I cannot give more particular messages, for the names are very difficult to spell – but I trust to you not to omit my compliments to every officer of my acquaintance in *our* regiment. I must, however, especially name my own quarter-comrades Von Bonkowski, and Von Heugel, of whose attentions I retain a grateful impression, often recurring in memory to Hagelstadt, Burg-Kremnitz, Nichel, and Schlunkendorf. Pray give me all the regimental news when you write. I shall not leave here till June – and, at all events, you shall hear from me before I move. We have our lodgings till 15th July, but shall not stay so long as that; and now, old fellow, God bless you, and send you all sorts of luck, and happiness, and sport, and promotion – everything you wish. May you pull out salmons, and many salmons pull you in, but without drowning you. I say, Tim, says he, if I was at Bromberg wouldn't we have fun; but that's over. So as Mahomet said to the mountain – 'why if I can't come to you, why you must come to me.' Farewell and Amen, says, my dear Johnny,

Yours ever truly,

Thomas Hood.

Rather better to-night.
Your box leaves here with this – acknowledge receipt of all.

752, Alten Graben, Coblenz, April 23rd, 1837.

From *Memorials* I 247–57
1/*Up the Rhine*
2/Probably Reynolds
3/Probably Beerman
4/Unidentified
5/Dilke, in *Up the Rhine* facing 93
6/In *Up the Rhine*, facing 307, 312 respectively
7/From *Verlobung*, betrothal, as the ensuing comments suggest. 'Von B' is possibly Von Bonkowski, referred to below, a comrade of De Franck.
8/Unidentified
9/Unidentified
10/*Frachtwagen*, a waggon, presumably carrying parcels
11/Thomas D. Rice caused a sensation with his act at the Surrey theatre in 1836.
12/In English, gander, a play on the name of their friend Wildegans
13/In *Up the Rhine*, facing 276

TO
PHILIP DE FRANCK

My dear Franck,
I quite forgot to ask in my letter for what I wanted. If you can spare it then, not otherwise, please to send me the book the old clergyman gave you on the march of military songs.
I mean that where he says his sweetheart is his belt, his knapsack, his firelock, &c., &c.; if you have it not, tell me the name of it.[1]
I have heard from London, and am happy to say Dilke is considerably better,

which is a very great relief to us. All concur in advising me to quit this; in fact, I feel sure that another winter and summer here would kill me between them.
So we are going – that's *decided* – on the 1st of June – a week earlier if we can get all our arrangements made. I am better, and feel quite pleased with the thought of leaving Coblenz, of which I am heartily sick – for it has nothing now to make us regret it, but the mere beauty of the scenery. We shall go to Ostend for the sea: if we do not like it to Bruges, Ghent, or Brussels, for as I do not expect to come to the Continent again, I mean to see a little of Flanders and France, should I be strong enough while there; and then we are so near we can pass over to England in a few hours whenever we like.
Dilke says he will not swear he *won't* come over to see us, though he had such bad luck in his visit to us here. There is a gentleman coming out shortly with the Comics, so I will send you one, and one for Prince Charles, if you like to send it.
By the time you receive this I hope you will have your box quite safe. Don't forget to toast some of your cheese, it makes famous Welsh rabbits. We sup on them four nights a week. I suppose, Johnny, all my fishing will 'suffer a sea change,'[2] and I must adapt my tackle for flounders, soles, whiting, cod, and mackerel.
As to wittles and drink, Coblenz is worse than ever. There is no Bavarian beer now, and no Westphalian hams! Deubel pulls a very long face at our going, and no wonder, for there are lists of 'lodgings to let' as long as your arm. I never saw so many before. I am riding out every fine day to gain strength, and bid good bye to the views. We don't take Katchen with us, who has been trying hard to go, as well as to be made residuary legatee as to all our things here – modest impudence!
Tim, says he, I saw a fight between men here the other night for the first time. It was good fun, two to one; and didn't they pull hair like *gals*, and then haul him down, and give him a good unfair beating while he lay on the ground! And didn't he go away, wiping his bloody nose, for good as I thought, but came back again with three or four allies; and the others, at least one of the others, was ready with a mighty big bit of wood; and didn't the women squall, and run out to see with candles, though it was hardly dusk; and didn't they screech like a knife on a plate, and lug the men about! Then the fellows all gobbled like turkeycocks – such explosions of gutturals! You know what thick voices the common people have. And then they began to fight again; and a lot of men, women, and children bolted up all sorts of streets, *sauve qui peut*. I don't know how it ended, so I won't say.
And now, old fellow, God bless you. I will write again with the Comic when it comes. The Dilkes desire kind remembrance to you; so does Jane, and Fanny ditto,

and Tom ditto ditto. Don't forget me to all the 19th, including the staff, and believe me from my top joint to my butt,

My dear Tim,
Yours very truly,

Thomas Hood.

752, Alten Graben, Saturday, 29th April, 1837.

From *Memorials* I 257–60
1/Carl Weitershausen *Liederbuch für deutsche Krieger und deutsches Volk* (Darmstadt 1830, 2nd ed. 1837) 367–8. Hood's translation of 'Liebessprache eines lustigen Soldaten' is in *Works* VII 246.
2/*Tempest* I ii 400

TO
WILLIAM ELLIOT

My dear Doctor,

Many thanks for your kind letter; it positively did me good. But you seem seldom to put pen to paper without that effect, whether in letters or prescriptions. I wrote a very brief notice of the state of my health to Mr. Wright.

The Germans drink low sour wines, and have a horror here of anything that *heats* them in the way of drink, such as Spanish wine, &c. Yet, in spite of this care, they are subject to inflammatory attacks very commonly. The grippe[1] here took that character very decidedly.

Fanny was obliged to have leeches on her face. Tom's was highly inflamed, and had a great discharge from his nose and behind his ear, which were very sore. Mr. Dilke's attack here was attended with strong inflammation. We have heard only yesterday of an English lady obliged to have leeches; in fact, there are standing advertisements in the town papers where leeches are to be had cheap. I *know* of three barber-surgeons who bleed; there may be more. The one who bled me in February is only just set up, and he told me he had bled eighty that month; one may say two hundred and fifty, between the three operators, with safety. Inflamed eyes are extremely common here, and there is a peculiar inflammation of the

whole face called the 'rose.' I dare say the causes may be found in the very great changes of temperature here, both abroad and at home. The sun is *very* much warmer than in England, and the winds are much colder.
It is dangerous to pass from the sun into the shade. Then in the houses their mode of building is the worst possible. This one is a fair sample. Below, a passage right through the house, with front door to the street, and back door to the yard, always open till after ten at night. From the middle of this passage a well staircase right up through the house, terminating in the garrets, where the high roofs are full of unglazed windows or holes, for the special purpose of creating draughts for drying linen. On this stair, or open landings, all your room-doors open; so that you step out of a close stove-heated room into a thorough draught of the street air. I tried it once by thermometer: the room was 60°, and outside 45°. The winters are very cold, and doubly so in these comfortless buildings. I used to fancy the Germans never cut their hair, by way of defence against cold in the head, but I saw two fight the other day, and the hair was of the greatest feminine use, namely, to pull at. My last attack of spitting blood came on the moment after going down the stairs; and the first time I came up them again I caught the rheumatism, and had leeches on my foot, which bled all night. So I am somewhat reduced, and the diet here is anything but nourishing. Take for example the present bill of fare: no fish ever, no poultry now, no game of course, never any pork, veal killed at a week old, beef from cart-cows and plough-bullocks, which when cold is as dry and almost as white as a deal board. The very bread is bad, poor wheat mixed with rye and inferior meals. The people are poor, and the ground is wretchedly over-cropped. It is a beautiful country indeed to the *eye*, but I shall not regret leaving it. There are no books within reach, and no society, which I need not to care about, for the torpidity or apathy of mind in these people is beyond belief. German phlegm is no fable; but you will have a book about them next half-year, with plenty of sketches. The communication, too, with London is so vexatious and slow (it takes above a month) as to be a serious evil to me. I had resolved on a change on this account alone, when my last illness clenched my decision. We are going to Ostend, where I shall be not only within reach of England, but hope to be benefited by the sea-air, which always did me the most marked good. I have tried in vain to master German, partly from its difficulty and partly from having only the intervals between my attacks for all I had to write or draw. But Fanny talks it fluently, and Tom understands it perfectly as well as English. Fanny is very well now; and Tom a fine hearty fellow full of fun, which his motley jargon makes very comic. The '*Jane*,' too, wears very well. For myself, I keep up my spirits on my toast-and-water, which is all I drink, save

tea and coffee, and seem rallying again. I have a sort of appetite, too, if there were anything worth eating.

I really cannot do as the invalids do here. Mrs. Deubel, our landlady, as the first luxury on recovering from the grippe, comforted her inside with a mess of dried bullaces[2] in sour wine! Head only tells half the truth, for instance, of the breeches maker, who ate a bowl-full of plums; but he doesn't hint that he swallowed all the stones. I *know* that's their way of eating cherries![3] I could tell you some strange stories. The mortality here has been great, but of young children it is painfully so all the year round. And no wonder – the other day a mother called in a barber-surgeon to save expense. The child had a rash – he put ice on the head – turned the red spots blue and black, and it died.

When we are at Ostend you will perhaps be tempted to come over and see us and the country.

The cities in Belgium are interesting, and all within easy reach. I think I shall make a strange sitting to an artist, who wants my portrait for next year's exhibition! I look more like the Rueful Knight that a Professor of the Comic.

Pray tell Mrs. Elliot that the man at Moselweis, whither we went by moonlight, who had only a bit of plum tart in his house, failed subsequently, as might be expected, but another has taken the gardens, and thay are as popular as ever. I hope it has not given her a taste for White Conduit House,[4] and the like. But it was a sample of our German manners and amusements.

I have not learned smoking yet; but hate it worse than ever, since I see its effects on the mind and the person. However, should I leave Germany, I have introduced angling and am the Izaak Walton of the Rhine, Moselle, and Lahn.

I shall write a less selfish egotistical letter when I get to Ostend, to tell you how it agrees with me, as well as some little anecdotes, &c., I have not now time or space to get in; besides being a little weary of holding my pen. I flag at times rather suddenly, of course from weakness. Jane promises to write too, when settled, in answer to Mrs. E.'s kind letter, to whom she sends her kind regards with mine; and Fanny begs to mingle – not forgetting Willy.[5]

I am, my dear Doctor,
Very truly yours,

Thos. Hood.

I was ordered lately a sort of slow blister on the chest, which would only stick on by help of strips of adhesive plaister.

The grippe seemed to cause a great deal of this humour here.

It has been a nasty malignant disease, infinitely worse than the influenza as we used to have it in England. The people have a great horror of what they call a nervous fever. They say the French brought it from Moscow. But I suspect the sour wines here are very bad, *per se.*

752, Alten Graben, Coblenz, April 29th, 1837.

From *Memorials* I 260–5
1/Influenza
2/Wild plums
3/I have not found the reference to plums in Head, *Bubbles from the Brunnens*, but in the section Journey to Mainz' he does refer to a 'poor creature' eating cherries, 'stones and all' (3rd ed., 300).
4/Tavern and tea garden at Islington
5/The Elliot's son

TO
JOHN WRIGHT

Private

My dear Wright.
I was going to write to you, when your last letter arrived – but I will still address myself to your former one first.[1] You will please to keep what I shall point out to you of this to yourself. – I was going to write a long account of my health to you with my plan of moving to Ostend that you might consult Dilke upon it, *if you found him well enough* – but in the meantime Jane has written to M^{rs} D & received an answer, in which D. approves of it, in fact I have a letter from himself – and as he has improved so much, I have written the long detail direct to *him*, instead of yourself. The reason I want you to keep it to yourself is – lest Baily should take any fright & suppose I am in a *bad way*. The truth is your first letter scared me, by informing me that the cuts were above a month in going – for in that case every set of cuts would take a month to draw – a month to go – & a month to cut = 3 months! – Enough, with the best health, to neutralize any efforts to be early. I was meditating a move therefore on this sole account, the difficulty of communication – & you may suppose the passage of the blocks here with the blocks I wanted, above a month again, only confirmed this necessity. But in the interim, whilst it was coming – I was again seized with a spitting of blood – only six weeks after the one before – which, being serious to apprehend if repeated so – set me thinking of searching whether the climate itself here was not in fault. For I am really contrary

to your supposition very moderate in what I drink. I have never taken grog of a night as a practise since I left England, & since my march in October I have left spirits off *altogether*. As for wine what I used to drink was only Moselle of 10 pence a bottle – & lately at one time I only took some ginger wine Jane made – & at the last attack I was on an allowance of 2 glasses a day. Mind – no beer which is so nasty here I can't drink it.[2] On strict inquiry into it I am convinced the diseases here are of a decided inflammatory character – which of course with the slow carriage makes *two* imperious reasons for a change. Dr Elliott says you were to show him a letter about me which you have not done – but I shall write a minute account of my health to him & enclose it open in this, so you can read it, seal it & forward it to him. I was very seriously alarmed, & the more as the Drs seemed more attentive than usual – but now that I know the cause, I am in good spirits – & expect great advantages not only in health but business by the remove. This illness has hindered my German book of course – but if you calculate, had I been well, it could not have been ready for May. I only got the fresh blocks on the 14 April, – & if I had sent them instantly back *blank* you would not get them till the 14th May – allowing me no time to draw nor you to cut them. I do not see any possibility then of being ready for 1st June – the more's the pity. But I shall not lose an hour. And *I* do not see the injury of one to the other book in the same half year – but think they may be made to help each other – by good manifestoes etc – supposing both to be early & one a month or two months before the other.[3] Why Bulwer is always coming out! And finally it cannot be helped.[4] I am glad you liked the drawings. You are right about them – they will require *engraving* – and I should like them well done. They are not like the comic cuts mere jokes – but portraits & facsimiles of the people etc & should be correctly done. I hope to make it altogether a superior book. I shall have another set of good ones to send you. You may show them to Harvey if you like – but mind – not J.H.R.[5] I had a rare bother about the box with the Customs. It had been opened at the frontier & they wanted to open it again here. But I beat em. Some wet had got in & the blocks were almost wet, & one of the bindings was a little stained by damp. I admired the style of the Prince's books. I did not venture any more than you to open the Prince's things they seemed so well packed, but sent them off as they were. And Franck's are gone too – with a bit of cheese.[6] It is very good & toasts capitally. An't it provoking for me, by chance we can get porter here just now – & I daren't touch a drop of it! with my cheese. I'm on toast & water – tho very low & weak. But I am getting right & as the weather is better ride out – The great comfort is I've no cough or pain at the chest, so I think my lungs are sound. I am delighted to think of the leaving here it is a beautiful country & cheap

– but I am worn out by these repeated attacks and delays, – & anxieties – & then it is most dismally dull. No one to converse with – I cannot see a book – or know what is going on in the literary world – the Athm̤ excepted – that *is* something. But the worst of the Ath is it makes me long to read some of the books it reviews. Then the diet here is wretched for an invalid – & the domestic comforts few. This Country is any thing but the land of wine & corn & milk & honey one would think to look at it & the people are hateful, I mean unbearable to Englishmen. – They hate us I am quite convinced. I was amused by Boz – but there is no great power in it. – Sam Weller is the best. It is all a sort of Tom & Jerryism,[7] – but a grade above in gentility – tho still vulgar. There never could be a greater proof of the want of perception in Theatrical people than the attempt to dramatize it – there isn't an atom of plot – very little story – & no passion. Yates's apology that it was very difficult as a subject & had therefore had only a few hours devoted to getting it up was perfect![8] Some of the designs are clever – for instance the dinner.[9] I don't think the popularity of Boz will last or that he has compass or range for any thing else. Jane desires her best thanks for them.[10] I have given up any idea of colouring my sketches except perhaps such a bit as that slop pail to show what it is.[11] And possibly the caps in some carnival figures to show they are the *tri-color*, emblem of Buonaparteism etc And now to your last letter. The first thing I must mention is your astounding news of Branston & Lake House. I would hardly credit my eyes. That he should be my successor after all thats past[12] – And Quinn too – a liar & thief, – I should think it won't & can't do. I suspect Old Hubbard egged him on to it.[13] Do you remember Quinn's account of the potatoes – from which I calculated we must have eaten 6 or 7 pounds apiece per day? Well – I don't despair now of taking Buckingham Palace some day! I made out all your letter but one thing & thats a poser – I defy the Devil to make out the name of the gentleman who is coming up the Rhine. We have made out or I have, that it is Ughlan.[14] It is quite a comfort to us to hear that Dilke is better – he is an old man tho' he says – & so am I. We were very uneasy about him. He says in spite of his sorry Rhenish trip he won't swear *not* to visit us at Ostend. Now that would be quite a practicable distance for you & it would do us both good. I have some projects I could concert with you there. – I fancy that I already sniff the sea & feel it bracing me. I once literally left my bed for the first time to get into the Brighton coach – & the next morning but one I was walking on the *shingles*. The sea is life to me. I propose to quit here about the first of June – sooner if I can – but there are some little arrangemts̤ to make first – & I must get my money from Berlin[15] – & moreover pick up some more strength. I think it will be the saving of me – I feel sure another summer & winter here would kill me between them. Whereas give me health, & I think I can retrieve all. I think my last Comic & the German cuts show I have lost no power – but can pen & pencil as well as ever, and I mean to lose no time. We talked with our landlord today about going. His naturally extra long face grew still longer – and he complained bitterly of the state of trade, want of money etc – and unluckily for him tho I could hardly get a place when I first came to Coblenz there is now a list in the paper as long as your arm of lodgings to let. I have been trying to learn German: – but it is very hard. I am too deaf to catch the pronunciation & when I do can't imitate it. And the grammar is hard & the construction too – the Germans are fond of long-winded sentences, & as the verb comes at the end you're very much bother'd. My Teacher is a Jew – a Dr. of philosophy – & talks English so I hoped for some conversation – but wherever we set out it ends in buying selling & bartering. He is going to leave Coblenz in about a month. We went all of us to tea there the other day – and ate up all their passover cakes but two – & they mustn't just now eat any thing else. My fancies now are rather piscivorous – I am thinking of skate, brill turbot dabs & flounders – & even what Jane once resented so a red spotted plaice.[16] I have wished almost like a longing woman at times for oysters, fancying they would revive & nourish me. Dilke will call me a humbug if I say there's little nourishment on the Rhine. But so it is. And it gets worse. Last year Bavarian beer was to be had – none this. Westphalian hams ditto –And yet – oh yet when I look at the Rhine it is a lovely country – and I love the beautiful. I shall see all I can before I go. But I can carry the scenery vividly in my mind. We have missed De Franck much. By accounts from him he likes Bromberg – it is a superb place for fishing – but after wishing for salmon, they are so large he's afraid to attack them – on account of his tackle. I expect there will be some droll work with the princes – as there are enormous fish in their lakes etc & they are unused to our tackle – the Germans fish by main force – We have a sea-fish they call May fish comes as high as here but we do not expect it this season – it is a very inferior sort of bass. I don't know whether Baily paid the freight to Rotterdam – if so I have paid it twice as it was charged here. I shall not take the bulk of my books, which I have here overland, to Ostend – but ship them direct in a case for London which Baily can keep for me, – or yourself. I had partly made up my mind to let the copyrights go – but with the commercial crisis its a bad time for selling – and it would injure the Comic – so that I shall be glad if Baily will manage it. Mrs. Dilke writes that there is some one else a friend of Green's coming up here I believe shortly. I am glad you like my Letter on Copyright. I have got the Athm. with the 2nd. part – I think remembering Tilt I have let off the booksellers very easily; I was glad at having such a subject in the Ath^m^.[17] – when I get nearer, I hope to be in print there more frequently – for here, things I should like to have my say on are gone by before I can come at them. Ostend will be next best to being in London. I have some thoughts of beginning a New Series with next Comic if I can hit on any novelty to distinguish it. I have a dim idea of one in my head. It is quite a relief to me to feel that I can account for my attacks – I have no doubt about it! – You will find my arguments in the Doctors letter. The weather is setting in warm. I am still getting & looking better – & not to throw away a chance shall stick to my toast & water till I leave. The heat here is sudden – & would try me if I staid thro June. Jane, who has conquered a little German for household use will have to learn a new Jargon. They talk I believe bad *Dutch* & French – but I expect English also. The cities are very interesting & easy to get to – famous pictures to be seen – so, if you contemplate coming I will reserve my visits to them for your Company. I have lots of funny things to tell you. When Dilke was here I did not get a single palaver with him. He was too ill to talk or to be talked to – & when better I was away to Berlin – So I should also stand some chance here of dying of a suppression of ideas. For the rest we are well enough. Jane is hearty – Fanny who was somewhat unmanageable we have got into good order – she is very clever – reads much & remembers it to good purpose. As for Tom he is a fine funny spirited fellow with an excellent temper & very strong. Yours that I knew must be getting into big boys. My godson an't much the better for his godfathers Christian looking after is he? And mine are all away from their godparents amongst Catholics and jews. Fanny makes crosses of wax – & Tom is very fond of passover cakes. Our maid is a Roman catholic but the easiest one I ever saw. She confesses only once a year & very seldom goes to mass – from shere indolence. She is the most phlegmatic being ever was.

> Should the whole frame of Nature round her break
> She unconcern'd would hear the mighty crack –[18]

provided it did not hurt herself. A fig for German Philosophy – it's selfishness. I've written to the Doctor – & you'll have it inside this. My hand aches so, & my head is so muddled that I cannot write more – So pray give our kindest regards to Mrs. Wright – & the same to yourself – I do now live in hopes to see you before very long, & so remain

My dear Wright Yours ever truly

Thos Hood

Pray dont forget me to E. Smith – & recommend to him in my name to hold his shoulders instead of his sides when he laughs. Did I ever tell you there is a young man over the way so like you, that in speaking of him we always call him not knowing his name – John Wright? I will try to fatten my face up for Mr. Lewis against he comes. God bless you. We shall see Miss Moore of Wanstead[19] as we go thro Belgium. Kind regards to Folkard Harvey & all friends. Tell Baily to beware of falling out of gigs during a commercial crisis or people may think he's *broken*. My next I hope will be from Ostend. Tell Dilke when you see him not to forget to enquire about the passports.

752 Alten Graben. [*30 April 1837*]

MS UCLA. Address: 'John Wright Esq[re]/ 4 New London Street / London / Angleterre.' PM: 'COBLENZ/30/4,' 'LONDON/4/MAY/1837.' Published in part in *Memorials* I 265–70. 'Private' is underlined three times.

1/Wright's letters, now in the Bristol Central Library, are dated 17 March and 20 April.
2/Wright had written: 'we all play the devil with our insides by *grog of a night* ... I know you have injured yourself by an abuse of spirits ... drink one or two glasses a day & this will suit your pocket as well as your health.'
3/Baily had written across Wright's second letter: "I do upon my word believe that a very serious injury be done to [the German book] & the Comic if they appear in one half year ... I shall be mortified ... if [the German book] is not ready by the 1st week in June.' *Up the Rhine* did not in fact appear until December 1839.
4/The whole of the letter up to this point is omitted from *Memorials*.
5/John Hamilton Reynolds. I cannot account for Hood's suspicion of his brother-in-law.
6/The contents of the parcel from Wright included fishing-tackle, copies of Hood's books for Prince Czartoryski, Count Wildenbruck, and Franck, and cheese for Hood.
7/A reference to Pierce Egan *Life in London* (1821), illustrated by Isaac and George Cruikshank, the main characters of which were Jerry Hawthorn and Corinthian Tom.
8/*Peregrinations of Pickwick* was performed at the Adelphi theatre on 3 April 1837. Frederick Yates 'apologized for the inevitable errors attending the first representation of a piece which had been got up with more than usual rapidity,' *Times* 4 April, 5.
9/Perhaps that facing 265 in the first edition, the work of Hablot K. Browne (1815–82), better known as 'Phiz.'
10/Wright had written: 'I have sent you as I thought you might like to see them the Pickwick papers as many as are out. Boz is making a great deal of money and has got the Town by the ear ... [He] has caught the town with his one string. I do not deny he has great merit for his fun and observation but I think he must be content to graze in one field and that a very small one if he attempts to jump out of it he'll never get out of the ditch on the other side. The Pickwick I present to Mrs Hood with kind regards and hope to give the rest by hand when completed.'
11/*Up the Rhine*, 253, uncoloured
12/Probably Robert Branston, Wright's partner in engraving the illustrations to the *Comic Annuals*, 1830–3. Wright's letters which touch on this business are quoted by J.C. Reid, *Thomas Hood* (1963) 133–4.
13/I have not identified Quinn and Hubbard.
14/The word was surely 'Coghlan'; Wright calls him 'a gentleman Rhine Author.' Francis Coghlan wrote *A Guide up the Rhine* (1837), published by Baily.
15/For the articles referred to in note 6. Their cost was £26.5.0.

16/Discussed in *Memorials* I 24–5
17/Hood's letter appeared in *The Athenaeum*, 15–27 April. At the time when he wrote, the author's copyright extended either for 28 years or for his lifetime, whichever should be the longer. Thomas Noon Talfourd was about to take up the question in parliament. Hood's claim, based on the nobility of literature and the respect consequently due to authors, was that their copyright should be made 'heritable property,' *Athenaeum* 1837, 305: *Works* VI 410.
18/Misquoting Addison's translation of Horace, Ode III, Bk III
19/Unidentified

TO
WILLIAM ELLIOT

My dear Doctor.
At last I have the pleasure of dating from this place, where we arrived safely on Tuesday last – very much fatigued, though we had come by easy stages, & been 10 days on the road. Indeed on my arrival at Liege – after a long very hot day's ride, I could scarcely speak – I have since thought, from over temperance – for a glass of porter at Brussels revived me amazingly – and unfortunately I could get no more afterwards. Except a little ginger wine, & even that not latterly. I had literally not touched wine spirit or beer for 4 or 5 months. However a day's rest now & then & the good bread & meat of Belgium as we proceeded brought me through – and here we are, located at about £4 per ann. more than at Coblenz, but with a £50 worth more of English-like comforts, great and small. We have even a very good spare-bed & room at your service should you feel inclined to a summer trip across. I have waited some days & purposely exposed myself to a smart sea breeze every morning in order to speak of its effect upon me – and really I cannot perceive any inconvenience from it to my lungs – and only an increase of appetite as to my stomach, which fortunately I am now able to gratify with something like wholesome food. I took care before leaving Coblenz to enquire of the Doctor there, as to the points contained in your letter, & he states as follows. That the first attack (about Feby twelve months) was the most serious – the later ones being more consequent on the grippe – that the blood came from the lungs –* was clear, & unmixed with other matter – & rather considerable in quantity. It is my own impression that the first time the blood was darker – latterly more bright & rather frothy. The first time I had been walking but not far – it was very warm & I returned with a feeling of great lassitude – drank a few glasses of French red wine – & in about ½ an hour, with a sort of slight cough, apparently only sufficient to clear my throat, I

* He perhaps stated otherwise before, not to alarm Jane.

discharged the blood, so freely as to come also through the nostrils. No cough previously – nor pain at the chest – nor thickness of breath – & only an occasional cough for 2 or 3 days afterwards which served to bring up stale clotted blood – unmixed with anything – but accompanied with a little phlegm, of the common kind, & no more than might be expected from the expectoration. I did not particularly examine but my impression is there was no pitchy matter like undigested blood downwards. I seemed to feel, or fancy, a relief from the discharge of blood – & up to the journey to Berlin never felt any pulmonary annoyance whatever. Indeed my lungs I considered my strong point – nobody could be freer than I had always been from coughs, wheezings, pains in the chest, short breath & the like – plenty of colds in the head but rarely even a sore throat. I still think it likely the first bleeding might not originate in the same part as the later ones. Then came the march to Berlin in Octr. last, when fainting from heat & the smell of stale tobacco in the night coach, I let down the window – & the wind was very cold. The next evening I was seized with stitchlike pains in each breast, that affected my breathing & speaking – they continued, but diminishing, 4 days, or so – & then I proceeded. I returned from Berlin apparently well & ruddy, but the 2nd day after getting home turned very pale with a constant physical depression, & lowness of spirits, so that I shed tears in reading, & even without cause – then came a violent cough, and I had shiverings on getting into the cold bed at night which almost took away my breath. I have little doubt this was grippe, as it immediately raged at Berlin – and at Coblenz it took a decided character in causing congestion of blood & hemorrhage. There was a deal of lancetting and leaching in the town in consequence. Then came the second effusion, not quite so much as the first – but, with the same symptoms. The other attacks followed at intervals, the grippe which the Dr. attributed the second attack to, seeming to linger in the system, with Fanny & Tom as with me, & of an inflammatory tendency – & during all these months the weather was dreadful & unseasonable – the temperature varying widely and suddenly several times a day. It is only since in the last attacks that I feel any uncomfortable consciousness of having a chest – by slight pains & not very frequent – generally on the right side about the nipple or thence towards the shoulder. The last time I had a sort of slow drawing plaster which produced a discharge not of water like a blister but water & matter, yellow – and some darkish – which lasted a fortnight & then healed under the spermaceti. This was put where I had felt most pain – which was very slight compared with that first felt on the road to Berlin. But except the usual coughing up stale blood – by which I mean a consistency to hang together – I have had no cough since – & can draw, now, a long inspiration without any pain any where. From these symptoms I derive hope that as yet the lungs are not seriously unsound – & consequently that with care & strict diet I may get over it ... I own I thought for a long time the blood must come from the stomach, partly because of the great weakness of the bowels & lower part of the body; & partly from the absence of all pain in the chest etc. You may judge how easily the blood comes, when I tell you that for want of better indications I have had doubts whether it did not come from my head or from vessels immediately in the throat. For instance the last time, on waking in the morning, I felt something rattling like phlegm in the throat. I hawked it up, & saw it was blood & then more followed in the same way. It ceased of itself – but at night after coming down the cold stairs it immediately came on again, & then I got bled. But in the intervals of the attacks I do not spit any blood – indeed I do not expectorate at all. A German Doctor at Gotha, to whom I described the pains in my chest, on my way to Berlin, thought it was cold, & *in the muscles* – indeed the pains seemed at times excited by motion of the arms or body. For the rest my bowels are more regular, not in extremes as they used to be – but I still suffer when a little tired from weakness in the lower part of the body & swelling about the groins – this after standing or walking comes on rather suddenly – all at once I seem to have passed the point of endurance – the bowels all seem to weight downwards – sometimes I have felt a sort of girdling tightness or drawing as of a string round my inside, – it seems almost to bend me forwards in walking – as if the suspenders of the bowels had given way, or that I wore my braces inwardly, & they were too slack. My legs also are weak. I am also a good deal troubled & inflated at times with wind which rolls about & rumbles but will not, & apparently cannot, quit. This, with total loss of appetite, & almost aversion to meat, was one of the original symptoms when I first came over – the dreadful spasms which I afterwards had o'nights seemed, so to speak, between the stomach & lungs – I could only breathe sitting upright – the least leaning on either side became very painful. Is it not probable – supposing the original disease to have been inflammation of the stomach – which was neglected or wrongly treated – that it might become chronic, & finally by sympathy affect the bowels below & the lungs above it? That would serve to explain my state perhaps. I ought to have mentioned that about the time of the last attack I had now and then headaches, with a sort of confusedness, – only comparable to the state after too much wine over night. Once or twice a little pain about the edge of the blade bone towards the spine. At present, that is to say, in common now, not at this mere particular moment, I have only very slight, & very temporary pain in the chest (right side) but no particular point or spot – generally between the nipple &

shoulder – seemingly most common when a feeling of fatigue. I do not cough at all nor expectorate, nor swallow phlegm, – & can draw & hold a long breath without any inconvenience or unusual sensation. My appetite is very fair – and I sleep well – often wakening, in the morning, however, rather low, & languid (but the weather is very warm) and I have occasional accesses of physical depression during the day–probably from slight indigestion, or flagging, or want of refreshment – for being very weak, all these things are very sensible to the feeling – and easily brought on, & not so gradually as in health. My tongue is clean, & no bad taste or fevered mouth – indeed I do not suffer under fever – I live temperately – & if I suspect any the least chill – or symptoms of common cold, I take care to promote perspiration.
I seem to bleed easily at a scratch or cut, & the blood is *bright red* & *thin*. My pulse as far as I can judge is good. Neither very weak nor very strong. I found the perpetual motion of the body from the jolting of the coach rather excites the blood – & causes rushing noises in the head – & in coach travelling I have invariably remarked it to produce distress to the bowels, an apparent looseness, or *false* inclination to stool – with bearing down – & protrusion of the anus. This is very marked – but the extreme sensibility and irritability of stomach that used to distress me is nearly gone. I eat much bread here & fish, – & a little meat. Some good wholesome beer too, brewed in the town & not strong I venture to drink: but no wine, though Bordeaux is cheap & good here. As to tranquillity of mind I believe anxiety may have had some share if not in creating, in aggravating the disease.
I am well aware of the potency of the action of the mind on the health, – & for that very reason, knowing that the best spirits were my best friends I have fought up against depressions, more cheerfully than might be supposed. But meaning to do that which is honourable & right – with the consciousness of doing all I could – & the confidence that my case was not irritrievable my heart has never acquiesced in melancholy attacks – tho I have had to struggle against the want of society & books. It has been much against my rallying in health, that the attacks have so abridged my time that when tolerably [well] I have had to work unremittingly to make up for lost time – & this haste adds much to the mental wear & tear. Whilst every delay was a positive loss as to the sale of my books. The long passages of parcels to & fro on the Rhine were also sources of great vexation anxiety & urgency, six weeks, each way, cutting deeply into the time for drawing printing & engraving. This I shall now be rid of – and the climate is at least a change for the better. I do not undervalue your advice as to the South of France or Isle of Wight – but the truth is I must not be in England but at the same time within easy & quick communication with it. To the present time I have only the negative comfort of not

having receded in my circumstances – should the new Copyright Act pass I have perhaps acquired something though not immediately available[1] – but as I have before now made as much in one year as would cancel all my liabilities, I see no reason to despair of yet returning to England (health allowing) in a year or two a free man. I feel sure but for illness I should ere now have been so – & perhaps now the sea, as it has done formerly will give me strength. And if I could but once begin to *cancel* – I believe it would do more for me than climate diet or anything else. In the mean time I have English-like comforts round me – my wife's care never fails – & my children are an amusement & relaxation to me. I draw & write with relish when well enough – & have a decently clear conscience & an old reliance in Providence. So you see my good Doctor, I do not mean to give myself over in any of my maladies till you do – & pray write to me at your leisure what you think & recommend in my bodily case. And I must beg one more medical favour of you – We spent two very pleasant days at the country house of Monsr. Nagelmacher a banker at Liege. The whole family are very amiable. Made. N. is highly accomplished – plays, sings – & paints in oil like a master. Valerie, about 10 years old, a most interesting child, made our Fanny very happy, – & Tom Junr. raced about the grounds till red hot – then slept – and then Da Capo. Some years since Valerie had a complaint in her throat – they call it – les glandes amygdales gonflées[2] – which a Paris surgeon removed by cutting. *But a small fragment remains.* Jane recollected a cousin of hers being cured of something similar, by some liquid or powder, applied on the end of a feather to the part – & Mad N is so anxious on the subject & we are all so taken with Valerie, that I have undertaken to ask a Doctor in whose skill I have reason to place the highest confidence whether from that fragment the disease is likely to recur – & also if there be any expedient, in that case besides cutting. Pray oblige me by ½ dozen lines on the subject when you write – & excuse this further appeal to your great kindness.

I will now give you a sketch of our departure from Coblenz. Beautiful as the Rhine is, I left its banks without the slightest regret. Coblenz I was particularly glad to turn my back upon – for it was associated with nothing but illness, suffering, privation, disgust, & vexation of spirit. I left not a single friend or acquaintance worth a sigh – Lieutenant de Frank being at Bromberg since October – & every thing I had to do with the people, especially at the end, was attended by circumstances of a kind almost to disgust one with human nature. The history of our last ten days would present only a series of petty robberies, just short of open force – lying, dissimulation, treachery, malice, hatred, & all uncharitableness.[3] First a shopkeeper took a shilling or its equivalent & swore it was only sixpence –

then the work girl stole a handsome book, a recent present from London to Fanny – then came a bill for half a year instead of a quarter – then our maid grumbled because as we were going away our tradespeople no longer tipped her – & then our landlord, knowing our witness was at Bromberg flatly denied a verbal agreement & wanted to make me repair etc. As a sample of his conscience he demanded 10 dollars, for whitewashing – I sent for a man who offered to whitewash the whole place for 4½ – & the rascal himself took 6. He moreover conducted himself so I threatened him with a gendarme where upon he retreated, & vented himself by shouting Dumm Englandërn – Stupid Englishers – from the top of his own stairs. Between our broken German & his broken French it made a tolerable farce. Then a civil functionary & his wife, fellow lodgers, condescended to all but beg some of our furniture & our stock of wood – & then a language master an old acquaintance came, & helped us to sell our goods, by buying some for himself thro a sham broker. This was a farce too – In fact they cheated me almost to the water's edge; for Jane called to pay a Bookseller a door or two from the packets office & he made her pay for a book we had never had. And finally Jane only discovered yesterday that at the very last of the packing, the maid, not the old thief that you saw but another, had abstracted a new unworn worked collar. This is but a sample of the usual style. In short with cheating & downright thieving I doubt whether we have economized much – at least we might have lived in England *in the same style*, without carpets & other comforts, for the same money. The very coat I started in, I was charged 11 shillings more for, than to my knowledge had been asked of a German. It is not pleasant nor even a pecuniary trifle to have to pay from 20 to 30 per cent *on your whole expenditure* for being an Englishman – & you cannot afford it – but it is still more vexatious to the spirits & offensive to the mind to be everlastingly engaged in such a petty warfare for the defence of your pocket, & equally revolting to the soul to be unable to repose confidence in the word or honesty of any human being around you. In aggravation I am persuaded that the English are no favourites with the natives. They are too independent for the serviles – & when not abject to German despotism the natives are Frenchified & Buonapartists. The proud poor Barons detest the English for their superior wealth – & talk who may of intellectual Germany, I have found none of their mental acquisitions or ability. I never met with a conversible being, – my doctor, a skilful man I believe & of rank in his profession, was in private but a bigotted Catholic a member of a sort of local Propoganda – Add to all, tho it never meddled with me seriously, there is a sense of discomfort & insecurity in living under a despotism – dependent on the whim of one man, or more properly perhaps on the state of his viscera. I was told, by one party, on complaining of the Coblenzers – Oh it was my fault – when I might have gone into good society. You would hardly believe this alluded to my declining the acquaintance of a family – the mother of which actually fought a duel with her lover – used to extort money from her husband by a pistol at his head – & was popularly accused of killing a daughter by throwing her down stairs! A little ago the commanding general of the Rhenish provinces, broke off his nephew's marriage even after betrothing (which is very rare in Germany) with a Colonel's daughter on account of her behaviour with other officers – this I supposed was good Society too – as it was certainly high – but nothing for us to covet. We knew one family – & the grown daughter would amuse herself the whole day with a child's puzzle. Indeed at their evening parties, they play at forfeits, blacking faces, and such intellectual amusements. I am afraid this may read like spleen but it is the truth. For Mrs. Elliott's amusement I will relate the last affair I heard of at Coblenz. A Miss L— had refused a young officer of the same regiment I marched with, – but after his departure wrote to him & accepted him. Since then there have been three duels on her account, between officers at Coblenz – & now to the utter indignation of all the militaires, she has given her hand to a Lawyer! Ex uno etc.[4] You will not be surprised to hear that as soon as I found that we were out of Prussia I threw up all our caps hats & bonnets with a mental vow never to enter the dominions of Frederick William again. Our entrance into Belgium was auspicious – on the very finest day of the season. The Belgian Douane opened a box or two, mistaking me at first – what an unwelcome compt. – for a Prussian – but passed all the rest. I could have smuggled very easily – but a genuine Prussian I understand gets well overhauled – & he deserves it as their own system is so rigorous. At Cologne we were so lucky as to get a return coach to Liege & the driver happened to be an excoachman of Monsr. Nagelmacher's so that we had not difficulty at all. At that House there was a German governess – & from near Coblenz and – don't it sound like prejudice? – she was as disagreeable as her country folk. We had a laughable description of her dignified descents to the kitchen to fetch her supper, & her dignified marches up again if it was not ready, – for she would not condescend to ask for it of servants. The latter all called her the Proud German.

Here we had two days rest. – then slept at Tirlemont – rested another day at Brussels – slept at Ghent, and came on here by the canal-boat. I saw nothing, being fatigued, of any place we passed thro – but the Cities are all highly interesting & at easy distances, so that when I get strong enough I shall go round to them. Brussels seemed a nice little city to live in. We like the aspect of this place – the sands are capital for the children who are as happy as can be with their shell baskets. I ought to tell you that little Tom was a capital traveller – ate drank & slept heartily – was always merry, & chatted & made friends with everybody – all the coachmen waiters maids etc. were in love with him – so that our trouble was less than might have been expected, with such a youngling. We had a very narrow escape from damp sheets at a Hotel at Aix which advertises itself as in connexion with the Emperor's Bath, & really the bedlinen seemed to have just come out of it. So we slept without – & the chambermaid had even the conscience not to show herself in the morning. In my state, such a mishap as a damp bed would have been serious ... I could not help remarking that we paid the dearest frequently at the worst hotels – as well as the best. The middle ones, being most reasonable & in essentials most comfortable. I found the wide *green* landscapes of Belgium very refreshing, & the rich clover fine corn & handsome cattle in the meadows, partake something of the air of a Land of Promise, after the delusive sordidness of Rhenish Prussia. The extreme cleanliness too as for instance between Bruges & Ghent, was a delicious feature after the German filth. But to enjoy them people should come from the Rhine to Belgium instead of vice versa, – now the general route of our tourists who go to Antwerp instead of Rotterdam & thence by the railroad to Brussels. It is no slight relief to me to hear English and French & even Flemish instead of that detestable gabble of gutterals which may account perhaps for the German partiality to turkeycocks. The people here are notoriously favourable to the English & seem civil good humoured & obliging. They also look healthy – I walked into the market on purpose to observe them, & saw only ruddy faces polished by the sea air. If they cheat us which is something I do not yet know they do it with more civility, & a better manner, which is something per contra. Our servant took a fancy to Tom & has brought him a little old family relic a china cup & saucer for his especial use, – & our landlady actually thinks for us & keeps adding little articles of comfort for our use, – tho I never saw lodgings so completely furnished – even to umbrellas. In my own little room I have a chamber organ should I get weary of grinding my brains – & the kitchen, little as it is, is complete even to an eightday clock. In fact I feel we are very lucky – for some old occupants have already applied for our apartments which speaks well for the people of the house – & the place is filling, & every day lodgings get scarcer. The King & Queen[5] are expected in a fortnight, & will live within 3 or 4 doors – so that I find we are actually at the Court End. There are a good many English & some foreigners – we shall have a few Germans by & bye to bathe so that I shall have an opportunity of seeing how they behave when away from home. Our friends Mr. Wright, Mr. Dilke & probably Mrs. D are to come over & visit us shortly, so that we have cards now with At Home upon them.

It is indeed but a step across compared to our late distance: – and I felt it quite a a comfort to reflect as I stood on the sand that there is but the sea & a few hours between me & England in case of extremity. I am none of those who do, or affect to, undervalue their own country, because they happen to have been abroad. There is a great deal of this Citizen of the worldship professed now a days, in return for which I think the English only get ridiculed by foreigners as imbeciles & dupes. Overweening nationality is an absurdity – but the absence of it altogether is a sort of crime. The immense sums drawn from England & lavished abroad is a great evil, added to other pressures at home – We read that last year, the Romans were starving on acct of the absence of the English deterred by the cholera – & if such be the effect of their absence on a foreign capital or country it must be injurious in as great a degree on their own. Thus Spitalfields weavers starve – & the waiter at the Belle Vue at Coblenz rides his own horse in summer, & in winter in his sledge in a cap of crimson velvet.

We are luxuriating on fish – it composes, with vegetables, my dinner, as often as not. For 6 cents we get as many shrimps as we can eat so that in addition to always dining, which was not often the case in Coblenz I always breakfast. I suffer rather from laziness after dinner when I have eaten tolerably – with a kind of wish for my tea or something to help my digestion – which I suppose is the only inconvenience from the disuse of wine. I sometimes since here, find myself irrisistibly attacked too by sleep in the afternoon, but I attribute it to the morning walk & the sea air, as it has been breezy weather tho fine ever since we came. I was never so strong or so stout in my life as after a six weeks at Hastings when I went to recover from rheumatic fever. I sailed daily fair or rough steering the boat myself, – & drank always on my return a large bowl of milk – with bread & butter by way of lunch. But my stomach was stronger then, – now I fear it would refuse the milk. Perhaps if I find the sea air affects me favourably I had better try the boating again which gives it in an intenser dose. Up to this point, & the last walk it blew almost a gale I have not felt any bad effect from the sea air – being out at least 2 hours each time. We think of Bathing for Tom & Fanny – they visibly are better already for the coast, indeed Tom looks quite handsome with his bronzed little face and white teeth & Fanny has acquired a good colour, – & there is no keeping them from the loaf. We are all in mourning here for the King[6] – that is to say we wear such black as we happen to have – myself not included, for I feel the heat so that I dress as lightly as I can – I have no doubt I pass for something extreme therefore in my politics as the mourning is very general here with the English. But like an old man I give up to comfort all dandyish fashion or forms that might interfere with my comfort, – & go in dishabille of green & white. Indeed the last two years have been as twenty to me in effect, and I almost feel as if on the strength of my weakness, I could give advise & dictate to young men, who were born no later than myself. However I hope to see you again before I am quite grey & childish, & in the mean time pray accept my felicitations on the satisfactory settlement of your brother, with my heartfelt thanks for the kind interest you have taken in me, & every best wish I can think of towards you & yours down to the last little unknown. Jane unites with me in kindest regards to Mrs. Elliott, & yourself & Fanny begs to add her love which Tom echoes.

I am my dear Doctor Ever truly yours

Thos Hood

Monday

39, Rue Longue / à Ostend. [*26 June 1837*]

MS Columbia. Address: 'Dr Elliot / Stratford Green / Essex / near London.' PM: 'OSTENDE/1837/28/JUIN,' 'LONDON/29/JUNE/1837.' Published in part in *Memorials* I 277–84. The letter is dated in another hand 27 June 1837, but Monday, to which Hood refers at the end, was the 26th.

1/Talfourd's bill, brought in on 18 May 1837, proposed the extension of copyright to 60 years after the author's death.
2/Tonsillitis
3/The last three characteristics occur in the *Book of Common Prayer*, 'Litany.'
4/*Ex uno disce omnes:* from one you may learn all.
5/Leopold I and Louise of Belgium
6/William IV died on 20 June.

TO
JOHN WRIGHT

My dear Wright,
You will see from the above address that we are not only safe here, but settled, after a prosperous but slow journey; nothing lost or broken but a little bottle of marking-ink, so that it was luckily performed, with the advantage of fine weather to boot. Our exit from Coblenz was worthy of the entrance: the farce did not, like many modern ones, fall off at the end. We had a famous row with our landlord. He rushed up his own stairs, and shouted from the top, 'Dumme Engländer!' And then Jane had a scrimmage with him. R— i[1] played the Italian traitor to both sides all the time. Finally, just on the gunwale of the packet, as it were, they gave us a

finishing touch; for Jane called to pay a bookseller on the road, and he made her pay for a number more than she had had.

As for Katchen, she cried at the parting point – partly, I suppose, because we did not take her with us (for she told all her friends she intended it), and partly because she was bidding farewell to good wages and to *enough to eat* – a case, by her own account, rather uncommon with servants in Coblenz. We had a fine trip down to Cologne, lodged comfortably, and took a coach to Liège, with an old coachman, oddly enough, of the very family we were going to visit. Next night at Imperial Aix, and the following one, after a long pull, and a fine, but tremendously hot, day at M. Nagelmacher's at Liège. He has a beautiful country seat an hour's drive from the city; but I was so exhausted with heat and fatigue I could scarcely speak, and kept my room all the evening, but rested there, and enjoyed the two next days extremely.

There are beautiful grounds, rhododendrons, hill, wood, and all quite to my taste, with a superb view. Moreover, one of the most amiable and accomplished families I ever met with. The lady paints in oils beautifully. I really took them for good Dutch pictures. A delightful sweet girl about ten made Fanny very happy, and Tom raced about like a young Red Indian, till he was half baked in the sun.

The Nagelmachers all speak French except Mademoiselle, so that Jane had to sit very like the matron of the Deaf and Dumb School, but she made up for it with our friend Miss Moore. We parted sworn friends with the Nagelmachers; ate and slept wretchedly at a dirty inn at Tirlemont; and the next night reached Brussels, where we rested the Sunday, too tired to stir out, except the children, who went to see St. Gudule.[2] Besides, it was wet weather. I started next day with a new coachman for Ghent. Slept at Ghent, and thence by trackshuyt (or barge) through Bruges to this place, where we arrived at seven in the evening in good style rather as to fatigue, after such a long pull with children, luggage, and bad health. I ventured to drink a glass of porter on leaving Brussels, which helped me up amazingly, as for four or five months previously I had not positively touched wine, beer, or spirit, till that hour. I then thought I might have held the curb too tightly, but there was no more porter to be had all the rest of the way. Jane, of course, is fatigued very much, but no more than was to be expected.

To do poor Fanny and Tom justice, they were models for grown travellers, ate and drank whatever came before them, slept when tired, waked all alive, talked and made friends with everybody – waiters, maids, coachmen, and all – so much so, that the coach was loaded with large bouquets of purple and white lilac, and other flowers: got into no scrapes except from exuberant fun, and came in at the end as fresh as larks, though almost roasted from sitting in the coach with their backs to the sun and no blinds.

Give my remembrance to all, and come as soon, and stay as long, as you can, Jane begs to say ditto, as I feel sure it will do me good, body and mind, to see friends.

Yours, ever truly,

Thos. Hood.

39, Rue Longue, Ostend, June 28th, 1837.

From *Memorials* I 271–4
1/Ramponi
2/Cathedral of Ste Gudule and St Michel

TO
JOHN WRIGHT

My dear Wright,

Do not forget to write yourself, whenever you mean to come, that we may meet you at the landing-place, and I trust it will not be long before we have that pleasure; and have the kindness to bring with you the articles mentioned at the end, chiefly books. I hope Mr. and Mrs. Dilke will come to see us in our new quarters, or we shall die of suppressed jokes, stories, and arguments we were to have had on the Rhine. We are just recovering from the fatigue of our journey – poor wretched travellers that we are – and I begin to enjoy myself as well as my weakness will permit.

We have now been here a week, and I have exposed myself to the sea-breeze to judge of its powers; and, as it has had no evil effect on my lungs, I begin to hope that they are not very unsound, and that in other respects for sea-side enjoyment there cannot be a better place.

The Esplanade is very fine, and the sands famous for our brats, who delight in them extremely. We munch shrimps morning and night, as they are very abundant, and quite revel in the fish. I have dined several days on nothing else, and it is such a comfort to think of only that strip of sea between us, quick communication by packets, and posts four times a week, that I feel quite in spirits as to my work, and hopeful as to my health. I am very weak, but otherwise as well as can be expected from such repeated attacks.

But I have moved only just in time, for I feel convinced the Rhine was killing me: between hurry, worry, delay, tedium, disgust, the climate, and the diet, and the consciousness, with all these disadvantages, of no very great improvement besides in health. I write a long letter by this same post to Dr. Elliot, with further particulars that I may have the benefit of his advice, how to live and keep alive.

I have now the comfort of thinking, that whatever I may do will not be long in reaching you, whether blocks or MS. It will even be possible here to see the proofs; not that I undervalue your kindness in that respect, but the German book would have unusual difficulties as to names, words, &c. I shall see some of the Germans here, as some come for bathing; and I propose, if strong enough, to take a trip, by-and-by, through the old Flemish cities, which are well worth seeing. Perhaps we may get together to one or two of them, as the communication is easy.

Bring with you such of the German cuts as are engraved, and arrange for as long a stay as you can, as it will do me good to converse a little about old times. The first news we had on arrival here was of the King's death, a kind old friend of mine.[1] I do not mourn for him visibly, for it is too hot for blacks; and the English here, who are all blacked at top, or bottom, or in the middle, no doubt take me for an extreme Tory or Radical. The King and Queen of Belgium come here in a fortnight; so that I shall be the neighbour of royalty, as they will live in our street, only three or four doors off. I am rather tired from writing at length to Elliot; and, moreover, feeling you are to come soon, I do not care to pen what I would rather say personally. So, with kind regards to Mrs. W., in which, with love to yourself and the boys, Jane and Fanny join, not forgetting my godson in particular,

I am, dear W.,
Yours ever truly,

Thos. Hood.

Tom, whom I have told of your hand, expects you, and even anticipates your appearance. You would laugh to see him walk with one arm trussed up like a fowl's wing, as he expects to see you.[2]

39, Rue Longue, Ostend, 30th June, 1837.

From *Memorials* I 274–6

1/Hood had dedicated to William IV the *Comic Annual* for 1832.

2/Hood's son notes that Wright had suffered an accident while shooting.

TO
JOHN WRIGHT

My dear Wright,

We find ourselves very comfortably settled now. If you come, there is a spare bed for you, and another for the Dilkes; so that if you should come together there is room for all. I am looking anxiously for your coming, as I think it would do me good, and give me spirits to finish off in style the books for this year. There are four mail packets come every week, and one Company's steamer. We have had famous weather, not one unfair day since we came; but if you prefer bad weather you can wait for it, though I think it will be late this year.

There are still a few things I should like to have: Talfourd's speech on copyright, Tegg's remarks on ditto, and Lamb's Letters.[1] I could perhaps make an article for Dilke of the latter, and weave into it some anecdotes, &c., of Lamb I was collecting before. It is published by Moxon.

I cannot make up my mind to write any particulars to you, as I look forward to the pleasure of telling them. I get the 'Athenaeum' regularly here on the Wednesday; and have been introduced to two people here, Colley Grattan[2] and – but the other I will show you, and then surprise you with his name.

I wish I could end here without having worse news; but our *début* here has not been in all respects lucky. Poor Jane has had a terrible sore throat, so much so, that I was obliged to call in a doctor; who gave her two grains of calomel only, but which seemed to revive all she had taken in her former illness, and in consequence she had her mouth in a dreadful state. A warm bath will carry this off, and we have one within a door or two; but she has had a relapse with her throat, probably from coming down too soon. I am assured it is *not* an affection belonging to the place, which they say is very healthy, and the people look so. Grattan has been here some years, and speaks well of it too. Poor Tom has had a most severe pinch with the street door, and has lost the nail of his finger; but let's hope this is all the footing we have to pay here.

And now, my good fellow, come as soon and stay as long as you can; and tell B— not to make me quite such an *Exile of Hearin'*.[3] And mind do not write to me any of your *poste restante* but to the address at the head of this. It will save postage if you bring your next yourself. I cannot help thinking that perhaps, as the French say, you *are* here next Saturday, in which hope I sign and *resign* myself, dear Wright,

Yours very truly,
Thomas Hood.

Saturday will be St. Swithin's day, so bring your umbrella. *That* puts me in mind of an impromptu on poor William the IVth.: –

'The death of kings is easily explained,
 And thus it might upon his tomb be chiselled –
"As long as Will the Fourth could *reign*, he *reigned*,
 And then he mizzled."'[4]

I am contemplating an ode to Queen Victoria for the 'Athenaeum.' You may tell Dilke I think Janin's last paper a capital example of political criticism.[5] I own I am curious to see T. Tegg's 'Remarks on Copyright;' so don't forget it. Pray poke up Dilke: and should he have any qualms about coming, scrunch them in the shell! You would do me a world of good among you; and I have never had a palaver with him yet. And it would not hurt *him*. Besides, he went to Margate some summers back, and it 'ain't to compare' with this for selectness and sea. I suppose, and hope, he is tolerably well. Unless you come soon, let me have a bulletin, rather clearer than those about the King. Why can't the Queen make me Consul here? I don't want to turn anybody out, but can't there be nothing-to-do enough for two? The King and Queen of Belgium are coming here. I rather think the Dilkes, who are very fashionable, are hanging back till they hear the Court is here, which makes Jane and me jealous. Mrs. Dilke need not bring a bit of soap with her, as they use it here; it is quite a treat to see the clean faces and hands. I *could* kiss the children here about the streets – and the maids too. I think the German men kiss each other so because, thanks to dirt, there is no *fair sex* there. Flemish contains many words quite English to the eye. Over the taverns here, you see 'Hier verkoopt *Man Drank.*' As we entered here, just under the words 'man drank,' sat a fellow with a tremendous black eye, quite as if on purpose to prove the text by illustration. But I am forestalling our gossip, so good bye. Pray attend to the business part of this letter, and do not neglect the pleasure part either.

Pray congratulate Moxon for me on having an article on his sonnets in the 'Quarterly,' where I never had a line though I write odes![6]

39, Rue Longue, Ostend, 13th July, 1837.

From *Memorials* I 285–8

1/Talfourd's published speech was referred to in *The Athenaeum* 3 June 1837, 402, and his edition of Lamb's letters was reviewed there a week later and on 8 July. Thomas Tegg's *Remarks on the Speech of Sergeant Talfourd* was also published this year.

2/Thomas Colley Grattan (1792–1864), writer, contributor to the periodicals, and author of *Highways and Byways* (1823). Left England because of pecuniary losses in 1828. Appointed British consul to the state of Massachusetts in 1839.

3/Baily. Hood is punning on the title of Campbell's song 'The Exile of Erin.'
4/'Mizzle' has two meanings, 'to drizzle' and 'to disappear suddenly.'
5/'Literature of the Nineteenth Century. France,' continued in *The Athenaeum* 8 July
6/Moxon's *Sonnets* was crushingly reviewed in the *Quarterly*, July. Hood himself was the subject of a disparaging reference in the October number, 484.

TO
THOMAS COLLEY GRATTAN

My dear Sir
A friend brought me over Lamb's Letters – and I thought you would like to see them. Pray keep them as long as you like.
Lamb was an odd man and a shy one. It was necessary to know him to understand him, – to understand him, to like him, – but *then*, you loved him. I was very intimate with him when his neighbour – we spent three evenings a week together at one house or other – and I found him an excellent friend as well as the best of critics. The book was therefore a treat to me. I saw him to his grave, – but as I have no intercourse with my old friends now but by letter, – they were as good almost as those of the living. Perhaps you did not know his sister, – a woman to redeem whatever's amiss, if there be any thing amiss, in the rest of the sex.
Pray accept our best thanks for your newspapers etc – which came very welcomely. I called one day en passant, to say so, but you were out.

Yours very truly

Thos Hood

T.C. Grattan Esqure

[*Ostend, July 1837*]

MS UCLA. Address: 'T.C. Grattan Esqre'

TO
ALFRED HEAD BAILY

Dear Baily, An idea struck me for the race paper, so I did it out of hand.[1] A tailpiece to the above effect would give it a finish.[2] But your plates are too artistical for my style – you might get it done on wood. I will do the other plate at first opportunity[3] – I am now as you may suppose very busy; and decidedly mending in health. – I hope therefore to have no delays in bringing out my books. I had Wrights letter with £5 the other day tell him – also bid him enquire at the Packet Company's before he sends much, – there is no opposition & somebody here told me they charge high. – We had a rare storm of hail big as walnuts the other day – the Chairmaker opposite was flooded – a man & boy were lost with a boat just off here – & a strange boy has been washed ashore. That is all the news of Ostend. I have a good deal to say but have not time before the mail is made up. But I shall soon write again. Our neighbour the King is coming on Sunday & the place is getting full. We have Romeo Coates here. – looking old enough to make one reckon ones own age. It does not seem such a very great while since he died on the stage.[4] Talking of dying on stages beware of shays – Wright tells me you still go like David with a sling.[5] It must be quite a new gig too, for[6] Hume to be thrown out. Sir Andrew too I see is out of *Wig*ton, – I thought he sat for *Tory*-ton. I see the Times here so that I know a little of what is going on over the water. Moreover there is a reading room I mean to belong to by & by but as the man said when his watch fell in the mud, my time is filled up. Mrs. Hood desires her remembrances.

I am Dear Baily Yours very truly

Thos. Hood

Tuesday. 23 minutes to 10 wind E.N.E. attended by a slight haze. Thermometer (Farenheit) 73° – Rain Guage 0 inches. Cumulus cirrocumulus etc etc. Time of High Water. 2 h. 15 ms. – barometer. Fair.

[*Ostend, 15 August 1837*]

MS UCLA. Address: 'Mess[rs] A.H.B / 80 Co / Lon.' The right hand side of this address has been torn away. PM: 'OSTENDE/16/AOUT/1837,' 'LONDON/17/AUG/1837.' Hood's note at the end of the letter indicates that he wrote it on Tuesday, 15 August.

1/Hood contributed 'The Ass-Race' to Nimrod's *Sporting*, published by Baily in December 1837. The article illustrated an engraving of Gainsborough's 'The Race.' 'Nimrod' was the *nom de plume* of C.J. Apperley.

2/*Sporting* 20

3/Cooper's 'Trout Fishing,' for which Hood wrote 'The Praise of Fishing' *Sporting* 111–14

4/Robert Coates (1772–1848), amateur actor, known as 'Romeo' from his performance in that part in 1810. He was hissed from the stage and, because of financial difficulties, obliged to live on the Continent.

5/1 Samuel 25:29. Baily had had a riding accident. Hood goes on to make a shorthand comparison between Baily's accident and the result of the General Election held in July. In the election Joseph Hume (1777–1855), the radical, was defeated. So was Sir Andrew Agnew (1793–1849), who stood for Wigtownshire. Hood had published an ode to Agnew in the *Comic Annual* for 1834, mocking his sabbatarianism.

6/MS reads 'to'.

TO
JOHN WRIGHT

My dear Wright,

I received yours this afternoon. Your account of your brother's family, and still more of the funeral, is very gratifying, and contains all the comfort that one could have under such an affliction: it must have soothed your feelings very much to witness such an unusual demonstration. A man is not all lost who leaves such a memory behind him. I am heartily glad your reflections have such a scene to rest upon, connected with him, to set-off against some of the bitterness of the deprivation.

You may be at ease about me, my health has not delayed the Comic; but I was so forward with the cuts, I thought it worth while to wait to send them *all* at once instead of by detachments; and accordingly I shall despatch them to you next week.[1] What a comfort to think that they will not have to be six weeks on the way! It makes a vast difference. I except the frontispiece. Did I understand you that Harvey would do one? His pencil is worth having – that there may be something artist-like; but if any doubt of delay say so at once, as I should in that case prefer knocking one off myself.[2] With regard to the two setters, do it by all means; the motto, 'Together let us range the fields,' is the best. Have it drawn according to your own idea of it.[3] You will find in the box a list of the mottoes, and the blocks will be numbered as before. I am in good spirits about it, as the 'Comic' will, must, and shall be earlier than common this year.[4] I will send an announcement in time for the Magazines.[5] And now for the fishing plate. I did not know there was such a hurry, so laid it aside; but I will take it up again. If I do it, it will come by *one of next week's* posts.[6] I do not know of anything more we want per parcel, unless you have a spare copy of the 'Tower Menagerie.'[7] Do not forget two or three copies of 'Eugene Aram' unbound, and one or two of last 'Comic.' But you had better see the Dilkes, for we have strong hopes of their coming out, and they would perhaps bring what we want.

Don't think of any beer; we get good here now. The poem in the 'Athenaeum' about Ostend confirmed us in our hopes.[8] I suspect it is written by Sir Charles Morgan (Lady Morgan's hub.), who has heard them talking of it.[9] I wish they may come, as there is a chance now of their enjoying themselves; and I should like to talk over German matters with him.

By the way, we have heard from Franck, who has been off into Silesia with recruits. He sent the money for the fishing-tackle; and our banker at Coblenz advised me that he received it, and sent it off on the 12th of last month; but it has never reached here yet. I suspect that post-office at Coblenz has kept it, so that they have even done me after leaving them. They tricked me once before. * * * For my part, I say, hang party![10] There wants a true *country party* to look singly to the good of England – retrench and economise, reduce taxes, and make it possible to live as cheap at home as abroad. *There* would be patriotism, instead of a mere struggle of Ins and Outs for place and pelf. Common sense seems the great desideratum for governors, whether of kingdom or family. I suspect the principles that ought to guide a private family would bear a pretty close application to the great public one; their evils are much of the same nature – extravagance, luxury, debt, &c. Thanks for your receipt: I may try it some day, but I am shy of stimuli. I do not suffer either under lowness of spirits; now and then I feel jaded rather, and indulge perhaps twice in a week in a single glass of sherry: my appetite is better than it used to be. I always eat breakfast now; so if I can but conquer the lung-touch, or whatever it is, I shall do. I think I have got a fair set of cuts, and have some good stories for the text of the 'Comic;' so that I am going on quite 'as well as might be expected.'

Are the other German cuts done? I have a hint to give you about the cutting the 'Comic,' – not to cut away my blacks too much, as they give effect. I am not sure whether some of the German cuts do not want black, but perhaps they *print* up more. I am so pleased with your ideas of the fables, I think I shall do them next after the German book, with nice little illustrations.

Jane is getting dozy, and so am I, for it is twelve o'clock; so I must shut up. Tom is very well, and talks of 'Mr. Light and Jim Co.'[11] Oysters are in here; that is to say, they send every one of them up to Brussels. I think I'll petition the King about it. My swallow seems disposed to migrate on that account to the capital.

Hang their shelfishness! confound their grottoes! I own I did look forward to the natives, but one cannot have everything in this world. As the 'prentices say, 'I'm werry content with my wittles in this here place!' Our kindest remembrances to yourself and all yours. God bless you.

My dear Wright,
Yours ever truly,

Thos. Hood.

There is a clergyman wanted (Church of England) for this place, salary £130 per annum. There's a chance for a poor curate! Tell Dilke of it.[12] It's a fortnight since I heard of it; perhaps it may be gone.

39, Rue Longue, Ostend, Saturday, 9th Sept., 1837.

From *Memorials* I 288–92, where the date is given as 10 September but, since Saturday was the 9th, I have corrected this.

1/Wright had written: 'and now my dear Hood 6th of September and no cuts or part of comic, do! do! for heavens sake rouse youself into determination to get on and be early, pray do! who knows what the difference may be in sale, old times may come again! Oh I do pray that your health is not interfering and yet I fear it for what else can in this important cause, so careful as you now are of your health I am sure your invention cannot be failing you,' MS Bristol Central Library.
2/The frontispiece was designed by Hood.
3/Wright suggested this subject and motto.
4/In fact, the *Comic Annual* was published on 29 November.
5/The announcement, dated 10 October, appeared in *The Athenaeum*, 4 November, 818.
6/Wright had warned Hood that the fishing plate for Nimrod's *Sporting* was wanted urgently: 'I who *know your ways* only tell you, if not commenced, to commence it and finish it and send it immediately'.
7/Edward T. Bennett *Tower Menagerie* illustrated by William Harvey (1829)
8/*Athenaeum* 2 September, 645: 'Cross not the Channel to Ostend,/ Your lagging pulse's pace to mend; / *Quodcunque Ostend-* is to me *sic*, / Makes me, like Horace, very (sea) sick.'
9/Sir Thomas Charles Morgan (1783–1843), MD, philosophical and miscellaneous writer, married Sydney Owenson in 1812. They lived in London from 1839 to 1843, during which time Sir Charles contributed to the *New Monthly Magazine*. Lady Morgan (1783?–1859), author, made famous by *The Wild Irish Girl* (1806). Both of the Morgans were friends of Dilke and wrote for *The Athenaeum*.
10/Wright had written: 'If you dedicate to the queen which I *would* advise avoid a hint at politics your own opinion would I know lead you towards Whiggism and I am by no means certain . . . that it is congenial with her feelings.' Hood did not dedicate to Queen Victoria (1819–1901) who had come to the throne in June.
11/Obscure
12/Probably a joke at Dilke's expense, a reference to his being no longer employed by the Navy Pay Office

TO
THOMAS COLLEY GRATTAN

Should you chance to have last Wednesday's Times, would you be kind enough to let me see it. I understand there are some verses in it under my signature, of which I am guiltless, and I wish to write a contradiction. These literary forgeries are too bad.

[*Ostend, September 1837*]

From Maggs Bros *Autograph Letters* no. 388 (Spring 1920) 105. *The Times* Tuesday 12 September 1837, 3, reprinted from *The Torch* a crude anti-government verse satire headed 'Petition to Her Majesty for preserving the Royal Stud at Hampton Court, by Thomas Hood.' Hood's letter of protest was published in *The Times* ten days later, p. 2: 'I have never written a line for the *Torch;* and, judging from its *pitch*, should be extremely loth to be *linked* with such a *burning shame* to literature.'

TO

JOHN WRIGHT

My dear Wright

This afternoon I sent off my box containing as per list 39 large cuts, making with Mr: Scott's 'Together let us range the fields'[1] the whole 48 for the six sheets. Put the steam on & we may hope for once to be early. I think while I am in the cue I will knock off a frontispiece without bothering Harvey. There are also 12 tailpieces by the box with 3 you have of Mr Scotts making half of those. It is an infinite comfort to me to think please God in a very few days they will be with you. I have got through them as easily as I ever did – and I think they are a fair set – & I am still fresh & full of running & in good spirits. I do believe that I am considerably better – & slowly mending. I have no bloody symptoms now. – To be sure I take great care in every way. – we have not heard a word from the Dilkes so live in hopes they may come next Saturday. Being so forward. I shall enjoy their company. – pray let them know I have sent the cuts. I shall now finish off the fishing plate for Baily, out of hand.

I am very much annoyed by that damnd Torch business. It is too bad. I that have not meddled with politics on my own account – & to be made to abuse *my own side!* I shall send with this or somehow a note to Barnes about it.[2] Such forgeries ought to be punishable as libels.

I congratulate you on *bee*ing so *busy* – which is very disinterested of me – but remember I'm a friend & so *cut* me as soon as you can. I suppose the Doncaster expedition[3] is a desperate try to retrieve – hit or miss – I am glad you liked my ass race – pictures are not easy to write to always, – I rather think I shall versify the fishing article. I have wondered much to see here about the street, two men carrying a large hoop with a net to it, always accompanied by a gendarme – I supposed for fishing in the moat, – but it turns out the net is to catch *dogs* – that are not muzzled. There's a new sort of sport for you! I think I must make a cut of it! – Then our police might really be called *Dogberries*. The King & Queen come back here tomorrow – not to stay. You see I know all about our Court movements. Today when I went down to the packet, I saw what I did not know you imported – a rare lot of live ducks & some geese – some hundreds, all going to make the voyage – regular birds of *passage*. And when one quacked they all went in chorus – no good omen for the sleeping on board, to say nothing of the passengers being all sure, if not of drowning, of a good ducking. Tom was delighted with the scene. I could not help fancying one of the baskets (a square as big as a table) full of live ducks would not make a bad raft in case of a wreck. You have had plenty of accidents lately with steamers. That wasn't a bad joke of the poor Apollo sticking on a bank all right with the Company of Baker's aboard – I think something like it will do for the Comic.[4] – What an *air-pump* poor Cocking was! – but if he had come down well we should have had too much parachuting – & friends dropping in to pot luck down our chimneys! I expect there will be a wreck some day with the aerial ship.[5] By the bye when our last accident occurred here I asked if there was not a life boat at Ostend. Yes said a sailor, – they sent over one from England – & one day they tried her & she upset & wouldn't right again, – but nearly drowned her crew. I have just read Back's account about a narrow escape he had[6] – he must have had *jam* satis of the ice. The ship seems actually to have tried to shake on it – how glad he must have been to quit the Terror for Terror firmer. I wonder, if Noah, ever sailed in the *Arktic* regions? – There is presumption he did – & maybe stirred up his beasts with the pole itself. I'll communicate this conjecture to the Philosophical Society[7] – & perhaps it will find *Backers*. An ode to Back will be a good subject.[8] He has not succeeded, & perhaps laments it – but for my part, if I were sent on such a freezy expedition I should try on purpose to make a *mull*[9] of it. It would comfort to be lukewarm in the cause. I happen to have a cold & I do believe its from reading his letter without taking the chill off. One's own fireside may be rather pokey, but its preferable to taking as Back says a 'departure from *Papa* Westra'[10] – with great odds against seeing that worthy old parent again. It is cold fun, sawing ice, even though you may be top sawyer for I presume there are no bottom ones, – and I can well believe the Captain when he says they were 'driven 14 miles to the eastward of Cape Comfort.' Well, Heaven forgive his Back-slidings for of course he had many – He must have had a blessed time of it – for middle watch, starboard watch or larboard watch every watch must have been pinch Back [11] – But my paper gets short, and I must leave joking to ask you seriously to remember me kindly to all – beginning with Mrs. Wright – & to believe that that *you* are far above zero with Dear Wright Yours very truly Thomas Hood Senior.

Burns seems to have foreseen the aerial ship – but with only two masts to it. He calls it the *Brig* of *Ayr*. Is Harman Dilsoon dead yet?[12] I will write his memoirs. Why is purchasing bacon-pigs like writing lives? Because it is Buy-hog-raphy. That's a very bad one but good enough for *bad*inage. Jane desires me to leave her a bit to herself – so Ill fence it off. Have you had any more windows broken? – they ought to be paid for – vide Pane's rights of man.

[There follow Jane's lines and a list of plates and tailpieces for the *Comic Annual* for 1838, to which Hood adds:] There is also another which should be marked J. & the name of which is not yet fixed.

I enclose a note for the Times. Put it in a Cover – to X. Barnes Esqre. & send it to the Times office.
Say on cover with T. Hood's Compts.

[Ostend] Tuesday 19th. Septr. 1837.

MS Morgan Library. Address: 'J. Wright Esqre./ 4 New London Street/ Fenchurch St./ London.' PM: 'OSTENDE/20/SEPT,' 'LONDON/21/SEP/1837.'

1/According to the attributions in the *Comic Annual*, this was designed by Hood; J. Scott designed several of the other plates.
2/Thomas Barnes (1785–1841), editor of *The Times*, educated at Christ's Hospital, member of Leigh Hunt's and Lamb's circle
3/Probably on the part of Baily, to the Doncaster race meeting, held 18–22 September
4/The *Apollo* sank 5 September. Hood did not make use of the episode in the next *Comic Annual*.
5/In these sentences there is a play on 'pump.' According to J.S. Farmer, *Slang and its Analogues*, the word means 'solemn noodle.' The first example of 'parachuting' given in NED is dated 1893. The 'aerial ship' is the Great Nassau balloon of Charles Green. He ascended in it from Vauxhall Gardens on 24 July, accompanied by Robert Cocking (b. 1776). When the balloon reached a height of 5000 ft, Cocking attempted a descent by parachute and was killed on hitting the ground.
6/'Return of Captain Back. Captain Back's own Narrative of the Voyage' *Athenaeum* 16 September, 687–8. Sir George Back (1796–1878) set out in June 1836 on an Arctic expedition in HMS *Terror*, returning in September 1837.
7/Philosophical Society of London, founded 1810
8/Instead, Hood wrote for the *Comic Annual* 'The Old Poler's Lament.'
9/Play on 'mull' meaning 'muddle' and suggesting 'mulled,' that is, 'hot'
10/Papa Westray, one of the Orkney Islands, Scotland
11/Play on 'pinchbeck,' alloy used in watchmaking
12/Unidentified

TO
JOHN WRIGHT

My dear Wright,
According to promise to B—,[1] I sit down to write to you to-day.

On the subject of my health, I feel somewhat easier, as it seems to give me better eventual hope. God knows! It has been a great comfort to me, and gone somewhat towards a cure, to feel myself within distance, and have such posting and sending facilities. The receipt of the 'Comic' cuts in three or four days actually enchanted me. Altogether, in spite of illness, I have done more this year. I feel I only want health to do *all*. I do not lose time when I am well, and am become, I think, much more of a man of business than many would give me credit for.

Now for your main subject; and I wish with you, we could talk it over instead of writing. There are so many points I should like to know something about. Such an idea as a periodical[2] it would have been impossible at Coblenz to entertain for a moment. Indeed, some months back I should at once have rejected the notion from sheer mistrust of my health. But I have now more hardihood on that score, and shall turn it well over in my mind. I have no doubt in the world that such a thing well done would pay handsomely, but I do not yet see my way clear. For instance, it is hardly possible for the first of January, seeing that the 'Comic' and the German book have to be done. Then there must be *two* numbers of the new work, for I would not start without a reserve in case of accidents, or the whole craft would be swamped in the launching. Moreover, the idea is yet to seek, as much, indeed all, would depend on the happiness of that. There is no end of uphill in working with a bad soil. Now I am not damping; but one must look at the probabilities and possibilities, and count chances. As for coming often before the public, – as I mean to do that anyhow, it goes for nothing. Nor am I afraid of its running the 'Comic' dry, fragmentary writing being so different, that what is available for one will not do for the other. So I shall seriously keep my eye on it, in the hope of some lucky thought for a title and plan. Such an inspiration would decide me at once perhaps. In such a case we must have a consultation somehow, as writing not only is unsatisfactory, but takes up so much time.

Please God I be well the year next ensuing, the 'Comic' will take up but one-quarter of my time, and I must have some work cut out for the rest. I fancy the fables for one thing, but that would be light. I do not think I fall off, and have no misgivings about over-writing myself; one cannot do too much if it be well done; and I never care to turn out anything that does not please myself. I hear a demon whisper – I hope no lying one – I can do better yet, or as good as ever, and more of it; so let's look for the best. Nobody ever died the sooner for hoping. I do not know that I can say more on the subject; it *must* be vague as yet. Of course, January is the most important; but if it *cannot* be done, I have no doubt of February, health being granted. But I would a thousand times rather talk over all these things instead of writing of them. I am glad to get rid of the pen and ink if I can, out of school-hours; and there is a sort of spirit and freshness about *vivâ voce* that on all joint affairs is much more invigorating than scribbling.

We are getting into the Slough of Despond about the Dilkes. No word from them since we wrote. It will be a disappointment if they do not come, as our hopes have been strong enough for certainties. And now, my dear fellow, I must close, for I am so tired I shan't add anything but Good night.

Yours ever,

T. Hood.

39 Rue Longue, Ostend, 16th October, 1837.

From *Memorials* I 292–4
1/Baily
2/Suggested by Wright

TO
JOHN WRIGHT

Dear Wright
Send me quantities as soon as ascertained. Going the pace – ain't I? Guess you'll like the Sidney Paper. I have now sent besides Carnaby & Angler – Patronage – Napoleon Review Right & Wrong – Animal Magnetism. The Forlorn Shepherd – which I hope have all come to hand. The letter for this was delayed a day by a storm here the mail didnt sail.

[*Ostend, October 1837*]

MS Morgan. This note occurs at the end of the MS of 'Review. The Rambles of Piscator.' It concerns pieces to appear in the *Comic Annual* for 1838.

TO
CHARLES WENTWORTH DILKE the younger

As for an Ode for the 9th it must depend on the inspiration.[1] If you have it at all, it shall be in good time – but I am very busy on the Comic, & today, at least, feel not in the best order for writing. Mrs Hood desires her kind regards with those of

Dear Wentworth

[*Ostend, 29 October 1837*]

MS BM. Address: 'C.W. Dilke (Junr) Esqre / Athenaeum Office / Catherine Street / Strand / London." PM: 'OSTENDE 1837/29 OCT,' 'LONDON/30 OCT 1837.' Published by Marchand 90. The letter is incomplete, with the signature torn off. In the early, lost part of the letter Hood must have explained the copy which he adds to this of a business letter from William Henry Harrison (1795–1878), author.

1/This sentence may be explained by a reference in the following letter to a dinner at the Guildhall on 9 November in honour of Queen Victoria.

TO
JOHN WRIGHT

My dear Wright,

In a hasty note to B—, I made an angry piece of work, which yours received to-day does not serve to unpick. I complained that, for want of *reporting progress*, I was at a loss to adjust my matter to the finis, and behold the fruit.

Had I known that the Song from the Polish and Hints to the Horticultural made some twenty-two pages instead of sixteen (as I reckoned by guess), I should hardly have written two unnecessary articles.

They were, in fact, the drop too much that overbrims the cup. But for them I should have come in fresh; but through those, and, above all, the nervousness of not even knowing if those two articles before had been received, I half killed Jane and half killed myself (equal to one whole murder) by sitting up *all* Saturday night, whereby I was so dead beat that I could not even write the one paragraph wanted for preface, whereby five days are lost.

I suppose there was a gale at Dover, for what you had on Saturday ought to have reached on Friday. I guessed the 'Hit or Miss' well enough, as I can count lines in a poem, but prose beats me, having to write it in a small hand unusual to me.[1]

Of course my sending a short quantity would cause a fatal delay, and I was hardly convinced even with the two superfluities that I had done enough. It is a nervous situation to be in, and I do not think you allow enough for the very shaky state of health that aggravates it. I am getting over it by degrees; but at times it makes me *powerless* quite. It is physical, and no effort of mind can overcome it – I could not have written the end of preface to save my life. Indeed, Sunday I was alarmed, and expected an attack.

I am rather vexed the 'Concert' will not be in, as I like it.[2] I think such *short* things are good for the book. Had it been in the palmy days of the 'Comic,' I should have given an extra half sheet; but now I can't afford anything of the kind. However, I am not sorry to have two articles to the fore. Should the re-issue be decided on, the 'Concert' will do for the first number, with a prose article I have partly executed.[3]

I think it is a very likely spec, and the best that can be done under circumstances. There is a tarnation powerful large class, who can and would give one shilling a month, and cannot put down twelve shillings at once for a book. I know *I* can't, and you would hesitate too.

I suppose you have heard of Dilke's opinion of the monthly thing. I quite agree with him, that because it *has been* done, is rather *against* than *for* the chance. The novelty is the secret. *Non sequitur* that something *like* —'s would do, because *his* has done.[4]

Whether *I* could not make a hit with a monthly thing is another question – but the more UNLIKE *to his* the thing is, the more chance. Now I do not despair of finding some *novelty*, which for the same reason as the re-issue of the 'Comic,' it might be best to do monthly: but as you must know that all depends on a happy idea, granting a *new* and lucky thought, I should start on it directly, and I shall keep it in mind, for I shall want something to fill up my leisure with.

We looked to have an account of the Guildhall Dinner – pray send the *fullest* one.[5] I think I can make use of it even yet. We don't see the 'Times' now Grattan's gone away.

However, one against the other, we don't miss them. As I expect a longer letter from you tomorrow, I shall shorten this. On the other side I repeat the end of the preface, for fear of the first edition not reaching you. It was sent *viâ* Calais; and please note, and tell me, when it arrived.

You will understand 'Potent, Grave, and Reverend Signiors'[6] to face the opening of preface, as if addressing them.

Take care of your cough, lest you go to Coughy-pot, as I said before: but I did *not* say before that nobody is so likely as a wood engraver to cut his stick.

Tuesday, 21st November, 1837. (New style.)

Pray send off a *very* early copy to Devonshire House.

It is only fair, as I have abused you, that I should thank you for seeing the 'Comic' through the press at all.[7] I forgive all your errors beforehand, as I know mistakes will happen. Pray accept, then, my sincere and earnest thanks for the more than usual trouble I fear I have given you, for I could not guide you much in the cut-placing. God Bless you.

Yours, dear Wright,
Ever truly,

Thos. Hood.

[*Ostend*] *21st November, 1837.*

From *Memorials* I 294–7

1/The three items mentioned above were in the *Comic Annual* for 1838.
2/'An Ancient Concert' appeared in the first number of *Hood's Own*: *Works* I 19–22. *Hood's Own*, appearing in thirteen monthly numbers from January 1838 to May 1839, was the 're-issue' referred to below, with the addition of some fresh material, particularly the 'Literary Reminiscences.' The work was accurately described on the title page as 'being former runnings of his comic vein, with an infusion of new blood for general circulation.'
3/Perhaps 'Black White and Brown' *Works* I 57–63
4/Probably a reference to Dickens's *Pickwick Papers* which appeared successfully in monthly parts, ending in October 1837.
5/The Queen dined at the Guildhall on 9 November.
6/The title of a plate, taken from *Othello* I iii 76
7/The *Comic Annual* was published on 29 November.

TO CHARLES WENTWORTH DILKE

My dear Dilke – This is to say that – I approve of the Agreement you have made in my name with Baily & C[o] 83 Cornhill London for the reissue of the Comic Annual namely that they will publish the proposed work and bear me harmless of all loss upon being Partners to the extent of one quarter of the profit – Please to forward this to the above parties as I defer writing till after the arrival of M[r] Lewis

I am Dear Dilke Yours very truly Tho[s] Hood

[Ostend] Dec[r] 1st 1837

Transcript in the Public Record Office. The agreement was for the publication of *Hood's Own*.

TO WILLIAM ELLIOT

My dear Doctor,
I have several times been on the point of writing to you; but firstly came a resolution to try first the effect of the place on me; secondly, the Dilkes; and, thirdly, the 'Comic.' Indeed, an unfinished letter is beside me, for (some time back) there seemed to be a change in the aspect of my case, to which I can now speak more decidedly.
I have done the 'Comic' with an ease to myself I cannot remember.
We are also very comfortable here. Fanny is quite improved in health, getting

flesh and colour, and Tom is health itself. Mrs. Hood, too, fattens, and looks well. I have got through more this year than since I have been abroad. I wrote three letters some months ago in the 'Athenaeum' on Copyright, which made some stir, and I have written for a sporting annual of B—'s. Also in January I am going to bring out a cheap re-issue of the 'Comic' from the beginning, so that my head and hands are full. I know it is rather against my complaint, this sedentary profession; but in winter one must stay in a good deal, and I take what relaxation I can; and, finally, 'necessitas non habet leges.'[1] I am, notwithstanding, in good heart and spirits. But who would think of such a creaking, croaking, blood-spitting wretch being the 'Comic?' At this moment there is an artist on the sea on his way to come and take a portrait of me for B—, which I believe is to be in the Exhibition; but he must flatter me, or they will take the whole thing for a practical joke. Of course I look rather sentimentally pale and thin than otherwise just at present. I must take a little wine outside to give me a *colour.* I have a little very *pure* light French wine, *without brandy*, which I take occasionally. I got it through B—, but do not drink a bottle a week of it – certainly not more. One great proof of its being genuine is, that it is equally good the second day as when first opened. French wine is cheap here: it only cost me, bottles and all, under fourteen pence per bottle.

We had an agreeable fillip with a visit from the Dilkes, accompanied by his brother-in-law and sister,[2] who have a relation at Bruges. It put us quite in heart and spirits, for we are almost as badly off here as in Germany for society. Not but that there are plenty of English – but such English – broken English and bad English – scoundrelly English!

To be sure, I made an attempt at acquaintance, and it fell through as follows. Coming from Germany with my heart warm towards my countrymen, and finding there was even a literary man in the same hotel, I introduced myself to Mr. G—.[3] He came here afterwards with his family, and we were on civil terms, exchanging papers, &c., till at last they even came to lodge underneath; but we never got any nearer, but farther off from that very neighbourly situation – in fact, we never entered each other's rooms, and they left without taking leave. There was no possible guess-able cause for this; but from what I have seen, and since heard, I rejoice it 'was as it was.' So I determined to stick as I be. The intercourse is so easy, we see a *friend* occasionally; for instance, Mr. Wright has been across to see us.[4] There is also a possibility of seeing an English book now and then. Nay, there is a minor circulating library two doors off, but Jane and I had such reading appetites, we got through the whole stock in a month, and now must be content with a work now and then – say once a month. But we go on very smoothly, and as contentedly as we can be abroad. Almost every Fleming speaks English more or less, and our lodgings are really very convenient, and our landlord and lady very pleasant people.

He is not an old man; but was a soldier, and marched to Berlin; and he is a carpenter *by trade*, but paints, glazes, and is a Jack of all trades. I have in my own little room a *chamber organ*, and I discovered the other day that he had made it himself, and he quite amuses me with his alterations, contrivances, and embellishments of the premises. He dotes, too, on children; and Tom is very fond of him, and of his wife, too, but declares he will not dance any more with Madame, because 'she fell down with him in the gutter, and kicked up her heels.'

He gets a very funny boy, with a strange graphic faculty, whether by a pencil or by his own attitudes and gestures, of representing what he sees. I have seen boys six years old, untaught, with not so much notion of drawing, and he does it in a dashing off-hand style, that is quite comical. His temper also is excellent, and he is very affectionate, so that he is a great darling. Fanny goes to a day-school, and is getting on in French, and improving much. So that I only want health at present to be very comfortable, and for the time being, I am better where I am than in London. I have as much cut out for me as I can do; and am quiet here, and beyond temptation of society and late hours, living well, and cheaply to boot. I seem in a fair way of surviving all the old annuals – most of them are gone to pot. My sale is nothing like the first year's, but for the last three or four it has been steady, and not declined a copy, which is something. The re-issue promises well. If I were but to put into a novel what passes here, what an outrageous work it would seem.

This little Ostend is as full of party and manoeuvring as the great City itself – or more in proportion. I verily believe we have two or three duels per month. There have been not a few about the minister at the Church – both parties having a man to support – and one gentleman actually fought three duels on the question. Some of us are very dashing, too; but it is a very hollow *Ostend-tation*. But I like the natives; they are civil and obliging, and not malicious, like the Rhinelanders. The English benefit them very much, and they seem in return to try and suit them. Indeed the prevalence of speaking English amongst the very lower class does them credit, and reflects disgrace on the 'Intellectual Germans' of the Rhine, who do not even speak French, which here is very general also. I believe this to be a very prosperous, happy, and well-governed country.

Their kitchen-gardening, I forgot to say, is very excellent.

The vegetable market is quite a sight; much of it better, and all as good as English.

And now I take warning to close. Jane is very anxious to explain to Mrs. Elliot that she has not been unwilling, but unable to write. I have written you but a stupid desultory letter, but hope you will get the 'Comic' about the same time, and that it may prove more amusing.

I am still rather languid, and have had to write besides on business: but having a spare hour or two, and something decided to say on my health, would not defer longer. I am unfeignedly glad to hear of your professional success, and also find from Dilke's report that I have to congratulate you on your brother's connection with Mr. C—.[5]

Pray give our kindest regards to Mrs. Elliot, and Fanny's love and Tom's, which is always overflowing to 'Willie;' and God bless you all as you deserve.

I am, my dear Doctor,
Yours ever truly,

Thos. Hood.

39, Rue Longue, Ostend, 2nd December, 1837.

From *Memorials* I 298–303

1/Necessity knows no law.

2/The Dilkes visited Hood in the fall of 1837; the sister and brother-in-law were probably Letitia and John Snook.

3/Thomas Colley Grattan

4/Wright's visit was probably in July.

5/Perhaps a wealthy patient of William's brother Dr Robert Elliot

TO
CHARLES WENTWORTH DILKE

Jane and I were very much concerned to hear so bad an account of Mrs. Dilke. We hope none of it is attributable to her trip. I can now sympathise in degree, leeches and all; but it is perhaps as well to have it, if possible, set to rights at once. Pray beg that she will send us word how she goes on. Jane laughed heartily at her description of the journey to Calais. But it served you right. Here our mail, charged with letters, with business public and private to forward, will stay in port if the weather is bad; but you, only for pleasure, must *set out* on a day when you were not to be *let out* upon, by your own confession, as if the devil drove you, and for what hurry? Why to wait at Dover for the worst fog ever known!!! Werdict: 'Sarve 'em right!'

Please to thank Mrs. Dilke for her kind message to me; and tell her not to be bothered with indexes, etc., to the 'Athenaeum.' I cannot help wishing for her sake that the little Doctor might be proscribed again, he might do much more good to her than he will, I fear, to Spain.[1]
What three hundred-power donkey wrote that tragedy in last 'Athenaeum?'[2]

[*Ostend*] *December 4th, 1837.*

From *Memorials* I 303–4
1/Probably a reference to Seoane
2/*The Cicisbeo. A tragedy*, author unnamed, was reviewed ironically in *The Athenaeum* 25 November 1837, 857–8.

1838

TO
PHILIP DE FRANCK

'Tim,' says he! 'hier ist ein brief mit my own hand geschrieben at last!' 'Time it was,' says you, – and so think I, considering our old comradeship; but I am not going to plead guilty to wilful neglect, or malice prepense. You know how my time is divided, – first I am very ill, then very busy to make up for lost time, – and then in consequence very jaded and knocked-up, which ends generally in my being very ill again. Neither of the three moods is very favourable for writing long, cheerful, friendly letters; ergo, you will conclude that I am at this present writing neither ill, busy, nor very jaded, which is precisely the case.

Your letter came while I was in bed, full of rising ambition, so I read it before I got up, – and how nicely the fellow timed it, thought I, to arrive on this very morning of all the days in the year! so I sit down to try whether I cannot hit you with mine on New Year's-day. You will like to hear all about me, so I shall make myself Number One. In health I am better, and in better hope than of late, for a complete revolution has taken place in my views on the subject. Hang all Rhineland, except a bit between Ehrenbreitstein and Pfaffendorf, and all its doctors. Old S—,[1] the Catholic, I verily believe knew no more about the case than the Jew B—,[2] but he is more taken up with the sort of little Propaganda there is in Coblenz, for converting Protestants, and getting Roman Catholics to leave their property to the Church, and walking in Corpus Christi processions, than with medicine or its ministry. For I hear he is a notorious bigot even in Coblenz, and I hate all bigots, Catholic or Lutheran. He told me my complaint was in the lungs; and I described the symptoms to Elliot, who rather concurred in his opinion, but of course from what he was told only, so I never touched wine, beer, or spirits, for several months, and in consequence ran it so fine, that on the journey here, when I got to Liège, I could scarcely speak. At Brussels I began to find out I had gone too far in my temperance, by the good effects of some bottled porter; and now here I am on a moderate allowance again, and even ordered to drink a little gin-and-water. So won't I toast you to-day, my old fellow, in a brimming bumper!

The doctor here is an experienced old English army surgeon, besides being used to London practice; and he said from the first he could find no pulmonary symptoms about me. The truth is, my constitution is rallying, as the Prussians did after

Quatre Bras, and is showing fight, the sea air and diet here being in my favour. You know what the Rhineland diet is, even at the best, while here we have meat quite as good as English, good white wheaten bread if anything better than English, and the very finest vegetables I ever saw. The consequence is I eat heartily good breakfasts, with fish, &c., and ample dinners: in fact, we have left off suppers simply from not caring about them in general. Sometimes we have a few oysters, and we eat shrimps, Tim, all the spring and summer through!

All this looks well, but by way of making surer, and for the sake of Elliot's advice, in which I have justly such confidence, I am on the point, Tim, of a visit to England, as Elliot's practice will not let him come to me. It must blow very great guns on Wednesday morning, or I leave this in the Dover mail on a flying visit to the glorious old island! It is a rough season, and Jane is a wretched sailor; and besides, cock and hen cannot both leave the nest and chicks at the same time, so I go solus. But she will go to see her mother, I expect, in the spring or the summer: for we have made up our minds to stay here another year, and perhaps two. It will be some time before I shall be strong enough to live a London life; and being rather popular in that city, I cannot keep out of society and late hours. At all events I am close at hand if wanted for a new ministry. Jane says she should not like me to be a *place*-man, for fear of red spots.[3]

Since the above I have been to England. I spent there about three weeks, and am just returned, full of good news and spirits.[4] Elliot came to me, and after a very careful examination, and sounding every inch of me by the ear, and by the stethoscope, declares my lungs perfectly sound, and the complaint is in the liver. He altogether coincides with my doctor here, both as to the case and its treatment, and my own feelings quite confirmed their view; so that at last I seem in the right road. But what long and precious time I have lost – I only wonder I have survived it! *You* must be a great lump of sugar, indeed, to sweeten such Rhenish reflections. The ignorant brutes!

The main reason why Elliot wanted to see me was because this place would be bad for the lungs, but it quite suits the real case as I must have *much* air, and cannot walk or ride much, or exert myself bodily. So sea air is good, and *sailing*, my old amusement, Tim, at which I was an adept, and shall soon pick it up again. I mean therefore to sail, and fish for my own dinner. So I have made up my mind to stay here for one or two years to come. We like the place, though it is called dull by gay people and those in health. But that just suits *me*, who am not strong enough for society; it is so near that those we care about do not mind coming, and as we have four posts a week, business goes on briskly. It is as good as English watering places in general, so I should gain nothing by going over. To tell the truth, I was not at all sorry to come back, for I have never been in bed before one or two in the morning the last three weeks. Of course we are very happy, for my death-warrant was signed if such blood-spitting had been from the lungs: it is not dangerous in this case. Between friends and business I had a regular fag in London, for there were such arrears: for instance, among other things, all my accounts with my publishers for three years to go through. They turned out satisfactory, and besides established the fact, which is hardly conceivable by those who are experienced on the subject, that the 'Comic' keeps up a steady sale, being, if anything, better than last year. All other annuals have died or are dying. Of course this is quite a literary triumph, and moreover I had to prepare a re-issue of all the old ones, which will come out monthly in future; you shall have them when complete at the year's end. Moreover my German book is to come out in the course of the year. I send you proofs of some of the woodcuts which are finished – you will recognise some of the portraits. Then I propose to begin a Child's Library, so I have cut out plenty of work.

We shall have plenty of visitors in the summer. How I wish it was not so far from Bromberg! But we shall have railroads, and all the world will go this way to the Rhine instead of Rotterdam. It is a nice little kingdom, and I like the people; they take very much to the English, and adopt our customs and comforts, and almost universally speak our language in this part. So you see, had the Luxembourg affair come to a head, I must have wished you a good licking.[5] What fun, if your 19th had been ordered down, and you had been taken, Johnny, with me for your jailer, and answerable for your parole! As to the Cologne affair, I think your king is perfectly right.[6] Fair play is a jewel, and an agreement is an agreement; but he is placed in a critical position, very – at all events a very troublesome one. It quite agrees with my prophecies. You know I don't meddle in politics, but I will give you my view of affairs. There will be a row in Hanover: it will not suit your king to have popular commotions so near home, so he will interfere to put it down, and finally hold Hanover for himself.[7] Then, as to Luxembourg, the French long to pay off the old grudge on you Prussians.[8] If you should get a beating at the beginning, I should fear *Catholic* (*French in heart*) Rhineland will rise; but if you Prussians like, you will keep Luxembourg to repay you for defending it *for the Dutch*. So the best thing for all parties is to keep the peace; and whatever you hot-headed young soldiers may wish, I think your king's prudence will keep us from war: and so long life to him! As for England, *we* Liberals must beat sooner or later; the money and commerce interests will beat the landed, who have too long had it their own way; and then no more corn-laws![9] Then if you Prussians be wise, you will encourage free-trade, and take our manufactures for your timber and corn, whereby we shall both profit.

But you abroad have a plan, on the supposition that the Tories will come again into power – so they may, but will never keep it, nor the Whigs either; there is a third party, not Radicals, but a national one, will and must rule at last, for the general, and not private, interests. I do not meddle, but look on, and see it quietly getting onwards towards a consummation so devoutly to be wished for.[10]

Leopold, whatever you may hear, is popular, and justly so, in this country, which is a more wealthy one than is generally supposed.

Bruges is a delightful little city, for anyone with an artist's eye. It is only fourteen miles off, and you can get there by the barge for a franc and a half. It is quite a gem in its way.

By the bye, I am going to try to paint a bit in oil: the artist, who took my portrait, has set me up for *matériel*. He has taken an excellent likeness of me, which is going to be engraved for the re-issue, so that I shall be able to send you a copy of my copy. Jane is quite satisfied with it, which is saying all in its favour. I am going to try to paint Tom's likeness, as we have Fanny's already. As I know nothing of the rudiments I expect to make some awful daubs at first, – may I say, like Miss A—'s?[11]

Jane told you of some articles I have written for a sporting-book, but we are not able to get the letter-press. The plates you will receive next parcel as a present from Jane. They are very good, and I know they will hit your taste. The plates I wrote to were the donkey-race, and of course the fishing. When I was in London I learned that Bond, our tackle-maker, has just wound up his line of life, leaving a good sum behind him. I inquired if there is extra strong tackle; so let me know what you want *directly*, and all shall come to you in one parcel, 'Comic,' sporting-plates, and all. You are at a distance that makes me cautious of carriage, or I would send the latter articles now.

I sent a 'Comic' to the Prince, *viâ* Hamburg, in a parcel of Count Raczinski's, or some such name, – the same who is publishing a gallery of German art.

You talk of my having 'a box out in the spring!' Why, man alive! the stewardess of our London packet fetches and carries like a spaniel every week between me and my publisher.[12] Your lost gorge-hook tickled me as much as it poked its fun into you. You must have rare sport, and of course do not regret the Rhine, Moselle, and Lahn. Do you ever drop in now? I should like to *Brake* my tackle with some of your large fish; but I am a prematurely old man, Tim, and past travelling, except on a short stage. I had fears I should perhaps disgrace my seamanship by being sea-sick, my stomach having become so deranged, but I held out; to be sure I had fine passages, although one fellow, a fox-hunter, was very ill. England seemed much the same as when I left it, but I was astonished by some of the hotel charges on the road being positively less than on the Rhine. The Dilkes dined with me; he is as well as ever, and they all desired their kind remembrances to 'Mr. Franks.'

I heard a good deal of H.O—.[13] He is still a bachelor, with about £13,000 a-year, – a nice sum, Tim, – and he *will* be richer. He spends it, however, like a good old English gentleman; keeps hounds, is very liberal to the poor, and is very much liked about the neighbourhood of W—.[14]

Old H—[15] is still dying. He sometimes gets my friend W— to write at his dictation to Richard D—, when he is on a journey, in this style: 'DEAR RICHARD – By the time you receive this, your poor brother will be no more. I died about noon on –,' and then W— breaks in, 'Why, my dear sir, but you are not going so soon?' 'Ah, so you think, but a pretty set of fools you will look when you see the shutters up. Send for Dr. S— directly!' And so forth; and in an hour or two afterwards, he is in his chaise at a coursing meeting! It is quite a farce, and W— imitates him capitally.[15]

Now I do verily believe that I am only alive, on the contrary, through never giving up. With such a wife to tease, and such children to tease me, I do not get so weary of life as some other people might – Lieutenants at Bromberg, for instance, in time of peace. Moreover, I am of some slender use. In the spring I wrote and published three letters on the state of the Law of Copyright, which made a stir in the literary world of London, and an M.P. borrowed my ideas and made a flourish with them in the House.[16] Moreover, a fellow attacked me and some others for our infidelity, &c., whereupon I took up the cudgels in a long poem, which delighted an old gentleman so much that he called it 'Hood's *Sermon*!'[17] You will hear of me next in orders, as the Rev. Dr. Johnny.

As for the 'Comic,' I did it this year with such ease, and at such a gallop, that I sent MSS. faster than they could acknowledge the receipt thereof. I never did it so easily before. The fact is, provided my health should clear up, and I get strong, I am but beginning my career. For the fun of the thing I must tell you that there has been a short memoir of me published. You will judge how well the author knows me when he says 'we believe his mind to be more serious than comic, we have never known him laugh heartily either in company or in rhyme.' But my methodist face took him in, for he says, 'the countenance of Mr. Hood is more solemn than merry.' The rest is a great deal handsomer than I deserve, and a proof how unfounded the notion is of envy and spite among literary men.[18]

And now I think I have told you everything about myself. Jenny is as thin as she has been for a long time; my last illness frightened her; indeed we have both had a fear we kept to ourselves, but of course she will now laugh and get fat. There is a treat too in store for her, for when the weather is fine enough she is going over to see her family, three years' absence is a trial to such a heart as hers. Luckily, she has no longer the dinner anxieties, and the wish and prayer for a 'new animal' that so worried her in Coblenz! I get nothing now that I cannot eat, and as to drink, I am quite a Temperance Society, though I am now allowed a little wine. To be sure she still sticks to her old fault of going to sleep while I am dictating, till I vow to change my *woman*uensis for *aman*uensis. And moreover she took the opportunity during my absence of buying a plaice *with red spots* – could not eat it after all – Verdict, 'Sarve her right,' when we can get plenty of turbot. Do you know one of our first freaks on coming here? There is a little library two doors off, and we sat down and read all its stock of books slap through. The bill came in. 'To reading 155 volumes – francs!'

Don't you wish you had been one of the *francs*, as you complain so of want of reading? We get newspapers, but have no society, save what we import, such as the Dilkes. There are lots of English here, but many of them outlaws; this is like

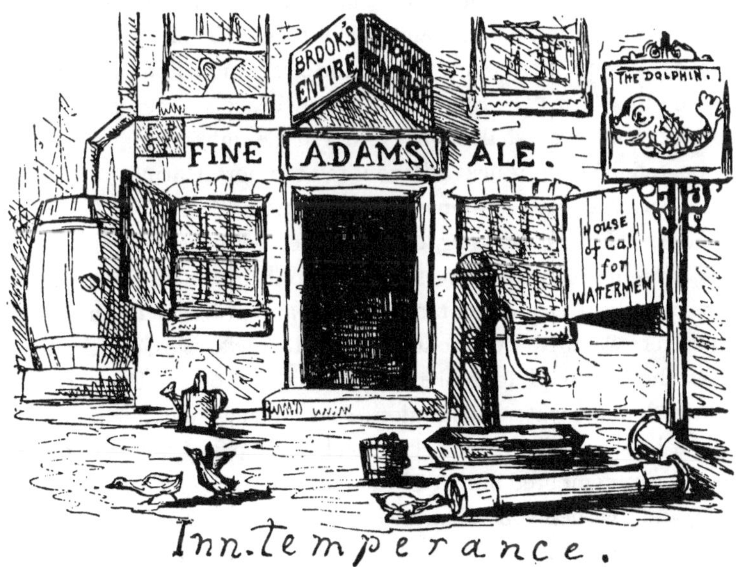

Inn.temperance.

Calais, Boulogne, &c., being a sort of city of refuge for gentlemen who won't or can't pay their debts.

We have plenty of military, and are consequently treated with abundance of duels. Our doctor knows and tells us all the news and scandal of the place. Fanny has been at a day school, but we have taken her home again, as she was being taught French in French, and consequently learnt nothing but an unknown tongue. I wish you could see Tom; to-morrow is his birthday (Jan. 19th), and he will 'take his *three*.'[19] He is very good-hearted and affectionate also, and quite a young 'Comic' for fun, and droll mischief. He has a famous notion of drawing for such a shrimp, and the other day came with his thumb and finger opened like a pair of compasses to measure his ma's nose to take her portrait. He is as strong too as a little horse, and always well. He makes us roar sometimes with his imitations; but one the other night was beautiful. He saw Fanny at her prayers, quietly slipped away, knelt down by his bed, clasped his little hands, and said gravely 'my love to pa, and my love to ma, and all my friends in England.'

I wish it might please one of the Princes to want a companion in a trip to England *viâ* Ostend, that you might see us all. I think we are set in here for at least another year.

It must be something very tempting to make me go to London as yet; it would kill me in a month. Indeed I am better already for being back. Even the pleasure is bad for me, as all excitement tends to urge the circulation, and cause palpitation. What do you think, Tim! Dr. Elliot says that my heart is rather lower hung than usual; but never mind, *you* shall always find it in the right place.

Tim, says he, tell me in your next all about my brothers in arms,– I guess I puzzle some people here with my Prussian officer's cloak. Suppose they seize me for a Luxembourg spy! But *àpropos* to my old comrades, who does not remember Wildegans, himself excepted? I saw some very long lines of his family flying southwards over the sea some two months back, and prophesied (and it is come true) some severe weather. Does he still feel kindly towards us, or have they cut off his breast, heart and all, to smoke, as they do thereabouts? Does he sometimes drink our health in the waters of oblivion? I am wicked enough to enjoy his being put over your head after all your tricks upon him; so pray congratulate him on his promotion. We remembered him at Christmas, over our pudding; Jane wished you both a slice, and I wished you a skewer. I suspect you do not often see 'Carlo,' but give our kind remembrances when you meet; also to 'Von Heugel,' and 'Von Bontonkonkowski,' as Jane says when she attempts his name.[20] That march is often a march of mind in my memory, and I am again at the Burgomaster's, or at

Wittenberg, or Schlunkendorf, not forgetting the Château, and the jack-fishing. I do hope my kind captain is as well as when he overlooked our sport from the window.

I have taken him of the *nose*, at his word, and drawn him. I think the sketches will prove how vividly I have remembered that frolic. I have made some of my friends laugh over it in description. I do not like to ask who may be gone, like the poor Major! You must not forget my respects to the Colonel.

I fear to ask about the translation of 'Eugene Aram;' it was in the most difficult style possible to translate into German; plain, almost Quaker-like; whereas the German poetical style is flowery almost to excess.[21] We are suffering from quite Bromberg weather here; it is like our first winter at Coblenz.

On resuming my letter this morning, I found my ink *friz* in the stand. But we have good coal fires and grates, though I almost scorch myself in getting warm. I told you of two children being frozen here, and this morning I heard that three more, all in the same bed, have been frozen to death at Bruges. I suppose, poor things, they had only an 'ofen,' not a grate.

I do not approve of your Private Plays. Officers ought not to be privates: but perhaps you play in such a style, that the privater the better. Of course *mein lieb-freund* Wildegans bothers the prompter. I would give a trifle to be within a hiss of your performance, to see how fiercely you would curl those moustaches of yours, which the Prince so properly made you dock. Jane and I agree, that in a sentimental, heroical, tearing, German part, you would be capital, remembering what a fine passion you were in once *with* Miss A. and *at* me and Wildegans.

Jane and I try to fancy a performance something as follows: – A house, pretty well lighted up, but with something of the look of a riding-school. In the centre box a stiff old governor, like a soldier preserved in ice. About seventeen ladies, in plenty of fur, and with rather blue noses, attended by fifty-one officers, twenty-five of them all in love with the same face. No gallery, but a pit full of fellows with a bit of yellow on their collars, and a fugleman, that they may applaud in the right places. Scene – the Brake; a gentleman fishing. Then enter a lady – to commit suicide by drowning. The angler humanely dissuades her, because she would frighten the fish, and they fall into argument on the romantic idea of suicide. The angler becomes enamoured, and requests the lady to hold his rod, while he kneels down and lays his hand on his heart. He protests he was never in love but seven times before, but had often been fallen in love with. The lady listens, and seems not averse to the match; but in striking awkwardly at a salmon, she snaps the top joint, and that breaks off everything.

Scene the second. The angler in his room smoking. A friend comes in, takes down a pipe from the wall, and smokes in company.

Scene the third. A pathetic interview between a lady and a lover with two swords on: she asks him if 'he can ever forget her?' and he answers 'yes.'[22]

Scene the fourth. A duel between the angler and his best friend, because the lady had broken his rod. They are parted by the lady's mother, who asks the angler to dinner, and promises him more brawn than *she* can eat.

Scene the fifth. A ball, with only one gentleman who can dance. He waltzes with them all in turn, and then drops down a corpse.

Scene the sixth. The ghost of the dancing gentleman appears: he forgets that he is dead, and is fetched by three little black boys with horns and long tails.

Scene the seventh. The angler at dinner with the old lady and the brawn. The old lady seems to admire him, and says 'he has good teeth!'

Scene the eighth. A gentleman comes on to sing a song, but can't, because he has parted with his '*bello*.'[23]

Scene the ninth. The Brake. The lady and the angler meet by appointment. He offers her his heart and a fine salmon, and she accepts the salmon.

Scene the tenth. A lieutenant in a rage because he is not a captain. He throws a set of somersets in trying to promote himself over his own head.

Scene the eleventh. The nine o'clock trumpet, and the play is snapped off like the top joint. The angler very crusty, because there was an embrace in scene twelve, and the young lady to be in love with him.

Talking of love, just imagine the following little dialogue after reading your last letter:

'I wonder,' said Jane, 'If he has ever lost his heart again?'

'I don't know,' says I; 'but he complains he has lost some lengths of his line.'

The salmon that won't take a bait must be a puzzler. My doctor is an Irishman, and if I see him before I close this, I will ask him if he knows anything on the subject. You know they have salmon in the Liffey, and many other rivers.

So you see I was right, after all, about the beavers in Germany – they are otters! But what a goose you are to shoot them! Otter hunting is capital sport, I believe, with dogs and spears. There is an account of it in one of Scott's novels – I think in 'Rob Roy.'[24] So there is a new variety of sport open to you. I will see if I can get any information about that, too. In the meantime, whenever you write, do not fail to give me any anecdotes as to fishes, fishing, or sporting in general, as well as any new jokes of your locality.

Whilst I was in London, the Royal Exchange was burnt down to the ground. A

great sensation was caused amongst the spectators by the chimes in the tower of the Exchange striking up in the midst of the flames with the very appropriate air of 'There's nae luck about the House.'[25] To make the coincidence more curious, there are half a dozen other tunes they play by turns through the week.
I hope the bank will take no advantage of it when people go there for money, for the cashiers might now say, 'We have got no Change.' Another practical joke was, that Wilson, the Radical bookseller, was the only Conservative, his shop being the only one that was at all left standing.[26]
Sad news from Canada of revolt and fighting. I earnestly hope that a timely redress of grievances, and they seem to have some, will prevent a struggle that would end, like the American war, in their loss to England.[27] The Spaniards seem to have acted like all other foreign states towards England, when money was concerned, – the legion broken up for want of pay, which the Spanish Government coolly cheats them of. That massacre of English prisoners by the Carlists was a brutal affair.[28] When we came here we travelled with a very nice, gentlemanly, elderly Irishman, whom we liked very much, and he took very much to us. I found out that he was a Catholic priest, very high in the Irish church. He had been to Rome, and spoke with disgust of the little that religion had to do with the civil wars in Spain – that it was purely political, and, in fact, Protestant princes patronised the Carlists. *Ainsi va le monde!* And I am very glad that I have had nothing to do with politics, though they try hard to identify me with some party or other. So, as I am no 'sidesman,' but only a 'merrythought,'[29] the leading reviews, Whig and Tory, have carefully abstained from noticing me or my works. This is funny enough in professedly *literary* reviews, and shows they are practically political ones. And the result is, I am going, I understand, to be reviewed by the *Radical* review, and, I hear, favourably.[30]
Some weeks ago some fellow or other on the Tory side wrote a poem against the ministry, and forged my name to it, and I had a skirmish on the subject. The fact is there is a set, who try to write down and libel all who are not Tories, neutrals like myself included; it is too bad, but they will sink of themselves at last from sheer want of character and principle. I am not afraid of them, and do not think they will care to attack me, as I am apt to get *the laugh* on my side. I was the more annoyed at the forgery, because it was addressed to the Queen. Are we not in luck, Tim, to have such a nice young girl to be loyal to; she is very popular, and does good by frequenting the theatres, &c. Her mother is very much respected, and has done her duty both to her daughter and to the nation, in a manner that deserves a statue at the hands of the English ladies.[31] But I must pull up or I shall have no

room for the messages. Tom sends his love to 'Fank, Vildidans, Tarlevitch, and Towski;' Fanny joins in chorus; and Jane sends her kindest regards, and says she has no chance of learning French here, there is so much English. There is plenty of *Flemish* too, but I can't *learn it;* and so must tell you in the mother tongue, that I am, my dear Franck, your friend ever, and in all sincerity, to the end of the line, and without a weak length in it.

Thomas, Tim, Johnny Hood.

P.S. Should you see 'Hood's Own' advertised in any of your northern papers, it is not my wife, but the re-issue of the 'Comic'. It is intended to be sent into Germany, as it will be as cheap as foreign editions. I will send you the inscriptions you desire in the parcel. When you write to the Princes, pray make my respects to them. I am very glad Prince Czartoriski had such sport, but you are all well off in that particular – whereas, in Britain, we have fished at them, till fish are scarce and shy. There is perch-fishing to be had here in the moat, and, I should think, jack somewhere in the cuts from the canals. I shall try next summer, and also at the sea fish, as a pot-hunter. There are good turbot and capital John Dory off the coast, and, I suspect, smelts in the harbour; they do angle for flounders a little. What is that fish you tell me of with a nob on his nose? Send me the German name if you know it. And what fish is a *wels?* I can't find it in the dictionary – a sort of sturgeon, perhaps. Many thanks for the *Lieder Buch.* We have had a good laugh over '*Ach Gretel mein taubchen.*' Tom took a fancy to it at first, and used to sing it. How Dr. Weiterhauser would stare to see my use of it!

What will you poor Germans do for victuals and drink? First, the doctors found out that your *würst* was a slow – no, active poison; and now a Düsseldorf chemist discovers that all your 'schnaps' and liqueurs are deleterious, from being made from bad potatoes. Then the Westminster Medical Society has proved that your German candles are arsenicated and poisonous;[32] and were there not edicts against your painted sugar-plums that poisoned the children? Not that I should care if all the Rhinelanders poisoned themselves or each other; they are not fit for their beautiful country; but I should not like it to spread further, as I like the other cousins, for example the Saxons. In justice to myself, I must say we have heard several English speak in our own style of Rhenish diet and the people; but they are not true Germans, only mongrels.

And now, Tim, have I not written you a long letter at all events? It will be as good as extra drill to read it all through at once. I fear I shall not soon be able to write so amply again, for I have great arrears of work, and shall be as busy in my little bureau as a Prime Minister, or at least a Secretary for the Home Department. Our severe weather continues; we all but stir the fire with our noses, and sweep the hearths with our shoes. I wish you would keep your own sort of winter at Bromberg; you are used to it, but I am not, and am sitting in the house in my snow shoes. Now then farewell, Tim. God bless you, and may you have good luck even in fishing. Take care of your liver, my old boy, in peace-time, and in war-time of your bacon; and always take a spare pair of breeches with you to the Brake for fear of falling in! Should you ever have thoughts of marrying, let me know, and I will give you some good advice. I have strong misgivings that those private theatricals will lead to something of that sort. As the children say, 'you may begin in play, and end in earnest.' Perhaps, whilst I write, the knot is tied, and you are in the honeymoon with it all running down your moustache! For anything I know, Carlo and Bonkowski have written to me to use my influence to prevent your chucking yourself away. I will go and get them translated to-morrow, and then perhaps you will hear from me again. You were always dying for somebody; but 'Philip! remember thou art mortal!'[33]

I have just heard that the London Packet (not a mail) is gone ashore. I wish she was wrecked at once, she is such a wretched craft. My portrait-painter was three days in coming over here – besides, I hate her very name, for reminding me of my own unseaworthiness, the *Liver*-pool! Whilst I was in London, all of a sudden there broke out here in Ostend, several attempts at robbery, that quite alarmed our quietude. A servant girl was knocked all down stairs by a fellow secreted in a room above. At Bruges there were several other attempts; some fellows, I suppose, from London or Paris. I have accordingly put night caps on my detonators, and I believe we have an extra military patrol. I wish they would rob me of my liver complaint: I would not prosecute. Good-bye for the last time; this is the end of my news, till we grow some more.

Rue Longue, Ostend, Christmas Day, 1837. [*finished 18 and 19 January 1838*]

From *Memorials* II 3–27, where it is dated in error, 'Christmas Day, 1838.' The letter was begun on Christmas Day, 1837, and continues, after a visit to England lasting three weeks, on January 18 and 19 1838.

1/Unidentified

2/Beerman

3/Reference to Hood's once warning Jane never to buy plaice with red spots, *Memorials* I 24. A 'placeman' was a person appointed to government service without regard to fitness.

4/Hood probably left Ostend on 27 December.

5/A territorial dispute involving Prussia, France, Belgium, and Holland: discussed in *Annual Register* (1838) 451. The controversy, principally between Belgium and Holland, ended in 1839.

6/On 20 November 1837 the Archbishop of Cologne had been arrested for acting on rigid Roman Catholic views in a way considered damaging to the Prussian state: *Annual Register* (1837) 345. He remained in detention for over a year.
7/Having succeeded to the throne of Hanover on 24 June, Ernest Augustus proceeded to suspend the liberal constitution. In his campaign against the constitution he was supported by the King of Prussia. However, Hanover was annexed by Prussia in 1866.
8/France held Luxembourg from 1795 to 1814. It was in the possession of Belgium from 1830 to 1839. Prussia seems to have benefited from the settlement of this last year.
9/The corn laws were only finally abolished in 1869.
10/*Hamlet* 3 i 63–4
11/Franck's lady-love at Koblenz
12/No doubt the safest way of transferring valuable materials was through the services of a friend or trustworthy acquaintance.
13/Perhaps this should be 'H. D—,' for Harman Dilsoon.
14/Perhaps Wanstead
15/Old H— and Richard D— are unidentified; W— is probably Wright. Of H— Hood's son notes: 'This gentleman is evidently the original of a character in "Up the Rhine".' The character is Richard Orchard, *Works* VII 11.
16/In the preface to his published speech Talfourd made a special point of 'the pleasure and benefit I have derived from Mr Hood's Letters on Copyright ... which are admirable for sense, spirit, and humour.' The letters appeared in *The Athenaeum.*
17/The old gentleman is unidentified. The poem to which Hood refers is the ode to Rae Wilson, published in *The Athenaeum* 12 August 1837.
18/*The Book of Gems. The Modern Poets* ed. S.C. Hall (1838) 254
19/It was Tom Hood's third birthday. He explains 'take his three' as 'an allusion to the old three-handed cribbage at Coblenz.'
20/Carlovicz, Bonkowski, and von Heugel, members of the regiment
21/Probably the translation of 'Eugene Aram' done by De Franck and Von Rühe. The finally published version was dedicated to the Prince Regent (1841).
22/Hood's son notes that the forgetful Wildegans had once gone on parade carrying both his own sword and Franck's.
23/Hood's son notes: 'This was Carlovicz, who gave me a little spaniel called Bello.'
24/The account is to be found in ch. 33.
25/The fire took place on 10 January.
26/Effingham Wilson (1783–1868), bookseller and publisher; his shop was at 88 Cornhill from 1809 until the fire.
27/The disorders began in Upper Canada on 4 December 1837, whilst Sir Francis Bond Head was lieutenant-governor. They were followed by the Durham Report (1839), laying the foundation for Canadian unity.
28/Discussed in *Annual Register* (1837) 303–4. In its war against the Carlists, a counter-revolutionary movement, the Spanish Government failed to take advantage of the support of a British Legion.
29/The wish-bone, or furcula, of a bird; NED gives no metaphorical usage of this word.
30/Hood's work was enthusiastically reviewed by H.F. Chorley in the *London and Westminster Review* April 1838. The article is initialled C.H., an inversion of Chorley's initials.
32/Victoria Mary Louisa, Duchess of Kent (1786–1861)
32/Reported in *Athenaeum* 6 January 1838, 14
33/Phocylides *Sententiae* 109

TO
ELIZABETH HOOD

My dear Betsey.

According to your invitation I write that you may hear from me, on Xmas Day. Mr Wright staid here, a much shorter time than we expected; but the truth is I have little time to write letters to any one except on business & I knew you would hear of if not from me through Mr Baily or Mr Wright. Since I have been abroad I have always been ill about six months out of twelve & not very well the rest, so that my affairs accumulate on my hands & I have to drive & hurry the rest of the time, & when not at work am glad to rest without pen or pencil in sight. This hardly gives my health a fair chance as I suffer of course from exhaustion after such extra exertion. The Comic is a tolerable job, for I do it all myself & till this year it has been quite as much as I can do – but since I have been in Belgium from better health & quicker communication I have been able to do more than the two preceding years. In the mean time the comic steadily maintains its ground tho so many of the other annuals are gone & going – all the rivals in my own line are gone, & I have again the field to myself. Indeed the present year the sale looks up rather than otherwise which is more than I could expect. I ordered a copy for you which you got of course. All I need to prosper, & which has hitherto delayed me, is health. But the change to this has done me good – & I begin to hope for a cure. But I left Germany only in time – where I was dying fast, & there is every reason to believe the Doctor there mistook my case. It first originated in inflammation of the stomach or liver for which I *ought* to have been bled but was not – & so it became chronic. Indeed it is a wonder it did not kill me at the first onset. Then it ended in spitting blood – not such as you have seen – but *a pint* at once – & one time a pint & a half – which my second German Doctor thought came from the *lungs*, & treated accordingly. Of course that was a very perilous case – but the English Dr here took another view & thought it came from the liver. But he had no opportunity of judging decidedly for I never have spit blood *here*, till about three weeks ago, & then only ⅓ of a cup full – but it enabled him to judge better, & every day shows stronger symptoms so that he is convinced it is from the liver – indeed the liver is palpably enlarged. I was sinking in Germany under wretched diet & wrong treatment – but the meat bread & vegetables are so very excellent here that I got an appetite, my constitution had fair play, rallied, showed fight, & by the bustle indicated the very scene of the conflict. I have never believed about the lungs all along. Now that the disease is known there is a chance for a cure – in fact I have made great progress in my health generally since I have been here. I eat heartily, – & got thro the Comic literally in a gallop. The D^{r} here is an experienced man & I think skilful & besides I have the benefit by letter of Dr Elliot's advice. But the diet does a great deal. – Instead of sour poor bad rye bread, sour small wine bad vegetables & wretched meat with execrable cookery, we have excellent white bread better rather than English, the best meat, good wholesome beer, – & the vegetable market is the finest I have ever seen, any where. The effect is very visible on us all. Fanny who was really delicate on the Rhine is quite hearty. – & little Tom grows both fast & fat. He is remarkably strong & well – quite boisterous with health, & admired wherever he goes. Jane has been very ill the last three weeks, but is now down stairs again – thro a miscarriage brought on by alarm & exertion at my last attack which came on suddenly. – Otherwise the place has agreed with her too. – We all like it very much & are as happy as we could be away from England. It is a nice quiet, very clean town – famous sands on which you may walk 30 miles on end, a fine sea, & a handsome esplanade, – ¼ of a mile long, – the country flat – but not I think so unhealthy as reported. The Ostend people & the market people all seem healthy & ruddy, & the children as fine as you would see any where. We have a very genteel nice lodging in a good street close to the sea – amply furnished in the English style with carpets, &c. Kitchen, two parlours – little study, and three bedrooms, no dearer than Coblenz where we had bare boards stoves & all sorts of discomforts. Indeed we live quite in the English style, & do not find it dearer than Coblenz. The people of the house very obliging nice persons – & the natives generally well disposed to the English, & all speak English more or less – some you would not know were flemings. Our servant for instance. Fish is often abundant & cheap – ½ a crown for a small turbot – others in proportion. Indeed tho we have very many scamps & outlaws here there are also respectables – ½ pay officers & their families for instance who come here for cheapness – for you get even luxuries at a moderate cost. I had not touched wine for 4 or 5 months but my D^{r} ordered me some to help my digestion – I took a part of a cask with him, a sort between claret & burgundy really *very* good, & including bottles & every thing not quite 14^{d} a bottle! In short we live as comfortable as we can be abroad, – & unless something very advantageous should turn up requiring my presence in England I have no idea of leaving this (providing it agrees with my health) for some time to come. I have work cut out to occupy me for the whole year to come, – there is a post 4 days a week, better than to some parts of England – & what should I gain by going over to double my expenditure. As for the rest, if it were necessary or desirable, I know there would be no difficulty at this very time in arranging for my return – parties in fact are ready on my behalf – but it is my choice to stay here. So I want no compositions or arrangements – granting me health I have no fear as to the rest, & when I come back, or before, all will be paid *in full.* I mention all this because you seem to be under a mistaken notion that I am *pining* to return. I was annoyed lately to hear that Miss Lawrance (the Goldsmith's friend) had been gossipping & talking about my anxiety to return, & that she knew parties would meet me as to terms &c.[1] I think it very unlikely she knows any one I am indebted to – so that it is mere idle gossip – but such stuff often makes mischief; & is annoying at any rate. What has Miss Lawrence or any body else to do with my affairs? Then as to Aunt Brown's[2] story of a gentleman coming with me from Hamburg it is a sheer *lie,* – I have never been near Hamburg – so could not come from it[3] – nor in England since I left it. I cannot guess what motives there may be at the bottom of such reports – but I do wish that such meddlers would confine themselves to their own affairs, which would prosper better & mine no worse, for the abstinence. *I* interfere in nobodys – nor do I ask or require assistance or advice for any one. My affairs are in due train, & nothing but my health has stood in the way of the fulfilment of my plans. I shall be glad therefore if you will stop all such nonsense decidedly from whatever quarter it comes. The rest is between ourselves – but you will be glad to hear that we are comfortable & prospects brighter than since we have been abroad.

I have just had my portrait painted, natural size nearly full length, by an artist come out expressly for the purpose. It is for Baily, & will be exhibited at Somerset House or Suffolk Stt.[4] It is a good likeness & a month or two hence will probably be at Baily's – where you will be able to see it – & what I am now like when looking my best. Jane is to have a Copy. I wish I could send you a portrait of Tom Junior. He is quite a baby in simplicity but a big boy in spirit, fun, & good humoured mischief. Dilke says he never saw so fine a temper & he is very affectionate – & tho I say it – very clever. He is very fond of drawing & for such a shrimp it is wonderful how well he makes out what he tries at. It is quite funny to see him sketching the whole family on the sand, on a colossal scale so that he is obliged to run from their heads to their legs. He is anxious to learn to read, & knows many of his letters. Fanny is tall, & will be pretty with auburn hair. She is very quick & clever too, & is learning French &c at a day school – Between the children we are never dull, – & we have had Mr & Mrs Dilke & his sister & her husband to see us, besides Wright – & now Mr Lewis the painter. So that we have had some society. Our landlord is a very pleasant man – very fond of children & a great favorite with Tom. A Jack of all trades, – but a Carpenter by rights. He paints, glazes, papers makes picture frames &c – and in my room I have a chamber organ made by him. We have a broken window & none of the regular glaziers will come & mend it because our landlord has been his own glazier. And he has been a soldier & marched to Berlin under Bonaparte besides! In the summer old Romeo Coates & his wife reside here. He has settled down into a gentlemanly old thin man, rather a beau – I have been introduced to him. Next summer the railroad will be brought down to us, so that the traffic will be tenfold. We have several times made trips to Bruges a beautiful quaint little old City about 14 miles hence, – you go in a passage boat by the canal for a franc & a half (15 pence). I shall make a tour of Belgium in the spring I think. You may do it all by railroad or canal — almost as cheap as sitting at home. The railroad will bring over the Londoners in shoals for it will be much the best way of going to the Rhine.

Since the above was written, I *have* been to England, for the first time and staid three weeks. The main reason was my health. Dr Elliot could not leave his practise or he would have come over – and he was very anxious to see me, to decide on my case, as an affection of the lungs would have made it improper for me to stay here. Besides as Doctors had differed so, the German one directly opposed to the one here it was important to know which was the right course as an error would be fatal. Elliot took great pains, & I am glad to say *entirely* coincided with the doctor here as to my case & its treatment. This is a great relief to our minds, as otherwise my death warrant was signed such bleedings from the lungs being extremely dangerous. He tried my back and chest thoroughly with the stethoscope & my lungs are sound. It is a diseased liver, of long standing, affecting the circulation & causing palpitation of the heart thro stoppage & congestion in the liver. The bleeding *not* dangerous. It will be very troublesome, having been mistaken & not treated at all so long – but luckily this place is good for me – sea air, to brace me – and I am to *sail* in summer, not being able to bear much walking or coach exercise – on acct of the palpitation & being very reduced & weak. But I am getting better knowing now how to treat it. But between bloodspitting & letting I got very low & left off *all* wine spirit & beer, whereas *some* was *necessary*, my digestion requiring help. Thus I have suffered severely thro those loggerheaded Germans. – You must not think it unkind I did not come to see you – as you may suppose I am not able to go about much at any time – but the stake was so great, that the utmost secresy was necessary. I was in lodgings, convenient for Elliot to come – & never stirred out the whole time: – indeed independent of safety I was fully engaged the whole time in preparing a reissue of the Comic, – & the moment it was done I returned.[5] Dilke Wright & Baily who had all to see me *on business* were all the parties that were in the secret – & if I had come to you I must have gone elsewhere, & so encreased the chance of the matter getting known. Arrangements are making to enable me at any time to come over openly when business requires tho we shall continue to reside here, both to save money & to suit my health. My portrait is thought an excellent likeness, – & is to be engraved so that you can have one by & by. It is gone to the engravers so you can't see it at Baily's as I proposed. I am not sorry to get back for I was never in bed till 2 or 3 in the morning, – and I feel better since I am back. I had fine passages to Dover & back & they did me good. I had amongst other things all my three years accounts to go through – they turn out quite satisfactory & the sale of Comic quite steady – but only sufficient for my yearly expenditure. Of course as I get better all extra works will go to pay off with – and there is not one shilling of fresh debt, since I left. So on the whole my prospects are considerably brighter & as I have now a chance of comparatively good health I have no fears for the result. We have just now extremely cold weather & of course you will share in it – two children frozen to death here – and three all in the same bed at Bruges. It is quite unusual here – where the climate is nearly the same as our own. I hope William is not travelling for it is hardly possible to bear it out of doors.[6] Our Doctor thought his ears were frostbitten. Thank heaven we are in a land of grates & coals instead of the horrid stoves or I should perish – as cold feet & hands are very bad for me, my circulation is so embarrassed. Today (19th) was Master Tom's birthday or as he calls it his Friday – Three years old. I am going to try to take his portrait in oil as the artist who took mine set me up for materials. You of course have seen the reissue of the Comic advertized as Hood's Own. It will be a very cheap work with a great deal of reading at a shilling a month. I have hopes of a decent sale. But the piracies now adays are infamous, for instance those on Boz & the Pickwick there ought to be some very summary process – it is of no use to bring actions against men of straw.[7] Jane will come over on a visit in the Spring or Summer. She desires her love to you & will write soon & in your letter will answer Jessy's to her at Coblenz. Fanny and Tom both send their love: – & give mine to Jessy & William. – & the short Bill or W. Junr. I have written a long letter as I shall not be able to soon write again, – I set to work again tomorrow very hard, on three or four different things, & hope to get through a great deal this year – among others a book on Germany with my March with the Prussian regiment. I have done between 40 & 50 cuts for it – a sort of Outlandish Whims & Oddities. God bless you all, with good health & all other goods.

I shall see you I expect this summer.

Your affectionate Brother

Thos Hood

[*Ostend*] *Sent off 20th Jany.* [*1838*]

MS. Bristol Central Library. Address: 'Miss Hood / 3 Guildford Street / Wilmington Square / London.' PM: 'OSTENDE 1838/ 23/ JAN,' 'LONDON/ 25/ JAN/ 1838.' The letter was begun on Christmas Day 1837 and continued on 19 January 1838.

1/Hannah Lawrance (1795–1875), an early friend of Hood when he lived in Islington. Hannah Lawrance contributed to *The Athenaeum* and published *Historical Memoirs of the Queens of England* (1838–40). She wrote a valuable article on Hood for the *British Quarterly Review* October 1867, 323–54.

2/Unidentified

3/Hood had dated the announcement of the *Comic Annual* from Hamburg: *Athenaeum* 1 October 1836, 708. He probably did this because he saw no reason to divulge his exact personal whereabouts.

4/Headquarters of the Royal Academy and the Society of British Artists respectively

5/The first part of *Hood's Own* came out on 25 January 1838.

6/Probably William Holt, the husband of Hood's other sister Jessy

7/Such piracies are discussed by John Forster, *Life of Charles Dickens* ed. J.W.T. Ley (1928) 101–2.

TO

CHARLES WENTWORTH DILKE

My dear Dilke,

I fear the bit on the other side is not good for any thing – as I am not at all in writing trim. Your letter found me yesterday with my head quite muddled with pain. I had struggled well with the very severe frost but the suddenness of the thaws upset me. I shall be well after a night's rest, as I barely winked till this morning. This ought to reach on Friday Mor^{ng}. – but our mails have been very irregular thro the blockade of ice. I Murphy'd this weather when I was at Blackheath. I am quite awake to the importance of something of *current* interest for the 2 next No^{s}[1] & in fact have been studying it. I shall well consider your suggestions which look likely ones. I will take care to be on time.

[*Ostend, February 1838*]

MS BM. Address, fragmentary: 'lke Esqre / Grosvenor Place / Pimlico / London.' Published by Marchand, 90–1. With the rest of the letter, 'the bit on the other side' to which Hood refers in his first sentence has disappeared. In the course of the letter Hood mentions Patrick Murphy (1782–1847), weather prophet. According to DNB, his name was prominent in 1838 as the author of the *Weather Almanack.* His prediction for 20 January was correct, and the *Almanack* ran to 45 editions. However, 'its sale very much fell off after the "nine days' wonder."' This comment may justify Hood's considering Murphy 'done up,' that is, worn out or ruined, as he does in the following letter.

1/Of *Hood's Own*

TO
JOHN WRIGHT

My dear Wright,

The books per *Stewardess* arrived in port Monday night, but are not delivered yet, thanks to that folly the Carnival, which plagues other houses[1] besides the Customs. In Coblenz it was kept up by the tradesmen. Here it is the Saturnalia of the lowest class. They have been roaring about the streets all the two last nights, our servant no doubt among them. She applied to be out two whole nights running (how your wife will lift up her eyes!), and insisting it was the custom of the place, we could not refuse. She masqueraded, too, as a broom-girl. The first night she got her mask torn, and to-day, after her second night, can hardly crawl with a swelled foot – maybe from a fight, nobody knows what, but it has given me quite a disgust. Neither Germans nor Flemings ought to Carnivalise – though the Germans have one advantage. I have heard very good singing in parts from the common people about Coblenz, but never did I hear such howling and croaking as here. They beat our ballad-singers in London all to sticks.

Now I think of it, was there ever a Flemish singer of any celebrity? I do not recollect one. How Rooke would enjoy 'Amalie's' popularity in Ostend![2] Shall I send him over a Flemish Rainer Family?[3] It would be at least a novelty. Murphy seems *done up* lately; but his very style, full of long mazy sentences, is quackish, and seems purposely mystified. I have thought of two cuts for him. Low Irish, with pots and sacks, looking out for a 'shower of *Murphy's;*' and 'the prophet a little *out,*' *i.e.* caught in a shower without his umbrella.[4] I think he doesn't understand the *Pour* Laws.

No local news, only another bloodless duel at Bruges. I have hopes our frost has gone – I noted some wild geese yesterday going back to the 'nor'ard,' and every one of them is a Murphy. Give my kind regards to everybody – I can't stop to enumerate, my head is so full of 'My Own.'[5] Take care of yourself, and when you dine, don't leave off hungry – leave off dry, if you like. I am, dear Wright,

Yours very truly,

Thomas Hood.

39, Rue Longue, [*Ostend*] *Feb. 28, 1838.*

From *Memorials* I 306–8

1/*Romeo and Juliet* 3 i 111

2/William Michael Rooke (1794–1847), wrote the music for *Amilie*, first performed at Covent Garden theatre, 2 December 1837. The opera had a long run and is highly praised in DNB.

3/The Tyrolese Rainer family sang in London in 1827. Presumably such a group would have performed well in Rooke's musical drama.
4/*Hood's Own* contains two anti-Murphy cuts, 'Wether Wise' at p. 96 and 'Rather out in the weather' at p. 130.
5/The second part of *Hood's Own*, containing these cuts, was ready at the beginning of March 1838.

TO
JOHN WRIGHT

My dear Wright,
I was very glad to have a few lines from you of cheering import, of which I have much need. I never had so little alacrity of body or mind, but you need never urge me, for it is only needlessly spurring a willing horse; I only wish that my power equalled my wish, but I have been almost 'lower than plummet e'er did sound,'[1] – like the weather, far below zero. I am now better, but by means so foreign to my recent habits, that like the little old woman I can hardly believe that I is I, for by medical advice I am drinking port wine daily. I am glad you like the Grimaldi cut, as I did myself, and I shall do as much as I can in that style, as I prefer it, and it is less trouble when I can do it.[2]
But I am not always in the cue; I have found more difficulty in inventing than in executing, my state allowing of the mechanical, but not of the imaginative; yet I have had some gleams. By the Stewardess you will receive another cut and tailpiece, the subject Female Spouting;[3] I think I shall be able to make a pleasant paper too on Grimaldi, an 'Ode to Murphy, or Moore's Ghost,' and the 'Bury Book.'[4] Be satisfied that for my own sake I will do *all* I can, and supposing you can wait till Monday, I do not despair of doing something worth while. In the meantime I will give you a selection to set up in type as before.
I am glad you are not out of heart, as I am not; there has been hardly time to get the thing well, *i.e.* universally known, and from this point it will go on improving, as I shall myself in health. By the bye, as an instance of a curious faculty I seem to possess, that I can hit off a likeness afterwards, though not if a person were to sit to me, I made such a resemblance of our servant's face when Grimaldi[5] called, that Jane recognised it, but unfortunately I blotted it out accidentally with a drop of ink, and could not get it again.
Thank goodness the weather is better, and I can, and do, get out; I am mending, and hope to rattle off the next No. as I did the 'Comic.' Why don't you come here

instead of going to Cheshunt, and we will take a trip to Bruges? Take care of yourself. I am vexed to trouble you so, but it won't last long.

I am, my dear Wright,
Yours ever truly,

Thomas Hood.

Àpropos – I want to patronise a poor self-taught *wood-cutter* here, in a very humble line; he only cuts butter stamps and moulds for ginger-bread; but when you send a parcel, if you have any worn out gravers or tools it would be a charity.

39, Rue Longue, Ostend, March 16, [*1838*].

From *Memorials* II 27–9, where the year is given as 1839, wrongly, since *Hood's Own*, referred to in the course of the letter, was issued in parts through 1838.

1/*Tempest* 5 i 56
2/*Hood's Own* 113
3/Unidentified
4/Hood is referring to 'The Elland Meeting," 'A Serio-Comic Reminiscence,' and 'The Apparition,' in *Hood's Own*, 97–103, 113–15, 129–30. He composed three epigrams and 'The Devil's Album,' 49–50, on *A Diary Illustrative of the Times of George IV*, supposed to be by Lady Charlotte Bury, published at the beginning of January 1838.
5/Joseph Grimaldi (1779–1837), clown and pantomimist. Hood addressed one of the *Odes and Addresses* to Grimaldi, and he wrote a speech for his farewell performance in 1828, the occasion of the clown's visit, referred to in the text. Dickens edited Grimaldi's *Memoirs* (1838).
6/In a note Hood's son refers to his father's skill in caricature as evidenced by sketches of Dilke and De Quincey. The former occurs in *Up the Rhine*, facing 93.

TO
JOHN WRIGHT

My Dear Wright,
I have just received 'Hood's Own,' and it looks like a good number. The cuts come capitally, including Scott's, which is a great acquisition. I am satisfied in print with the Elland article and Grimaldi: I had partly written some verses for the latter, but luckily did not risk going on with them, or all might have hitched. It was not my fault but my misfortune, for I had been finishing the Elland article all night in bed, and was copying out the Murphy when the last minute arrived for the mail. I did afterwards hope you would guess the case, and 'take the very bold, daring, presumptuous liberty,' perhaps, of getting the ghost off the stage as you could.[1] I have read of one, that would not go off, being hustled away by the

performers. But bygones must be bygones; it might have been worse. There are better than two sheets of a 'Comic Annual.' I was shocked to see no more advertisements, and parodying a note of B—'s,[2] I might write 'I am not the man to say *Die*' – but, by the Lord Harry, you must get me fresh advertisements; *that* will give me fresh vigour to work on the letter-press and cuts! By the way, as you say, the notices get very frequent and favourable; they ought to be saved, as it might be advisable to print them some day in an advertisement, as they did formerly with the Athenaeum. A thing that gets frequent and favourable notices ought to move, if properly pushed. Has B— done anything abroad? Brussels is particularly full, – – Paris, – America. – .There are plenty of English to buy *cheap* books, and with so many cuts, it cannot be pirated. I do not think the field has been even yet properly beaten, and a one-shilling book is the very thing where a twelve-shilling one would not do.

For the next Number, I propose 'Hieroglyphical Hints,' – a paper on the dismissal of the yeomanry with the old 'Unfavourable Review,'[3] that you had a hand in turning into a libel on Mrs. Somebody and her close carriage. I think of writing something from a black footman on the Emancipation question.[4]

I get my papers very irregularly. For instance, I have not yet had last Sunday's 'Dispatch'. This is bad, and might be very unfortunate, as in the charge against me of plagiarism. Pray tell B— to blow up that 'd—d boy that puts papers in the wrong box,' and please then desire said boy to row his master for sending wrong advertisements. I mention this for B—'s sake, as well as my own, because he must be badly seconded in other cases as well as mine.

I am quite satisfied and pleased with your arrangement of No. 3, and only regret, my good fellow, I have to give you so much extra trouble. Do go out of town and refresh! Poor Rooke! How Amalie's nose is put out of joint! for of course you will now sing nothing about Herts, Essex, Middlesex, and Kent, but 'This is my eldest daughter, Sir!'[5] Take care of her now you have got her, at last. Some infants are squatted on, like the 'spoiled child.'[6] Mind, and whenever Mrs. Wright looks fatigued and sedentary, take care to hand her a chair. Now and then, a child is turned up with a bedstead, but that could not happen, if the maids slept in hammocks. Mind how you nurse her yourself. Never toss her up unless you are quite certain of catching her, a butter-fingered father might become wretched for life in a moment. Don't let her go up in your study among the wild young men. What do you think of her for our Tom? Don't give her a precocious taste for lots o' daffy;[7] or a box at the Opera. You ought to know better than dream of operatising, yourself such an invalid. I have never d—d or t—d out since at Ostend, and am going, to-morrow, for the first time, but only to my doctor's, and if anything happens, he will be at hand.

How do *all* the boys like the Gal? Poor things! I never knew a *dozen* brothers, but *one* sister managed to tyrannise over 'em all. Have you got a dictionary name yet? If I might propose, I should say christen her 'Mary Wollstonecraft,' as the supporter of *Female Wrights!*[8]

You must not be out of heart about your cough, – of late years the spring has brought an almost certain influenza in England as elsewhere. Easterly damp winds are the cause. I have been teazingly coughing, and Jane is wheezy, but what proves it to be *influenzial*, is that Tom, Junior, is as hoarse as a crow. How should we weak ones hope then to escape! For he is a young horse for strength, and indeed, has adopted from 'Nimrod's Sporting,' the name of 'Plenipotentiary!'[9]

There is a genteel blot, as the clerk said, on my scutcheon. That comes of foreign paper. Jane, at the other side of the table, is grumbling at it too. Thanks for the fishing-tackle, – all right, – and gone to Bromberg. I wish the Prince Radziwills would go to the Coronation[10] and bring Franck with them. But, no! Prussia, and Russia, the two great enemies of England, are to colleague together in a family party instead. There is a great conspiracy there, or I'm mistaken, but it will fall through, – say I Murphy'd it. For Mrs. Wright's benefit, I must tell you now, the finis of our maid, Mary. She insisted on two whole nights' leave at the Carnival, as being customary, and came home each morning between seven and eight, so done up she could hardly stand. At last, one evening there came by a jolly, roaring set of Carnivalities that quite set her agog the moment she heard the *singing*, if it might be called so! She *took* leave *instanter*, came home next morning, jaded to death, and had occasion to *take some soda!*[11] Of course we paid her off on the spot, and have since learned she used to *persecute* a waiter we called *Cheeks* (ask Lewis about him), and go out on the sly, and drink brandy-and-water with him. She was seen at the Carnival with petticoats up to her knees, bare-legged and be-ribboned, in the character of a broom-girl. Won't Mrs. Wright bless her stars there is no Carnival in England? Greenwich fair is next to it as performed here. And even the respectable people join in it, the tradespeople and all, and the children of the gentry go about in character, – some of the *banker's* here did, for example. By the bye, did I ever tell you of an incident the other day. There was going to be a grand religious procession, and a fine gilded car, or chariot containing a figure of the Virgin, which was to be filled with angels, represented by children with spangled wings, &c., and our landlord, who was engaged in preparation for it, came to borrow Tom *for an angel!* Just fancy Jane's great horror and indignation, – I could hardly appease her by suggesting that it was a compliment to his good looks.

And now, I must shut up: I will send as much and as often as I can. Give my comps. to B—, and tell him to get a whole No. of advertisements. Seriously, we must both stir our stumps, and I do my best.[12] What would he say now the Copyright Bill is coming on again, to reprinting my letters as a pamphlet, as proposed before?[13] What wouldn't I do if I had health and bodily strength? Pray for that when you pray for me, for without it, what a clog to one's wheel!

And now, God bless you and yours, including Miss Wright – only think of a *mile* of daughters! there is a family of Furlongs coming to live here, whereof *eight* are daughters – 8 furlongs = 1 mile.

Give my kind remembrances to all friends of ours, and believe me,

Dear Wright,
Yours ever truly,

Thos. Hood.

Two more commissions! *What* a bother I am; but would you let somebody inquire where to get it, and send me two packets of *vaccine matter* by the stewardess next Saturday, and a German grammar for Fanny, with plenty of exercises for young beginners; and pray thank E. Smith kindly for the seeds he was *sow* kind as to send. Is anybody coming out a Maying?

Ostend, April 5, 1838.

From *Memorials* I 308–14. In the relevant portion of *Hood's Own* the cuts on 108, 125 appear to be the work of another hand than Hood's.

1/*Literary Gazette* 7 April 1838, 214, quoted concluding stanzas to 'The Apparition,' the 'Murphy' here referred to. The *Gazette* explained that the stanzas had been omitted from *Hood's Own* through an accident in the press.

2/Baily's

3/*Hood's Own* 161–8

4/'The Black and White Question' 145–52

5/Apparently compliments to Wright on the birth of a daughter

6/*Whims and Oddities* facing 59

7/Gin

8/Mary Wollstonecraft Godwin (1759–97), had published her *Vindication of the Rights of Women* in 1792.

9/A celebrated race-horse, depicted in *Sporting*, facing 120

10/The coronation of Queen Victoria took place on 28 June 1838.

11/As a cure for a hangover?

12/A glance at the end pages of the following issues shows that the advertising position did not improve. Dilke wrote to Hood on 21 April: 'I have just been laughing over [your letters] and never

so heartily as at yr indignation – Think of Baily being kicked about Blackheath by a respectable palefaced gentleman in spectacles. You know my opinion of Baily therefore I need not repeat it – but as a Bookseller you must use him, and therefore be gentle, I said from the first that *he* could not get advertisements and the result proves it,' MS Bristol Central Library.
13/Talfourd's bill received a second reading on 25 April 1838, but was withdrawn on 28 June. The letters were not reprinted.

TO
MRS ANNE MATHEWS

Dear Madam,
I feel much flattered by your request, indirectly conveyed to me, that I would contribute some sketch to the Memoirs you have in preparation. It would give me great pleasure to do so, but, unfortunately for myself my acquaintance with M[r] Mathews was so limited, and transient, that I could not do more than add my mite to the public award which always attended on his inimitable performances. Still should my memory furnish any trait worthy of your purpose I shall make a point of communicating it, –

I am Dear Madam
Yours very respectfully

Tho[s] Hood

[*Ostend, 1838*]

MS Osborn. The letter is dated in another hand 1838. The first two volumes of Mrs Mathews' *Memoirs* of her husband, the actor, appeared at the end of this year, and the last two towards the end of 1839. There is a passing, amiable, reference to Hood at III 463 and note. There is no reference to his brief connection with Mathews.

TO
CHARLES WENTWORTH DILKE

But I'm a low-lived, ungenteel, villanous, blackguard Radical. There is a deep stigma on the Have-nots trying to take from the Have-somethings, but what ought to be the stigma on the Have-everythings trying to take from the Have-nothings? Chorley has proclaimed me a '*Liberal*.'[1] I don't mind being called at once a Moderate Republican.[2]

[*Ostend, 4 June 1838*]

From Dilke *Papers of a Critic* I 55, which dates it, commenting: 'Hood writes on Mr. Rowland Hill's postage scheme, and on the uses of franks by rich men.'

1/Hood had been described in this way by H.F. Chorley in the *Westminster Review* April 1838, 125.
2/Perhaps the following sentence, also printed in *Papers of a Critic* I 55, belongs to this same letter of 4 June 1838: 'I am sick of my species. What can be more disgusting than the Emancipationists getting a victory by a *manoevre*, having God, the Bible, and reason on their side, and then the House rescinding its own resolution.' These tortuous proceedings took place on 22 and 28 May 1838.

TO
JOHN WRIGHT

My dear Wright,
I was disappointed at not receiving the 'Hood's Own' per *Liverpool*, not from eagerness to see the dear original's reflection,[1] but I was anxious to see how the Introduction read. I have seen it partly in to-day's 'Athenaeum,'[2] and it reads decently well. I shall want a 'Progress of Cant,' and also some old 'London Magazines' from J.H.R.[3] I am struggling to get early this month with my matter so as to give you as little trouble as possible. The weather has been up to to-day very so-so. I have had only one sail, and it did me such manifest good, that I quite long to get to sea again, but either there is no wind, or rain with it. You will be glad to hear I am getting better slowly. I wish, my dear fellow, you may be able to give as good an account of yourself. Pray send me a full and particular *bulletin.*[4] And, in the meantime, please to present my best thanks to Mrs. Wright for the cane, and tell her it is quite a support. I seem to walk miles with it.

Did I give you the history of a steamer built at Bruges? They quite forgot how she was to get down the canal, and they will have to take down the brickwork of the locks at a great expense – some 1500 francs instead of 25; all along of her width of paddle-boxes. Well, the other day, 10,000 people assembled to see her launched; troops, band, municipals, everybody in their best; and above all, Mr. T—, the owner, in blue jacket, white trousers, and straw hat. So he knocked away the props and then ran as for his life, for she ought to have followed; but, instead of that, she stuck to the stocks as if she had the hydrophobia. Then they got 200 men to run from side to side, and fired cannons from her stern, and hauled by hawsers, but 'there she sot,' and the people 'sot,' till nine at night, and then gave it up. She has since been launched *somehow*, but in a quiet way quite; she looked at first very like an *investment* in the *stocks*, and I should fear her propensity may lead her next to stick on a *bank*. The only comfort I could give, was, that she promised to be *very fast*. To heighten the fun, the wine was chucked at her by a young lady who thought she was going; I know not what wine, but it ought to have been *still* champagne. And now, God bless you and yours, take care of yourself, and mind and send us an account of how you feel, and what your doctor says of you. The vicissitudes of such weather try us feeble ones. I am anxious to know whether you think your new doctor's course has produced any marked effect. Don't B—[5] mean to come, or don't he not? If he and Mr. S— would make the trip together, it might be pleasanter, and we have accommodation for two, and especially a *tall* one for B—, for whom an accommodation bed ought to be like an accommodation bill – the longer it runs, the better. When you see Rooke, pray thank him handsomely in my name for 'Amalie'[6] – though I do not quite find the airs suit my compass. What Jane has said about F—[7] please to make me a partner in – and tell E. Smith that our *Sandy* soil has *Scotched* the flowers, so that he wouldn't know them for his seedlings. But Jane is very proud of them, as they are very good for Ostend. Our festival of Kermesse has begun, and will continue for a fortnight, and then we are to have the King and Queen next month, when your royal gaieties are over and gone. What does Dymock think of being cut out of the pageant? I suppose he will pretend that he 'backed out.'[8] I shall try if I cannot have a verse or two about the Coronation.[9] I want to know if any distinction was shown to Art, Science, or Literature on the occasion. Was the P.R.A. there?[10] Had the live Poets admissions to the Corner? What became of the V.R. at the Prussian ambassador's? He seemed only to compliment Frederick William with initials.[11] How wonderfully well the mob behaved; but then, to be sure, they are not Tories! I am glad they cheered Soult.[12] And now I must shut up, and believe me, dear Wright,

Yours ever very sincerely,

Thos. Hood.

39, Rue Longue, [*Ostend*] *July 3, 1838.*

From *Memorials* I 314–17

1/Hood's portrait was published in this June number of *Hood's Own*.

2/30 June 1838, 456–7

3/Hood doubtless needed these items to help in the literary reminiscences which he was preparing for *Hood's Own*, and which he had begun with the Introduction here referred to.

4/Wright himself appears to have been ailing.

5/Baily. Mr S— might be the Scott referred to in the previous letter to Wright.

6/Rooke must have sent Hood a score of his work.

7/Possibly Folkard. I do not know what Jane said.
8/Until the time of George IV the King's Champion of the family of Dymoke took part in the Coronation ceremonies on horseback, backing out of the royal presence; this piece of business was dropped at the coronation of Victoria. One of Hood's *Odes and Addresses* was addressed to the Champion.
9/Hood did not versify on the Coronation.
10/The President of the Royal Academy at this time was Sir Martin Archer Shee. I doubt whether special attention was paid to him at the coronation.
11/According to *The Times* 29 June 1838, 7, the Prussian embassy, unlike many of the other illuminated buildings of the capital, was not embellished with the initials of the Queen.
12/Maréchal Soult (1769–1851), representative of France at the coronation

To
PHILIP DE FRANCK

I say Tim,
If you are dead, write and say so; and if not, pray let me hear from you. Perhaps you were killed at the taking of Spandau[1] – or are you married – or what other mortality has happened to you? or have you had the worst of a duel – or taken a fancy to the Russians and gone to St. Petersburg? Perhaps some very great 'Wels' has pulled you in – or have you been to Antonin?[2]
The chief purport of this letter is to inquire about you, so you must not look for a long one – but we are getting uneasy, or rather too uneasy to bear any longer your silence – fearing that in the unsettled state of Prussian and Belgian relations, the intercourse may have become precarious.
I sent you a box containing your fishing-tackle, a 'Comic,' some numbers of 'Hood's Own,' and the sporting plates, which I calculated ought to reach Bromberg about the 20th of April. It was directed to Lieut. von Franck, 19th Infanterie Regiment, Bromberg en Prusse, with the mark

H

I paid the carriage to Cologne, and sent a proper declaration of the contents. Jane, at the same time, wrote per post to announce it, with an especial request for an acknowledgment of its arrival; so that we begin to fear that neither the box nor the epistle has reached its destination: pray write and let us know; because, in case THE *case* has stuck at Cologne, I will write from here, and you send inquiries for it from *there*, *i.e.*, Bromberg.

We are going on as usual. I am getting better, but slowly; my monthly work, and the very bad season, having been against me. I shall be better when I get to sea, but till last week I have been unable to boat it; we have had fires within the last ten days. Springs are, I suspect, going out of fashion with black stocks. Jane and the 'kin' were on board with me, and I wish you could have seen the faces and heard the uproar they made. It was an ugly, long, narrow craft enough, for a short sea; three lubberly Flemings for a crew, and myself at the helm. Jane groaned and grimaced, and ejaculated, and scolded me, till she frightened the two children, who piped in chorus. Tom, like a parish clerk, repeating after his mother, with the whine of a charity boy in the litany, 'Oh, Lord!' &c. &c., and then very fiercely, 'Take me home – set me ashore directly! Oh, I'll never come out with you again!' and so forth. So we have parted with mutual consent, so far as sailing is concerned, which is very hard, as I cannot take out any other ladies without Jane, the place being rather apt to talk scandal, – and one of our female friends here is very fond of boating. For my own part, I have been lucky enough to get a capital little boat, built under the care of an old English shipmaster, and his property – all snug, safe, and handy – so that I mean to enjoy myself as a marine.

In the meantime, Jane has made a voyage to England and back, which I shall let her relate. She had fair weather out and home, and prefers a dead calm to a living storm. I suppose I must take to sea-fishing, as there is some fresh-water fishing, but the canals are too much of thoroughfares to my taste, who enjoy the contemplative man's recreation – only with one companion. I sometimes wish for the Lahn.

It was odd enough – but on our return from Bruges fair in the barge, an English family came with us on their way from Coblenz, where they settled in the Schloss Strasse just before we left. He gave the same account of the people as I do, and was a fisherman – but caught nothing but dace.

England is all alive now with the Coronation. Why did you not egg on one of the Prince Radziwills to visit Her Majesty *viâ* Belgium, with yourself in his *sweet*. I read the other day that some of the 30th were come to Luxemburg. When our railroad shall be finished, it will only be two days' post from Cologne to this – and I have just taken my lodgings for another year – *Verbum sap.*

We expect several guests this summer from England – one of Jane's sisters and a daughter amongst the rest[3] – and we know *a* FEW *people* here – but the majority are not worth knowing, being of the scamp genus.

We still have an undiminished liking to the place, which suits our quiet 'domestic habits,' though it is notorious as dull, amongst the *notoriously* gay.

We know enough to be able to get up a rubber when we feel inclined, besides 'taking our three.'[4] I get excellent Bordeaux here, and bought a cask with my Doctor, only thirteen or fourteen pence English per flask, whereof on the last 23rd May, I did quaff one whole bottle out of a certain Bohemian Goblet to my own health, not forgetting the donor of the said vessel, which has a place of honour in my sanctum.

What a bore it is, Johnny, that you are not in the Belgian service; most of its garrisons are near, it would be but a holiday trip to come and see you. Were I, as I once was, strong enough for travel, I should perhaps beat you up even at Bromberg *viâ* Hamburg. But I shall never be strong again – Jane got the verdict of our friend Dr. Elliot, that the danger of the case was gone, but that as I had never been particularly strong and sturdy, I must not know expect to be more than a young old gentleman. But I will be a boy as long as I can in mind and spirits, only the troublesome bile is apt to upset my temper now and then. We are all a little rabid at present, for after having fires far into June, the weather has just set in broiling hot, and the children do not know what to make of it.

The faces of Tom and Fanny are like two full-blown peonies, or two cubs of the brood of the Red Lion. Tom is a very funny fellow. The people of the house try to talke to him, and as they speak very bad English, he seems to think that they cannot understand very good ditto, and accordingly mimics them to the life. You would think he was a foreigner himself when he is talking to them. Fanny is learning German and French, and makes up by her quickness for some idleness.

She is very much improved, and gets stouter, as she was too thin, whilst Tom gets thinner, as he was too fat; as for Jane, all my London friends said she had never looked better, so that I doubt the policy of walking out with her, for it makes me look worse than I am.

You will judge when I send you a proof of my portrait, which is to be in the next number of 'Hood's Own,' on the 1st July. It is said to be very like.

I have no news to give you; but there are plenty of rumours. Of course you were at the grand review at Berlin. Tell me all the particulars you can, and of your fishing, in which I take great interest, though now but a sleeping partner. I quote at the end of this a few words about Salmon. I expect a friend out here on a visit, who is very fond of the rod. By the bye, I must not forget to tell you, that the other day, which proves there must be some sort of fishing, my Doctor was called out of his bed in the morning by an Englishman, who mumbled very much, and on going to the door, found him with a hook, and not a little one, through his own lip. He had been tying it on by help of his teeth, and by a slip of the line had caught himself, genus *flat* fish. Being a Belgian hook, like the German, with the shoulder at one end and a barb at the other, it would not pull through; but had to be cut out. Lucky he had not gorged it. *My* leaf is full,[5] so God bless you says,

Yours, Tim,
Ever very truly,
Johnny.

Kind regards to Wildegans.
Tom, Junior, sends his love to you and Carlovicz and Wildegans. He said to his mother this morning, 'I love you a great way;' so he can love as far as Bromberg. It has just occurred to me, that there may be a reason for your silence I never thought of before. You are promoted and in the first pomp of your captainship, and too proud to own to us *privates*. If that is not the reason, I can think of no other with all my powers of imagination. Perhaps it is your D— Douane that always bothered my own packages. I hate all Customs, and not least the Prussian. I wish all the officers would confiscate each other. Sometimes this hot weather, I should like a glass of Rudesheimer, one of the few things I care for that is Rhenish – Bow, wow, wow!

39, Rue Longue, à Ostend, July 3, 1838.

From *Memorials* I 317–23
1/This took place in 1813.
2/Estate of the Radziwills, in the province of Posen.
3/A reconciliation seems to have taken place, though it is not clear to whom Hood is referring and the visit does not seem to have been made.
4/See 356 n19.
5/Hood's son notes that the other leaf was left for his mother to write on.

TO
PHILIP DE FRANCK

My dear Franck,
I have been laid up again, but this you will say is no news, it happens so often. A sort of bastard gout, without the consolation of being the regular aristocratic malady as if I were an aristocrat. By the way, I almost rejoice *politically* in the results of your own illness, you were always an abominable Tory, but now must needs be a moderate *wig*.[1] But as Gray says:

'To each their evils – all are men
Condemn'd alike to groan.'[2]

You (to speak as a fisherman) complain of your hair line, and I of my gut, which I fear has some very weak lengths in it. I hardly go ten days without some disagreeable indigestion or other, which is the more annoying as here the victuals are really good. Moreover, I am, in a moderate way, a diner-out; for instance, the day before yesterday at the Count de Melfort's, whom I had known previously by his book, the only one that ever coincided with *my Views of the Rhine.*[3]
In fact in spite of keeping quiet, I am a little sought after here, now I am found out. A friend of Byron's wanted to know me the other day, but I was laid up in bed; and now Long Wellesley (Duke of Wellington's nephew), my old landlord is here, and asking after me.[4] Luckily, there are so many lame men here, I am not singular in my hobble, for though I have got rid of the rheumatism these ten days, the doctor gave me a lotion with cantharides[5] therein, that has left me a *leg*acy of blisters. Then again what an abominable swindling season! The winter embezzled the spring, and the summer has absconded with the autumn.
A fig for such seasoning, when the summer has no Cayenne, and in July even you wish for your ices, a little mulled. I have only managed to keep up my circulation by dint of sherry, porter, and gin and water; and nine times out of ten, had it come to a shaking, I should have given you but *a cold right hand.* That is one of my symptoms. In the meantime the Belgians are bathing daily, but I observe they huddle together, men and women, for the sake of warmth, at some expense to what we consider decency. As for Jane she is very willing to believe that winter is absolutely setting in, as an excuse for wearing her sables.[6] They are very handsome, but no thanks to you on my part, considering a hint that I have had, that it is a dress only fit for a carriage! I don't mean, however, to go so *fur* as to set up a wheelbarrow. Many thanks however, for your views of our old piscatory haunts, which cannot lead one into any extravagance, for here there is no fishing. It is another Posen in that respect – but mind do not go and marry for want of better amusement. Talking of aquatics, a pretty discussion you have got me into by your story of the beavers on the Elbe. I have repeated it, and been thought a dupe for my pains – indeed I began to believe you had hoaxed me, but only this very afternoon I have found a Confirmation of the Baptism in a book of Natural History.
In the Berlin Transactions of the Natural History Society, 1829, is an account of a family of beavers, settled for upwards of a century on a little river called the Nuthe, half a league above its confluence with the Elbe, in a sequestered part of the district of Magdeburg.[7] There! To be candid, I always thought you mistook for beavers the Herren Hutters, or gentlemen who always wear their castors.[8] But why talk of keeping on one's hat to a man, who can hardly keep on his own hair? Methinks

instead of sables you ought to have bought of the Russian merchant a live bear, to eat up the little boys that will run after you, as they did after Elisha, crying 'Go up, thou baldhead!'[9] Of course the Radziwills, who made you so retrench your moustaches, will be quite content with you now; but I hope you will not slack in your correspondence in consequence, although I must expect to have more *balder*dash out of your own head. As for Wildegans, he will forget that you ever had any hair, and will take you for some very old friend of his father's, or perhaps for his grandfather.

For my own part as promotion goes by seniority in your service, I do hope you may have an opportunity of taking off your hat to the king, who cannot make anything less than a major of such a veteran. In the meantime you cannot be better off than in the 19th, which has so many Poles to keep yours in countenance; you see how little sympathy I profess, but having fancied you killed, wounded, or missing, in some riotous outbreak, I can very well bear the loss of your *locks*, as you are upon the *key* vive!

Moreover sickness is selfish, and invalids never feel acutely for each other.

The only feeling I have on hearing of another patient in the town, is a wish, that, whilst about it, he would take all my physic. When I can make up a parcel worth sending you, you shall have a copy of my face, to hang on the gallows for a deserter, if you like. Tim, says he, either I shall get over this liver complaint, and be a portly body, or the liver complaint will get over me, and I shall die like a Strasbourg goose.[10] How lucky I should have a decent interval of health for that march to Berlin! I often recall it, Tim, trumpet-call and all, and wish you were one of *our* military.

I do not know how the Belgian question goes on, but would not advise you to attack us, for in case of a reverse, your Rhinelanders are not the firmest of friends to fall back upon. Your Posen Bishop is a donkey for his pains; a Needle, if it enters a piece of work, ought to go through with it.[11] For my part I like fair play. I would have everybody married, and blessed, how they please, Christian or Jew. Privately I really believe marriages between Jews and Catholics would make capital half-and-half, one party believing too much, and the other too little.

I wear no mitre, but if you should wed a Polish Jewess, you shall be welcome to my benediction. But there has been a precious fuss about nothing. You say the Bromberg ladies, old and young, were very kind during your illness, and sent you nourishing food. You have omitted to mention whether they considerately masticated it beforehand. Yes? Of course you will have some fishing at Antonin. Pray present my best respects to the princes. Were I as young as I am old in health,

I would come and beat up your quarters at Posen, but my travelling is over, in spite of steam and railroads; so, if we are to meet again in this world, I am the mountain, and you, Mahomet, must come to it.

My domestic habits are very domestic indeed; like Charity I begin at home, and end there; so Faith and Hope must call upon me, if they wish to meet. And really Faith and Hope are such ramblers, it will be quite in their line, so with all faith in your friendship, and a hope we may some day encounter in war or in peace,

I remain, my dear Johnny,
Your true friend,

Tim.

Tom, Junior, sends his love and says, 'if you will come he will give you a kiss, *and teach you to draw.*' Vanity is born with us, and pride dies with us; put that into German by way of metaphysics. Give my love, when you see him, to the King of Hanover, and God grant to those he reigns over a good umbrella. I have many messages in a different spirit, which you will be able to imagine, for my old comrades for instance, Carlovicz. You do not mention 'Ganserich,' has he *forgotten* to exist; say something civil – as becomes a civilian – to the rest of your militaires on my behalf; you will see the colonel I guess, or are you the colonel yourself? It would be fatal now to your hair to have many go over your head. Have you ever tried currant jelly to it? Thank Heaven you require no passport, or how, as Heilman said, would you get 'frizze?' Shall we send back that hair lock you gave to Mrs. Dilke? No news except local, and you would take no interest in our abundant scandal, as you do not know the parties. To me it is very amusing, there is so much absurdity along with the immoralities; it is like an acted novel, only very extravagant. You know that this is one of the places of refuge for English scamps, of both sexes. But the parson and I do not encourage such doings, we are almost too good for them.

Ostend, August 20th, [*1838*].

From *Memorials* I 323–9, where the year is given as 1837

1/Franck presumably had a fever which resulted in the loss of some of his hair.

2/'Ode on a Distant Prospect of Eton College'

3/Edouard de Melfort *Impressions of England* (1836) II 164–8

4/William Pole Tylney Long-Wellesley, Earl of Mornington (1788–1857), married the heiress of Wanstead in 1812. As a result of his financial extravagance Wanstead House was demolished in 1822. Wellesley presumably retained the property, including Lake House where Hood had lived. In the preface to *Tylney Hall*, when it was reissued in 1840 (p. viii), Hood denied a connection between Wellesley and his novel.

5/The pharmacopoeial name of the dried beetle or Spanish fly, used as an external counter-irritant, producing blisters
6/Hood's son notes that these were a gift from Franck.
7/*Verhandlungen der Gesellschaft Naturforschender Freunde* I 325
8/'Beavers' is a pun involving the animal and the hat; 'castor' is another word for beaver hat. The Moravian sect built the town of Herrnhut in Saxony.
9/2 Kings 2:23
10/Since the second half of the eighteenth century Strasbourg geese were fattened to make *pâté de foie gras*.
11/The Archbishop of Posen was arrested during the year for his opposition to mixed marriages. The 'needle' is presumably metaphoric.

TO
JOHN WRIGHT

My dear Wright,
Take care and do not get drunk with your Prussic acid.
I wish you better health in a glass of sherry. I am concerned to hear you still suffer with your throat, but have hopes of your medical advice, as Elliot concurs.
His offer is very kind, and pray avail yourself of it at need, as I have reason to know he is sincere in his kindly professions. I think also he has *very* great skill. For myself you will be glad to hear that I am at last taking a change I think for the better: partly from better weather, but greatly I think from the occasional use of a warm sea-bath, and partly, B—[1] says he thinks, I am wearing out the disease. Time I did, says you, or it would have worn me out.
Something perhaps is due to a slight change of system, but I almost flatter myself, there is a change for the better. I have done without my doctor for an unusually long time, partly from being better, and partly from knowing how to manage myself; I have left off Cayenne and *Devils*,[2] and such stimulants recommended by B—. I begin to think as they are supposed to be bad for liver complaints in India, they ought not to cure them in England, and referred to Elliot, who said 'No,' very decidedly.
But I have no great faith in the principles of my doctor here, though some in his skill, but without the first, the last goes for little. He shook my opinion lately when I had rheumatism, by giving me cantharides in lotion, which favoured me with a sore foot for weeks. It looked like making a job. I now eat well and have much less than before of those depressions, though hurried and well worked. The baths I do think *very highly* of. Should you see Elliot, ask him; you might run over here for a fortnight, they are almost next door and cost little. *Think of this seriously.* I *have not*

felt SO WELL FROM THE 1ST JANUARY, *as during the last ten days:* accordingly I am getting on, and, at the present writing, have a sheet of cuts, besides those sent, and some tail-pieces drawn.[3] I expect next packet (on Tuesday), to send you a good lot; they promise to be a good set, and I find the pencilling come easier, which is lucky, as they are to your mind too. So I am throwing up my hat, with hope of making a good fight.

I doubt whether the first article will be on the Coronation, which is *stalish,* but seem to incline to 'Hints for a Christmas Pantomime, personal, political, (not that party), and satirical.'[4]

The baths I have in the house before going to bed, – no fear of cold. I strongly recommended them for Mrs. Dilke, and suspect they have gone to Brighton with that view; we have been very anxious about her.

I hope to send with this 'the Reminiscences,'[5] but if not they will be certain to come with the cuts on Wednesday; I am so full swing on the drawings, I hardly like to leave off to write. You say you are short of prose, but there is all 'Doppeldick.'[6] We heard to-day from Franck: he is well, and back, to his great joy, at Bromberg and his fishing; he has at last caught a salmon of eleven pounds. He tells me a sporting anecdote of a gentleman he knows, that will amuse you, as it did me. He was shooting bustards, of which there are plenty near Berlin. They are shy to excess, but do not mind country people at work, &c.; so seeing a boy driving a harrow, he went along with him, instructing him how to manoeuvre to get nearer. At last, wishing to cross to the other side of the harrow, he was stepping inside of the traces, as the shortest cut, when at that very instant the horses took fright, and he was obliged to run, with the gun in one hand, taking double care between the horses' heels, and the harrow, which occasionally urged him on with short jabs[7] from the spikes. It might have been serious, but just as he was getting tired out, the horses stopped at the hedge; the gentleman, besides the spurring, having his breeches almost torn off by the harrow. Franck wants me to draw it, and truly a flogging at *Harrow* School, would hardly equal it for effect.

Wellesley went back to Brussels to-day; I declined dining with him, but he sent me venison twice, some Wanstead rabbits, birds, and a hare. We have been up the railway to Bruges in forty-six minutes, Brussels in six hours for nine francs! Tell B—[8] to think of this. Count Edouard de Melfort wrote a book 'Impressions of England;' he is a cousin of the Stanhopes:[9] the family are to stay here the winter, and as we like him and her, and they seem to like us, they will be an acquisition for the winter. They sometimes drop upon us, as he calls it, and we drop upon them. As to local news, lots of scandal, as usual; I could fill a whole Satirist[10] with our own town-made. I think the idea of 'The Heads' a good one, but do not like the specimen either as to the head, or the style of the writing;[11] and now God bless you. I must to work again, and leave Jane to fill up the rest. Kindest regards to Mrs. W— from

Your ever, dear Wright,
Very sincerely,

Thomas Hood.

N.B. My hand aches with drawing, I am going to bed for a change.
Pray put in again the advertisement of Harrison's Hotel in 'Hood's Own,' and keep it standing to the end;[12] kind regards to everybody all round my hat.[13] We had a complete wreck, close to the mouth of the harbour, such 'a distribution of effects,' no lives lost, but such a litter, as Jane would call it. The cook's skimmer was saved, at all events, for I saw it.
There was a soldier shot to death at Franck's last review – putting stones in the guns! The confusion on our rail is great, one may easily go on the wrong line; two of our party at Bruges were actually in the wrong coaches, but were got out in time; I shall make some fun of this. We have had the Nagelmacher family from Liège, and Miss Moore, lodging for a fortnight on the floor below, but they are gone again.
How goes on the Amaranth, or off rather?[14] And have you seen the Bayaderes?[15]
Our new opposition steamer is come – 'The Bruges' – a very fine boat. But how will the fish like the railroad, seeing they now have such facilities for going by land, there will be many more fish out of water; who can calculate the results in future, of railroads to bird, beast and fish – besides man? We have begun fires in my little room, quite snug. Tom is going into trousers for the winter, and is very proud of it. He complained the other day that 'Mary washed all the *flavour* off his face.'
Well, I must shut up; I have done a good day's work, and leave off not very fagged, but rather cocky, as the tone of this will show. Give me but health and I will fetch up with a wet sail, (but not wetted with water). Who knows but some day Jane will have a fortune of her own, at least a mangle. Has your mother sold her mangle?[16]
I admire Harvey's 'Arabians' extremely.[17]

[*Ostend*] *Saturday, 6 p.m., Oct. 13th, 1838.*

From *Memorials* I 329–34. Though the letter is there dated the 10th, Saturday (the day given) was the 13th.

1/Presumably Hood's Ostend doctor
2/Highly seasoned dishes, or their hot ingredients
3/For the *Comic Annual* for 1839

4/Hood is referring to his plans for the next *Comic Annual*, which did not, in the end, include the 'Hints.'
5/Published in *Hood's Own*
6/'The Domestic Dilemma,' *Hood's Own* 436ff. Doppeldick is the last name of the main characters in the story.
7/*Memorials* has 'jobs.'
8/Baily
9/Presumably the aristocratic family which included Philip Henry, Earl Stanhope (1805–75), styled Viscount Mahon (1816–55). Mahon was historian, advocate of copyright reform, friend of Sir Robert Peel, and collaborator in helping Hood obtain a government pension in 1844.
10/Sunday newspaper (1831–49), ed. Barnard Gregory
11/A reference to *Heads of the People* (1840), drawn by Kenny Meadows, 'with original essays by distinguished writers.' Hood must have been sent a sample of the illustrations and text. The work was first published in monthly parts, beginning towards the end of 1838. The first three numbers were reviewed in *The Athenaeum* 26 January 1839, 68.
12/This advertisement appeared only in number 6.
13/Catch-phrase of the time
14/An annual edited by T.K. Hervey and published by Baily; Hood contributed to it.
15/Indian dancers who performed at the Adelphi theatre in early October
16/Catch-phrase of the time
17/E.W. Lane's translation of the *Arabian Nights' Entertainments*, with illustrations by William Harvey, was published this year.

TO
JOHN WRIGHT

My dear Wright,

I have no immediate occasion for writing, but hoping that my chance letters may be as agreeable to you as yours are to myself, I sit down partly for your sake and partly for mine own, as it is pleasant to exchange the pencil for the pen. I have just sent you off nine more principal cuts: in my list I have put 'Off by Mutual Consent' and 'All Round my Hat' as principals, and so you can make them, should I not send you others in lieu by the packet that leaves here on Saturday, when I hope to send you all the drawings, tail-pieces and all; exclusive of frontispiece, which I should be really glad if Harvey would do for me, however slightly, I sending an idea for it, as I am very short of time.[1] The effect of 'Hood's Own' has been to somewhat hinder the 'Comic', by preventing that quiet *fore*thinking which provided me with subjects, but I have done wonders on the whole.

The 'Comic' is always *a lay miracle*, and done under very peculiar circumstances; perhaps being used to it is something, though the having done it for so many years, and having fired some 700 or 800 shots, makes the birds more rare, *i.e.* cuts and subjects. But somehow it always *is* done, and this time apparently by a *special Providence*. God knows what I did, for the 'Hood's Own' was the *utmost* I could do. Strange as it may appear, although little as it is, it amounts probably on calculation to half a 'Comic,' as to MS. But I literally *could do no more*, however willing; the more's the pity for my own sake, for it was a very promising spec. For the rest I feel precisely as you do about 'My Literary Reminiscences,' but the fact is all I have done, I hoped to do in one or two numbers. For instance, the very last time I was thus thrown out.

As usual, I had begun at the end, and then written the beginning; all that I had to do was the middle, and breaking down in that, you had but a third of what I had intended. It was like a fatality. Moreover I never wrote anything with more difficulty from a shrinking nervousness about egotism.

But although declining to give a life, I thought it not out of character to give the circumstances that prepared, educated, and made me a literary man – which might date from my ill-health in Scotland, &c. Should I be as well as I am now, I hope to fetch up all arrears in Nos. 11 and 12: and it may be advisable to give a supplement, as, after December, I shall be free of the 'Comic,' and it may help the volume of 'Hood's Own,' with literary letters from Lamb, &c. &c. &c. This is my present plan, and perhaps the 13th No. would partly help to sell up the whole. But advise on this with B—,[2] &c. In the meantime you will have a good batch for next No.: allowing me as long as you can, perhaps the whole first sheet, and more afterwards. This I know to be mine own interest – I would not have B— lose *on any account*, much less on mine. With letters, &c., I could fill a good deal when I am once clear of the 'Comic' – about which I am in capital spirits. I think I have a good average set of cuts, and some good subjects for text. But above all, as the best of my prospects, and for which I thank God, as some good old writer said, 'on the knees of my heart,'[3] is the, to me, very unexpected improvement in my health, which I truly felt to be all I want towards my temporal prosperity. The change has been singularly sudden for a chronic disease. I wish I could hear as good news of Mrs. Dilke as this, which I beg of you to convey to them. Pray say that as far as I can judge, a radical change for the better has taken place. I have some thoughts, as a finisher and refresher after the 'Comic' (both for body and mind), of dropping in on them for three or four days – in which case you will *not* have further advice. I want to talk over the German book with him, which I shall most assuredly soon get through, health permitting, in the course of February or March.

I do most seriously, comically, earnestly, and jocosely tell you that 'Richard is himself again,'[4] and therefore you need not, Hibernically, have any fears on Tom's account: which last word reminds me of your kindness in going through all mine – for which I thank you as earnestly, as I know you have been engaged on the work. You must occupy yourself much on my behalf, and I can make you no return but to say that I feel it, which I do, very sincerely, or I should not take so much to heart as I do, the good effects of Prussic acid on your complaint, and wish the three drops which would kill any one else, could render you immortal, at least as long as you liked to be alive. But it does seem, or sound an odd remedy, like being revived by the 'New Drop.'[5]

I am writing a strange scrawl, but my hand is cramped by drawing. Otherwise, 'I am well, *considering*,' as the man said, when he was asked all of a sudden. Sometimes I feel quite ashamed of these bulletins about my carcase, till I recollect that it is too far off to be of interest merely as a subject. Seriously I believe I am better, and if I enforce it somewhat ostentatiously on my friends, it is because I have achieved a victory unhoped-for by myself!

To allude to the battle of Waterloo, I should have been glad to make it a drawn game, but I think I shall escape the Strasbourg pie after all.[6]

The above was written some time back, and given up from sleepiness. I have now yours of the 19th. Glad you like the cuts – I think they *are* a good set. To-day, or to-night rather, have sent off three more large, which if you take in 'Off by Mutual Consent,' will make up the six sheets. Also three more tail-pieces, in all forty-eight and eleven. A dozen more tail-pieces will do.[7] I wish Harvey would do the frontispiece, I am so very short of time.[8] Methinks the lines

'Mirth, that wrinkled Care derides,
And Laughter holding both his sides,'[9]

would supply a subject. The 'Reminiscences' I must send you on Saturday by the '*Menai;*' our post comes and goes so awkwardly.[10]

Thank God, I keep pretty well, – a day or two back rather illish, but took a warm bath and am better, wonderfully, considering my 'confinement.' After the Custom-house stoppage, no fear for some time of any hitch. It only cost three shillings, as the woman says.

I hope Mr. C.[11] will not forget the books I wrote for, by next Saturday's boat. Pray send me proofs, rough or anyhow, of all the cuts you can, as they help me in writing. Do not forget this. Bradbury's proofs will do.[12] It is getting very wintry, and I and the fires are set in – in my little room. You talk of a grand Christening Batch – but what is to be the name of 'my eldest daughter, Sir?' Tom exclaimed pathetically this morning, 'I wish I had *none* teeth!' He is cutting some that plague him! He draws almost as much as I do, and very funny things he makes. He picks up both

Flemish and French. We went to a French play the other night, and I was much amused by an actor very much *à la* Power.[13] It set me theatrically agog again. Perhaps – who knows? – I may yet do an opera with Rooke! In the meantime, I shall some day send you the piece that was accepted by Price, with a character for Liston, for you to offer to Yates. Jane is going to write, so I make over to her the other flap. We were much rejoiced to hear good news of Mrs. Dilke, as we had not had a word. Pray tell Dilke how much better I have been, and take care of yourself, and believe me, with God bless you all,

Yours very truly,

Thomas Hood.

What a capital fish a dory is! We had one for dinner t'other day. Good – hot or cold.

[*Ostend*] *November 22nd, 1838.*

From *Memorials* I 334–9

1/The frontispiece of the *Comic Annual* for 1839 was the work of J. Gilbert.

2/Baily

3/Unidentified

4/Phrase interpolated by Colley Cibber into *Richard III* 5 iii

5/'The scaffold used at Newgate for hanging criminals; which dropping down, leaves them suspended,' Francis Grose *Classical Dictionary* (3rd ed. 1796) ed. E. Partridge (1931)

6/Hood feels that he is getting over his liver complaint (379 n10). In the struggle for health, he has been fighting his Waterloo and is surprised at seeming to have won the victory.

7/The *Comic Annual* for 1839 contains 23 head and tail pieces.

8/An advertisement in *The Athenaeum* 15 December 1838, 901, declared that the *Comic Annual* would 'positively be published on 20th December.' A week later, on 917, the *Comic* was promised for the 29th, but it was reviewed in the same number. The *Literary Gazette* reviewed the *Comic* on the same day, 'as yet a little roughshod and only partially in form.' On 19 January *The Athenaeum* gave the *Comic* a second notice, though it was 'delayed somewhat beyond the Publisher's promise.' A week later, p. 57, it was advertised for publication on the 30th.

9/Misquoting Milton, 'L'Allegro' 31

10/An advertisement in *The Athenaeum* 22 December, 917, announced that number 12 of *Hood's Own* was postponed until 31 January, in order 'to enable the Author better to complete his Literary Reminiscences.'

11/Unidentified

12/Bradbury was the printer of the *Comic Annual.*

13/Tyrone Power (1797–1841), Irish comedian, popular from 1826

1839

TO

CHARLES WENTWORTH DILKE

My dear Dilke,

Yours, in Times for the Barnes, – Verbum Sap.

By dint of turning a Common boatman, I have got rid of the dregs of the Influenza – at the expense of the skin of my nose, – my left temple – & cheek bone.

I shall not say more or I shall not be conversible at your dinner.

My love to the Dilkes, & as Elliston used to say whether 'in the House or out of the House'[1]

N° ( ) *Fenchurch Street* [*early 1839*]

MS BM. Published by Marchand 91. The date given is a tentative one. Marchand points out that Fenchurch St was the business address of John Wright, and he died at the end of this year. Hood came over to England early in 1839, in order to try to settle his affairs with Baily.

1/The signature is torn out.

TO

JOHN WRIGHT

My dear Wright,

You will be surprised to hear from me again; but the weather and a bad cold made me resolve yesterday to go *viâ* Dover, besides preferring mail *versus* equinoctial gale. I shall go therefore Monday or Tuesday. Should the weather improve, I shall perhaps see you ere then. We ought to meet once more, at least, to settle the balance, and close the accounts up to Christmas, for good.

I observe on referring to your last, you seem to blame me, and say, all might have been settled on Sunday, 'if I had only done as you wished.' I do not know what you wished me to do; but the result ought to convince you that B—[1] never had any serious intention of going on, or he would have been here, as he said he should, during the week, whereas he has never been near me; so that in one sense, as you say, I have done nothing by coming to town, except arranging the accounts, and for which I ought not to have had to wait a single week, instead of three. In short, I have been trifled with most abominably. However, you must acknowledge that it is no fault of mine if I and B— have not gone on together. *Between ourselves*, I am convinced he wants money, and never contemplated any farther advance, or the possibility of our going on, or he would at least have treated me with common civility by coming here. As for the 'Hood's Own' account not affecting the question, I disagree with you, and think it *does* most essentially. I was extremely surprised, after hearing the assertion of £300 loss, to find only 66, nearly 20 better than last account. Now it is my opinion, and also Dilke's, that it is yet a very good spec, and might reasonably be expected to realise £200 or so, as a volume, if we were to give 13 numbers, and I write a good spell for it with the autograph letters, &c.[2] But that I cannot now answer for, as I must at once write for money, for my own need. By the bye, did you settle with the 'Heads of the People' publishers, or shall I write to them direct, to know the terms they propose?[3]

Perhaps, if it improves, I shall see you to-morrow.

I am, dear Wright,
Yours very truly,

Thomas Hood.

[*Pimlico*] *Saturday*. [*March 1839*]

From *Memorials* II 1–3. Hood is about to return to Ostend. He is disappointed with Baily's accounts and the sales of his works. Hood himself seems to have been responsible for the delay in publication of *Hood's Own*, and possibly for that of the *Comic Annual* (see 385 nn 8, 10). In England Hood stayed with his friend Dilke in Pimlico.

1/Baily
2/A loss on the parts of *Hood's Own* was eventually compensated for by a profit on the volume, which on 7 October 1840 came out at just over £70. However, number twelve was again postponed, until the beginning of March.
3/*Heads of the People*, published by Robert Tyas, first appeared in periodical form at the end of 1838; Hood did not contribute.

TO
WILLIAM ELLIOT

My dear Doctor,
I fully intended to have had the happiness of spending an evening at Stratford before my departure from London, but thanks to a number of vexatious and unjustifiable delays in business, I was at last obliged to cut and run to save time,

leaving all the pleasures I had promised myself to the future.

For instance, I longed to see all your children, but I fear now they will all be a year older should I meet them. But it was very kind of you to come to Pimlico; and I rejoice at it, as I think you and Dilke will know and like each other. Pray tell Mrs. Elliot that I acknowledge my debt, and owing her a visit, will pay it for my own sake the very first opportunity.

I was fortunate in a very fine passage across, but have been very poorly since my return; the voyage to London did me *very* great good, so much so that my foot healed two or three days after my arrival. But – I need not tell you how – I was well worried when in town (all booksellers are alike), and my foot got worse, and at this present writing is as bad, or nearly, as ever; my great anxiety to get my foot healed is for the sake of air and exercise, and besides I shall have to work pretty hard ere Midsummer.[1] Unluckily we have such a bad coast, bad boats, and bad boatmen, I cannot sail; but I mean to take a trip to Dover and back now and then, or perhaps to Havre, as there is a boat from here just begun running. Poor Jane has not been very well through fatigue and anxiety; Fanny is pretty well, but Tom has been troubled a little in cutting his back teeth.

He was very delighted to see me back, but I suppose I did not romp with him quite equal to his expectations, for after a day or two, as I was sitting reading, he said with an arch look at his mother, 'I do wish my pa would come home.'

I was a good deal fatigued by my night journey in the Dover mail, and no doubt looked invalid enough. So the cabin boy placed a basin in at my feet at starting, and I caught him watching me intently throughout the passage, evidently not a little wondering that only 'the sick gentleman' wouldn't be sick. To make the case more marked, a very fierce looking foreign officer, well moustached, was pitiably 'reduced to the lowest terms,' and had all the fight, as well as everything else, taken out of him. These are strange constitutional differences – my own viscera, for instance, have been so long deranged, I cannot imagine how they could be proof against the malady. By the bye, did I ever tell you of my Italian teacher at Coblenz, and his emetic? He took it over night, but after an hour or so, feeling very comfortable, he began to get very uncomfortable, so he drank a quantity of tea which staid with the emetic; still more uncomfortable because he was so comfortable, he then took warm water at intervals which made him as comfortably uncomfortable as ever.

Then, getting a little nervous, he took some wine. No discomfort, except the comfort. Then warm water again. Still only mentally uncomfortable, till finally, having spent the night in this manner, he comfortably took his breakfast, which acted as the sailors say, 'like a *stopper* over all.' That was a stomach to delight Franklin, for as poor Robin says,

'Get what you can,
And what you get, hold.'[2]

I wonder none of the quack doctors have got up an infallible nostrum against the sea malady.

It would be sure, one would think, of a *sail*. One can almost fancy a little dialogue.

Passenger. 'Well, Doctor, I have tried your seasick remedy.'

Doctor. 'Well, – and how did it *turn out?*'

Thank heaven, the twenty-four articles are signed[3] and we are at peace. I have no desire to move again, except to England.

My prospect of that coast is somewhat clearer, as my health seems radically better, and, in the meantime, I have learned to like even Ostend. It seems to agree with me in spite of my foot. Moreover, as I learned when in town, I am far from fit yet for a London life. Summer is before me, and I do not mean to throw it away by late hours and dissipation, but to try, by a regular system, to get a little a-head in health. I am not desponding, but such annoyances as the present, weaken, and lower, and worry me, particularly as I have as much to do as a strong person could get through.

And now, God bless you all, and prosper you in every way. Pray give our kindest regards to Mrs. Elliot. Mrs. Hood, alias Jane, shall, and will write some day, but she is so much of a nurse that, like her patient, her pen is obliged to leave undone many things that should be done, – for instance, the last Number of 'Hood's Own.'[4]

I am, my dear Doctor,
Yours ever, very faithfully,

Thos. Hood.

Have you read the account of Photogenic drawing or Lightography?[5] Moore saw 'History *write* with *pencil* of *light*,' but now light itself draws without any pencil at all. 'Tis a mercy light does not write; but perhaps even that will be done hereafter, and Phoebus will not only be a patron of poets, but a poet himself, and deal, like me, in Light literature.

Jane, who has some maternal vanity, when she heard of the sun drawing pictures, said, 'so does *my* son!'

39, Rue Longue, Ostend, March 31, 1839.

From *Memorials* II 29–33

1/When Hood was in England, on 12 March, he agreed to hand over to Baily 'the M.S. of the German Book on the 1st June 1839,' MS Public Record Office.

2/Benjamin Franklin *Poor Richard's Almanack* ed. Ben. E. Smith (New York 1898) 60. According to 2n 'an English comic almanack, "Poor Robin," furnished the suggestion of "Poor Richard."' *Old Poor Robin* continued publication from 1664 to 1828.

3/Settling territorial differences between Belgium and Holland

4/This was finally advertised as 'now ready' in *The Athenaeum* 11 May, 345, together with the complete volume. Baily's figures indicate the declining sales of *Hood's Own:* Pt 1, 10,000; Pt 2, 5,000; Pt 3, 4,000; Pts 4–8, 3,000; Pts 9–11, 2,000; complete volume, 750.

5/Perhaps that in *The Athenaeum* 23 March 1839, 223

TO

PHILIP DE FRANCK

Tim, says he, I am only able to write at short length, having more work for my pen and less time to do it in than ever. I have had a sad nine or ten months of it, almost always ill, and then having to do everything in haste by day and night. I think my liver complaint is tolerably cured, and I have not spit any blood for a very long while, but the *curing* has half killed me. I am as thin as a lath and as weak as plaster. Perhaps I have no blood left to spit.

As to my leanness, look at the portrait. Tim, says he, I was over in England about three months ago at Dilke's, where I spent three weeks; but though I am quite at home there, I came back to Ostend very willingly; late hours and company do not agree with me yet. Will they ever? God knows.

Another year will set me up, or knock me down, – the wear and tear of my nerves, &c., cannot last longer. By the bye, this very day I am forty, – and you will have to drink my health out of a certain Bohemian Goblet, given to me on a certain birthday. As you cannot pledge me in it yourself, I will cheerfully be your proxy, provided the wine be good. As Béranger sings –

> 'Dans un grenier qu'on est bien à vingt ans!'[1]

But then I am two score, and sometimes am ready to call them the Forty Thieves, having stolen away all my youth and health.

Look at the picture, Tim, I do not quite look so ill as then, but I am as weak as gin-and-water without the gin.

Since Jane wrote, I have found your list and procured what tackle you wanted. But, moreover, I have had the good luck to meet with some *here,* which I jumped at, and send, good or bad, with some flies and hooks I had by me. For fear of plunder, I send a list signed by me, in the box.

All the tackle you will be so kind as to accept from me – with my best wishes towards the fisherman, and the worst towards the fish – except the gentle-boxes,[2] which Tom junior (I will not call him my 'son and heir,' as you have neither son nor hair) is desirous of sending you. He says, 'The gentles have not only a little house, but a yard to walk about in.' I did not expect an improvement in a gentle-box, but you see there is a little tray to roll them into and select from. I guess you will enjoy the Pickwick – it is so very English.
The mark on your box is And put in your note-book, Tim, that in future you must direct

À MONSIEUR T. HOOD,
La Rhetorique,
Rue St. FRANÇOIS,
À Ostende.

(*Your* 'St. Franck,' if you 'haven't a devil' instead.)
A longer letter next time from,

Dear Johnny,
Yours ever very truly,

Tim.
[*Ostend*] *May 23rd, 1839.*

From *Memorials* II 33–5
1/A line echoing phrases in Béranger's poems 'Le Grenier' and 'La Jeune Muse,' *Oeuvres complètes* (Paris 1834) III 126, 51
2/Boxes for bait; gentles are maggots.

TO
JANE HOOD

My own dearest & best.
You will have wondered at not hearing from me, – & still more as no packet went for Bradbury[1] – all of which I have to explain. It is a mingled yarn I must spin of good & bad.[2] I was getting on so well that knowing its importance at present on many accounts, & as Mrs Dore[3] was writing I would not hinder myself. – for it is not always I have the power to compose, which I was enjoying. – In fact I was

rejoicing in my progress, – & the only reason I did not send a packet was this, that what I had written was farther on in the book, & wanted some previous matter to connect it, & as Bradbury's had a sheet to go to press with & ½ a sheet besides set up I was afraid of locking up their type. The last thing I did was the story of the man who overhears the Devil repeating the fatal word.[4] This was finished on Wednesday night but not posted for the above reason. – And so I went to bed about eleven, – well pleased with my work, but no sooner in bed than I had one of my old rheumatic attacks in my foot. A sudden change to very cold wet weather I think brought it on. You know what those attacks are. Your desire that I should wish for you & not wish for you literally came true. I missed the comfort but was hardly sorry you were not present to be distrest by sufferings you could not relieve. I groaned all the night thro in agony without intermission & on Thursday morning about 10 put on leeches which relieved me *a little*, soon after from sheer exhaustion I feel asleep, but almost immediately woke up again with a most violent cramp in the same leg. The only remedy is to walk about on it, – but with my foot all swelled & inflamed I could not put it to the ground & could only wait, till the cramp went away of itself. You may suppose the double anguish was intolerable in fact it quite convulsed me – & when the cramp was over I had the other pain all day – with only one short doze – At night it was worse than ever, & I got no relief but by repeatedly putting it in hot water – & then only for the moment. It was so dreadful I made Mary sleep in the children's room, for I thought I should be delirious. It abated a little in the day, but I was so weakened I was less able to bear it, but got a little sleep in the evening & in the night – the pain only left me this morning – & I still cannot move my foot freely. But it is so far over & gone, though I am suffering from exhaustion. I waked several times in the night quite in a dew of perspiration. Tomorrow I shall be up I expect in my own room. Mary nursed me very attentively – & the children were *very* good. Poor Tibby made herself very useful, & Tom did his best at nursing, tho it consisted in cuddling up one of my hands & keeping it warm with every thing he could wrap round it. – I seem doomed to have this trial once a year, – thank god it only comes like Xmas. But I am not out of spirits for in other respects I have been unusually well & getting on. I am glad the Dilkes like the book & have hopes of it myself[5] – I shall make it 12/s. & it will have nearly or quite double the letterpress of the Whims & as many cuts. As for the Hood's Own, I think there may be more than Baily owns to yet – 75 for me & 25 to him ie £100 is so very like a round number. From the sale I should have expected more – But I shall see in Jany. by the acc[ts]. As to Wright it did hurt me very much to find he had had the letters & not noticed them – but I have got over it.[6] From

what Folkard said to me when I was in London, I suppose there has been a sort of failure in London St[7] Write to me all the news you can.
I hope the back stock will sell well as its of high importance to me – to clear off Baily's Balance. Would to God I could get a-head but last year was a fatal one. My present attack & the getting over it convinces me if I needed conviction of the wanton wickedness of the Cantharides. The Major as usual has been very kind, calling twice a day to see me[8] – & I have had an interview in bed, with Made & M & Mrs Dore. Madame offered to come & nurse me or do any thing in her power. Mrs D is pretty well – she has not heard, – but expects, to a certainty Miss D will come on the 23rd By the bye, The James Watt is coming in lieu of the Liverpool which is to be repaired. The Watt is a fine vessel, so that you can come by that, instead of the Menai. Glad as I shall be to see you dearest, whilst you are there settle all if you can – & especially as Baily wants you to stay. Don't fret yourself about *me* – now this is over, I expect to go on very well, – as I take all care of myself. A little parcel will come by next Stewardess for Miss Nicholson[9] who will send to Dilke's for it. Mrs D has had a very satisfactory account from Ypres. Mr Pyne[10] has not sent yet but I shall not forget the matter. It is the small Crabbs dictionary at 7 or 9 shillings he wants.[11] Mind & ask about Scott's Works for the Nagels.[12] I shall send a good packet for press on Tuesday – I shall think of nothing but getting out my book. Baily might advertise it for early in Novr[13] – say the 10th. Does he think any cover, would be advisable, like Hood's Own for instance? beyond mere boards?[14] –
I do beg you will see Elliot, – it is as great a concern as any thing else, – & you are apt to forget *yourself*, dearest, when other matters are in hand. Don't over fatigue yourself but use those little flys.[15] Come back to me well & you will find me so or make me so, my best. We shall do well yet, & weather the point if my health keeps as it promises. I shall go out to sea again. Trawling is over & long line fishing begun. He[16] does not stay out all night but goes one day & puts down his lines – returns – & goes & takes them up the next. That would suit me very well. Thank you dearest for the herrings – they were excellent.
News of Capt Spooner[17] – they went to Capel first for some days & he dined out, lost his way home (drunk of course) & spent the whole night in a ditch! The day I dined at the dM's[18] we all drank your health in Champagne — but I escaped the ditch. Never a line from Mrs Lindo the note must have miscarried.
The Count has brought me the following which I copy just as it is

'100 yds of the Chintz
50 yd of lining glazed – the colour that may suit the Chintz *pink* I prefer.
50 yds of Zeno for (inner) curtains for windows. Dear Mr Hood beg her to

mention the amount she will have to pay & I will leave you a Draft on Coutts before I go.'

They go I rather think on the 24th.
Mrs Dore begs you will bring her two boxes of the Calomel & rhubarb pills. I will attend to the coal man &c. – Don't forget some Magnesia – I am quite out of it.

6 Oclock. Yours dearest, with the money, safely come to hand. – As Mrs. D was dining at the de M's, & there was so much concerned Made – I sent on your letter there to her. I will add any message. I am glad you enjoyed the Theatre so well. I am very much better & have just sent Mary for some socks as I shall be in my own room again tomorrow. I suspect the attack was coming on, when I was so low, – & working hard hastened it. I am glad that it is over as I shall go on with fresh spirit. I have even done a little this evening – so let that comfort you – I did not spring up again so easily, before. The kin are just going to bed & send plenty of loves & kisses. We have plenty of fish. I had a small turbot today, but cannot eat yet – but Tom & Fanny gobbled it all up. No local news except the Leith Hay's[19] are going to give a party.) All in the bracket[20] was written since what follows.
I feel so much better that I shall go to work again this evening. It will not hurt me as getting on is the greatest comfort I have. The Children bless them are so good & agree so well, it is quite delightful. Mrs D takes them out every fine day. They both send love & kisses in abundance. Tom has drawn me with the leeches on & says I roared like Dilke. You may tell Mrs. Dilke I mean to lay up my Uncle in earnest at Coblenz – & let Frank go on his march whilst the old Gent. recovers.[21] How useful them Dilkes are to me as suggestions. It does me good to hear of them or from them. Pray give my love to them & say I now do hope we may all meet someday on this side of heaven. Also the Elliotts & ask his consent to the Dedication.[22] I am glad your mother liked the trifle. Of course you have put your father up to the glass – it should be distilled water & filled so as to enter the tube a little.[23] Remember me kindly to Willm Dilke if you see him.
Is it true Lockhart is to marry Miss Coutts Burdett? *Bawbees!*[24] That cheating steward wrote a note to me for a new order & said Messrs B. had made no objections – but only wanted an order for the sum. How he could make 13 times come to above £2 is more than I know – I have done nothing but let them give him what is fair – say 30s/.
And now again & again God bless you my own dearest & best Jane – I am getting well. Observe how much better I write than at the beginning of this letter. Take care of yourself & do not attempt too much. You want physical power as well as I.

Your own ever & ever Tho Hood (written & blotted in bed)
God bless you my own – enjoy yourself as much as you can – you may be easier about me now this is over than before. It was CRUEL suffering but I could not describe to them without laughing that cramp – for I was pirouetting about on one leg & the other drawn up in such a twist, as only Grimaldi used to effect. Or remembering I was only in my shirt I must have been somewhat like Oscar Byrne[25] in his short tunic, & making as many grimaces. Luckily I was alone, for I must have bundled out of bed, had Hannah More been present.[26] *Don't* tell Mrs Dilke or she will never lend me a spare bed again. Mary has brought me up a twofold supper on one plate – on one side a roasted apple – on the other some nondescript stripes (tripe)[27] – . I ate the apple – & *looked at* the tripe – Verbum sap. She is very attentive so bring her something. God bless you again. I am going to settle. it's ½ past 10.
I forgot to say I shall want 4 Hood's Own – (in the vol) you had better send them p Stewardess as I suspect you will be loaded. NB. Dories are coming in tell the Dilkes. – the other day I, Tom & Fanny had a little one apiece. I must wait for Sidney Smith till I'm richer – perhaps they will reprint it at Brussels.[28] Mother Rogers[29] has not sent my books yet – I bide my time.[30] As to the Farce the best way will be by a notice to C. Mathews.[31] Mind, it was *accepted* by Price, but stopped by his stoppage.
(Bulletin.) 'Huzza! I can move my toes!'

[*Ostend*] *Saturday* [*19 October 1839*]

MS University of Bristol Library. Published in part in *Memorials* II 35–40. Address: 'Mrs Hood / Care of C.W. Dilke Esqre / 9 Lower Grosvenor Place / Pimlico / London.' PM: 'LONDON/ 21/ OCT/ 1839.' The letter was written on the Saturday preceding the 21st, that is, the 19th. Business trouble had obliged Jane to visit England, where she arrived on 9 October.

1/Printer of *Up the Rhine*
2/*All's Well that Ends Well* 4 iii 67
3/Friend of the Hoods in Ostend. Hood is presumably including his letter with her's.
4/In *Up the Rhine* 131–49
5/*Up the Rhine*, announced in *The Athenaeum* 7 December, 934, as to be published in a few days
6/Perhaps letters which he had not acknowledged
7/4 New London St, Crutched Friars, was the address of Wright and Folkard, engravers.
8/In her letter to Hood of the 10th Jane refers to Major Opie, MS Bristol Central Library.
9/Apparently a friend in England
10/Possibly William Henry Pyne (1769-1843), painter and author
11/An edition of George Crabb's *Dictionary of General Knowledge* was published in 1839 at 7 shillings.
12/Probably the Nagelmachers
13/This must be a mistake for December, the reading of *Memorials* II 38.

14/The cover of *Up the Rhine* was fancifully decorated.
15/Four-wheel hackney coaches
16/*Memorials* II 39, gives the name 'Backer,' an Ostend acquaintance.
17/Unidentified
18/De Melforts
19/Unidentified
20/The lines from '6 Oclock ...' to '... give a party.' are bracketed in the margin of the letter.
21/Characters in *Up the Rhine*
22/*Up the Rhine* was published without a dedication, in spite of Hood's request to Elliot.
23/An obscure practical joke, such as Hood was fond of
24/A mere rumour
25/Oscar Byrne (1795?–1867), ballet dancer
26/Hannah More (1745–1833), religious writer
27/Hood's son notes: 'The Dutch servant's idea of the English word "tripe!"'
28/Sydney Smith's *Works* had been published on 29 June.
29/Unidentified
30/The first example of this phrase given in NED is dated 1853.
31/Charles Mathews the younger (1803–78), actor, undertook the management of Covent Garden theatre on 30 September 1839.

TO
CHARLES WENTWORTH DILKE

My dear Dilke,
As regards Boz, his *morale* is better that his material, though that is often very good; it is *wholesome* reading: the drift is natural, *along with the great human currents and not against them.* His purpose sound, with that honest independence of thinking, which is the constant adjunct of true-heartedness, recognising good in low places, and evil in high ones, in short a manly assertion of Truth *as* Truth. Compared with such merits, his defects of over-painting, and the like, are but spots on the sun.
For these merits alone, he deserves all the successes he has obtained, and long mav he enjoy them! As for Jack Sheppard, the test of its value is furnished by the thieves and blackguards that yell their applause at its slang songs, in the Adelphi. Can the penny theatres so unceremoniously routed, produce any effects more degrading and demoralising? From what I have heard of *their* pieces they were comparatively mere absurdities to such positive Moral Nuisances.
The 'Inland Navigation' was also interesting. I like to see scientific theories thus justified by practice. Brains are better than brute force after all![1]

I am very glad you like my German book so far. I think I have kept old Orchard true to himself;[2] but I fear it is vastly unlike the character of that pig-headed, purblind, bigotted being, an English agricultural country gentleman; a species identified with Corn Laws, No Popery, 'Bible, Crown, and Constitution,' and all other creeds and opinions that are sown by narrow instead of *broad* cast. However a man, with Death constantly before his eyes, would probably be more honest, and tolerant.

Talking of Germany, I have just heard from Franck, who desires his remembrances to you and Mrs. Dilke. He is now in Silesia, making, or at least superintending the manufacture of guns. Possibly Russia and Prussia have some joint war game in view, with a very blind reliance on bayonets, by number, and a great ignorance of their own real position. The death of the King, made prudent by reverses, if it were to happen at this juncture might precipitate the dénouement. But with a plot in his army, and the Circassians, I should think Nicholas had enough to do at home. The moral effect of that brilliant affair in India at this crisis will be great.[3] 'If England to herself would be but true;'[4] if Englishmen would but seek their own good in the national welfare, instead of the reverse; if, instead of attributing her past greatness to old systems of misrule and corruption, because they were contemporaneous, they would but see that she flourished in *spite of them!* But alas! like the blind young gentleman in the 'Tatler,'[5] the more you couch them, the more they will blunder and mistake one thing for another. He took the cook, didn't he? for his sweet-heart, and the postman for his father.
Apropos to Germany how very C—ish are the letters from Berlin and Leipsic![6] How he jumps from the Turk's turbans, by a *Volti subito*, to the crotchets and quavers.

'With rings on his fingers and (bells on his toes?)
We shall have *music* wherever he goes!'

I defy you, editor as you are, to make a more apt and characteristic quotation; poor dear editors, when the new postage begins, how you will be pelted by penny letters![7]
Tom and Fanny are quite well, poor dear things, they are the only comforts I have in my goutiness, namely, by making them sit still because I can't walk about! And that is such a comfort (if you ask the philosophers) to crusty people. My poor legs! I must go and stick them in the sands, as the piles are, to get *mussels* to 'em! By the bye I am going to have some for supper; they don't swell me, as they did your Mussulman,[8] and they would only improve *my* figure if they did. Poor Mary, she tries to nurse and suit me, only when I had no appetite, the weakest stomach, and worst digestion, she brought me a bullock's liver to tempt me! But she does her

best, which is more than Lord Camelford did.[9]

My landlord has just sent me up a prospectus he has received from Frankfort, inclosing shares of a lottery for the grand estate of Gross Zdekau[?], in Austria! To gull John Bull I reckon. I guess they won't get much out of the close-fisted Belgians. I remember such a lottery before for a princely estate somewhere in Germany, and the prince won it himself! How *very* lucky! But you know, Dilke, the Germans are so honest! For instance I read this day in the 'Life of Höltz,' 'It occurred to me to give lessons in Greek and English, for the purpose of earning something, and taking the burthen off my father; I gave daily five lessons; but I have not been paid by half my pupils. Some have gone away, and others show no intention of paying!'[10]

Mind that's a German's own account of German honesty, and not mine, Von Dilke! But what an ungrateful dog I am! The first thing Franck saw in a Silesian circulating library was 'Tales from the Works of Thomas Hood, translated by Gustavus Sellen, Leipsic,' (seven of the 'National Tales').[11] 'Now I am sure,' says Franck, 'you never wrote them, firstly because I never heard you mention them, and secondly they are not at all like you, they are much too sentimental, and as high-flown and flowery as the Germans generally write their novels!' That's what I call translation, not merely done into the German language, but into the German style, and German feeling.

The first thing I have found do me any good, was a bottle of porter, so I have continued it, three glasses per day, eschewing all other drinks: luckily it's very gettable here, and I think it helps me to fetch up my long arrears of sleep; in case I don't, I have little Tom for a bed-fellow till Jane returns. Only the sick, and sleepless, and spiritless can know the comfort, the blessing of a familiar voice in the long dreary night. Mind I don't wake him up on purpose, but, even if I did, his good temper would excuse it. Being waked in such a way is a sure test of temper, if ever you want to try Mrs. Dilke's. *I* rouse up very well, and patiently, particularly about ten in the morning. I am living in a sort of world before time. Tom has managed to stop the works of my watch, the Black Forest clock has stopped of itself, and there is a Dutch clockmaker's over the way, but it's dark, – I guess it's about half past ten, but it may be two in the morning, so I'll shut up. My kindest regards to Mrs. Dilke (I shall write next to her,) to Wentworth, and to William if in town. God bless you all, saith,

Dear Dilke,
Yours ever very truly,

Thomas Hood.

P.S. Mrs. Dilke, if you are a happy woman, and don't want to be a 'widder,' read all Dilke's letters and notes *first*. The Count de la P—[12] will call him out, but don't let him go out, any more than his Arnott's stove.[13] If anybody inquires after the editor, say 'Mr. C—'s in Germany, but I don't exactly know where, it begins with a B!' Good bye. 'God Bless.'

You need have no remorse about this letter. You would not have had such a long one if I had not actually despatched a packet by this very night's steamer for Bradbury.[14] As the boys say from school to their fathers, 'I am getting on very well in my writing!' and at this present somewhat ahead of the printer.

Ostend, November 7th, 1839.

From *Memorials* II 41–6

1/In these paragraphs Hood is commenting on *The Athenaeum* 26 October, which contained a review of Ainsworth's *Jack Sheppard*, comparing his work with that of Dickens, and an article on 'New System of Inland Transportation' 803–5, 812. The performance of *Jack Sheppard* at the Adelphi Theatre is berated in *The Athenaeum* a week later, 830.
2/The character of Richard Orchard in *Up the Rhine*
3/In Afghanistan British troops captured 'one of the strongest places in Asia' *Annual Register* (1839) 344.
4/Misquoting *Hamlet* I iii 78
5/Number lv
6/These letters, signed H.F.C. (Chorley), appeared in *Athenaeum*, 5 and 26 October, 2 November, 762, 810, 828.
7/The penny post was introduced 10 January 1840.
8/Reference obscure
9/Thomas Pitt, second Baron Camelford (b 1775), was killed in a duel with a Mr Best in 1804.
10/Ludwig Heinrich Christoph Hölty *Gedichte* (Hamburg 1783) xiv. This passage had been quoted in the *London Magazine* November 1821, 520. Hood perhaps read it in one of the volumes sent over by Reynolds.
11/Gustav Sellen was the *nom de plume* of Ludwig von Alvensleben (1800–68).
12/Unidentified
13/A smokeless grate, the invention of Neil Arnott (1788–1874)
14/Part of the material for *Up the Rhine*

TO
CHARLES WENTWORTH and MARIA DILKE

Dear Dilke,

I should think C— would not part with *his* autograph, but I think it very probable that M— appropriated one.[1] After the 'Gem' was done, a silver cup, or something, was sent to Sir Walter,[2] and there may have been a letter springing out of that to me, as editor. I feel sure I have kept *all* mine. I should like to know the fact.

You were quite right about my advertisement, but it *was* a difficulty I have not yet got over. I am toiling hard for the 25th, but it *is* such weather![3] It's a wretched climate in spring, autumn, and winter: such damp, unwholesome fogs. Our paved yard has been sloppy wet the last week, without a drop of rain. Plenty of low fever and dysentery in the town: yet it is better than inland, for we *have* the sea.

I am *so* glad you haven't seen the Bruges casket *yet*.[4] I would get Jane to copy out a criticism on that, too, but there isn't room. Besides you threaten to print, – wherefore I shall send nothing but cutting-up strictures on the 'Athenaeum' in future, which you may extract in it *if you like*.

You talk of my being meant for a painter, – Tom *is*; t'other day he cut a great notch out of his hair. 'How came you to do that?' asked his mother. Says Tom, as grave as a judge, 'for a *paint-brush*!' There's early bias for you! Now I must go to work again. It will be my waking dream, *our* Belgian Tour. Kind regards to Wentworth, and love to all.

Ever, dear Dilke,
Yours very truly,

Thomas Hood.

My Dear Mrs. Dilke,
I owe you a letter!
Yours very truly,
Thomas Hood.

P.S. – Eleven at night.

La Rhetorique, Rue St. François, [*Ostend*] *Nov. 18th, 1839.*

From *Memorials* II 46–7

1/Alexander Cooper provided the illustrations for *The Gem*, and William Marshall published it.
2/Scott. Hood published a letter concerning this business in *The Athenaeum* 23 November 1839, 894, strongly insinuating that a letter addressed to him from Scott had been misappropriated.
3/*Up the Rhine* was advertised in *The Athenaeum* 16 November, 878, to be published on the 25th.
4/Either the reliquary of St Ursula in the Museum of the Hôpital St-Jean, or that in the Chapelle du Saint Sang

TO
WILLIAM ELLIOT

My dear Doctor,
I ought to have written to you before, but I am terribly hurried in getting out my book, having been thrown back by the weather of this uncertain climate. The truth is, I cannot quite make out your meaning, or your wish in your note to Mrs. Hood about the dedication. If you mean to imply that I should look out some more illustrious personage, or great man, who might have patronage, I have no hopes or desires of that nature, but prefer inscribing my books to parties I respect and esteem, or have a regard for, – such as yourself.

But perhaps you are averse to having your name brought before the public in that way; in any case, do not scruple at once to object, if you *feel* any objection, and I will not be too inquisitive about your reasons. May I beg your answer *by return of post* – a few lines will suffice, as I know how your time is occupied with business.[1]

Mrs. Hood is hardly settled enough to pronounce upon herself yet. Tom is as well as can be. Fanny has had a slight attack of the low fever peculiar to the place. I am convinced that at times I have suffered from it too; for instance, during the last ten days, when we have had the wind from the land, bringing from the low ground and marshes such damp fogs, that our yard has been continually as wet as after rain. It acts on me by producing great lassitude and general torpor of the functions, circulation, and digestion especially. It produces generally a peculiar effect on the tongue, as in Fanny's case, which Mrs. Hood described to you. She has now a slighter relapse of it, through going again to school. A girl of eighteen or twenty lately died of it; for a long time her tongue swelled too big for her mouth. A great mystery is made of it, for fear of frightening away the English, who spend some £2000 a year in the town. But it is well known by the natives, who will all tell you the remedy, though they deny the disease. I got the truth partly from my reading, and partly from my old boatman, a German. It is called the Koorts,[2] and is very prevalent about Walcheren. Our old doctor having retired from practice, we have had a new one to-day – a younger man. He said Fanny's complaint arose entirely from atmospherical causes, the late cold, damp weather, and when asked if it was not Koorts, at once acknowledged it. But this is the first time that we have had it admitted. I seriously think when my time is out here, of going either to England or into France on this account; it occasions serious hindrance, for at such times I cannot write, or even think; but when the yard is dry, and the sky clear, or a frost, I do both. The changes are so marked, and I have watched so attentively, I have no doubt of the fact. What is worse is, it creates a necessity for more and stronger wine than is good for me, to counteract the lowness, &c. I have lately been trying to drink the Bordeaux, which is very good and pure here, in lieu of other wine. I like it; but it seems to me that it *makes too much blood.* I should try to leave them all off in a better climate. But in the meantime I must do the best I can. My wife sends her love, and hopes Mrs. Elliot and the baby are going on better than could be expected. Pray accept also the congratulations of,

Dear Doctor,
Yours very truly,

Thomas Hood.

La Rhetorique, Rue St. François, à Ostend, November 23rd, 1839.

From *Memorials* II 47–50

1/The work was not dedicated to Elliot, despite the salutation at the head of the letter on 406. *Up the Rhine* was advertised as to be published in a few days in *The Athenaeum* 7 December 1839, and was reviewed there on that day.

2/Flemish for fever

TO
MRS MARIA DILKE

My dear Mrs. Dilke,

As I always came to your parties with a shocking bad cold, I now write to you with one, which I have had for three days *running*. But it was to be expected, considering the time of the year and the climate, which is so moist that it's drier when it rains than when it don't. Then these Phlegmings (mind and always spell it as I do) – these Phlegmings are so phlegmatic, if it's a wet night, your coachman won't fetch you home, and if it's a cold one, your doctor won't come; if he does, ten to one you may forestall his prescription. If it's a sore, a carrot poultice; if an inward disorder, a carrot diet. I only wonder they don't bleed at the carotid artery; and when one's head is shaved, order a carroty wig. The only reason I can find is that carrots grow here in fields-full.

Well, my book is done, and I'm not dead, though I've had a 'warning.' The book ran much longer than I had contemplated, and I've left out some good bits after all, for fear of compromising Franck and my informants. It has half as much writing again as the 'Comic,' and I told B—[1] to consult Dilke about the price, as it has five sheets more paper and print than the Annual.[2]

We thought this week's 'Athenaeum' much duller than the one before it; it hadn't such a fine hock flavour. I read the review six times over, for the sake of the extracts; and then the extracts six times, for the sake of the review.[3] If that isn't fair-play between author and critic, I don't know what is. I have been prophesying what will be Dilke's next extracts. We go on as usual at Ostend. Tell Dilke there are some other 'friends' staying at Harrison's,[4] a Captain B., *alias* K., and Sir W.J., said to be of large fortune. But what a residence to choose!

I heard also of two young men obliged to fly from the troubles at Hanover;[5] but it turns out that they have robbed or swindled a Chatham Bank. So we don't improve. A Colonel B. has done W. out of 100£, and an English lady, in passing through, did the banker here out of 78£. Then an Englishman shot at his wife the other day with an air-gun; and Mrs. F. will not set her foot in our house again, because I gave her a lecture on scandal-mongering; and the doctor has done Captain F. in the sale of some gin; and the Captain talks of calling out the doctor for speaking ill of his wife; and the De M.s[6] are gone; – a fig for Reid and Marshall, and their revolving hurricanes![7] We Ostenders live in a perpetual round of breezes.

I must now begin to nurse poor Jenny, who has had no time to mend and cobble her own health for soldering up mine. The children, thank God, are very well, and very good, and 'so clever!' The other day, Jane advised Fanny to talk to C— (about her own age) to subdue her temper. 'Oh,' said Fanny, 'she is so giddy, it would be like the Vicar of Wakefield preaching to the prisoners!'[8] Tom has taken to his book *con amore*, and draws, and spells, and tries to write with all his heart, soul, and strength. He has learned of his own accord to make all the Roman capitals, and labels all his drawings, and inscribes all his properties, TOM HOOD. He is very funny in his designs. The other day, he drew an old woman with a book: 'That's a witch, and the book is a Life of the Devil!' Where this came from, Heaven knows. But how it would have shocked Aunt Betsy! The fact is, he pores and ponders over Retsch's 'Faust,' and 'Hamlet,'[9] and the like, as a child of larger growth.[10] But he is as well and jolly and good-tempered as ever; and as he is so inclined to be busy with his little head, we don't urge him, but let him take his own course. So much for godma and godpa.

I cannot write more at present, as Mary is in the room, and she is a great listener. God bless you all!

Yours ever truly,

Thomas Hood.

P.S. – I shall thank Dilke for the two vols. of the 'Athenaeum' when I write to *him*, which will be after the tail of my review. The discovery at Trèves, &c., is stale – I mean the window story – six years old at least. Puff of the K. of P. to gull John Bull of some money.[11]

P.P.S. – I forgot to mention that I had a little duel of messages with my 'scandal-mongering' acquaintance the other day. 'Pray tell Mr. Hud,' says she, 'that I have no doubt but his complaint is a *scurrilous* liver!' (schirrous). So I sent her my compliments, and begged leave to say that was better than a 'cantankerous gizzard!'[12]

Ostend, Dec. 17, [*1839*].

From *Memorials* I 339–43, where the year is given as 1838

1/Baily

2/Dilke replied to this ten days later: 'According to your suggestion Bayly first sent and then came to consult me respecting the price – but it was obviously too late to alter it. The book had been advertised every where at 12/- – it was then the 19th or 20 and the wholesale houses might and I think would have chosen to consult their correspondents before they fulfilled orders under such circumstances, and then would have lost the *season* and the year,' MS Bristol Central Library.

3/*Up the Rhine* was reviewed in *The Athenaeum* 7 and 21 December 1839.

4/Hotel at Ostend. I have not identified the 'friends.'

5/Dispute between the king of Hanover and his subjects

6/De Melforts. I have not identified the persons previously referred to.

7/The views concerning 'the law of storms' of Colonel Reid and J. Marshall are referred to in *Athenaeum* 7 December, 925.

8/Goldsmith *Vicar of Wakefield*, ch. xxvi

9/A reference to the works of Moritz Retzsch (1779–1857). His illustrations of *Faust* appeared in an English version of 1820, and of *Hamlet* in a version of 1828. Retzsch also illustrated Schiller's *Fridolin* (1824), *Fight with the Dragon* (1828) and *Song of the Bell* (1834).

10/Dryden *All for Love* iv

11/Discussed in *Athenaeum* 7 December, 928: 'Many relics of Roman architecture, are now, thanks to the King [of Prussia]'s wise munificence, among the lions of Treves; and the supposed door-way in the old wall, proves to be an upper window of the Thermal Baths.'

12/Hood's son notes: 'My father mortally offended the elderly maiden afterwards by a mischievous peace-offering of those brown "wizzen'd" stony apples, that go by the uncharitable title of "medlars."'

1840

TO
ALFRED HEAD BAILY

I have looked through the Accounts as well as the time permitted. I find some errors but none of such consequence but might have been set right as proposed by an hours conference with Mr Carty –.

[*Pimlico, 18 February 1840*]

Dated transcript in the Public Record Office. The legal documents there include this and other quotations from Hood's letters as evidence in the case of *Hood* v *Baily*. In mid-January 1840 Hood 'came to London to get his accounts. He was five weeks at Dilke's and then, with much trouble, he returned with only a part,' *Memorials* II 77–8.

TO
ALFRED HEAD BAILY

There is another serious point which must greatly determine our going on together, vizt, the Accounts now that Wright is gone,[1] and all such matters depend on myself I cannot afford to lose valuable time through such delays as occurred 12 months ago, and I am sorry to say have been repeated this present year – I was seriously disappointed and displeased to find myself still unfurnished with the needful Statements to this hour in February 1840; – I have never received accounts of 'Hood's Own' altho' the 1st No was published in February 1838, and the last about June 1839, for of course it cannot be supposed that mere Memorandums of 'No so and so. – sundries – so much – ' can be received as accounts. In short I require business like and mercantile accounts – I have written to Mr Carty[2] to this effect and desired him to let me have them by the return of the Stewardess – My own experience in a Counting house tells me that with the vouchers and books before me I could make out such accounts and correctly too in a few hours and there can be no excuse for delays of weeks not to say months. This is a point so important to be understood that I ought to have mentioned it along with money matters but I could not foresee at that time that the accounts sent after me by Mr Carty would be so incomplete –

I am yours faithfully. T. Hood. – To A.H. Baily Esqre

[*Pimlico, February 1840*]

Transcript at the Public Record Office, with the previous item. The reference to 'the Stewardess' indicates that Hood is writing just before his return to Ostend.

1/Wright died suddenly at the end of 1839. It is a pity that Hood makes no further comment on his friend and helper.

2/Presumably Baily's assistant

TO
ALFRED HEAD BAILY

Dear Baily I duly received the Account on Saturday and your Letter on Friday last

[*Ostend, 4 March 1840*]

Dated transcript at the Public Record Office

TO
WILLIAM ELLIOT

Dear Doctor and Dedicatee.
I was much disappointed at not seeing you all as I intended before I left London but you would hear from the Dilkes how it happened. I have certainly not been better in health generally, since I have been abroad than during those weeks in town which makes my present attack the more striking. It was however so well defined & the causes seem so clear to me that I will give you a full true & particular account of it. I was unusually well in London, good appetite, & a total absence of all my usual symptoms a yellow tongue, cold feet & cold right hand. I had a cold as every body had, & a cough with it, but not frequent – & not the slightest trace or tinge of blood in the expectoration. I set off in good spirits, had a good journey & a very fine passage from Dover, feeling on landing very well. But the very second day here I began to feel unwell cold feet, the cold right hand & my appetite fell off. At the end of the week I was taken with a spitting of blood, which with three exceptions has recurred daily ever since – full a fortnight. Generally in the evening – & often but not invariably soon after eating or drinking. At first the blood bright red, rather frothy – with a good deal of mucus or slime somewhat like melted gum arabic – afterwards mixed with black clots of blood & thick dark blood apparently stale, or that had been congested. Sometimes a clot of discoloured brownish & once greenish mucus – Now see the sketch at the side.[1] The spitting was always

preceded and announced by a sort of a rattle or drawing of a fluid, at the point A below the ribs quite at the side (right), on drawing in my breath. After some two or three respirations came a sensation in the throat or windpipe, urging me to cough to get up the blood which once or twice at first came rather freely so as to get thro the nostrils. Sometimes the cough was rather violent but like what is called a stomach cough. In the beginning the cough caused pain in the direction marked red. It almost felt as if some parts there cohered also some pain about the liver B – One night, in the early part of the illness in particular I could not lie at all on my right side there was such soreness & tenderness of the liver & part marked red. NB. No pain ever at A. I had next day 10 leeches on at the red part, & its vicinity – & especially at C which seemed the worst part. At times the pain seemed to extend across the centre D. As I got better the pain left the upper part E but lingered at C – But that went, I could lie again on my right side & had no pain in coughing. Not a frequent cough but occasional – sometimes still for 2 or 3 hours – & apparently only to bring up pieces of coagulated blood. Little or no phlegm expectorated. During the spitting a good deal of pulsation – the heart disturbed – & at all times a sound of rushing, & pulsation in the head. Sometimes head ache often an inclination to it, & muzziness especially in the morning when I wake with a parched mouth & tongue, uncomfortable & unrefreshed. A feeling as if I had committed excess overnight – but throughout the whole time I have drunk only toast & water barley water gruel & tea – food bread & butter, toast, now & then a bit of sole or whiting & twice some boiled chicken. But generally no desire for food – digestion & bowels torpid – Irritation of the nose as from disordered stomach. Note no embarrassment of breathing except just before spitting when the accumulation of congealed blood seemed, at the red part to inconvenience by pressing on the neighbouring lung. No pain or shoot on drawing & holding my breath which I can do as well as any one. I had a spitting this morning, in bed before getting up, followed by head ache, blood in quantity a small teacup full mostly thick – some bright red. But I ate pretty well of boiled chicken at dinner & then fell asleep for two hours – woke with head better but still a rushing sound in it. No blood since morning – & have only coughed some ½ dozen times during the day to bring up clots. The Dr. I called in at first said it was a congestion & gave me something to take every hour. He did not think it the lungs. But finding the bleeding to continue and fearing he was only temporizing as Belgian Doctors are apt to do with palliatives, I latterly called in an old man, Chef of the Hospital here, to a consultation. He thought from the appearance of the blood it was the lungs– but appointed yesterday to meet & examine me with the stethoscope etc. After a thorough trial they both concur that the lungs are perfectly sound – that the blood comes from the liver by the stomach, or from the stomach itself, that I have a predisposition to hemorrhage, from weakness of constitution, & overuse of calomel. (German & Belgian physicians are very averse to calomel) & one added that the cold & damp of this climate in this season are very unfavorable to me. They recommend tonics & I am taking some every 2 hours, but cannot trace the result yet only beginning at noon today. They call it, the disorder, in French Hematemèse. Now even in name, I think all this concurs with your own conclusions. I should have told you too they remarked my heart being placed unusually low, – that there was no disease in it, but the more liable to disturbance from its greater proximity to the affected parts. My own impression is that both stomach & liver are wrong – & this attack has been from the evil influence of the climate on old chronic disease. – I am convinced the tendency of this climate in the winter season is to torpify by its chilly moisture the functions in general, hence peculiarly obnoxious to languid or irregular circulation, sluggish bowels, & bad digestion. There is a decided endemic here called the Koorts, which seems to act in this way – on the stomach especially as shown by the peculiar affection of the tongue. Fanny has slight attacks of it she is the next weakest – & begins with languor – pain in the head. Ostend is bad enough, but moreover the prevailing winds bring down at this season malaria from that horrid marshy country about Walcheren. It does not suffice to clothe against it – you breathe it, and from the badly constructed houses even in doors, – I have no doubt Jane's face & our Maid has only just taken her head out of wrappers, are from the same cause. We cannot use our lower rooms for damp – & live up stairs. Except in a hard frost the yard is always wet from a cold sweat from the earth. I have no doubt it torpified the functions, struck in the cold I had & caused congestion. It is curious that in London I read a medical report on the diseases of the Cornwall miners, & amongst them the effects of what they call cold damp, & immediately recognized the symptoms as my own here. Headache – drowsiness – chilliness & derangement of stomach & digestion. When I had finished my book, I went out one day here to dinner. In a coach, but I had to pass thro the lower rooms & an open passage all steaming with damp. Immediately after dinner I was suddenly seized with a most violent headache. My mouth filled with blood I know not how, without hawking or coughing, as if from the gums, & I fell asleep heavily for three hours. In short I believe at such seasons the climate here is very bad indeed. The natives are not proof against it. There is a young girl I know of spits blood like me but oftener & in greater quantities – & I know of a young lady dying of the Koorts not being able to close her mouth for months for the swelled tongue. Unfortunately one of the very worst things, for my case, is here I believe a necessary evil – the use of spirits or strong stimulants. By the bye, the water here is I suspect almost as unwholesome as the air. Luckily the better season is coming of which I shall avail myself for my Belgian tour – & then I have determined to remove – if not to Paris perhaps to Dieppe – England is impossible at present.[2]

I hope you got your book early & liked it. When you write let me know *when* you received it, there have been such gross neglects in that way I am looking into them as well as other abuses. You will be glad to hear the first edition 1500 went off in a fortnight. The second has paid its expenses & is henceforth profit.[3] But all this it has done for itself. I fear if I have an honest I have otherwise a very bad publisher. Hoods Own ought to have cleared me of my difficulties, but there as I can now trace, the climate went against me. The very same thing as now occurred in 1838 about this season. I left Blackheath in tolerable health, and broke down immediately on my arrival here. The same with the Comic towards the end of that year – when I had to stop nearly at the end from sheer physical prostration. I got thro the Rhine book thanks to some bracing beforehand by boating – but it is a dangerous coast & I cannot get out to sea when I most need it. I am getting too tired to write more – Give my kind regards to Mrs Elliot –

God bless you all. I am
Yours ever very truly

Thos Hood

I take care to keep warm feet in bed by a water bottle – & when the spitting is bad put them in hot water

[*Ostend, 4 March 1840*]

MS Yale. Address: 'Dr Elliot / Stratford Green / near Bow / Essex. / England.' PM: 'OSTENDE 1840/ 5 MA,' 'LONDON/ 6 MAR 1840.' The date given by me is that of Jane Hood's accompanying letter.

1/The sketch is of a torso with areas labelled from A to E.

2/Because of the pressure from Hood's creditors. It is not known what kind of a settlement he came to with them when he did return.

3/According to a MS in the Public Record Office, the first edition of *Up the Rhine* made a profit of £222, whilst the 2nd edition of 1000 copies showed a loss of £5 by 7 October 1840.

TO

WILLIAM ELLIOT

Dear Doctor,

I feel deeply obliged in the lowest depth, and deeper still, for your prompt and kind letter. I have just translated it to one of the Belgian Consultation, and hasten to give you the result.

Now, here was a striking proof of the ill effect of the climate. Though the weather looked so beautiful, the earth was in one of its cold sweats: at three o'clock the whole placed was wrapped in a white mist, and our paved yard as wet as after rain. It is quite curious to watch the phenomenon. From the yard a flight of about twelve or fifteen steps leads to the second floor. You literally see the damp ascend, step by step, till the whole flight is wet. To natives and residents in health this may not prove so obviously injurious; but to invalids, and especially coming into at this season, its effects are very marked. I have just heard of a case like mine.

An old retired sea captain has been lately in London for medical advice. The doctors sent him home well; and the very day after his return he was seized again, and is now laid up in bed. The family say they are now convinced it results from the climate: a conclusion they would be loth to come to, as they have a good business here, and the suffering uncle is a principal partner.

Moreover, Mr. D—,[1] a strong man, returned from fox-hunting in England last Friday, and is now taken with a sore throat, and unwell, and attributes it altogether to the same cause. As to myself, I am a perfect hygrometer, and for a wager could tell, by my feelings alone, whether the stones in our yard were wet or dry. I can perfectly, I think, understand the peculiar effect of the air on me as on Sunday.

* * * However, whether the lungs be touched or not, I shall follow your instructions as if they were; though I could hardly help smiling at a part of them – where I was 'to be mum and very still;' it sounded so much like an exhortation from *a Friend* to turn *Quaker*. But, in reality, I find no difference in my voice, it is as strong as usual, and I read aloud your letter from end to end without the slightest inconvenience.

In the Walcheren low fevers (akin to the effects of this air), bark I believe was the great specific: and in the same way the tonics may do me good. * * *

Till I get over the blood-spitting, I sit wholly in my bed-room; it looks to the west and is better secured. My own room is not very air-tight, and the windows front the east, and in spite of fire I feel its evil influence. The ground-floor is uninhabitable – it drips with damp!

Without all these means and appliances (hot bottles, baths, &c.), I find great difficulty in keeping warm extremities. I even cover my hands, and, like Sir Roger de Coverley's literary ancestor in the picture, write sonnets with my gloves on.[2] For, alas! I cannot follow up one of your rules, and give up all work. Throughout I have been obliged to puzzle through very ill-kept and tardily-rendered accounts – – a harassing job enough – and I know its ill effects on me; but *necessitas non habet!* But I leave all such matters to talk over with you by word of mouth, some day. Really I was half-inclined to come across by to-day's packet to see you, feeling it a serious case if I should happen not to be in the right course. But I gave up the idea as very inconvenient just now, and in some respects a risk. I was obliged to leave London suddenly, or I should most certainly have come to Stratford, as I had planned. If I did not write from Grosvenor-place, it was only from fear of taxing your kindness, remembering the great distance, and how you are engaged. I was exceedingly disappointed that I could not drop in on you, and show you my boy; he is a fine healthy fellow, very good, and almost reads. He behaved most manfully on his travels, by sea and land, and was quite a gallant in London, as perhaps the Dilkes told you.[3] Fanny is more delicate, but very good and very clever. With tolerable wealth I could be very happy, for my prospects are far from hopeless, indeed far otherwise – in fact, looking up. Poor Jane does not mend much; but her anxiety and fatigue about me are against her, probably the climate also. But I hope in autumn to quit Ostend, that is to say, I *must;* for another winter would assuredly kill me.

I was amused by a remark of old Dr. Jansen's (for he is quite a veteran). I said my sedentary profession was against me. And when he understood it was literary, 'Ah!' said he, with a glance at a thin, yellowish face, 'a *serious* writer, of course.' Akin to this, I one day overheard a dispute between Tom and Fanny as to what I was. 'Pa's a literary man,' said Fanny. 'He's not!' said Tom: 'I know what he is.' 'What is he, then?' 'Why,' says Tom, 'he's not a literary man – he's an invalid.'

They have made me an honorary Vice-President of the African Institute at Paris.[4] Oddly enough, the day afterwards two black gentlemen came here in a ship on their way to Havannah. They caused some speculation in the town, so I gave out that they were a black deputation to bring my diploma.

I must now follow your rule, and go to bed. Our Carnival is fortunately over (the maskers of the lower class were dreadfully noisy), and we can sleep o'nights.

God bless you all. My wife's love to Mrs. Elliot and my kind regards along with it. Your united healths in a tumber of Vitriolic! As I know your time is precious, do not trouble yourself to answer this, as there seems nothing of consequence to reply to; and, in the meantime, I shall follow your rules.

I am, dear Doctor,
Yours ever very truly,

Thomas Hood.

P.S. Can my spitting blood have ceased because I have *none* left? What a subject for a German romance, 'The Bloodless Man!'

[*Ostend*] *11th March, 1840.*

From *Memorials* II 51–5

1/Unidentified though perhaps the husband of Mrs Dore, mentioned elsewhere

2/In Steele's *Spectator* no. CIX, or rather, 'he sits with one Hand on a Desk writing, and looking as it were another way, like an easie Writer, or a Sonneteer ... he would sign a Deed that passed away half his Estate with his Gloves on,' ed. D.F. Bond (Oxford 1965) I 451.

3/Hood had taken Tom with him to England.

4/L'Institut d'Afrique was 'founded in 1838 to aid the civilisation and colonisation of Africa,' *Galignani's New Paris Guide* (Paris 1846) 94. I do not know why Hood received this honour.

TO
ALFRED HEAD BAILY

the accounts will I think pretty well answer the purpose but they must be postponed for more pressing matters.

[*Ostend, 12 March 1840*]

Dated transcript in the Public Record Office

TO
WILLIAM ELLIOT

Dear Doctor,
I write again to report progress, especially as it seems to be favourable. I have had no regular return since this day week. I began on Wednesday last to follow your directions closely, in all but the silent system;[1] which I found in some degree impracticable, my signs being constantly inadequate or misunderstood; but I have spared my lungs as much as possible. Luckily for me, the weather changed to fine

about Wednesday, the wind going round to west and south-west. I felt during that time much better, but yesterday and to-day the wind blows north and east again, the ground is wet, and I feel it like a conscious hygrometer.

This discomfort consists in no pain, but a general feeling of languor or lassitude, and more or less drowsiness.

I attribute this solely to the change of the weather, for neither yesterday or to-day have I felt so well: cold feet and *the cold hand*. I was free from this during the finer days, but think the low fever is particularly consequent on the climate. I knew an English family in Rotterdam, and one of the daughters suffered so continually from low fever for two years, they were obliged to move up to Coblenz. Now in London, though eating heartily, and living well (but on joints, which I prefer to made-dishes), I was particularly free from any symptoms of bilious derangement, indeed better generally than since I went abroad. And I think this luckily gave me strength to struggle with the present attack, by which I am less beaten down, than might otherwise have been expected.

But I feel sure now mere fine weather would bring me round. A friend of ours the other day visited the Hospital here, and one of the Sisters of Charity, who was nursing, told her that during the present season, February and March, the number of their patients is doubled, compared with any other period.

Several circumstances have concurred probably to bring on my attack; not only cold damp weather, but for the last six weeks two hundred men have been employed in clearing out the moats round the town. The sewers flow into them – the tide does not – and they have not been disturbed before, perhaps for many years. When I came I saw heaps of the black mud, etc., on the sands, to be washed away by the sea.

Besides this it turns out that our water has been failing (it is always bad enough), and latterly we have been drinking the very grouts of our well. At present we have none, and are obliged to beg and borrow. We use some sort of filter, but I believe the water here to be very unwholesome, and know the Belgians from up the country have a horror of it.

By the harbour there is a house where water is sold, which is brought from the interior in barges: it is used for the shipping. I presume because the Ostend water will not keep!

As for the air I am persuaded that its miasma acts upon me more immediately, and perniciously, than you could credit, unless it were at once brought under your notice. As a sample of the damp, and its penetrating nature: in the latter autumn, I remember our butcher saying that the meat hanging in his shop was literally saturated and dripping with water! When I am well enough, I mean to inquire into the cases so numerous at the hospital; the peculiar effects of the malaria on myself make it a subject of great interest. A lady friend of ours here in delicate health, has her good and bad days so regularly with mine, that we corroborate each other like two good barometers.

I am told the chemists here make all their preparations very strong.[2] Ten drops of their vitriolic acid quite suffice for a tumbler of water.

What is the test for Epsom salts and oxalic acid? I got some sulphate of magnesia, but a fresh supply to-night tasted so unusually hot or acrid in the throat, that I was afraid to go on with it.

Directly the weather is settled enough, I shall take a sail. The voyage to England does me so much good always, I half incline some day to go over to Dover by mail, and return the next morning. I should not get further, for I cannot well stand long coach journeys. As for the south of France or Italy, it is far, far away to go with a family, bag and baggage; and the uncertainty of my working days, from illness, renders a prompt communication with London imperatively necessary.

I should think that Dieppe, or some other such place answerable to our own coast, on a chalk cliff, might suit me. I used to be very well at Brighton. I do not think mere cold hurts me, if it is not combined with damp. By the way, should authorship fail me some day, don't you think I have studied enough and dabbled in my own case to set up for a Quack? Talking of cases, a Liège banker's wife was here last summer for health. On asking her what ailed her, she told me her doctor said she had 'too good a digestion.' I could not help answering: 'Oh! if that's all, *I* will undertake to cure you of that!'

Did I tell you of the panic here at Christmas. A Mr. and Mrs. R—[3] were stopped, all packed ready for a flitting without paying. The creditor here has his choice, so Mr. R— was put in Bruges jail; but it ought to have been the lady, for she incurred all the debts. Then a major and his family went clear off. The Belgians got frightened, and put an execution in at Sir —'s. Next, a man came to Ostend, took lodgings, won a horse at a raffle, rode out one morning, and never came back. There was quite a panic! Since then they have sent a Colonel B— to Bruges, and now a Mr. D—. We are getting quite select!

I have hopes to-morrow will be fine. How I shall enjoy the sight of the first butterfly: I shall not feel safe till then. Jane sends her love to Mrs. Elliot, and God bless you all! From,

Dear Doctor,
Yours very truly,

Thomas Hood.

What a droll notion of a Greek lately appealing to the Tribunal at Athens to move for a new trial *in re* Socrates! The Court refused to enter on the matter.[4] It might have reversed the verdict on the philosopher, but who could unpoison him?

La Rhetorique, à Ostend, Wednesday, [*18*]*th March, 1840.*

From *Memorials* II 56–60, where the date is given as the 19th. However, Wednesday, the day given, was the 18th.

1/Method of prison discipline

2/Hood's son notes: 'Probably because the damp atmosphere diluted the nostrums sufficiently as they stood on the shelves.'

3/Unidentified, as are the following persons

4/Reported in *Athenaeum* 14 March 1840, 214

TO

CHARLES WENTWORTH DILKE

I am a little Job in afflictions, but without his patience ... The silent system did not answer at all. Jane and I made but a sorry game of our double dumby, for the more signs I made the more she didn't understand them. For instance, when I telegraphed for my nightcap she thought I meant my head was swimming, – and as for Mary, she knew no more of my signals than Admiral Villeneuve of Lord Nelson's.[1] At last I did burst out, fortissimo, but there is nothing so hard as to *swear in a whisper*. The truth is, I was bathing my feet, and wanted more hot water, – but as the spout poured rather slowly, Mary, whipping off the lid of the kettle, was preparing to squash down a whole cataract of scalding. I was hasty I must confess; but perhaps Job himself would not have been patient if *his boils* had come out of a kettle.

[*Ostend, March 1840*]

From Dilke I 57–8. Hood refers to the 'silent system' in the previous and the following letter.

1/Villeneuve was Nelson's opponent at the battle of Trafalgar (1805).

TO
WILLIAM ELLIOT

My dear Doctor,

Many thanks for your very kind letter.[1] I am happy to tell you, that I have had no return of the blood since I mentioned. I am more than ever convinced the great evil is the climate; and it appears to be characteristic, as of Holland, &c., that when once the climate gets hold of you in such a way, there is no remedy but to leave it. It is my belief that this place, the height of summer excepted, cannot be good for any one; but that for any peculiar complaint or predisposition, it is one of the very worst that could be selected.

I see that Marryat, speaking of the diseases most common in America, mentions those of the marshy parts, as ague, and 'congestive bilious fever.'[2] Moreover, in reading the new 'Sporting Magazine,' I came across an article which seemed to have a curious bearing on the subject – the 'Diseases of Hounds,' and in particular, kennel lameness – a sort of rheumatism – and the yellows, a kind of jaundice. These it attributes to their kennels being built on a sandy soil, giving several remarkable instances. It says that rain does not penetrate deeply into the earth, and consequently sooner evaporates; whereas wet sinks into the sand deeply, and is given off again in a constant but imperceptible manner. This is very perceptible, for our sands are beautiful to the eye, and look dry; but thrust in a stick an inch or two, and the hole is instantly filled with water: only the immediate superficial surface is dry; below is sand and water intermixed. I have seen a curious effect from this. When at high water in roughish weather a wave runs on the dry sand, the pressure forces up the water from beneath the apparently dry sand in little fountains one or two inches high! The fluid we drink here is all rain-water, more or less recent, which has thus been stagnating in the sand; at the best from the roofs and gutters! It smells strongly, and even tastes of the soot; but some of it (from our well, for instance) must be putrescent, it smells like stinking fish; and the plates, &c., which have been washed in it are at all times disgustingly strong of it.

I perfectly understand your description of my case, and have not the slightest doubt of your being right. What I mean to say is, there is no lung disease, *i.e.* original. This mischief is in the stomach or liver; and I can imagine how that may affect the lungs, or any other neighbouring part, as an embarrassment or stoppage in the Strand would affect bridges or any other laterals.

I continue to take the drops, but with some misgiving that the water does me as much harm as I derive benefit from the drops. Just now it is execrable, and with the soot in it ought to give one the 'sweeps' disease.'[3]

Your kind invitation is a very tempting one in every way.[4] For the mere benefit of your opinion, I was half tempted to run across for a week; but, in reality, the voyage and change of air always do me so much good, and so promptly, that, instead of seeing me indisposed, you would be almost inclined to think half my complaint must be hyp – or sham. I almost suspect it is the belief of some of my non-medical friends. For instance, how well I was at Dilke's! You know better; but still, you could not see an attack.

I never had even an inclination to spit blood in London. Then at Dilke's I used daily to let the fire go out; whereas here I am perpetually scorching my boots to keep my feet warm, and cannot keep my hands out of my pockets for cold. Moreover, my mind always derives benefit from the change of scene, and a little society; and altogether I am better always for a trip to England. But there are too many lions in the path[5] for me to think of it at present. In the meantime, I will follow your rules as closely as possible, and if I can but hold on till the fine weather sets in, I hope I shall get over these attacks whilst I have to remain at Ostend.

My principal suffering at present is that after dinner, however light, – a bit of fish, for instance, whiting or haddock – I feel a great discomfort, not easy to describe, a compound of sinking and yet oppression; sometimes a little drowsiness, languor, lassitude, and a craving, not for wine in particular, but some assistance, either stimulus or warmth. I longed for my tea, for example, but find coffee still more comforting, and have it directly after dinner. It seems to me to be the first process of digestion is so weak. I take no other liquids save toast or barley-water.

I will try to be as dumb as I can; but then I have as many impediments to silence as there are sometimes to speech. I wish I *could* rest from work: but I have just finished an article for the new Sporting Magazine.[6] But then at the worst of my attack I was *obliged* to write business letters, and go through troublesome accounts – neither a pleasant nor a profitable labour of the pen.[7] I am so sleepy, I must not transgress another of your rules, but e'en to bed at once.

So, God bless you all. With kind regards from us to you both,

I am, dear Doctor,
Yours ever very truly,

Thos. Hood.

La Rhetorique, Rue St. François, à Ostend, March 29th, 1840.

From *Memorials* II 60–4

1/Dated the 27th, in the Bristol Central Library

2/'Michigan, Indiana, Illinois, and a portion of Ohio, are very unhealthy in the autumns from the

want of drainage; the bilious congestive fever, ague, and dysentery, carrying off large numbers,' Marryat *Diary in America* (1839) III 263.
3/Hood may be referring to 'dreaded "chimney-sweepers's cancer"' caused by 'soot cached in the unwashed folds of the scrotum,' Geo. L. Phillips *England's Climbing Boys* (Cambridge Mass. 1949) 5.
4/To visit Elliot privately
5/Predatory creditors
6/Hood's contributions appeared in the April and July 1840 numbers of the *New Sporting Magazine*, between 253 (April) and 49 (July).
7/Towards the end of March Hood relinquished his connection with Baily. In spite of what Hood writes here, at the beginning of April, in Jane's words, he 'left Ostend alone ... as we could not directly leave the place, having engaged our lodgings for a year. He stayed a week at Dilke's,' *Memorials* II 78.

Distant Relatives.

AT HOME AGAIN April 1840–May 1845

1840

TO
JANE HOOD

My own dearest and best,
I could not write yesterday to you, nor can much to-day. I came here on Monday evening, and fortunately for me, for in the evening, or rather at night, I had a very bad attack, spitting more blood than ever at once, except the first time at Coblenz. The Doctor watched it, and meant to bleed me, but it went off. Tuesday morning it returned; and, by way of saving blood, he took some from my arm, till I was rather faint. I am now better, but am obliged to keep silence and remain in bed. It will be a comfort to you, dearest, to know I am here with all skill and help at my hand, and every comfort and care. A brother and sister could not be kinder to me than they are; only *one* other *could* nurse me more tenderly and affectionately. So pray do not be anxious on my account. I am now better, body and mind. The Doctor says he has now no doubt on my case, that I am as he expected to find me, and the affection is what he supposed it to be, aggravated by the largeness of my heart. The more to give to you, love!

The weather is fine, but with a cold east wind, though I do not suffer from it under an English roof in an English bed. I am hoping you had fine weather for your Bruges trip, which would do you all good. Dilke, if he can, is to come here to-day to see me. Poor Mrs. D.[1] wrote me such a storm of wind, to account for my not hearing from you on *Wednesday*, thinking I was worrying myself. I have written to quiz her on her hurricane, as *there was no post.*

I quite regret that I was prevented from bringing Tom here; he would have been so happy. There is a little fellow, full of fun, about his own age, and a little girl, so like what Willie was, it struck me in an instant. They are all very well. I am a sort of melodramatic mystery, I suspect, to some of the boys, associated with many basons and blood! The two little ones have visited me in my room, and this morning brought me in the Comic Annual to *amuse* me! To the little things I must look a very odd personage, for I have been unshaven since last Saturday, and am almost a *sapeur.*[2] But I avoid all exertion, and keep in bed, in hope of discounting the attack. It is rather trying to my patience to be so laid up – passive, when I ought to be active.

They have a nice garden here, and a paddock. I take a look out of my window sometimes, and invariably find my eyes resting on Shooter's Hill.[3] A blue hill is a novelty after our flats. Then the quiet is quite delicious. I do not hear a sound. Now the Rue St. François is almost as noisy as Cheapside, with railway-trucks and fish-barrows. I feel very English-like here; that is as good as saying I feel very comfortable!

The young Dilkes are expected back soon; they are at Henley-on-Thames. They are to live in Sloane Street. We have had a deal of fun, Mrs. Dilke and I, about the haste of the wedding, that the cake was put in a very quick oven, &c. I told Mrs. Dilke they ought to have put it in the papers thus: – '*Suddenly*, on such a day, at St. Luke's, Pimlico.'[4]

Mrs. Elliot has just looked in, and desires her love to you. I know you will give them credit for all kindness, but it is really delightful, and I am so very comfortable; it must help my getting well, for it soothes my mind, which else has enough to fret about. But I turn my thoughts into the pleasantest channels I can, none more so than yourself and the children. I think of you continually, and, however well off, must pine and long for your faces and kisses. God bless you all, again and again! Do let me hear from you soon that you are better, and let us get well, body and mind together. I long to write more, but am forbidden.

Stratford, [*9*] *April, 1840.*

From *Memorials* II 64–7, where the letter is dated 14 April, but this must be wrong, since its contents indicate that it precedes the letter following, postmarked 13 April. On the basis of the chronology of the first paragraph, I suggest that the letter belongs to Thursday, 9 April, and amend the date accordingly. Hood returned to England, but fell ill at once, and was looked after by Dr and Mrs Elliot at Stratford. Jane and the children eventually followed him, but it was a very nerve-wracking time.

1/Probably Mrs Dore

2/The Belgian sappers must have been noted for not shaving.

3/The Elliots' home was at Stratford, east of London, south of Hood's old home at Wanstead. Southwards on the far side of the Thames, were Greenwich and Blackheath, and, to their east, Shooter's Hill.

4/Dilke married Mary Chatfield on 30 March 1840.

TO
JANE HOOD

Monday. I am doubtful whether from *here* this can reach you on Tuesday.

My own dearest love.
As you seem so anxious about me, I write though it should prove but a few lines to make you more easy. You have no doubt been alarmed by my writing from bed, where indeed I still am – but not from inability to rise but as a measure of precaution, that the parts may heal – as I am still spitting up the stale blood. But I have had no fresh attack since the bleeding in the arm. I suspect had I been bled at first at Ostend instead of going on for 14 days spitting it would have averted all this – but the Dr says they probably thought I had no blood to spare – & he only bled me to save blood in the end. He seems to think that the great cause is in the heart, itself, more than the liver, & that in future I must live very orderly & quietly[1] as free as possible from agitation or mental annoyance. Alas how difficult for any of us to escape! He is very earnest for my returning to England, – as the best climate for mind & body – & at this moment there are many inducements *before my eyes*. It is a lovely sunny day – imagine me, in bed with the window open, looking over their garden, across the country so green with its meadows & hedges & Shooters Hill beautifully blue in the distance! It looks lovely – & yet my heart's in the *Low*lands my heart is not here[2] – & I feel how many other conditions are necessary to my dwelling in England. In the meantime let it console you that I am enjoying English comforts – my bed when it had not been made for 3 or 4 days was more comfortable than any littering down abroad. My great misery is to lie here doing nothing either in work, or arrangements for I must not speak, but too little for business, – and I feel great anxiety lest you should be annoyed by those lucre loving Ostenders – it costs me a great effort to keep off such thoughts – & only by dint of reading can I manage it – but my spirits are pretty good, and I trust I shall soon be up again. But by the present sacrifice of time as of blood I hope to save in the end by avoiding any risk of relapse. You are right about my cravings I do long for the old familiar faces[3] & for the young ones too & the dear sweet voices & the loving kisses – There is no place like home[4] – especially for the sick or sorrowful. Yet is this the next thing to one's own house & in one respect better in which we must both take comfort. I have great hope the extreme care & skill I am treated with must do me *permanent* good. The kindness and attention of both the Dr & Mrs E are delightful – she brings me every thing herself, – & forestalls all my wants & wishes. I have daily visits too from the children. Willy, now a fine lad, likes to come

& talk a little – he found me out but of his own accord kept the secret. In fact he knew me again! They have such a nice house & garden! On Thursday Dilke came to see me & dined here & Mrs D I expect will come this week. D said I was better than he expected to find me. (I can hardly write with these steel pens) I have just been reading Dr James Johnson on Travelling, Climate, & the effects of malaria abroad – which seems to quite account for my own case.[5]

I find if I close shortly it will get off today – so I must finish. Of course I have no news had I time – beyond what I have told you of myself. I am grieved to hear of your bad cold – of course it was from the early journey – but the jaunt would cheer you up a bit. As you cannot nurse me take good care of my other self, – & above all do not fret about me – but let us meet again happy & well on both sides.

I wish I could write to my dear good children – bless them. Kiss & hug them fondly for me – I know what a comfort they must be to you. – As for yourself, think do & feel all that can make you comfortable – rely on my love as I do on yours & look only forward to our meeting. The Dr has just been up to me & I am going on he says quite well. Again & again God bless you the servant is waiting to take this so I conclude, my own dearest & best

Your own ever affectionate husband

Thos Hood

Love to Mrs Dore I am sorry she is ill with her heart too. I promise you faithfully to let you know should I be worse so that when you do *not* hear from me you may be at ease.

[*Stratford, 13 April 1840*]

MS Bristol Central Library. Published in part in *Memorials* II 67–9. Address: 'Thomas Hood Esqre/ La Rhetorique/ Rue St François/ à Ostend.' PM: 'LONDON/ 13/ APR/ 1840.'

1/Hood's son notes: 'we children were brought up in a sort of Spartan style of education, and taught the virtues of silence and low voices,' *Memorials* II 67.

2/Misquoting the first line of Burns's song, 'My heart's in the Highlands'

3/'The Old Familiar Faces,' the title of Lamb's poem

4/In the refrain of John Howard Payne's 'Home, sweet home!'

5/Johnson *Change of Air* (1831) 124–7

TO
JANE HOOD

My own dearest & best love

Recollecting that you could not otherwise hear till Tuesday I cannot deprive you so long of what I know will be such comfortable news for you, as my being much better. Fortunately the weather has been beautiful – on Tuesday I had my bedroom window open nearly all day – on Wednesday for the first time I came down stairs, and took a turn in the garden. Yesterday I was out in it for a still longer time – and the fresh air really seems fresh life to me. Good air acts as potently on me as bad. Yesterday for the first time I spat without stale blood. I walked a good deal in the garden yesterday & do not feel so weak as I expected from such loss of blood & low diet. I take no meat – only light puddings, with tea coffee & the vitriolic lemonade[1] as drinks. Oranges, & Lemonade made with isinglass – biscuits & sponge cakes – There you have my diète. In answer to your query I have the Doctors dressing gown & altogether manage very well. The rigour of my silence is relaxed a little & I am beginning to make acquaintance with the kin. William — George & Gilbert are nice boys – then little Dunstanville, about Tom's age, Jeanie a year older & the baby – a girl. They all look so well & happy it is a pleasure to be amongst them. Such regrets that I could not bring Tom here last time – Dilke has talked of him to them a good deal. By the bye it seems to me, being fine & a holiday I may possibly see something of the Dilkes today – as she talked of coming. Tell Tibby & Tom, being Good Friday I breakfasted to-day on regular hot cross buns. I shall long for their letters as I have done for their dear faces & gossip – for you may suppose, I have had many lonely hours in bed – for being forbidden to talk, it was no use having any one to sit with me. But now comes the hardship. As I get better, my mind gets anxious and I long to be doing – Whilst it was impossible I submitted, – by dint of reading I kept my mind quiet – & have been tolerably patient – but now that I can get down & walk out tho but a little all the urgency of my affairs returns on me in spite of myself – but I must banish them or I shall be thrown back again. Nothing could be more unlucky & ill timed for me than that panic at Ostend[2] – it is the Belgians now that most hang over my mind – for here I am quiet & feel safe.[3] Moreover I fear it will require *time* & great difficulty to find a new Publisher to do what I want.[4] One comfort is I have enough stock &c for security to offer. I told Dilke of the new mistake of £10 who said it was most extraordinary – he evidently believes Baily to be *dishonest* – in fact he said as much. The Dr says B. always spoke to him about me as if taking such interest, he thought him quite a friend. But perhaps the £10 is not B's mistake after all. You talk of 10 coming before you went to London. What was the date of your going? The acct in his accts stands thus. *1st October* £10 18th £15 – 24th £10 – 26th £15 – Novr 7. £10 – in all 60 which when I read over to you, you said you had in London – & so misled me – Perhaps the 10 on the 1st Octr is what you allude to, as coming before you went to London – in which case he is correct. Let me know to a certainty before I tax it in going thro the accts. You can remember at all events whether the first sum you recd in London was 10 or 15. – I greatly fear owing to my illness that Baily & Carty knowing there must be a transfer will have employed the delay in making up the stock to suit the accts I am quite fretted to think of the result of Up the Rhine which was & ought to have been a hit – a poor £150 – but its my belief if it had come to 500 or £600 B. could not have paid me. I think, he is in a bad way, & really has no money or he would not have let me go so profitable as I must be to an *unscrupulous* Publisher.[5] The worst is wherever I go there will be an enquiry of what the last book did – & in spite of any promises to the contrary, as Dilke says – every one of them will go and make enquiries of Baily. But a truce to business for the present. In your next tell me have any letters come – & have you heard from Folkard. I fear that last affair is settled & you will never have the letters. Perhaps I shall manage to see him.

I am sitting opposite my open window & by help of Shooter's Hill can tell which way lies Ostend. I seem to have the pigeon's sight but wish for the pigeon's flight along with it towards home.[6] It is a strange feeling for me to wish myself out of England – but I am a man without a Country. But thankful I have a home. My hope is this attack may enable Elliot to judge & put me on a good plan for the future. But I had rather my liver had been worse & my heart better – as I know I am foredoomed to wear & tear that is worst for the last. One thing is certain I *must* live with great care & quiet or my life will be the forfeit. That infernal climate has poisoned my whole blood I feel sure & I shall long feel the consequences even if we remove from it.[7] By this time with *fair play* I ought to have been free of care – but I will think of my blessings not my curses.

I must not write a great deal more or I shall lose my lounge in the garden. I have got to dress & the post goes from here about 3. I dine between one & two. I mean to try to write a ballad or something whilst I am here to fetch a little money – but my mind as well as my body as yet feels very languid. I take for granted JHR. has not sent the Sporting Magazines & I take equally for granted that as *I have done the article* I now shall not have them.[8] I should like some Sardines for the Elliots but do not know where to have 'em left. The Stewardess mustn't go near Bailys or

anybody's known to me. Perhaps Mrs E. can tell me of somewhere in the City.
I did not tell you there has been strange work in the Literary Fund – embezzling of money &c. People who had given £10 & so forth at the anniversary said not to have paid – but on being applied to, *had* paid – & some of their cheques I believe paid in to Jerdan's banker – traced.[9] Amongst others a £10 cheque of Baily's paid for Maxwell[10] who was a steward. Jerdan has *resigned his seat there* so we may presume Verdict Guilty. What a set they are. But don't mention it, as I suppose what Dilke tells me ought to be secret. So much for Charities that profess to do good by stealth. The copyright Bill is I fear dead & gone – or crushed to pieces by party politics.[11] I have seen the 2nd No of Boz which contains a story of London in the olden time, more in Miss Lawrences style than his: This is a great mistake, his strong point was every day & now aday life.[12]
Now I must shut up tho I feel very loth to finish & tho fine it is so windy I am almost willing to make it an excuse as I can enjoy the air up here. Besides whilst I am writing to you I feel less alone – or at least more at home. But every other comfort I have here – & all that kindness can do or think of. There is no country like England – no people like the English after all. (It is too windy to go out so I shall continue.) It blows much more since I began.
NB. Shake up my inkbottle daily – you will see this is not very good.
I am not surprised at Blackwood wanting to go to New Zealand. There are simple savages there to take in & plunder.[13] The application to the Major plainly shows me the terms they have been on any *speeches* to the contrary notwithstanding. Miss will go back & blarney her Mother – but Ostend will be the wholesomer. I only hope Blackwood will well take in the Sweetloves[14] &c. No news from Mr Pyne of course. The Major must begin to doubt on that business as I do. I don't think he feels so easy as he used about Belgian debts. My pens (steel) & ink are so bad it is quite a labour to write – I must get some quills. So you must not take fright at my scrawl. It is the best I can manage unless the vitriol water I have put in mends my ink. My pen ought to run to say all I feel towards you – for I think of you incessantly – it helps to make me well, so comfort yourself that you can nurse me in that way if in no other. I do hope you will take care & nurse yourself now I am off your hands for it will be of no use my getting well unless you do. It will be like a paralysis of one side. I often wish you could drink out of their porter barrel here – it looks so good – My dinner is just come, – a batter pudding boiled.
I can see the smoke of the steamers going up & down the river & it sets me longing – This time I hope to come home direct. It is odd but all three times I have returned to Dover. But I fear a month lies between now & *then* for I dare not return

if well without the needful – it would be the signal for all demands. But for this world's gear, how happy could I be in spite of ill health. I half suspect the sickness of my heart has been from hope deferred.[15] But time & the tide wear thro the roughest day.[16] So pluck up your spirits dearest & best & let us hope still. It is better at all events than despairing – if you were but as near as you are dear to me, I think I should feel little ailing now. If it but please God to spare you my bairns sound & well I will not repine at the rest. – In the meantime lay my love & all other comforts to your good heart – & kiss & hug our dear children for me & tell them to give you plenty in return for me. The wind has lulled & I am going to take a walk – so God bless you again & again my own dearest & best. – & my own dear good Children I will answer their letters. Love to Mrs D[17] & kind regards to the Major.

Your own ever affectionate husband

Thos Hood

[Stratford] Good Friday [17 April 1840]

MS Bristol Central Library. Published in part in *Memorials* II 69–72. Address: 'Thos Hood Esqre/ La Rhetorique / Rue St François / Ostend.' PM: 'STRATFORD/AP 17/1840,' 'PAID/17 AP 17/ 1840.'

1/Presumably a medicinal drink

2/The panic must have been that of Hood's Belgian creditors, who no doubt feared that he intended to evade them by staying in England permanently. Hood eventually decided to do just this.

3/Hood felt safe in the seclusion of his friend's home at Stratford (see 430).

4/That is, take over from Baily

5/There is no evidence of grounds for Hood's suspicion.

6/'The first pigeon races of record were held in the early part of the nineteenth century in Belgium' (1818), W.M. Levi *The Pigeon* (Columbia S.C. 1941) 49.

7/Medical opinion seems to have been not quite as strong as that of the patient himself. When application was made for a government pension on Hood's behalf in 1844, Elliot certified that Hood suffered incidentally from 'an aguish susceptibility to the atmospheric changes, occasioned by exposure to malaria in Holland': Reid 237. Reid discusses Hood's ill-health in general, and Clubbe gives a modern medical opinion, 230–1.

8/Through Reynolds Hood had contributed 'Fishing in Germany' to the *New Sporting Magazine* (April). The conclusion of this article and 'An Autograph' appeared in the July number. Hood is complaining that, having submitted the article, his dilatory brother-in-law will not send him the printed version.

9/The anniversary of the Literary Fund was celebrated each year; in 1839 it took place on 8 May.

10/William Hamilton Maxwell (1792–1850), Irish novelist. He contributed to Nimrod's *Sporting* (1838) and wrote the *Life of the Duke of Wellington* (1839–41), both works published by Baily.

11/Hood had been active in the cause of an extension of copyright. With thirty-two other authors he signed a petition presented to the House of Commons by Talfourd on 27 February 1839. He also supplied an individual petition which was not presented because 'too richly studded with jests.' However, it was published in *The Athenaeum* 29 June, 485–6, and by Talfourd in the printing of his *Three Speeches* 141–4, which Hood himself reviewed in *The Athenaeum* 8 February 1840. The bill was

defeated, largely by parliamentary indifference.
12/Dickens's *Master Humphrey's Clock* was published in 88 weekly parts, beginning 4 April 1840.
13/Presumably this Blackwood was an English resident of Ostend. The major referred to in the next sentence is probably Major Opie of 395 n 8.
14/Unidentified, as is the 'Pyne' following
15/Proverbs 13:12
16/*Macbeth* I iii 147
17/Mrs Dore

TO
JANE HOOD

I find my position a very cruel one – after all my struggles to be, as I am, almost moneyless, and with a very dim prospect of getting any, but by the sheer exercise of my pen. What is to be done in the meantime is a question I ask myself without any answer but – Bruges jail. At the very moment of being free of Baily, am I tied elsewhere, hand and foot, and by sheer necessity ready to surrender myself that slave, a bookseller's hack!

[*Stratford, April 1840*]

From *Chambers' Encyclopaedia* (1888–92) v 768, where Baily is misspelt with an 'e'. I surmise that this excerpt belongs to the letter which Hood sent between the last and the following, in which he advised Jane against joining him in England.

TO
JANE HOOD

I am very sorry my own dearest & best to have been the cause of disappointing you, – but I only told you what my own impression was on the subject of y.r coming. I must confess I almost wished afterwards that you should come in spite of it – your heart seemed so set upon it. I do not either undervalue the comfort you would be to me tho I hardly see how you could well help me in business matters: – and I should be anxious about the kin in the absence of both of us. As regards myself I am mending tho very slowly – I have not deceived you about my state – I do not spit even stale blood now – but I am very weak, & languid – often low & nervous – as you may suppose, – as up to this I have never eaten any animal food or had any drink save tea & coffee. But the Doctor thinks it the best & safest course & evidently proceeds very cautiously as I have no doubt a relapse now would be very serious. I could, but don't fret a good deal at the delays & loss of time – & in spite of all my efforts at times am much disturbed to think that nothing is doing. I try to write a trifle but cannot from prostration of mind & body – Up till now indeed I have been sadly troubled with beatings & noise in the head. I am getting better – but it takes time. Yesterday I had a ride out for the first time with the Doctor, past Lake House, as far as Old Roundings & back – it did me good – the weather is still fine luckily – and is all in my favour. – But I have not been yet to town – nor do I yet feel equal to business – my nerves are shaken & my spirits are low generally – tho I keep as tranquil as I can. But it frets my heart to remain thus passive – in fact I cannot go on so much longer but must exert myself at all hazards. The worst is I cannot stir, but I must ride everywhere – I have seen nobody yet, nor let any one know I am in town & must therefore repeat my caution to you. I have a strong notion my danger last time was thro Longmore & Martyn.[1] – I have recd your letter by post – but not the children's which I hope to have in the course of the day – I will answer them both – & am going to send down to Thames S^tt^ for the Sardines. I have had a note too from Mrs Dilke. She says D talks of coming here soon. He met Baily who observed that the Stewardess had left off coming. I got D to ask for any thing at Bailys & he has got the two watches & a note that was lying there from the Ed. of Dispatch[2] – as I thought he says he *had not* my books – which was the only reason they were not noticed. A very civil note. He says 'You must be aware that there are Publishers who pursue courses not very conciliatory with respect to criticisms on their publications' – Exactly so – Maxwell's Wellington to wit!

Mrs Elliot (the D^r^ is out) has begged me to give you the warmest invitation – I do not know what to say. If I were merely selfish it could instantly be 'Come' – I must leave it to your own resolve, whether you can come comfortably & can feel secure about the children – for I see you are fretting yourself ill about me. Perhaps you could save me some trouble in enquiries &c – at all events I will try to think so & I know you will try to make it so – but all must depend on your own feelings of what you are equal to & how you can manage. If it would but help to shorten my stay here I would say come at once that I may the sooner return with you – for in spite of all the kindness & comfort here, the constant sense that I ought to be elsewhere & active makes it like being bedridden or in a prison. You will understand what I mean – for I have every comfort & care under this roof.

Of course if you come you will come here first, – I have no notion when you will arrive – My dinner is coming – and I have only time to say God bless you own best & dearest, & my dear Fanny and Tom. A thousand kisses amongst you all. –

I am
Your ever affectionate Husband

Thos Hood

The Dilkes have not seen the J.H.R's.
The Anniversary dinner of the Literary Fund is shortly. I wonder if Jerdan will be at it.[3]
I bore the sight of L. House very well, till passing the front & looking up at that bedroom window the recollection of so much misery suffered there came over me like a cloud. It is all doing up smart – How beautiful it looked over the Chigwell Hills – but a great deal of timber is cut down in the park & the church stands out bald & ugly.
Bring Wellesley's pamphlet with you.[4]
Give my love to Mrs D – [5] & I hope she will not let herself be worried by humbugs or bugbears. Pray, pray, if you do come be particular about the children.[6] I shall long to get back again. The tray stops me. God bless you. Kind regards to the Major. I am glad my news got first. I suppose it will be in next Athm.[7]

[*Stratford, 23 April 1840*]

MS Bristol Central Library. Published in part in *Memorials* II 76–8. Address: 'Madame Hood / La Rhetorique / Rue St François / à Ostende.' PM: 'STRATFORD/AP 23/1840,' 'D/PAID/23 AP 23/1840.'
1/Presumably they would have betrayed him to his creditors. Longmore was Hood's brother-in-law. Martyn I have not identified.
2/Editor of the *Weekly Dispatch*, founded 1801
3/Hood wonders if Jerdan will attend the Literary Fund anniversary dinner after the scandal of last year, reported on 427.
4/Perhaps W.L. Wellesley *A Word to the Belgians* (1839)
5/Mrs Dore
6/Jane wrote later: 'at a few hours' notice, leaving the dear children in care of our friend here [presumably Mrs Dore], I set off to London in the middle of May ... On my arrival in town, I had to do my best in business matters, which Hood was too ill to do,' *Memorials* II 78–9. Having lost confidence in Baily, Hood resolved to withdraw his works from the publisher's hands. Reynolds, acting as his solicitor, wrote to Baily to this effect on 19 May. On the following day, Baily refused to give the works up. Jane explained the situation later when she wrote: 'On his return to England his Publishers accounts were so incorrect that he resolved to remove his works elsewhere when Mr Bailey retained them *all* on the plea that he had a quarter share of *one* – The "Hoods Own" – instead of a quarter share of the *profits only*,' *Keats Circle* ed. H. E. Rollins (1948) II 471. The situation was made even worse when on 22 May John Follett, one of Hood's creditors, attached the works in

Baily's control. Hood did not learn of the attachment until 18 June. Six days before, his bankruptcy had been officially docketed, and the next day a fiat was issued against him.
7/I do not know what Hood is referring to here.

TO
CHARLES WENTWORTH DILKE

Jane has been busy in a mercantile way – a perfect Tim Linkinwater[1] in petticoats: I have been as useless as Mother Nickleby in trowsers. I have been very low; but how can one have any animal spirits without animal food? Of course I have not fattened, except that some calomel flew to my face and gave it something of the shape of William the Fourth's. I am become a Pythagorean, not only in my diet, but my feelings, and wonder how anyone can eat meat. For instance, Jane has just lunched on a piece of cold beast. I therefore beg leave to thank you all the same for your wish for me at your dinner on Monday, but I don't eat bullock or hog. Not but that some ladies, and even delicate ones, make a 'Long Lane' of their 'red' ones – that is to say, a thoroughfare for the cattle out of Smithfield. But though I am not exactly in Paradise, *my* feeding is more consistent with that of our innocent first parents. Then, for drink, I taste the pure rill, and not the juice of squashed grapes, that Germans have danced in up to their *hocks*. In short, I have left off being carnivorous, and am nice as to my liquids.

Stratford [*May 1840*]

From *Memorials* II 76–7
1/Clerk in Dickens's *Nicholas Nickleby* (1839)

TO
D.A. AGNEW

Sir
In answer to your request for my Autograph, I beg leave to refer you, for *a printed one*, to the pages of the next Number of the New Sporting Magazine

With friendly Compts. to Auld Reekie, Auld Lang Syne, Auld Robin Gray,[1] & the rest of your Aulder men, I am

Sir, Your mo obed^{t} Servt.

Thos: Hood

D.A. Agnew Esqre

8 New South Place / Camberwell New Road / 15 June 1840.

MS Cameron. I have not identified Hood's Scottish correspondent. The address is that of Hood's first London home after leaving the Elliots'.

1 /Title of a poem by Lady Anne Lindsay

TO
RICHARD BENTLEY

Dear Sir
Will you have the goodness to inform me when at the latest it will be likely you will require the new Preface to Tylney Hall?[1]
I am sorry that I could not fulfil my intention of writing an article for your present No. [2] – but imperative demands on my time & indisposition prevented me. I am even seriously doubtful whether an arrangement – otherwise perfectly satisfactory, can now be carried into effect. The cruel position in which I have been placed by Mr Baily, with circumstances thence arising since I saw you will too probably make it necessary for me to accept any engagement which will secure me a sum in hand for an indispensable purpose.[3] I feel that some explanation is due to you – which shall be forthcoming in due time. Nothing less than urgent be assured would cause an alteration in my plans that will be a matter of regret to

Dear Sir
Yours very truly

Thos Hood

8 South Place / Camberwell New Road. / Monday. [*June 1840*]

MS Bodleian. The letter is dated in another hand. Richard Bentley (1794–1871), publisher, partner of Henry Colburn, 1829–32

1 /Hood sold the copyright of *Tylney Hall* to Bentley, who brought out the novel in his standard edition. The new preface is dated July 1840, and the novel was advertised for sale at the beginning of August.

2/Bentley also published *Bentley's Miscellany* (1837–68), to which Hood here refers; he never contributed to the magazine.
3/The detention of her children, referred to below

TO
RICHARD BENTLEY

My dear Sir
In answer to your note you shall at once have the explanation required – trusting to your honour not to mention the circumstances unless released by myself. In the mean Mr. Dilke who has known all my affairs from the first could vouch if necessary for the facts.
There is much more to tell properly, than can be put into writing – but the main fact is that since I saw you my children (for whom I sent) have been detained in Belgium, for some debts owing there – which would have been paid out of the means in Baily's hands. Neither my wife nor myself can return there, both being liable by the Belgian law – & I only ascertained yesterday that our Ambassador had no power to interfere. They must be obtained by process in the Belgian Courts, or the payment of the money (£150). – All my books etc are there too. It was never thought possible that a boy & girl of 5 & 9 years old could be detained – it is not perhaps legal – but they are in the people's power & I am doomed just now to feel how might overcomes right. It has become therefore a matter of strict necessity for me to seek for present money to release my children. Nothing less urgent would have altered my views. The arrangement for the Miscellany was entered upon with perfect good faith on my part, – it would have suited me & I had no other engagement. My fears not my wishes prompted what I wrote to you – indeed I would now rather consider it, as a thing postponed than given up. But it would only make bad worse to deceive you with promises not likely to be fulfilled. Till this heavy anxiety be removed from my mind & the natural effects on health such as mine I feel too sure I could not carry out that arrangement or indeed any other.
It was in reality the anxiety & vexation from this cause which alone prevented by making me ill, your having an article for your present number. I sincerely looked forward to it as the commencement of a connexion likely to be mutually beneficial in no small degree but my course is now painfully imperative. You are now in possession of my exact position; & will see that I have been governed against my will by the tyranny of untoward events. I acknowledge & deeply regret the awkwardness of the position for yourself – but it has been quite involuntary on my

part, & I have had none but the most straightforward intentions. But you will feel as a man & especially if you be a father the nature of the demand upon me. I have given you the earliest notice of them that I could, when other means had failed on which I calculated. – & once more be assured it is a matter of unfeigned regret & disappointment to myself. For these reasons instead of this letter I should have come up to Burlington Street, – in the hope that on consultation we might hit on some scheme to meet the exigency of the case – for instance I would undertake a novel – as well as the articles in the Miscellany – or the intended Sequel to 'Up the Rhine' – if you would make me an advance on them – but I am obliged at present to be very careful of too much bodily fatigue. My most obvious course would be to write some book off hand to bring me a sum – but such a course would necessarily set aside every thing else. I have thus no alternative – however unwelcome – for I did flatter myself that as no mean addition to your host I could make myself useful to your Miscellany, & in return should derive equal advantage from you as an Ally. These were my sincere views, – & I can only say that if you would come forward to my help, you would find them earnestly acted upon by

Dear Sir
Yours very truly

Thos Hood

8 New South Place / Camberwell New Road. [*June 1840*]

MS Bodleian. The letter is dated in another hand. Apparently Hood had made an arrangement to contribute to *Bentley's Miscellany*, but the need to free his children from his Belgian creditors meant that he must have money immediately. Where this came from is not clear, though Hood may have made use of the sum he got from Bentley for the copyright of *Tylney Hall*. According to Jane, writing on 13 August 1840, 'we could not return for the children till about a month ago': *Memorials* II 79.

TO
ALFRED HEAD BAILY

Sir
I have had handed to me your accounts purporting to be made up £5 in my favor I also find in the Cash account to same date the interposition of a sum of £15 a payment which I mean to state most distinctly was never made to me – so much for the amendments in red ink. I can perfectly understand your anxiety to foist up[1] by

any means an apparent balance against me as the only excuse you could have for detaining my property: Even such an amount as you claim if a just one would be disgraceful enough as a plea for keeping the whole of my Books &c. in your hands but I deny your balance and repudiate your accounts – Those accounts will undergo a thorough sifting elsewhere but in the meantime intending to make a public use of them I require to know definitely whether you deliver the said accounts as deliberate and final statements by which you mean to abide. Unless therefore I hear to the contrary within three days from the date of this I shall treat the accounts now furnished as the figures by which your Character for rectitude and Mr. Carty for Clerkship are to stand or fall I am Sir

Yours Thomas Hood – Mr. Alfred Head Baily

10 Adam Street / 31st. July 1840

Transcript in the Public Record Office. Hood is writing from the address of J.H. Reynolds, who was acting as his solicitor. At about the time of this letter Hood came to a publishing arrangement with Henry Colburn, for the latter's *New Monthly Magazine* for August contained the first of a long series of contributions from Hood's pen. He did not cease contributing until September 1843. On 13 August Jane Hood wrote that her husband 'is now engaged to publish with Mr. Colburn, and is writing articles in the " New Monthly Magazine," which are then to be collected in a volume.' Hood interpolated in her letter: 'I have made a capital arrangement with Colburn,' *Memorials* II 79, 80. In the September number of the *New Monthly*, the first of four parts of 'Miss Kilmansegg and her Precious Leg' appeared.

1/Stealthily arrange; the phrase does not occur in NED.

TO
WILLIAM ELLIOT

My dear Doctor,

We were very much disappointed at not seeing you on Monday, but could easily divine the cause; something *akin* to what keeps us from Stratford – except that your time is essential to the lives of others, and mine to my own living. We have, however, been seriously intending to come over: for I felt sure you would be pleased to find me so much improved physically, if not morally, in spite of adverse circumstances – the long run of wet weather for one. I only mention hard work – which, like virtue, brings its own reward – as something besides, that my health has to get *over* – and then the *season* of the year – and yet it seems steadily to improve! Your brother[1] appears to have hit upon some medicine very congenial, if it be not that the very sight of him does me good (the only doubt I have of *your* medical *skill*), for an 'Elliot' has always been one of the best exhibitors[2] to a heart out of order. I will not enter on details, which probably your brother has given; but to me there appears to be a decided change for the better. And in return for the general interest you take in me, you deserve to know that matters are looking up – there is, and will be, a struggle of course; but from every quarter they say that I am writing better than ever, and I get on very comfortably with Colburn. Perhaps you saw my skirmish with B— in the Athenaeum; the exposure of my private affairs was on his part malicious, but being falsely given, has only ended in his own discomfiture and dishonour. He could not answer my charges, and did not, which people will understand.[3] The final settlement of this affair is all that is necessary to clear up my mental weather. For the rest, I may suffer with what is called Society, because, like many others, I do not pretend to be a rich man; but as I never sought the herd, they are welcome to shun me, as they did the bankrupt stag in the Forest of Amiens.[4] After all, 'As you like it,' is the great secret, and I like it well enough as it is.

N.B. I mean to come to Stratford for all this moralising; and as all my complaints have a periodical character, most probably between this 'New Monthly' and a new 'New Monthly;' or from the 24th of this to the 1st of next month. But you had better prepare Willy for my coming in a common-place way, not so melodramatically as when I seemed to have been committing suicide with your assistance.[5]

If I were such a centaur as George is, I would oftener mount myself and trot over to see him; but Willy is much more of a locomotive than I am; what a frisky engine he would be on the Eastern Counties railway?

Dunnie and Jeanie will have grown like two cucumbers into quite another species, and May into a May-pole. Give my love to them all: my own 'population' are very well, and now having filled my half I give up the pen to Jane, that she may write to Mrs. Elliot, to whom please give my kindest remembrances, and say that, having taken again to meat, I am more stoutly than ever,

Yours and hers very truly,

Thomas Hood.

Camberwell, Nov. 19th, 1840.

From *Memorials* II 80–3

1/Dr Robert Elliot lived conveniently near Camberwell, at Denmark Hill to the south.

2/Hood uses the word in its medical sense as indicating one who administers a remedy.

3/Hood initiated this skirmish with Baily which continued through three numbers of *The Athenaeum*

3–17 October 1840, 767, 792, 829. Hood declared in his first statement that he had renounced his connection with Baily 'as religiously as one renounces the devil and all his works.'
4/Should be 'Arden': *As You Like It* 2 i 29ff; Amiens is one of the followers of the exiled duke.
5/When he was being bled by Elliot

TO
HANNAH LAWRANCE

My dear Miss Lawrence
Pray accept my best thanks for your handsome Volumes which from your known research taste and ability will be sure to afford me some very interesting reading as soon as my leisure will permit me such enjoyments. In the mean time my little girl has begun to make acquaintance with the Queens as eagerly as if they were fine 'live ones, in their Birthday plumes.
By an odd coincidence I lately alluded to you in a review of Humphrey's Clock in the Athenaeum, so that to speak annualish, your Books however welcome as Keepsakes were not necessary as Souvenirs.[1]
As regards my return to England – & let me thank you for your kind congratulations – it has probably lengthened my days. Change has visited me as well as any old neighbourhood, only that instead of being built upon, I have been pulled down. My health has been so shattered in foreign parts that it would not be a bad bargain for me to change constitutions even with Spain. A long course of absolute Pythagoreanism & teatotalism, only lately relaxed has shrunk me from an Author to a Pen – and a very bad one to mend. In such fast *go-ahead times* as the present it is my peculiar misfortune to be tormented by *slow* fever – induced by my residence in Flanders – with, from the same cause, a dash of ague in whatever ailment befals me – and when it rains I sympathize with the damp like a salt-basket. On these accounts, I keep house so closely that my most extravagant outgoings do not exceed a journey to town about once in two months.
Otherwise it would give me much pleasure to call in Vincent Terrace[2] – Turks as the inhabitants must be to have conquered Rhodes.
It may happen for you, nevertheless, to come some day in this direction in which case, speaking for 'self & Partner' we shall be most happy to see you. The New Road leads from Camberwell Common to Kennington Ditto – & we are uncommonly near the centre from each. We are sure to be here, or in the vicinity for some time to come because my case requires watching & my friend Dr Elliot

resides on Denmark Hill. Pray present our kind remembrances to your Mama & believe me

My dear Miss Lawrance
Yours very truly

Thos Hood

8 South Place / Camberwell New Road [*November 1840*]

MS Morgan Library. In the course of the letter Hood refers to a recent review by him in *The Athenaeum* 7 November 1840, 887.

1/References to the annuals, *The Keepsake* and the *Literary Souvenir*

2/Hannah Lawrance's address, off Colebrooke Row, Islington, where Lamb had lived. I cannot explain the next sentence.

TO
WILLIAM BRADBURY?

PRIVATE

My dear Sir.
Mr Dilke was here yesterday & told me of what had passed relative to the plates etc in your hands.
I wish you to have as little trouble or annoyance as possible – you ought indeed to have had none – but it is no fault of mine. The manner in which Mr Baily treats your own claim against him is quite in character: – of course you could compel him to pay you but he would never dare to let the transaction come to such an issue. His present attempt seems to me to throw some light on a former one to take the printing of Hood's Own out of your hands.
I should think you would feel satisfied from Mr. Dilke's showing, that Baily has no claim on the property – but if you still have any reluctance to part with it to my order, I shall be quite satisfied with the following arrangement – that you shall lodge the plates & blocks etc somewhere, *out of the City*, so that they should not be attached by the same Creditor as before – which may probably be attempted.[1] I should say Moxon – who offered to hold my stock before would do so by the blocks etc. Or you may know some party who would take charge of them – till you feel yourself secure in giving them up. This arrangement it seems to me would be satisfactory to both parties. But perhaps you are already satisfied on the subject of Bailys proprietorship in Hoods Own. For the rest, his mock balance is only £68 –

which if correct is amply covered by the stock he has in Cornhill. But the truth is, I do not owe him a shilling – as can be proved from his own accounts. Indeed he was so hardly put to it to get up even this apparent balance – that in his Midsummer account he inserted a debit of Cash £15 *which I never had* – as I can prove from documents. Indeed if correct – being charged in October – it ought to have appeared in the preceding Xmas account. Considering that these gross attempts all admit of *proofs* – the infatuation of the perpetration seems to me truly Brobdignagdian – and I cannot help thinking that Baily must be the personage mentioned by Lord Chesterfield as 'Folly at full length.'[2] Seriously if you knew all the wanton injury & suffering inflicted on me by that scoundrel you would not only think that I ought to have redress but that he ought to meet with punishment – But he is now nearly ripe for a full exposure, at the hands of

Dear Sir
Yours very truly

Thos Hood

After this week I shall not be at the address I have given you, being on the point of removal.

8 South Place / Camberwell New Road, / Monday [November 1840]

MS UCLA. On 20 May 1840 Baily had given instructions to Bradbury and Evans, the printers, not to give up to Hood the stereotype plates, the woodblocks, or any part of Hood's stock in their possession. In October they refused to give up the plates to Baily himself. This letter seems to refer to this refusal, so I suggest that the recipient is William Bradbury. I do not know what happened to the plates ultimately.

1/A reference to John Follett's attaching of Hood's property in the hands of Baily, on 22 May 1840 (431 n 6).

2/Chesterfield, 'On the Picture of Richard Nash'

TO
UNKNOWN CORRESPONDENT

I got the printers to remove all my property out of the city – which they have done – now it cannot be attached.

[Camberwell] November 1840

Cutting from a dealer's catalogue at UCLA. The note seems to refer to the substance of the previous letter.

TO
CHARLES DICKENS

My dear Dickens
Your kind letter arrived very opportunely, when I was laid up in bed, for it served to give me great pleasure in the midst of great pain. I am confined, as you know, to slops, but of course had committed some excess, – having that Teatotal Gout – the Rheumatism – in my foot.
As to the Review – as in the Grand Reviews at Coblenz – the beauty of the country that was passed over was a sufficient reward.[1] That it was written with a kindly feeling towards you, is true: for books which put us in better humour with the world in general must naturally incline us toward the Author in particular. (So we love Goldsmith for his Vicar of Wakefield) – Add something, for the sympathies of the Bruderschaft, – and that I felt you had been unfairly used in a certain Critique – & you will have the whole Animus. Yet I was critical too, & found all the faults I could pick.
My opinion of your Works is a deliberate one: – and in spite of an early prejudice that Boz was all Buzz. Some illchosen extracts which reached me abroad, with the rumour that one of the Prominences was a stage coachman & the other a Boots (what grammar!) led me to think that the Book was only a new strain of Tom-&-Jerryism – which is my aversion. So strong was this notion, that I did not properly enjoy the Work itself on a first perusal, or detect that 'soul of goodness in things evil'[2] the goodness of Pickwickedness. I afterwards read it several times with encreased delight & finally packed off the whole set to a friend, a Prussian Officer, but English by birth & feeling, that he might enjoy its Englishness – to my taste a firstrate merit.
Go on, and prosper! – and I wish it most sincerely, though no man in England has so legitimate a right to envy you, for *my* circulation is so bad that I can hardly keep my hands warm, and I wish I could only get *one* Subscriber, gratis, to *my* Periodical – an Aguish Remittent. I wish Baily had a copy of it, with the rest of Hood's Own! – Amen.
I am lodging out here partly for the sake of the air & partly to be near a skilful medical friend who is 'watching the case.' But some happy day, Lord knows when, I will certainly come, Lord knows how, & see you in Devonshire.[3] I drop the Terrace, because to *me* you are a county or two distant, so many things as weather, health & leisure must concur, to allow such expeditions. I have not been to Dilke's for months. Indeed as a domestic Author, I beat those of Douglas & the Iliad –

Home[4] – Homer – Homest. – and if ever I go mad – (as you did)[5] – I feel persuaded that I shall fancy myself some piece of household furniture – most probably a chair. In the meantime I heartily grasp & shake the hand you autographically held out to me, & embrace your friendship with my whole heart. A friendship that promises to endure, if from nothing better, thro the mere difficulty of falling in, & consequently out, with each other. And yet a better friendship than that of the Society of Friends, who are not on speaking terms at their meetings.
By the bye the last time I saw you, I was on a very happy errand, & you of course on a pleasurable one – mine to Ostend to fetch home my dear Children – yours to Ramsgate or Margate – the two steamers paddling for some time, side by side.[6] May all our approaches be under as happy auspices.
Should you ever take an airing into Surrey, you would be sure to find about 100 yards nearer London than the Red Cap, at Camberwell Green, a Mr. Robinson's house in Union Row – and you would be certain to find me in it – & to receive literally such hospitality as *a Country Mouse* can afford – viz bread & cheese. The last friend that dined with us had the Canary.[7]
Pray present my Respect to Mrs. Dickens, & believe me Bozitively

Yours ever very truly

Thos Hood

C Dickens Esqre

2 Union Row, / High Street / Camberwell [December 1840][8]

MS Huntington. Published by Whitley HLQ 392–4. Charles Dickens (1812–70) had already published *Sketches by Boz* (1836), *Pickwick Papers* (April 1836–November 1837, monthly parts), *Oliver Twist* (February 1837–April 1839, in *Bentley's Miscellany*), *Nicholas Nickleby* (April 1838–October 1839, monthly parts), and *Master Humphrey's Clock* (April 1840–November 1841, weekly parts). This last incorporated *The Old Curiosity Shop* and *Barnaby Rudge*. Dickens also edited *Bentley's Miscellany* (January 1837–January 1839). After a severe illness in the autumn of 1841, he sailed for America, 4 January 1842. The result was *American Notes* (October 1842). *Martin Chuzzlewit* appeared in monthly parts (January 1843–July 1844), *A Christmas Carol* at the end of 1843 and *The Chimes* at the end of 1844. Dickens set out for Italy in July 1844. He paid a swift visit to London in December and returned in June 1845, after Hood's death.

1/Hood reviewed volume 1 of *Master Humphrey's Clock* in *Athenaeum* 7 November 1840; Dickens was moved by Hood's appreciation. The unfair critique to which Hood refers may have been that in *Fraser's Magazine* April 1840.

2/ *Henry V* 4 i 4

3/Dickens lived at 1 Devonshire Terrace, Regent's Park, across the river from Hood at Camberwell.

4/John Home *Douglas* (1756)

5/Dickens denied the rumour of his madness in the Preface to *Master Humphrey's Clock*; Hood welcomed the denial in his review.
6/Hood brought his children home towards the end of June.
7/Either wine or pet bird
8/Hood has moved to a new address in Camberwell.

1841

TO
THOMAS NOON TALFOURD?

My dear Sir.
The weather frightened me – having lately lost some fifteen ounces of blood from the lungs – or I should do myself the pleasure of calling upon you instead of writing. But the renewal of the Great Question and the declared opposition of Mr Warburton[1] urge me to offer any little help within my power. As the owner of a number of copyrights, – and a sufferer by lax notions of the rights of Authors, & of the nature of literary property, – I have some claim to be heard. If you think then, that a Petition to the following effect would be useful to the cause, perhaps you will have the kindness to furnish it with the requisite formalities & then to present it in my name.
Showeth

That yr Petitioner instead of disposing of his Copyrights has retained the majority of them in his own hands. That the said Copyrights are chiefly under six years old. That yr Pr has never sold or assigned any portion of the said Copyrights to his late Publishers, Messrs Baily & Co of Cornhill.

That nevertheless the said Messrs Baily & Co have virtually appropriated the whole of the said Copyrights by detaining all the stereotype plates & woodcut blocks, belonging to the same as well as all copies of the said works that were on hand.

That as regards one Work called Hood's Own a pretended one quarter share was made the pretext for appropriating the other three fourths of the property. That the plea for keeping the rest of the works – twelve in number – was a false balance of about £60[2] – whereas the accounts, which are full of one sided errors and omissions, have been examined by a competent accountant who is ready to vouch that a correct balance would place at least £50 to the credit of yr Petitioner.

That yr Pr believes that the said Publishers must have been greatly supported comforted and encouraged in such appropriation by the anomalous Laws of Literary Property, which, treating it as neither freehold nor copyhold, must tempt the unscrupulous to lay hold.

That your Petitioner humbly conceives that his works are as much his own, &

ought to have as much protection, as if they were iron-works, alum works, water works, gas works, or any other works whatever.

That yr Pr therefore prays that the Bill introduced by Mr Serjeant Talfourd may pass into a law

etc etc.[3]

I send you, at the end, a *brief* of the particulars, that you may have the *facts* – which I am ready, if necessary, to prove and illustrate before a Committee. For after all what has Baily done, but anticipated the universal pirate – forestalled the time when Hood's Own would be Any Body's Own – & started a few lengths ahead of our precocious Executor in Cheapside? He has only acted with Tegg-rity instead of integrity.[4] As for Mr Warburton, he would swap Pegasus any day for the Trojan Horse, & then not for a Homeric Relic, but to cut up into timber. I wonder what are his opinions on the Corn Laws – there are certainly gentlemen in your House who set their faces against Cheap Bread – but even at the author's expence are decidedly for Cheap Books – as if it were desirable to see the public like a misshapen dwarf, – with a little belly & an enormous head.

You will, I know, acquit me of any selfish motives in urging a personal case. But I feel strongly that Literature and its professors have had more than their share of public neglect & the world's contumely – that Authorship has been treated like a slave ship, & a writer, as a black-&-white fellow somewhere between a buckra[5] man & a nigger. There is now I believe or was lately under repair at the public expence a certain splendid Mansion formerly conferred on a celebrated military Hero & his descendants as a national acknowledgment of his services & a perpetual memento of his brilliant victories. Literature, too, has had its achievements which have shed an everlasting lustre on our country – but where its Blenheim – its Strathfieldsaye?[6] Far be it from me to begrudge either Duke his Palace & Estate – but fain, fain, fain, would I see only a cottage & a paddock entailed on some distinguished Author – & held by the honorary tenure of delivery, yearly, a play, or still better a yearly volume (it need not be the Comic Annual) to the Sovereign. But alas! the greatest honour ever conferred on an Author – a peerage – was bestowed on Bubb Doddington – and then not for writing his Life![7]

The Blue Ribbons of Literature are as mere juggles as those which come out of the mouth of a Conjurer – Even the very few appointments hitherto allotted as its portion are already going or gone. The Examinership of Plays has passed from an Author & Dramatist to an Actor[8] – & my mind misgives me that the Laureateship at the next vacancy, may fall to a Portrait Painter.[9]

Even public Compliments, on which Authors have a strong moral lien, are witheld from them. Considering who are the parties destined to profit by their remains – it would be but a suitable acknowledgment – a becoming expression of that sort of gratitude, which consists in 'a lively sense of future favours' – were the Company of Stationers to present their Freedom in a golden box to Messrs Wordsworth Southey Campbell Moore Rogers & a few others. But in spite of 1800 Christmases that Boxing Day has yet to come.

So much for the honours paid to a literary man, during his life – if it can be called life, that so often has hardly a living. He writes for bread – & gets it short weight. For money – & receives the wrong change. For the present – & he is pirated. For the future – and his Children are disinherited for his pains. At last he sickens, as he well may, & can write no more. He makes his will – but as regards any literary property, might as well die intestate. His eldest Son is his heir – but the Row[10] administers. And so he dies – a beggar perhaps – with the world in his Debt. Being poor of course – he is buried with less ceremony than Cock Robin. Had he been rich enough he might have bought 'snug lying in the Abbey'[11] of the Dean & Chapter of Westminster: – but even then, true to the same style of treatment, they would have put him – were he the greatest & best of Poets, – where the mother puts her least & worst of Children – namely into a *Corner!*

There is a sketch for you – not at all exaggerated – for our Country is illustriously disgraced by the biographies of its literary men. For the least of us are men – but all your Warburtons & Co want is to have our brains at a cheap rate, as if they were sucking at the heads of so many shrimps!

The plea, for cheapness, *at the author's expence* is a disgraceful one. Think what a placard, it would be for the national Window – to have written up in the largest & brightest of Letters

Great Bargains in Books – Unexampled Distress of the Manufacturers!!!

This is a mercantile view – but there are authors by profession – men who write for bread – & why should it be brown? Even those who write for fame, may have famous appetites of another kind – & why should they not have famous dinners? Because their property is in *boards*, – not in *planks?*

For my own part I set a very high value on the right – founded on common principles of justice – the right of making a testament & disposing of my Works hereafter as now, according to my own will. Why should lapse of time, which confirms other proprietors in their possessions oust me from mine? – Possibly I might like to leave my copyrights to some learned or scientific Body. – perhaps to bequeath them to one Publisher in preference to another, – for instance Mr Colburn instead of Mr Catnach – Messrs Longman & Co. – instead of Mss Stockdale.[12] But

even that power is denied to me. An Author is worse off than an alien – or labours under greater than Jewish disabilities.[13] He is called one of the community – but who will dare to say that he is treated 'like one of the Family?'
In the History of England there is a case which has always been reckoned a very hard one – but which strictly resembles that of an Author suffering under the law of Copyright. I allude to Sir Walter Raleigh – & the iniquitous sentence by force of which *14 years afterwards* – the old term of copyright – his head was cut off from his posterity.
But I am trespassing on your valuable time – & have no doubt come to the end of your patience, as well as of my own paper – and besides *you* do not require either suggestions or urging from

My dear Sir Yours ever truly

Thos Hood.

2 Union Row. / High Street / Camberwell / Tuesday. [*January 1841*]

MS Cameron. Talfourd (1795–1854), author, lawyer, and politician, was granted leave to bring in his copyright bill again on 27 January 1841. Thanks to the powerful eloquence of Macaulay and 'the attractions of dinner' (Wordsworth's phrase), the bill was defeated on the second reading nine days later: *Letters of William and Dorothy Wordsworth: The Later Years* (Oxford 1939) III 1065. In the summer Talfourd lost his seat and the copyright cause was taken up by Mahon.

1/Henry Warburton (1784?–1858), philosophical radical, supporter of the Anti-Corn Law League
2/'70' crossed through
3/Talfourd had included an earlier, less personal petition by Hood in his *Three Speeches*, published by Moxon (1840).
4/Thomas Tegg (1776–1845), bookseller and publisher, celebrated for cheap reprints, abridgments, and the distribution of remainders. His address was 73 Cheapside. Tegg wrote against Talfourd's copyright proposals (1837, 1840).
5/White
6/Blenheim is the seat of the Duke of Marlborough and Strathfieldsaye that of the Duke of Wellington.
7/George Bubb Dodington (1691–1762) was created Baron Melcombe for political services in 1761. His *Diary* was published in 1784.
8/George Colman the younger was examiner from 1824 to 1836. He was succeeded by Charles Kemble, who was in turn followed by his son John Mitchell Kemble. The last was appointed on 24 February 1840.
9/In fact, the Laureateship passed in 1843 from Southey to Wordsworth.
10/Paternoster Row, home of booksellers
11/Sheridan *The Rivals* 5 iii
12/Catnach published broadsides and chapbooks at Seven Dials, and Stockdale published *inter alia* Harriet Wilson's *Memoirs* (1825).
13/A bill to allow Jews to hold corporate offices was introduced 9 February 1841; the bill would benefit in particular David Salomons (1797–1873), as yet not entitled to serve as alderman in the city

of London: his name recurs in Hood's biography. The bill was read a second time, 10 March, but was defeated in the Lords, 11 June. A Jewish Disabilities Removal Act was finally passed in 1845. Salomons became alderman in 1847, Lord Mayor of London in 1855, and a baronet in 1869.

TO
CHARLES WENTWORTH DILKE

No K this month. I was too ill to finish it. The long run of wet floored me at the last. A sample of my Belgian breakdowns.[1]

[*Camberwell, January 1841*]

From Dilke I 55–6. Hood is referring to the fact that he did not contribute an instalment of 'Miss Kilmansegg and Her Precious Leg' to NMM January 1841.

TO
OCTAVIAN BLEWITT

Mr. Hood presents his Comp[ts] to Mr Blewitt, and begs to acknowledge the receipt of his note and the enclosure, – & will forward a letter for the Committee in the course of tomorrow – (Friday)

[*Camberwell*] *Jany. 14. 1841.*

MS Royal Literary Fund. Published by Lane KSJ 57. Octavian Blewitt (1810–84) was Secretary of the Literary Fund from 1839 until his death. The letter referred to follows immediately. When Hood's financial circumstances became very difficult (see 450 n 8 below), Richard Harris Barham and Dilke applied for help to the Literary Fund on Hood's behalf. However, the following letter shows that Hood felt able to refuse it proudly. He had to swallow his pride a few months later.

TO
THE COMMITTEE OF THE LITERARY FUND

Gentlemen,
I have to acknowledge the receipt of a letter from your Secretary, which has deeply affected me.
The adverse circumstances to which it alludes are unfortunately too well known – from their public announcement in the Athenaeum by my precocious Executor and officious Assignee.[1] But I beg most emphatically to repeat that the disclosures so

drawn from me were never intended to bespeak the world's pity or assistance. Sickness is too common to Humanity, and Poverty too old a Companion of my Order, to justify such an appeal. The revelation was merely meant to show, when taunted with 'my Creditors', that I had been striving in humble imitation of an illustrious literary example[2] to satisfy all claims upon me – and to account for my imperfect success. I am too proud of my profession to grudge it some suffering. I love it still, as Lord Byron loved England, 'with all its faults',[3] and I should hardly feel as one of the Fraternity if I had not my portion of 'the Calamities of Authors.'[4] More fortunate than many, I have succeeded not only in getting into print, but ocasionally in getting out of it, and surely, a man who had overcome such formidable difficulties may hope & expect to get over the commonplace one of procuring bread and cheese.

I am writing seriously, Gentlemen, although in a cheerful tone, partly natural & partly intended to relieve some of your kindly concern on my account. Indeed my position at present is an easy one compared with that of some eight months ago, when out of heart, and out of health, – helpless, spiritless, sleepless, childless. I have now a home in my own country, and my little ones sit at my hearth. I smile sometimes, & even laugh. For the same benign Providence that gifted me with the power of amusing others, has not denied me the ability of entertaining myself. Moreover as to mere worldly losses I profess a cheerful Philosophy which can jest 'though China fall'[5] and for graver troubles, a Christian faith that consoles and supports me even in walking through something like the Valley of the Shadow of Death.

My embarrassments and bad health are of such standing that I am become, as it were, seasoned. For the last six years I have been engaged in the same struggle, without seeking, receiving, or requiring, any pecuniary assistance whatever. My pen & pencil procured not only enough for my own wants, but to form a surplus besides – a sort of Literary Fund of my own, which at this moment is 'doing good by stealth'[6] to a person, – not exactly of learning or genius, – but whom, according to the example of your excellent Society, I will forbear to name. To provide for similar wants there are the same means & resources – the same head, & heart, & hands, – the same bad health – and may it only last long enough! – in short the same crazy vessel for the same foul weather but I have not thought yet of hanging out my ensign upside down.[7]

Fortunately since manhood I have been dependant solely on my own exertions – a condition which has exposed & enured me to vicissitude; whilst it has nourished a pride which will fight on, & has yet some retrenchments to make ere it surrender.

I have now Gentlemen, described circumstances & feelings, which will explain and must excuse my present course. The honourable and liberal manner in which you have entertained an application – that a friendly delicacy concealed from me[8] – is acknowledged with the most ardent gratitude. Your welcome sympathy is valued in proportion to the very great comfort & encouragement it affords me. Your kind wishes for my better health – my greatest want – I accept and thank you for with my whole heart – but I must not & cannot retain your money, which at the first safe opportunity will be returned. I really do not feel myself to be yet a proper object for your bounty. And should I ever become so, I fear that such a crisis will find me looking elsewhere – to the earth beneath me for a final rest, and to the heaven above me for final justice.

Pray excuse my trespassing at such length on your patience, and believe that I am with the utmost respect

Gentlemen

Your most obliged & grateful Servant

Thos Hood

2 Union Place / High Street / Camberwell [15 January 1841]

MS Royal Literary Fund. Published by Dilke I 58–60. The letter is annotated: 'Mr. Thomas Hood / returning the Grant of £50 / Voted Jany 11. 1841 / Recd Feb. 10th 1841. / Registrar.'

1/A.H. Baily in *Athenaeum*, 10 October 1840, 792

2/The example of Sir Walter Scott who in January 1826, after the failure of his publishing connections, 'resolved not to become a bankrupt, but to carry on the business for the benefit of his creditors,' DNB.

3/Byron, 'Beppo' xlvii, quoting Cowper, 'The Task' II 206

4/The title of a work by Isaac D'Israeli (1812)

5/Pope, 'Moral Essays' II 268

6/The same, 'Epilogue to the Satires' 136

7/As a sign of distress. Compare Hood's last letter (686).

8/The application had been made by R.H. Barham, whose testimony was confirmed by Dilke. The latter wrote that Hood 'has been for months in extreme ill health, & that about ten days since he was so bad that for many hours his life was in danger. For some months too he has been in great pecuniary difficulties [and] I can certify that within these few days, he has been in want of even a few shillings:' K.J. Fielding 'Hood and the Royal Literary Fund' *Notes and Queries* December 1953, 534.

TO
UNKNOWN CORRESPONDENT

I shall finish Miss Kilmansegg this month. It is *not* her brother who is come over as Envoy from the King of Hanover.

I am Dear Sir Yours very truly

Thos Hood

[*Camberwell, January 1841*]

MS Rylands. The fourth and last part of 'Miss Kilmansegg' appeared in NMM, February 1841. I have not traced the envoy, but Professor John Clubbe, in the notes to his edition of Hood's *Selected Poems* (Cambridge, Mass., 1970) 362–3, discusses the associations of the 'Hanoverian Kielmanseggs' with the English court.

TO
CHARLES WENTWORTH DILKE

Dear Dilke,
You will be glad to hear – that I have killed her at last, instead of her killing me. I don't mean Jane, but Miss Kilmansegg; and as she liked pomp, there will be twelve pages at her funeral. She is now screwing in at Beaufort House; and being a happy release for all parties – you will conclude it is a relief to me, especially as I come in for all she is worth. Love to all, and no more news from

Yours very truly,

T. Hood.

[*Camberwell, January 1841*]

From Dilke I 56. Hood refers in the letter to Beaumont House, where NMM was printed. The last part of 'Miss Kilmansegg and Her Precious Leg' was published in NMM February 1841.

TO
WILLIAM ELLIOT

Dear Doctor,
I am able at last to sit down to write a few lines and report progress. For, at last, I have killed her, instead of her killing me; not my wife, but Miss Kilmansegg, who

died very hard, for I found it difficult to get into the tone and story again after two months' interruption.

I am pretty well again, and, as a proof, walked to town and back yesterday with Tom and Fanny, but feel to-day as if I had for the second time been learning to walk, which had become a strange exercise to me. But I hope to put myself on my feet, if this weather should continue. Now for news.

You will be gratified to hear that, without any knowledge of it on my part, the Literary Fund (the members of the Committee having frequently inquired about my health, and the B— Business, of Dilke), unanimously voted me £50, the largest sum they give, and, setting aside their standing rules, to do it without my application. I, however, returned it (though it would have afforded me some ease and relief), but for many and well-weighed reasons.

I am, however, all the better for the offer, which places me in a good position. It was done in a very gratifying and honourable manner, and I am the first who has said '*no.*' But I am in good spirits, and hope to get through all my troubles as independently as heretofore.

We have much more comfortable lodgings, and the busses pass the door constantly, being in the high-road 50 or 100 yards townward of the Red Cap, at the Green. I have a room to myself, which will be worth £20 a-year to me, – for a little disconcerts my nerves.

Jane, if not literary, is littery, – in the midst of two years 'Times,' and 'Chronicles,' and sixty volumes of 'New Monthlys,' cutting out extracts towards a book of Colburn's.[1] Pray offer this as her excuse for not writing to Mrs. E—. I know of no other news of the literary kind, save that Lady C.B—[2] is in the sanctuary (for debt) at Holyrood. We all send our loves to you all. If the weather lasts, I shall hope to come over some day to see whether Dunnie and Jeanie have learned to cry yet. Jane is not over well (if there be such a state), for she has had a great deal of fatigue lately, the moving being in a hurry. The rest well, or weller. Jane will have some small adventures to tell Mrs. Elliot when they meet. I shall only say that one was at a Court of Requests, and the other at the House of Correction.[3] God bless you all,

From, dear Doctor,
Yours ever, very truly,

Thos. Hood.

2, Union Row, High Street, Camberwell, / Feb. 1, 1841.

From *Memorials* II 86–8.

1/Book unidentified

2/Perhaps Lady Charlotte Bury (1775-1861), novelist

3/I have not tracked down Jane's adventures.

TO
PRINCE ALBERT

May it please Your Royal Highness,

The greatest literary honour that can befal a poem is its translation into a foreign language, particularly the German. That such a distinction had been conferred on any verses of mine has only just been made known to me by the receipt of a volume from Bromberg, with a request to me, to forward the copy, which accompanies this, to its high destination.

Under other circumstances I should have shrunk from such an intrusion; but being thus unexpectedly brought under your Princely notice, let me crave permission to offer the respectful homage and loyal congratulations of the English author of 'Eugene Aram.'

I have the honour to be, &c.,

Thomas Hood.

[*Camberwell, April 1841*]

From *Memorials* II 93. Albert of Saxe-Coburg (1819–61) married Queen Victoria in February 1840. For the contents of Hood's letter see 456ff.

TO
PHILIP DE FRANCK

Tim, says he, I thought you had hung up your hat, says he, and in fact *I* have nearly done so, once or twice, on the everlasting peg!

Long as it may seem to you, dear Franck, since I have written, the time has been short enough for all I have had to do in it. I do not remember ever having so many events crammed into the same space. Between law, literature, and illness, I have been living in such a hurry that, often and often, for repose of body and mind, I have wished myself fishing again, with the other 'chubby' fellow, on the banks of the quiet Lahn; so I have thought of you, Johnny, if I have not thrown a line at you, for which I have always wanted either leisure, or health, or spirits; for it were ungracious to write merrily for the public, and vent the blue devils on my private letters. Moreover I have had so little of pleasant to communicate; but I will waste no more time, or space, on explanations. We really have not time to play at cribbage; and Jane, I suspect, has quite forgotten how to 'take her three.' I suppose she told you of the serious attack I had at Stratford; since then I have had two attacks, one a bad one, for I lost altogether about fifteen ounces: indeed I feel sure another month in Belgium would have done for me.

Ostend and the sea-air, are healthy enough in summer, but the rest of the year it is an unwholesome place, especially in the spring. The easterly winds, which then prevail, bring the malaria from Walcheren, and the Dutch swamps. It is ascertained that if you have once been affected by malaria, it will give an agueish and intermitting character to your future complaints. Of this I am a living instance, for I have regular bad days (Tuesday and Friday), with an extreme sympathy with wet weather, when I *give* like an old salt basket; this pleasant tendency I shall most likely enjoy for the rest of my days.

But the English air has so braced the fibres, that the blood-spitting now stops at once; whereas in Belgium it kept returning every second or third day. But mine is a complicated case, and there is affection of the heart. Luckily I am excellently off for advice, as Dr. Elliot's brother, who is also a physician, resides within a quarter of a mile, and visits me two or three times a week to watch the case; if not cured, I think the progress of the disease is stopped. Camberwell is the best air I could have.

Oh! Johnny, after all my Utopian drinking schemes of London porter, and sherry, I have not drunk a glass of wine for twelve months, and as for porter, have been disa*pint*ed of even a pint of England's entire!!! not even a glass of small single x, vulgarly called 'swipes.' For *four months* I never tasted animal food! Zounds! as I used to say on cattle days,[1] one thing would now make my misfortunes complete – to be tossed by an ungrateful beast of a bullock!

But I have now returned to beef and mutton, and how delicious they are here! What a taste of the fresh green English pasture! None of your German 'bif sticks,' with no more gravy in them than walking sticks, but real rumpsteaks out of Smithfield oxen, that have never ploughed or dragged a cart (don't you call it the *speise cart?*), juicy as the herbage, and done to a turn on the gridiron by 'neat-handed Phillis.'[2] Jane and I are just going to have one for supper on purpose to tantalise you; can't you fancy it in your land of fried saddleflaps?[3] You would like a bit I guess, even *after the old lady* (you remember the old lady and the bit of brawn), but I won't set you against your apple soup and goose sausages; so no more about

English suppers, or all the other good things in this land of untrussed plum puddings. Glad am I to be back in it! For your sake I will not regret Germany, but I do bitterly repent having staid so long in Belgium; it was a serious loss of time, health, and money.

I am now engaged to write some 'Rhymes for the Times,'[4] and then think of a two volume novel. Afterwards if I get strong enough, I shall begin a new series of the 'Comic Annual.' I have never been able to send you my book called 'Up the Rhine,' it has been reprinted in English at Leipsic, and is sold on the Rhine I understand; some day I must send you a box. I suppose 'to Hamburg' will be the best way. My literary reception on my return has been very gratifying. They say I am as well as – or better than – ever.

By the bye, I made one or two articles out of your sporting information, especially the Pirsch Wagening, and had the drawings engraved.[5] You shall have them also. Didn't you enjoy Pickwick? It is so very English! I felt sure you would. Boz is a very good fellow, and he and I are very good friends.

So much for literary news, and now for domestic. My health requiring me to live very quietly, and regularly, we are no gayer than at Coblenz. But then for the soberness indoors what a bustle without! London was always a place pre-eminent for business, to which is now added *bussiness*. *Buss* (plural *busses*) is the short for omnibus,[6] which is anything but a *short* stage, for it carries twelve inside and four out. We live on the high road, – fancy some fifty of these vehicles running backwards and forwards all day long. The same in the other suburbs. A buss goes as fast, Tim, as ten droskys,[7] and will take you three or four miles for sixpence, which is cheaper riding than at Berlin. To be sure, omnibusses, I suspect, kill horses, but the droskys kill time! Everything in England goes at a pace unknown abroad; I think even the clocks and watches! The very butchers seem riding trotting matches against time. When I first came to England I thought everybody's horse was running away. But there is a vast increase of smoking shops since I left, and that may eventually make us slower. Well, it may be a cockney taste, but I like Lunnon, where everything is to be had for money, and *money is to be made*, which gives it some advantage over even cheap places. Besides, living quietly as we do, positively we do not spend more than we did abroad, where some things are cheaper, but others are dearer than in England. And then the tax (universally levied on the English) brings the countries to a par. The English I think are finding it out. I have tried to open their eyes. As to myself, I scarcely go to town above once a month – we are about three miles from St. Paul's, so that it is a walk for the children, and then we buss back, after a stroll to look at the shops, which are as good as an Exhibition. Very rarely I dine out – they dine too late for me at seven, and a cold ride through night air lays me up for a month. I am grown, Tim, quite an old man, and an invalid for good, and am as thin as two Wildeganses. Jane is thinner, and not so strong, but is not like me a teetotaller. '*Dam* my blood,' as I say to the doctor, when I want it *stopped* – I wonder where it all comes from! I seem to be like those little red worms they bait with for gudgeon, with only blood and skin. And for all my temperance nobody gives *me* a medal! One hot evening last summer as I walked home I could have murdered an old fish-woman who stood drinking a pot of porter *out of the cool pewter!* why couldn't she drink it in the tap-room, or at the bar, out of my sight? I fully expect next dog-days[8] to have the Hydrophobia. But enough of myself. Have you heard yet in your remote out-of-the-way parts of the Daguerreotype?[9] How I wish by some such process I could get a picture of us all – the family group just as we are – to send you; then you would have me quite as ill-looking as my portrait, and dressed for warmth in a pea jacket and blue trowsers (my Ostend boat-costume). Jane as usual, but looking rather less puzzled than when she had to contend with foreign money and Germany cookery. Don't you perceive it? Fanny tall and fair, Tom tall and dark, a good deal like a squirrel without a tail. He has fagged very hard at his books with his Ma till he can master the fairy work of 'Midsummer's Night's Dream,' and is particularly delighted with Bottom the weaver. It's very funny to hear him reading to himself, and laughing. Having some dim notion of mythology, he stopped short in the middle of a frisk to ask, 'Is there a god of romps?' Fanny is very literary too, so that I have two critics, of ten and six years of age. I have been writing to prove that the rum and *tobacco* that Robinson Crusoe *drank* for his ague would have poisoned him,[10] whereupon Tom told me that if I killed Robinson Crusoe, *he wouldn't praise my works!* The other day he talked of a lady in Italics (hysterics), and at cards, called out 'now, we must make a puddle!" (*i.e.* a *pool*). He and Fanny are full of odds and ends, fairy tales, and plays, and travels, and in their games it all comes working out like beer from a barrel. We are all going to the play on Saturday, and shall have, I expect, plenty of *after-pieces*[11] in consequence. Tom knows something of Scripture too, for we have a figure of Joan of Arc, and he says she is the wife of *Noah* of *Ark*.

As to the books, in the beginning I thought that you had perhaps drawn up a manual of Infantry manoeuvres, then that the Princes at Antonin had edited some work on hunting, or fishing, and next that your father had composed some rules for the management of large families. Jane would have it that you had written a play for the Bromberg theatricals, and Fanny guessed that you had written a novel, something like Charlotte and Werter. In short we supposed a dozen different works from as many authors, even going so far as to imagine that Wildegans had been putting into verse his 'Recollections of the Rhine.'[12] Even the sight of the book did not set me right, for I exclaimed 'Oh! Colonel G—'s book,' but 'I thought a lie.'[13] And now how can I express my delight at knowing the whole truth? Jane says I looked as if I was turned to red and white with pleasure! I am sure she turned from red and white to all red, and looked as happy as if I had been transported instead of translated. But the next moment I was horrified, for I saw your name, 'Von Franck,' as one of the translators! No fear had I on account of my friend Mr. Rühe, his habits qualified him for the work, but 'odds triggers, and blades!' (as Bob Acres says)[14] a Lieutenant of the 19th Infanterie regiment! Oh! Jane! (here I fairly groaned to think of it), Oh! Jane! We know from Dr. Weitershausen's book what sort of work a *Prussian soldier* will make of poetry! Zounds! he will put Eugene Aram into 'parade breeches.' Yes, he will make him *march* up and down (see verse 7) '*rechtsum und linksum*,' the bludgeon will be the stick of a *heerpauk*, and the booty regularly packed in the *tornistor*. Confound him! it will be no more like Eugene Aram than Commis-brod[15] to muffins and crumpets, – all Brown Tommy and Brown Bess![16] I actually cried *dry*, for I was too shocked to shed tears at the picture.

But this comes, said I, of your young whiskered Sword-Blades that sigh so for war, and because it is peace, and no other butchery stirring, they must go and murder Eugene Aram, as well as Daniel Clarke![17] For he knows, the *Blut Egel*, that in spite of all his swagger and curling his moustachios, there is not going to be any '*Krieg*,' except, perhaps, between the New Zealanders and the Esquimaux. And sure enough when I looked into the German version, in the very beginning, I found the game of cricket turned into *Ball Spiel;* which I suppose means playing with bullets or cannon balls, or as we call it, Ball-Practice. If I had understood German, that confounded military verse would have deprived me of all courage to read further; but luckily I recollected Mr. Rühe, who would make the matter more fit to be read by *civil*ised people. He had not been educating his ear for rhythm, and musical verses by manufacturing and proving muskets, carbines, and blunderbusses. A '*Neisse*' way of getting a *nice* ear for harmony! He is not a man of blood (as the Quakers call soldiers) and will not make every verse like a '*blut-würst*,' as if it had been written in East India, namely at *Barrack*-pore. He, Mr. Rühe, will know better than to make Eugene Aram a blue and red usher at the military school in Berlin, just because Von Franck was drilled there, and, what is better, he will make the repentant murderer read his Bible instead of his 'Scharnhorst,'[18] or 'Astor on Fortifications.' He will model the verse on something more musical and varied than that everlasting Rub-a-dub-dub below the walls of Ehrenbreitstein. In short, thank Heaven, Mr. Rühe will *translate*, and not *recruit* me into the German service; and leave me to be tried by a jury of critics instead of a court-martial! Such were my misgivings when I saw your name in the muster-roll (I beg your pardon, the title page), though Jane, from her dealings with French money in Belgium, thought at first it was the price of the book in francs. When I explained it, she literally screamed with surprise, and exclaimed, 'What, Franck turned literary! Then take my word for it, Hood, he has married Bettine the authoress.' And she was as frightened as I was for Eugene Aram, though for a different cause, namely your extravagant passion for fishing. 'Franck must be very much changed,' she said, alluding to the first verse, 'if he leave you one of the "troutlets in the pool." ' And in point of fact, on referring to your German, you do make them jump *here* and *there* as if, at least, you had *hooked* them. Lord knows what you have made of my 'Calm and Cool Evening,' but I suppose instead of one solitary beetle as in 'Gray's Elegy,' there is a whole flight of cockchafers, *because they are such good baits for chub*. Of one thing I can judge, for I have measured with a straw, and some of the lines are rather long, as if you had thrown them as far as you could. Moreover, I asked Fanny, who is the best German scholar in the family, to give me an account of the thing, and she said, that Eugene Aram 'played' with the old man before he killed him, and then struck till he broke his *top-joint*. That when the body was full of *gentles* it was thrown into the stream for *ground-bait*, but unfortunately the water dried up, and so the body was put into a heap of bran, and the wind blew away the bran, &c. But I cannot depend enough on Fanny's acquaintance with the German language to feel sure of such a translation; perhaps it may not turn out quite so fishy as she represents. Mind, however, that should it not prove to be full of ram-rod and fishing-rod I shall attribute that merit to your coadjutor, for even Tom asked when he heard that you had been translating it, 'Did Mr. Franck do it with his sword, and his schako, and his moustachios on?' (as if the last ever took off!) I am quite convinced that he thought you were doing some exercise. Tom inquired too, *why your* version had not the pictures, and I told him it would not suit your way of telling the story. But a truce to banter, I will now be serious at turning over a new leaf: seriously then, dear Franck, I feel sure that your part in the business has been a 'labour of love;' and I could not but be pleased to see our two names, as Winifred Jenkins says, under the same '*kiver*.'[19] The highest literary honour that a poem can receive is its translation into a foreign language, particularly the German. You

may therefore estimate how much I feel myself indebted, as an author, to Mr. Rühe. Of the closeness of his version I can judge, but the beauty of it I must unfortunately only relish through the testimony of yourself and others. Yet it is a droll fact, Tim, that I understand twice as much German as I did in Germany; perhaps what I cropped there, has become digested by after-rumination, as the cows become more intimate with the cud. However, the fact is plain.
I have always felt it as a reproach that I, a literary man, had not mastered that literary language; but such an illness as mine dissolves more than it resolves – it even impairs my memory, and particularly as to names, dates, and technicalities, in which I am at times a perfect 'Wild-goose.'[20] Still there is another point on which I am able to speak – the 'getting-up', as we call it, of your little work; and really, as to typography and paper, it seemed the very best specimen of the German press that I have met with. The binding, too, has been much admired, and especially pleased me by a sort of outlandish look, that made me feel, at a glance at the outside merely, that I was translated. To-day being Good Friday, and therefore the postal arrangements more early, will not allow me the pleasure of writing to Mr. Rühe, but which I shall do next week. In the meantime, I will keep shaking the friendly hand, which he extends to me so *hand*somely, and drink his good health in the strongest beverage that is allowed to *Tea* Hood. Pray tell him this from me, and that I really rejoice in the accession of such a member to the Freundschaft.
By the bye, I will send you here a joke I lately made on Prince Albert's breaking in through the ice when skating, Her Majesty pulling him out again with her own royal hands: –

On a Recent Immersion.
'Long life and hard frosts to the fortunate Prince,
And for many a skating may Providence spare him;
For surely his accident served to convince
That the Queen dearly loved, tho the ice *couldn't bear him*.'[21]

'Tim, says he,' I shall set about getting your fishing tackle or making you up a box, *viâ* Hamburg; but you cannot have the tackle by the time you propose, for, look you, to-day is the 9th (your precious almanack says the 90th, and I suppose with your regiment it is the 19th). As to the *two last* 'Comics,' Tim, you *have* had them, for there have been none since. 'Up the Rhine' was in lieu of one of them, and there has been no other. I shall be most happy to send my face and the 'Eugene' in English for Mr. Rühe, and some other trifles besides; but there will be some delay; for, thanks to that B— (would he were tried at Bailey Senior, as we genteelly call the Old Bailey!), everything is locked up at law, even my mock countenance. He has almost un-Christianised me, for at times I have been on the point of cursing him in the terms of the awful curse of Ernulphus – for which you must consult Tristram Shandy.[22]

Amongst other things, you shall have the *Pirsch Wagening* article, and two piscatory dialogues – one on the Netze, and the other the Brake – which I made out of your letters, and have really sketched the places very like the originals, considering that I have never been there! As all English reading will be welcome, you shall also have my New Monthly Magazines; but N.B. with my articles cut out for reprinting, which you will get some day in a volume. Jane is horrified at my sending out 'Up the Rhine;' she says it contains so many quizzes on the Germans. But, as *you* know, I quiz by preference my best friends, and it is in favour of the Germans that they can afford to be quizzed. It may seem a paradox, but only respectable people are quizzable; nobody dreams of quizzing good-for-nothings and blackguards: and if 'age commands respect' (you remember your copy-book), so it commands quizzing. Nothing is more common than to hear of an Old Quiz – generally a very respectable elderly gentleman or gentlewoman, but something eccentric. Long life to *you*, Tim, and when you are sixty, look out for a good share of quizzing! I shan't be alive to do it, but I'll bequeath you, Tim, as a good subject to some first-rate hand in the line.

This reminds me to wonder what you are going to be *put out of the army* for, for that is the way that we in England interpret the threat of a young officer's *retirement*. Have you been drinking Moselle out of a black bottle, like Captain Reynolds of the 11th Hussars?[23] Jane thinks the 19th have been ordered to shave off their mosquitoes (she means moustachios), and you won't submit to it; and Fanny supposes you are weary of wearing a 'cap' without 'tain' to it. For my part, I can only guess at military feelings, and should think it would be very disagreeable to leave the army without having killed anybody; indeed, I think it is a reflection very likely to lead to suicide, or killing yourself. A civilian, indeed, would point with great satisfaction to a sword that had never hurt man, woman, or child, since it became a blade; but a warrior's sentiment, I presume, must be the very reverse – more in the style of Körner.[24] Mind, I'm not wanting you to go and kill anybody, that I may write another poem about murder, but only speculating philosophically on the different feelings of civilians and uncivilians.

Apropos of fighting, are you not sorry, Tim, to find that the knife has come so much more into vogue among our lower orders? There seems to have been a sort of vulgar chivalry about pugilism, after all, when a man struck another fairly, as the Irishman said, 'with nothing in his hand but his fist.' But I suppose all sorts of fighting are coming in, for Quakerism is clearly going out. Few of the second generation in Quakers' families are friends. You had the great Mrs. Fry at Berlin.[25] Well! none of the junior Frys are Quakers. There is a great deal of humbug about them – one fact is admitted by a very clever writer of their own body, that they are particularly worldly – a money-getting and money-loving people. I rather think if the law would allow them to refuse taxes, to serve in the army, &c., &c., we should have plenty of Quakers. I have lately been quizzing them a little,[26] and am at open war, as I have been with all canters, here called saints, – and there is an unusual quantity current of pious cant or religious bigotry.[27]

The Tories got up in England, for party purposes, fanaticism against the Catholics, and a cry of 'the Church in danger:' now, what is called 'High Church of Englandism,' the higher it is carried, the nearer it approaches to Popery. I predicted the result, that it would end in making a sort of Pope of the Archbishop of Canterbury, and now there is actually a schism in the High Church party at Tory Oxford, a Popish-Protestant section writing in favour of celibacy, images, &c., &c. But we have no fear of your turning a Protestant monk. Perhaps, when Amanda comes to Bromberg, you will get by degrees (of comparison), to think that Miss Besser[28] is Miss Best, and if you once think that, you are safe from Puseyism, *i.e.* celibacy. Pray give my love to her; if we were nearer I might choose another word, but at this distance, even her Mamma could not object to the affection, – Jane don't! And now, in spite of her remonstrances, I must tell you what happened last night, after I had written most of this letter. I was looking out of the window, at nearly dark, when a female figure stepped out of a coach, ran about six yards like a crab, *i.e.*, sideways, and then fell flat, what the wrestlers call a fair back-fall. If you have ever seen any mosaic, you can fancy a figure inlaid, as it were, in a dark ground.

It was Jane just returned from her mother's. You will be glad to hear that her fall was broken by an inch or two of Camberwell Road mud, after a providential shower of rain. I suppose it was the same feeling that induced Eve to make poor Adam as begrimed as herself, but the moment I appeared, Jane threw herself into my arms, and took care to make me quite as dirty. She was not hurt, though shaken. As she came home in the dark, so as not to see the steps of the coach, I pronounced the usual verdict, – but perhaps you have not heard of that story – an inquest on the body of a woman, who had been killed by her husband. She was a notorious cat, and when the coroner asked the jury for the verdict, the foreman gave it in these words, 'Sarved her right!'

And now, Tim, *how's your mother?* I must be thinking of shutting up this letter,

don't you wish you may get it? but I must ask you before I close, *has your mother sold her mangle?* which I suppose will puzzle you *and no mistake!*[29]
I shall lose the post if I do not stop at once, so God bless you Johnny, alias Tim; what suspicious characters we should be for the Old Bailey with so many names! The horn is blowing, and the eil-wagen is going out of the yard, and my stomach is full of parsnips, hot-cross-buns, salt fish and egg-sauce, but my heart tells me that I am,

Dear Franck,
Your loving friend,

Thos. Hood.

Camberwell, Surrey, April [*9–*] *13, 1841.*

From *Memorials* II 93–111. Although the letter is dated 13 April, in the body of the letter, on 459, Hood indicates that he is writing on the 9th.

1/Presumably cattle market days in Koblenz
2/'*speise cart*,' pun on 'die Speisekarte,' the bill of fare; 'neat-handed Phillis,' Milton ,'L'Allegro,' 86
3/The only example of this word given in NED is dated 1844.
4/'Miss Kilmansegg' had been published under this heading.
5/Two articles on 'Fishing in Germany' were published in the *New Sporting Magazine*, April and July 1840, and 'Shooting the Wild Stag in Poland' in NMM December 1840: *Works* VIII 72–90, 134–45.
6/The word first introduced in 1829
7/Droshky, Russian four-wheeled vehicle
8/The hottest and most unwholesome time of the year, midsummer
9/Published by Daguerre this year, and discussed in *Athenaeum* 26 January 1839, 69
10/'The Friend in Need,' NMM April 1841, *Works* VIII 48, *Robinson Crusoe*, 28 June
11/Afterpiece, farce or smaller entertainment after the play
12/Ironical, in view of Wildegans's poor memory
13/Book unidentified
14/Sheridan *Rivals* 3 iv. Acres does not actually utter this oath, but a dozen like it.
15/Ammunition-bread
16/'Brown Tommy' was 'ammunition bread for soldiers' and 'Brown Bess' 'The old regulation musket:' J.S. Farmer *Slang and its Analogues* (1890–1904) I 338, VII 152.
17/Aram's victim
18/Prussian general, author of *Militärische Taschenbuch* (1792). I have not traced Astor.
19/Smollett *Humphry Clinker* letter of 18 July
20/Reference to Wildegans
21/The accident occurred on 9 February 1841.
22/Sterne *Tristram Shandy* III 10, 11
23/On 18 May 1840 Captain Reynolds had a bottle of Moselle 'in its original black-bottle state,' instead of a decanter, placed on the mess table. As a consequence of this offence against etiquette his commanding officer, the Earl of Cardigan, had him arrested. Cardigan fought a duel over the business on 12 September, and was tried for this crime before the House of Lords on 16 February 1841. He was found not guilty on a technicality.

24/Karl Theodor Körner (1791–1813), patriotic German poet
25/Elizabeth Fry (1780–1845), philanthropist, visited Berlin in April 1840. Her work at Newgate had been made fun of in *Odes and Addresses*.
26/'The Friend in Need,' NMM March and April 1841
27/'My Tract' *Memorials* II 113–20
28/Perhaps a girl-friend at Koblenz
29/Hood's son notes that these are 'slang sayings in vogue at the time.' NED dates an example of the first 1838. The second, Farmer, giving the date 1837, calls 'A retort forcible,' *Slang and its Analogues*. The third, with the date 1836–7, NED calls 'at one time the commonest piece of "chaff" used by London street-boys.' The fourth NED dates as early as 1818.

TO
OCTAVIAN BLEWITT

Mr Hood presents his Comp[ts] to Mr Blewitt & requests him to have the kindness to lay the enclosed before the proper meeting. Below is a new address –
2 Union Row
High Street
Camberwell

25th May 1841

MS Royal Literary Fund. Published by Lane KSJ 57; 'the enclosed' is the letter which follows.

TO
THE COMMITTEE OF THE LITERARY FUND

To the Gentlemen of the Committee
of the Literary Fund.
Gentlemen
You may conceive the extreme pain with which I revoke my former decision. My views and feelings as then expressed are still unaltered; but unexpected combinations have occurred which compel me for the sake of others to seek and accept the aid you so handsomely offered to

Gent[n]
Your most obed[t] Servant

Thos. Hood

[*Camberwell*] *25 May / 1841*

MS Royal Literary Fund. Published by Lane KSJ 57. Hood had been declared insolvent on 13 May 1841. This letter is endorsed: '9th June 1841 / £50:0:0 granted / T. Crofton Croker / Registrar.'

TO

THE COMMITTEE OF THE LITERARY FUND

To the Gentlemen of the Committee
of the Literary Fund
Gentlemen.

The feelings I endeavoured to express when you so generously tendered me your assistance have left me little to add on the actual receipt of your bounty. Pray accept, once more, my most grateful thanks for your kindness, & your continued good-will towards me. It cannot but be gratifying to find that so many strangers are my friends, at a time when friends are proverbially apt to degenerate into acquaintance & acquaintance into strangers.

The present opportunity tempts me to explain why my former renunciation of the money should have been followed so speedily by an application so much at variance with my professions. There was, however, no affectation of independence – indeed, during the last twelve months my earnings will cover my very economical expenditure. The truth is, that an unforeseen case occurred when the sum would be of service so important as to overcome my scruples – or rather it made their sacrifice a matter of duty towards others. But my former sentiments and views remain unaltered – for my vessel is no crazier, my clouds no blacker & my 'sea of troubles'[1] no rougher than before. It is true that I have heard from Leicestershire that I am in prison, – and from Brussels that I am insane. My difficulties have again been paragraphed in public journals[2] – and my 'destitution' has been cried about the Exchange, or rather in the neighbourhood of Cornhill.[3] Nevertheless I am happy to assure you Gentlemen, that as yet my only confinement has been to my bed, and that my madness must have originated in some other brain, or at least Head.

It is not improbable that the unwarrantable publicity thus given to my private affairs may again provoke or compel me to further disclosures – But such a statement I repeat will be purely explanatory. It will be in fact my humble contribution to Literary history, & serve to show that my present cruel position is not due to the improvidence & careless habits as generally imputed to Authors (for my proper pecuniary difficulties I could have overcome) but to the fraudulent practices of a dishonest agent.

I have the honor to be
Gentlemen
Your very grateful & obedt. Servt.

Thos: Hood

[*Camberwell, June 1841*]

MS Royal Literary Fund. Endorsed: '19 / Mr. Thos. Hood/ £50 / Read Nov. 10. 1841 / for Registrar / Jno Bruce.' Published by K.J. Fielding, 'The Misfortunes of Hood: 1841' *Notes and Queries* December 1953, 535–6.

1/*Hamlet* 3 i 59

2/Fielding notes that 'Hood may have had in mind the *Argus*, 7 February 1841, which remarked: "THE LITERARY FUND. – A subscriber informs us that the old system of favouritism is adopted in relieving applicants, and that in one instance lately it has been carried to a most unwarrantable excess. We shall enquire into this; the donors must not be Hoodwinked." '

3/Baily's address

TO
JOHN LEECH

Have you done any more drawings? I have just sent a part of the poem to the printers.[1]

A remark was made by a person on the drawing of the 'Marriage' that the balustrade seemed composed of decanters. On reflection, it seems to me, if the case be so, it would be advisable to alter them. My old foes the Canters are always on the look-out for a hole in my coat ... The Man is fair game – but the *place* is not – and the carpers are ingenious enough to make out some association of decanters with the *Communion wine*. Verb sap.[2]

I was pleased to see a complimentary notice of some of your 'Pencillings' in the Athenaeum.[3]

[*Camberwell, 1 July 1841*]

From Maggs Bros. *Autograph Letters* no. 332 (Christmas 1914) 47; the date is given in the catalogue. John Leech (1817–64), comic artist, worked for *Bentley's Miscellany*, NMM and *Punch*, begun 17 July 1841. He later illustrated Hood's *Whimsicalities* (1844).

1/'Miss Kilmansegg,' published in the *Comic Annual* for 1842

2/The drawing in question appears in *Comic Annual*, facing 76.

3/*Athenaeum* 3 July 1841, contains a review of Captain Pepper's *Written Caricatures*, with favourable reference to its illustrations by Leech.

TO

JOHN LEECH

Dear Sir.

The Count now is the Man. – Wouldn't he bear a little more whisker in the 'Wedding'? The Clergyman's hair seems to have been got up by special license – & with some of the grease you told me of. Sir Jacob cries 'City!' as plainly as if he stood behind an omnibus – with something of the look of a sucking pig in its second childhood. That bridesmaid as sweet as a young pea, & in excellent contrast to Miss K! Rupertino looks – as he ought – pretty *Bob*-ish.[1] – As to the 'Friend in Need'[2] I think I mentioned to you my idea for an illustration – Robinson Crusoe (see chapter 17) lying dead with Dog, Cat, & Poll wandering.
Perhaps the Finding of the Dragon would make a subject – (Chapter v) making the bones gigantic & the workmen Lilliputian. [The following as illustrating *yourself*. Seneca with a Leech on, – vide p. 530]
In Miss K – perhaps the Count having a '*Strange Gentleman* home to dine' – page 67[3] – or 'Death & the Lady'. p. 271
If any more occur to me I will drop you a line.

Yours very truly

Thos Hood.

2 Union Row – High Stt / Camberwell [*7 August 1841*]

MS Cameron. Address: 'J. Leech Esq / 66 Judd Street / Brunswick Square.' PM: '1841/AU 7/PD.'

1/In good spirits. Hood is referring to the cut facing 76 in the *Comic Annual* for 1842.

2/Also in the *Comic Annual*, though the 'idea for an illustration' does not appear to have been realised. Hood is in fact referring to ch. XIX of 'The Friend in Need,' and, in the passage in square brackets, to ch. XVII.

3/This is illustrated facing 96.

TO

WILLIAM and GEORGIANA ELLIOT

My dear friends,

It was only a semi-official visit of S—'s.[1] Still a very good chance – perhaps having spitten so much blood away, I am not quite so sanguine as Jane. Time will show. Seriously it would be comfort at last, and, I think, go far to cure me of *some* of my ailments. Should I get appointed, be sure the editor will come and show himself at Stratford to receive your congratulations. God bless you all; kisses for all my little dear friends, and love to the big boys.

Yours most truly,

Thomas Hood.

[*Camberwell, 31 August 1841*]

From *Memorials* II 121–2. The first part of this letter (dated) was written in high spirits by Jane Hood, *Memorials* II 120–1. Dickens had been approached to replace Theodore Hook as editor of NMM, published by Colburn. When he refused the offer, Hood was approached. On 2 September 1841 Jane wrote to the Elliots again, informing them that Hood was appointed. He was to receive £300 a year, 'independent of any articles he may write, which are to be paid for as usual,' *Memorials* II 123.

1/Probably William Shoberl (d 1853), son of Frederic Shoberl, and Henry Colburn's assistant

TO

JOHN LEECH

Have the goodness to let me know how many drawings are done – and if you have finished with Miss Kilmansegg?

Also please to let me know what verse the drawing of a 'Leg or a Wing' is intended to illustrate.

[*Camberwell, September 1841*]

From Maggs Bros. *Autograph Letters* no. 333 (spring 1915) 52. Hood is referring to the *Comic Annual* for 1842, illustrated by Leech.

TO
WILLIAM ARMSTRONG FOLKARD

Are you to have all the Cuts to do. Have you any in hand. Did you get two of mine I sent last week. I am all in the dark ...

[*Camberwell, September 1841*]

From Maggs Bros. *Autograph Letters* no. 421 (spring 1922) 123. According to Sotheby, Wilkinson & Hodge, *Catalogue* 5 December 1921, 58, four letters from Hood to Folkard from 2 Union Row, High Street, Camberwell were sold to Maggs. It is probable that this and the following letters belong to this group. The illustrations for the *Comic Annual* for 1842 were engraved by Folkard and Orrin Smith.

TO
WILLIAM ARMSTRONG FOLKARD

I send you two more drawings of mine ... Keep the remains of the black bottle as *black* as it would seem to Lord Cardigan ... In the Pig one, the man's eyes are not strictly natural but let them stick as they be. Keep the black puddings black.[1]

[*Camberwell, September 1841*]

From Maggs Bros. *Autograph Letters* no. 421 (spring 1922) 123
1/The cut on 229 of the *Comic Annual* for 1842

TO
WILLIAM ARMSTRONG FOLKARD

private

Dear Folkard
Mr Leech has been to show me three more drawings & is gone on with them to Marlbro Street. *You had better send as soon as you can for them*, as some may find their way to Smiths – who has not yet done his.
The Leg or Wing cut Mr Leech has taken to make some slight alteration in it & you will have it back. Take care of the female head in it which is very nice.

Mind – the proof of the puppy cut send to *me.*[1]
I send a messenger on purpose that you may not lose time in going – or sending.

Yours very truly

T: Hood.

[*Camberwell, September 1841*]

MS UCLA. 'Marlbro Street' is Henry Colburn's address. Colburn published the *Comic Annual* for 1842, the illustrations for which are the subject of this letter.

1/On the title-page of the *Comic Annual* for 1842. The *Comic* was announced as ready as early as 30 October 1841.

TO
UNKNOWN CORRESPONDENT

Madam.
I am much obliged by the offer of your Stanzas, which are so far from 'prosy,' that, but for the reality, and dreadful nature of the subject, – & the risk of shocking the feelings of some relative, – it would have given me much pleasure to have inserted them in the New Monthly Magazine.

I have the honour to be
Madam
Yours very obediently

Thos Hood

[*Camberwell,*] *3rd Novr 1841.*

MS UCLA

TO
WILLIAM LAYTON SAMMONS

My Dear Sir, – I am much flattered by your persevering partiality to my Whims and Oddities, Annuals, and Comic Almanack, – which last, however, is not mine, but an imitation.

It would have gratified me to have seen you in the '*New Monthly Magazine*,' as well as in the '*Omnibus*,' so as to have been able to say with Fluellen, 'there is Sammons in both,'[1] – but Turkeys, Pigs, and Plum Puddings,[2] are better in plates than on paper. Even the celebrated 'Reading Sauce' does not do for mere perusal.

I am, dear Sir,
Your's very truly,

Thos. Hood.

Mr. W.L. Sammons, 3 Springfield Place,
Lansdown, Bath.

17, Elm Tree Road, St. John's Wood, / 3rd December, 1841.

From *Sam Sly's African Journal* 14 August 1845, communicated to me by Mr W.J. Carlton. Hood is writing from his new address north of the Thames, whither he had moved towards the end of 1841. His correspondent is William Layton Sammons (1801–82), man of letters, who emigrated to the Cape in October 1842 and set up *Sam Sly's African Journal* (1843–51).

1/*Henry V* 4 vii 33

2/According to *Sam Sly's African Journal*, 'This article (most unsuitable for the *N.M. Magazine*, but written in a merry mood) in the chapter of accidents, will be found in *Van de Sandt's African Almanack* for 1845.'

TO

HORACE SMITH

Since we last met, I have gone thro' many vicissitudes, and have once or twice been at Death's door, but fortunately did not go in. Thus, paradoxical as it may sound, I have been in too serious a case for serious poetry, but now my spirits are better, expect to be able to write something in the graver line.

For an answer whether your communication would be acceptable, I refer you to the magazine. Some objections having been made to the title, and time not allowing a reference to the author, I ventured to make an alteration which I hope you will excuse ...

Thos. Hood.

[*St John's Wood, 4 December 1841*]

First paragraph from Anderson Galleries, *Library of the late Adrian H. Joline* pt. VI, 17 and 18 May 1915, 24, and Maggs Bros. *Autograph Letters* no. 381 (Autumn 1919) 87. The first gives the fuller address and the date, the second identifies the recipient as 'Mr. Smith.' I have given the second version. In the letter, Hood also mentions 'a contribution by his correspondent to "the Magazine".' In NMM, December 1841, Smith began contributing his 'Short Rides in an Author's Omnibus.' The second paragraph is taken from an excerpt from an unidentified catalogue in the Berg Collection, New York Public Library. It carries the same date, and relates to the same subject.

TO
HORACE? SMITH

My dear Smith, I am sorry to tell you that it is utterly out of my power to put in an appearance to-morrow night. But I enclose a trifling contribution ...

[*St John's Wood, 1841*]

From Anderson Galleries *Selection of Rare Books* no. 1250 (20 November 1916), 46. According to the catalogue, this note is accompanied with a signed MS of 'The Dream of Eugene Aram.'

TO
LAMAN BLANCHARD

The pleasure I have derived from your writings makes it very gratifying to me to find that we are imbarked in the same craft ...

[*St John's Wood, December 1841*]

From Bertram Rota *Autograph Letters* catalogue 134 n.d. 9. The catalogue entry contains the note: 'Watermark 1841 ... This must refer to a new periodical to which both were contributors.' Blanchard's first contribution to NMM after Hood became editor appeared in January 1842, 102. Laman Blanchard (1804–45), journalist, connected with *The Examiner*, friend of W.H. Ainsworth, committed suicide. His *Sketches of Life* (1846) was published with an introduction by Bulwer-Lytton who sympathized with such struggling men of letters as Blanchard and Hood.

TO

CHARLES DICKENS

Dear Dickins.

As you are going to America, and have kindly offered to execute any little commission for me – pray, if it be not too much trouble, try to get me an Autograph of Sandy Hook's.[1] I have Theodore's.

Yours very truly,

Thos. Hood.

My boy does *not* wait for an answer.

17 Elm Tree Road / [St John's Wood] Saturday [25 December 1841]

MS Huntington. Published by Wm. P. Frith *John Leech* II 187. This letter was written before Dickens' departure for America on 4 January 1842. On 30 December Dickens inscribed to Hood a copy of *Barnaby Rudge*: 'From his friend and admirer'; in Berg Collection, New York Public Library. Hood reviewed the work in *Athenaeum* 22 January 1842.

1/Sandy Hook is a point off the coast of New Jersey at the entrance to New York harbour.

Marry time Supremacy.

1842

TO
J.T.J. HEWLETT

My dear Sir.
I am very glad that you relished *my* Oxford Sausage[1] & its seasoning. The truth is, the Controversy – ridiculous in itself – has given rise to a host of minor ones still more absurd; and the serious agitation of very comical questions. For instance there was a grave discussion the other day in Essex, by a party of Ministers – whether the Clergyman & his Congregation ought to repeat certain parts of the service together, or the last ought to give him a start, – & how much. If they split on such trivial matters we shall have as many sects as Churches & Chapels.
A whole drum of figs for the Oxford Herald & its attack on you.[2] I am of opinion that such criticisms review themselves. In the mean time I am happy to be able to give you a set off. The other day Miss Lamb (Elia's sister) was here, an excellent old creature, with as much masculine sense as womanly feeling – she is mad occasionally, but in her lucid intervals enjoys as much intellect as many who have their wits all the year round – Well, she highly praised some paper in the Magazine which she said had caused her to shed tears, & on my enquiry, turned to your story of poor Matt.[3]
Should you come to town again, I hope you will do me the favour of calling on me – & taking pot luck – till now my house has been such a hospital as (lucus a non lucendo) to preclude hospitality. In the meantime I wish you all good things, in your very distressed neighbourhood, as it must be, to combine *Want & Age.*

I am My dear Sir
Yours very truly

Thos Hood

17 Elm Tree Road / St John's Wood / Monday. [January 1842]

MS Texas. Joseph Thomas James Hewlett (1800–47), novelist, was born in London and educated at the Charterhouse, whence he was expelled. He then studied at Worcester College, Oxford. The background to Hewlett's quite extensive correspondence with Hood is filled out in the *Gentleman's Magazine* April 1847, 441: 'Shortly after he had graduated, he took holy orders, married an amiable but portionless bride [his cousin, Charlotte Elizabeth], and was appointed Head Master of Abingdon Grammar-school. Here Mr. Hewlett's troubles began; his wife was a perpetual invalid, unable, moreover, from want of tact in management, to keep his house in order ... Mr. Hewlett failed at

Abingdon, and retired thence, about the year 1839, to Letcombe Regis – a healthful village among the Berkshire downs, near Wantage. Here ... having for his next-door neighbour the kindest of country squires – Mr. Goodlake ... Mr. Hewlett laboured with his pen to eke out the slender stipend his curacy yielded him ... In the year 1840 [he was] presented ... to the living of Little Stambridge, near Rochford ... Essex.' There a rectory had to be built, 'to the diminution of the poor Rector's small annual income.' His wife died in August 1842. 'The effect of the unhealthy climate of Essex upon Mr. Hewlett was speedily discernible.' He died, leaving nine children. This account in the *Gentleman's Magazine* seems to be wrong in one particular. The first evidence in Hewlett's correspondence with Hood indicating that he had moved to Essex does not occur until 1844, see 595. Hewlett was the author of *Peter Priggins, the College Scout* (1841), edited by Theodore Hook, *The Parish Clerk* (1841), *Poetry for the Million* (1842), *College Life* (1843), *Parsons and Widows* (1844), and *Great Tom of Oxford* (1846). He contributed to NMM. Hewlett is discussed by his great-grandson Jocelyn Brooke, 'An Oxford Novelist of the Forties' *Nineteenth Century* (June 1948) 341–51.

1/Thomas Wharton's original *Oxford Sausage* was published in 1764. Hood's 'The University Feud' appeared in NMM January 1842. It concerned the controversy over who should be elected Professor of Poetry at Oxford, James Garbett or Isaac Williams. Garbett won, and this seemed to be a check to the Tractarian movement.
2/The *Oxford Herald* 8 January 1842 attacked the 'highly repulsive and immoral tendency' of Hewlett's fiction.
3/In NMM January 1842, 17–31. B.W. Procter about this time called Mary Lamb 'this poor old soul, with her excellent heart and fine intellect;' his remark is quoted in *The Athenaeum* 24 December 1892, 890.

TO
J.T.J. HEWLETT

My dear Sir
The landrails[1] did their duty by the Rabbits – and the Clerks 'wot give themselves hares'[2] allowed one at least to reach its destination. It was young tender & well shot, – and has been completely eaten & thoroughly relished. And moreover *we* drank your health in a bumper –
The rabbits were fine ones & reminded me vividly of my own little burrow mongering at Wanstead. But I shall never again shoot any thing – unless a Burglar – in which case you may look for a hamper.
The last day's sport I had was with a Poor Law Commissioner, for company, & didn't he give the poor birds their gruel! As for 'shooting Folly as it flies'[3] the notion is ridiculous – Folly don't fly – it only flaps and flutters & thinks it does. But it's quite as good fun to knock it down sitting – for example on a mare's nest.
I hardly knew how to take your announcement of a *17th* child,[4] till *fancy* suggested to me that those who have to do with *priggin's* are '*family men*'.[5] (By the bye, there

was one of the cloth with me last night who spoke very highly of Peter.) For my own part I often feel grateful, for having but a pair to feed & drive. A quiver full of them might be very useful in the ancient wartimes – but nowadays the enemy at the gate is a dun. – and every Child is not a Banker.

I am sorry to hear that you are unwell, & still more so to receive so bad an account of your lady. But after spitting blood from the lungs for six years I am more sceptical than formerly about consumption. As to the 'nasty stuff' the less, it seems to me, the better. Luckily one of my best friends is a very skilful physician – who at different times & in most critical circumstances has saved my wife's life & my own. Under his care, a severe diet & a cheerful heart have pulled me through: – 'Never *say* die' is a capital rule. I think if I had but given myself over, – the die would have been cast.

Well, many thanks for the 'articles'[6] – one of which has been inserted, as aforesaid, & very much liked – and a place is booked for the others.

Mrs Hood desires to be kindly remembered to you.

Yours very truly

Thos Hood

17, Elm Tree Road / St. John's Wood / Monday [*early 1842*]

MS Texas.

1/Presumably a pun involving corn-crake and railway

2/Quotation unidentified

3/Pope *Essay on Man* i 13

4/A misreading or a joke; Hewlett had only nine children.

5/Slang terms; the phrase means, those who have to do with folly are thieves.

6/Hood is probably referring less to Hewlett's contributions to NMM than to the rabbits mentioned at the beginning of the letter.

TO

PHILIP DE FRANCK

Tim, says he,

You can't be a Jew or you wouldn't live in Ham.[1]

I made cock-sure of you, when you did not answer our last letter, that you were coming with the king; why didn't you? I think it will make me disloyal to Frederick that he didn't bring you.[2]

However write soon, and I will send to you what has long been made up, and let me know what tackle you want. I have a 'Comic' for you, and for Mr. Rühe, with a letter, and one for Prince Radziwill, to your care. It has come meanwhile to a second edition.

As editor of the New Monthly Magazine, I stand higher than ever; there was great competition for it, but I did not even apply, and was therefore selected. If you can give me any genuine German information at any time, it will be very serviceable, anything *new*. You will find in the 'Comic' your account to me of the stag shooting at Antonin,[3] &c., the Harrow Story, and so on; so that if you can give me any more sporting, it will be acceptable. I shall be highly honoured by any from Their Highnesses; you will also receive 'Up the Rhine,' which you have perhaps seen already, as it was reprinted at Leipsic. This is such a short month for editors I must not write more.

I believe, thanks to our dear Dr. Elliot, I have got over the blood-spitting, but England has a capital climate after all, as is proved by the life-tables.

Mind, come and see us, and won't we have some fun? God bless you Tim, says

Your faithful friend,

(in great haste), Thos. Hood, E.N.M.M.!!!

P.S. There are several very nice young *English* ladies in this country quite disengaged; I do not know how many exactly, but will answer for five or six.

[*St John's Wood*] *February 20th, 1842.*

From *Memorials* II 126–7

1/Hood's daughter notes that Franck was now stationed at Hamburg.

2/The King of Prussia visited England from 22 January until 4 February 1842.

3/'Shooting the Wild Stag in Poland' *Comic Annual* for 1842

TO
HENRY COLBURN?

My dear Sir.
I am sorry to say I have been unable to finish the Schoolmistress to my own satisfaction. The fates have been against it – for last night we had a domestic Conflagration. The Maid set fire to her bed – and I had a narrow escape from being done brown or black. I quite enjoy, this morning, to find myself so raw & am

My dear Sir
Yours very truly

Thos Hood.

My best thanks – for the DArblay

[St. John's Wood, April 1842]

MS editor. The first two parts of Hood's 'Schoolmistress Abroad' appeared in Henry Colburn's NMM March and April 1842. The third and final part did not appear there until June. Throughout this period the magazine contained accounts of the first few volumes of Mme D'Arblay's *Diary and Letters*, published by Colburn.

TO
WILLIAM JOHN BRODERIP

Sir
I have read with much pleasure your Second Chapter of Owls – and beg leave to suggest that there is a curious burrow-mongering Bird – some sort of Owl? – which *lodges* with the Prairie Dog in S. America. If I am right you may like to insert a paragraph about it in the proof.

I am Sir Yours very rheumatically

Thos Hood

I have the pleasure to say that I know, & have a very favourable opinion of the Gentn with whom you have placed the young Hooks.[1]

17 Elm Tree Road / St. John's Wood / Monday. [*18 April 1842*]

MS Cameron. Though the letter itself is dated the 19th in another hand, Monday, the day given, was the 18th. William John Broderip (1789–1859), lawyer and naturalist, magistrate at the Thames police court (1822–46), one of the original fellows of the Zoological Society, formed in 1826. His contributions to NMM and *Fraser's Magazine* were collected in *Zoological Recreations* (1847) and *Leaves from the Note-book of a Naturalist* (1852). In this letter Hood refers to the article published in NMM May 1842, 90–101.

1/The Hooks may be the children of Hood's solicitor St P.B. Hook, who took over from Reynolds in June 1841. I have not identified the gentleman.

TO
J.T.J. HEWLETT

My dear Sir

Your letter found me at the fag end of a rheumatic fever, that sets in with the inveterate East Wind, in the beginning of April. Today, is my first appearance down stairs. – (ie 5th May)

I will not condole with you on an event which must have been a release and a relief to both parties – there are circumstances under which life is neither desirable by, nor to be desired for the sufferer.[1] And you must both have undergone much slow misery, in so long a space as seven hopeless years. As to your young ones nine are a serious charge – I find two quite enough – but one does *somehow* get thro most formidable difficulties, and weather storms, in which apparently the craft was doomed to founder. I venture to say no man has gone thro a severer struggle for the last eight or nine years than myself – contending with wretched health, difficulties, dishonesty, & the treachery & misconduct of some who ought to have been friends & allies – but to my astonishment I find myself alive, whilst better lives, in the assurance phrase, have fallen in – & moreover continuing to rub on without losing ground. And I verily believe I have not been beaten, because I would not despond – but entertained the spirit hinted at in the preface you allude to.[2]

As to Colburn, I do not know whether he be in earnest but he said to me, personally, to the same effect as a paragraph in last N.M.M. written by one of his understrappers – (Literary Report first page in the number) that he does not intend to publish much till the introduction of single copies of foreign reprints is prohibited. Perhaps an excuse for drawing in. Otherwise I should think a cheap edition of Peter[3] would do well in the quarters you mention.

And now in answer to your question I shall be very happy to see you whenever it may suit you to take such pot luck as I can afford – if you will let a hearty welcome eke out my poor entertainment. We will treat you, as the advts say, 'as one of the family'. For my part, I shall enjoy a gossip with you over a glass of wine.

I am glad to tell you that amongst my own friends I find your papers very much relished. Could you make any thing whimsical of the following case which once came under my notice? A really clever and classical College Man banished to a curacy in a Berkshire village. Lord of Manor non resident – gentry none – nothing but bumpkins & clodpoles with whom he could not associate. Thrown thus on himself – he sprouted into all sorts of eccentricities – took to mend his own stockings & make his own shirts – became a regular Guy, to look at – as absent-minded as the Revd George Harvest[4] – & so shy that if he saw a gent coming to call he bolted into his garden or fields & had to be regularly run down. To conclude, as if not knowing what to do with himself married his servant, an elderly woman, and a fortnight afterwards – took a walk to some where & never came back or was heard of afterwards. Now & then as if in spite he would preach a sermon to his hawbucks[5] about as intelligible to them as N0 90[6]
My Schoolmistress[7] is partly founded on fact – but I have been in queer dilemmas myself in a foreign country from not knowing the language –
Wishing you better health, better luck, and whatever may conduce to your comfort under your bereavement I am My dear Sir

Yours very truly

Thos Hood

Drop me a line when you are likely to come.

17 – Elm Tree Road / St John's Wood. [*5 May 1842*]

MS Texas
1/Hood is referring to the death of Mrs Hewlett.
2/Perhaps the Preface to *Hood's Own*, *Works* I viii–xiv
3/Hewlett's *Peter Priggins* had been published by Colburn in 1841.
4/Unidentified
5/Country bumpkins
6/This last sentence was added in the margin. Newman's *Tract 90* was published in 1841.
7/'The Schoolmistress Abroad,' begun in NMM March 1842

TO
PHILIP DE FRANCK

Tim, says he, what a dreadful fire! The English will sympathise strongly with the Hamburgers, who are their old commercial allies. The city must be a long time in recovering from such a calamity.[1] I sincerely hope no friends of yours have suffered.

I got all the fishing tackle six weeks ago, along with it I have sent two *glass baits*, the last invention and novelty, one of which is for yourself, and the other please to present for me to the Prince.[2] The little leaden caps are to put on the line at the head of the bait, as without the cap the fish would not spin.
Yesterday a sporting clergyman dined with me, and I was glad to hear him say, that he has tried the glass bait, and it is *very killing*. I also send for yourself an imitation gold-fish. It appears that there is something in the colour or taste of the gold-fish, that renders it irresistible to other fish, as a bait. They are quite mad after it. It appears to me to be intended to be sunk with a weight, and pulled about under water, or else to float on the top; but they say it is taken in any way.[3] I send two 'Comics' (one for Mr. Rühe), and the 'Up the Rhine' for yourself. If you can easily get me a copy of the German Edition of 'Up the Rhine,' published at Leipsic, you can bring it when you come. There is a recent difficulty about sending letters in packets or parcels, so I must write to Mr. Rühe per post. And now observe, the box will be sent in a day or two after this letter. It is directed to Mr. F. Weber, Breiten Giebel, care of Messrs. C. J. Johns & Sons, Hamburg, and marked with PvF. Thank God I seem to have got over my old complaint; but I have suffered much from rheumatism. It has been very general amongst people here, the east wind having blown inveterately for a whole month. I was quite disabled, but luckily I had a whole magazine in print beforehand, what you would call in *reserve*.
I congratulate you on your promotion, and the success of your application to the King:[4] of course you will now marry for want of something to do. And now, Johnny, I must say good bye, for I am crippled with the right arm, as well as right foot. To aggravate these evils our drawing room overlooks Lord's Cricket ground, and I see the fellows playing all day, add to which, once or twice a week, a foot-race for a wager. But it is of the less importance, that I can only write a short letter, as we are to see you this summer. Your best way would be by Hamburg packet direct to London. God bless you, Tim, says he,

Your faithful friend,

Thomas Hood.

I forgot to say I thought a new fly-line would be useful to you, and so send one for your acceptance. The two Sporting Magazines contain two articles of mine on fishing in Germany.[5] Our merchants in two days have subscribed £7500 for the Hamburgers, and are going to send them shortly £10,000. I am glad of this.

Good bye,

Tim H.

17, Elm Tree Road, St. John's Wood, May 11th, 1842.

From *Memorials* II 132–4
1/A great fire at Hamburg took place 5–8 May 1842.
2/Prince Radziwill
3/Hood's son notes: 'The very taking gold-fish bait described in the letter was, with the directions for its use, the sole invention of my father. It was carved in two halves, out of deal, painted and joined with gum, so that after a short immersion one half would detach itself and float away, leaving the other attached to the line, and inscribed (by an encaustic process, with a hot knitting needle) with the words – "Oh! you April fool!" that month being the season when it would probably be first used.'
4/Perhaps an application for retirement
5/*New Sporting Magazine* April and July 1840 *Works* VIII 72–90

TO
WILLIAM GASPEY

Sir
I am much flattered by your intention of quoting from me in your Lecture on the Living Comic Poets – & your request that I would point out to you such piece or pieces as I may conceive to be best adapted to your purpose. I must, however, remind you that Authors have always been considered to be but *puny* Judges of their own works;[1] and my modesty forbids me to think I am better qualified for the critical Bench, at my own trial, than the other Members of the profession. The selection must therefore be left to your own taste & judgement; should you still persist in your intention, after a closer examination of my claims, as an exciter of the risible muscles. To be candid, I have always fancied like Mr Liston, & other so called comedians, that my performances in the serious line were the most worthy of the public approbation.[2] In fact, I have more than once thought of testing my powers in the tragic, by the composition of a Tragedy in Five Acts. If you will take the trouble to refer to the titles of some of my more popular effusions you will find that 'Farewell Nancy Gray' was a *Pathetic Ballad* – so was 'Mary's Ghost' – and the Dream of Eugene Aram, although generally taken as a joke, was certainly intended to be a serious production. My Portrait alone, if you saw it, would indicate that my forte is pensive.
Still, I should be happy, as you desire it, to send you some samples of what might be called my levities; but that my whole stock has been disposed of except a solitary copy, or rather set.
To turn from self – pray accept my thanks for the offer of your M.S. which I regret to return to you: it would have read better, it seems to me, when the change that

came over the spirit of our lamps[3] had been more recent. As to your little volume of Poems it would perhaps come under a general review of Poetry lately published, which is in contemplation – tho not certain of execution. I will at least promise to read the book & am

Sir Yours very obediently

Thos Hood.

W Gaspey Esqre

17 Elm Tree Road / St Johns Wood / 17 June [*1842*]

MS Huntington. Wm Gaspey (1812–88) was the author of *Poor Law Melodies* (1842), to which Hood refers at the end of the letter. I do not know the manuscript to which he also refers.

1/Swift, 'On Poetry:' 'Put on the Critick's Brow, and sit / At Wills the puny Judge of Wit.'

2/Lamb discusses Liston's 'natural bent to tragedy' in his 'Biographical Memoir,' *Works* ed. E.V. Lucas (1903–5) I 253.

3/The phrase is adapted from Byron, 'The Dream' iii, but I do not understand the point of Hood's remark.

TO
DOUGLAS JERROLD

Dear Jerrold,

Many thanks for your Cakes & Ale,[1] & for the last especially, as I am forbidden to take it in a potable shape. Even Bass's, which might be a Bass relief, is denied to me. The more kind of you to be my Friend and Pitcher.

The Inscription was an unexpected & really a great pleasure; for I attach a peculiar value to the regard & good opinion of literary men. The truth is, I love Authorship –, as Lord Byron loved England – 'with all its faults'[2] – and in spite of its calamities. I am proud of my profession & very much inclined to 'Stand by my order.' It was this feeling, & no undue estimate of the value of my own fugitive works that induced me to engage in the Copyright Question[3] – Moreover I have always denied that Authors are an Irritable Genus,[4] except that their tempers have peculiar trials, & the exhibitions are public instead of private. Neither do I allow the especial hatred, envy, malice & all uncharitableness[5] so generally ascribed to us – & here comes yr Inscription in proof of my opinion. For my own part I only regret that fortune has not favoured me, as I could have wished – to enable me to

see more of my literary brethren, around my table. Nevertheless as you are not altogether *Home*'s Douglas I hope you will some day find your way here.
Allow me to thank you also for the Bubbles & to congratulate you on your double success on the stage – being I trust Pay and Play – not the Turf alternative[7]

I am Dear Jerrold
Yours very truly

Thos Hood

17 Elm Tree Road / St John's Wood, / Friday [July] (1842).

MS New York University Libraries. Published by Blanchard Jerrold, *Life and Remains of Douglas Jerrold* (1859) 274. Douglas William Jerrold (1803–57), friend of Clarkson Stanfield and Samuel Laman Blanchard, author of the successful comedy *Black-eyed Susan* (1829), contributor to the periodicals, including *Punch*. He edited the *Illuminated Magazine* (1843–5).

1/Jerrold's volume with this title was published in March 1842 and was dedicated to Hood.
2/*Beppo* xlvii, quoting Cowper *Task* ii 206
3/Hood published two further letters on 'Copyright and Copywrong' in *The Athenaeum* 11 and 18 June. Their subject was copyright domestic and international. With regard to the first, Mahon had introduced a new bill in the House of Commons on 3 March. In the debate in committee on 6 April the radical Wakley attacked Wordsworth; this led to a comment by Hood in NMM May 136. However, Peel suggested an amendment of the length of copyright to forty-two years or life plus seven years. In this form the bill was finally passed by the Lords on 24 June. The Act remained in force until 1911.
4/Horace *Epistles* 2 ii 102
5/Phrase adopted from the *Book of Common Prayer*, Litany
6/*Bubbles of the Day*, performed at Covent Garden Theatre, March 1842. *The Prisoners of War* had been first performed at Drury Lane in February.
7/I have not traced the phrase Hood uses here.

TO
J.T.J. HEWLETT

My dear Sir:
I have had a regular paving stone of a good intention in my mind ever since the magazine was finished to write & book myself for Wantage – but so many slips & obstacles have come on the rail that the line has never been clear before me. Moreover I have not been quite in travelling trim – for the vibration of a locomotive is apt as the doctors say to squablificate the fluids of delicate people, & my claret[1] hath so much of port in it as to be no better for shaking. And I am sorry to say

that I do not yet see my way being tied here till after Monday next – & then the New Monthly will be waxing old again – my only chance being to get very forward with it in the interval. All this is very tantalizing to me – who know your kind invitation and welcome to be no idle compliment & can believe, besides how beautiful you & nature look at this season. – & how the rabbits must want at Wantage to be shot. Not that I should *now* be more *fatal* to them than our Oxfords etc to the Queen. How pleasant for Prince Albert – it is like riding with a target! I would not have such fellows as Francis & the rest hung – but tied up, & ball-practised at by an awkward squad.[2]
I am glad to hear that your trip did you good – and beg to congratulate you too on your improved terms as well as better health. The Pubs. seem more inclined now-adays to *advance* backwards, like the Champion's horse, & lay the blame on the 'Foreign Piracies'.[3] – I never hear of a new attempt on her Majesty's life but I think the fellow must be a poor author who wants to be comfortable in Bedlam or Newgate – or another & a better world[4] – The last shot – Dean – or Bean – you see, wrote verses.
Now if I should *see* my way clear – & provided you do not in the mean time send me word that it will be inconvenient or uncomfortable, I will write on Saturday & say whether or not I shall put myself into the 2 o clock train this day week – Tuesday 12 Instant. If so I will bring a Comic with me which I have had for you some time but did not send it, taking the chance of your returning from Dover via London & hoping in that case to see you. But you passed thro like a Meteor.

I am
My dear Sir
Yours very truly

T Hood:

Mrs. Hood desires her remembrances – & hopes on your railway the passengers are not locked-in.[5]

17 Elm Tree Road / St. John's Wood / Monday. [*4 July 1842*]

MS Texas. Hood is writing after the threat against his life of Queen Victoria made by John William Bean, 3 July 1842, and before getting under way with NMM July. The days given by Hood fit the dates which I have supplied for this and the following letters.
1/NED gives 'Pugilistic slang, Blood.'
2/A correspondent signing himself FLAGELLATOR wrote in *The Times* 7 July 1842, 5: 'Had Oxford been hanged, there would have been no Francis; and because Francis has been reprieved, there will be a host of Beans.' Oxford made his attempt on 10 June 1840, Francis followed on 30 May 1842, and Bean flourished an unloaded pistol in the direction of the Queen on 3 July.

3/ Hood had spoken on the subject of international copyright at a meeting in the Freemasons' Hall on 30 June.
4/Kotzebue *The Stranger* I i
5/On 21 May and 7 June this year Sydney Smith wrote two stinging letters on this dangerous practice to the editor of the *Morning Chronicle*.

TO
J.T.J. HEWLETT

My dear Sir.
This is to say that on Tuesday, if I do not arrive according to your direction, by the two o'clock train, you may conclude that I am sick, dead, or arrested for shooting at Her Majesty whichever may be most agreable to your notions of

Dear Sir
Yours very truly

Thos Hood

P.P. Hewlett, Esqre [1]

[*St John's Wood*] *Saturday Morning* [*9 July 1842*]

MS Texas.
1/P.P. for Peter Priggins, Hewlett's pseudonym

TO
MRS GEORGIANA ELLIOT

My dear Mrs Elliot
Here we are again – the Babes in the Wood of St John – all safe & sound. Jane having successfully bussed her children all the way home – but a little fatigued from getting her baggage so far without any *porter*.
You will be pleased to hear that in spite of my warnings & forebodings I got better & betterer, till by dining *as the physicians did*, on turtle soup, white bait, & champagne,[1] I seemed quite well. – but I have always suspected the Doctors' practice to be better than their precepts: – & particularly those which turn down *Diet* Street. The snug one dozen of diners, however turned out to be above two – (in fact 27) two others, Talfourd & Macready,[2] being prevented. Jerdan was the *Vice* & a certain person not very well adapted to *fill* a chair – was to have occupied

the opposite *Virtue*, but on the score of ill health I begged off, & Captain Marryat[3] presided instead. On his right, Dickens, & Monckton Milnes the poetical M.P.[4] – on his left Sir John Wilson[5] – T.H—& for my left hand neighbour Doctor Elliot*son*[6] – which seemed considerately contrived to break my fall from Stratford. The Kelso man was supported by Foster & Stanfield the painter.[7] Amongst the rest were Charles & Tom Landseer.[8] Tom two stone deafer than I am & obliged to carry a tube – Father Prout & Ainsworth – these two men at paper war,[9] wherefore some six, including a clergyman, were put between them – Proctor alias Barry Cornwall & Barham, otherwise Ingoldsby, Cruikshank & Cattermole[10] – a Doctor Gwynne or Quin,[11] & a Revd Mr Wilde[12] who greatly interested Dr Elliotson & myself, a tall very earnest looking man, like your Doctor, only with none of his Sweet William colour but quite pale – & the more so for long jet black locks – either strange natural hair, or an unnatural wig – He was silent till he sang, & then came out such a powerful bass voice fit for a cathedral organ, – to a song of the olden time, that between physiognomy, costume, vox, & words, the impression was quite black-letterish – I had never seen him before but seemed to know him *traditionally*, somewhere about Cromwell's time. Nevertheless some of his reading had been more modern & profane – for when we broke up, he came & shook hands with me to my pleasant surprise – for I seemed to have ascended to antiquity whilst only aiming to descend to posterity.

Well, we drank 'the Boz,' with a delectable clatter, which drew from him a good warm hearted speech, in which he hinted the great advantage of going to America for the pleasure of coming back again – & pleasantly described the embarrassing attentions of the Transatlantickers, who made his private house & private cabin particularly public. He looked very well, & had a younger brother along with him. He told me that two American prints have attacked me for my Copyright Letters in the Athenaeum – so I shall procure them as a treat for 'Jane'. Then we had more songs. Barham chanted a Robin Hood Ballad – & Cruickshank sang a Burlesque Ballad of Lord H— & somebody unknown to me gave a capital imitation of a French showman. Then we toasted Mrs Boz – & the Chairman & Vice & the Traditional Priest sang the 'Deep deep Sea' in his deep deep voice – & then we drank to Procter, who wrote the said Song.[13] Also Sir J. Wilson's good health – & Cruickshank's & Ainsworth's – & a Manchester friend of the latter sang a Manchester ditty, so full of trading stuff that it really seemed to have been, not composed, but manufactured. Jerdan as Jerdanish as usual on such occasions. You know how paradoxically he is *quite at home* in *dining out*.

As to myself – I had to make my *second maiden speech* – for Mr Moncton Milnes

proposed my health in terms my modesty might allow me to repeat to *you* but my memory won't – However I ascribed the toast to my notoriously bad health & assured them that their wishes had already improved it – that I felt a brisker circulation – a more genial warmth about the heart, & explained that a certain trembling of my hand was not from palsy or my old ague – but an inclination in my hand to shake itself with every one present. Whereupon I had to go thro the friendly ceremony with as many of the company as were within reach – besides a few more who came express from the other end of the table. *Very* gratifying – wasn't it? – tho I cannot go quite so far as Jane, who wants me to have that hand chopped off – bottled – & preserved in spirits. She was sitting up for me – very anxious as usual when I go out – because I am so domestic & steady – & was down at the door before I could ring at the gate, to which Boz kindly sent me in his own carriage.[14] Poor girl! – what *would* she do if she had a wild husband – instead of a tame one?
In coming home Dickens volunteered to bring Mrs Dickens to see us on Tuesday or Wednesday, but I shall be obliged to put them off till next week – as I shall be at Wantage – so that it seems probable I shall be able to *fix* them for an evening – & then of course you will come – unless you should be at Don't Want-age.
The children, stuffed with happy remembrances of Stratford *Le Beau*,[15] send their loves wholesale & retail; and as Jane & I can unite in that, we do –

I am My dear Mrs Elliot
Yours, & the Doctor's, very truly

Thos Hood

We hope Dr Robert will dine with us at the Hoskins's[16] tomorrow. If he does, won't we quiz him about the new carriage, & exhibit a wife to be taken, as the medicals say, in an appropriate vehicle? He ought not to have that great Cupid's hand with a dart in it on his harness for nothing. I asked Jerdan last night about Agnes's marriage & he confirmed the rumour. God bless you all

T.H.

17 Elm Tree Road / Monday. [*11 July 1842*]

MS Yale. Published in *Memorials* II 135–9. The letter is dated in another hand.

1/Hood is describing a dinner he attended in honour of Dickens on his safe return from America. The dinner took place at J.J. East's Trafalgar Tavern, Greenwich, which specialised in the food and drink named.
2/William Charles Macready (1793–1873), actor and manager
3/Frederick Marryat (1792–1848), naval captain and novelist

4/Richard Monckton Milnes (1809–85), poet and politician, M.P. from 1837, worked for the Copyright Act, helped Hood in his last months, and published Keats's *Life and Letters* (1848). Created Lord Houghton 1863.
5/Sir John Wilson (1780–1856), general, had taken Dickens's house during his absence abroad.
6/John Elliotson (1791–1868), physician
7/John Forster; Clarkson Stanfield (1793–1867)
8/Charles Landseer (1799–1879), historical painter, brother of Thomas (1795–1880), engraver. They both illustrated Hood's *Laying Down the Law* (1843). Their younger brother Edwin became the most famous. Thomas Landseer, deaf and shy, also lived in St John's Wood: Chas. Dickens *Letters* ed. M. House and G. Storey (Oxford 1965, 1969) I 601, II 256.
9/Francis Sylvester Mahony (1804–66) wrote for *Fraser's Magazine* under the pseudonym of Father Prout. He also contributed to *Bentley's Miscellany*. William Harrison Ainsworth (1805–82), novelist. He had published Hood's *National Tales* (1827). Ainsworth's *Jack Shepherd* appeared in *Bentley's*, which he edited (1840–1). He published his own *Magazine* (1842–53) and then the *New Monthly*. Ainsworth had quarrelled with Bentley and relinquished his connection with the *Miscellany* at the end of 1841, setting up his own *Magazine*. George Cruikshank had also quarrelled with Bentley and attacked him in the first number of *Ainsworth's*. As a response, Prout ridiculed Ainsworth in *Bentley's* February 1842. *Ainsworth's* replied in April and May, and Prout continued the controversy in the May number of *Bentley's*. Open warfare was over by the time of Hood's letter.
10/George Cattermole (1800–68), water-colour painter and book illustrator
11/Frederic Hervey Foster Quin (1799–1878), homeopathic physician, popular in London society
12/Unidentified
13/Hood may be referring to 'The Sea' from Procter's *English Songs* (1832) 1–2.
14/Hood may have enjoyed the scene which Dickens describes: 'Cruikshank was perfectly wild at the reunion, and, after singing all manner of marine songs, wound up the entertainment by coming home (six miles) in a little open phaeton of mine, *on his head*, to the mingled delight and indignation of the metropolitan police' *Letters* ed. Dexter (1938), I 471.
15/Pun on Stratford-atte-Bowe
16/Perhaps a misspelling of Hopkins. Manley Hopkins (1817?–97), father of the poet, became a friend of Hood and dedicated to him his volume of poems *The Philosopher's Stone*, published at the end of 1843.

TO
MRS GEORGIANA ELLIOT

My dear Mrs Elliot.

You tell me that a Friend of yours, and a Lady, wishes to have my Autograph, – two reasons so potent, that I ought to send a couple – one from each hand.

À propos of Autographs, it appears to me that the least use to be made of them has hitherto been overlooked. For the Doctor's sake I will endeavour to explain. If not officially required, like Sir H. Halford or Sir James Clark,[1] to issue a public report on the state of his Patients, no doubt he has often been called upon for a Certificate of good or bad health. Now it is my opinion, that a Document of the kind, instead of being penned by the Physician, should be given under the hand of the Patient – in short that the Invalid ought to write his own Bulletin. For my own part, I cannot imagine that any thing from the Medical Attendant could be so satisfactory to the world at large, or the private circle, as such announcements as the following:

Almost gone T. Hoo
Very bad indeed TH.
A little better TH
Getting Well TH
Quite stout again Thos Hood
Better than ever!
Tom Hood[2]

Pray tell your Lady Friend that if along with her Album she should keep a Hortus Siccus,[3] I am almost thin enough for that also.

I am My dear Mrs Elliot
Yours ever very truly

Thos Hood

[*St John's Wood, July? 1842*]

MS UCLA. I have been unable to date this letter, but it is inserted here because it belongs in spirit with the preceding letter to the same correspondent. Note that the following letter to Dickens belongs to the same date as the last to Mrs. Elliot.

1/Physicians to Queen Victoria

2/These lines are written in appropriately shaky and stronger hands, and are followed by a playful drawing of two heads in profile.

3/Collection of dried plants

TO
CHARLES DICKENS

My dear Dickens.
Only thinking of the pleasure of seeing you again, with Mrs. Dickens on Tuesday or Wednesday, I never remembered till I got home to my wife, who is also my flapper, (not a young wild duck, but a Remembrancer of Laputa) that I have booked to shoot some rabbits, – if I can – at Wantage in Berks. A Reverend friend called 'Peter Priggins' will be waiting for me by appointment at his rail-way station on

Tuesday. But I must & can only be three or four days absent, – after which the sooner we have the pleasure of seeing you the better for us.
Mrs. Hood thinks there ought to be a Ladies' Dinner to Mrs. Dickens – I think *she* wants to go to Greenwich seeing how much good it has done me, for I went really ill, & came home well. So that occasionally the Diet of Gargantua seems to suit me better than that of Panta*gruel.*
Well, adieu for the present. Live, fatten, prosper – write, & draw the mopuses wholesale thro Chapman & *Haul.*[1]

Yours ever truly,

Thos Hood

C. Dickens Esqre

17. Elm Tree Road / St John's Wood—/ Monday. [*11 July 1842*]

MS Huntington. Published in *Memorials* II 139–40. This letter fits in closely with the chronology of the previous letters to Hewlett and Mrs Elliot.

1/Chapman and Hall were Dickens's publishers from 1836 to 1844.

TO

CHARLES WENTWORTH DILKE

Dined every day with a regular old English squire – Goodlake – the famous breeder of greyhounds.[1] Lounged delightfully, and had what I have been longing for: a lie on the grass. No such green Turkey carpets abroad, Dilke. Then, for company, a Mrs. *Smiley*, of *May Fair.*[2] What isn't there in a name? God bless.

[*St John's Wood, July 1842*]

From Dilke I 56. Hood is here describing his visit with Hewlett.

1/Among 'The chief promoters of the sport of coursing in modern times,' according to C.J. Apperley in *The Oracle of Rural Life* (1839) 71, is 'Thomas M. Goodlake, Esq., of Letcomb Manor, Berkshire, editor of the *Courser's Manual.*' Letcomb Manor was near Hewlett's home at Wantage.

2/Unidentified

TO
J.T.J. HEWLETT

Dear Sir

I plead guilty: I ought to have written to you before & had plotted a letter but the Magazine interfered with my intention.

On receipt of your last I was just setting off again out of Town, having spent a week with my friends the Dilkes – & returned on Saturday night. On Monday I was in Marlboro Street, – & found there the enclosed – addressed to me.[1] It is evidently from some enemy of yours or mine – or both. However I send it as you may be able to recognize the handwriting. I propose to have a cut at him in the Gallery so as to be only understood by himself.[2] As to the article in question I have reason to believe it has been especially liked – Colburn himself had heard it commended – I have said, tho', nothing of the note to him. Better not.

I heard of your flying visit to town & was wondering at its brevity: – Now I am sorry to learn its cause; but hope ere this you have returned to those 'effervescing draughts,' which are *not* made up at the Apothecary's. I was glad to hear your article had arrived, – in proof your head no longer sympathised with your stomach – your mucous membranes with the other brains.

For myself I came back so improved that Mrs H. hardly knew me till the end of the month had pulled me down a little. Indeed the fine air of your downs, deserves to be bottled & sold by the dozen. – It certainly acted very favorably on my Belgian marsh fever – and if ever I am asked for a prescription for the ague I shall recommend Port wine & Bark-shire.[3]

On my last excursion I had a little dangling – it should be *d*angling – for little fishes, – and some how or other '*caught the eye*' of a large one – I mean literally, – found the organ on my hook – enjoying 'a bad look out'.

N.B. Did not try the 'cold Water Cure'[4] like Mrs Smiley. Only worm bobbing of course – for as to throwing a fly – I think a strong one could throw *me*. But I found it very pleasant to play Piscator again, and almost fancied myself *Walton* on Thames.[5]

Are there any hopes of soon seeing you in Town? I am not likely to be in country again – but set in for at home – where if you like chops & changes we can give you a chop & change your plate. In the meantime give my love to all your Girls & boys – & please to distribute my kind remembrances amongst the Smiley family, & the Squire[6] – not forgetting some canine compliments in Dog Latin to the long & the short bow wows. Tom Junior was delighted with my account of them but won't believe in the Squire's Tree Champaigne – he says nothing but real pain was ever got out of birch.

I am My dear Sir
Yours very truly

Thos Hood

Mrs Hood desired me to present her kind regards to you.
Take care of the note enclosed – as we may between us trace the hand.

17 Elm Tree Road / Tuesday. [*August 1842*]

MS Texas. In the course of the letter Hood refers to a response of his own which appeared in NMM, October 1842 (note 2).

1/Office of Henry Colburn, publisher of NMM. The enclosure to which Hood goes on to refer has not survived with his letter.
2/NMM October 1842, 280: 'ANONYMOUS. Some gentleman – if he be a gentleman – has favoured us with a letter without his name. Will he now oblige us with his name – without a letter?'
3/Bark was used in the treatment of ague.
4/ The cold water cure was a fashionable medical treatment about the time of Hood's letter. It was originated in Germany about 1829 by Vincenz Priessnitz. Hood satirically reviewed R.T. Claridge's *Hydropathy or the Cold Water Cure*, an account of Priessnitz' method, in NMM March 1842, *Works* III 373–82.
5/A play on the name of the author of the *Compleat Angler* and that of the town on the river.
6/Goodlake

TO
HENRY COLBURN?

Mr. Barrows [...] Railroads', & to see the whole of them before deciding – especially as there is a strong personality in the present portion. I send a note for him to that effect.
It is impossible to judge from the skeleton notes of what the 'Bright & Dark Places in an Irishman's Life' may turn out – Correspondents must show us the building not a brick of it. I return his note, as addressed to you.
I hope you have escaped the Cholera which every one almost has had a touch of. I have been unwell the last three or four days but it is gone off again. I see by

today's paper the death of poor Longman – another proof that two legs are better than four.

I am, – My Dear Sir Yours very truly

Thos Hood

[*St John's Wood, 30 August 1842*]

MS George Milne and E.L. McAdam jr. The letter probably refers to NMM of which Hood was editor, and Colburn publisher. 'Mr Barrows' may be John Henry Barrow (d 1858), a miscellaneous writer. Thomas Norton Longman, the publisher, died on 29 August 1842, after falling from his horse.

TO
WILLIAM SHOBERL?

Dear Sir
Please to send by Bearer any Books or letters for me: I proposed having the pleasure of calling in Marlboro Street today but was deterred by the complication of wet & east wind. However I shall be down tomorrow morning, as there are M. Steward.[1] & some other matters to mention to Mr Colburn.

I am Dear Sir
Yours very truly

Thos Hood

I have sent a making up[2] for Mr Gough.

17. Elm Tree Road / Tuesday. [*1842*]

MS Massachusetts Historical Society. This is another business letter concerning NMM.
1/Possibly Mrs Isabella Steward (d 1867), author
2/Presumably a completion of materials for the sake of the printer of NMM employed by Charles Whiting of Beaufort House.

For letter to Shoberl which follows this one, see 686.

TO

J.T.J. HEWLETT

Dear P.P.

I ought to have written to you before – but I have been very busy and very bothered: a little unsettled beside in health by the sudden changes from hot to cold – east winds, hail, rain, & 'donner und blitzen!' – Nevertheless thanks to my late rambles, I am very well again, for me – & have been so complimented on my good looks that Colburn is urgent for my Portrait in the Magazine.

I return Mrs Hughes's note.[1] She is evidently a lady of a strong mind & a good heart – the more gratifying the very handsome terms in which she speaks of me. Pray tell her that I take her 'cellar metaphor' as a very high compliment – it made me feel like a Magnum. Perhaps it was as well we did not meet, for she would only have seen a pale thin Author – the reverse of full bodied.

I hope, that ere this your muco-gastritis is over & gone – & your blue devils to the black one. Dreadful is that enforced temperance which forbids us the animal spirits. Mine are apt to get sometimes far below proof – in spite of my philosophy which is 'tho thin as an eel be merry as a grig.' But as Mrs Hughes says 'le bon tems viendra' – and if you only get to be Bishop of Single Gloucester and I, Master of the Penny Rolls, we shall always have bread & cheese.

Since we met I have heard of more drops shed into the 'Clear Stream'[2] including some of Miss Lamb's. You may call that paper your *Cry-teary-on* – & your writing fluid *Hink* illae lachrymae.[3]

I have no news to tell you. Cricket is over at Lord's, & the flag seems to have scored some of the notches – or else the wind has tattered it. Miss Portis is still single.[4] Tom Junior is well of course. Mrs H is so so – and Fanny has been so but isn't so now. Walnuts are in &, what is better, wine isn't out. The Queen is gone to Scotland – and I am not – tho I have an Aunt & Uncle in Fife[5] & scores of Scotch cousins in the Carse of Gowrie. Our only excursion has been to the Zoological Gardens where I saw, – how tantalizing for an Author – ! – more *rhino*[6] than a man could put in his pocket – let alone the ceros.

Pray give my love to all at the Parsonage & my regards & remembrances at the Squireage. I would be more particular but that unless I close directly this letter will be *post*humous.

I am Dear P.P.
Yours very truly

T.H.

17 Elm Tree Road / St John's Wood / Monday. [*12 September 1842*]

MS Texas. In the letter Hood refers to Queen Victoria's departure for Scotland, 29 August. In his first paragraph he seems to refer to the weather of the Wednesday previous to the day of his letter. According to the Meteorological Journal for Wednesday 7 September 1842, the direction of the wind at 9 a.m. was from the east. The evening of that day was marked by 'Thunder and lightning, accompanied with very heavy rain,' *Athenaeum* 8 October, 870.

1/Mrs Mary Ann Hughes, friend of Scott, Southey, and Ainsworth, grandmother of the author of *Tom Brown's Schooldays*, lived at Kingston Lisle, Berks, close to Wantage.
2/Phrase introduced in Hewlett's 'The Five Incumbents,' NMM August 1842
3/Terence *Andria* I i 99
4/Unidentified
5/Mr and Mrs Keay
6/Slang, ready money

TO
GEORGE HUNTLY GORDON

Dear Sir.

I beg to assure you that I have forgotten neither yourself nor your 'definite article.' On the contrary, dining lately with a Mr *Hunter Gordon*, the name, to my dull hearing, was so identical with your own, that I could not help asking him, with some wonder, 'what had become of the trumpet?' To be sure, you *looked* rather a different man, but I allowed for the changes of time, & perhaps a new *stamp* from your unfortunate accident. I ought to say by the way that I sincerely sympathised with you on that mishap, for I am quite deaf enough myself to be run over, except that to do it, a horse must come up to my room, I go out so seldom.

I have read with much pleasure the paper by your friend Dr McCabe – but unfortunately the subject is too polished for the Magazine. It seems written with great fairness, & unusual freedom from party spirit, and I even agree with his conclusions, which confirm my own impressions from a residence in Belgium. But such an article would be out of place in the New Monthly.

Pray accept my best thanks for the offer of it & believe me

Dear Sir Yours very truly

Thos Hood

H Gordon Esqre

In the absence of directions from you, I have enclosed the M.S under cover for 'G.H.G. Esqre at Mr Colburn's.

17 Elm Tree Road / St John's Wood / Monday. [*September 1842*]

MS UCLA. George Huntly Gordon (1796–1868) was deaf; he transcribed the MS of Scott's Waverley novels for the press in order to preserve the secret of the authorship. William Bernard Maccabe (1801–91), author and historian, settled in London about 1833 and wrote for the *Morning Chronicle* and *Morning Herald*. He was later employed in the Stationery Office.

TO
GEORGE HUNTLY GORDON

Dear Sir
I am so little acquainted with the Periodicals in general as to be unable to name the one most likely to be suitable for your Friend's paper. I could much more easily enumerate the Magazines which are not in its line – e.g. The 'Evangelical' The 'Railway' – & the Magazine in Hyde Park. Perhaps the article would do for Fraser, Blackwood or the *Foreign Quarterly*.
I am much gratified by your kind & flattering expressions as to my peculiar consolations under a partial loss of hearing. I am not in fact quite so deaf as the man who will not hear, & my ears, like my razors, are sharper at some times than at others. But the sense is often dull enough to make me so – especially in company with strange voices.
It ought to be some comfort to you, in your Stationery Office, that its *Quires* are not vocal – which would certainly be tantalizing: – And remembering how the Millions are learning to sing, *in Chorus*,[1] your privation will, perhaps, hereafter, be quite enviable.

I am
My dear Sir
Yours very truly

Thos Hood

I sent one of those long snaky tubes to a deaf female friend in the country: but it was not approved. She could not bear, she said, to put it to her ear, it reminded her so strongly of the 'Serpent tempting Eve.'

G.H. Gordon Esqre

17 Elm Tree Road / St John's Wood / Friday [*September 1842*]

MS UCLA

1/John Pyke Hullah's system of teaching singing was growing in popularity. 'The first great choral meeting of [his] classes was held ... at Exeter Hall' on 13 April 1842, *Annual Register*, Chronicle 71. Hood celebrated 'More Hullahbaloo' in NMM October.

TO
ELIZABETH BARRETT?

Dear Madam
With many thanks, I beg leave to return to you the M.S.S you have been so good as to offer to the N.M. Magazine.
Whatever promise they contain, as the blossoming, and fruition of the bud has been forbidden, it seems unadvisable, in my humble judgment, to present such immature offerings to the public– bad critics, sometimes of even the riper productions of genius.
Pray accept my most sincere wishes for your health & comfort, prompted by some very agreable, & some sad recollections of Brighton, & believe me to be

Dear Madam
Yours very truly

Thos Hood

Mrs Barrett.

17 Elm Tree Road / St John's Wood / 5 October. [*1842*]

MS editor. The attribution is very tentative. Elizabeth Barrett (1806–61), author of 'Cry of the Children,' 1843, married Robert Browning 1846.

TO
CHARLES DICKENS

Dear Dickens.
Can you let me have an early copy of the American Notes, so that I may review it in the New Monthly?[1] – Is it really likely to be ready as advertised?[2]
I aim this at Devonshire Place, supposing you to be returned,[3] for with these winds tis no fit time for the coast. But your bones are not so weather-unwise (for ignorance *is* bliss) as mine.

I have had Mr. Goderich (Peter Parley) here disclaiming the American right to alter English works, and denying the practice. He is to address a letter to me[4] – but I doubt whether he can get over the Boston Petition[5] & Mathews's comment.[6] He came to me with an introduction from Grattan, once a *Colley*flower[7] of literature, now our Consul at Boston. Did you notice Grattan's speech at the Ashburton Dinner when his health was drunk as the Representative of English Literature – whereupon he so handsomely dropped all allusion to Authors & Authorship & played the Diplomatic?[8] He deserves I think an American Note? I knew something of him in Belgium – nothing very pleasant, as far as our intercourse was concerned. I should have asked these questions by word of mouth, – in Devonshire Place – but the weather has kept me in doors. It is no fiction, that the complaint derived from Dutch Malaria seven years since, is revived by Easterly winds. Otherwise I have been better than usual, and 'never say die.' Moreover I have left off Panta*gruel*ism and take wine.

Don't forget about the Yankee Notes. I have had but one American friend & lost him *thro a good crop of pears*. He was a son or brother in law of Van Buren's[9] & paid us a visit in England, whereupon, in honour of him, a pear tree which has never borne fruit to speak of within memory of man, was loaded with 90 dozen of brown somethings. Our Gardener said they were a *keeping* sort & would be good at Xmas, whereupon as our Jonathan was on the eve of sailing for the States we sent him a few dozens to dessert him on his voyage.[10] Some he put at the *bottom* of a trunk he wrote to us, to take to America but he could not have been gone above a day or two when all *our* pears began to rot – *His* would of course by sympathy, & I presume spoilt his linen, or clothes, for I have never heard of him since. Perhaps he thought I had *done* him on purpose: & for sartin, the Tree, my accomplice, never bore any more pears, good or bad, after that supernatural crop.

Pray present my respects for me to Mrs. Dickens. How she must enjoy being at home, & discovering her children after her Columbusing & only discovering America!

I am Dear Dickens
Yours ever truly

Thos Hood.

Do you want a motto for your Book? – Coleridge in his Pantisocracy days used frequently to exclaim in soliloquy – 'I wish I was in A-me-ri-ca!' Perhaps you might find something in the advertisements of Oldridge's *Balm of Columbia*[11] or the American Soothing Syrup. Qy. Gin Twist?

17 Elm Tree Road / St. John's Wood. / 12. Octr [*1842*]

MS Huntington. Published by Whitley HLQ 396-8.

1/In his reply, written the next day, Thursday, Dickens promised to bring 'the American book, next Monday. It will not be in the hands of any other friend I have, until Tuesday.' Dickens hoped to bring with him Mrs Dickens and 'Professor Longfellow of Boston ... who, admiring you as all good and true men do, wants to know you.' These quotations from Dickens' letter and those which follow are from a transcript kindly sent me by Mrs Madeline House. Henry Wadsworth Longfellow (1807–82), poet, stayed with Dickens in London 6–20 October 1842. On the 17th he called on Hood. Hood reviewed *American Notes* in NMM November 1842.

2/*American Notes* was advertised in *Athenaeum* 8 October, 879, as to be published on the 19th.

3/From Broadstairs. Dickens replied from 'Devonshire Terrace.'

4/Samuel Griswold Goodrich (1793–1860), the American publisher, was an opponent of international copyright. Dickens proclaimed him 'a scoundrel and a Liar.' Hood had attacked Goodrich in *Athenaeum* 18 June, 545. Now he gave him an opportunity, which he did not accept, to reply in NMM: Goodrich, *Recollections of a Lifetime* (New York 1856) II 302–3.

5/As early as 1838 the citizens of Boston had presented to Congress a petition in favour of international copyright. Dickens carried to Washington a memorial signed by prominent American authors which was presented on 30 March 1842. A convention of booksellers, meeting in Boston, formulated a petition against copyright which was presented on 13 June. Hood is here surely referring to the second of these petitions. The matter is discussed by Aubert J. Clark *The Movement for International Copyright* (Washington 1960) 47, 68 and W.G. Wilkins *Charles Dickens in America* (New York 1912) 248.

6/Whitley notes that Cornelius Mathews (1817–89), American author, 'supported international copyright. He spoke on the subject at a dinner given to Dickens in New York on February 18, 1842.'

7/A pun involving Grattan's second name, Colley

8/Grattan's speech was reported in *The Times* 26 September 1842, 5–6. Though much applauded as the spokesman of literature, he only touched on the question of international copyright. Dickens considered Grattan 'a very false and time-serving fellow. He lives by those qualities, and is worth nothing but contempt.'

9/Martin Van Buren (1782–1862), president of the United States 1836–40

10/Jonathan: slang name for an American.

11/Hair-restorer

TO

J.T.J. HEWLETT

Dear Peter.

It's now my turn to ask – are *you* dead? Has that Muco-*Gas* – (some affection of the *lights* I suppose) – really carried you off? Poor fellow! I had better hopes of you – To think of my outliving you, with my spitting of blood, with an attack of which I have just been visited after a cessation of 12 months. Thanks to the blowed & blasted (NB not vulgar but in this case strictly appropriate terms) Easterly winds. But *I* am better, & *you* – who knows? All I am afraid of is that you are not *write*. If he is not able to hold pen, thought I, at least he might send me, in lieu of his whole hand the fist with Peter's thumb-mark. What can be the cause of this portentous silence? Has the Squire for want of Justice business committed you? Or as birds are in, have you shot yourself like a Cockney? Or have you, after an extra bottle of champagne, buried yourself, by mistake, instead of a Parishioner, with Mrs *Smiley* for Chief *Weeper?* Who knows? *I* don't. Have you rashly (Sir W Scott spells it *Rashleigh*[1]) tried to walk up to Town on the line & been caught by the train up in the way you shouldn't go, – or are you in process of translation per se into Essex – or were lost in that last steam bother with your favorite boat called the Ile of Thanet because it goes like ile – and so, salt-Peterfied in the German Ocean?

I have been living in hopes of some day seeing you walk in to partake of pot *luck* or pint ditto as might happen, but no such *luck*. In the mean time here comes Dickens today to bring his American Notes & enquires after the gentleman who came with me to Broadstairs, & who had evidently made a favourable impression on the said Boz. Whereupon I made up my mind to write to you at once, to know if you are in this world or in a better – *or in a worse* – (whichever you like)

Saturday night I was at a Party of Literati – amongst them a Persian, (in costume) a regular *Kuzzilback*,[2] whom I especially elected to take wine with, to his evident surprise. But hadn't I a good reason for the preference – that as there is always good beer at the *Red Cap*,[3] of course the wine would be superior? That's *my* last – but to return to yourself – if you an't dead, or whether or not, just drop me a line, to say so – & if there is any prospect of soon seeing you, – If you are likely to make a visit to London within 3 weeks or a month I propose to have a meeting of a few friends, Dickens, Dilke, etc etc, & should like you to be one.

I only slightly noticed the Anonymous letter, – coz why? I don't like Colburn to know there are objections made, well or ill founded – My own impression is that the letter came from a Canter – but it is as well not to allow a Publisher to suppose, or say, that one is *unpopular* even with them. Verb. Sap.[4]

Give my love to all at the Parsonage – & the best of Compliments that are *not* compliments at the Squireage. Of course you are looking very brown now, at Letcombe – we have today looked very yellow with a regular London fog, which obliged me to light candles to shave by. However I made the best of it & told an American[5] that they had no such fogs in their country, which was a very safe brag. Dear me – it was thicker than I am! & yet I am

Yours corpulently

Thos Hood.

P.S. I am happy to inform you that the postage between us if you send via France is decreased by nearly 50 per cent.

Peter Priggins Esqre

NB. Yours just received. Many thanks for y^{r} considerate kindness. I am rather late this month, and shall be bothered with proofs about the 25-26 27. But if you don't mind em I don't. I shall be better able to enjoy y^{r} company on the 31st But come when & whenever you like.

17. Oct^{r} [*1842*]
17. Elm Tree Road.

34

MS Texas

1/Rashleigh Osbaldistone in Scott's *Rob Roy*
2/J.B. Fraser had published *The Kuzzilbash: a Tale of Khorasan* (1828).
3/Presumably the Persian was wearing a red cap; this was the name of the public house near which Hood had lived in Camberwell.
4/NMM October 1842, 280. Hood's note is given on 492 n 2.
5/Longfellow

TO JAMES SHERIDAN KNOWLES

Dear Knowles.
I had your paper, – read it, – & returned it within a day or two of my receipt of it, to Mr Colburn. – (before he went to Brighton.). Since then I have enquired about it, & understood that he had written, or was about to communicate with you on the subject. Hearing no more of it, I concluded you & he had not agreed as to terms. I will make a point of asking about the paper on Monday, but *you* had better also send him a reminder. I am

Dear Knowles
Yours very truly

Thos Hood.

J.S. Knowles Esqre

17 Elm Tree Road / St John's Wood / Saturday. / (Guy Fox) [5 November 1842]

MS editor. James Sheridan Knowles (1784–1862), dramatist

TO
J.T.J. HEWLETT

Dear P.P.
I return Colburn's note – or rather Shoberl's. I must not drop in on him again yet, for twice in one week would make him connect me with the 'conspiracy.' Nor do I think he would mention the matter if I did, for he seemed rather alarmed by hearing from Mrs. H. that I had been to the 'Nucleus' alias Garrick.[1]
I hope to send you the bit o writin on Monday – so will pull up now, – wanting to get a little ahead of the Magazine.

Yours ever truly

T.H.

[*St John's Wood*] *Saturday Morning.* [*5 November 1842*]

MS Texas. The date is conjectural, 'the bit o writin' to which Hood refers perhaps being 'the note' of the following letter and Monday.

1/The nucleus of the conspiracy at the Garrick Club. I do not know what the conspiracy was.

TO
J.T.J. HEWLETT

Dear P.P.
I return the note. The proposed public explanation would certainly be an aggravation of the mischief.[1] However, I hope your negociation with Colburn will end happily, for I should like you still to sail in the same craft with me.
We had some fun on Saturday night, & were sorry you could not join. Harvey came with Misses Portis & Robinson[2] – 13 in all besides ourselves. There was some singing – a good deal of laughing – with two Acted Charades – Guido Fawkes & Cold-Water-Cure, which went off like fireworks. Supper – & a bowl of punch. Being a Birthnight, – which is a sort of Benefit – I acted & sang!!! out of my usual line of parts. The intended Entertainment of our Neighbours the Clergy Orphan School was less fortunate – their grand display of fire works in Lord's Ground was postponed – not pork[3] – all the boys & girls having the measles. Sick transit!
I must now go Boz-hunting again – & wish I may catch him!

I will send you a verse or two as soon as I can find a few, & will write with em in a day or two. Meanwhile I'm

Yours very truly

Thos Hood

[*St John's Wood*] *Monday.* [*7 November 1842*]

MS Texas. The letter is dated to fit the reference to Jane's birthday which was 6 November; Saturday, Guy Fawkes' day, was the 5th.

1/Perhaps arising out of the anonymous letter mentioned on 500.
2/I have not identified these women.
3/The meaning of this phrase is not clear.

TO
J.T.J. HEWLETT

Dear P.P. (Qy Piety Parsonified?)
According to yours just received I shall expect you to take your mutton, if it an't beef, with me on Monday or Tuesday. Drop me a line when *you* know to let *me* know which, & what hour will suit you. If you think Barham would eat a plain dinner with us, & waive ceremony, you would perhaps be so good as to arrange it with him – forewarning him, of course not to expect sharks fins, edible bird's nests, & other foreign luxuries & dainties – washd down by Burgundy Claret & Champagne – but a plain dinner dressed by a very plain cook with only the liquidations of port & sherry, ginnums & O.dD.[1] – in short something like the hospitality of a Hospital, when the patients are recommended a moderate diet. But perhaps you would prefer a tête a tête – for business All I have to say is, arrange it as will best please you – *& let me know what, how & when.*
As to the Millions of Poems I will listen to *a few* of them with great pleasure, & afford my very best advice, & not flatter.[2] Your mockery of me I dont care* a Kus for – if it mislikes me I will retaliate with an *imitation sermon* that will do your business. But don't close yet with Colburn as to ½ profits. Take a sum at once & if he will give you £50 for the book, *I will edit it for £100.*
I feel so like a greyhound myself that your kicking one seems quite brutal & personal. Besides she is only answerable for the *pur* – the *loining* being supplied by the mutton

* I like to spell cus with *K* because it's *harder* than C.[3]

itself. As good says you as half the quibbles-in-law by which thieves are sheltered. Àpropos of long Dogs, please to tell the Squire with my compliments that he and all his brother Coursers are Dunces to spell Ashdown without an H.[4] We always *hash down* our Hares the second day, if not demolished the first – & our cook would spell the place properly. Dear Tom I believe prefer'd them *brown jugged.* I dote on Etymology –

It's fine weather – i.e. fine & cold, but it suits me for it braces. Till when I remain

Yours in haste.

T.H.

Mrs H. says with her Compts that you promised her a book – not of Sermons.[5]

[*St John's Wood, November 1842*]

MS Texas

1/Farmer *Slang and its Analogues* defines 'ginnum' as an old woman fond of gin! The second should perhaps be O.D.V. for brandy: Eric Partridge *A Dictionary of Slang* 5th ed. (1961).

2/Hewlett's *Poetry for the Million* must have been published soon after the date of this letter, for it was reviewed in NMM January 1843.

3/The first use of 'cuss' given in NED is dated 1848.

4/The Ashdown (Berks.) coursing meeting was established in 1780. Hood's reference is timely, since the Ashdown Park Cup was run for in the February and November of each year, and this year the November meeting took place on the 14th.

5/The book was perhaps Hewlett's *College Life*, published towards the end of December 1842.

TO

J.T.J. HEWLETT

Dear P.P.

From what I learn Colburn has been *very much annoyed* about the announcement of your name etc, but says it was entirely through Shoberl. Mrs H. told him about the Bishop.[1]

Has he given any answer to your proposition to him? If not don't be hasty. *I* should of course be very sorry to lose you as a contrib and coad – but besides from all I hear & have heard Bentley is a very queer customer, however liberal *at first* – but this is really verb. sap.

Have you any guess yet whether you shall be able to come tomorrow?

My head-ache went off shortly after getting home – it was from the dramatic gas not the vinous.

I am
Dear P.P.
Yours very truly

Thos Hood.

17, Elm Tree Road / St John's Wood / Friday [*November 1842*]

MS Texas

1/For example, in *The Athenaeum* 17 December 1842, 1096, *College Life* was advertised as by 'J. Hewlett, M.A. Late of Worcester College, Oxford.' Perhaps Hewlett's bishop objected to the publication of his name as a novelist.

TO
WILLIAM ELLIOT

I went to Dickens this morning but could not catch him.

[*St John's Wood, 11 November 1842*]

From Myers & Co *Autograph Letters* no. 313 (1936) 37, where the date is given. This note belongs with the following letters to Dickens and Elliot, the second of which gives us a date to work with.

TO
CHARLES DICKENS

My dear Dickens.
Just read the enclosed, & if your voice and interest are not otherwise bespoke, it would really oblige me could you give them in favour of Mrs. K.[1]
Dr. Elliot is a Physician well known & in extensive practise. He brought my wife, almost miraculously thro a desperate illness at Wanstead – & myself thro the most dangerous of my attacks in his own house. He & she are indeed of those good people after your own heart, & of whose existence one might be sceptical but for such living examples. They have been as brother & sister to me, & if a man can have *two homes* my second one is in their house. So you see I have good cause to wish to meet their wish in this matter – & it may fortunately happen that you are not especially interested for any candidate.

You will meet the Elliots one day, if, as I hope you, and Mrs. Dickens will spend one sociable evening with us, & a few friends, The Dilkes &c &c. Is it likely you will have an open night for this purpose in the beginning of next month?
I called lately in Devonshire Terrace, during a morning ramble with Mr. Hewlett. My purpose was chiefly to congratulate you on the success of yr. American book, of which privately I have heard the highest commendations, – I hope you did not dislike the notice in the N.M.M.[2] I could not pretend to a review, or to extract much – the dailies and weeklies having *sweated* your *Notes* as if they had been *Sovereigns*.[3] We are all dying now for Mrs. Dickens's notes –

Our kindest regards to her.
I am
My dear Dickens
Yours very truly

Thos. Hood.

Last week there were some sheets stolen of a work printing at Beaufort House[4] – for the use of a rival publisher. I thought we should have a touch of the American system here. Then there are those American Notes by Buz advertised from Holywell Street[5] – of course a piracy. It is hard for an individual author or Publisher to have to proceed agt. men of straw.[6] There ought to be a Literary Association for the Suppression of Piracy – a fund subscribed by Authors Booksellers & friends to letters – and of which to proceed agt. the very first offender – similar to the provincial Associations for the persecution of Felons. Eh?[7]

17 Elm Tree Road / Friday [*11 November 1842*]

MS Huntington. Published by Whitley HLQ 398–9. This was perhaps written on the day before the following letter.

1/'Mrs. K' (Mrs. Kennion) was a candidate for the post of matron at the Sanatorium, Devonshire Place House, New Road, of which Dickens was a patron. This institution was opened on 6 April 1842, in order to look after 'Sick Persons of the Middle Classes': prospectus in the British Museum. See the following letter.

2/NMM November 1842, 396–406

3/To sweat a sovereign is to lighten it by attrition: the periodicals have made fraudulent use of Dickens's *Notes* for their own benefit, in the process reducing their value.

4/Place of business of Charles Whiting, who printed NMM for Colburn

5/'Of unsavoury reputation, the whilom Booksellers' Row of Dickens' day, a "narrow, dirty lane" which ran parallel with the Strand ... occupied chiefly by vendors of books of doubtful morality,' Francis Miltoun *Dickens' London* (Boston 1904) 125–6.

6/Men of no substance

7/Whitley refers to a comment in *The Athenaeum* 26 November 1842, 1016, asking why authors and publishers do not unite against literary pirates, and to a report in the *Literary Gazette* 20 May 1843, 337–8, concerning a 'meeting for the formation of an Association for the Protection of Literature,' at which Dickens presided.

TO

WILLIAM ELLIOT

Dear Doctor.

I have but just heard from Dickens who has been out of town,[1] I suspect, hunting for a locality for his next tale. At least he was twice in the country when I called lately. I am sorry to say his interest at the Sanatorium has been preengaged. It appears to me that Mrs Kennion has come rather late into the field, & Dickens implies that the candidates are very numerous. Here follows his answer.

'I can't state in figures (not very well remembering how to get beyond a *million*) the number of candidates for the Sanatorium matronship but if you will ask your little boy to trace figures in the beds of your garden beginning at the front wall, going down to the cricket ground, coming back to the wall again, and "carrying over" to the next door, & will then set a skilful accountant to add up the whole the product, as the Tutor's Assistants say, will give you the amount required. I have pledged myself (being assured of her capability) to support a near relation of Miss Edgeworth's; – otherwise I need not say how glad I should have been to forward any wish of yours.'

He adds 'We shall be more than glad to come to you on any evening you may name' – so that we shall hope to see you all together, so soon as I have got thro this Magazine, into the thick (& thin) of which I am just wading.

In the mean time I have written to Dilke on the chance that he may know some of the Sanatorium Committee – & Jane is writing to your Brother to know if he has any voice in the New Camberwell Church organ – that is to say, in the commission. Nothing but canvassing – which reminds me of Berlin wool work, & that recalls Mrs Elliot. Pray tell her Jane has some new patterns. She commissioned Franck to send her some for *slippers*, but wrote the word so badly that he asked what new English articles were *dippers*. However the patterns came – at least as far as the front gate, by the Parcels cart, & then went away again – for not living near any shop we sometimes run quite out of change, & in the whole house could not muster 3s/6d for carriage & duty! However she has obtained them at last, & I really think her head has been wool gathering ever since.

I suppose your Brother's accident happened during his idleness at Cheltenham – or

was it about the date of the new family vehicle? When I told Jane of it, she directly said ' I have a great mind to go over & see him, about the Camberwell organ' – for which read, the organ of Curiosity. The 6th was her birthday, and we had a few young friends and performed two Charades – so we are pretty well.
Give our love to all, – including the new Grammar-school-boy. Of course he can tell now what mood *May* is in. Jeanie I know is the Potential. I am Dear Doctor

Yours very truly

Thos Hood.

Have you seen the advt of Dr Laycocks mystics, in the Lancet?[2] Or that headed Chemia Antiqua, in yesterday's Athenaeum offering to a select number of Pupils, premium 200 guineas, an induction to the Hermetic Science – and a shy with the Philosopher's Stone!!![3]

17 Elm Tree Road / St John's Wood / Saturday Evening [*12 November 1842*]

MS Yale. Published in *Memorials* II 143–6. The letter is dated in another hand.
1/In Cornwall
2/Dr Thomas Laycock speculated on 'Periodicity in the Phenomena of Life' in *Lancet* 29 October 1842, 160–4.
3/*Athenaeum* 12 November 1842, 961

TO
CHARLES DICKENS

My dear Dickens.
Will the 6th. of Decr. suit you to spend an evening with us – ? If you, or Mrs. D, should happen to be engaged, we will name another date, to get sociable on.
I ought to tell you of two remarks from two Publishers, but to one effect – viz, that, in reference to the proposed association for the defence of Copyright, the Authors being most interested ought to pay Double!!! How fond they are of profitable practical jokes!

Yours ever truly

Thos Hood

C. Dickens Esqre

17 Elm Tree Road / St John's Wood / Monday [*November 1842*]

MS Huntington. Published by Whitley HLQ 400–1

TO
J.T.J. HEWLETT

Dear P.P.
Dickens will & can come on the 6th so all is right – but we want the Number of the Smileys & the right spelling of the name. Also, if the son be Mr Andrew, or Mr Andrews? – Or *What?* A line by return of post will oblige me – to make no mistakes. I hope you arrived safely at Letcombe with Miss Hewlett, alias Charlotte, & that therefore she does not repent her Tower of, or to, London.
I am in the thick of the Magazine – & have just received *the sheet in which you stand* to make *quite correct.*
Ergo

Yours very truly & hastily

Thos Hood

17 Elm Tree Road / St John's Wood / Nov. 22nd [*1842*]

MS Texas. The signature of this letter ends with an elaborate twirl.

TO
CHARLES DICKENS

Dear Dickens
Perhaps you did not observe the following in the papers.
Dr. Imray pubd. a Cyclopedia of Popular Medicine intended for domestic Use – sometime in 1841.
In May 1842 Tegg brought out a Cyclopedia of Medicine intended for Domestic Use, of 502 pages of which 384 copied verbatim from Imray. His Honour the Vice[1] satisfied himself of the piracy by reading the Chapter on Cholic – & granted the injunction.[2]
After Teggs insolence about Copyrights & Authors,[3] this fact ought to be published as widely as possible.
I sounded one or two Booksellers yesterday about the association, & oddly enough, on seeing Longman Junior,[4] G.P.R. James[5] had been there just before on the very same subject – & Longman showed me a paper on which the plan was sketched.

So I said what you & I thought of it, & offered to cooperate.
No answer required.

I am Dear Dickens Yours ever truly

Thos Hood.

C. Dickens Esqre

17 Elm Tree Road / Tuesday. [*22 November 1842*]

MS Huntington. Published by Whitley HLQ 399–400. Whitley's notes are followed below. In his second paragraph Hood is drawing on a newspaper account, such as that of *The Athenaeum* 19 November 1842, 993. If Hood is indeed using this account, then his letter belongs to the following Tuesday, 22nd.

1/The Vice-Chancellor, Sir Lancelot Shadwell

2/Unfortunately, Tegg won his case.

3/In 1837 Tegg had issued his *Remarks on the Speech of Sergeant Talfourd*, adversely criticising Talfourd's attempt to strengthen the copyright laws.

4/Thomas Longman (1804–79)

5/George Payne Rainford James (1801–60), novelist and historical writer

TO

ROBERT ELLIOT

Dear Doctor,

Altho the winter has not exactly set in, I have volunteered to break some ice, in which you have hitherto preserved a certain secret, & of which some mutual friends at Stratford have given us a hint.

Of course you have had your note of invitation for the 6th to Jane's party – she has already received promises from Dickens, Ainsworth, Miss Pardoe,[1] Peter Priggins, Forster, & expects Procter, Ingoldsby – Sir C. & Lady Morgan – Poole (the Author of Paul Pry) & some others. If you know therefore of any young lady who would like to see a few of our literary lions and lionesses, we should be most happy to see her, particularly if she should happen to be a namesake of Mrs *Hemans* & a word from you to *authorize* it will produce a regular *article* from Jane to that effect. I am glad to say the Stratford-not-upon-Avon Elliots are coming with Manley Hopkins,

& some of the Wards[2] out of Chancery. What a pity the Barnes's are not within reach! – to be at our first bit of gaiety.
If the INFLUENZA will let you, *do* drop us a line by return of post, & believe us*

Dear Doctor (for self & Partner)
Yours very heartily

Thos Hood.

[*St John's Wood*] *Friday Evening*. [*November 1842*]

* Not editorially but domestically.

MS Harvard. Published by Lane KSJ 51–2. Hood is inviting Elliot to his party of 6 December 1842.
1/Julia Pardoe (1806–62), author
2/The first reference to Frederick Oldfield Ward, who later helped Hood greatly in the publication of *Hood's Magazine*. Ward was a friend of other poets. Landor wrote him, 'Your kindness to poor Hood ought to exempt you from all calamities,' Rylands MS, and Browning considered him 'a capital fellow, full of talent and congeniality,' *Letters of Robert Browning collected by T.J. Wise* ed. T.L. Hood (1933) 30. In 1838 Ward published *Outlines of Osteology*, and he later earned the soubriquet of 'the Louis Blanc of Sanitary Reform' *Engineers and Officials* (1856) 84. G.H. Lewes called him 'the *Times* thunderer on sanitary matters – and, a remarkable man to boot,' Rylands MS.

TO
CHARLES DICKENS

Dear Dickens.
Your Cornwall trip reminded me of a Romance of Real Life which I have heard, & may afford you a hint.
A certain London architect was engaged to the Daughter of a wealthy market gardener, near town; but during a journey in the West of England was smitten by the extreme beauty of a young lady whom he saw, at a first floor or second floor window in a country town – She was the daughter of a Surgeon, & was kept a prisoner, almost to her chamber, by her father. The Architect thinking her illused became interested in her behalf – then desperately in love, & forgetting his betrothed in London – ran away with the West Country girl & married her. It soon appeared that she had not been under restraint without reason – She was a very pickle – spent every thing, & ran her husband deeply into debt – giving him cause besides for jealousy. Her husband wishing for children – she at last palmed off a baby on him, which was sent to nurse, – till about a year old, when as the pseudo Father was passing, or going to the woman's house he heard her beating &

rating the little one very harshly. He immediately went in & reprimanded her – when in the height of her passion she let slip that the brat was none of his & subsequently confessed in explanation that she had been bribed by his wife to *lend* the child, but that 'the trick had been played off long enough.' Other hints induced him on his return home to search his wife's room for letters, – instead of which, in a drawer, he discovered a full suit of widows weeds (new) & naturally inferred that he was to be got rid of by poison – He accordingly turned off his wife – to whom perhaps he made no allowance of money – or probably she became utterly abandoned, – for some years afterwards, a friend, on a tour in the West of England, recognized her* *working in the Cornish mines.*

The incident of finding the mourning I have used in the National Tales[1] – but the story is true, & some of the parties were known, I believe, to my wife's mother. The name of the Architect, was Nash, – whether *the* Nash[2] I know not.

No answer required – Mrs. Dickens says you are very busy or Bozzy – both will do. I'm buzzy[3] – in the head, to think of so short a month as Decr. will be to

Yours ever truly

Thos Hood

Of course your American little dog will pirate some English ones bark. Try him some day with the first proof sheet of Chuzzlewit.[4]

17. Elm Tree Road / Thursday. [*November 1842*]

*chiefly by her remarkably long & beautiful hair.

MS Huntington. Published by Whitley HLQ 395–6. In his last paragraph Hood is referring to the December work on NMM.

1/In 'Baranga' *Works* v 429

2/John Nash (1752–1835), designer of the Marble Arch, Regent's Park, Regent's Street, and other squares and terraces in London

3/The first example of the word used in this sense given in NED is dated 1871.

4/The first monthly part of Dickens's *Martin Chuzzlewit* was issued in January 1843.

TO
CLARKSON STANFIELD

A faction of a few friends has increased into a party – to meet here on Tuesday, 6th Dec ... will you join in the Plot? – to the great pleasure of

Dear Stanfield, Yours very truly, Thos. Hood.

[*St John's Wood, November 1842*]

From Myers & Co. *Autograph Letters* no. 287 (June 1932) 10

TO
CHARLES DICKENS

My dear Dickens
'The more the merrier' – which I suppose is the reason of such a mob of mourners at an Irish Funeral.
Many thanks therefore for your friendly additions to our little edition of a party. We shall be most happy to see Mrs. Dickens's sister[1] (who will perhaps kindly forego the formality of a previous call from Mrs. Hood) and as to Maclise[2] I would rather be introduced to him – in spite of Mason on Self Knowledge[3] – than to myself. Pray tell him so much – & give him the 'Meet'.[4]
I fancied one day that I saw coming out of your house a younger Brother[5] who dined with us at Greenwich – would he object to come with you? – but I will not suggest, Mrs. Hood having just desired me to send you the enclosed,[6] which you must consider, on both sides, to comprehend.

Yours ever truly

Thos Hood

C. Dickens Esquire.

17 Elm Tree Road / St John's Wood / Thursday [*1 December 1842*]

MS Huntington. Published by Whitley HLQ 401

1/Georgina Hogarth (1827–1917)
2/Daniel Maclise (1806–70), artist, came to London in 1827, contributed portraits of literary men to *Fraser's Magazine* (1830–8). Friend of Dickens from 1838. The hitherto unpublished sketch of Hood, used as a frontispiece to this edition, was doubtless made about this time.
3/John Mason's work, first published in 1745, appeared in many editions until 1846.

4/In reply to Dickens's letter of 30 November *Letters* ed. Dexter, I 491–2
5/Frederick Dickens (1820–68). Whitley gives Alfred, but Mrs Madeline House kindly points out the 'younger Brother' here is more likely to be Frederick, who was in charge of the Dickens children while their parents were in America.
6/The enclosure has not survived with the letter.

TO
J.T.J. HEWLETT

Dear P.P.
I was in hope of seeing you again before your exit;[1] but such fogs are solid excuses. Did I understand you to say that you sent two Copies of the Poetry for the million for me – or one for me & one for Colburn – or was there one written in for Mrs. *H.*? Tell me the rights that I may set them to rights. I have received one – not written in at all.
I will send you an Athm. if a review in it – but do not build on it – for Dilke has his own views of things & will not be swayed – so it depends on how he himself may relish the thing.[2] I shall get a notice in this month any how – but Colburn's reviews cramp me sadly in that matter, look at the mass of them last month. But I shall bespeak space for it.[3]
Have you had any notices elsewhere, and good? – I see nothing, save Herald, Athm. & Weekly Chronicle. –
The party from all we hear went off well. We are bespoke for Twelfth Night to Dickens's – Xmas Day – Doctor Elliots – tomorrow to Mr Wards – Saturday & Wednesday to Dilkes. – That is *gay* for *us*.. With love to all

Yours very truly

Thos Hood

Don't forget this is a plaguy short month ending in the 23 – after which Gwynn says 'no printing.' so your article as soon as you can will oblige me and T.H.

17 Elm Tree Road / St. John's Wood. / Thursday. [*8 December 1842*]

MS Texas

1/After a visit to London
2/Hewlett's *Poetry for the Million* was unenthusiastically reviewed in *Athenaeum* 10 December 1842.
3/A review of *Poetry for the Million* appeared in NMM January 1843.

TO
MRS MARIA DILKE

My dear Mrs Dilke. I am very glad to hear that you think the party went off so well. Of course next day we were rather snoozy[1] gapey and indolent & like the wild Beasts after Bartlemy Fair, very tame indeed.[2] Tom excepted who ought to have been dozey but was as brisk as a bee. So much for youth. I lay in bed very late like Watts's Sluggard[3] & made my reflections on the guests – What good spirits you were in & how frisky the Editor was – with a deal of dance left in him when he went. Then that very popular Punch!! for which every body must have been better – & how well your boy waited – but I beg pardon for you were described below stairs as '*the lady with the Page*'. (I'd make Dilke indulge me in a double number of such pages) And all the servants lauded him so that our boy grew jealous & said 'you'd better lap him up in gold paper.' – Another young lady, who had no page, was not so happily described as *the lady who tumbled up stairs*. Then they had never heard such singing – Jane (the servant) thought herself I suspect within sound of the angelic quire – for she is of a decidedly pious turn. Marian's[4] voice made quite a sensation – every body was asking me about her – & then Mr Hook was so taken with your singing, he said it was one of the best ballad voices he had ever heard. So I think you may come next time as the Countess of Essex – only don't come from Antwerp or you won't come at all, – like the Countess de Melfort, who was *missed* thro *fog*. However, the thing seemed really to go off well & all *parties* to be pleased[5] – and it will be well if with Colburn's puffing propensity his Editors party does not get into the Post. But now comes a preciously short month and I must work double tides – that Xmas revelries may not be cut short. That's the way in which we Editors must go from gay to grave from lively to severe.[6] – ie from cheerful guests to dull contributors, from a Bayle Farm Féte to Squampash Flats.[7]

I shall tell *you no* more that something may be left to talk over when we see you – which however is impossible thro so much fog: – not to mention streets, parks, &c. hardly more solid. –

I hope you all got home safe, & that Mrs Wentworth was no worse for the weather. I meant to go out to day but am afraid of losing myself – & don't like to be my own link boy. –

NB. Your note just arrived which I leave Jane to answer having to write a little Ode to whist – a Sonnet on hearing a lady sing – Stanzas on witnessing a quadrille – and Punch, a reverie.[8] I am My dear Mrs D. Yours very truly

Thos Hood.

[*St John's Wood, December 1842*]

MS BM. Published by Marchand 82–4

1/The first example of this adjective given in NED is dated 1877.
2/When William Hone visited Bartholomew Fair in 1825 he saw both Atkins's and Wombwell's menageries, though he did not comment on the tameness of the animals: *Every-day Book* (1826) I 175, 1197.
3/Isaac Watts *Moral Songs*, 'The Sluggard'
4/Unidentified
5/Dickens was one of the guests who enjoyed the party, for he wrote on 7 December: 'A party and some hot Punch – made hotter inside of me by dancing, last night – has rather impaired my memory today,' *Letters* I 493.
6/Pope *Essay on Man* iv 380
7/Boyle Farm was the site of a famous society fête which took place in 1827. Squampash Flats was Hood's own name for a desolate colonial outpost, 'Letter from an Emigrant,' *Comic Annual* for 1830, *Works* I 23.
8/Imaginary poems

TO
J.T.J. HEWLETT

Dear P.P.

We *all* wish you *all* a right merrie xxx mas! (The same with my Compliments to the Squire –)

I have written a brief notice of your book & sent it direct to the Printers so if it should not appear it is not my fault – but Colburns had set down 12 pages for their reviews & I have already reduced them to 9 – but I suspect he will give an extra 1/2 sheet.[1] I like the introduction to your 'Widders.'[2]

Barham called here Thursday or Friday, & said Mrs Hughes was in town – if you see her offer my respects to her & good seasonable wishes. Also to the Haywards. We are all off on Monday to Dr Elliots at Stratford, Essex – where we shall pass best part or all of the week.

I have written more than usual this month – an Etching Poem – & The Defaulter, a prose story[3] – & yet I am done today as far as I am concerned! *Spry* for me![4]

Yours very truly

Thos Hood

Did you notice in the paper the marriage of The Ramsgate Snowden?[5] Ask yourself seriously tomorrow, as an Author, whether you do not prefer 'solid pudding to empty praise?'[6] I have taken to drink punch & find myself the better for it. Tom Bowling![7] We shall not forget you tomorrow in our *pot*ations & of course shall make a *pint* of Charlotte's good health & happiness.[8]

Decr. 24th. 1842/ 17 Elm Tree Road

MS Texas

1/NMM January 1843 finally contained only eight pages of reviews, nearly two of them occupied by Hood's review of his friend's *College Life;* he also noticed Hewlett's *Poetry for the Million.*
2/NMM January contained the first number of Hewlett's 'The Widows' Almshouse.' I have not identified the Haywards mentioned in the next paragraph.
3/NMM January, 1–7, 117–128
4/A pun on 'pray' and 'spry,' meaning quick of movement
5/13 December 'At Ramsgate, T.H. Grove Snowden, esq. to Sophia, younger dau. of the late Hugh Sandford Harrison, esq.:' *Gentleman's Magazine* February 1843, 198. Snowden was probably an acquaintance common to Hood and Hewlett.
6/Pope *Dunciad* i 52
7/Hero of a nautical song by Charles Dibdin
8/Hood is here echoing a sentence in *Poetry for the Million*, 38, where Hewlett wrote: 'We wish [the M.P.] luck – *pot* luck or pint *luck* ... as his model, the great comic Perennial himself would say.' The Perennial is Hood.

TO
CHARLES DICKENS

Dear Dickens
As you are so busy the following advt. in todays Herald may escape your notice.
Now Ready. Tenth Edition 1s/.
Parley's Library Vol 1. contains every incident in Master Humphrey's Clock – the whole of the Curiosity Shop & Barnaby Rudge.
Cleave Shoe Lane Fleet Street Lee & Haddock printers Craven Yard Drury Lane.
All good wishes from us all to you all. Just setting off to spend a few days at Dr. Elliots Stratford.

Yours ever truly

Thos Hood

[*St John's Wood*] *Decr. 26th.* [*1842*]

MS Huntington. Published by Whitley HLQ 401–2

1843

TO
WILLIAM ELLIOT

Dear Doctor,
We did not forget the wedding-day, but drank the health of the pair, with earnest wishes for their long and lasting happiness; of course they are now in the midst of 'honey and B's:' Bliss, Brighton, Baths, Billows, and Beach.
I thank you for your congratulations on my gout, but fear it is 'no such luck,' I am more likely to have the cold aguish rheumatism. I have got rid of the 'agony point' of the game, but the progress seems very slow – in accordance with other sluggish characteristics, my foot continues swelled, and so tender I can hardly put it to the ground; I don't believe therefore it can be a *long-standing* complaint like the gout. You do not say how Mrs. Elliot got over her fatigue, so we hope it was not worth mentioning. Give all our loves to all, and pray tell Dunnie and Jeanie they will hear from me as soon as I can write a good *foot.*
I am, Dear Doctor,
Yours every truly,
Thos. Hood.
[*St John's Wood*] *Thursday night,* [*12 January*] *1843.*

From *Memorials* II 150–1. Robert Elliot, William's brother, was married on Wednesday, 11 January 1843.

TO
J.T.J. HEWLETT

Dear Peter
I have received yours, but time presses, & *Mag* forbids *gossip.* –
I went to Essex & spent a week there, happily as regards comfort & hospitality but miserably in respect to health, – the old ague revived from the very first day, I had regular shivers all the morning & fever all night, till on the last I was slightly delirious. I was better on getting home but have never been well since, & for the last fortnight have been laid up with my foot – *I* say Rheuma*tiz* but my Doctor

says Rheuma*tisn't* – but Gout! You may guess how this has driven me for time – besides cutting me out of half my parties including Dickens's on Twelfth Night. And worst of all makes Jany. a very short *New Month*, – & my article not yet done! It was neither of *my* D^r. Elliots at Wantage – One cannot leave his practise; & his brother is spending his honey moon at Brighton. They have a namesake I believe in the profession.
So much, just to account for my silence, I am in the middle of proofs & *making-up* with Gwynn, not that we have fallen out – but to make the articles fall in.
Kind remembrances to all at Letcombe, from

Yours truly & hastily

TH.

Any chance of your soon visiting Lonnon?
Rev^d. J. Hewlett
P.P. Esqre.

[*St John's Wood*] *Wednesday.* / *Bednesday.* [*late January 1843*]

MS Texas. Dated on internal evidence

TO
MRS MARIA DILKE

My dear M^rs. Dilke.
As Jane has written so awkwardly, for a correspondant, I mean to try my luck, and to ensure our letters not crossing shall return you your own with my comments in a different ink.
'Dilke has been very ill the last four or five days – *Yes, with the Athenaeum up to Friday*[1] – not able to get out of his bed – *no, he was always an inveterate you know what* – but yesterday there was a great change for the better – *& whoever laid the first stone of the Great 'Change Dilke no doubt was at the feast*[2] – and today is so fine he has gone out for a little drive *he ought to have walked* – and as that is the case – *a very mild one,* – I think I may venture to ask you & Hood *nothing venture nothing have* – & one or two more to join us in a family dinner on the 18th – Wentworth's Birth day – *Wentworth – what, a family dinner for one child!* – a ¼ before 6-*nonsense-he's 7 if he's a day* – do come if you can – *what an if!* as we really want to see you – *a bit of ground bait to get us to bite!*

Are you going to Colburn's on Tuesday? *Of course – it would be a day after the fair on Wednesday.* We have had an invitation to meet Lady Morgan & a few literary friends – *and a blue Hare?*[3] but Dilke *of course* is too unwell – *si sick omnes!!!*
I want to get a walk – *Walker!* that I know you will excuse my saying more than my kind love to you all &
Believe me yours ever
M.D.
(*No God bless – think it's a forgery*)

S.P. Let me hear from you soon – *Who hinders you?*
Yours ever truly
Thos Hood.

P.S. Many thanks for the order – We'll be sure to come – but mind & keep places for us – two – *dress circle* – FIRST ROW.

P.P.S. The last paragraph is in the wrong ink which ought to have been RED. *I am not accustomed to be* READ *in M.S. but in print.*
Jane would add her hand but from haste only puts her finger.[4]

17 Elm Tree Road [*February 1843*]

MS BM. Published by Marchand 84–5. The italicized passages in this letter were written by Hood in red ink. The letter can be dated by the reference to Wentworth Dilke's birthday, 18 February.
1/*The Athenaeum* was published on Saturday.
2/Prince Albert laid the foundation stone of the new Royal Exchange on 17 January 1842.
3/Presumably to go with the blue stockings
4/There follows a finger print.

TO
J.T.J. HEWLETT

Dear Peter.
Did you see that the other day a boy was taken up for picking pockets, & gave his name as 'Peter Priggins'?
After that, many persons would not write to you, but after a few days' hesitation, you see, I have got over my qualms, & resume the intercourse.
As you will conclude from this missive, I am *not* dead – but I have been very unwell, & could not revive the weather continued so favourable – to illness. Moreover I have been *very* busy at short notice not only in getting out the Mag – but with extra

affairs – including overtures for accommodation of all differences from my old Pub. Baily but which ended in humbug, so I am now going to law with him in right down earnest – if he dares go into Court all the Authors ought to make cause with me for the fun's sake & muster in the Hall. There would be some very queer proceedings, & accounts to show up.

While on business, pray remember the curtailed month & let me have your paper as early as you can.[1]

I wish I *could* go down to Letcombe but, to use a strong word it is *him*-possible – but Mrs H joins with me in acknowledgment & thanks for your kind invitation. When are you likely to be in town? I thought you never staid so long in Berks.

I write these few lines in haste to relieve your anxiety as to my death – not that you can have any expectations from it – but perhaps you intended a Funeral sermon.

Love to all
I am Dear Peter
Yours very truly

Thos Hood.

17 Elm Tree Road / Tuesday. [*February 1843*]

MS Texas. The overtures with Baily to which Hood refers were made in the third week of January 1843 and came to nothing on the 21st.

1/NMM March contained a continuation of Hewlett's 'The Widows' Almhouse.'

TO
EDWARD MOXON

My dear Moxon –

I have read the M.S. which certainly shows up or rather shows down the great Savage very effectively – a great part of the paper however having no reference to the attack on Wordsworth, which by the bye I must get to read. However, I fear I must not meddle with the matter, by insertion of the article in the New Monthly – not that I should mind personally a bit of pen & ink skrimmage – on behalf of Wordsworth versus Landor – but it has been my aim as Editor of a Mag – to avoid all controversy with other mags. – and I know Colburn, if I were willing, would be very averse.

In the mean time I sincerely hope & trust that Landor's attack will do no more harm to Wordsworth or his fame than the assault of Wakley.[1] My own notion of the probable truth is, that the Poet will be asked again to the Duchess of Sutherland's[2] or Windsor Castle, & that he will have another son (if there be one) made a Stamp Commissioner[3]

I am My dear Moxon
Yours ever truly

Thos Hood.

[*St John's Wood*] *Wednesday* [*February 1843*]

MS UCLA. Walter Savage Landor's 'Imaginary Conversation' between Southey and Porson, critical of Wordsworth, appeared in *Blackwood's Magazine*, December 1842. Perhaps Moxon sent to Hood the mock 'Imaginary Conversation' by Edward Quillinan, who referred to the 'Incomparable Savage' as 'a more formidable critic than Wakley.' This eventually appeared in *Blackwood's*, April 1843: 535, 536.

1/In NMM May 1842, 136–7, Hood had defended Wordsworth against the attack made upon him in parliament by the radical Thomas Wakley (1795–1862).

2/Harriet Elizabeth Georgiana, Duchess of Sutherland (1806–68), granddaughter of the fifth Duke of Devonshire.

3/Wordsworth's son William had in fact succeeded his father in the office of Stamp Distributor in the summer of 1842.

TO UNKNOWN CORRESPONDENT

My dear Sir
I was ill all day yesterday in bed or you should have had the Poem – I am down again today & at work at it getting on better, now that the Magazine is off my head – but it is certainly not in a state to show to *Judges*.

I am Dear Sir,
Yours very truly

Thos Hood

I must have another *nights* work at it – which is better than two *days*.

[*St John's Wood, February 1843*]

MS Huntington. Hood is surely here referring to his poem 'Laying down the Law,' published in NMM June 1843. See 524 and *Works* VIII 308–11. The poem illustrated Edwin Landseer's picture of the same name, in the possession of the Duke of Devonshire; the picture was painted in 1840 and engraved by Thomas Landseer three years later.

TO
CHARLES WENTWORTH DILKE

Dear Dilke
Moxon was here today & says Lord W. Lennox came to him about a novel – that he said *he only gave a sort of outline & heads of chapters & others filled them up*. I have no doubt after the exposé he will declare the true writer – I have strong suspicions of Shoberl being the man.
He wrote to me decidedly as from Lord L – ending with a proposal to call on me to know whether I was willing to comply '*with Lord L's request*.' Lord Lenox wrote to me that he did not authorize the application tho he had named me as the person he should prefer to write a preface – but that Shoberl shd have applied as from Colburn. I wrote to ask Shoberl if he was authorized by Colburn & he wrote that he was NOT but had '*applied of his own accord!*'
I have not seen the book yet – & have said nothing at Colburns of the discovery – but from the above have concluded that Shoberl was the true plagiarist, & wanted to entrap me into an apparent sanction of the work.
Yesterday morning I swore my affidavit in the Common Pleas, & shall have news tonight how the other party meet it, – we are going to a[1]

[*St John's Wood*] *Wednesday*. [*15 February 1843*]

MS BM. Published by Marchand 86–7. This and following letters (to 52) deal with the minor scandal of *The Tuft-Hunter*, a novel by Lord William Pitt Lennox (1799–1881), published by Colburn, and in part a plagiarism of Hood. The novel received a trite recommendation in NMM February 1843. The critic of the *Literary Gazette* 11 February, 82, described it ironically as 'written by the scion of a noble family, and not by a hack *littérateur* more conversant with the art of making up and sticking together.' There is thus some doubt, shared by Hood, as to whether in fact Lennox compiled the work.

1/The rest of the letter is missing.

TO
CHARLES WENTWORTH DILKE

Dear Dilke,
The Tuft Hunter appears to be one of the grossest cases possible. I have only seen the 1st Vol from a Library – & stumbled on passages taken from Sir W. Scott. Compare pages 243-244-245, 246 with St Ronans Well – pages 3-4-5-6-13- (Vol 34 of Fishers Edition of the Novels)

I have just received a note from Shoberl in reference to his former ones – he marks it '*Confidential*' which I interpret 'No word of this to Mr Colburn.' He encloses a letter from Lord L to him (Shoberl) dated 18 Jany – which confirms Lord L's to me viz – that the *suggestion* about me & a preface was to be made to Colburn. Shoberl did *not* consult Colburn but comes to me as with a direct request from Lord L. This I think convicts S. of the Authorship, by his personal interest in the scheme.
We passed your end of Grosvenor Place this morning – but as it was between 4 & 5 we did not drop in.

[*St John's Wood*] *Thursday.* [*16 February 1843*]

MS BM. Published by Marchand 87

TO

J.T.J. HEWLETT

Dear P.P.
Tom Junior, thank God is well, & has I think as much life in him, as our united vitalities. My left temple – bless him! – has been *green* for a week – the dear boy! – from his weight overbalancing me, – precious fellow – & sending me headpiece against mantelpiece – But I did not get my bust tho my caput was so marbled. I am so lame *to boot* in one foot that I am forced to wear a shoe & as I cannot stand walking or walk standing must either ride or sit at home. Wherefore I am very domestic in my habits. However the frost suits me it is so bracing – & then on Wednesday night we had such a nice long cold ride to a party at Camberwell Grove – (not to see the Beauty though)[1] that we went in very genteel – for we were *iced*.
Tuesday in Common Pleas I swore my 'Davit against Baily. So the fight is begun. Persuaded Mrs H to go back the whole length of Elm Road for 'a very good shilling' to pay for the oath. Would rather have sworn *at* Baily – but was afraid of the penalty. Saw lots of wigs & wondered if Judges & Counsel ever have colds in the head.
You know Landseer's Doggish Picture of 'Laying Down the Law.' – Well, I have written some dogrel verses to go with the print – & the moral is 'For what is Law –, unless poor dogs can get it
Dog-cheap?'
I have directed your Widows to be *set up* in the printing business & hope they will

prosper. In a day or two, no doubt, they will be more *composed* than at present. But od's tombstones how you have carried off the family like a plague – Babby – Father – Father in Law – Mother in law – Husband[2] – odds Shovels! how fond you Clergy are of funerals! Trust me, as I *am* sickly – for coming to be defuncted at Letcombe! While you are in this humour! –

Seriously I have no prospect before me for months to come but of fagging with pen & pencil to make up for lost time. Many thanks nevertheless for your kind invitation – I will enjoy it, in fancy, & get Jane to help me by playing some Berkshire air – for instance the Birks of Aberfeldie.[3]

Shall not we soon see you and Joe? –

All here send loves, & hope Charlotte is happy at Minehead

We have not seen the Smileys nor nobody since our Party as I have been so laid up – but I am going to take a round in a fly, – a regular day's work of calls.

I am
Dear P.P.
Yours ever truly

Thos Hood

P.S. I have advised as the commercials say a barrel of oysters to go by this day's (Saturday's) train to your station – and as they will be strangers to you, I request you to *take them in.*[4] The gale has prevented their coming in – so I shall send on Monday or Tuesday instead

My respects to the Squire – & Remembrances to all Berks.[5]

17 Elm Tree Road / St John's Wood / Saturday. [*18 February 1843*]

MS Texas. The reference to the weather in the first paragraph helps to date the letter. According to the 'Meteorological Journal' published in *The Athenaeum* 4 March 1843, 211, it was frosty between Monday 13th and Saturday 18th February.

1/Hood published 'The Camberwell Beauty' in NMM February.

2/These deaths occur in Hewlett's contribution between pp. 367 and 372 of NMM March.

3/Scots air, words by Burns

4/This sentence has been crossed out. The wording of the second half of the sentence is reminiscent of *Hamlet* I v 165.

5/The letter is illustrated with two little sketches and a final scroll.

TO
J.T.J. HEWLETT

Dear Peter.
Think of the date & you will see I must write in haste & briefly.[1] –
The oysters did not go till yesterday – 'because they were not good before' – so pray let me know candidly their quality that I may know whether I may trust the man in future.
I must shortly give you a bit of literary gossip – such a mess with Lord W. Lennox's novel – the Tuft Hunter! Plagiarisms of whole paragraphs from the Antiquary – St Ronan's Well – Tylney Hall – 12 pages from the 'Lion' by Chorley – and plunderings besides I understand from H. Smith – James Mrs Hall – & Bulwer! To complete the thing *I* one of the copied was applied to, for a Preface, by Shoberl as a direct request from Lord L – who says he only suggested it – & the burthen of said Preface to be Copyright & Literary Piracy! My impression is Lord L has paid or employed somebody to write the book, who has sold him – but query – who got it up. My guess was *Shoberl* – who seemed so anxious for the Preface – and a pretty position I should have been in! I have been very angry and rather amused but as yet all is dark & a mistery hangs over *the* party. He must be equally dishonest & stupid, – for he takes even half sentences as if he could not construct a whole one! I never recollect such a Phanomenon during my literary experience! However I have had a correspondence with Shoberl Lord L, & Colburn about it – & some *fun* out of it. As the thing appeared fix'd on a 'literary friend' of Colburn's I ventured to exculpate *you* in spite of your suspicious name P. *Priggins!*
R.U. coming up to town some day?

Yours ever

T.H.

[*St John's Wood*] *Friday* [*24 February 1843*]

MS Texas
1/Because of the schedule of NMM

❦❦❦❦❦❦❦❦❦❦❦❦❦❦

TO
CHARLES WENTWORTH DILKE

Dear Dilke
You have done it very well – the thing shows itself up, or you might have been perhaps severer upon it.[1] – Lord L. is a fool, but the other is a thorough rogue, & double traitor,[2] – the *system* deserves denouncing – however I have thundered a bit at the attempt to connect me with it – and am having my fun out of Colburn. Last night, in a sort of scheme of the contents of the Magazine I quietly inserted my own first article on the list, – as 'The Literary Daw' – they will be in a regular stew about it – & I mean to say if he does not like it, I can use it elsewhere.
Also as Lord L. has said the thing was done by one of Colburn's 'literary friends' & he has admitted it, – I have urged on him the propriety of giving up the man, & not leaving the slur amongst the Authors & Authoresses of his acquaintance, going thro the list – beginning with Lord Londonderry[3] – Morgans Bulwer H Smith, Lady Blessington &c &c &c. And as he did not like my fixing it on his Clerk, I have guessed again, from the ignorance of the work, borrowing half sentences even that it must *be the porter!*
In the meantime as the fellow gets off scot free & I have not had the slightest[4]

[*St John's Wood, February 1843*]

MS BM. Published by Marchand 88

1/Lennox's *Tuft-Hunter* was reviewed with cool irony in *The Athenaeum* 25 February 1843. At the suggestion of Hood, *Punch* treated the plagiarism on 11 March, 106, 109.
2/Hood seems to be suggesting that Shoberl was Lennox's ghost-writer.
3/Charles William Stewart, third Marquis of Londonderry (1778–1854). Colburn had published his *A Steam Voyage to Constantinople* in July 1842.
4/The rest of the letter is missing.

TO
CHARLES WENTWORTH DILKE

Dear Dilke,
The note we want is one that Day & Hughes[1] wrote to you, to say they thought it as well to state the reason for declining your proposal was that the stock was attached.

Mrs Dilke sent me a copy of the note but without the date – it must have been I think in *July* 1840.[2]

I am Dear Dilk.[3]

C.W. Dilke Esqu

17 Elm Tree Road / Monday [*early 1843*]

MS BM. Published by Marchand 92. The letter probably belongs to the period of litigation to which Hood had referred above, 524.

1/Baily's solicitors

2/It was 18 June.

3/The rest of the name and the signature are torn out.

TO

UNKNOWN CORRESPONDENT

My opinions on the neglect of Authors by the State, & their anomalous position as a class, were recorded in 1836 in some letters on Copyright in the Athenaeum ... [nothing since has altered opinions.] To be sure the Legislature has conceded to us a little longer lease of our own freeholds ... I cannot recall any public compliment to Literature – or its professors. Royal patronage there has been none ... [The remedy in their own hands] The enormous increase of readers must confer greater importance & influence on the writer ... [urges more unity of action, denies] all uncharitableness so commonly imputed to our irritable tribe[1] [peculiarly exposed to wrong ... & the world's contumely] ... should have formed a 'Bruderschaft' [for mutual support & defence] ... the more the world forgets his high calling the more the literary man ought to remember it [& then would rank *above* those equivocal blessings to Humanity, the Soldier & the Lawyer] & be placed between 'the Priest & the Physician.'

[*St John's Wood, 2 March 1843*]

Taken, with the date '2 March' and the phrases between square brackets, from Winifred A. Myers *Autograph Letters* no. 3 (1960) 31–2. I do not know the occasion of this letter. According to the catalogue, Hood goes on to regret that he cannot dine at the Freemason's Tavern (Great Queen St, Lincoln's Inn Fields).

1/Horace *Epistles* II 2, 102

TO
WILLIAM BRADBURY

My dear Bradbury,

Pray accept my best thanks for the Froissarts,[1] I am really obliged for them. Mrs. Hood begs me to add her best acknowledgments for the flower books.

I suppose the form of giving up my blocks was gone through yesterday, but if no inconvenience to Evans, I shall be glad if he will keep them a little longer: I never had any objection to the custody, and we may have more to do with them.

By way of variation of work I am drawing a little. I hope to hit on something worth sending. Such a lovely day up here! I have been trying to whistle like a blackbird, and have some hope of getting into the daily papers as a harbinger of spring heard in St. John's Wood.

Everybody now seems to have his monomania, (you have your D—) a spectre ominous as the Bodach Glas, in Rob Roy,[2] to the Highland Family. Couldn't 'Punch'[3] make something of Sir Robert going to the House in a cuirass for fear, with his back marked thus for a shot?

Yours very truly,

Thomas Hood.

P.S. There seems such a panic I should not wonder at some Irish gentleman shooting himself for fear of being shot.

What do you think of a little Guide-book, to be called 'Every man his own McNaghten?' But I beg your pardon, I forgot you are a marked man, and will not see any joke in the thing. Only take care that D— does not steal any of your type to cut into slugs; it would be so very unpleasant to be shot through the head with your own Small Caps.

17, Elm Tree Road. [*March 1843*]

From *Memorials* II 131–2. The letter can be loosely dated from the fourth paragraph and the postscript: on 21 January 1843 Daniel McNaghten shot Edward Drummond, Peel's private secretary, mistaking him for the minister. On 3 March he was tried and acquitted on the ground of insanity.

1/An edition or plates which I have not been able to identify.

2/Actually Scott's *Waverley* lix. I have not identified Bradbury's 'D.'

3/*Punch* had been wholly owned by Bradbury and Evans since 24 December 1842. Hood contributed odds and ends of writing and drawing to it from March 1843.

TO

J.T.J. HEWLETT

Dear P.P.

I did not send back the Critique because I looked for you every day – with Joe – & when your article did not come supposed you meant to bring it. A precious fellow he is, that reviewer of yours. – some private grudge I should think.

I have had all sorts of extra business on my hands – made Baily give up my blocks about 800 of em – & am now going to put him into Chancery.[1] But I defer gossip till we *meat*, & with love to all rest Dear P.P. Yours ever truly

Thos Hood.

Revd J. Hewlett.

17 Elm Tree Road / Saturday / 1. April. [*1843*]

MS Texas

1/Though Hood proceeded against Baily under the equitable jurisdiction of the court of Chancery, the case seems to have remained unfinished at Hood's death.

TO

WILLIAM JOHN BRODERIP

My dear Sir,

I admire, and shall have much pleasure in again reading, your seasonable poem in the 'New Monthly;' it breathes not only of spring, but the spring feelings which inspire true poetry.[1] I am glad to hear of more 'Recreations' for the next number, being partial to Natural History, and certainly preferring it, as no doubt you do, to the Unnatural Histories called novels, romances, &c., in the present day,

I am, my dear Sir,
Yours very truly,

Thos. Hood.

17, Elm Tree Road, St. John's Wood, April 6th, 1843.

From *Memorials* II 148–9

1/Perhaps Broderip's 'Molly Bann,' NMM April 1843. His 'Recreations in Natural History' appeared in NMM throughout this year.

TO
WILLIAM ELLIOT

Dear Doctor,
Accept our heartiest congratulations.[1] We were delighted to see your note, for we were getting very anxious, but did not like to write on that account; I am not made Laureate,[2] or I would write an ode on the occasion.
Jane will come as soon as Mrs. Elliot is well enough to see her. She is servant-hunting, so I am obliged to be, what she calls, her 'manuensis.'
I did go last night to W—'s,[3] being in fact pretty well, in spite of the east winds. I have been working hard with pen and pencil, besides some extras on my hands, such as Lord L— and B — .[4] I must not write more, except that we all join in love to you all, and Jane says it's beautiful weather for babbies, only they can't walk out; and the printers will keep Easter holidays, and the editors can't, in consequence. What is the title of the new article in your Magazine?
If you find him *de trop*, there is a chance for you in Boy's distribution.[5] Raffles are epidemic. So are monomaniacs. The comet is an intermittent.[6] The aërial carriage is flying gout, a lame affair![7] The income tax will be chronic:[8] and I am,

Dear Doctor,
Yours ever truly,

Thos. Hood.

17, Elm Tree Road, St. John's Wood, / Thursday, April 13th, 1843.

From *Memorials* II 149–50
1/Probably on the birth of a child
2/Southey died on 21 March 1843 and was succeeded as Laureate by Wordsworth two weeks later.
3/Perhaps Ward
4/Certainly Lennox and Baily
5/'In 1843 was promoted Boys' Fine Art Distribution,' offering many prizes and benefitting art: C. L. Ewen *Lotteries and Sweepstakes* (1932) 300–1.
6/Observed on 17 and 18 March by Sir John Herschel
7/The subject of an article in NMM April, 544–9
8/Peel had reintroduced the income tax in the previous year. This year's budget was brought in on 8 May.

TO

WILLIAM ELLIOT THE YOUNGER

Dear Willie,

You owe me no thanks, the book is in better hands than mine. I have not the organ of constructiveness, and made sure that by the help of the sledges at the foundry, you would hammer more out of the volume than I could.

Till lately, such was my ignorance, I thought the Engineers were the Fire Brigade. And even yet I do not rightly understand what you make at those factories along the river-side, except a noise, enough to render the Thames fishes deaf, as well as dumb. Of what use then could such a book be to me, who have no more notion of engineering than a Zoological monkey of driving piles? I hastily read a few pages, but understood little, except about fastening cross beams with two ties, which, being like a counsellor's wig, seemed to me the legal way. The railroad matter was quite beyond my comprehension, especially the necrological mode of laying down sleepers, which I should have thought belonged to medical practice. I hope you have no hand or finger in the construction of the Flying Fly at Blackwall;[1] some people insist rather inconsistently, that it will never ascend because it is a bubble, but you engineers know best. By the bye, your operations at Dover[2] do the profession great credit, you beat the doctors hollow. Give your father as much Dover's powder[3] as he pleases, and see if he can mine into a gouty foot, and blow out its chalk. I rather think I have an engineer amongst my correspondents. He signs himself *Screw*-tator, constantly quotes from Dr. Lever,[4] and speaks of carrots and turnips as *wedge*-ables. He even dines, I am told, at a French house, that he may ask for a *pully* instead of a chicken.[5]

Good night! I would write more, but I have scientifically lighted my candle, and am going mechanically to bed,

Yours, dear Willie,
Very truly,

Thos. Hood.

Talking of Engineering, it is strange that Brunel never calculated on one great use of the Thames Tunnel,[6] namely, to give the Cockneys at Easter a *hole* holiday. I forget how many thousands of Londoners had a *dry-dive* under the river. Some day, I predict, the tunnel will become a great water-pipe. And I'm a prophet.

I foretold in last month's Magazine, that *the Comet would blow up the Waltham Abbey Powder Mills.*[7]

17, Elm Tree Road, St. John's Wood, April 21st, 1843.

From *Memorials* II 151–3. Hood's daughter notes that this 'letter is addressed to Dr. Elliot's eldest son, who was being educated as a civil engineer. My father had sent him a book on the Steam Engine, forwarded to him in his editorial capacity.'

1/Perhaps the subject of the article on Mr Henson's 'Aerial Steam-Carriage,' NMM April 1843
2/On 26 January 1843 'A vast mine was sprung at Dover, to blow up the Rounddown Cliff ... the object being to make a roadway instead of a tunnel, for the South-eastern Railway' *Annual Register* 'Chronicle' 9–10. Thus the engineers 'beat the doctors hollow,' as Hood says, in removing obstacles to improvements.
3/Celebrated medicine, named after Thomas Dover M.D. (1660–1742)
4/Possibly Charles James Lever (1806–72) M.D., novelist, or John Charles Weaver Lever (1811–58), leading South London medical consultant
5/Hood is merely punning here, not referring to an actual correspondent.
6/Marc Isambard Brunel (1769–1849) and his son Isambard Kingdom Brunel (1806–59), civil engineers, were together responsible for the Thames Tunnel. Though work on the tunnel began in 1824, it was not opened to the public until 25 March 1843. By the end of April nearly half a million people had visited the work. Hood had published an 'Ode to M. Brunel' in the *Comic Annual* for 1831, *Works* I 38–40.
7/Hood had briefly discussed the appearance in the skies over London of a comet in NMM April 562. He is here mocking false prophets by linking it with a mishap at Waltham in which seven men were killed. This accident took place on 13 April.

TO
ROWLAND HILL

My dear Sir ...
I have seen so many instances of folly & ingratitude similar to those you have met with, that it would never surprise me to hear of the railway people some day, finding their trains running on so well, proposing to discharge the engines.

I am, my dear Sir,
Yours very truly,

Thomas Hood.

R. Hill, Esq.

17 Elm Tree Road, St. John's Wood. 1st May. [*1843*]

From Rowland Hill and G.B. Hill *Life of Sir Rowland Hill* (1880) I 479. Rowland Hill (1795–1879) and Hood were friends of old standing, according to Eleanor C. Smyth *Sir Rowland Hill* (1907) 179n. Hill, despite his work for postal reform, was dismissed from the Post Office at the end of 1842. In April 1843 he circulated the correspondence leading to his dismissal 'to the members of the Mercantile Committee, and some others of my friends,' Rowland Hill and G.B. Hill I 484–5. Hood received a copy with the request: 'Can you do anything for Penny Postage in your Magazine?' (Transcript in the possession of Mr J.M. Cohen). The above is part of Hood's reply. He doubtless informed Hill that NMM was no place for such a discussion.

TO
CHARLES WENTWORTH DILKE

Have you the *Quarterly*? I am rather anxious to see the article on 'Theodore Hook.' I suspect the Tories grudge the *New Monthly* very much to a Liberal editor, who can allow such latitude as our friend Sir Charles Morgan requires now and then.

[*St John's Wood, May 1843*]

From Dilke I 55. Lockhart's article on Hook, to which Hood refers here, appeared in the *Quarterly Review* May 1843.

TO
CHARLES WENTWORTH DILKE

From my bed room where I am nursing myself for a spasmodic attack of the lungs. – sharpish, but I am getting all right.

My dear Dilke.
Happening the other day to pick up an odd Vol of an old book amongst some waste paper, I have extracted & enclose a few amusing paragraphs which may help to make up with, in your column of odds & ends. – If you like them I have noted a few more for extract.
I have just got your note, & am much pleased that you liked the articles. Thanks for the No which reads capitally. – I hope Liction has a great increase of business. – I am looking out for another little book to do but send off these to be with you early –
I will write to the Secy, & shall like to be on the Committee – if it be but necessary to attend occasionally –

With joint kind regards to [you] I am
My dear Dilke

[*St John's Wood, May 1843*]

MS BM. Published by Marchand 92–3. Hood is probably referring at the end of this letter to an Association for the Protection of Literature, a meeting for the formation of which took place at Messrs Longman's on 17 May 1843, with Dickens presiding. The signature is torn out.

TO
CHARLES DICKENS

private

My dear Dickens.

I send you a letter I wish you to lay before the Association. I do not care to be a Committeeman, but feel convinced there was a juggle. There are plenty of the trade would object to *me*, for I have published what I thought of them. Colburn as likely as any, who on the publication of my *last Copyright Letter* attempted to call me to account for writing in the Athm.[1] I had all along told him I should write there & had done so, *till then* without an objection.

I understand Baily intends to call a number of Booksellers to give *their interpretation* of our agreement. Let him. I hardly think the Court or the Jury will take their verdict.

I am unpopular with the 'Publishers & sinners' (that's my emendation of the Gospel –) because in advocating their rights I have not forgotten their neighbors'. So be it – amen.[2]

As to Baily I mean if my lawyers will let me – perhaps if they won't – to plead my own cause in spite of the legal proverb.[3] I should like to cross examine one or two, of the Pubs & Sinners. But I have such *proofs* of fraud I fear he will not come into Court.

As to the society they knew that you & I & Dilke should pull together, in the Committee. However I can act as a Free Lance – help the society if I see fit, & if not, like an Irish Partisan I'll co-operate against it. In the mean time it seems to me that they have declared for the Integrity with a sneaking kindness towards the *Tegg*rity of Literary Property.

Goodbye. Hope you are all too well as usual. We are just so well that we might be better, which is *very well* for us.

I am aware of all your kindness about Colburn. Someday – I don't know when, we will meet I don't know where, & go thro I dont know what, on that subject. In the meantime good bye, & God bless you all, & hang the Aristocrats French or English, who do not prefer Charles Dick – to Charles Dix.[4] Mrs. Hood is gone to the Girlery (pronounced *gal*lery) of The Freemasons Hall to hear, see, & eat & drink all she can. I cannot spare time or money for the arts tho I love them & the Professors – & particularly Stanfield for coming uninvited the other night. I shall believe hereafter in Godsends & windfalls. Is he really a son of Mrs. Inchbald's[5] – she who produced, you know, 'Nature and Art'? Forster is a good fellow too, seeing that while Dilke roasted Colburn Forster would baste him: – quenching the burning shame of the Tuft Hunter, with the cool atrocity of Cavendish. Who knows but that as Lord Lennox found himself a Shoberl, – a Shoberl might fancy himself a Neale?[6] Since that first affair, & the second, who but must believe in Transmigration – of a lord into his own *Hack* – & a naval writer into a *shark*. A great Pub – into any little reptile you like – or don't.

T.H.

17 Elm Tree Road / Saturday [*20 May 1843*]

MS Huntington. Published by Whitley HLQ 402–3. Hood here discusses the Association mentioned in the previous letter. Jane's visit to the gallery of the Freemasons' Hall may have been on the occasion of the anniversary dinner of the Artists' Benevolent Fund which took place this year on Saturday, 20 May.

1/Hood is here referring to his two letters on 'Copyright and Copywrong' in *The Athenaeum* 11 and 18 June 1842.
2/Baily had written in *The Athenaeum* 10 October 1840, 792: 'Mr Hood's character may be left to the appreciation of all or any of the respectable publishers who have had literary transactions with him, before I had, and got rid of him one after the other.'
3/Unidentified
4/Whitley notes that this is an 'allusion to the barely concealed piracies' of Dickens's works.
5/Elizabeth Inchbald (1753–1821), author of *Nature and Art* (1796)
6/*Cavendish* by William Johnson Neale (1812–93) was published anonymously by Colburn and Bentley in 1831 and reissued ten years later. According to Bentley's *List of Publications*, under the date 25 November 1831, the secret concerning the authorship was long concealed.

TO
CHARLES DICKENS

Dear Dickens.
I have not been able till now to thank you, for doing all that was right and kind, as to the Association.
If you remember the arrangement of bodies at the first meeting, at the lower end of the table were the Publishers Longman, Murray & Colburn, but off from the rest by Dilke, and I think Turner.[1] The proposition originated with that Trio. I do not

believe Murray, whose Father is the only gentleman, in the line, I have met with. I have already told you about Colburn & my Copyright letters in the *Athenaeum*, & as to Longman, considering that when the idea of such a Society occurred to me, I called and proposed the thing to *him* (a compliment not impaired by Mr. James having anticipated me) I feel warranted in saying that he has shown himself deficient not only in the courtesy of a gentleman, but the common civility of a Tradesman.

By way of experiment I sent to the Printer an announcement of the association – coupled with the bare fact of my retirement from it – & he has suppressed it. Confirmation strong as holy writ[2] of my impressions both as to him & a section of the Society, which has only now to order a seal, with a motto from Rolla's address to the Peruvians. – 'Such Protection as Vultures give to Lambs – covering & devouring them.'[3]

And so ends a matter, for the present, which annoys me but little on personal grounds, for I trust I can afford, in fame at least, to be unpopular with a few booksellers. – but oh the littleness to which some human souls reduce themselves. – as if Heaven would not have room for us all.

Well, – Good bye & God bless you all,
Yours fraternally,

T. Hood

17 Elm Tree Road / Tuesday. [*May 1843*]

MS New York. Published by Whitley HLQ 403–4. Hood continues his discussion of the literary Association.

1/Possibly Sharon Turner (1768–1847), historian and business associate of John Murray. I do not know what the proposition was to which Hood refers. The elder Murray died in June 1843, so his son (1808–92) was probably at this meeting.
2/*Othello* 3 iii 327–8
3/Sheridan *Pizzaro* 2 ii

TO
DAVID MACBETH MOIR

I am a confirmed invalid for the rest of my life; and, like Dogberry, 'I have had my losses too.'[1] All such losses time may amend – except that of my health. But, in spite of that conviction, I am no hypochondriac, and make the best approach I can to what is called 'enjoying bad health.' It has concerned me to find that, in the same interval, you have not been without your afflictions. But, in all domestic bereavements, I comfort myself with the belief that love, in its pure sense, is as immortal as the soul itself – not given to us in vain; but to form a part of that eternal happiness which would not be complete without it. It has pleased God hitherto to spare me trials of the kind. I have one son and one daughter – good, clever, and affectionate; and I feel strongly that my domestic happiness has kept me so long alive.

[*St John's Wood, June 1843*]

From Moir *Poetical Works* (Edinburgh 1852) I lxv–vi. David Macbeth Moir (1798–1851), poet, novelist, and contributor to *Blackwood's Magazine*. This letter was written in acknowledgment of a copy of Moir's *Domestic Verses*, published May 1843.

1 / *Much Ado about Nothing* 4 ii 82

TO

RICHARD HARRIS BARHAM

My dear Sir

Is there any hitch in Marlboro Street?[1] I have had a note thence, today, implying that you are 'making up your mind.' I hope you will do so before I make up the Magazine, & so that we may both jingle in the same time.

My stiff knee is relaxing, so that I shall be ready to unbend in your society, as Colburn proposes, whatever day & hour may be fixed.

I am My dear Sir

Yours very truly

Thos Hood

Revd R. Barham.

17 Elm Tree Road / St John's Wood / Monday. [*June 1843*]

MS Harvard. Published by Lane KSJ 49. Lane suggests that the letter was written before 13 June 1843. Richard Harris Barham (1788–1845), author of *Ingoldsby Legends*, schoolfellow of J.H. Reynolds and Richard Bentley at St Paul's School, minor canon in St Paul's Cathedral, contributor to *Bentley's Miscellany*. At the beginning of 1841 Barham had applied to the Literary Fund for help for Hood.

1 /Where Colburn published NMM, to which Barham contributed 'The House-Warming!' July 1843

TO
WILLIAM JOHN BRODERIP

My dear Sir
I have never yet acknowledged your considerable information, for my editorial guidance. Pray accept my thanks.
I shall be very happy to receive the Natural History you propose for the next number.
My Tiger story was founded on a dream, in part – and partly derived from observation of wild animals in our menageries.[1] The murder, you alluded to struck me particularly. The poor Woman's name Rosa Stuyk – or Rosy – seemed vividly to place before me one of those plump florid frows I have seen in Holland, – & then the blood made such a *display* of itself – inside & out, of the house, upstairs and down, on ceiling & floor!
À propos of murder I have seen abroad a ridiculous illustration of a passage in Shakspeare –

> 'Murder will speak
> With a most miraculous organ–' [2]

A series of pictures, on board, exhibiting the several stages of a barbarous assassination, to which a gaunt fellow pointed, in turn, with a rod, while he chaunted the narrative, accompanied by an organ.
Charles Lamb once said to me that the most knowing man in the world was one who had done a Murder, & had not been found out: – for example Eugene Aram, during the 14 years that he was unsuspected.[3]

I am
My dear Sir Yours very truly

Thos Hood

17 Elm Tree Road / St John's Wood / 3 July. [*1843*]

MS Folger Library. The year is added in another hand.
1/'The Longest Hour of My Life,' NMM May 1843
2/*Hamlet* 2 ii 589–90
3/Eugene Aram (1704–59), linguist and murderer, subject of Hood's poem (1829) and Bulwer's novel (1832)

TO
HENRY COLBURN

My dear Sir.
I send with this Sir C. Morgan's paper for the printer. Also the M.S said to be Mrs. Gore's[1] – a thing of shreds & patches[2] of which I can make no use.
I had a note also from Mr. Broderip, & expect one of his Nat.Hist. papers this month. Mr Hardman has promised one in a week.[3] I hope we are likely to have one from Major Campbell.[4] So many persons I have sounded seem in favour of my 'Irish Rebellion' that I mean to do it & most probably my star-paper, as oddly enough I am going to dine today at Richmond to meet Francis Baily the distinguished Astronomer[5] & hope to get some information from him to the point. He is the uncle of Baily the Publisher with whom my Trial come on Tuesday next. A show up of some very dirty business. I have also a Bill in Chancery to make him go into his accounts – which are 3 or 4 years old. I am also to meet Braham.[6]
I was vexed to hear last night from Leech that he has not yet recd. instructions about my volume. He is slack now, & would be able to take pains with the drawings.[7] Pray attend to this, as it is impossible for me to continue writing such things as I am writing for such returns. I am doing my very best. – & think it should be our mutual policy now by a brilliant push, to go right ahead of the other Magazines. I have some views on this subject I will call next week, for a consultation.
By the bye, I was much surprised by a note from Miss Lawrance, saying that Mr. Shoberl was to apply to me for an article of hers & had promised her 10gs. per sheet. Now Miss Lawrance is a very old friend of mine & *many* months ago sent the article in question, or rather part of one, which I told her would be *too long*. (I am not anxious for *long* articles but short ones, so as to have variety as in the last number) I intend therefore to return the article direct to the Authoress from whom I received it, – & so far from desiring any interference of Mr. Shoberl in my department, shall be content to know of his existence merely by such public report of him, as that in the Atlas of last Sunday.
I mention this less on my account, for I can right myself, than your own, for *no* man, of literary standing will put up with such meddling. Besides you and I have a common interest in the N.M.M, which bids me point out the evil. You are continually in scrapes for which I do not blame *you* – but those about you – or rather one of them whom I have never scrupled to name. Preferring permanent connexion & friendly ones, I give you frankly my opinion on matters which others would pass over. I not only see, but hear much, which enables me to offer advice. For example, I observed something last night, which, perhaps, will convince you

of the propriety of keeping the management of the Magazine strictly between yourself & me & the Contributors. Mess[rs] Patmore, Williams & Shoberl have quite enough to occupy them in their own departments, if properly performed, without trenching on mine. But I shall meet you soon, & talk over all private matters.

I am My dear Sir
Yours very truly

Tho[s] Hood

H Colburn Esq[re]

17 Elm Tree Road / Friday. [*7 July 1843*]

MS New York. In the course of the letter Hood refers to *The Atlas* of Saturday 1 July 1843, 412–15. This would suggest that the letter was written as early as 7 July. *The Atlas* reported the case which Colburn brought in the Court of Queen's Bench against the owner of the newspaper for libel over his publication in NMM of 'Ellistoniana.' In the course of the trial, Wm Shoberl testified that he had worked for Colburn for 14 or 15 years. He stated that his father wrote *Frederick the Great*, though the work was credited to Thos Campbell. Amid laughter Shoberl was questioned concerning Colburn's puffing, and it was suggested that this might be the work of Hurst or Williams. Colburn was awarded 40 shillings in damages.
Hood probably refers to contributions to NMM August 1843 which contains Sir Charles Morgan's 'Pills for Politicians,' Mrs Gore's 'The Orphan House of Brussels,' one of W. J. Broderip's 'Recreations in Natural History,' and 'The Two Brothers,' probably by Frederick Hardman, with 'Extracts from my Indian Diary,' perhaps by Major Campbell. Hood's 'Repeal of the Union' – perhaps the 'Irish Rebellion' referred to in the letter – appeared in the September issue.

1/Mrs Catherine Gore (1799–1861), novelist
2/*Hamlet* 3 iv 102
3/Frederick Hardman (1814–74), journalist
4/Robert Calder Campbell (1798–1857), 'a graceful writer of the minor prose and poetry of our time' *Athenaeum* 23 May 1857, 664
5/Francis Baily (1774–1844), founding member of the Royal Astronomical Society
6/John Braham (1774?–1856), singer
7/For *Whimsicalities*, to be published by Colburn

TO

J.T.J. HEWLETT

Dear P.P.
Should I be well – a proviso necessary with me – for I have just been three days in bed[1] – I shall like very well to go with you to Gravesend – & on board the

cetaceous ship – tho it seems to me y[r] friend *Whales*ly[2] would be the appropriate companion. Of course we shall see you & Joe here, before hand. Let me know when it is fixed.
Is your article done? – You see that Barham has joined our corps. He & M[rs] & Miss B. called here yesterday, but unluckily I was not at home, ie in bed. Love to all from

Yours very truly

Tho[s] Hood

Rev[d] J. Hewlett. Gossip when we *meat.*

17 Elm Tree Road / S[t] John's Wood / Thursday. [*July 1843*]

MS Texas, following the publication of Barham's contribution to NMM July 1843
1/From his bed, 18 July 1843, Hood wrote a letter to the secretaries of the Bazaar Committee for the benefit of the Manchester Athenaeum: MS Osborn, *Memorials* II 153–7. I have not reprinted the letter here, because it was clearly intended for publication.
2/Perhaps Francis Pearson Walesby (1798–1858), editor of Johnson (1825), professor of Anglo-Saxon at Oxford (1829–34), probably referred to below, 617, as a contributor to HM

TO
CYRUS REDDING

My dear Sir.
I am sorry you should have had the trouble of sending for your M.S. which I kept here, to forward, as we are neighbours.
I beg you to think that I have no disinclination to the M.S. itself, from the slight glance I have taken at it, – but from a cause you allude to in your former note – the Continuations moving through periodicals – I cannot see an opening for a series of any length. – I am dependent on the movements of Mr Colburn who sometimes takes a mass at once like Barnaby[1] – P. Priggins etc. and consequently cramps me as to room.

I am
My dear Sir,
Yours very truly

Tho[s] Hood

C. Redding Esq[re]

17 Elm Tree Road / Friday Morning. [*July 1843*]

MS Boston Public Library. Published in part by Cyrus Redding *Fifty Years' Recollections* (1858) II 373–4. Cyrus Redding (1785–1870), author, working editor of NMM (1821–30). Redding comments: 'I sent Hood an article, and it duly appeared [NMM June 1843, 161–73]. I then sent him a specimen of another that would occupy a double space.' This is Hood's reply.

1/Mrs Trollope's *The Barnabys in America*

TO

CYRUS REDDING

Dear Sir.

I am sorry you had to send for the M.S.S – but *you* can imagine what it is to be unwell & late at the end of a month.[1]

I am indeed so much an invalid, that my walks are few & far between[2] – there never was such an *in-Keeper* – wherefore if you will favour *me* any day with a visit, 364 to one, I shall be at home. I am Dear Sir

Yours very truly

Thos Hood

C. Redding Esqre

17 Elm Tree Road / Tuesday. [*July 1843*]

MS editor. Published by Redding *Fifty Years' Recollections* (1858) II 374–5, after the previous letter.

1/Hood is presumably referring to Redding's own editorial experience.

2/A phrase used by Thomas Campbell *The Pleasures of Hope* ii 378

TO

MANLEY HOPKINS

My dear Sir,

I must accept with pleasure any mark of your kindness.

As to the size of your book, a thin volume is more likely to get thro the narrow opening for such things, in these prosaic times, than a thick one: – but ought you not to publish with *Smith & Elder*, in mere compliment to the partnership in which it has been hinted to me, you are to engage?

Please to present my kind regards to your Mama, sister & such of your family as I have the pleasure of knowing. When I can find time enough, which I trust will be on this side of eternity, I hope to satisfy my curiosity about *Savage Gardens*,[1] whether like the Zoological, or a far west Wilderness inhabited by wild Red Men.

I am
My dear Sir
Yours very truly

Thos. Hood

17 Elm Tree Road, / St. John's Wood. [*July 1843*]

MS Hopkins family papers. Hopkins dedicated to Hood *The Philosopher's Stone and Other Poems*. The volume, published by G.W. Nickisson at the end of 1843, is the occasion of this letter. Hopkins married Kate Smith, 8 August 1843. I should think the relation to 'Smith and Elder' is merely a punning one.

1/Hopkins's address

TO
SIR CHARLES MORGAN

Dear Sir Charles
I have carefully read Mr Mariotti's paper,[1] – the subject is not a very fortunate one – the Catastrophe repulsive – and the tone of the Artists discourse might be obnoxious to the many who would boggle at a defence of suicide even by a maniac. It is however well written, and I think the Author might very well be a contributor to the New Monthly:– (the next Nº of which I ought to forewarn you is already more than provided for). If Mr M would favour me therefore with another paper, it is needless to say that it would afford me very great pleasure to be able to recommend it to Colburn. It should be sent to me direct – or at any rate addressed to me by name, whereby it would escape the opinions of Messrs Shoberl, Patmore[2] etc. who, probably, have already passed sentence on the present M.S.
I was prepared by the result of enquiries in L.G. Place[3] for the death of Mrs Savage. I had once the pleasure of meeting, & vividly remember her, as one to be universally liked by her acquaintances & loved by her intimates.
Mrs Hood begs to offer her kind regards with mine to Lady Morgan, with our regret at her affliction. I am

Dear Sir Charles
Yours very truly

Thos Hood

Sir C. Morgan.

17 Elm Tree Road / St John's Wood / Friday [July 1843]

MS UCLA. Lady Morgan's niece Olivia Savage died, 1 July 1843. Sir Charles himself died after a fortnight's illness, 28 August this year.

1/Luigi Mariotti was the pseudonym of Antonio Carlo Napoleone Gallenga (1810–95), Italian author, journalist, and patriot. According to Gallenga himself, *Episodes of My Second Life* (1884) II 148–9, Hood printed an article left by him in Hook's hands and encouraged its author 'to send many more, which were equally accepted.' However, identifiable articles by Gallenga only appeared in NMM in September and December 1843 and October 1844. It looks as though Gallenga may have submitted another paper according to Hood's polite suggestion and this was published after Hood gave up the editorship in August.

2/Peter George Patmore (1786–1855), father of Coventry Patmore, the poet, was Colburn's reader and adviser.

3/Lower Grosvenor Place, the address of Hood's friend Dilke

TO
WILLIAM BRADBURY

Dear Bradbury

I was very glad to see that you injunctioned Marshall[1] – an old Pirate – & hypocrite. He pretended to be so pious that when I edited the Gem for him & offered an *original* letter of Lord Byron's *unprinted* – he said sooner than have a letter of Byron's in his book, he would burn the book in his fire. But he had no objection to filch my name afterwards for pretended Comic Annuals.

This is to say if you will send me a block of the proper size I think I can draw a Cartoon for you. The two you have had were very good – I mean those of Leech & Meadows. I have no wood by me big enough.

Just suggest to Jerrold who is a theatrical man. – I should say a dramatist, – the Proposal of a Joint Stock Company, to write for *Webster's Prize* as a speculation.[2]

Many thanks for your care as to the Stereotype plates. We shall both be glad when that affair is settled. It might have been two years ago when an arbitration was proposed on my part with the amt deposited as security. Nothing could be fairer – & I only want justice between man & man. But I will not have it referred to *booksellers* – as I do not want to have it decided by *Authors*, but by important men. Since then the case has become much blacker, & I am quite content to abide by a fair trial.

Mrs Hood told me you thought of coming up – I shall be very happy to see you, or both (I mean Evans)[3] if you will be content with a plain dinner & a bottle of port or sherry at a day's notice

Yours very truly

Thos Hood

17 Elm Tree Road / St John's Wood / Thursday. [*20 July 1843*]

MS UCLA. The full-length cartoons by Leech and Meadows to which Hood refers appeared as the first of a series in *Punch* 15 July 1843, 23, 27, so his letter may belong to the following Thursday.
1/This was reported in *The Times*, Wednesday, 19 July 1843, 6. On the previous day Bradbury and Evans obtained an injunction against Marshall, restraining him 'from transferring to the title-page of ... *Punch's Steamboat Companion*, the frontispiece ... which is printed on the first leaf of each number of Punch.'
2/In June 1843 Benjamin N. Webster (1797–1882), manager of the Haymarket Theatre, offered £500 for a comedy.
3/Frederick Mullet Evans, Bradbury's partner

TO
CHARLES DICKENS

My dear Dickens,
Make any use you can of my name, or me, for the purpose you mention.[1] I would add my purse, but unluckily just now there is nothing in it, thanks to B—.[2]
Many years ago, when I wrote theatrical critiques for a newspaper,[3] I remember pointing out a physiognomy, which strongly prepossessed me in favour of its owner, as indicating superior intelligence. It was that of poor Elton, who was then undistinguished amid a group of dramatic nebulae. The name brought him vividly to my memory, along with the scene of the tragedy, which is familiar to me. In fact I once passed in very calm weather *between* the two Fern Islands, on one of which was a lighthouse, and the man in charge, possibly the father of Grace Darling, waved his hat to us.[4]
How touching that description in the newspapers of the two children, prattling unconsciously of trifles, whilst the vessel was going down under them![5]
I have been intending to write to, or call on you, but besides B— *v.* Hood, I have been ill, and in consequence, my article for this month is not *yet* finished. That will be a sufficient excuse with you for my non-attendance to-night at the Freemasons'

Tavern. But it is of the less consequence as my feelings being so entirely in unison with yours in this matter, you will be able to speak not only your own, but those of

Yours ever truly,

Thos. Hood.

17, Elm Tree Road, St. John's Wood, Wednesday. [*26 July 1843*]

From *Memorials* II 157–8. Dickens's letter, to which Hood is here replying, was written on the same day, Wednesday, 26 July.

1/Dickens headed a committee to relieve the seven destitute children of Edward William Elton, the actor, drowned on 19 July in the wreck of the *Pegasus* steamer near the Fern Islands (now called Farne). Several theatrical benefits were held on behalf of Elton's family. For that at the Haymarket on 2 August Hood composed an address which was delivered by Mrs Warner and was afterwards sold as a pamphlet.
2/Baily
3/Hood wrote theatrical criticism for *The Atlas* newspaper in 1826, *Works* x 548–80.
4/William Darling, keeper of a lighthouse on the Farne Islands, and his daughter Grace Horsley (1815–42) carried out a heroic rescue on 7 September 1838.
5/The children were passengers on board the *Pegasus*. There is reference to them in the *Annual Register* (1843) 90.

TO

HANNAH LAWRANCE

Confidential.

My dear Miss Lawrance.
I write in haste a few lines to put you on yr guard, by telling you of the arrangements for reviewing in the Magazine. I undertook to review all books except Colburn's own with the puffing of which I of course desired to have no concern. They are *done* by the persons of the establishment, – Patmore, Williams[1] or Shoberl. If you see the Mag. you will know what wretched things these reviews are. As to mine they are few and far between. I get few books and those appear to be the *refuse*, what is not worth the while of somebody else to keep.
I do not mind your saying you have understood from me afore time, or have detected from the style that I write the reviews, except of C's books. If he would give you 10 gs a sheet to review his generally (not *one* only) I should rejoice for I am ashamed of them at present or should be were it not pretty well known that I have

no hand in them. Pray give my Comp^{ts} to your Mama & believe me My dear Miss Lawrance

Yours very truly

Thos Hood

17. Elm Tree Road / Friday. / [*August 1843*]

From Jerrold, where most of the letter is published in facsimile facing 370. The facsimile must be abbreviated, for the last two sentences of the first paragraph, not present there, appear in Jerrold's printed version of the letter, 370. I do not know whether Hannah Lawrance undertook the reviewing to which Hood refers in the letter.

1/Possibly D.E. Williams, author of *The Life and Correspondence of Sir Thomas Lawrence* (1831), published by Colburn and Bentley

TO

J.T.J. HEWLETT

Dear P.P.

I told Mrs Colburn/last night/*yesterday* that for want of a job you had *buried yourself* – in the country. But she objected, that you are expected *up* next week. If the news be true, come on or before Tuesday – we shall have a few friends in the evening – a sort of extempore party.

Love to all from Yours very truly

T.H.

Thank goodness the *short* months are over. The last half killed me. If we don't hear we shall expect you.

17 Elm Tree Road / Friday [*August 1843*]

MS Texas. It is placed here because it seems to fit with the following letter.

TO

J.T.J. HEWLETT

Dear P.P.

You must have wondered at not hearing from me – but ever since you left I have been *confined* with a rheumatic foot, & *going* any where was out of the question. I have only yesterday been able to get out of slippers.

And now the Magazine is *on* again, so that I have no prospect of the pleasure I proposed, – for next month if I can manage it I must go to Scotland.
Mrs. H. desires her kind regards & thanks for the Autographs.

I am Dear P.P Yours very truly

Thos Hood

Revd J. Hewlett.

17 Elm Tree Road / Saturday [*August 1843*]

MS Texas. Hood looks forward to his visit to Scotland in the following month.

TO
PHILIP DE FRANCK

My dear Johnny,
What a noise you have made about my silence. Why didn't you write in the interval? You, you, you, who have half-pay for doing nothing, whereas I am only half paid for doing everything. Besides I have to write, till I am sick of the sight of pen, ink and paper; but it must be a *change* for you to scribble a bit after your fishing, shooting, boar-hunting, and the rest of your idle business at Antonin. Besides you know what leisure is, I don't. Why, for one half the month I have hardly time to eat, drink, or sleep, to say nothing of twiddling my moustaches, if I had any, or sucking myself to sleep with a German pipe. How unlike you, who have so much time that you can hardly know how to kill it, you, who, however you may wish for war, can lie, sit, or stand, yawn, and snore, in such profound peace, that if you are not all overgrown with duck-weed, like a stagnant pond, it's a wonder. What indeed! why couldn't you write to yourself in my name? which would have improved your hand and your mind, and kept your English from getting rusty. For you have no correspondence, you know, like mine, with dozens of poetical ladies, old and young; and prosaic gentlemen; and if you do write articles, the Editors have refused them, for I have never met with any in print. But it all comes from your ignorance, and your living in that calm phlegmatic country, called Germany, where you travel through life in slow coaches, with the wheels locked, and have no notion of the railway pace at which we wear ourselves out here in England, or at least in London, and then go off, Bang, by apoplexy, like dry gunpowder, whilst *you* die fizzing and whizzing at leisure like 'Devils.' I don't mean

Satans or old Nicks, but the wildfire so called at school, if you can remember so far back, or if you ever '*wented*' to school, of which your strange grammar sometimes suggests a doubt. Seriously, my dear Johnny, you cannot imagine the hurry I live in, like most of my contemporaries, but aggravated in my case by frequent illness, which makes me get into arrears of business, and then, as the sailors say, I have to work double tides to fetch up my lee-way; or, I might have said, to scratch my figure-head with the cat harpins by way of splicing the mainbrace, for you know, you inland lubbers know nothing about ships or nauticals. I could show you a German engraving of a ship with four masts, not set up in the middle, but along the side; the vessel by way of finish sailing stern foremost, at ten knots an hour. Sometimes at the end of the month, I sit up three nights successively, Jane insisting on sitting up with me, so that we see the sun rise now and then, as well as you early birds in Germany. Then we are obliged to visit and be visited, which we shun as much as we can, but must to some extent go through, as I am a sort of public man. Mind, this does not mean keeping a public-house, as you may think from the sound, and your oblivion of English. My position therefore entails on me some extra work; for example this last month I was made a Patron of the Manchester Athenaeum, and wrote for them a long letter on the benefits of literature, which has been printed;[1] and on the back of that job, a poetical address delivered at the Haymarket theatre, at the benefit for the seven children of an actor, just drowned in the wreck of a steam ship.[2] But of all, the hardest work is writing refusals to literary ladies, who *will* write poetry, and *won't* write it well. I wish you would come and marry a few of them, which would perhaps reduce them to prose.

Well, besides all these labours, I have had on my hand two law-suits, one at law, and one in equity or Chancery, and which will be decided at the end of the year. So you see, Johnny, I have not been silent through idleness.

In reality, I have begun one or two letters, but could not finish them while they were fresh, besides which we have had dreams of seeing you: so that, one morning, when your king was over here,[3] I did say to myself, 'there *is* Franck!' for a Gog, about your height, in a Prussian military cloak, actually came down the hill opposite; and, as we do not live in a thoroughfare, we supposed you must be coming to the house. A graver figure that followed I guessed was Mr. Rühe; but you were not you, and Rühe was not Rühe. As the dramatist says, 'I had thought a lie.'[4] Well, I suppose you will come some day, when Jane is a palsied, blind, old woman, and I am in my second childhood, sucking a lollypop, and 'uppards of ninety.' At present, we are only in a ripe middle age; but she wears best, as you may suppose, when I tell you that, only this spring, we had a party at which she danced! and what is more, with the Sheriff of London[5] for her partner (whose official duty it is, you know, to superintend all 'dancing on nothing'), and he said that she danced very lightly, considering that she was not hung.

So, you see we *are* alive, if not kicking,[6] which will comfort you for the present. In a post or two, you will have a longer and more particular letter: and, in the meantime, we do not ask for your reasons for not coming, which we suppose to be as good as our own for not writing. We give you credit for the best intentions, and shall live in hopes of seeing you long before you are a colonel.

Fanny is very well, and so is Tom junior, and both send their love to you. My messengers being absent, they are going with great alacrity to carry this to the post, having read your melancholy letter, and being persuaded that you were going into a consumption beyond the cold water cure.

Jane is gone to town, or she would have had a finger in this; but she will have a hand in the longer epistle, of which this is the *avant courier*. But, mind, it will not be quite so big as to come by that heavy after-post-wagen that carries packages instead of packets. In the meantime she sends her love to you.

I have but a moment more before post-time;[7] and then, when I have done, I shall go and take a look out of the drawing-room window at Lord's Ground, where the Eton and Harrow scholars are playing their annual match at cricket! Does not that sound English to you, old fellow? or have you forgotten that there are such things in the world as bats and stumps? I should like to knock your bail off with a ripping ball! I tried to make a match up the other day, but had two doctors in my eleven, who had so many patients to bowl out that they could not come to the scratch – if you know what that is![8]

I am much flattered by the kind remembrances of the 19th. Pray offer my respects to their officers, with my thanks for the honour they have done me in their memories.

God bless you! and
Believe me, my dear Franck,
Yours ever very truly (but rather rheumatically),

Thomas Hood.

17, Elm Tree Road, August 14th, 1843.

From *Memorials* II 159–64
1/Reprinted in *Memorials* II 153–7
2/Edward William Elton, see 546
3/The King of Prussia was in England from 22 January to 4 February 1842.

4/I have not identified dramatist or quotation.
5/The Sheriff of London and Middlesex this year was F.G. Moon, the printseller. Part of his official function was to superintend hangings.
6/The first use of the phrase 'alive and kicking' given in NED is dated 1860.
7/The first use of this word given in NED is dated 1845.
8/The crease, that is, the place where the batsman receives the ball in cricket.

TO
JOHN BRITTON

My object in going to *Ham* was to get sketches of some of the trees, etc. by Harvey. By the bye, there must be *a Ghost, at Ham House.* Miss Costello[1] once meant to inquire concerning it, and I sent her this, –

'Never trouble Ham House, or its inmates at all,
For a ghost, that may be but a sham,
But seek in a sandwich that's cut at Vauxhall,
For the true *apparition of Ham.*'

[*St John's Wood, August 1843*]

From John Britton, *Auto-biography* pt I (1850) 95–6n. Hood's poem 'The Elm Tree,' published in NMM September 1842, 'was suggested by a visit to Ham House' *Works* VIII 177. In September 1843 Hood told Dickens that the poem was to appear separately, illustrated by Harvey (554) but nothing came of this. Britton himself wrote that on the occasion of the visit to Ham House Hood wrote 'one of his extraordinary poems for No. 1 of *Hood's Magazine.*' 'The Haunted House' appeared there, but it was not illustrated by Harvey.

1/Louisa Stuart Costello (1799–1870), author

TO
JOHN BRITTON

Dear Sir
Thanks for the orders – if I can get away we are going to the Private View.[1]
I begin to think we shall have a harvest after all. – at least I feel a little riper this weather.

With our kind regards to Mrs Britton I am
Dear Sir
Yours very truly

Thos Hood

J. Britton Esqre

17 Elm Tree Road / St John's Wood / Friday [*August 1843*]

MS British Museum

1/The first use of this phrase given in NED is dated 1852.

TO
CHARLES DICKENS

My dear Dickens, I have at last a little leisure to write to you, taking it for granted that in the meantime our friend Forster has given you the particulars of the split with Colburn,[1] and as that little man is at Broadstairs, perhaps he has given you some little particulars too, including some little falsehoods. So I will just give you the history of that precious document he showed to Forster, and which he dares to call an agreement. [He goes at great length into his dealings with Colburn, speaks of the document (signed by him in respect of an advance of £150) as] containing all sorts of undertakings, & provisions – 'hard ones,' as ship biscuits – things never contemplated – sold cold, cautious people will say I ought not to have signed – but the little Shylock knew where to have me, nearest the heart. I had been ill for months – on the brink of death – with my children, both very young, in a foreign country among unfriendly people ... But nothing should induce me to write for him now, under the new management, for no successor in the Editorship is appointed – it is to be 'done in the house,' like some people's washing – that is to say the Editorship successively held by Campbell, Bulwer, Hook, & myself, will sink into the hands of Mr. Shoberl, the author of a 'Guide to Greenwich'[2] ... You will be glad to hear that I have made an arrangement with Bradbury to contribute to 'Punch' – but that is a secret which I cannot keep from you. It will be light occasional work for odd times ... I have written a long rigmarole, & something too much[3] perhaps of my own affairs, but I wish you to know something of them, because it is too much the fashion to ascribe all the difficulties of literary men to their improvidence, mismanagement, etc. etc. – whereas I have been involved in unusual complications, & subject to extraordinary crises when one cannot act by rule. Nine years since, I was embarrassed by the misconduct of other parties, but I can show that since then, in spite of desperate health, I have made more than I have spent & even paid off some arrears.

[*St John's Wood, 5 September 1843*]

From Sotheby, Wilkinson and Hodge *Catalogue of an Important Collection of Autograph Letters* 21 May 1890, 21–2. Hood has suddenly decided to give up editing and contributing to NMM. His own ill-health no doubt increased the strain of the work, and made him more irritated with the interference of Colburn and his subordinates in the management of the magazine. Colburn was still to publish Hood's *Whimsicalities* at the end of the year. There remained open to Hood the possibility of publishing in *Punch*, and in the new year he brought out his own periodical *Hood's Magazine*. The immediate need was for a holiday. It is around the date of the holiday (560) that this and the following letters to Dickens and Leech can be grouped.

1/John Forster had acted as mediator in the dispute between Hood and Colburn. In a letter dated 14 August Forster wrote that Colburn 'accepts your resignation of the Editorship (as he phrases it)': MS Bristol Central Library. In 1846 Thackeray commented on Forster: 'whenever anybody is in a scrape we all fly to him for refuge. He is omniscient and works miracles,' *Letters* ed. G.N. Ray (Cambridge, Mass. 1945) II 252.

2/William Shoberl's *A Summer Day at Greenwich* was published by Colburn in 1840.

3/*Hamlet* 3 ii 72

TO

CHARLES DICKENS

My dear Dickens.

I have made up my mind to be off this week to Dundee, thence to Edinbro, & home by Leith.

Will you therefore oblige me with a line of introduction to Lord Jeffrey & Professor Napier[1] – with both of whom I believe you are intimate. I may be able to write an occasional review in the Edinbro. I believe Mrs. Hood told you I had an idea of reviewing Chuzzlewit – but I have resolved to have nothing to do with the N.M.M. under the present management, – & for certain reasons, I cannot well do it in the Athenaeum but might in the Edinbro.[2]

I long to have a talk with you on matters in general, & but for the other trip should have taken a day at Broadstairs on purpose, for we have never yet had a regular gossip – or comparison of 'Notes.'

Hurst told me the other day Colburn had left Broadstairs, for he did not like it. Perhaps he met *you* in his walks.

He is going to bring out my papers in two volumes, with Leach's designs – for I told him if he did not now, I should by & bye have some books of my own coming out.

The Elm Tree Poem is coming out per se, illustrated by Harvey.[3]

I have two other Poems, planned some time since, rather favorite subjects, and to be illustrated, like the German ones, Fridolin – The Song of the Bell – The Fight with the Dragon &c.[4] I think these would be likely to suit Chapman & Hall. I suppose you got my long letter the other day, – directed to Broadstairs. –

Goodbye & God bless you all says
Yours ever truly,

Thos Hood

C. Dickens Esqre

17 Elm Tree Road / St. John's Wood. Monday. [*11 September 1843*]

MS Huntington. Published by Whitley HLQ 405–6. Before Hood's visit to Scotland, 558. Dickens's interesting reply to this and the earlier letter is in the Berg Collection, New York Public Library, and is published by Shelley 359–61. Dickens sent Hood letters for Jeffrey and Napier. He wrote that he was still at work on *Chuzzlewit.* He shared Forster's view that the agreement with Colburn had been disgraceful to the last, though he regretted that Hood had flung up the editorship of NMM and the offer of 30 guineas a sheet. He recommended that Hood apply to Bentley, since 'editing a mag. is valuable.' Dickens also wrote: 'your supplementary note gave me a pang such as one feels when a friend has to knock twice at the street door, before anybody opens it.'

1/Dickens's note to Macvey Napier (1776–1847), editor of the *Edinburgh Review,* is dated 12 September 1843, and included in his *Letters* (ed. Dexter) I 539. Napier was professor of Conveyancing at the University of Edinburgh from 1824.

2/Whitley comments: 'Hood seems to have broken a long connection with Dilke and the *Athenaeum.*' Why the break took place unfortunately remains obscure. Hood was certainly very sensitive in personal and business relations from this time until his death.

3/This scheme did not materialize.

4/Schiller's 'Fridolin,' 'Lied von der Glocke,' and 'Kampf mit dem Drachen' had all been translated, and illustrated by Moritz Retzsch. Hood put forward his own version of the last poem as 'The Knight and the Dragon' in *Up the Rhine, Works* VII 139–49, and his variation upon 'Fridolin' as 'The Forge,' NMM July 1843, *Works* VIII 291–307.

TO
JOHN LEECH

Dear Leech –
It has been decided to bring out the two Volumes together. Mr Hurst will therefore send you the rest of the matter – & you must reserve the 10 (ten) remaining cuts to illustrate that portion (the 'Elm Tree' is reserved for a separate pubn) for example 'News from China' – The Defaulter Confession of a Phoenix – 'Mrs Gardiner' – 'Camberwell Beauty' & the longest of the papers – that the distribution may be equal[1]

I was glad to hear you were out of town – for of course you are enjoying this fine weather. I start with Tom Junr on Wednesday for Scotland, which you know is in the North – but not quite at the Pole.
I suppose you are at Ramsgate. It is a nice place. If you shut your eyes you can walk right over the Pier – or bang against the cliffs, or off them, – whichever you like. You may treadmill[2] yourself for exercise up & down Jacob's Ladder[3] – & if you relish such sea insects – peg well at the shrimps.[4] On a clear day, if you understand French, you can see their coast: and it may concern you to know that a vast number of leeches are imported from France – I believe via Dover. The sea for some miles round Ramsgate is salt – cheap for pickling – & you may chalk your blocks gratis – a saving of flake white. When you want to wash there are two basins – let Mrs L have the inner one the water is not so rough. But do not dream like a Cockney of sitting in the harbour, for it is not a bower except for Tritons. And do not put on your best trowsers when you go shrimping. Perhaps if you look sharp you may catch a crab – but if an old one remember that 'crabbed age & youth cannot live together'[5] – so kill him & eat him. If lucky you may by chance pick up a few very tiny shells which you may keep till they grow big enough for the mantel shelf – if fond of marine gardening you can go & roll the sands & weed the beach & plant your walking stick, & water your shoes. If you bathe & swim out – don't get into the wrong machine – and if you have any boating beware of getting 'squamp'd,' – which is one form of the Cold Water Cure. Some curious people ascend the Pharos on the pier, but it is light-headed – & therefore, like a monomaniac, ought not to be trusted. – others pick shell fish from the masonry which is very muscular – but boil a silver spoon with them, or you may be spoonily poisoned. Many persons are very ill on the sea-voyage, – & if you were sick in going down you may be sure of sickness coming up. A coach & horses is the best preventive. NB. Talking of the Preventive – the Coast *Block*ade is not for drawing on – as you may imagine: but there is a great Bank called the Goodwin which you may draw on, if you have any cash in it – The head partner is Mr David Jones. This being all I have to say on business, except kind regards to Mrs Leech, I am

Dear Leech

Yours very truly

Thos Hood

J. Leech Esqre

17 Elm Tree Road / St John's Wood [*11 September 1843*]

MS Princeton. Dated in another hand. At the head of the letter is a sketch of a leech applied to a human foot, inscribed 'A Rechabite.' The Rechabites (Jeremiah 35:5–6) refused to drink wine.

1/Hood is referring to his *Whimsicalities* (1844).

2/The only example of this verb given in NED is dated 1899.

3/'Near the north end of the west pier, is an elegant flight of steps, called *Jacob's Ladder*,' *New Ramsgate, Margate, and Broadstairs Guide* (Ramsgate n.d.) 7.

4/'PEGWELL BAY, famous for its shrimps ... a short distance south of Ramsgate,' *The Journey-Book of England: Kent* (1842) 134

5/Shakespeare *Passionate Pilgrim* xii

TO
D. HURST

I do not at all like the design – it is more vulgar than funny.

[*St John's Wood, September 1843*]

From Myers *Autograph Letters* no. 348 (1947) 33. Hood writes concerning his *Whimsicalities*, probably to Daniel Hurst (1802?–70). A Hurst was one of Colburn's assistants, and from 1854 Daniel Hurst published with Henry Blackett at 13 Great Marlborough St.

TO
WILLIAM HAZLITT

Sir,

I have so often enjoyed the conversation and writings of your Father that, predisposed to look favourably on your own MS., it would have given me great pleasure to find you a contributor to the *New Monthly Magazine*.

You would therefore have heard from me sooner but for an uncertainty, which is resolved by my renouncing my own connexion with the *New Monthly*.

I am, Sir,
Yours very truly,

Tho. Hood.

I return your paper for your own disposal, as there is no successor appointed to the Editorship, which is to be managed, I understand, 'in the house' or by the publisher and his clerks.

W. Hazlitt, Esq.

17 Elm Tree Road, / St. John's Wood, / Tuesday. [*12 September 1843*]

From William Carew Hazlitt *Four Generations of a Literary Family* (1897) I 240. William Hazlitt (1811–1893), only son of the essayist, author in his own right. Hood is writing after having given up the editorship of NMM.

TO

JANE HOOD

Here we are safe and sound, red and brown, my own dearest, after an excellent passage; Tom tolerably sick most of the first day and night, and I too, once! but am much better for it. I was very much out of sorts when I left, and we had a very rolling swell, added to which, about a steamer there is a smell of oil and smoke mixed, which particularly offends my sense. We saw little, being obliged to go outside of Yarmouth Roads in the night, so that yesterday morning we were out of sight of land, and only got a distant view of Flamborough Head.

Luckily there was a whale blowing, to Tom's great delight. We have made a very good passage, arriving here about seven this morning.

But imagine yesterday, while finishing our dinner, down came into the cabin a gentleman we had never seen before, announcing, 'Ladies and gentlemen, I don' know whether you are aware of it, but we are all in imminent danger: the fires are out, and the captain don't know where we are; the ship is sinking, and you will all be at the bottom in a few minutes.' At first I was a little alarmed, not hearing what he said, for I had left Tom on deck, who was too squeamish to come below, but thinking, when I heard better, that he was some fool who had got frightened, I went up, brought Tom down, and said with a laugh to the passengers, 'then my boy shall go down in good company!' – for some looked scared. Luckily the prophet of ill-luck did not go into the ladies' cabin, where many of them were sick, or we should have had screams and hysterics. It turned out that he was insane.

I remembered seeing the man rather mysteriously brought on board at Gravesend, and shut into the captain's private cabin on deck. It seems, after a day there, he got violent, and insisted on coming out. All the rest of the evening he did nothing else but go about addressing everybody, and particularly the captain, in a style that shocked weak nerves: – 'We are all going (throwing up his hands), you will be all at the bottom in a few minutes, and no one left to tell the tale. She is settling fast forwards! Captain, captain, do you know where you are? Are you aware that the fire is out? Look, look forward there, she is going down. Good Heavens! and nobody seems aware of it, and *you* (to me) won't care about it, till you are making a bubble in the water! Good Heavens! what day is it, sir? (to another), Thursday!

no such thing, sir, it is Saturday, but no matter, it is your last day! And what a destruction of property, this fine vessel and all her cargo.'

He harped a good deal on this, for it was said he had lost his own property. The steward meanwhile dogging him all over the ship, lest he should jump overboard; but in the evening they got him in again, and locked him up, and he is safe landed. You may tell Dr. Elliot that he would have charmed a phrenologist, for whenever he was not waving his arms, or holding them up in despair, the fingers of both hands were behind his ears on the organ of destructiveness, *i.e.* the wreck.[1] This is not a joke, but fact: it was a very remarkable action.

We have put up, *pro tempore*, at an hotel; we have had breakfast and a ramble. I could not find R.M—, but left my card at the G—s:[2] it was so early they were not visible. We shall go down by a train to the North Ferry, cross by the boat to the South Ferry, where there is an Inn, at which I shall put up. In the meantime, if you write on the receipt of this, direct 'Post Office, Dundee.'

I will let you know directly my plan is formed, how long I shall stay here, or at the Ferry. Tom has been very good and happy, and looks a good deal better already; I feel very much better, and those on board, who remarked my illness, congratulated me on the change, so it must be visible at all events.

Dundee, at first sight, was much altered in one respect, owing to the march of manufacture. To the east a remarkably fine crop of tall chimneys had sprung up in lieu of one, – all factories. But I suspect that have been going too fast. The harbour much improved, otherwise much as before; filthy morning gutters, and plenty of bare legs and feet. Luckily the Post Office is next door, so that you will be sure to get this in good time. The boat was very handsomely and commodiously fitted up: a number of separate little rooms, in each two beds; Tom and I had one to ourselves; it contains window, lamp, washstand, towels, water at will from a cock, in short very different to the 'Liverpool' and the like. And we were all very sociable, so that the time did not seem long.

I did not go to bed, as I like my head high, and slept both nights on one of the sofas. You may now make yourself quite easy about me, I feel that I shall be much better for it; I sadly wanted a change, and this is a complete one. I have banished all thoughts of bookery, and mean to take my swing of idleness, not always the root of all evil. As soon as I get settled at the Ferry, however, I shall finish the article on Temperance by the help of whiskey-toddy, but that need not be put in the paper.[3]

The weather promises to be fine, in which case we shall spend as much time as possible out of doors.

I am glad to see Tom looking quite himself again; he is quite a Spaniard already, red and brown. He sends his love to Ma and Fanny, and promises plenty of drawings, for he began on board with his sketch-book. God bless you, my own dearest. Do not fail to drink your port wine. Love to dear Tibbie.

Your own ever,

Thomas Hood.

Dundee, Friday Morning, Sept. 15th, 1843.

From *Memorials* II 166–70

1/According to the phrenologists, the organ of destructiveness is located above the ear. I do not understand Hood's last phrase here.

2/M— stands for Miln, G— for Gardiner.

3/Perhaps a reference to 'Mrs Burrage. A Temperance Romance,' published in HM January 1844, *Works* IX 57–76.

TO
JANE HOOD

My own dearest. I received yours the day before yesterday: – having had to send for it to Dundee. On Friday we came here to the Ferry & I engaged a bed – but my aunt[1] would not hear of it, and made me come to her house at once, where we have been ever since. Very nice house & garden, & we are made much of & very comfortable. Tom is as happy as can be, & they are much taken with him. All goes right as to that: they seem to have been sickened with the shyness, oddities &c, of W. Holt.[2] By the bye on Monday came a very strange & artful letter from Betsy, – could she have heard of my being here – she does not allude to it – but take no notice of this – I will tell you more when we meet. My Aunt says she wanted her aye to be singin hymns, & brought some wafers with texts on them – but that's not religion – & indeed both she & Mrs Holt seemed to rely oe'r much on their own good works. She says there is a Mr Gray a rich man at Dundee who says I'm the first man of the age & begged when I came to let him know & he would make a party to meet me. I do not know if this will fall out. I have seen Mr Gardiner – his wife is dead – but could not find R. Miln.[3] I have made a sketch for you that will give you an idea of the prospect from here of the mouth of Tay. It is a noble river.

We are living on the fat of the land[4] – Tom has milk porridge – baps cookeys, jelly &c – & I have good small ale & whiskey – & both are much the better, – greatly so in looks. I shall go by a steamboat from here to Leith some day this week, so you must not write again to Dundee, but to the P.O. Edinboro – You had better send the slippers, if not already sent, *direct* post paid to Mrs D. Keay, Rose Cottage –

Ferry Port on Craig
By Cupar
Fife N.B.

On Sunday I went with my Aunt to hear her minister, one of those who have seceded, & preaches, in the school room, but at the same time thro a window into a large tent adjoining – a temporary accommodation whilst a new Church is building, in opposition to the old one – something in the spirit of the old Covenanters. The minister & family take tea here at 5. which will shorten this. He & I get on very well.[5]

I hope you explained to Dickens that I *could not* write under the present management – I *would* not for any consideration. As to the teetotal paper, if possible I wish it could have been deferred for an application from Bentley, instead of being offered – but you must be guided by circumstances.[6] I hardly think Dickens understands the how & why I resigned – that it was impossible to go on – & that as the result shows that set meant to have it sooner or later in their hands. Colburn will repent *yet* – I foresee – & perhaps not long after the next reviews.

I have had a letter from Hurst with a few of the cuts – he says Colburn agrees to 16 gs for the new matter[7] and I am to have an answer about the Elm Tree. –

I write very hastily expecting every minute to be summoned to tea. I am looking at a hill out of the back window covered with sheaves for it is the middle of harvest. Tom is off, for the two ministers boys are coming & he has made a crony of one already. – He send his love to you & Fanny and Mrs Dore & says you are to make yrself comfortable about him for he is very happy, & I can add very good. I am sorry to miss dear Mrs Dore but I think I should have been very ill if I had delayed. I eat & drink pretty well but sleep very badly still. However the time is short as yet for much improvmt I found my Uncle & Aunt better than I expected – & the place really a very nice comfortable one, – they had seen my Manchester letter[8] – & altogether I stand high, as well as T. Junior. Aunt has given him a silver pencil case of her brother Robert, who was a Scholar at College – for she admires his reading & his spirit – tho they have of course some *misunderstandings* between English & Scotch. They talk of W.H. as half witted & that he was afraid to go near a sparrow. I expect to be much delighted with Edinbro, and shall most likely go from here Friday or Saturday – but there will not be time for you to write here again, so direct *there*, if you write before Wednesday – as probably I shall return by Saturday week's packet. And now God bless you dearest, kiss my dear Tibby for me & give my kind love to Mrs Dore – perhaps I shall see her on her return from Cheltenham. – We have beautiful weather – but E. winds. Perhaps you have written – I shall send to Dundee tomorrow to know – but from this side the boats are not frequent. – & the ferry opposite Dundee is three miles off – a long pull there & back. Take your port & drink the health of

Your own affectionate

Thos Hood

[*South Ferry, near Dundee*] *Wednesday.* [*20 September 1843*]

MS Dundee. Published in part by Elliot 142–5. The letter is dated in relation with the preceding.
1/Mrs Keay
2/Probably William Holt, husband of Hood's sister Jessy
3/Hood's old friend died on the following day.
4/Genesis 45:18
5/William Nicholson (d 1890) took part in the setting up of the Free Church of Scotland in May 1843. He resigned his living at Ferry-Port-on-Craig and later formed a congregation at Hobart, Tasmania.
6/Hood may be referring to 'Mrs. Burrage. A Temperance Romance.'
7/Simply the preface to *Whimsicalities*
8/A public letter to the Manchester Athenaeum, *Memorials* II 153–7

TO
JANE HOOD

My own Dearest,
We parted with my aunt and uncle this morning, – they came with us in an open fly to the Ferry, where we separated on the very best terms. I dine to-day with Mr. G—,[1] (he has lost his wife years ago) – sleep to-night in Dundee, and tomorrow, per steamer, to Leith.
I think I shall leave Leith for London to-morrow (Saturday) week.
You must not come to meet me, the hour of arrival is too uncertain. I am very much better, and Tom visibly fatter, and both in good spirits. I must shut this up, as Mr. G— dines early. Love to Fanny. God bless you, my own dearest and best.

I have got slippers and all, and am sending them off to the Ferry. I shall have much to tell you when we meet.

Your own affectionate

Thomas Hood.

Dundee, Friday Morning. [*22 September 1843*]

From *Memorials* II 172. Dated in relation with the preceding.

1 /Gardiner or Gray: see 560.

TO

JANE HOOD

I have not been quite able to make out, my own dearest, about my letters to you; it appears to me that one of them has missed.

I wrote from Dundee, then from the Ferry, and then from Dundee again. I have not been able to write from here till now, there is so much to see, and so much ground to be got over. In one thing I have been unlucky, that it is the Long Vacation, and most of the lions are out of town; Wilson thirty miles off, Napier gone too.[1] I left my letter for him, and also for Lord Jeffrey,[2] who has just sent me an invitation to dinner to-morrow at his seat, three miles hence. Otherwise, I was partly resolved to return by to-day's steamer, instead of Saturday's, which will now be the one. Do not write again, therefore, lest I miss it. I went to Chambers's and saw William; Robert, the one I knew,[3] lives at St. Andrews, thirty miles off. Mrs. W. is in bad health, but I drank tea with them. He showed us all over his establishment; everything, binding, &c., done on the premises; and sent a younger brother, a very nice fellow, to show us about. We went up to the Castle, saw the very little room where James I. was born, – half the size of my room, or even less, – from the window, the house where the Burking was perpetrated.[4] He led us to some of the back slums, and Tom saw the shop where the rope was bought to hang Porteous; still the same family in the same line in the shop.[5]

Saw the Advocates' Library, Old Parliament House, and the anatomical museum of the Surgeons' Hall. I am delighted with the city, – it exceeds my expectations. You must go with me to the Edinbro' panorama when I return. Yesterday we took a cold dinner at three, and then drove to Musselburgh, as Blackwood said Moir was not likely to come to Edinbro' shortly.[6]

Such a kind welcome and delightful people – he and she; nice children. Tom and the boys got very sociable. About six miles from here – staid three hours with them – took very much to each other. We are in comfortable quarters. For the sake of society we live in the travellers' room, and dine at the ordinary. As one of the results, on Sunday there dined a very strange man, – long beard, matted hair, &c., – but spoke English. Thought he was the *Hebrew* Professor at the College – turns out to be Alexander Groat, the proprietor of John o' Groat's, with about £700 a-year – a great oddity. But he has been very civil to me, given me an order to see the Antiquaries' Museum, &c. I save one of his orders for an autograph.

We live on the best of Scotch victuals; haddies for breakfast and supper, whiskey-toddy, &c., &c. Tom enjoys it very much. I shall not fail to bring home some 'sweeties' for the Elliots and others. The weather is beautiful, and I mean now to ramble all day, and see all I can; so you must not expect me to write again. I look longingly up at Salisbury Crags, and Arthur's Seat, but 'who can tell how hard it is to climb?'[7] I don't think I shall manage it, but mean to try, some cool evening.

I am sleeping better again, but wish I had brought my pills. I went to one shop, and the man was, he *said*, out of galbanum. Went to another, who said he had it, but gave me something else. However, I am much better from the constant air and exercise. I do not find, however, that I can settle to write, but am growing ideas I suppose. I shall perhaps write something about my trip to Edinburgh in my book.

I think I could make a funny burlesque of Willis' Pencilling style, only the characters visited to be imaginary Professors, &c., &c. They would enjoy it *here*.

I think of looking to-day at the Canongate, Holyrood, and Heriot's Hospital.

Tom saw a cannon ball, that was fired at the Highlanders from the Castle, sticking in the wall of a house. He has almost filled his sketch-book after his own fashion. I am in good spirits, and hope to have some fun before I go; but I am disappointed about Wilson, and think he will be sorry too.[8] Last night we had a party of travellers at the hotel, singing Scotch songs, &c., to Tom's great amusement. It is much better this public room, than moping in a private parlour.

A bookseller in the town, with a famous collection of autographs, has sent to ask for mine, so I am going to call on him this morning.[9] If I do but keep as I am now, I shall get on; the bracing air does me infinite good. I have indeed been surprised to find how far I can walk, being on my feet great part of the day. I shall reserve a bit of room in case of a letter from you when the post comes in, and therefore stop for the present. Give my kind love to Mrs. D—.[10] I should have liked to have seen her, but for this invite of Lord Jeffrey's, but feel now that I ought not to leave. Give my love to Tibbie; and Tom sends his, and kisses to you all.

God bless you, my own dearest and best,
Your own affectionate

Thos. Hood.

Edinbro', Wednesday Morning, 27th. [*September 1843*]

From *Memorials* II 172–6

1/Compare Scott's *St. Ronan's Well* xxv: 'Edinburgh, which is a tolerable residence in winter and spring, becomes disagreeable in summer, and in autumn is the most melancholy sojourn that ever poor mortals were condemned to ... no inhabitant of any consideration remains in the town; those who cannot get away, hide themselves in obscure corners ... The gentry go to their country-houses.'
2/Francis Jeffrey (1773–1850), critic, editor of the *Edinburgh Review* (1802–29), took his seat on the bench and became Lord Jeffrey, 1834. He lived at Craigcrook, just outside Edinburgh.
3/Robert Chambers (1802–71), publisher, author of *Vestiges of Creation*. William Chambers (1800–83), publisher. William recalled Hood's visit in *A Long and Busy Life* (1882) 64–5: 'At this time [Hood] was pale, thin, and emaciated, but retained his liveliness of manner, and smartness of repartee.' I do not know who is meant by 'a younger brother' in Hood's text.
4/In 1827–8 William Burke (1792–1829) and William Hare carried out their multiple murders in Log's lodging house, in Tanner's Close, beneath the Castle on the north side of the West Port.
5/John Porteous was hanged by the mob in 1736. Scott described the affair in *The Heart of Midlothian* vii: in the West Bow 'the booth of a man who dealt in cordage was forced open, a coil of rope ... was selected ... and the dealer next morning found that a guinea had been left on his counter in exchange.'
6/In his letter of 12 September Dickens had recommended Moir as 'a very fine fellow'; Hood had probably met Robert Blackwood (d 1852).
7/Beattie's 'The Minstrel' I
8/Dickens had asked Hood to give Wilson 'a hundred greetings from me.'
9/See the following letter.
10/Mrs Dore

TO
WILLIAM FINLAY WATSON

For W.F. Watson Esq[re] Edinbro.

'Then gie's *yer hand* my trusty fere'[1]

Considering the above as a Scotch mode of asking for an Autograph, I have great pleasure in complying with the Request, and with the utmost regard & respect for Auld Lang Syne, remain his admirer

Most retrospectively.

Thos: Hood

Edinbro –/ 28 Sept[r] 1843.

MS NLS, bequeathed with over three thousand other autographs by the recipient, William Finlay Watson (d 1881), bookseller.

1/'Auld Lang Syne': 'And there's a hand, my trusty fiere! / And gie's a hand o' thine!'

TO
WILLIAM FINLAY WATSON

My dear Sir.

Many thanks for your present, which will be a pleasant remembrance of my visit to Auld Reekie, & its Reekiebites; whom Father Matthew,[1] I perceive, hopes to turn into Rechabites.[2]

I hope the Professor will ask him to one of the Noctes.[3] Not that I am a Drunk-hard (NB the true spelling of the word) I like Temperance, and always put a little water in my grog.

Perhaps, – who knows? – between Professor Wilson & Father Theobald, the vexatious difference may be settled between the Moderates & the Immoderates – as to Spirits as well as Spirituals. A consummation devoutly to be wished.[4]

I shall return to London, or at least steam in that direction tomorrow, so well pleased with Edinboro, – some of your ancient Scots I believe, spell it Edenborough, paradisaically, – that at some future time, you may perchance see me again – especially if you will look in here tonight & take a glass of toddy – which I have learned should be pronounced toadey, – with

Dear Sir

Yours very truly

Thos Hood

My laddie desires his love to all in your flat. If Tom Junior *cuts no great figure*, – at least he can *carve a little mouse* – as you saw last night. – It used to be reckoned a mountainous effort to give birth to such things[5] – so he may yet prove a genius. He is as delighted as I am with your Town – but in a different way – for instance, I think he will regret the Cowgate for the sake of the milk.[6] In London we have but the ghost of that luxury.

I have a bad cold in my head, if it be not a Scotch mist – for it is very like it, – but I suppose toadey drinking, which is far preferable to toadey eating, will cure any of your national complaints.

T.H.

Edinbro. / Friday Eveng [*29 September 1843*]

MS NLS. Published in part by W. Forbes Gray, 'A Budget of Literary Letters' *Fortnightly Review* March 1928 345–6.

1/Father Theobald Mathew (1790–1858), Irish 'apostle of temperance,' paid a successful visit to London in August 1843.

2/Jeremiah 35: 5–6

3/The series of 'Noctes Ambrosianae' by Professor John Wilson and others in *Blackwood's Magazine*

4/*Hamlet* 3 i 63–4

5/Horace, 'Art of Poetry' 139

6/A mere pun; the Cowgate is a street in Edinburgh.

TO

MR and MRS D. KEAY

Dear Uncle & Aunt,

Here we are, safe & sound, after a capital passage in 43 hours from Leith; the weather so quiet & the boat so easy, we had no squeamishness even, but were free to enjoy agreable society & good fare. There were a little boy & girl on board, who served for play-fellows for Tom, – besides the stewardess's scissors, which enabled him to cut out steam-ships, cats, dogs, and horses: – instead of making a fort of your pump, or picking up pebbles. So we got on very well.

On reaching Dundee, I found a letter enclosing your slippers, which I forwarded to the Ferry, & hope you liked them. I called on Mr Gray but he was away from home. You would see from a paragraph in the Dundee Warder, that I visited the Watt Institution.[1]

Unfortunately there was thick weather on our voyage to Leith, so that I lost much of the scenery of the Firth, as well as the first sight of Edinbro, which, as I could judge on my return, must be very striking. I was delighted with Auld Reekie & my reception there: – but unluckily it was vacation time & Professors Wilson & Napier were in the country. However I had an invitation from Lord Jeffrey, and dined with him at his country seat Craigcrook about 3 miles from the city. I also rode out, with Tom, to Musselburgh to make acquaintance with Mr D.M. Moir, a surgeon, & well known author. I was very much pleased with him & his family – & there were some fine boys with whom Tom was very soon quite at home. I have corresponded with Mr Moir for many years, but never met him before.[2]

In Edinbro we saw Holyrood, the Castle, the Anatomical Museum, the Advocates Library &c &c, & altogether my visit to Scotland has been very gratifying to my feelings as well as beneficial to my health. Tom made several friends at Edinbro,

& amongst the rest some ladies who sent him a *short* cake, which of course he wished had been a *long* one, of their own making.

I found my family quite well, – and had the pleasure of seeing our Friend from Belgium, who had been detained longer than she expected.[3] My Wife was delighted with the improvement in our looks – & much amused with Tom's account of his Travels. His memorandum book, by the time we got home was quite full. You will be glad to hear that we brought home every thing, without loss or damage – including the Venetian wine glass, in which I shall drink your health, I trust, very often.

I have been very much tempted since my arrival to start off to Manchester, having had a very pressing invitation from the Committee to be present at the Grand Evening Assembly at the Athenaeum, – but found too much to do at home. Otherwise I should no doubt have made some valuable acquaintance.[4] Indeed for the next six months I shall be extremely busy, as it is the briskest season of the year. Betsy has not been at our house during my absence – she will perhaps come on Saturday. I conclude that poor Mrs Holt is in much the same state, and as I told you have little hope of her ever being otherwise under so much mismanagement. My wife desires her love, & thanks for your kindness to her boy, who by his own account was very happy & comfortable, & is loud in praise of cookeys, jelly, and porridge – not forgetting the beautiful milk & butter. We rather turn up our noses at our breakfasts, for even the haddies are better farther north. Fanny unites in love & thanks, for your presents, – & Jane (my wife) is much pleased with those pretty mats – the silver pencil case she has put away till Tom is older, to take care of it. We all wish there were a chance of seeing you or my Uncle in London – Travelling now is easy to what it used to be – but we are none of us very young – and I almost fear my journeyings are pretty well at an end. I shall sit still at home, for the future, I suspect, like an old young man. I am

My dear Uncle & Aunt Your affectionate Nephew

Thos Hood

17 Elm Tree Road / St John's Wood / Thursday 5th October [*1843*]

MS Dundee. Published, with the omission of the sentence concerning Mrs Holt, by Elliot 148–50.

1/The paragraph is quoted by Elliot 151.

2/Only one letter to Moir before this date survives.

3/Mrs Dore

4/The occasion is described in *The Speeches of Charles Dickens* ed K. J. Fielding (Oxford 1960) 44–52.

TO
LAMAN BLANCHARD

I have only just received by the post your kind note of the 25th September, which has afforded me very great pleasure. Proud of my profession, and loving it 'with all its faults,' I delight in the friendship of my literary brethren; and especially enjoy their writing, their conversation, and society. Hence my chief regret in leaving the New Monthly has been at losing the company of those who, like yourself, have been so long associated with me in its pages ... I have received several other testimonials of good will from the Bruderschaft, highly gratifying to my feelings; and proving that we poor authors are much better fellows amongst ourselves than the ignorant have supposed.

[*St John's Wood, October 1843*]

From Douglas Jerrold *Works* 2nd ed. (n.d.) v 62. Hood is replying to a flattering letter from Blanchard in which he expressed regret at Hood's resignation of the editorship of NMM. Blanchard's letter is in the Folger Shakespeare Library.

TO
CHARLES DICKENS

My dear Dickens.
I called twice on you today, wanting a word of knowledge, perhaps, & advice from you.
Your report of Cunningham & Mortimer,[1] added to Barham's who says that they placed a blank paper before him to fill up with his own terms, induced me to ask them if they would like me as a Contributor. I heard from Cunningham to say Mortimer was absent & today got the enclosed.[2]
Now you told me that Ainsworth was out of the Editorship – Barham asked Mortimer, who said Ainsworth was not Editor, – they had *none* – & Hurst of Colburn's told me that Ainsworth had not been editor for months, – but it was reported that Blanchard was Editor. All this makes Ainsworth's note a very odd one.
It seems to me as if Mortimer, the money'd man? is going to withdraw – & Cunningham, Ainsworth & Blanchard are to carry on the Mag – & are anxious to make use of me. At any rate the terms won't do – & I do not like the aspect of

things. Blanchard is very much in with Colburn, Patmore, & the Marlboro Street gang.[3]
My *notion* is to see *Mortimer* tomorrow & know the rights of it – to decline the thing – & reopen an old arrangement with Bentley. Mortimer will be there at 10 A.M.
I have had it proposed to me by a man with means[4] to start a new one. It is rather tempting for I have never had fair play in the N.M.M. & think I could do something – if left alone to do it.
But my present object is to ask whether you know any thing of the Ainsworth affair, & to have your view of it.
I called on my return from Scotland but could not catch you. I was delighted with Edinburgh – but unluckily it was vacation time & the Professors Napier & Wilson were absent. But I had the pleasure of dining with Lord Jeffrey, at Craigcrook, who sent his love to you – & spent a very happy evening with Moir, – delighted with him. Tom Junior accompanied me. I am much the better for my trip in various ways.
Today in passing thro Lincolns Inn Fields I called on our friend Forster & was shocked to hear he was very ill – but could not make out exactly how – for they said he had undergone an operation – & his complaint was rheumatic. I shall call again tomorrow on him.
My wife is doubtful whether her answer to Mrs. Dickens, about the *new* Dilke,[5] ever reached its destination – for another note, posted at the same time & place, did *not*.
If you can conveniently – two or three lines will help me in making up my mind.
– A propos of Colburn's – the result shows that from the beginning the Patmore Shoberl & Williams trio had resolved on being sub-over Editors – & that if I had not resigned I should have been resigned. God bless you – Jane joins in kind regards.

Yours ever truly, Thos Hood

C Dickens Esqre

17 Elm Tree Road / Thursday Evg [*19 October 1843*]

MS Huntington. Published by Whitley HLQ 406–8. The letter from Ainsworth to which Hood refers at the end of his second paragraph is dated 19 October. Perhaps this letter of Hood's belongs to the same day.

1/Hugh Cunningham and John Mortimer, publishers of *Ainsworth's Magazine*. The title page of vol. III (January-June 1843) carries both their names, but that of vol. IV (July-December) has only the name of Mortimer.

2/Ainsworth offers Hood '16 guineas per sheet – the highest terms the Magazine can afford, and higher than are given to any other contributor. Of course you retain your copyrights.' The letter is

published by S. M. Ellis *William Harrison Ainsworth and His Friends* (1911) II 70. The original is in the Berg Collection, New York Public Library.
3/The tone of this sentence contrasts strongly with that of the previous letter to Blanchard.
4/Edward Gill Flight offered financial support to Hood, so that he could set up his own magazine, but the support quickly proved to be inadequate.
5/Hood's friend's grandson, another Charles Wentworth, was born 4 September 1843.

TO
WILLIAM HARRISON AINSWORTH

Dear Ainsworth.
Your note rather astonished me, for I knew long ago that you had sold the Magazine[1] – & no less than three parties have since told me that you had ceased to be Editor. I therefore wrote to the Publishers. But in whatever character you so handsomely open your arms to me, the terms mentioned put any embracing on my part quite out of the question. Besides, to be candid, I do not quite like the unsettled state of the establishment.
Since I wrote to Messrs C & M. I have had propositions from a man of means & literary propensities to start a *new* Periodical – it is rather tempting, for I should like to show what I could do with such a vehicle, – without those *skids* on the wheels, in *uphill* work too, that helped to disgust me with the New Monthly.
I wonder how Colburn saves the Editorship if he is going to reduce the price of his Puffing Machine?
I should be very happy to accept your friendly invitation to meet Blanchard – but for the rest of the month I shall be engaged night & day almost with business. I have two volumes of my papers preparing for publication – with other matters to arrange.

I am
My dear Ainsworth
Yours very truly

Thos Hood

Mrs Hood desires her kind remembrances.

W.H. Ainsworth Esqre

Friday Morng / 17 Elm Tree Road / St John's Wood [*20 October 1843*]

MS Bodleian, dated in another hand
1/Hood was evidently misinformed.

TO
J.T.J. HEWLETT

Dear P. P.

Where am I – ? – *Here* & shall be till Xmas when my lease is out. And then I shall have a box somewhere in this neighbourhood. I have no expectation of being from home *any* week this year.

You were not much surprised I dare say at the split with Colburn. We have never been comfortable together – from the same causes that annoyed Hook as you know. And Redding who was here, the other day, says what broke up Campbell's Editorship was the interference of the *subs*. The result proves the thing – for now the Mag is to be conducted by Williams Patmore & the illustrious Author of a Guide to Greenwich![1] rather an Anticlimax after Campbell Bulwer & Hook. C. offered me an advance but I will not write on *any* terms under such a management[2] – & you may perhaps see me Editor of Bentley's – or a Periodical of my own – still more likely. They played me a dirty trick last month with the Anti Mathewite paper which was evidently meant to appear as mine, to the public.[3]

By the bye I may as well tell you the rights here of a matter the result of which may have been attributed to me. Hurst asked my advice about your Welsh Proposition – I mean as to Rebecca – I understood it to refer to 7 numbers of the Mag & said I thought before 7 months the subject would be settled, & the riots over & Becca dead and buried – But that for 2 or 3 numbers it was a good subject & would even warrant some extra expense of a journey of the party to the spot who was to write it.[4] – This was *precisely* my opinion, as given – neither more nor less. Love to all.

Thine truly

T.H.

17 Elm Tree Road / Saturday. [*21 October 1843*]

MS Texas. This letter belongs with the previous group.

1/William Shoberl

2/According to John Forster, 14 August, 'he still offers to advance you on account of the forthcoming volume, 50£,' MS Bristol Central Library.

3/First article in NMM October 1842, 145–51, not by Hood.

4/Rebecca was the name of the supposed head of the 'anti-turnpike conspiracy,' a symptom of agrarian discontent, which troubled South Wales throughout this year.

TO
RICHARD BENTLEY

Sir.
Having resigned the management of the New Monthly Magazine, & dissolved my connexion with Mr Colburn, I am looking about me for other engagements, & before deciding on any propositions elsewhere, should be glad to know if you feel inclined to treat with me for the Editorship of the Miscellany.

I am Sir
Your most obedly

Thos Hood

R. Bentley Esqre

17 Elm Tree Road / St John's Wood / Saturday [*21 October 1843*]

MS Bodleian. Dated in another hand

TO
RICHARD BENTLEY

Sir.
The tenor of your note, & a report which has just reached me, compel me to say that I should never have dreamt of offering my services as Editor of the Miscellany, *with a knowledge that Mr. Wilde, or any other gentleman, had the management of that periodical.* I understood the office to be vacant, the party who had filled it having received a foreign appointment. Under this impression, & having paid off Colburn, I took the opportunity of offering my cooperation, – the loss of which you were once pleased to consider as a grievance.

I am Sir
Yours most obedly

Thos Hood

R. Bentley Esqre

17 Elm Tree Road / St John's Wood / Thursday [*26 October 1843*]

MS Bodleian. The argument follows on from the previous letter, so I have dated it the 26th.

TO
CHARLES DICKENS

My dear Dickens.
I only received Bentley's answer last night – he 'feels obliged by the offer I was so good as to make, but has not the remotest idea of making any alteration with regard to the Editorship of that publication.'
A gentleman who has just left me says that Lever told him that Bentley had quarrelled with four of his writers (including Lever himself). Are the Publishers & Sinners going to write as well as edit their own Periodicals?
Look at today's Herald under the head 'Marlborough Street –' Colburn at the Complaint of Colonel Davison, – Another charge of fraudulent agreements! – and Mr. Shoberl the 'Managing Man.'[1]
I was very glad the other day to receive a few lines from Forster though written in bed. I have been trying vainly to get to him – & have no messenger.
As for myself – I don't feel damped *through* yet – perhaps I shall be able to start a literary cab of my own.

Yours very truly

Thos Hood

C. Dickens Esquire.

17 Elm Tree Road / St John's Wood / Thursday. [*26 October 1843*]

MS Huntington. Published by Whitley 408–9. The discussion follows on from that in the previous letter. In his third paragraph Hood refers to the *Morning Chronicle*, 26 October 1843.

1/The item is reported in *Morning Chronicle* 26 October 1843, 7. Charles J.C. Davidson in vain sought the return of the MS of his work just prior to its publication by Henry Colburn. John Blackwood wrote 20 December: 'Colburn's last feat in the art of puffing a book (viz., by causing Colonel Davidson to have him up at the police court for his MS, and then publishing the book within three days) has excited the admiration and envy of the whole trade. [Dickinson] thinks Bentley will commit suicide from vexation that the master-thought had not occurred to him first,' Mrs Oliphant *Annals of a Publishing House* (Edinburgh 1897) II 356.

TO
WILLIAM ELLIOT

Dear Doctor.
I have been *mean*ing to come down to Stratford, with my Scotch news for you and Mrs Elliot, & my sweeties for Jeanie & May – but I have been in quite a whirlpool

of business, which has kept me revolving[1] round home – first my two volumes from the New Monthly to prepare for the press, with tedious waitings on Colburn, – (law with Baily as well as literature) – & finally negociations about to close for a New Periodical! HOOD'S MAGAZINE. to come out on 1st Janry!!! So, I cannot keep the news from you, but write at once to tell you what is likely to be.
My fortunes seem subject to *crises* like certain disorders – on or about Xmas I am to dine with you – turn out, & get a new House, – come to issue with Baily, & start with a Periodical under my own name. NB. There are folks with money to back it. I shall be rather better paid than with Colburn – & have a future share if the thing becomes a property.
Colburn is sick, & I believe sorry – and yesterday I had an offer to write for Jerrold's Mag.[2] on my own terms – the project having got wind. This looks well. So do I, people say, for Scotland did me good in various ways. I think if I could live in a monument on the Calton Hill[3] I should keep pretty well.
There is a sort of rage for periodicals in our Row – at least Jane, who has been engaged for the last three years in writing one *Childish* article,[4] is thinking of starting a *Monthly Juvenile.* You may safely take it in for it won't take *you* in beyond 2 or 3 numbers. It's very innocent – I have read one little bit, & can truly say it wouldn't hurt the babby. I only hope it may not prove one of the Fallacies of the Faculties. *Mine* is sure to do – & Jane feels Hen-sure of hers. But who would have thought of her keeping 'a Public!'
She sends her love & means to get to Stratford as soon as she 'is out' – whether she means bodily or bookily I cannot tell. I suspect she has a plot to ask Manley Hopkins to write for the 'rising generation'.
Tom & Fanny have given her some hints how children ought to be brought up: & of course Dunny, Jeanie, & May have some notions of their own on the same subject.
God bless you all. These here all unite in love to those there – with Dear Doctor
Yours ever truly

Thos Hood.

Jane desires me to say she hopes she may put down your name among her *prescribers.* I suspect she means subscribers – but must refer you to her 'prospecticusses' in print. Pray tell Mrs Elliot to tell Thomas not to send away any Hawkers with books in numbers[5] – it may be US.

17. Elm Tree Road / St John's Wood / Tuesday Night [*7 November 1843*]

MS Yale. Published in part in *Memorials* II 177–9. The letter is dated in another hand the 8th, but Tuesday was the 7th.

1/A blot over 'vo' is annotated 'Excuse boluses'.

2/*The Illuminated Magazine*, begun in May 1843

3/In Edinburgh, at the east end of Princes Street, surmounted by the incomplete and empty National Monument, Nelson's monument, and monuments to Dugald Stewart and Playfair.

4/I have not been able to identify this work; it may be one of Hood's jokes.

5/An interesting indication of a technique of selling the serial works popular at the time.

TO

MAY ELLIOT

My dear May,

I promised you a letter, and here it is. I was sure to remember it; for you are as hard to forget, as you are soft to roll down a hill with. What fun it was! only so prickly, I thought I had a porcupine in one pocket, and a hedgehog in the other. The next time, before we kiss the earth we will have its face well shaved. Did you ever go to Greenwich Fair? I should like to go there with you, for I get no rolling at St. John's Wood. Tom and Fanny only like roll and butter, and as for Mrs. Hood, she is for rolling in money.

Tell Dunnie that Tom has set his trap in the balcony and has caught a cold, and tell Jeanie that Fanny has set her foot in the garden, but it has not come up yet. Oh, how I wish it was the season when 'March winds and April showers bring forth *May* flowers!' for then of course you would give me another pretty little nosegay. Besides it is frosty and foggy weather, which I do not like. The other night, when I came from Stratford, the cold shrivelled me up so, that when I got home, I thought I was my own child!

However, I hope we shall all have a merry Christmas; I mean to come in my most ticklesome waistcoat, and to laugh till I grow fat, or at least streaky. Fanny is to be allowed a glass of wine, Tom's mouth is to have a *hole* holiday, and Mrs. Hood is to sit up to supper! There will be doings! And then such good things to eat; but, pray, pray, pray, mind they don't boil the baby by mistake for a *plump* pudding, instead of a plum one.

Give my love to everybody, from yourself down to Willy,[1] with which and a kiss, I remain, up hill and down dale,

Your affectionate lover,

Thomas Hood.

17, Elm Tree Road, St. John's Wood, / Monday [*November 1843*]

From *Memorials* II 196–7. To Hood's friend's youngest daughter. In view of the seasonal references in the letter to wintry weather and coming Christmas, November seems a more likely date than April 1844, that given in *Memorials*.

1/Hood's son notes: ' "Willy", at that writing, being very tall for his age, and May, his youngest sister, *not* very tall for her age.'

TO
CHARLES DICKENS

My dear Dickens.

You will have wondered at not hearing from me; but the truth is after receivg your note, about Chapman & Hall, it struck me, that in case the arrangement for my Magazine was completed I ought to throw my new ballads into the periodical. As you will see by the enclosure, the Magazine is to be –[1] I shall still publish the Elm Tree as I proposed but not so soon as I intended – & C & H may not think a single one worth their attention. I have had quite as much – & a bittock – to do as fits my powers, you will suppose, and am still hard at work.

I am besides in all the anxieties of my Trial with Baily which comes on this week. Make Tom Pinch turn Author, and Pecksniff become a Publisher.[2] I have done my collected papers in 2 vols – for Colburn. Much I shall get by them *now*.

All our loves.

Yours very truly

Thos Hood

C Dickens Esqre

17 Elm Tree Road / Monday. [*4 December 1843*]

MS New York. Published by Whitley HLQ 409. Dickens' reply to this note was written on Thursday, 7 December.

1/In his reply Dickens commended the prospectus of HM. It is published in *Memorials* II 186–9.

2/The monthly parts of *Martin Chuzzlewit* began to appear in January 1843 and continued until July 1844.

TO
J.T.J. HEWLETT

Dear P.P.
By this time you will have received a Prospectus from Mr Flight, and some account from our friend Harvey of the progress of the Magazine. From the short notice, I have had plenty to do – (or too much rather with my two Vols to get clear off[1]–) preliminary, which must be my apology for not writing sooner. I will now give you a slight sketch of our views. Our quantity will be 7 sheets, – 2/6 price – & in each number we propose to give a very good plate as *a work of art.*[2] It has been generally agreed by those concerned or consulted that we should avoid Series or Continuations, against which there has grown up a strong prejudice from the badness of so many of them – the feeling against them has become very general; & makes us anxious for *independent* articles. – the more so, as not being Pubs. we cannot dispose afterwards of a three vol. story or novel. All of which I doubt not you will see the *proper-priety* of and concur in.[3] At all events let me have *your* views – and a scheme of what you could do for us – of course retaining your Copyrights, for the reason given above – as I do by my own.
We are up to our eyes in Bills – Prospectuses etc – as you may suppose, with daily *meets* & drinks. By the way, perhaps, you are likely to *come to town* shortly, which would be better than *espistling* – if so let us know.
I am middling well considering that my trial with Baily comes on this week, & you know the nervous uncertainties of the law. I expect to see ½ the trade arrayed against me Colburn & all.

All here send their love to all yours.
I am Dear P.P.
Yours very truly

Thos Hood

How do you like the Prospectus?

Revd J Hewlett.

17 Elm Tree Road / St John's Wood / Monday. [*4 December 1843*]

MS Texas. Hood looks forward to the publication of HM, January 1844.
1/*Whimsicalities* was advertised as now ready in *Bent's Monthly Literary Advertiser* 11 December 1843.
2/This plan was adhered to in the first three numbers of HM.
3/This plan broke down in the March number with the publication of the first part of Moir's 'Recollections ... of Gideon Shaddoe,' and in the May number with the publication of the first four chapters of Hood's 'Our Family.'

TO
UNKNOWN CORRESPONDENT

Dear Sir.
If you were the Bearer of the book last night why did you not come in? I should have been glad to see you.
I have given up Colburn's some months ago – but as per enclosed Prospectus have a coach of my own.

In haste Yours very truly

Thos Hood

17 Elm Tree Road / St John's Wood / The 5th Decr 1843.

MS UCLA. Hood refers in the letter to the prospectus of HM.

TO
J.T.J. HEWLETT

Dear P. P.
As all was so satisfactorily settled when you were in town you had better refer the subject of your last to your next visit to London. Flight is very poorly with influenza, & as you may guess I am as busy as *two* bees. – So send us a crack paper as soon as you can, & there is no doubt of the liberal being done hereafter. We don't care for names, so that you can use any signature you like, or don't like which will not compromise you with Colburn.[1] He is very savage I guess. Did you observe Patmore's letter in last Athm & Gazette? I suppose he is angry at *not* having the Editorship instead of Shoberl.
I told Flight of your wish for more Prospectuses & he undertook to send em. All is going on famously.

In haste
Dear P. P
Yours very truly

Thos Hood

Revd J Hewlett.

17 Elm Tree Road / Monday Night [*11 December 1843*]

MS Texas. Hood refers at the end of his first paragraph to *The Athenaeum* of the previous Saturday, 9 December 1843, 1094. In the letter Patmore denied being editor of NMM.

1/Hewlett's 'Great Tom of Oxford' appeared in HM January 1844, under his usual *nom de plume* of 'Suum Cuique.'

TO
UNKNOWN CORRESPONDENT

Dear Sir
After mature deliberation (without any reference to the merits of your M.S) it has been decided that it is not desirable to have articles in the Magazine from a party so generally known to be connected with Mr Colburn's establishment – an objection, the force of which, on reflection, you will no doubt perceive.

I am Dear Sir Yours very truly

Thos Hood

17 Elm Tree Road / Friday [*December 1843*]

MS Cameron. I place this letter here, because it was written after Hood undertook to publish HM and before he moved to Devonshire Lodge, in the same district of St John's Wood, at the end of the year.

TO
MARK LEMON

My dear Sir.
I send the Song of the Shirt – Will it be too grave for Punch? If not there may be some more of it. I have been too unwell to send it before – & too busy to copy out the farce – but you shall have all in time – Almanack included[1]

Yours very truly

Thos Hood

1 Adam Street[2]*/ Wednesday.* [*December 1843*]

MS UCLA. Mark Lemon (1809–70), editor of *Punch* from 1841 until his death. 'The Song of the Shirt' appeared in *Punch* 16 December 1843. Since by this time Hood addressed Bradbury, the publisher of *Punch*, by name, I am sure he is here writing to the editor.

1/*Punch's Almanack for 1844* was advertised at the end of the 1843 volume, 268.
2/Address of the office for HM

TO

THE EDITOR OF THE SUN

Sir.

Permit me to thank you for your very flattering remarks on some verses of mine in Punch, called the 'Song of the Shirt.'

I have derived an unusual gratification from the reception of those lines by the Journals – as evidence that my *intention* has not been altogether without effect.

I am Sir

Yours very truly

Thos Hood

Office for Hood's Magazine / 1. Adam Street. Adelphi [*20 December 1843*]

MS Bodleian. The letter has a printed letter-head, and is dated December 1843 in another hand. *The Sun* quoted 'The Song of the Shirt' on 16 December 1843, dealt with it in a leading article three days later, and published Hood's letter, dated 'Wednesday,' on Thursday the 21st.

TO

EDWARD WILLIAM WATKIN and PETER BERLYN

Gentn

Please to accept a trifling contribution to the library of the Manchester Athenaeum, from

Gentn

Yours very truly

Thos Hood

E. Watkin Esqr

P. Berlyn Esqr

Office for Hood's Magazine / 1. Adam Street. Adelphi [*21 December 1843*]

MS Manchester Reference Library. Address: 'E. Watkin Esqre/ P. Berlyn Esqre/ Athenaeum/ Manchester.' The letter has a printed letter-head, and is dated in another hand. The Manchester Athenaeum had been 'established in 1836, to furnish intellectual recreation for the youth of the middle classes,' *Spectator* 5 October 1844, 945. Hood had wittily and wisely declined an invitation to patronise a Bazaar held by the Athenaeum in July this year: this letter was printed and sold there, and is reprinted in *Memorials* II 153–7. Watkin and Berlyn were officials of the Athenaeum.

TO

MR RAMSAY

Sir

I do not want to see sheets 1 and 2 again. You print so very correctly it would be a mere loss of time to have revised. Get the sheets to press as soon as the cuts come. I have sent a message to the engraver.

Yours

Thos Hood

[*St John's Wood, December 1843*]

MS University of Liverpool. Address: 'Mr Ramsay.' I have not identified this person but he was presumably printing HM. The letter is dated in another hand 1845, but I feel that it may refer rather to an early issue of HM.

1844

TO
SAMUEL PHILLIPS

My dear Sir,

I cannot tell you how much your letter shocked and grieved me; for being strictly a domestic man myself, finding my comfort for many evils in the bosom of my family, I can the better imagine and sympathise with such a bereavement.[1]

The only comfort I can offer to you, is the one which I have found most consolatory under the loss of dear relatives, the belief that we not love in vain; that so surely as we must live, having lived, so must we love, having loved; and that after some term, longer or shorter, but a more vibration of the great pendulum of eternity, we shall all be re-united. In the meantime let us *endure* as bravely as we can for the sake of others.

You may guess by the number, which comes with this, how I have been occupied, writing very hard with the prospect of fighting very hard, for there is every appearance of a trade combination against us. But the first number seems very well liked. The plate I may commend as very beautiful, knowing something practically of engraving.[2] I need not say, when you feel well enough to resume your pen, how happy I shall be to receive a paper from you. We have agreed not to have any serials (as, not being booksellers, we can do nothing afterwards with the copyright),[3] but each article independent of another.

I would not trouble you with this, but that, without any *selfish* view, I would earnestly recommend you, from my own experience, to resume your pen. I have had my share of the troubles of this world, as well as of the calamities of authors,[4] and have found it to be a very great blessing to be able to carry my thoughts into the ideal, from the too strong real.

I am writing hastily, which you will, I know, excuse; for you must be well aware of what a Christmas month it has been for editors, and the 31st on a Sunday! And I have another short one before me with only twenty-eight days; I hope I shall survive it. Thank God my blood keeps within bounds.

Mrs. Hood desires her kind regards, and believe me to be, my dear sir,

Yours very truly,

Thos. Hood.

My new home is at Devonshire Lodge,[5] New Finchley Road, St. John's Wood, where I shall be most happy to see you; it is just beyond the 'Eyre Arms,' three doors short of the turnpike. The Magazine Office is 1, Adam Street, Adelphi, and I am sometimes there of a morning. I just see I have made a mistake about twenty-eight days, I was thinking of the No. for February.

1, Adam Street, Adelphi, Jan. 1st, 1844.

From *Memorials* II 192–4. Samuel Phillips (1814–54), journalist, author of *Caleb Stukely* (1844), suffered from consumption.

1/I do not know what member of Phillips's family has died.

2/An illustration of 'The Haunted House,' by Thomas Creswick (1811–69)

3/I do not see why not being able to take advantage of copyright as the publisher of HM by later issuing serials in book form would inhibit Hood from publishing them in the first place. In fact, HM contained serials, such as Hood's own *Our Family*, begun in May.

4/Title of a book by Isaac D'Israeli (1812)

5/Hood's son notes that his father gave the house this name 'in remembrance of the exceeding generosity and kindness' which he received from the Duke of Devonshire. This is Hood's first letter from the new address.

TO SAMUEL PHILLIPS

Wishing you whole horse-powers of health, – & happiness to match I am My dear sir

Yours very truly

Thos Hood

S. Phillips Esqre

[*St John's Wood, January 1844*]

Transcript UCLA. In spirit akin to the previous letter

TO MARK LEMON?

The great man of Great Marlborough Street[1] is very sure, on my assuming the right of speculating with my own brains ...

He has since done worse – for in default of Humourists for his Humorist,[2] and not being able to write an article himself he has dreamt one – a 'legend by Ingoldsby.' It is not advertised in London, where the trick would soon be detected, but I have seen it, as No. 3 of the contents of the New Monthly Mag[3] ... What will become of poor Authors when a Colburn is equal to a 'Tale of *Fiction*?'

But if there were no Colburnism – if all the world could be quite correct, and no humbug, half the vocation of Punch and his fellows would be gone. May I hope to derive the same sort of sport in hunting him thro' all his wrigglings and doublings into dark holes and dirty corners ...

What would you have done as a Wild Irish Girl if all the world had been one Quaker? Eh! Lady Morgan?[4]

[*St John's Wood, 5 January 1844*]

From Maggs Bros. *Autograph Letters* no. 272 (November 1911) 37. The date is given in the catalogue. The ellipses indicate gaps in the transcript. The reference to *Punch* makes me suggest Lemon as the possible recipient.

1/Henry Colburn

2/A reference to the *New Monthly Magazine and Humourist*

3/The March number of NMM in fact contained Barham's legend 'The Lord of Thoulouse,' so Hood's suspicion was unjustified.

4/Hood is comparing *Punch* with Lady Morgan. If the world had been wholly pure, then there would have been no room for the wildness of the lady or the satirical wit of the magazine.

TO

CHARLES DICKENS

Dear Dickens

I send you a copy of the Mag. There is a dead set against it I suspect in the trade for not a showboard is to be seen nor will they put it in their windows. It was ready on Saturday morning but there was a story got up & told at all the shops we asked at that it would not be ready till Saturday Night or Monday[1] – H. Cunningham said he had been told so at the office which was false but Chapman & Hall said the same tho they had had a parcel sent them in the morning!

Colburn has refused three letters addressed for me to his care – & they came to me endorsed 'not known to Mr. Colburn' this is so dirty a trick I have advertised it. What a set they are. Yours very truly in haste

Thos Hood

All good wishes from us to you all. – I am often at 1 Adam St. if you should be that way.

'No connexion with the Scavangers.'[2]

Devonshire Lodge / New Finchley Road / St John's Wood [*January 1844*]

(just two or three doors short of the turnpike beyond the Eyre Arms)

MS Huntington. Published by Whitley HLQ 410. The letter is written after the appearance of HM January 1844.

1/In fact, HM was advertised in the periodicals for publication on the 1st, that is, Monday.

2/Hood is here distinguishing himself as an independent writer and editor from the predatory booksellers.

TO

WILLIAM HARVEY

My dear Harvey,

I SENT you the Magazine. There is a dead set against it in the trade, not one will they put in a window or hang on showboard. But we shall beat them. I have the press on my side.

Now we have determined on a woodcut number for our 2nd, and we want you to do one in your very best style, and to get it engraved in the very best ditto, to do you all justice – Thomson,[1] or if he could not, perhaps Williams[2] – but *you* had better see to that – so as to show you off best. The great thing is time, in which you must not deceive yourself, as it is imperative on us to forestall the other Mags. this month. But that is between ourselves. I can give you a subject at once, which may save you some trouble – my own Modern Belinda – if you take to the subject. You can draw it your own way – perhaps introducing the same accessories. We want a capital specimen of Harvey, as I think we have given of Creswick. Pray let me know your mind as early as you can, and get it forward. We shall not haggle about terms or be Cradocky.[3] Only let us be *sure* as to *time*, by not deceiving yourself about it.[4]

We shall do very well, – but rather a hard fight of it at first with the trade. All send love to you.

Yours very truly,

Thos. Hood.

W. Harvey, Esq.

[*St John's Wood, January 1844*]

From *Works* IX 149. Written after the publication of HM January 1844.

1/Probably James Thomson (1788–1850)

2/Joseph Lionel Williams (d 1877) engraved Creswick's illustration of Hood's 'The Haunted House' which appeared in the first number of HM.

3/Perhaps a reference to F. M. Cradock, bookseller, 48 Paternoster Row

4/According to Hood's children, Harvey was applied to too late. The February plate was invented by Hood and engraved by Williams. It illustrated Hood's poem, 'The Lady's Dream,' the lady being his 'Modern Belinda.'

TO
J.T.J. HEWLETT

My dear Hewlett

First mark my new Home.
Devonshire Lodge.
New Finchley Road
St John's Wood.

It is just beyond the Eyre Arms three doors short of the 'Pike right hand side. And now to the purport of my note. The chief thing is to beg your paper early – as we wish to be *before* the others. We were ready on *Saturday* morning – but every shop said *Monday* or Saturday night. It was a dodge. In fact there is a dead set against us by the trade – which is *flattering* in one sense – as they *fear* us. They will neither hang up a board nor put the book in a window – nor take one they can help.

Colburn has pulled off the mask – & returned 3 letters for me directed there 'as not known to Mr Colburn'. What a fool! It will only damn him, for I have advertised the fact. And if he gives me any more cause I'll 'Rae Wilson' him.[1]

'He may or may not kiss the rod
But if he don't Ill lay it on by –'

Byron[2]

Your article is very much liked. The trade be damn'd – we'll show em what Authors can do.[3] But pray be early. Kind regards from all &

Yours very truly

Thos Hood

Lines on being unknown to Mr Colburn.
(Enclosed to Hurst)
For a couple of years in the columns of Puff
I was reckon'd a passable writer enough,
But alas! for the favours of Fame! –
Since I quitted her seat in Great Marlboro Street
In repute my decline is so very complete,
That a Colburn don't know me by name!
Now a Colburn I knew, in his person so small
That he seemed the *Half* Brother of no one at all,
Yet in spirit a Dwarf may be big:
But his mind was so narrow, his soul was so dim,
Where's the wonder if all I remember of him
Is – a suit of boy's clothes & a Wig![4]

[*St John's Wood, January 1844*]

MS Texas

1/Hood had attacked Rae Wilson in an ode published in *Athenaeum* 12 August 1837.
2/Byron *Don Juan* i 206
3/The *Derby and Chesterfield Reporter* 12 January, welcomed HM which appeared 'without the puffing aid of booksellers.'
4/Hood also sent a copy of these lines to Dilke and Barham.

TO
RICHARD HARRIS BARHAM

Office 1 Adam Street Adelphi.
and
Home Devonshire Lodge
New Finchley Road
St. John's Wood.
'like a Bird in two places at once!'[1]

My dear Sir.
Herewith you have a sample of the quality of our Magazine. We shall have rather an uphill fight for having no connexion with the trade, they are making a bit of a set against us. But we mean to 'do or die' – & rather consider it a compliment to our prowess. Colburn, to begin has thoroughly committed himself by refusing to take in letters addressed to me at Marlboro Stt. by strangers, sending them adrift endorsed 'Not known to Mr. Colburn'. I am therefore relieved of all delicacy towards him, & beg to say at once, that, should your time allow, & your inclination prompt you to give us your help, I think you would find the connexion a pleasant one in every respect.
A line from you, or a look in – at the office – if you will make an appointment will oblige,

My dear Sir
Yours very truly

Thos. Hood

Revd. R. Barham.[2]

Seriously, the miscarriage of a letter might be of such vital importance to *third* parties, I cannot imagine *a Man* could be guilty of such an act as Colburn's towards his most mortal enemy.

[*London, January 1844*]

MS Harvard. Published by Lane KSJ 50–1
1/Part of a saying attributed to Sir Boyde Roche (1743–1807)
2/There follow Hood's 'Lines on being unknown to Mr Colburn,' given above.

TO
MESSRS SMITH AND ELDER

Dear Sirs,

If you think the 'Spirit of the Age' a likely book you may send it for review in my new Periodical.[1] You can refer to the notices of Dickens's Xmas book – & '*Life in the Sick Room*' – for the sort of review we shall have of worthy books[2] – & as we have no works of our own to puff exclusively like Colburn – Publishers may expect fair & impartial notices – in fact all the help we can give to meritorious works.
The first Number of our Mag. appears to have made a very favourable impression, & our resources of every kind make me confident of success. In the mean time we shall be obliged by your good offices for standing on the same ground as Bentley Colburn etc *who only sell their own* – we expect to have the support of the respectable & independent Houses – in spite of the opposition which some parties interested in their own periodicals may set up. For example it was very generally reported that the Mag. would not be ready till Monday whereas it was ready on the Saturday Morning. But these tricks will only injure the characters of the dealers in them, like Mr Colburn's refusal to take in letters addressed to me under the plea of 'not known to Mr Colburn' – And I have *since* had a letter from his Cashier to my private address! Fine fun with him by & by: – for our motto is your national one Nemo &c[3] & tho we prefer peace & good will amongst men, & especially all engaged in Literature, we are ready to fight.

Please to drop me a line about the book & believe me
Dear Sirs Yours very truly

Thos Hood

1 Adam Stt Adelphi / Tuesday [*9? January 1844*]

MS University of Rochester Library. To George Smith (1789–1846) and Alexander Elder (1790–1876), publishers, both from Scotland.

1/Hood wrote a playful notice of R.H. Horne's *New Spirit of the Age* for HM April *Works* IX 201–4.
2/Dickens's *Christmas Carol* and Harriet Martineau's *Life in the Sick Room* were reviewed by Hood himself, HM January *Works* IX 77–88, 93–103.
3/The motto of the Order of the Thistle, *Nemo me impune lacessit*

TO
WILLIAM BRADBURY

Dear Bradbury –
I send some copy & have lots more, so put that forward, & the Oxford Article *first* that the Author may correct his proof while in town at Adam S^{tt}.
We are going on quite as well as can be expected – the trade has decidedly combined agin us – particularly in the country. But from letters received it will turn ag^{t} themselves for the public will be indignant at being dictated to what they shall or shall not receive. We have almost all the public press at our back, & such notices as Booksellers cannot buy!
I have not forgotten Punch – but have been first unwell & then bothered for a subject. When one occurs *in my line* to Lemon tell him to suggest it. –[1]
Why don't you come up these fine days? – Three doors short of the 'Pike (right hand) beyond the Eyre Rooms – to which busses every half hour from Silver X[2] Charing X?

All good wishes to yourself & Evans
If ever you leave Newington[3] – live up here. Capital air –
Yours very truly

Thos Hood

[*St John's Wood, January 1844*]

MS UCLA. In his first paragraph Hood probably refers to J.T.J. Hewlett's 'The Installation' HM February 1844.
1/Hood's last contribution to *Punch* appeared 16 March, 118.
2/Public house
3/Suburb of London, south of the Thames, east of Lambeth

TO
CHARLES MACKAY

My dear Sir.
Wo do pay for Poetry – at least for such as yours. Have the goodness to tell me – (as there be other proprietors) what arrangement would be agreable to your own expectations: – as both the pieces are in that editorial pigeon-hole, where articles

are laid, to be hatched in print.[1] And whether your name is to be appended. We do not lay any stress on the signature, if the stuff be good.
Please to let me have a line at your earliest convenience, as we mean to be early, & believe me

My dear Sir Yours very truly

Thos Hood

What have you to do with 'Remorse?' – Did *you* kill Mrs Donally?[2] – Or have you thrown poison, for a joke, into the Thames and its tributaries,[3] & hocussed the Londoners as well as the fish?

C. Mackay Esqre

1 Adam Street Adelphi / Saturday. [*27 January 1844*]

MS New York. The letter is dated in another hand 'Jany 1844.' The specific date is suggested by the reference to Mrs Donally in the postscript of the letter. Charles Mackay (1814–89), poet and journalist.
1/Mackay's contributions were published in HM from February 1844.
2/Mrs E. Donally, 'an inveterate drunkard,' committed suicide by jumping off Waterloo Bridge on 23 January 1844: *Times* 27 January, 7. This event took place after her husband had threatened that because of her ways he would kill himself.
3/Title of a book published by Mackay in 1840

TO
J.T.J. HEWLETT

Dear P.P.
Flight could have told you why you had not a proof as well as I could without much going out of his 'department': – viz that your proof lay directed for you at 1 Adam Stt whither you were to return but didn't. Afterwards it was too late to send as I was making it up. I don't think you will find any mistakes in it – at any rate not worse than the one in the N.M.M where the shot dog leaps 5 *yards* high – a devil of a leap even for Leap Year! Your Commemoration is very much liked – 'The narrative is skilfully sustained throughout' says the 'Sun'.
I should have written before, but have been very unwell & jaded – such queer weather! Flights, E. & T.[1] dined with me yesterday. The Mag is going on well – capital notices – the difficulty is to get them to customers in Glasgow etc – the

people want them but the trade are wilfully *backward* in *forwarding* them. I have had letters, signed & anonymous, of complaints from parties to that effect. –
Are you likely to be up again soon? Mrs H. has something to say so I resign the other side to her, & am

Dear P.P Yours very truly

Thos Hood

P.P.P.P.P.P.P.
I have just had a nice kind letter from Mrs Hughes

Devonshire Lodge / New Finchley Road / St John's Wood Tuesday. [*6 February 1844*]

MS Texas. At the end of his first paragraph Hood quotes from *The Sun* 1 February 1844.
1/Edward Gill and Thomas

TO
H. RENSHAW

Dear Sir.
I send a list of the Country Papers, which gave us good reviews – some of them may not be worth sending copies to – you will be able to judge. Please to forward a Copy – by post will be as cheap perhaps as any way – to Revd. J. Hewlett Little Stambridge, Rochford Essex (a contributor – 'Peter Priggins')[1]

I am
Dear Sir Yours very truly

Thos: Hood

Devonshire Lodge / New Finchley Road / Thursday [*8 February 1844*]

MS Cameron. Renshaw was the publisher of HM. Possibly Henry Grundry Renshaw (1806–84), medical bookseller, 356 Strand. The list to which Hood refers follows the letter. The last of the papers which I have seen is dated 26 January 1844.
1/This last sentence is crossed through.

TO
HENRY FRANCIS CARY

Please to take note of the above address where I shall always be most happy to see you.
I feel much gratified and flattered by your very kind contributions to the Magazine: I beg to say that in all cases the copyright belongs to the Author: whom we also desire to remunerate, for the use of the articles, on a scale to be determined by an understanding between the parties.
I am vexed at the error in your last paper: but there is so much extra labour in the starting a new Periodical that some omissions are natural. You will however duly receive a proof, if not already sent, of your present article.
You will find it a very pleasant ride here when you take an airing, & you can scarcely fail to find me at home.

I am, My dear Sir,
Yours very truly

Thos. Hood.

Devonshire Lodge / New Finchley Road / St John's Wood [February 1844]

Transcript made by Mr R.H. King, who informs me that in the opening part of the letter, not transcribed, Hood provides Cary with directions for finding his house. Cary's reply is dated 19 February. I have not been able to identify his contributions to HM.

TO
J.T.J. HEWLETT

Dear P.P.
Flight himself was the authority for your being paid. I have had about ½ mine. The only other is Mackay some three guineas.
The keeping aloof from me was part of a premeditated plan. When the Number was late he turned round on me & made it a pretext for being off – for he knew he could not go on. I tell you he has not yet paid for No 1 – & Bradbury's are obliged to sue him. Stationer not paid either, & he has been changing all, Printers etc, to get cheap, & credit.[1] Look at the paltry paper of the last wrapper compared with 1 & 2. As to his not hindering my writing, by coming, he did hinder it, by boring notes of the quantity wanted etc – & by making a mull at the printing office by his meddling. I sent Mr Phillips to him as third party, & wish you could hear his

report of him.[2] First he wanted 3 sheets deposited with him as a security to put in, if not ready by a certain day. Very good. Then he wanted six, & to have the selection – in fact to be Editor. But not giving any pledge how or when he would fulfil his own engagements. In short a regular shuffle. I could not get my letters or packets from him even – but his brother I suppose advised him better & they came last night p carrier. I had sent the boy repeatedly for them. He in fact sets me at defiance – and even wanted to deny that I was to have any thing for Editorship. Luckily I have it down in the estimates. But who would believe that – he being sole Proprietor. In short as I have told his brother I never met with a man of so small a mind, so bad a temper & so little principle. What right has he to speculate with other people's name, fame, brains, & time – ready to receive if he wins but not to pay if he loses? We know what such fellows are called on the Turf. His conduct, too long to describe now, has left me no alternative. I shall place my claims in my lawyer's hands & advise the Contributors to do the same.[3] For my own sake, as he has compromised me with the public I shall explain the whole thing in a New Prospectus & appeal to the support of the press.

The thing promises capitally – contributions are flowing in & from various indications I am making a stir. So you had better send your paper *here* at once – for I have no doubt of going on, & am preparing a number, with a new name, for a fresh start. My name never stood higher than it does now; I mean now to have better terms & a share in the property.[4] Flight meant to come in to a good thing very easily it appears. Phillips saw *both* Brothers yesterday & could get no satisfactory answer – so that they will hear next from my attorney. I meant seriously if he had detained my letters any longer to have had him up at a police office. Some dated the 9th – an abominable blackguardism.

You *must* be in a nice confusion – but why don't you come here in your way to Essex?[5]

Mrs Hood sends her kind regards. I am going to dine today with three M.P.'s.[6] – a sign of the times with

Yours very truly

Thos Hood

Did I tell you I meant to begin a Novel in the Mag? – I think it will be a capital card – & the drawing by Landseer the number after or so.[7]

Revd J Hewlett.

Devonshire Lodge [*St John's Wood, March 1844*]

MS Texas. Hood refers in his second paragraph to the third number of HM March 1844.

1/Jane Hood wrote: 'The first alarm we had, was [Flight's] quarrelling with Bradbury and Evans, the printers, about payment. This was on the 27th of January; he then got another man in February, who could not manage it; and on the 12th, he engaged another, who had new type to buy, and could not begin to print until the 16th ... The worry laid Hood up; and all these things of course prevented the Magazine coming out in time,' *Memorials* II 195.

2/John Blackwood reported probably in March: 'I dined on Friday last with Phillips. Thomas Hood was there, a very quiet fellow, evidently in the most miserable health. He is in a dreadful fix with the man who is associated with him in the unhappy magazine, so I daresay it will speedily come to a close. He has applied to Phillips to arbitrate. P. says the other fellow deluded Hood with the notion that he had money; it turns out that he had only £100, which he has never produced, and grabbed the money received at the office as it came in,' Margaret Oliphant *Annals of a Publishing House* II 366.

3/Jane Hood provides a relevant comment: 'Hood will be obliged next week to compel Mr. [Flight] to pay him – he owes him nearly £100. Of course it has been a sad blow to us, and crippled us for the present. This man's behaviour has astonished us, having started apparently with such plenty. His house is his own, and brings him in, let off in chambers, £400 a-year!' *Memorials* II 195.
The straits to which the Hoods had been reduced are shown in a poignant letter from Jane to Bradbury about this time: 'Will you do me the very great kindness to see Mr Dawe of Serjeants Inn Fleet Street and induce him not to proceed against Hood for another week – till we have turned us round a little – as Mr Flights not paying the £100 has distressed us extremely –Mr D – gave me at my entreaty till last Saturday and I am in great anxiety lest he should put an execution in – TODAY, which would disgrace us here so – I am sure I do not overvalue the kindness and friendship you have shown as well as Mr Evans in making this request – We are going today to put the affair of Mr Flight in Mr Hooks hands – My husband is not up and does not know I am writing as I thought of it in the night – He had your note yesterday and will be very glad to have a talk with you tomorrow – If you can spare time to set my mind at ease – the boy will wait as long as you like – to bring me word – You could assure Mr Dawe how we are situated which would have more effect than coming from me if I went –' MS *Punch* office. According to F.O. Ward, writing to Bulwer on 12 July, the £100 was due to Hood for editing and contributing to the first three numbers: MS Lady Cobbold.

4/Jane commented: 'there will be no difficulty in getting another partner,' *Memorials* II 195.

5/A reference to Hewlett's removal from Berkshire. His new address is given in letter to Renshaw, 8 February 1844.

6/Jane wrote on the same day: 'Hood dines to-day at Dr. Bowring's ... He knew him well years ago in the "London Magazine;" and he wrote ... to ask Hood to meet Bright and Cobden on business. *I* think to engage him to write songs for the League ... This comes of the "Song of the Shirt," of which we hear something continually,' *Memorials* II 195–6. Bowring himself wrote: 'The anti-Corn Law League was desirous of making him their poet-laureate ... but his death put an end to any such arrangement,' *Autobiographical Recollections* (1877) 63.

7/Hood commenced 'Our Family' in HM May. The Landseer may be Thomas, but I have not found the drawing.

TO
FREDERICK OLDFIELD WARD

PRIVATE

My dear Ward.

I have come to the conclusion that a number for 1 April cannot be brought out.[1] Sunday next being the 31st the last of the month or publication day would be *Saturday*. No printer could be got to undertake it, perhaps, if the whole matter were ready at this hour – which of course it is not. This materially alters the case. As there *must* be a break in the publication, – there *must* be a sort of new announcement for a fresh start, which might include a full explanation – showing that in spite of a new title – the spirit of the work would be kept up by the same Editor & contributors.

In fact it is my *Name* that sells the thing – not the word Magazine or Miscellany. And whatever I might produce, with my name, would induce the same Subscribers. Would *one* give up a Periodical on being informed it had lost Mr Flight the Publisher?

I am convinced his Copyright is not worth a dump – that he has none to transfer. That the mere identical name besides does not signify – he has no right to it by purchase or otherwise & if he had it would not be worth 5 per cent – to say nothing of the thing I regard with utter repulsion – paying a man for swindling. You will see that the impossibility of bringing out this month & avoiding a 'solution of continuity' – most materially lessens the importance of buying off any litigious opposition. There must be a new start – & a new announcement. Under this view a new title, but still Hood would not damage me – and I am convinced were I even to use the old one he could *not* get an injunction, he has by Letter given it up – but in point of fact never made good his right to it by fulfilling the bargain in the first instance.

Just ask if he has entered himself Proprietor at Stationer's Hall & on what grounds. And get a statement of what stock there is: – by which we shall get at the real sale. Under this view I am not disposed to give even 5 p Ct but let me know what you have done.

I take for granted that they are going to smash – but this must be done in one of three ways. By composition, which fails if one holds out & I think I know of more than one who will. By the Insolvent or Bankruptcy Court: in either of which I should most determinately oppose – & see how far the thing has been, or not, a swindle. And I owe it to my professional reputation to set the public right, as to my capabilities as Editor of a Periodical so impugned by Flights' falsehoods! I have been grossly involved in a speculation, to the risk of my own name, by a fellow who knew he was insolvent, & deliberately traded on the labour & means of others, to receive if he won but not to pay if he lost. Under these circumstances if they give up the stock to me in satisfaction of my claim well & good – otherwise I shall proceed – the transfer of their pretended copyright I do not consider worth a pin.

Yours very truly

Thos Hood

I *say* nothing about thanks – but feel a good deal.[2]

Devonshire Lodge / New Finchley Road / St John's Wood. / Sunday. [*24 March 1844*]

MS UCLA. The date is indicated at the beginning of the first paragraph.

1/Ward wrote to Bulwer on 12 July 1844: 'I have little experience & connection in the literary world, never having written in a magazine – much less edited one, till I began in March to help Mr Hood': MS Lady Cobbold.

2/Ward recalled in July that HM 'was on the point in March of being dropped when I succeeded, by the greatest good-fortune, in finding a wealthy capitalist – Mr Spottiswoode the Queens printer – to carry it on ... [Spottiswoode] gives Mr Hood 25 guineas a month for Editing it – & 20 guineas a sheet for what he writes in it – paying all the other expenses. Two-thirds are his property – the other third Mr Hood's – but it is not yet producing anything beyond the expenses – which indeed are very large – between £2000 & £3000 a year. Indeed, counting everything, the expenses still somewhat exceed the receipts. Mr. Spottiswoode consented to carry it on for 12 months on trial, reserving to himself the right of discontinuing it supposing at the end of that time it should not have reached a paying circulation': MS Lady Cobbold. Ward is referring to Andrew Spottiswoode (1787–1866), head of the house of Eyre and Spottiswoode, Queen's printers.

TO FREDERICK OLDFIELD WARD

Dear Ward.

I am quite inclined to avert any loss to Mr Spottiswoode that I can, & to meet his views: giving him credit for the liberality & gentlemanly feeling you attribute. But I must & ought to know more – for example the Copyright? – What does *that* include – my Novel?

I remember something of Mr Rowcroft[1] – he offered to controul me to Mr Flight. I cannot but think under all the circumstances, no time would be lost by your coming up to me for an hour, & talking it over – you have plenty of M.S. to go on with – & I could give you a quantity more back with you. *That* will be the way to convince me you are acting *kindly* & for the best. Yours ever

Thos Hood

[*St John's Wood, March 1844*]

MS Fitzwilliam Museum. After the proposed involvement of Spottiswoode as business supporter of HM

1/Possibly Charles Rowcroft (d 1856), author

TO

CHARLES DICKENS

My dear Dickens.

I cannot say how delighted I was to learn from my friend Ward that you had promised me a little 'bit o' writin' to help me to launch afloat again. It has been a cruel business & I really wanted help in it: or I should not have announced it – knowing how much you have to do. I am certainly a lucky man & an unlucky one too – for Spottiswoode is far better than the first promise of Flight. By the bye I have heard one or two persons doubt the reality of a Pecksniff – or the possibility – but I have lately met two samples of the breed. Flight is most decidedly Pecksniffian[1] – as Ward says he is so confoundedly *virtuous*. After telling two parties he was going to fail his brother who is a partner corroborating – after excusing himself from giving me up the stock for his debt to me, as he had promised because it would be preferring one creditor he turned round & said he was not only not going to fail but had never said so! On the back of this he now says if all will not take a composition there will be a friendly fiat. He *cried* to Ward, & begged him to get him a situation of only a guinea a week as he was a ruined man – & then served *a writ* – not a summons – on Ward for 18 Copies we had had of the back stock! – less than £2. And then when Ward went to settle this, Flight said Pecksniffishly – Now Mr. Ward, let me ask in the whole of our intercourse on this business have I behaved in any way inconsistent with what you think is right & proper. Why said Ward I really cannot think how you could reconcile to your conscience to say & do – so & so.

Conscience – said Flight – Sir, I have lived too long in the world to be *a slave to my conscience*! Was not this capital?

Just let me know by a single line per Bearer how much space I shall leave for you, – as I will leave the first sheet open – not to hurry you.
I hear that you are going to learn on the spot to eat Italian macaroni.[2] For God's sake take care of the Malaria – I am suffering still from a touch of the Dutch pest, 10 years ago. Last week I dined at Tom Landseer's & was taken so ill on the road home, walking, I was obliged to get a policeman to assist me – & after all I suspect he thought it a strange case of drunkenness – the Gent. having all the use of his faculties – but unable to walk without support.
Mrs. Hood unites in kind regards to yourself & Mrs. Dickens. Our new house is in a road that is a nice drive when you take an airing. verb. sap.

Yours ever truly

Thos Hood

How is Forster? I heard lately that he was ill again.

C. Dickens Esqre

Devonshire Lodge / New Finchley Road / St John's Wood/ Monday. [*1 April 1844*]

MS Huntington. Published by Whitley HLQ 410–12. On 26 March 1844 Dickens wrote circumspectly to Ward that he would contribute to the next number of HM 'if it should be in the hands of Mr. Spottiswoode,' *Letters* (ed. Dexter) I 587. This promise was advertised in the April number, and in May there appeared Dickens's 'Threatening Letter'.

1/Referring to the character in *Martin Chuzzlewit,* appearing in serial form at the time of Hood's letter. The only example of this adjective given in NED is dated 1874.

2/Dickens left for Italy on 2 July.

TO

FREDERICK OLDFIELD WARD

Dear Ward
Enclosed is the paragraph of your note.
I am writing, with a hard pen – as hard as I can. Prose & Poetry. One paper from a Contributor has come in. I have all but done a poem on 'the Bridge of Sighs' – ie Waterloo, and its Suicides.[1]

Yours ever truly

Thos Hood

F.O. Ward Esqre

Devonshire Lodge. / New Finchley Road [*St John's Wood*] */ Wednesday* [*10 April 1844*]

MS Rylands. Hood's 'The Bridge of Sighs,' to which he refers in the letter, was published in HM May 1844.

1/Waterloo Bridge was particularly attractive to suicides (see 592).

TO
J.T.J. HEWLETT

Dear P.P.

The way we came out last month was this. A very active friend of mine Mr Ward entered into a treaty for me with a really wealthy party, who undertook to go on with me for two months at any rate: So Ward & I set to work, & I being really helped instead of hindered – as by that old humbug in the Adelphi,[1] got out the thing in time. As every body who knows any thing of periodicals says it has done wonders, I have no doubt the Capitalist will go on, & take to it. Blackwood says we sold more than any Mag ever did at starting.[2] I have some capital things in prospect.

As to Flight, he is the greatest shuffle & humbug & ass I have ever met with; & the greatest liar. He told *two* parties he was going to fail & his brother confirmed it. He *cried* to Ward, who was to try & get him something of a situation if only 'a guinea a week'. Was to give up the stock to me for my claim – then said he could not do that, as it would be preferring one creditor – now turns round & says he never said he was going to fail, in short says & unsays every thing. Came & wanted to sell the back stock, & now out of spite apparently, is selling it in the neighbourhood at low prices – In fact the most contemptible animal I was ever introduced to. He threatens me with a cross action, – for I have had a writ served & mean to proceed – & talks of an action for libel! If he behaves like a rogue I will say so & if he tells lies I will contradict them. He has not even paid most of the contributors for the first number even – one a poor blind girl in Ireland.[3] But I'll make him. He dare not show his face in court in a case so like a swindle.

You are all right therefore as to the two months & I will let you know then, how it is to go on. I should say for the present N° therefore you had better send an Old Tom paper; I will send your N° p post – but in the hurry I have not got one *here* to forward. You will see a good lot of ad*vts* in it.

I expected to have seen you in your passings thro London to & fro – especially as I heard of your dining at Mr Wainewrights.[4] When are you to be in town?

Yours very truly

T.H.

Revd J. Hewlett.

Devonshire Lodge / New Finchley Road [St John's Wood] / Thursday. [11 April 1844]

MS Texas. After the publication of HM April 1844.

1/The wealthy party is Spottiswoode, the humbug, Flight.

2/The sale was of 1500 copies, a modest number. The Blackwood was probably John (1818–79), see 596.

3/Frances Brown (1816–79), poet of Donegal

4/Unidentified

TO

C.E. RAWLINS

Sir.

Pray convey my best thanks to the gentlemen of the Council of the Anti-Monopoly Association of Liverpool for the honour they have done me by an Invitation to the Banquet on the 12th with my regret that my literary engagements will not allow of my absence from London.

I have at the same time to acknowledge a very handsome compliment to my small efforts in a great cause.

I have the honour to be
Sir Your very obedient Servt.

Thos. Hood

C.E. Rawlins Esqre.

Devonshire Lodge [St John's Wood] / 11 April 1844

Transcript Mr J.M. Cohen. Rawlins was secretary of the Liverpool Anti-Monopoly Association (1842–7).

TO
J.T.J. HEWLETT

Dear P.P.
I shall know definitively about the Mag. tomorrow when I am to meet the party. I must not name him yet – but he is of undoubted wealth & respectability –. If he takes to it the thing is certain. As to Flight he & his brother, in the Law List, are *partners*.[1] The brother as great a shuffle as the other. How could the Mag. ruin them when they have comparatively paid nothing. He gave Hardman a bill which of course will end like yours. And he has paid about 3 guineas to Mackay. Nobody else. Not paid Printer for 1st No, – only a part – & I believe not the stationer. On the other hand by his stock on hand, stated by Renshaw at 2600, – he must have sold say 3 or 4000, at 2/– & received some £350, as much as he has paid, I should think in cash. Now he & his brother distinctly proposed to give up the back stock to me in lieu of my claim: and as certainly afterwards receded on the plea they were going to fail & must not prefer any one. When I mentioned this to Mr Phillips (Caleb Stukely of Blackwood)[2] he said how did you know that? The Flights told me they were going to fail, *in confidence*. But I suspect they hoped he would tell me, – & my notion is it was merely a dodge to deter me from proceeding, so I have told my lawyer to go on. Flight now declares he never said he was going to fail! I have heard a rumour of his being a money-lender – & my nephew[3] who helped in the office at first says the great part of Flights business seemed with bills.[4]
As to his being victimized & people sympathizing with the literary man, they do, with the literary men & women, upon whose brains and names a couple of adventurers have speculated, to receive if they won, & not to pay if they lost. If Flight is insolvent now, he must have been so when he began the things. – On what ground was he to be the proprietor, but as Capitalist paying all? We among ourselves could have speculated with our writings & popularity & kept the property, with the chance of dividing, besides the pay, some 1000 or 1200 a year. But to show what he is more plainly we had 18 copies of his back stock – & sent daily to Ward for the amount. I said 'set it off agt my account'. Well, he has actually not *summoned* Ward but issued a *writ* against him for the amount, some 40 shillings.[5] This is sheer blackguardism.
The fact is he came to Ward, after he had said he was going to fail & offered to sell the stock to us. Ward asked, if we buy it, do you intend to pay the Contributors with the money. Whereupon F very grandly took out his watch & said if I offer

this watch for sale to you have you any concern to know how I came by it. Why under the circumstances said Ward, since you ask me I should like to know whether I was not purchasing stolen goods. So you see the impression he makes on those who have to do with him. My own notion is that he has means, but will shuffle & sham poverty, ruin etc, any thing to sneak out of paying – & I am *acting* on this belief. There are the House & the pictures up stairs at any rate. As to failing he could not pass Bankruptcy or Insolvent Court with such an opposition as I could set up. His last printer is very indignant, for Flight let him actually buy new type for the Mag. when he knew he could not pay him.
I ordered your Mag: to be sent *by post*, & hope you will have had it by this. You had better do a Chapter of Old Tom, that in case of the Mag going on you may continue the thread – or rather bell-rope.[6]
Your daughters were here yesterday but I was in bed, getting rid of the Influenza & did not see them. When you can come, we can have the whole story about Flight – the details are too long to write.

I am Dear P.P
Yours very truly

Thos Hood

I have done a Poem for the Mag some say beats the 'Shirt,'[7] but I don't think it. If the moneyd man, does take to it – we will have a capital campaign.

[*St John's Wood*] *Monday.* [*15 April 1844*]

MS Texas

1/*The Law List* 1844 names among London attornies Edward Gill Flight, 1 Adam Street, Adelphi, and among country attornies, Edward Gill Flight and Thomas Flight, Bridport, Dorset.
2/*Caleb Stukely* appeared in *Blackwood's*, February 1842–May 1843.
3/W.A. Longmore, referred to by Jerrold as in touch with Hood before this time
4/The Flights carried on business at Bridport as money scriveners, that is, lenders.
5/In law, a summons apprises a defendant that an action has been begun against him and cites him to appear to the action, whereas a writ is a formal court order, directing a person to act in a certain way.
6/HM May 1844, contained Hewlett's 'The Election.' Old Tom is the bell at Christ Church, Oxford.
7/'The Bridge of Sighs'

TO
J.T.J. HEWLETT

Dear P.P.
Thanks for the letter.[1] I will just show it to Ward & then return it to you. What a regular hypocritical old Scoundrel! He never coveted the company of literary men! – no, nor talked of *a cold game supper*, with Bulwer etc at which he was hardly worthy to sit etc etc etc. I think you heard something of that. As to what he says of me, it will deserve answering when he can show if I had never brought out N° 3 at all, how that would justify his 'duplicity & defalcations' as to N° 1. However he must explain in some Court or other, for I am proceeding, & others will, Hardman for one. I shall begin in the Court of Requests on behalf of poor Miss Browne the blind Irish Girl, & have it *reported*.[2]
In the meantime the Mag is all right, as you will know when I tell you the party I saw yesterday & my future Co-partner is Mr Spottiswoode the Queen's Printer, – a man of undoubted respectability & *large* wealth. He lives in Carlton Terrace. He undertakes to pay all, – which is enough. And we shall have the trade with us thro his relationship to the Longmans. So write away & send me a crack article Old Tom for this No as soon as you can – & the thing is sure, if we all do our best. Mind & *come* as soon as you can – as there is much to talk over.
I am writing in great haste for I have a great deal to do for this No including the first Chapter of my novel[3] – & have had to run about – besides running with the Influenza.

I am Dear P.P.
Yours very truly

T.H.

I will enquire into your Mag not being sent – but we have been dismally hurried & there have been necessarily some sins of omission.
Flight has done all he could to spite & injure. I met two subscribers, neither of whom had recd their N° *3*. That was *his* fault. But he knew he must give up & did not care.

Revd J. Hewlett.

[*St John's Wood*] *Wednesday.* [*17 April 1844*]

MS Texas. Two days after the preceding letter.

1/Perhaps a letter from Flight to Hewlett

2/There is no evidence of Hood proceeding against Flight in this way.

3/The first chapter of 'Our Family' appeared in HM May.

TO
FREDERICK OLDFIELD WARD

Dear Ward.
Here is Tennyson's address. Alfred Tennyson Esqre 6 Belle Vue Place – London Road – Cheltenham.[1]
I meant to tell you last night that on Tuesday Smith Junr.,[2] of Smith & Elder the Booksellers, came up here with an application to publish the Mag. if I was not engaged. This looks well. He said Fraser is going down & Bentley ditto but very fast. So I shall hope we are to catch what they lose.

I am Dear Ward Yours very truly

Thos Hood

Devonshire Lodge [St John's Wood, April 1844]

MS UCLA

1/Alfred Tennyson (1809–92), first Baron Tennyson, poet, did not contribute to HM.
2/George Smith (1824–1901) late in 1843 assumed temporary control of the publishing department of his father's firm. He published R.H. Horne's *New Spirit of the Age* (February 1844) and Mrs Baron Wilson's *Our Actresses* (June). Hood refers to both of these works. Smith's offer concerning HM came to nothing.

TO
H. RENSHAW?

You cannot have a better advt for the Athenaeum than the one in the papers, with the threatening letter and the Novel. I think it would be well to push it also in Punch ...

[St John's Wood, April 1844]

From Maggs Bros. *Autograph Letters* no. 370 (Autumn 1918) 78. The *Athenaeum* advertisement of HM appeared there on 4 May 1844, 395: the magazine will contain 'C. Dickens's Threatening Letter to Thomas Hood' and 'The Commencement of "Our Family," by the Editor.'

TO
J.T.J. HEWLETT

Dear P.P.
I write in haste to say don't take the 2/3. He paid Bradbury's – or they agreed to take 10s/– in the pound. And he told Ward lately there would be an offer of 10s/– in the pound & if not accepted there would be a friendly fiat. I believe it to be a dodge to pay as little as possible. As to the fiat he couldn't pass for if he owed £2000 the mag. affair was a swindle – as he must have been insolvent at the time. But they are full of tricks – my lawyer tells me T. & G. Flight have just dissolved partnership, into which they only entered about Xmas I believe. Now this appears very like a shuffle – Is it not likely that G. will take the debts & make over the property to T. In the meantime he has withdrawn his action against me – which of course he only brought to bully me & my action agt him would have come to issue by this – but he got it put off till June or July by taking a Special Jury – which I am told would cost him about 10 guineas expences. He can't face these things in a Court Insolvent or Bankrupt. I don't believe in his inability & mean to stick to him.
Your paper did not appear in a short hasty advt – chiefly of the new things – but it did in the others. I do not think it is quite so brisk as some of your others but of course you have been very unsettled.
I cannot make out about the Magazines for I gave the address to Renshaw & told him to *post* them. I will remind him. We have a capital No this time & I think shall now be all right: but Flight is doing the spiteful as far as he can by keeping back the list of subscribers.
I have had the Influenza very heavily & the cough has shaken me terribly.
When are you likely to be up? Yours very truly

T.H.

Take care of that letter of Davies's.[1] I have proceeded agt him for Miss Browne by writ.

Revd J. Hewlett.

Devonshire Lodge / New Finchley Road [*St John's Wood*] / *Saturday* [*11 May 1844*]

MS Texas. Hood is discussing Flight's bankruptcy. The dissolution of the partnership between the brothers took place, 25 April 1844.

1/Unidentified

TO
W. POTTER

Sir.

I should have replied sooner to your request, for my autographs, but for the prolonged indisposition of my usual Amanuensis, who writes a much better hand. In his absence you will perhaps make shift with this specimen of my own performance.

I am Sir

Yours most obedtly

Thos Hood

Epigram.
When would-be Suicides in purpose fail –
Who could not find a morsel though they needed –
If Peter sends them for attempts to jail,
What would he do to them if they succeeded?

T.H.

Devonshire Lodge / New Finchley Road / 12th *May 1844.*

MS University of Liverpool Library. Address: 'W. Potter Esqre/ Nunnery Cottage/ Wellington Road/ Foxheth Park/ Liverpool.' The epigraph appended to this letter was published in HM November 1844. It refers to Mr Justice Maule's condemnation of Mary Fowley (16 April) for the murder of her child. She had attempted to kill herself at the same time. The sentence was later commuted.

TO
FREDERICK OLDFIELD WARD

private

My dear Ward.

Phillips is out of town beyond reach, in point of time – I promised in that case to read the Proof for him carefully & having read the M.S. already will do so, knowing the thing: You shall have it first thing tomorrow morning with the reserve articles & whatever you want. I am writing, but not in good cue, for my mind is sadly distressed by causes hinted to you. My wife was out all day yesterday, & encouraged I suspect by some of her family has taken up a position of defiance that must lead to our severance – Nothing less than that she will not account for what she has received, nor come to me for Cash in future. I cannot even learn what she took up from Renshaw – nor any thing what became of it. Of course such a position, for my own sake & my Childrens I must not suffer – & unless she gives way my mind is made up. But it is very fatal to me in working as you may suppose. This for your own bosom. Of course she must have no money without my order.

Yours affectionately

Thos Hood

I almost give up hopes of recovery with such trouble before me. My shortness of breath seems coming on again. I have been on the eve of writing to Dr Elliot to say his care of me is in vain.

[*St John's Wood, May 1844*]

MS University of Illinois. Hood's wild comments here are no doubt a product of his sickness.

TO
WILLIAM ELLIOT

My dear Doctor.
A sudden & strange change has occurred which my own feeling tells me was critical –
After you left I had taken only a cup of tea & my naptha,[1] & was quietly reading in bed, at about 8 o'clock when suddenly I felt an internal jerk or crack, I cannot tell where, it took me so by surprize – not stronger than the snapping of a thread – & without pain. But immediately afterwards I felt my water coming spontaneously from me but gently – accompanied by a sort of general bodily perturbation. It was less marked by the palpitation of the heart than by a sudden rushing & ringing – but with a very fast *beat* to the middle – in my head: – which before in the spasms had been quiet. At the same time I struck out in a violent perspiration: – there was evidently some great momentary struggle going on, with all the rush of renewed action. I cannot describe it better than as general physical perturbation – so great I could not think what was going to happen – then came various active feelings in parts that had been torpid – & then a large quantity of wind escaped, each way – & I afterwards had a motion.
But there was a sensible relief to the whole system – & I have since had rumblings,

grumblings, & symptoms of wind & fluid stirring – even in the chest – which before had seemed inactive & solid. I can now draw a long breath much more freely – & the stomach rises & falls with a more natural action. At supper I had some crab & have suffered no inconvenience – I found myself looking at the crab while being dressed with something like greediness: I ate for the first time with appetite. But what is curious at the same time I became thirsty, as suddenly – which I have not been before, but on the contrary have taken only one instead of my usual cups of tea. It was quite a longing for a draught – which a tumbler of cold water with a little sherry in it scarcely satisfied. I have since felt altogether easier & lighter – & can draw a long delicious sigh. My pulse is stronger – but not fast – & the whizzing in my head continues but less loud, with a billing sound that beats the time. The other noise is continuous. My heart quieter. There has been something very noxious in the weather – a dairyman here has lost about 14 cows – he describes the disorders to have been in their lights.[2]

By the bye Jane meant to ask you but forgot – if my lights began to burn with so much naptha how they were to be put out? I comforted her by telling her that as she might know by the name *nap*tha was only a soporific –

I am writing this at 12 in bed – so that if no more be added you will conclude that I have gone on well thro the night – as this must be posted before 8 & I shall I hope be asleep. The relief is very marked. I do not pretend to explain – but is it not possible there might be some obstruction or adhesion, released partly by your all sounding at me – a sort of shampooing?[3]

But there might be some cause still more occult – I heard of a man who died from an orange pip getting into his vermiform process.[4] I have hopes now of Hoods Magazine No 6.

I have given the best account I could & exaggerated nothing. I was particularly struck by the sudden recovery of my thirst as if I had picked it up from the floor. I am glad to say I am gaping & feel sleepy, – so Good night & all good days follow it: God bless you – I know my comfort will be a comfort to you both. I have suffered this time severely – but enjoyed my bad health too – for the mere sight of you does me good – Love to all I am Dear Doctor Yours ever very truly

Thos Hood

[*St John's Wood*] *Tuesday Night* [*14 May 1844*]

MS UCLA. The letter is dated in another hand 15 May 1844; the 15th was a Wednesday.

1/Used as an external application for removing pain

2/Lungs

3/Hood was examined by three doctors, the Elliots and Archibald Billing (1791–1881). The last is included in DNB as a distinguished physician 'of high general culture.'
4/Worm-like process extending from the first part of the large intestine

TO
MARK LEMON

Dear Lemon
I am much better tho not allowed yet or indeed able to leave my bed. About five weeks ago I was struck by a very cold wind in walking home from T Landseer's near here, where I dined. It proved to be inveterate influenza, – complicated by my heart being faulty, & an old marsh complaint, that made a periodical of it, with spasms. I lost my breath so once or twice I felt & looked I am told very like death. One comfort is my three doctors between them could not discover any really unsound place in my lungs. My breath is now lengthening, my cough all but gone – & my chief complaint is weakness – but that is gigantic. But I am notorious for rallying at the worst – so I hope in a day or two to be on my legs.
Last Punch's cuts very good. Chuny capital – & Brummel ditto. When you think of a subject likely to suit *me* let me know.
I understand entre nous that the Puck[1] people applied to Thackry – but he said he was too well used in Punch to join them. The proprs are safe in that feeling which is general.
Give my kind regards to B & E.[2] I hope to see them soon. The Mag. is going on very well – rose 90 last No & a good many advts come in.

I am
Dear Lemon
Yours very truly

Thos Hood

There was a consultation of three Doctors on Tuesday so for once I suppose I have been *serious*.

[*St John's Wood, 20 May 1844*]

MS Harvard. Published by Lane KSJ 52. Written after the issue of *Punch* referred to in the second paragraph, 18 May 1844, 213, 218.

1/This comic periodical flourished 6 May–15 June 1844. Thackeray was a regular contributor to *Punch* at this time.
2/Bradbury and Evans, publishers of *Punch*

TO
ROBERT ELLIOT

Dear Doctor,
Put on six leeches yesterday, on the pit of the stomach (my stomach ought to be all *pit* by this time): the bites bled a good deal. I slept at night but was very exhausted.
Great noises in the chest when I swallow, as of renewed action. Heart quiet, and pulse stronger; beat equal and not too fast. I think it is a turn for the better; but I am dreadfully reduced. I find brown bread and honey a good diet.

Yours ever affectionately

T. Hood.

P.T.O. A pleasant party to you. To-day is my birthday – forty-five – but I can't tell tell you how old I *feel*; enough to be your grandfather at least, and give *you* advice! viz. don't over-polka[1] yourself.

Epigram on Dr. Robert Elliot, of Camberwell.
Whatever Doctor Robert's skill be worth,
One hope within me still is stout and hearty,
He would not *kill* me till the 24th,
For fear of my *appearing* at his party!

[*St John's Wood*] *May 23rd, 1844.*

From *Memorials* II 200–1. Written on Hood's birthday.
1/The polka was introduced to London in 1842. The first use of the verb 'to polka' given in NED is dated 1859.

TO
FREDERICK OLDFIELD WARD

My dear Ward,
Thursday night was a dreadful one – & prostrated me completely – with suffering added to which *deep vexation.* My nerves gave way at last.
To counteract this, & on a calculation of my own I took last night instead of morphine, a good dose of mulled port wine – my plan has so far succeeded I got some hours sleep – & feel a little stronger & my nerves more composed. But I want

to see you as soon as you can & also the Doctor – perhaps you will drop him a line & post it to say so.

Yours affectily

Thos Hood

[*St John's Wood, 25 May 1844*]

MS Columbia. 'The Echo' in HM June 1844, 615, reported that Hood struggled through sickness until Thursday, 23 May, when the effort to 'sketch a few comic designs ... was followed by a wandering delirium of utter exhaustion.'

TO
FREDERICK OLDFIELD WARD

Dear Ward
I am much the same, a middling night: – no spasm: but restless. I am so glad you did not come last night – I was selfish enough to forget the distance – but your presence has been a comfort to

Yours affectionately

T:H:

[*St John's Wood, 26 May 1844*]

MS Columbia. Probably written after the last. Hood was so ill that Ward largely managed HM, June–September 1844.

TO
CHARLES DICKENS

My dear Dickens/
I must write at last, in lieu of coming as I have hoped, leaning on a *hanker*, for day after day – but a severe course of influenza, with a strong cough, has so shaken the little physical power I possessed, that I can hardly stand, & certainly cannot go, without a go-cart. I have indeed had a foretaste of dying, in a terrible shortness of breath at night. I never felt touched in the wind before, but know now that I have lungs. What a comfort! À propos to which let me again cry to you to beware of the

Italian malaria. My ten year old marsh malady has throughout aggravated the other by aguish chills & fitful fever.[1] And what's worse it isn't catching, so that you can't give it to any one you don't like.

But for this Influenza I should certainly long ere this have had an outfluenza to grasp your hand & thank you for your great kindness, which I feel the more from knowing by experience how many obstacles there must have been in the way of it. Thanks to that & similar backing I shall now, I think turn the corner, – and in the meantime the pinch has not only shown me, in a very gratifying way, the sincerity of some younger friends, but has procured me an accession of new ones, quite enough to console & compensate for the defection of certain old Pecksniffian ones. For example Ward who has slaved for the Magazine like an enthusiastic sub-Editor.

Your paper is capital – I had been revolted myself by the royal running after the american mite, & the small-mindedness of being so fond of an unmagnified man, or child. I cannot understand the wish to see a dwarf *twice*.[2]

At Coblenz I saw two – natural Curiosities for they were Brothers, – one about 40 years old – not at all deformed except that his face was a little large in proportion – he was a clerk in the war office, & frequented an ordinary at the Hotel near me – where he had a miniature set of plates knife & fork &c. His brother was a flower & miniature painter at Dusseldorf, & looked like a child, for he wore a straw hat, little frock coat, & his hair in long curls down his back. But he was manly enough to be found locked in a room, with some one, to fight a duel about a lady! I think neither of them was taller than my Tom, then three years old.

The two Queens henceforward ought always to look thro the wrong ends of their telescopes & opera glasses.

I have arranged matters with Spottiswood & hear a very good account of him. A very bad one of Flight. He has withdrawn a cross action agt. me: but I have to sue for my money – no mite to me – nearly £100. He offers 2s/3d in the pound – & if all be true was insolvent when he undertook the Magazine.[3] Once more, accept my thanks, & believe that I am deeply sensible of your kindness, and as largely obliged as helped by it. I long to see you & have a gossip on things in general: but cannot say when I shall get abroad. Give our kind regards to Mrs. Dickens – is she to go Romeing with you – & have a row (pronounce it roe) with you in a Gondola? – I am

My dear Dickens
Yours ever very truly,

Thos Hood

By the bye, – as Chuzzlewit approaches its end[4] did you ever say any thing to P. Napier about the Edin. Review?[5] It was unlucky I did not see him, or I could have spoken myself. My reason for reminding you of this is that *the Athenaeum is closed against me* – whereof when I see you.[6]
I have lately made the acquaintance of a Doctor Alex. Blair, a great friend of Professor Wilson's – do you know him?[7]

Devonshire Lodge / New Finchley Road [St John's Wood] / Tuesday. [May 1844]

MS Huntington. Published by Whitley HLQ 412–3. Thanking Dickens for contributing to HM May 1844, 'Threatening Letter to Thomas Hood, from an Ancient Gentleman.' Dickens' letter is dated 23 April.

1/Ominous allusion to *Macbeth* 3 ii 23
2/Dickens ridiculed the attention paid by Queen Victoria to 'Tom Thumb,' Charles Sherwood Stratton (1838–83). He was brought over to England by P.T. Barnum in January 1844 and was a great success, receiving invitations to Buckingham Palace. There he enchanted both the Queen of England and the Queen of the Belgians.
3/Flight's fiat in bankruptcy was dated 20 May.
4/The publication in parts of *Martin Chuzzlewit* came to an end in July 1844.
5/Hood hoped to contribute to the *Edinburgh Review*, but nothing came of this ambition.
6/I do not know the cause of the disagreement between Hood and Dilke which must have led to the closure of the *Athenaeum* against him. The following letter to Dilke is friendly.
7/Blair looms large in the biography of Wilson.

TO
CHARLES WENTWORTH DILKE

I burn without getting warm. I wish I were the ham between two buttered slices of bread, well mustarded – that seems like warmth. But this wind is keen enough to *cut* sandwiches. I could cry with cold, only I'm afraid of the icicles. I wish that in settling other *Eastern* questions, they had deposed this wind. I confess, for two nights past I have wished for a little 'warm-with,'[1] but the only bottle I am allowed is at my feet, and even then, only warm water – without. I almost fancy myself a gander sometimes, and web-footed. My stomach is like a house where the washing is done at home – all slop, hot-water, and tea. So I stop. I'm so cold and washy, I'm only fit to correspond with a frog. Give my love to all, but you had better *mull* it.

[St John's Wood, June 1844]

From Dilke I 57. The Eastern question, to which Hood refers, concerned eastern Europe. It was discussed during the visit to London of the Emperor of Russia, Nicolas I, 1–9 June 1844.

1/Order for spirits and water, 'the "with" refers to sugar,' J. Redding Ware *Passing English of the Victorian Era* (n.d.).

TO

SAMUEL PHILLIPS

My dear Phillips

I have had Dr. Elliot with me since dinner which has occupied me. He thinks I am better, but forbids me to leave bed – my best place in this weather.

When I see you we will talk over the project.[1] One point has occurred to me. There was a great stress laid on the Athenaeums independence of booksellers – none being in the proprietary – but the influence of publisher's *advertts* is very evident. And in disclaiming *influences* take care to repudiate those of friendship & the reciprocity system – that a work will be tested by its intrinsic merits, not on party principles – or with reference to the dogmatic opinions of an Editor or the tenets of a *clique*.

My cough has been quicker, and I am rallying – the very sight of my dear good Doctor does me good – better than mesmerism.[2]

The Reviews have all spoken well of the Ghost Seer.[3]

I have done 10 drawings for next number – so I am not quite idle.

Yours ever truly

Thos Hood

[*St John's Wood, June 1844*]

MS Massachusetts Historical Society.

1/Seems to be connected with HM. The drawings to which Hood refers at the end of his letter were included as cuts in HM July.

2/Mesmerism, from Anton Mesmer (1733–1815), was a topic of general public interest about this time.

3/Unidentified

TO
FREDERICK OLDFIELD WARD

My dear Ward
I continue better – & the wind has changed & I have had my window open – The sycamore is no longer emetical[1] – What a day for Ascot !– without any Running Rain![2]
You haven't sent the Frazer?[3] I will look over Wolesby's[4] list more carefully by the morning. Most of them, it appears, are very stale – e.g. Life of Louis Phillippe – a poor book, I have had it these 9 months[5] – Slick the Attaché is old too.[6] Howitts *German* book I should like to do myself.[7] Twiss Life of Eldon ought to be good book, but it is not ready I suspect.[8] I hope Wolesby is not strong Tory. Our actresses I dare say will be sent by Smith & Elder when ready.[9]
I have done three cuts on the wood today and shall send them per boy tomorrow to the wood cutter. Perhaps with some more.
It is funny Wolesby talking of 'novelties' with such a list of stale books. Please not to write to Broderip – pro tem.
If Cooper's Ashore and Afloat is new it might do.[10] But I do not see why we should turn Retrospective Reviewers and go back to old wares. My notion is reviews of novelties, with good extracts – for our readers before they can generally get the books thro circulating libraries. I will send George tomorrow for the Fraser.
Dr. Toulmin's[11] verses are weak & come to 'a bad end.' They certainly will not do. The Mag. has a poetical reputation we must not undermine. A little and good. I am certain that readers are more disgusted by indifferent poetry than by bad prose. Yours affectionately,

F.O. Ward Esq. T. Hood

[*St John's Wood, June 1844*]

From Adrian H. Joline *Rambles in Autograph Land* (New York 1913) 146. The first part of the letter appears in facsimile after p. 144. The letter coincides with the Ascot race meeting, 4–7 June 1844, to which Hood refers in his first paragraph.

1/As it was held to be

2/The horse referred to is 'Running Rein' which won the Epsom Derby on 22 May but was subsequently disqualified.

3/*Fraser's Magazine*

4/The second letter of the name looks like 'a' in the facsimile, but Joline transcribes it 'o.' The name may be that of Francis Pearson Walesby.

5/G.N. Wright's *Life and Times of Louis Philippe* was noticed in the *Literary Gazette* 6 August 1842.

6/Haliburton's *The Attaché; or Sam Slick in England* was advertised in *The Athenaeum* 8 July 1843, 640.

7/William Howitt's *German Experiences* was published 25 May 1844.
8/Published 4 July
9/Mrs C. Baron Wilson's *Our Actresses* was published 10 June.
10/Cooper's *Ashore and Afloat* was advertised in *The Spectator* 15 June, 574, as just published.
11/If 'Dr.' is in error, then the name may be that of Camilla Dufour Toulmin (1812–95), later Mrs Crosland, miscellaneous writer.

TO
FREDERICK OLDFIELD WARD

George[1] waits.

Dear Ward
I am better – have dressed today for the first time I hope tomorrow to get down the stairs. But I am so feeble – I think I must go to the Zoological to value it. Till I see the elephants & rhinoceros, I can hardly estimate my weakness. But I have continued to make 6 or 7 tailpieces, etc. on the wood. I have not sent them to Linton[2] that you may see them before they go. The nerve of my hand is still good – it always was – & I draw steadily. I have an idea for an article on Joinville so send the book. I have made a cut for it.[3]

All other matters I defer to oral comm[n] – with
Yours affectionately

T:H:

[*St John's Wood, June 1844*]

MS Columbia. The convalescence indicated in the previous letter is advancing.
1/Presumably a servant-boy
2/William James Linton (1812–98), engraver
3/The Prince de Joinville's *Note on the State of the French Navy* was published 15 May 1844. He was attacked by Thackeray in *Punch*, 1 and 15 June, 234, 252.

TO
H. RENSHAW?

Dear Sir.
I continue mending. I have just sent off two more designs for the woodcutter.
Please to apply for the following for review in the Magazine.
Howitts German Experiences (Longman)

Farming for Ladies (Murray)[1]
I have been down stairs & in the garden – so am no longer an *in-keeper*.

Yours very truly

Thos Hood

Devonshire Lodge [St John's Wood]. Friday [June 1844]

MS Yale. Hood's improvement in health continues.
1/Advertised in *The Athenaeum* 6 July 1844, 611

TO
J. T. J. HEWLETT

Dear P.P.
Do not be later than you can help with your M.S. as it is a short month. I am sorry to hear of your loss by the Romford Bank: – authors *are* to be victims ever. As to Flight the docket I hear was struck by a builder for £600 a debt of course as old as the occupation at the Adelphi.[1] Hook told me also that he owes Swynfer Jervis[2] £1000 – & after that has the impudence to have said he was ruined by the mag. I expect there will be some queer disclosures I mean to attend & prove & if possible examine him, & the attorneys for the fiat are said to be very shrewd sharp fellows & have traced assignments etc etc. Of course J. Flight is to walk off with the assets & E. G. is to take the debts. But I hardly think the Creditors will stand a dissolution of partnership just before the break, & *after* they had told Ward they should fail. I can swear that E. G. told me he & his brother had but one purse between them.[3]
I have got down stairs & into the garden – very weak still for I am not allowed to mend too fast for fear of a relapse. I have had a very narrow escape indeed – & can hardly believe that I am alive –
Many thanks for the poultry – but do not think of it – we can get every thing of the sort here – & half my diet is fish.

Yours very truly

Thos Hood

What a mess the £500 Prize Comedy being damnd! What a ridiculous false position for all parties Webster – Judges – & Mrs Gore.[4]

Devonshire Lodge [St John's Wood, June 1844]

MS Texas. Written after the failure of the Romford Bank, 6 June 1844, to which Hood refers in his first paragraph.

1/The creditor petitioning against Flight was Johnson Hanke, builder.
2/Unidentified
3/Flight had been declared bankrupt. In the letter Hood writes 'J.' for 'T.' Flight.
4/The competition for the prize comedy was won by Mrs Gore with her *Quid Pro Quo*. The play failed in performance on 18 June.

TO
THOMAS RESEIGH

Dear Reseigh,

Nothing is nearer to my will or farther from my power than getting, & dining, out. I have got no farther yet in either than the garden & a fowl's merrythought.

It would give me great pleasure to accept Mr Rolts kind invitation & still more to hear Mr Bacon's masterly reading of the Song of the Shirt[1] – But I have been too near singing the Song of the Swan, & too recently, to admit of such delights. In truth I hardly feel quite yet out of the Valley of the Shadow – or much more than a shadow myself. Pray say this to our friend & explain how slowly I am compelled to mend – so slowly that I'm *darn'd* if I know when I shall be *mended.*

I am wondering nevertheless with pen & pencil, in spite of the MD's who ordered me to do nothing, but I found it so hard to do, I preferred writing & drawing. Besides which for all my ill-looking-ness there is one man coming to draw me[2] – and another to model me – as if I were fat enough to *bust.*[3] Luckily I am capital at sitting just now, & not bad at lying, as to walking or standing, I am as feeble almost as a baby on my pins, which by the way have dwindled into needles.

I am
Dear Reseigh
Yours very truly

Thos Hood

Devonshire Lodge / New Finchley Road / Tuesday Night [*June 1844*]

MS UCLA. Written during Hood's illness, though he was still capable of 'writing and drawing' for HM. According to Jerrold, 396–7, Thomas Reseigh was 'one of his later friends, confidential clerk to a city firm of solicitors,' and largely responsible for the Memorial Fund collected after the poet's death.

1/If Rolt is John Rolt (1804–71), knighted in 1866 and appointed lord justice of appeal the next year, then Bacon might be James Bacon (1798–1895), appointed judge 1869 and knighted 1871.
2/Perhaps Maclise
3/The bust by E. Davis was exhibited at the Royal Academy in 1845.

TO
WILLIAM MAKEPEACE THACKERAY

I thank you exceedingly for your generous opinion.[1] It has been a huge success. Perhaps on some other occasion when my health is better and I am not so worried over money matters I may set the Thames on fire.[2]

[*St John's Wood, June 1844*]

From Maggs Bros. *Autograph Letters* no. 516 (Spring 1929) 103. William Makepeace Thackeray (1811–1863), novelist, studied at Cambridge where his friends included R.M. Milnes and Tennyson. He contributed the 'Yellowplush Correspondence,' 'Catherine,' and the 'History of Samuel Titmarsh and the Great Hoggarty Diamond' to *Fraser's Magazine*. He also contributed with both pen and pencil to *Punch*. His first great novel, *Vanity Fair*, appeared in 1848.
1/Thackeray praised 'The Song of the Shirt' in *Fraser's Magazine* June 1844, 704.
2/Hood's conclusion seems a mere colloquialism.

TO
FREDERICK OLDFIELD WARD

Please send me Patmore's Poems.[1]

My dear Ward
Your article will do very nicely – I think you might extract with a comment at p 98, what is very true as to our bonnes[2] if they are bonne. There is a bit at p 85 on Fairy Tales rather unsixteenish.[3] Beauty & the Beast, & some others are worth hundreds of our damnd untrue true books for unchildrenizing Children[4] As it gets latish you had better send all you can to compose – for example your paper – Mrs Lindon's – & Hardman's will come today, I presume to Renshaws. I wonder that Broderip & Miss Lawrance have not sent yet.[5]
It was very unlucky that your note came just 5 minutes after George had set off to the city on Saturday. I meant to send him yesterday morn^g^ in time for Milnes, but by some misconception he was gone to church.

I send the Poem – the word '*bothers*' is not poetical or artistical – the author should alter it in his proof – as you can suggest to him.[6]
Would you have me do the Cartoons or not? Would it annoy Milnes or DIsraeli?[7]
I continue mending slowly but very weak. Yesterday it blew northerly – & the sycamore tree was worse than ever, the leaves had become dried like paper, in that posture, & when there did not blow any wind, the leaves looked as if there did.
Today it is South-West again. From what I see of it in the Athm. I think I can make a good notice of Howitt's Germany.[8]
None of the MSS sent will do: Some of them beyond all reasonable length. I think it very bad to have 'continuations' – & do not like 'series' – (we have one already) ergo if you can let us have independent papers from Titmarsh[9] I should not like to be pledged to a series.[10]

Yours affectly

Thos Hood

Bulwer's letter is very kind one.[11]

[*St John's Wood, June 1844*]

MS Osborn. Hood is writing about HM July 1844.
1/Published at the beginning of June 1844
2/Maids
3/HM, July 1844, contains 'Sensations of Sixteen. By a Very Old Man,' which is largely made up of extracts from the recently published *Impressions and Observations of a Young Person during a Residence in Paris*. This is the article by Ward to which Hood is referring, though the pagination is not that of the magazine.
4/A view shared by Lamb, Wordsworth, and Coleridge: see Lamb's 'Witches, and other Night Fears,' and R.D. Havens *The Mind of a Poet* (Baltimore 1941) 388–90.
5/The August and later issues of HM contain articles signed H.L., presumably for Hannah Lawrance.
6/Hood is perhaps referring to a phrase in Andrew Winter's 'July' which appears in HM as, 'there's something in the earthly man/ That poses one.'
7/I am not sure what cartoons Hood is referring to. He is afraid of HM falling under the influence of the Young England party. See n.10.
8/*Athenaeum* 15 June 1844, 544
9/Thackeray, who began a series in *Punch* as 'Our Fat Contributor,' 3 August 1844
10/As well as making these comments, Hood insisted on contributing the editorial 'Echo' to the July number of HM. The number itself was variously received. Though the *Weekly Chronicle*, 6 July, 2, was pleased to find Hood surrounded by 'the young intellect of the day,' *The Britannia*, the same day, 427, commented: 'The only fault of a capital number is, that there is somewhat too much of Young England in it.' A private individual who felt the same way was John Ruskin who wrote to Ward on 26 August: his 'friend the author of Modn painters ... is ... at present far too much engaged to think of writing in any periodical. Were it even otherwise – he is not, I think, the man you want, for he would, I am persuaded shrink from associating himself in any way with the

efforts – or the opinions – of "Young England" – He has an infinite horror of novelties *as such,*' MS Rylands. The Young England movement, a revived Toryism, began in 1842 and was led by Disraeli with Manners, Smythe, and Cochrane. 1844 was their triumphant year. Milnes, mentioned in Hood's letter, 'fluttered uneasily around the group, hesitating to commit himself': W.F. Monypenny and G.E. Buckle *Life of Benjamin Disraeli* (1910–20) II 195.

11/On 1 July Ward wrote to Bulwer: 'Mr Hood is better, but still wretchedly weak & infirm. I try to prevail on him to rest – but he assures me that financial reasons compel him to write. My impression is that he cannot live long. Under favorable circumstances he might hold out a few years – but harassed as he is by pecuniary & literary cares nothing is more probable than a relapse; – which might, & I believe would, prove fatal': MS Lady Cobbold. On the day that Ward wrote this gloomy and truthful prognostication, Hood wrote three fanciful letters to the son and daughters of his medical adviser and friend (see the following letters).

Ward's letter to Bulwer contains the first reference to seeking a pension for Hood. He wrote: 'I have thought of applying to the Government for a pension for him.' He goes on to complain bitterly about Hood's unrewarded suffering, then apologises and concludes: 'what is written must go – & I hope you will forgive it. You would, if you had seen him, night after night, struggling whole hours for breath.' Bulwer's immediate reply must have been favourable, for Ward wrote again on the 12th: 'The incurable nature of Mr Hoods disorder would certainly weigh strongly ... on the side of granting the aid – and that *without delay* ... A diseased heart is a very active enemy – working night & day with terrible despatch. My own secret conviction is that we are already too late – and that the extent of our success, even if we succeed, will be, to smooth in some slight degree the harsh passage to the tomb.' Ward considers that 'a public petition signed by a number of literary men might ... establish a troublesome precedent – which Sir R. Peel would desire to avoid. I can conceive Sir R. Peel, as a gentleman & a man of honour, feeling happy to listen, on a question of this sort, to the representation of a political opponent, eminent in letters.' Ward is of course thinking of Bulwer himself. Bulwer went so far as to suggest that Ward should take up the matter with Lord Francis Egerton. Accordingly Ward approached Egerton through Milnes, and received an encouraging reply. Ward decided to forward to Egerton the material he had prepared in support of Hood's case. He wrote again to Bulwer, asking what a suitable form of petition would be, and then sending a couple of versions for improvement: 'I never tried harder to do a thing well – & (perhaps for that very reason) I never felt so dissatisfied with the result. With such a crowd of calamities as encompass Mr Hood there must be the materials of an appeal that should carry every thing before it.' Later in the month Bulwer sent Ward a formal letter in support of Hood's claim. He felt 'sanguine of success, both from the distinction of the claimant and the character of the Minister': MS Rylands. Presumably Ward was the principal author of 'The Case of Mr Thomas Hood' submitted to the government and now in the BM. He concluded eloquently: 'Mr Hood's *genius* is recognised as of the highest order ... – his *diseases,* complicated and incurable, require rest for their alleviation, render him liable to sudden death, and limit to a very few years at the utmost his chance of life: – *straitened* means oblige him to work, when he should be recruiting his shattered frame by repose: – and *debts,* occasioned by misfortunes which no prudence of his could avert, aggravate all his other calamities.'

TO

DUNSTANVILLE ELLIOT

My dear Dunnie,

I have heard of your doings at Sandgate, and that you were so happy at getting to the sea, that you were obliged to be flogged a little to moderate it, and keep some for next day. I am very fond of the sea, too, though I have been twice nearly drowned by it; once in a storm in a ship, and once under a boat's bottom when I was bathing. Of course you have bathed, but have you learned to swim yet? It is rather easy in salt water, and diving is still easier, even, than at the *sink*. I only swim in fancy, and strike out new ideas!

Is not the tide curious? Though I cannot say much for its tidiness; it makes such a slop and litter on the beach. It comes and goes as regularly as the boys of a proprietary school,[1] but has no holidays. And what a rattle the waves make with the stones when they are rough; you will find some rolled into decent marbles and bounces: and sometimes you may hear the sound of a heavy sea, at a distance, like a giant snoring. Some people say that every ninth wave is bigger than the rest. I have often counted, but never found it come true, except with tailors, of whom every ninth is a man.[2] But in rough weather there are giant waves, bigger than the rest, that come in trios, from which, I suppose, Britannia rules the waves by the rule of three. When I was a boy, I loved to play with the sea, in spite of its sometimes getting rather *rough*. I and my brother chucked hundreds of stones into it, as you do; but we came away before we could fill it up. In those days we were at war with France. Unluckily, it's peace now, or with so many stones you might have good fun for days in pelting the enemy's coast. Once I almost thought I nearly hit Boney! Then there was looking for an island like Robinson Crusoe! Have you ever found one yet, surrounded by water? I remember once staying on the beach, when the tide was flowing, till I was a peninsula, and only by running turned myself into a continent.

Then there's fishing at the seaside. I used to catch flat fish with a very long string line. It was like swimming a kite! But perhaps there are no flat fish at Sandgate – except your shoe-soles. The best plan, if you want flat fish where there are none, is to bring codlings and hammer them into dabs.[3] Once I caught a plaice, and, seeing it all over red spots, thought I had caught the measles.

Do you ever long, when you are looking at the sea, for a voyage? If I were off Sandgate with my yacht (only she is not yet built), I would give you a cruise in her. In the meantime you can practise sailing any little boat you can get. But mind that it does not flounder or get squamped,[4] as some people say instead of 'founder' and 'swamp.' I have been swamped myself by malaria, and almost foundered, which reminds me that Tom junior, being very ingenious, has made a cork model of a diving-bell that won't sink!

By this time, I suppose, you are become, instead of a land-boy, a regular sea-urchin; and so amphibious, that you can walk on the land as well as on the water – or better. And don't you mean, when you grow up, to go to sea? Should you not like to be a little midshipman? or half a quarter-master, with a cocked hat, and a dirk, that will be a sword by the time you are a man? If you do resolve to be a post-captain, let me know; and I will endeavour, through my interest with the Commissioners of Pavements, to get you a post to jump over of the proper height. Tom is just rigging a boat, so I suppose that he inclines to be an Admiral of the Marines. But before you decide, remember the port-holes, and that there are great guns in those battle-doors that will blow you into shuttlecocks, which is a worse game than whoop and hide – as to a good hiding!

And so farewell, young 'Old Fellow,' and take care of yourself so near the sea, for in some places, they say, it has not even a bottom to go to if you fall in. And remember when you are bathing, if you meet with a shark, the best way is to bite off his legs, if you can, before he walks off with yours. And so, hoping you will be better soon, for somebody told me you had the shingles,

I am, my dear Dunnie,
Your affectionate friend,

Thomas Hood.

P.S. – I have heard that at Sandgate there used to be *lob*sters; but some ignorant fairy turned them all by a *spell* into *bol*sters.

Devonshire Lodge, New Finchley Road, St. John's Wood, / July 1st (1st of Hebrew falsity). [*1844*]

From *Memorials* II 208–11. The recipients of this and the following two letters were the young children of Hood's friends Dr and Mrs William Elliot. They were on holiday at Sandgate, Kent.

1/Proprietary schools, which flourished at this time, were the outcome of like-minded people banding together to form joint stock companies to run the schools in the way they desired.

2/Proverbial expression

3/Small flat fish

4/Probably making fun of Dunnie's mispronunciation

TO
JEANIE ELLIOT

My dear Jeanie,

So you are at Sandgate! Of course wishing for your old playfellow, M.H.[1] (he *can* play – it's work to me) to help you to make little puddles in the sand, & swing you on the gate. But perhaps there are no sand & gate at Sandgate which in that case nominally tells a fib. But there must be little crabs somewhere, that you can catch if you are nimble enough – so like spiders I wonder they do not make webs. The large crabs are scarcer. If you do catch a big one with good strong claws, & like experiments you can shut him up in a cupboard with a loaf of sugar, & see whether he will break it up with his nippers.

Besides crabs, I used to find Jelly fish on the beach – made, it seemed to me of sea calve's feet – & no sherry. The mermaids eat them I suppose at their wet water-parties, or salt soirées. There were *Star* fish also, but they did not shine till they were stinking, & so made very uncelestial constellations. I suppose you never gather any sea flowers but only sea weeds. The truth is Mr David Jones never rises from his bed & so has a garden full of weeds like Dr Watts's Sluggard – Oysters are as bad – for they never leave their beds, willingly, tho they get such oceans of cold pig.[2] At some sea sides you may pick up shells, but I have been told that at Sandgate there are no shells, except those with passive green peas in them, & lively maggots. I have heard that you bathe in the sea which is very refreshing, but it requires care for if you stay under water too long, you may come up a Mermaid – who is only half a lady with a fish's tail – which she can boil if she likes. You had better try this with your Doll, whether it turns her into half a doll-fin.

I hope you will like the sea. I always did when I was a child which was above two years ago. Sometimes it is so brisk & makes such a fizzing and foaming I wonder some of our London cheats do not bottle it up & sell it for ginger pop. When the sea is too rough, if you pour the sweet oil, out of the cruet, all over it, & wait for a calm, it will be quite smooth – much smoother than a drest sallad.

Some time ago, exactly, there used to be about the part of the coast where you are, large white birds with black tipped wings that went flying & screaming over the sea, & now & then plunged down into the water after a fish. Perhaps they catch their sprats now with nets or hooks & lines. Do you ever see such birds? We used to call them Gulls – but they didn't mind it.

Do you ever see any boats or vessels? – And don't you wish when you see a ship that Somebody was a sea captain instead of a Doctor that he might bring you home a pet Lion, or lap Elephant – ever so many Parrots, – or a Monkey, from foreign Parts. I knew a little girl who was promised a baby Whale, by her sailor brother, &

blubbered because he did not bring it. I suppose there are no whales at Sandgate, but you might find a seal about the beach or at least a stone for one.[3] The sea stones are not pretty when they are dry – but look beautiful while they are wet, & one can always keep sucking them. If you can find one pray pick me up a pebble for a seal. I prefer the red sort, like Mrs Jenkins's brooch & earrings, which she calls 'red chameleon'[4]

Well, how happy you must be! Childhood is such a joyous merry time I often wish I was two or three children! But I suppose I can't be or else I would be Jeanie & Dunny & May Elliot. And wouldn't I pull off my three pairs of shoes & socks & go paddling in the sea up to my six knees. And Oh how I would climb up the down & then roll down the ups on my three backs & stomachs. Capital sport only it wears out the woollens, – which reminds me of the sheep on the downs. And little May, so innocent, I dare say[5] she often crawls about on all fours, and tries to eat grass – like a lamb. Grass isn't nasty, at least not very, if you take care while you are browzing not to chump[6] up the dandelions. They are large yellow star flowers, & often grow about dairy farms, but give very bad milk.

When I can buy a telescope powerful enough I shall have a peep at you, I am told with a good glass you may see the sea at such a distance that the sea can't see you. Now I must say good bye, for my paper gets short – but not stouter.[7] Pray give my love to your Ma, & my compliments to Mrs Hall[8] – & no mistake I remember me my dear Jennie as

Your affectionate Friend

Thos Hood.

The other Tom Hood sends love to every body & every thing.

P.S. Don't forget my pebble: & a good naughtylus would be esteemed a curiosity.

Devonshire Lodge / New Finchley Road / July 1st [*1844*]

MS editor. Published in *Memorials* II 211–14

1/Master Hood?

2/To give cold pig is to awaken by pulling off the bedclothes: Eric Partridge *Dictionary of Slang* (5th ed. 1961).

3/Perhaps Hood means: to use for a seal.

4/Win Jenkins is a favourite character of Hood's in Smollett's *Humphry Clinker*, but I have not traced the phrase quoted. Chameleon = cornelian?

5/MS reads 'she.'

6/The first use of this verb given in NED is dated 1855.

7/Presumably a reference to the colloquial 'short and stout'

8/Perhaps Mrs S.C. Hall

TO

MAY ELLIOT

My dear May,

How do you do, and how do you like the sea? not much perhaps, it's 'so big.' But shouldn't you like a nice little ocean, that you could put in a pan? Yet the sea, although it looks rather ugly at first, is very useful, and, if I were near it this dry summer, I would carry it all home, to water the garden with at Stratford, and it would be sure to drown all the blights, *May*-flies and all!

I remember that, when I saw the sea, it used sometimes to be very fussy, and fidgetty, and did not always wash itself quite clean; but it was very fond of fun. Have the waves ever run after you yet, and turned your little two shoes into pumps, full of water?

If you want a joke you might push Dunnie into the sea, and then fish for him as they do for a Jack. But don't go in yourself, and don't let the baby go in and swim away, although he *is* the shrimp of the family. Did you ever taste the sea-water? The fishes are so fond of it they keep drinking it all the day long. Dip your little finger in, and then suck it to see how it tastes. A glass of it warm, with sugar, and a grate of nutmeg, would quite astonish you! The water of the sea is so saline, I wonder nobody catches salt fish in it. I should think a good way would be to go out in a butter-boat, with a little melted for sauce. Have you been bathed yet in the sea, and were you afraid? I was, the first time, and the time before that; and dear me, how I kicked, and screamed – or, at least, meant to scream, but the sea, ships and all, began to run into my mouth, and so I shut it up. I think I see *you* being dipped in the sea, screwing your eyes up, and putting your nose, like a button, into your mouth, like a buttonhole, for fear of getting another smell and taste! By the bye did you ever dive your head under water with your legs up in the air like a duck, and try whether you could cry 'Quack?' Some animals can! I would try, but there is no sea here, and so I am forced to dip into books. I wish there were such nice green hills here as there are at Sandgate. They must be very nice to roll down, especially if there are no furze bushes to prickle one, at the bottom! Do you remember how the thorns stuck in us like a penn'orth of mixed pins at Wanstead? I have been very ill, and am so thin now, I could stick myself into a prickle. My legs, in particular, are so wasted away that somebody says my pins are only needles: and I am so weak, I dare say you could push me down on the floor, and right thro' the carpet, unless it was a strong pattern. I am sure if I were at Sandgate, you could carry me to the post office, and fetch my letters. Talking of carrying I suppose you have donkeys at Sandgate, and ride about on them. Mind and always call them 'donkeys,' for if you call them asses, it might reach such long ears! I knew a donkey once that kicked a man for calling him Jack instead of John.

There are no flowers I suppose on the beach, or I would ask you to bring me a bouquet as you used at Stratford. But there are little crabs! If you would catch one for me, and teach it to dance the Polka, it would make me quite happy; for I have not had any toys or play-things for a long time. Did you ever try, like a little crab, to run two ways at once? See if you can do it, for it is good fun; never mind tumbling over yourself a little at first. It would be a good plan to hire a little crab, for an hour a day, to teach baby to crawl, if he can't walk, and, if I was his mamma, I *would* too! Bless him! But I must not write on him any more – he is so soft, and I have nothing but steel pens.

And now good bye; Fanny has made my tea, and I must drink it before it gets too hot, as we *all* were last Sunday week. They say the glass was 88 in the shade, which is a great age![1] The last fair breeze I blew dozens of kisses for you, but the wind changed, and I am afraid took them all to Miss H—,[2] or somebody that it shouldn't. Give my love to everybody and my compliments to all the rest, and remember, I am, my dear May,

Your loving friend,

Thomas Hood.

P.S. Don't forget my little crab to dance the Polka, and pray write to me soon as you can't, if it's only a line.

Devonshire Lodge, New Finchley Road [St John's Wood], July 1st, 1844.

From *Memorials* II 214–17. According to Maggs Bros. *Autograph Letters* no. 343 (Spring 1916) 65, this letter had the added attraction of being enclosed in a Mulready envelope, the first penny postage envelope issued by Rowland Hill in 1840, with an attractive, elaborate design, used briefly but caricatured by Leech in *Punch* and abandoned.

1/According to the Meteorological Table in the *Gentleman's Magazine* July 1844, 112, the temperature on 23 June reached 81 at noon.

2/Unidentified

TO
FREDERICK OLDFIELD WARD

My dear Ward

I send you the best list I can of my writings.[1] They make no great show in the Catalogue, Small fruits & few, towards what you will call my literary *dessert*. You must trust, I fear, to my negative merits. For example:

That I have not given up to party even a *party*ciple of what was meant for mankind,[2] womankind or children. It is true that I may be said to have favoured liberal principles; but then they were so liberal as to be *catholic* – common to Old, Young, or New England. The worse chance of my reward from powers political who do not patronise Motley – but would have their very Harlequins all of one colour, – blue, green, or orange: any thing but neutral tint.

I have not devoted any comic power I may possess to lays of indecency or ribaldry. 'I *stooped* to truth,' as Pope *stoopedly* says '& moralized my song.'[3]

I have never written against religion: any thing against Pseudo Saints & Pharisees, notwithstanding. Some of my *serious* views, were expressed in an Ode to Rae Wilson in the Athenaeum.

I have never been indicted for libel.

I have never been called out for personality.[4]

I have not sought pleasure or profit in satirizing or running down my literary contemporaries.

I have never stolen from them.

I have never written *anonymously* what I should object to own.

I have never countenanced, by my practice, the puffery, quackery & trickery of modern literature – even when publishing for years on my own account. In short though I may not have reflected any very great honour on our national literature, I have not disgraced it. All which has been an infinite comfort to me to remember when lately a *critical* illness induced a *Retrospective Review* of my literary career. Now, in the days when the Father of a certain Friend of ours was made a superannuated Postman, in his cradle, at £70 a year[5] – even such negative merits as mine, in Literature, might have deserved a pension, but in these times of retrenchment & Political economy, towards the unpolitical, I sincerely believe, as I told you before, that my strongest recommendation, would be what would prevent my insuring my life, but aid me in purchasing an annuity – the moral certainty that I can last but a very few years. *That* is indeed the *sole* consideration that could induce me to accept any thing of the kind, as it might enable me to make some slight provision for my children – whom I am but too sure to leave, like the children of literary men in general, to a double lament, – for the author of their being, & for his being an Author.

Personally – I am not very sensitive on the score of poverty since it has been the lot of many of those whose names I most do venerate. The reproach clings not to them but to the country they helped to glorify: My debts & difficulties indeed cost me trouble & concern: but much less than if they had been the results of stark extravagance or vicious dissipation. At the very worst, like Timon, 'unwisely not ignobly have I spent',[6] – & even that to a small amount. But like Dogberry, I have had losses[7] – & been weighed down by drawbacks I should long ago have surmounted but for the continued misconduct & treacheries of others: – called friends & relations. Only, it provokes & vexes me that my position countenances the old traditional twaddle about the improvidence &c. of authors, want of business habits, ignorance of the world &c &c. Men can hardly be ignorant, in particular of what they professedly study – & as to business, authors *know their own*, as well as your mercantiles or traders, & perhaps something of accounts besides. That they do not thrive like those who seek for money & nothing else is a matter of course: nor can they be expected to prove a match for those whose life long study has been how to over reach or swindle. Their Flights have been in another direction. Their contemplations, turned towards the beautiful the just & the good. They are not simple spooney victims – but martyrs to their own code. To cope with Bailys, & Flights, one must be not merely literary men, but literary scamps – rogues – sharks – sharpers. Authors are supposed too often to be mere ninnies, and therefore plucked, especially: in wit men, but in simplicity mere children. A vulgar errour. The first fellow who took me in, victimised also no few friends in trade, bankers & bill brokers – To my next mishaps I was no party, – being abroad, & the tricks played without my knowledge. Baily, a bookseller, had necessarily long odds in his favour, against an author, by the force of position, – & with the law to help him, which whatever may be said protects the wrong doer – Witness my barren verdict – & yet costly.[8] Flight, you know – a practised pettifogger, & money lender to boot. And yet after all, much as I have suffered from it, I do not repent my good opinion of my fellows. – There is a faith in human goodness, to renounce which altogether is, in its kind, an impiety. It is a total loss, when a man writes up, over his heart 'No Trust' – one had better lose a few hundreds more, than keep such a 'pike.[9] For my own part I would rather be done brown a little than go black – for fear of it.

I have entered into this matter, partly because it may seem that with my popularity I ought to have done better, – & partly because I am jealous of the honour of

Authorship, & do not think we are so imprudent, unwise, ignorant of the world, unbusinesslike &c &c &c as we are reported. I could prove, that on the whole, I have earned more than I have spent, – & but for dead robberies should be a living Croesus – at least for a Poet.[10]

I must stop to save the post. Come as soon as you can & let us have a palaver on things in general. I am getting on faster in health than in writing or drawing – for I eat drink & sleep well – take all the air I can, & greedily as a man may well do, who gasped for it, in 16: hour spasms, a week or two ago. I am almost spectre enough, for the Phantom Ship, but too weak to work my passage. However I will not strike, – my colours, (yellow & white) must be hauled down for me.[11] Meanwhile I fight on as well as I can – at the very worst, when all is lost, I can *blow up the Magazine*. God bless you Yours affectionately

Thos Hood.

Pray convey to Sir E.L.B.L. my deep sense of his kindness – I will, myself, as soon as I am strong enough for it. I always stood up for the good feeling of the Bruderschaft in spite of the old calumnies about the irritable genus &c &c &c & lo! the proofs.[12]

Vanbrugh House [*Blackheath*]. *Tuesday* – [*July 1844*]

MS Lady Cobbold. Published by Lord Lytton *Life of Edward Bulwer* (1913) II 63–6. Early in July 1844 Hood removed to Vanbrugh House, Blackheath, for convalescence. (The house was named after its architect.) In October Jane reported: 'He went to Blackheath for two months when he was well enough for removal from home': *Memorials* II 227. On 12 July Ward wrote to Bulwer: 'I have taken Mr Hood to Blackheath, a gravelly soil where he may sit in the garden in the pure air all day. He has promised not to write for a week – & is I think better:' MS Lady Cobbold.

1/For the sake of the pension application
2/Goldsmith's criticism of Burke in 'Retaliation' 32
3/Pope, 'Epistle to Arbuthnot' 341
4/Personal abuse
5/Unidentified. Postal reform at this time was less concerned with nepotism than with the rates at which the mails were charged.
6/*Timon of Athens* 2 ii 175
7/*Much Ado About Nothing* 4 ii 82
8/Hood, represented by Serjeant Talfourd, had gained a verdict against Baily in the Court of Common Pleas on 15 February. However, as Jane pointed out in August, 'being a contract [the Judge] was compelled to refer to the Judges in Banco – which will be settled in Septr – But the delay of 3 or 4 years has ruined the property': *The Keats Circle* ed. H.E. Rollins (1948) II 472.
9/Turnpike. Presumably a sign with the legend 'No Trust' would be welcome to the traveller, since it would indicate that the road was not controlled by a trust enforcing tolls.
10/Here Hood gives a list of his works.
11/Compare Coleridge's account in 'The Ancient Mariner' of the phantom ship and its crew:

Her locks were yellow as gold:
Her skin was as white as leprosy,
The Night-mare LIFE-IN-DEATH was she.

12/Ward sent this letter to Bulwer, warning him not to be deceived by the 'jocose style.

TO

FREDERICK OLDFIELD WARD

My dear Ward.

Enclosed are the mottoes & Proofs of cuts.

I am getting on much better with my pen & no worse with my knife & fork – & shall therefore fill up my cavities physical & literary.

If possible let us avoid extra & night work this month – give the printer making-up for more sheets. Mine & one of the shorter articles will certainly fill the first sheet.

I don't think the eagle's neck being single signifies – they might take it for the swan with Two if I altered it.[1]

I am going to dine with Dr Elliot on Monday at Blackwall[2] to meet his brother from Scotland. I am curious to see whether in such a locality, for feasting, he *can* forbid me iced champagne, – (a cooling draught?) & cold punch. Which reminds me of an occurrence yesterday, like the French Pic nic to which every body brought a pigeon pie. Jane brought me the last Punch, which I offered to Hoskins,[3] who pulled one out of his pocket – purchased on my account – & then a visitor brought a Punch for him. There is no other news here except that two more gooseberries have burst from overripeness. Better, than boilers of Greenwich steamers.

The east wind, parched me terribly till yesterday afternoon with slow fever – but today I am all *write* again: my own room is cooler, & there may be a blackbird whistling in the garden, but if there is, I don't hear him. Perhaps the butterflies sing – only I'm deaf: which as I am recommended quiet, is a mercy. Give a hint of vocal butterflies to Winter – & of melted butter ones if he is going to describe the hot weather.[4] There are three cows in the paddock opposite, and I distinctly see, that I don't hear them low. By the bye none but a deaf man, can be truly fond of dumb animals. Crops as before – only since the P.O. disclosures[5] the taters are uncommonly waxy: – and the apple trees keep discovering gravitation, by means of windfalls. Raspberries make nice easy thimbles if you don't work with them – & starlings frequent the field next the Park.[6] I wonder, when you slit their tongues with a sixpence, if they discuss the currency question. School began today – so tomorrow I can beg a whole holiday, for the boys – I have offered my services as a teacher of ignorance: & drawn up a prospectus, which you must *not* put in the advertisements of the Magazine. I have called today on the Gladstones[7] – how much better than going to the Grave stones! – A serious joke I have made on purpose for those who expect me to be funny.

I stick to my temperance – except as to tea of which I drink so much that if it went to my head I should certainly have a pigtail[8] – Hoskins manures a radish bed with my grouts. I am trying to rise early & am up to every thing about 9. But I eschew *up* the Hill & heavy papers. There was a boat came down, safe last night with 1100 passengers.[9] Another, with only six & the Athenaeum, – foundered – & what's worse can't be weighed. By the bye don't come down, even with Owen Jones[10] – he will want to visit his brother at the bottom. I am glad he patronises – the Magazine – but I hear that Partridge, next September, don't like Number Six.[11] Remember me kindly to him notwithstanding.

Yours affect^ly^

T:H:

I am nervous about Lord J Russel: don't let him in – if he is political.[12]

[*Blackheath*] *Friday*. [*26 July 1844*]

MS Fitzwilliam Museum. The reference to Blackwall in paragraph four links this with the following letter, probably dated by its recipient.

1/A reference to Hood's comic illustration in HM August 1844, 120

2/East London, on the north bank of the Thames, then the site of the Brunswick and the Artichoke taverns, noted for whitebait dinners

3/Probably the other tenant of Vanbrugh House

4/Andrew Winter's poems on the months appeared in the August and September numbers of HM. This might be Andrew Wynter (1819–76) who later wrote several books and contributed to *Once a Week*, *Fraser's Magazine*, the *Quarterly*, and the *Edinburgh Review*.

5/On 14 June Sir James Graham, the Home Secretary, was accused of having broken open the seals of the letters of Mazzini and others. 'Seals' accounts for 'waxy' in the following phrase, but the joke seems thin.

6/'The brick towers of Vanbrugh House ... overlook the east wall of the park,' *Pictorial Guide to Greenwich* (1844) 25.

7/Unidentified

8/Hood prefers China tea.

9/A letter in *The Times* 2 July, 6, feared the consequences of overcrowding on Greenwich steamers to the number of seven or eight hundred passengers.

10/Owen Jones (1809–74), architect. In 1842 he published *Designs for Mosaic and Tessellated Pavements*, with an essay by Ward.

11/I do not understand this reference.

12/Explained by 'The Echo,' editorial notes in HM August, 208: 'The article on the Leader of the Opposition [Lord John Russell], which was announced for publication in our present Number, is unavoidably deferred.' Ward later attributes the article to 'Mr Madden author of Ireland & its Rulers,' 639. In HM June, R.O. Madden was named as the author of 'The Irish Attorney-General, Right Hon. T.B.C. Smith, M.P.' This was probably Richard Robert Madden (1798–1886), author of *The United Irishmen* (1843–6). According to the DNB Madden spent these years in Lisbon as correspondent of the *Morning Chronicle.*

TO
WILLIAM ELLIOTT

Dear Doctor
I am so curious to see with what sort of face you can forbid me such cooling draughts as iced champagne & cold Punch, at such a notorious feasting place as Blackwall, – (after a glimpse too of Greenwich Hospitality, –) that I shall be sure to meet you, at 3 o'clock – I was going to say, amongst the other Pensioners – but as yet I only know the pen part of it.

Love to all
Yours ever & ever

Thos Hood

I have had a little more spinning material in me, the last few days, & have nearly done three chapters:[1] but you needn't tell Sir Robert.[2]

Vanbrugh House, [*Blackheath*] *Friday* [*26 July 1844*]

MS Cornell University. Published in *Memorials* II 218. Perhaps the meeting to which Hood refers in the letter was concerned with the medical report signed by Elliot on 23 July 1844 and submitted to the government together with 'The Case of Mr Thomas Hood,' MS BM. The MS of the letter is dated, perhaps in another hand, 26 July, whilst the *Memorials* version is dated the 20th, and that in *Works* x 420, the 23rd.

1/Of 'Our Family,' being serialised in HM
2/Sir Robert Peel (1788–1850), Prime Minister (1841–6), despite his cold exterior, noted for his generous feelings and sense of humour

TO
FREDERICK OLDFIELD WARD

Dear Ward,
Better begin making up, with the 2d sheet to save time, leaving the 1st open for me – The Unknown Singer by Hardman 18½ will do best to begin 2d sheet which it

will fill up – and run over. That sheet can then be worked off which will save time. We want Poetry. If Winter's is ready, follow Hardman's with it. NB. Contribs. must not take so late in the month – they ought to be 'all in' on the 20th We must try & save night work & extra charges. Broderips must come in this month – it will divide at '*with the air of a Martyr.*' 9th line at top of 3rd slip. How sly of you not to show me the Britannia's review!

Yours affectly

T:H:

Phillips's sea side lore will come today.
[*Blackheath, July 1844*]

MS Columbia. Reference is made in this letter to HM August 1844, which contained 'The Unknown Singer,' an episode of 'Sea-Side Lore,' the first part of 'Ballads and Broadsides,' ending with 'with the air of a martyr,' and Andrew Winter's poem 'August.' *The Britannia,* to which Hood also refers, commented, 6 July, 427, 'The only fault of a capital number is, that there is somewhat too much of Young England in it.'

TO
WILLIAM MAKEPEACE THACKERAY

My Dear Thackeray, – I am grieved to hear of your ill-health, and sincerely trust that before many days intervene you will have thoroughly recovered.[1] I fear that so far as I myself am concerned King Death will claim me ere many months elapse. However, there's a good time coming,[2] if not in this world, most assuredly in the next. Always yours,

Thos. Hood.

[*Blackheath, 4 August 1844*]

From Jerrold 380, where the letter is dated.

1/By 22 August 1844 Thackeray had recovered sufficiently to be on his way to Grand Cairo. He returned by way of Paris, February 1845. Perhaps from there he wrote to Hood, apologising for the delay in replying to a later note: 'By this post I have sent you the cuttings you wrote about ... You cant think how glad I am to learn that you are once more well again: and I pray heartily that you will continue to remain well. Your letter of some weeks' ago paind me hugely: the one that I am now answering has pleased me not a little. More power to your elbow! and more lustre to your already famous name!' Thackeray also sent Hood an inscribed copy of Anthony Pearson *The*

Great Case of Tithes (1754). Both letter and book are in the Berg Collection, New York Public Library. The letter is not included in Thackeray's *Letters* (ed. Ray).
2/The phrase seems to have been popular about this time. Hood also uses it in the following letter.

TO
SHIRLEY BROOKS

I say at once that I will with pen and purse do all I can. Goodness knows that I my own individual self have suffered enough from illness; and I certainly have not been wholly unacquainted with poverty. However I believe in the good time coming, and between you and me I do not think it far off.

[*Blackheath, August 1844*]

From Charles B. Shaw, 'This Fellow of Infinite Jest' *Poet Lore* XL (1929) 276. Charles William Brooks (1815–74), journalist and dramatist. Shirley Brooks was his *nom-de-plume*. He wrote in *Ainsworth's Magazine*, the *Morning Chronicle*, and *Punch*. I do not know the cause to which Hood is referring in this letter.

TO
FREDERICK OLDFIELD WARD

I should be an ingrate indeed to forget the storm when you came on board, or the prompt services rendered to the vessel & myself in distress by your zeal & activity ... My very confidence in your good intentions & my estimate of your former services impel me the more forcibly to prevent you from neutralizing them & undoing what you have done, by pointing out where & how you might harm me or the Mag. by a mistaken course. My personal position & literary views are of course best understood by myself, & no one would regret it more than F.O.W. if he damaged either for want of knowledge on the subject. Especially I value a certain literary standing & peculiar reputation earned by many years of care & labour, & which might be seriously compromised in as many days if I hesitated to point out to you any proceeding that endangered them ...
[Hood objects strongly to the notice of a sermon by Dr. Hussey, as being] *A High Churchman's attack on the Dissenters* who are especially given to the religious tea parties, etc., he denounces.[1] I am sure it will be taken so – and I am in the way to know – & that to allude to that sermon with commendations will offend every Dissenter who reads the Magazine, in all probability one half of the subscribers.

Now as 'Hood's' is not the 'Church of England Magazine,' this would be running a needless risk. You are as neutral as I am in a controversy between Church & Chapel & as to our 'giving our support to the cause of sound manly & genuine religion,' I must smile as surely as some quizzers will grin & others will look grave at the notion of advocating so serious an interest in a frisky article on the Polka. A combination quite as incongruous as 'tea and bible' ...[2]

As to the calico test,[3] I do not hold that a female must necessarily be a modest one tho' tied up to the neck in a sack, especially if she jumps in it – her modesty may be dubious, but she is decent. But there can be no doubt of the immodesty of one who goes half naked. Now if your argument was intended to be as given in the 'Explanation,' you did not clearly state it in the article, where it certainly reads like a recommendation to carry the costume & capers of the public Ballet into private life. If I understand your sliding scale of Modesty, the most delicate may dance in the shortest petticoats, & the purest of all in fig leaves ...

Yours just received – and thank you for a good laugh, though a quiet one as the old Trapper's[4] – at your Purity taking refuge with the Nubians – who go naked for full dress, and skin themselves I suppose for dishabille. Why, of course there is no harlotry amongst them, as there can be no fashion where there is no costume. But admitting them chaste – on traveller's authority – what becomes of the High Art & the Dancing? I never heard that they were famous as Terpsichoreans.[5]

But no doubt like other savages they have their perouettes, entrechats, & ronder les jambes & surpass Cerito as much as they *outstrip* her.[6] I think I see you taking a mud stall, in the sand pit, at their bare Ballet, & paying for it in cowries!

By the bye, there was once a German student who thought proper to go to a Masquerade in Berlin, in a flesh colour tight suit, a la Nubian – but the King, a patron of the Ballet, respected his purity so little, as to send him to the guard-house.

As to Coleridge's village, doubly remarkable for the simplicity & purity of the inhabitants & for the men & women bathing higgle de piggeldy together[7] – did the great Samuel Taylor mean to applaud? or wonder? or simply to mystify with pure nonsense? At any rate, you must show me that the purity prevailed in consequence not in spite of such wet socialism. Or it might be the exception to the rule. For according to general experience such a Hog's Norton & Hog Washing ought to have produced what Liston called 'poly-piggamy'.[8]

You remind me that Eve 'as example of perfect purity did without even a fig leaf.' Yes, but if she polked[9] she also did without a circle of spectators, including perhaps a few of Young France, as goatish in their propensities as in their beards, as lax in their morals as in their collars, as loose in their lives as in their trowsers. And you shall be welcome to dance naked on the same terms. But I rather think your Ballet, high artistical as you please, would soon give over their exhibition if limited to one couple & no spectators. If a Figurante were now to dance naked, as Eve, it must be with the same view of charming a circle of Beasts. A Young World nudity & a Young France purity are very different things. Remember – we do not live now in Hermit Pairs in Paradise, but in society – with a Belle Assemblie[10] dress circles – and Drapers' Gardens.[11] These are my opinions. But I may be wrong. I only wonder in that case, that where so much Purity & High Art go together no Painter or Sculptor within my acquaintance or to my knowledge has coveted a figurante for his wife, & think it a shame the Royal Academy does not invite the whole Corps de Ballet to their Annual Dinner & especially when so many of the ladies from mere devotion to Art & Artists would willingly sit, on the 'Hamiltonian System' as models to the students.[12]

And after all, who are to strip? The masses – or only a select few – only the lovely & symmetrical & artistical – or who so conceit themselves? A, or Anne, may be chaste but clumsy – B, or Betsy, delicate minded but dumpy and dowdy – C, active and fond of dancing but ugly – F, feminine in feeling but fat & fubsy. Must they therefore cover up? Must only Grace, Beauty, & Agility *go cool* whilst Fat swelters & Fubsy faints? If so, may there not be an exclusiveness in Polka as in Piety – & a monopoly of nakedness as of righteousness – a Socialism that is Selfishness at bottom ...

[*Blackheath, August 1844*]

From Maggs Bros. *Autograph Letters* no. 349 (autumn 1916) 60–1. The letter shows that Hood and Ward differed on how the magazine should be run. In August 1844 Ward wrote to Bulwer asking for his advice: 'Do you think the sketch of the Premier in the last number was of a nature to give a magazine a political character? I had engaged its author – (Mr Madden author of Ireland & its Rulers) to write one like it on Ld J. Russell – but Hood was so nervous about the danger of giving a political character to the magazine that I withdrew it [see 634 above]. I feel satisfied that unless you address people on subjects affecting their interests & the real facts of daily outward life, you can hardly expect to have any extensive sale for a magazine': MS Lady Cobbold. Hood's concern about the running of the magazine is shown in a letter from Jane to Ward probably belonging to this month: 'Please to send him proofs & all information you can about the Mag – as he will else get restless and desire to return home – and its very important that he shall remain at Blackheath during this fine weather he is so much better for the change': *Keats Circle* ed. H.E. Rollins (1948) II 472.

1 / *The Times* 14 August 1844, 6, is pleased to reprint a sermon by Thomas John Hussey, delivered 'at Chelmsford about a fortnight ago, whilst ... discharging his duties as chaplain to the High Sheriff of Essex.' Hussey objects in particular to the loose modern use of the word 'religious': 'there are religious parties, excursions, tea-drinkings, bazaars, tickets of salvation, and draughts upon the bank

of faith.' *The Times* leaves 'these remarks to be digested as they best may by the religious meddlers at Exeter-hall.'

2/In his article Ward wrote: 'Little Bethel has been losing ground ever since Boz gave Stiggins that ducking under the pump. "Tea-and-bible" is found out for a dilute sort of religion after all; and keen noses have smelt something very like gin in all that piety-and-water,' HM August 1844, 167.

3/Ward had written: 'Is villanous calico better to behold than woman's graceful neck? ... Away with this pinchbeck purity – these millinery morals! We refuse the calico-test,' 173.

4/Unidentified, probably mentioned in Ward's letter

5/Maggs has 'Zerpsichorean.'

6/Fanny Cerito (1821–99), star of the ballet, whose return to Her Majesty's Theatre had been welcomed in *The Athenaeum*, 11 May 1844, 435. The company there had introduced ' "La Polka," the present rage of French dancers,' a month before: *The Athenaeum* 13 April, 341.

7/Coleridge's letter had been published in *Gentleman's Magazine* March 1836 and in NMM August, but in the second the passage under discussion was omitted.

8/Phrase untraced

9/The first use of their verb recorded in NED is dated 1845.

10/*La Belle Assemblée* was the title of a periodical which flourished intermittently between 1806 and 1832. From the latter year until 1836 appeared the *Court Magazine and Belle Assemblée.*

11/'Attached to the [Drapers'] Hall is a pleasure garden, in the heart of the city, and which is free to the public,' *Pictorial Handbook of London* (1854) 335. 'It was for a long time looked upon as a fashionable promenade in the afternoons and summer evenings,' A.H. Johnson *History of the Worshipful Company of the Drapers of London* (Oxford 1914–22) III 448.

12/James Hamilton (1769–1829) had developed a system of teaching languages. His plan was 'to teach instead of ordering to learn,' DNB.

TO

WILLIAM ELLIOT?

Ward has heard from Ld F. Egerton[1] that he has laid the matter before Sir R.P. who has sent for me £150 from Royal Fund for similar purposes, ad interim, & will consider the case.[2] Ward seems sanguine that Sir R. feels favourably – but the thing will read two ways – it might be a mode of softening a refusal so I do not build. Please not to mention it.

I have resumed the Mag: Ward's last article on Camberwell fair is harmless – but French at the end – sentimental about a Boothia Infelix.[3] I send his apology or explanation of the Polka for all whom it may concern.[4]

[*Blackheath, September 1844*]

From Maggs Bros. *Autograph Letters* no. 469 (autumn 1925) 83. I suggest that the letter is addressed to Elliot, since it is written in the same spirit of intimate friendship as the letters known to be written to him about this time. The letter is written after Hood resumed control of HM in September.

1/Francis Egerton (1800-57), first Earl of Ellesmere, statesman and poet, MP (1822–46). He was very active in public life, but also described in the *Complete Peerage* (1910–40), v 55n as a shy and grave book-collector.
2/On 22 August 1844 Egerton reminded Peel of the application on behalf of Hood. The Prime Minister replied the following day.
3/Boothia Felix in the North West Territories of Canada, discovered by Sir James Ross, 1829–33. Hood considered the fair more suitable for satire or reprobation than for sentiment.
4/'The Polka' appeared in HM August 1844, and 'Camberwell Fair – Towards Midnight' in September.

TO
FREDERICK OLDFIELD WARD

Dear Ward.
I do not dispute your/calculation/statement – but my '5 months' referred to editing a periodical not to the date of your work on Osteology.
Sketches of Ministerial & Opposition leaders must, would, & ought to be political – especially from an Irishman.[2]
You must have misunderstood me if you thought I approved of the dropping 'Comic Miscellany'[3] – unless at the top of the page & of that I thought better.
I disapproved of much besides the 'tea & bible,' – including the latter part, which I only saw in print.[4]
You *may* be right about the signature & the reprint:[5] but I certainly made the objection before the Explanation was written which was printed with it.
You still do not say whether the Atlas extracts were from the objectionable parts.[6]
The many others, London & provincial, I ought to have seen but have not.
Mrs Hume[7] may be a subscriber, but surely not on account of the Polka when her note said she differed with you, on it. In a dose of brimstone & treacle[8] what do you consider as 'mixing it fair?'
As to Winter extracting from Keats – 'a living ass is *not* better than a dead Lion'[9] – *as a Poet*. And why Phillips *next time*? – he should have preceded, – (but Self first!) especially if Winter admired the Poem. And with that I strop & sheathe my razor, rejoicing with you that neither party has cut the other, in the encounter.
Tomorrow at nine say ¼ before. Not a minute later, to run me out of breath, which is shortish.
Are you ever sick? If you are I will advise you what to give up.

Yours ever affectionately

Thos Hood.

[*Blackheath, September 1844*]

MS Osborn. Continuing the quarrel with Ward

1/Ward had begun editorial work for HM in March 1844. His *Outlines of Human Osteology* appeared in 1838. Ward's letter, to which this is a reply, does not survive.
2/See 639.
3/Sub-title of HM
4/See 637, 640.
5/See following letter. 'A footnote signed Editor' occurs in HM, August, 166.
6/Hood is referring to the extracts from Ward's 'Polka' article in *The Atlas* 17 August 1844, 552. The *Weekly Chronicle* 4 August, 3, commented favourably, considering the contribution 'as sparkling and crisp a bit of writing as we could wish to read – just the style for a light magazine article.'
7/Unidentified
8/The first example of this phrase given in NED is dated 1863.
9/Ecclesiastes 9: 4: 'a living dog is better than a dead lion.'

TO
FREDERICK OLDFIELD WARD

My dear Ward
I have to remind you that my letter which has annoyed you was in reply to a rather unnecessary epistle of your own – after a recommendation from yourself 'not to write, but talk about the matter.'
I am sorry that you are offended at being called a chick in Authorship & inexperienced – & beg to withdraw those expressions. You are a literary fowl full fledged with four feathers, and a veteran Editor of five months' old. On my own plumage & standing it would not become me to insist, but I may say briefly they are such as would exempt me in this case at any rate from 'editorial jealousy' – an imputation that might as well have been spared. Of course I have considered my own responsibility & experience as of some weight & authority, but have not needlessly interfered with your management, nor at all, except when my 'lifelong example' & the character of the Magazine were likely to be compromised or altered. Thus I presumed as 'Editor in Chief' to protest against a series of political articles to which you had somewhat rashly pledged yourself – telling me that you did not care for my Prospectus – wherein I had elaborately disclaimed such subjects.[1] I also ventured to resist a proposed alteration of the very title of the Magazine by dropping the 'Comic Miscellany', a descriptive addition deliberately adopted & expressly intended to indicate what had been a prominent & popular feature of Hood's periodicals. And lastly I took the liberty of objecting to certain passages in the Polka but with so little success that even two words of it were not given up to me. Nay more you made me sanction the article by a footnote signed

Editor – as if of my writing, & have retained that footnote in your reprint in spite of my remonstrance. If in these acts I have overstepped the proper duties of a party repeatedly alluded to in print by yourself as 'Editor in Chief' & responsible by name and character to the public, my anomalous position would indeed be strange enough a new chapter in the Curiosities of Literature. As to my Polka polemics, subsequent events have proved that my misgivings as to that paper were well founded. All who have spoken in my hearing have condemned it – enough to your own conviction to induce you to say that 'it should not happen again'. Here the matter might naturally have dropped, but on the very slight encouragement of an extract in the Atlas, – not taken I venture to say from the objectionable parts – you revoke your concession – stick to it that the Polka had done good or no harm – attribute to it a rise in the sale, more probably in spite of it, and stigmatize all my friends, & your own, who differ from you, as Puritans – a nickname surely as offensive from its association with canters & hypocrites as the phrase I borrowed from the poultry. Taken with the context you will find that expression to have been used in a fraternal spirit – perhaps something in the style of an elder brother in literature – but not more so than our respective ages would justify. You have yourself invited my criticisms, as from a senior, on your writings, and I have given them fairly. But I shall be wiser in future, and remembering that you accepted my praise of Camberwell Fair, & rejected my censure of the Polka, will take care to administer my brimstone & treacle without the brimstone.

Of another contributor I shall speak more freely. I have given my reasons to you for not liking his last effusion,[2] & will now show cause for not holding out much encouragement in that quarter. I observe that he has again quoted his own Poem in the Weekly Chronicle not content with his own good character of it the week before.[3] It is therefore evident that in Andrew Winter's opinion Andrew Winter is *the* poet of Hood's Magazine – a conviction he might privately enjoy without much harm except to himself – for nothing is more fatal to progress in a young writer than too much self-satisfaction with his performance. He will never climb much higher who fancies himself at the top of the tree. But besides such public criticism is unfair to other contributors – for instance Phillips – whose Poem is worth a long hundred of Winter's, – far more eligible for quotation – if to advantage the Magazine – as addressing the Feeling, not the Fantastic.[4] Now here is a case where a true friend might 'wholesomely take the conceit' out of a young aspirant – for I need not tell you that some two or three pages even of good poetry – but the fruits of slow & painful elaboration – will hardly constitute a Poet. A Bard or a Bird with one feather is still callow. Here – for the sake of others I am jealous – as well as reasonably sensitive on certain points, such as my literary character & abstinence from politics. I am not anxious I confess by health or inclination, after a long neutrality to be associated with English Party – or the philosophy of Young France – the Social Owenism[5] of Fourrier – Nubian Purity – or the conversion of the Great Globe itself[6] to a great Fancy Ball. Having read of my Uncle Toby,[7] I can allow other men their Hobbies, but may reasonably object to being obliged to ride behind upon them. But it is time to end my homily, provoked by your own crow of defiance – rehoisting the Polka flag, with the Atlas extract, & parading your new auxiliaries, Owen Jones & his naked Nubians. Having flourished my own standard & answered your cheer I am *now* willing 'to drop the whole subject' – agreeing with you that after all that has passed between us any difference would be most unfortunate & unseemly. Difference of opinion of course excepted, for I will not suppose you so ungenerous as to expect the surrender of my judgment & convictions to you, in consideration of your good services to the Magazine under difficulties or those which you continue to myself. If it *could* be so – a man, of an independence of spirit, would at once decline a friendship so identical with the common patronage of the world.

[*Blackheath, September 1844*]

MS Cameron. Hood here takes up points made in the preceding letter. However, the phrases he refers to at the beginning of the second paragraph must come from another letter which I have been unable to locate.

1/Hood's firm disclaimer is to be found in *Memorials* II 187–8.

2/'September' in the September number, Winter's last contribution

3/*Weekly Chronicle* 1 September, 4, and 8 September, 6. It sounds as though Winter was a contributor to that newspaper.

4/Phillips was the author of the only unsigned poem in the September number, 'The Husk and the Grain,' about a widow whose husband is now translated to heaven.

5/The first use of this noun given in NED is dated 1870, from the social reformer Robert Owen (1771–1858). Charles Fourier (1772–1837) held similar views. 'Nubian purity' presumably refers to the primitivistic element which Hood feared in their thought.

6/*Tempest* 4 i 153

7/In Sterne's *Tristram Shandy*

TO
WILLIAM ELLIOT

My dear Doctor ...
I have left Vanbrugh House, for good. It was impossible to stay longer with comfort; all we have suspected has been confirmed with worse additions. I am now convinced that we were pressed[1] to come there to keep up appearances & give a sanction; but they have so little self-restraint we became unwelcome, as witnesses, and our treatment became ambiguous accordingly, or rather there was 'no mistake about it.' Jane from her sense of propriety, and quickness of ear, a complete nuisance.
Saturday at midnight, a decided row upstairs, a medley of angry voices. Mrs. H.[2] above all exclaiming she would not stay in the House to be talked to by such a blackguard. Then a rush of feet downstairs & a door barred. The Housekeeper told Jane in the morning that there was no butter in the house, & Father & Son pulled the mother out of bed and downstairs, declaring she should fetch it from Greenwich ... The poor creature has been most vilely used. Her father is dead, & she had £150 to receive for which H. is struggling. He is in difficulty, but money is evidently lavished on Miss S whose keep[3] as an Artist would say is 'out of all keeping' whatever she has herself. The wife says the trio will get her money & then break her heart, perhaps her neck. For they seem to me to have become reckless; and she is frightened to death. Probably the concern will break up and then Hoskins & the girl will go off together ...
I have resumed the Magazine reins, not without some difficulty and skermishing with Ward, who I foresaw would very reluctantly give up the box. Luckily he is somewhat diverted elsewhere this month by lodging hunting. He might help me much in the way you suggest, but unfortunately he will not easily admit any 'supervision and superintendence' from the nominally 'Editor in Chief.' I have only interfered where necessary – not always successfully – & even then he has evidently grudged his concessions and repented of his repentance.

[*St John's Wood, 14 September 1844*]

From Maggs Bros. *Autograph Letters* no. 459 (spring 1925), 122–3. The date is given in the catalogue.
1/Perhaps by Ward and the other occupants of the house beside Hood himself who proved uncongenial to the virtuous and invalid poet
2/Hoskins
3/Maggs has 'dup.' 'Miss S' unidentified

TO
FREDERICK OLDFIELD WARD

Dear Ward.
Glad it is not *Bottle* Street, which I am forbidden to enter. Have you a long lease, – for of course in *Cork* Street you mean to be a stopper? You will be near your Friend Fisher who I think lived thereabouts, in some angle, if he has not taken to Hungerford or Billingsgate or some other piscivorous locality.[1]
I am pretty well & working through some epistolary arrears,

Yours affectionately

Thos Hood

Don't forget Rowland Hill: I knew a man who removed from Whitechapel to Bayswater, per penny post.

Devonshire Lodge. [*St John's Wood, September 1844*]

MS Osborn. The postscript may be a devious request for Ward to resume their correspondence after their quarrel over HM.

1/William Fisher, artist, lived at 4 Cork Street, Bond Street. This was probably the portrait painter of that name (1817–95).

TO
SAMUEL PHILLIPS

My Dear Phillips,
What the devil do you mean? Have you no concern for the nerves of editors – the nourishment of magazine readers? It may be horse-play to you, but death to us. What business had you in the saddle at all? Have I not said in print, that sedentary persons have never a good seat? Is it not notorious that authors from Coleridge down to Poole are bad riders? And you must go proving it again by being run away with; not by vanity, in a very writer-like way, but by the brute quadruped, never well pick-a-backed by seamen and the literati. Do you want a hole in your head as well as in your lungs? And are you not contented with the *Neck*, crying 'lost, lost,' but you must break your own?[1] Is your head no better than a common pumpkin, that you must go pitching on it, and grazing the 'dome of thought and palace of the soul?'[2] I think I see you getting up – not content with expectorating blood – spitting mud! And, plague take you, all through trotting on an earthly

roadster, when you might have been soaring so celestially on Pegasus, after his feed of 'husk and grain.' Do you really expect, though you die of riding, that you will get an equestrian statue for it at Trafalgar Square, Cockspur Street, or in front of the new Exchange?[3] Not a bronze poney! Nor will you get a shilling a sheet the more from 'Hood's' or 'Blackwood's,' no, nor from any of the Sporting Magazines, for going at a gate without hounds or fox! And a father too, with a baby and a boy, and a young lord to bring up![4] And a friend, with such friends as a Blair, a Salomans, and a Hood, and all the Pratts,[5] to expose himself to be kicked out of such society by a hoof. Oh! Philippus, you deserve a Philippic – and here it is! Seriously, I am glad you escaped, and hope 'you will not do so any more.' If you must run risks, do it as I do, on two legs, and at a walk – for such invalids, a damp clothes-horse is danger enough – or if you *must* go pick-a-back, get acquainted with some sheriff that can lend you a quiet nag.

I am come back here from Vanbrugh House for good – much better; and have resumed the driving of the Magazine. I am sorry to have had the last of the 'Sea-side Lore:'[6] but your beautiful poem was some consolation. It has been much admired by my friends. Don't get too proud with your Marchionesses for the muses. My bust is modelled and cast. It is said to be a correct likeness: two parts Methodist, to one of Humourist, and quite recognisable in spite of the Hood all over the face. To-morrow I take a trip to Calais, for a day only, with Fanny, for the sake of the voyage and sea air. We are a brace in need of bracing, as you know. If I can catch a sea-horse, I will, for you to ride in the Race of Portland.[7] Ward accompanies to edit the main sheet, and return the whole Packet if unsuitable. I only hope he won't be sick without 'Notice to Correspondents.'

Pray for us, and for peace, for if a war breaks out while we are there, the Magazine will be as bad as blown up, and I might as well be cased *full*-length in plaster of Paris.

By the bye, have you read the 'Mysteries of Paris?'[8] Very bad! Or the 'Amber Witch,' which is very good?[9] Or do you read nothing but Burke and Debrett to the young Peerage? Do you like my novel?[10] or do you prefer Rookwood for the sake of the ride to York?[11]—advertises 'Revelations of London,'[12] in imitation of the Parisian mysteries, of course! Won't they be very full of the slang of the Rookery? The mere idea gives me the *Back-Slumbago*![13]

Write soon, and tell me how you like your new position, and how you live. Aristocratically enough I guess, and spitting nothing under high blood. Your stomach a mere game bag, or pot for the preserves, eh? And some fine day you will come and triumph over us with your corpulence, and 'Phillips me like a three-man beadle.'[14] For you drink the choicest of wines of course – your smallest beer old double X ale. What a change for an author! And then you lie I warrant in a down bed, with such sheets! every one equal to forty-eight pages of superfine cambric, margined with lace and hot-pressed with a silver warming-pan! Nevertheless come some day and see us – some day when you are ordered to live very low, and then perhaps our best holiday diet may be good enough for you. We are very poor and have only seventy-two thousand a-year (pence mind, not pounds), and our names not even in the Post-office Directory, much less the Court Guide![15] Well, if it isn't too great a liberty, God bless you! Mrs. Hood hopes you will forgive her offering her kind regards; and Fanny and Tom presume to join in the same. And if you would condescend to present my kind regards and respects to Mr. Salomans, it would exceedingly oblige,

Dear Phillips,
Yours very truly, and hoping no offence,

Thos. Hood.

Devonshire Lodge, New Finchley Road. [*St John's Wood, September 1844*]

From *Memorials* II 219–22. The reference in the first paragraph to Coleridge suggests Coleridge's description of himself, in the midst of his youthful military experiences, as 'a very indocile Equestrian' *Collected Letters* ed. E.L. Griggs (Oxford 1956) I 66. Phillips's poem 'The Husk and the Grain,' referred to in the same paragraph, was published in HM September 1844.

1/I do not understand this passage.
2/Byron *Childe Harold's Pilgrimage* II 6
3/Since December 1843 Trafalgar Square had contained an equestrian statue of George IV. At Charing Cross, at the end of Cockspur Street, stood an equestrian statue of Charles I. Wellington's statue was 'inaugurated' on 18 June 1844, and the Exchange itself was opened on 28 October.
4/Hood's daughter notes that Phillips was 'tutor of the son of the Marquis of —.'
5/Unidentified
6/Completed in HM September, where it is preceded by the poem probably next referred to, that is, 'The Husk and the Grain'
7/Current off Portland, Dorset
8/A translation of Eugene Sue's novel was reviewed in *The Athenaeum* 27 April.
9/Wilhelm Meinhold's *Mary Schweidler: the Amber Witch*, published in English on 3 August
10/'Our Family,' appearingly serially in HM
11/Book IV of Ainsworth's novel, published in 1834, is entitled 'The Ride to York.'
12/Published in *Ainsworth's Magazine*
13/John S. Farmer *Slang and its Analogues* (1890–1904) defines the term back-slum as 'generally applied to the dens and rookeries of the criminal ... classes.'
14/ *2 Henry IV* I ii 215
15/If the Hoods are not named even in the *Post Office Directory*, this indicates how very poor they are. Hood had playfully reviewed the *Directory* in HM January, complaining about the omission of the entry 'authors' from it, *Works* IX 128.

TO
EDWARD WATKIN and PETER BERLYN

Dear Sirs,
I should sooner have answered your obliging letter, and the flattering invitation which it conveyed, but my state was so precarious, that it seemed presumptuous, without a *morning* certain in September, to speculate on a *soirée* in October. It would indeed afford me very great pleasure to be present at the meeting on the 3rd, but really I have not 'man' or 'chest' enough for Manchester; and, as for Mr. Disraeli,[1] might as well hope for an introduction to Ben Ledi or Ben Nevis! For me all long journeys, save one, are over. Recent experimental trips have shown that I am barely equal to water-carriage, and then 'with care,' like brittle glass or frail crockery. No slight hardship, while steam and rail afford such facilities for locomotion, to be compelled to renounce travelling! – to be incapable of physical activity just when young England is promising parochial May-poles and county Cricket. The truth is, I am a confirmed invalid, and almost set in for still-life – a condition irksome enough, and which would be intolerable but for the comfort and consolation I derive from the diversions of authorship and the blessed springs of Literature.
Fortunately the head – that has a mind to it – may travel without those pantings, which beset spasmodic lungs: the thoughts can expatiate without such palpitations as result from the excursions of the legs. Forbidden to walk, there is the run of the library; but I have already described the advantages of books and reading, by help of which even the bed-ridden may enjoy a longer range than Captain Warner's.[2] Suffice it, that experience and suffering have confirmed my former views;[3] that, if anything could aggravate the evil of becoming what the Scotch call 'a puir silly body,' it must be a poor silly mind, incapable of wholesome exercise, without appetite for intellectual food, or the power of digesting it.
And, as age and accidents to the human machinery will impair the strongest horse-power of health, whilst the fairest mercantile endeavour may fail to secure a fortune, I would earnestly forewarn all persons within reach of my counsel – especially the young – to provide against such contingencies by the timely cultivation and enrichment of that divine allotment, which it depends on ourselves to render a flower-garden or a dead waste – a pleasure-ground visited by the Graces and frequented by the Fairies, or a wilderness haunted by Satyrs.
But I need not dwell longer on these topics. You will have a chairman, who, inspired by his father's spirit, will discourse so eloquently of the pursuits and

amenities of literature,[4] and the advantages of the Athenaeum, that every leg in the hall will become a member. In brighter colours than mine, he will paint, to the 'new generation' of your busy city, the wholesome recreation to be derived from Science and Art – the instruction and amusement to be gained from works of Philosophy and Poetry, of History, Biography, and Travels; and last, not least, the infinite relief, amidst commercial occupations, of alternating matters of *Fiction* with *Fact*ory.

Pray accept my warmest wishes for the success of your *soirée*, and the permanent prosperity of your institution, and
Believe me, dear Sirs,
Yours ever truly,

Thomas Hood.

Edward Watkin, Esq.,
Peter Berlyn, Esq.,
Honorary Secretaries,
Soirée Committee.

Devonshire House, New Finchley Road, St. John's Wood / October 1st, 1844.

From *Memorials* II 224–6. For Watkin's name I have followed the spelling of the MS letter, see 581. This letter was read aloud by Richard Cobden to an audience of 3,200 at the *soirée*.

1/Benjamin Disraeli (1804–81), first Earl of Beaconsfield, MP since 1837, later Prime Minister. At Manchester, though the meeting was non-political, Disraeli was accompanied by Lord John Manners and George Smythe, members of the Young England group. Whilst in the north, he visited the homes of Lord Francis Egerton and Richard Monckton Milnes. Elsewhere Hood mentions Smythe and Young England, and Egerton and Milnes both helped in getting him the pension from government.

2/On 20 July 1844 Samuel Alfred Warner (d 1853) demonstrated the capability of his 'invention for destroying ships at sea,' *Annual Register* 'Chronicle' 77. According to DNB, Warner invented an 'invisible shell' and a 'long range,' a balloon used to drop the shell.

3/Expressed in *Memorials* II 153–7

4/Isaac D'Israeli (1766–1848), author of *Curiosities of Literature* (1791), *Calamities of Authors* (1812), as well as *The Amenities of Literature* (1841)

TO
MR and MRS D. KEAY

Dear Uncle & Aunt,
I have delayed writing, to send the First Volume of my Magazine which you will receive shortly after this: my own papers are marked in the index. I only was able

to resume the management last month – the four numbers previous were managed for me by a friend. You will see by the opinions of the Press, bound up with the Volume, that I have very good friends of all parties.
My illness in the Spring was very severe – spasms, & gasping for breath for 12 hours at a time. I had a very narrow escape, and am still very weak & much shattered, as I must not live well, for fear of spitting blood, & exciting the heart. I had three physicians. Indeed I am particularly fortunate in that respect, as two of my best friends Dr. Elliot & his brother are both very skilful practitioners. But I shall be obliged to remove from my present House – the clay soil is not good for me – I must be on gravel, high & dry, I derived much benefit from being at Blackheath near Greenwich, & lately from a trip to Calais for the sea air. I took Fanny with me who is suffering in a milder degree from my complaint – marsh fever. Tom is as usual; he goes to a day school, & gets on very well & he & his Master are very fond of each other. One of my correspondents, a naval surgeon,[1] has brought him a Brazilian monkey – as big as a squirrel, which is a great favourite for its size.
What a pity I was not Foreign Secretary instead of Lord Aberdeen, & Tom Junior Captain of the Royal Yacht, as then we might have looked in at the Ferry, in our way to Dundee.[2] As it is, there is as little chance of my going to Scotland as of your coming to London. My vehicle for the future is a hackney fly – or an arm chair.
By the bye I have been sitting lately for my bust to be done in marble for exhibition at the Royal Academy. The likeness is said to be very good. If I could travel, I should go to Manchester, having had a very handsome invitation to a grand meeting of 3000 persons at the Athenaeum; but the vibration of the railway, for so long a journey would be too wearisome for my loose bones. If balloons were manageable they would suit me best.
I have heard from Betsey that Jessy is so much better there is a probability of her being soon at liberty, & her husband talks of placing her in a boarding house.[3]
But I have great misgivings about her continuing well – her treatment at first was not judicious, & the cure is most easy in the early stage. Her boy is at boarding school. As for Betsy she goes on in her usual way getting more odd in her ways as she grows older: so that she will be a Curiosity at last.
Pray give my kind remembrance to Mr. & Mrs. Nicholson & thank him for his kind letter, which I ought to have acknowledged but was too unwell at the time & have since been overwhelmed with arrears of business from my long illness. I was sorry I did not meet them when they were in London, but hope for better fortune next time.
Our weather is fine & I am pretty well in spite of the Magazine & having to sit up

all one night last week to complete the work. But it will be easier in future. I hope you are both well & setting in comfortably for the winter; with a stock of mountain dew[4] for the cold days & nights. I am obliged to be content with good fires – which is lucky for the Monkey as it comes from a hot climate.
My wife, Fanny, & Tom unite with me in love to you both. Please to send me a line on receipt of the parcel – as if it does not reach you I will enquire after it.

I am Dear Uncle & Aunt
Your affectionate Nephew

Thos Hood

Devonshire Lodge / New Finchley Road / St John's Wood / 2nd October [*1844*]

MS Dundee. Published, with three omissions, by Elliot 152–4
1/Robert Douglas, who died in 1844
2/The Queen visited Dundee, 11 September 1844.
3/Hood wrote in 'My Tract' (1841), 'my poor sister has been excited by a circle of Canters ... into a religious frenzy, and is at this moment in a private mad-house,' Jerrold 408.
4/Whisky

TO
WILLIAM FINLAY WATSON

My dear Sir
I owe you many apologies for my delay in returning your paper. The truth is I have been but half alive – & for the last five months only writing etc by proxy, whilst I have been seeking for health & strength elsewhere. I have only just resumed the box & reins of the Magazine & of course found awful arrears to get through: – &, reduced to half speed instead of high pressure, am still in arrears.
The original M.S. of the Song of the Shirt is I suspect destroyed. I cannot find it. Ditto as to the Bridge of Sighs: – If I can discover a Scrap of Keats I will enclose it – but I fear not, as I did not know him personally. The sonnet in the Mag. was sent me, *copied*, from his M.S.[1]

Tom Junior is very well & desires his kind regards to yourself, & the ladies, with those of
Dear Sir Yours very truly

Thos Hood

— Watson Esqre

I fear there is no chance of my seeing Auld Reekie again, my travelling must consist of very short stages in future. I have been on the very edge of this world if it has an edge, & was slipping off into the next, but hitch'd somewhere. I find that I had made a Copy of the Bridge of Sighs, which, as it may suit your purpose, I enclose. The Scrap I send is genuine Keats – tho without his name – from Mrs. H's Autograph Book.[2]

Devonshire Lodge / New Finchley Road / St John's Wood / 8 October [*1844*]

MS NLS. Address: 'W.F. Watson Esqre./ 52. Princes Street/ Edinburgh/ NB.'

1/HM September 1844, contains Keats's sonnet beginning 'Life's sea hath been five times.' This deviates from the MS, 'Time's sea hath been five years.'

2/An adjacent MS contains Keats's sonnet 'On sitting down to read King Lear once again,' and is inscribed, 'sent me by Thos. Hood with MS. of Bridge of Sighs.'

TO
DAVID MACBETH MOIR

My dear Sir.

On my return from a trip to Calais, for the benefit of the sea air, I found your welcome note, & the Poems, just in time to get them into the Number.[1] Many many thanks for your kind remembrances & good will to the Mag which I ought sooner to have acknowledged, but I only resumed my task last month, with sad arrears to get thro without even my usual pony[2] powers of physical strength. In fact my life now is made up of alternations of effort & exhaustion. In such cases, where all cannot be performed, our friends are apt to come in for our postponements, their indulgence being more certain than that of strangers.

Last May I was at death's door – on the very threshold – all but walked in & left my mortal dust on the mat. I gasped for breath, in spasms, for 12 hours at a time, feeling, probably, very like a fish with too much air. Disease of the heart, my Esculapions say, aggravated by old Marsh Fever, producing a state similar to the ancient Sea Scurvy. Indeed so sensitive am I become as to Malaria that a minute or two on the drawbridge over Calais moat sent me home to the inn with sore throat.

But for this last shake I should have indulged hopes of revisiting Edin – & of course – Musselborough – But I am more sedentary than ever, some would say *chairy* of myself, so that sitting for my last bust lately seemed hardly beyond my usual still habits. Luckily, I have always been a domestic bird, & am therefore, not so

wretched from being incapable of passage. Still I should prefer health & locomotion, – riding here & there, to & fro – as you do – because others were ill & I was not. How you must enjoy walking to set a broken leg!
What is the Commemoration of Burns? Here it is a Bonfire on the 5th of November.

Since the foregoing I have dined, & being in consequence a better man, in strength, it just seems to me that by a *miraculous possibility* I may some day revisit the North, & enjoy one or two of those jaunts you hold out to me. Perhaps I may even be able, like Prince Albert, to deer stalk *out of a castle window*, or like her Majesty, be up at the death of a *Bag* otter.[3] So keep your wheels well greased, *till then*, & look to your linchpins, & give your horse or horses a few beans, & keep all your patients alive, & present my distant regards to Professor Wilson – & Doctor Blair, if you know him – I believe, & so does he, that he is somewhere in Edinburgh – but we are not quite sure.
Tom Junior is very well & joins heartily in kindest remembrances to yourself Mrs. Moir, & all the young folk:

I am My Dear Sir
Yours ever truly

Thos Hood

D.M. Moir Esqre

Devonshire Lodge / New Finchley Road / St John's Wood / 8 Octr [*1844*]

MS NLS

1/'Three Gaelic Melodies,' HM October 1844
2/As opposed to 'horse.' See 659.
3/Occasions described in *The Times* 24 and 26 September, 5, and 1 October, 4. *The Times* of the last date commented: 'It is questionable ... whether the otter, after so long a confinement in a close box, could have preserved the requisite spirit to afford a really fine hunt.' NED does not give bag otter, but gives '*Bag-fox*, a fox brought alive in a bag to be turned out before the hounds.'

TO
PHILIP DE FRANCK

Dear Johnny,
'Jack's alive!' Three doctors could not kill me, so I may live a year or two. But I almost went a-fishing in Lethe for forgotten fishes. You talk of my excess! Why, I am hardly allowed table-beer and water, and never go out to balls! Now you are

in the 'John-d'armes,' you ought to come and take a lesson of our new police,[1] who are almost as military as yours, and more civil I suspect. If you want a job, you shall mount guard at my Magazine and fight all my duels. Editors get into them now and then. I will write to the Prince. Tom says, he should so like to see you in green and gold, you must be so like a beetle!

[St John's Wood, October 1844]

From *Memorials* II 227–8, where the letter is dated.
1/Inaugurated by Peel's Act of 1829

TO
DOUGLAS JERROLD

Dear Jerrold.
I'm alive. Are you? If so the Bearer, Mr Moore,[1] wishes to make to you a literary proposition & has asked me for an introduction. I should think what he wants would suit your leisure if you have any. I have a little – Why don't you come some day & see

Dear Jerrold
Yours very truly

Thos Hood

I have been ¾ dead & even yet have not got back my animal ones from the world of spirits.

D Jerrold Esqre

Devonshire Lodge / New Finchley Road / [St John's Wood] Monday. [21 October 1844]

MS editor. The letter belongs with the following group, the first of which provides a date.
1/J. C. Moore, publisher of the *Novel Times* (1844–?)

TO

HORACE SMITH

My dear Sir.
I have been requested to introduce to you Mr Moore, who has some literary proposals to make to you: and therefore sent him to Brighton – but you are become

more Shakespearian & less Marryatian in your locality.[1] Are you going to finish, where gentle Will began, with Deer stealing? And are you too busy stalking for writing a novel, (the errand of Mr. Moore to you) – not in any given number of volumes, but, a more sensible plan, in one two or three – more or less, according to subject & inclination. If so, he is not unlikely to prove your man. I have been all but dead last Spring – which is a great comfort – it makes one so alive to being alive.

Mrs. H. unites with me in kind regards to yourself, Mrs. Smith, & family.

I am
My dear Sir
Yours ever truly

Thos. Hood

H Smith Esqre.

Devonshire Lodge / New Finchley Road / St. John's Wood / 22d. Octr. [*1844*]

MS Folger

1/Perhaps Smith has moved temporarily from Brighton by the sea, associated with Marryat, inland, to Stratford-on-Avon.

TO
FREDERICK MARRYAT

My Dear Sir,
I have been requested to introduce to you Mr. Moore, who has some literary proposal to make to you, which, as 'The Naval War with Young France' has evaporated,[1] you may have leisure to entertain. I believe he wants a novel, not necessarily a three-decker, but in one, two, or three vols., according to the subject or the author's inclination – to my thinking, a very sensible latitude.[2]

I am, my dear sir,
Yours very truly,

Thos. Hood.

St. John's Wood, / Oct 22, 1844.

From Florence Marryat *Life and Letters of Captain Marryat* (1872) II 172–3

1/Hood is perhaps referring to the controversy concerning the relative naval strengths of Britain and France which centred upon the Prince de Joinville.

2/Miss Marryat notes: 'The proposal made was that Captain Marryat should write a book, in three volumes, for a periodical about to be started, and called "The Novel Times." Nothing further, however, was done in the matter, as he himself maintained to Mr. Moore that his name would "do *the publication more harm than good.*" ' The first volume of the *Novel Times*, published by J.C. Moore, contains 'Things Old and New' by G.R. Gleig, and 'Letters from the Orient' by Ida, Countess Hahn-Hahn, translated by Samuel Phillips. The work commenced publication in weekly parts on 30 November 1844. In an advertisement in *The Athenaeum* 23 November, 1080, Marryat is referred to as a potential contributor, as well as G.P.R. James and Mrs Norton. In an advertisement in *Bent's Monthly Literary Advertiser* November, 170, Jerrold and Marryat are referred to as contributors.

TO
MRS ANNA MARIA HALL

My dear Mrs Hall.
I have long contemplated a visit to the Rosery,[1] but you may imagine how often my intents good bad or indifferent must be frustrated by my very capricious state of health. I should have been delighted to learn personally that you are quite recovered.
The Bearer, – Mr Moore has some literary proposition to make to you & has asked me for an introduction, I believe he wants some 'Tales of the *Hall*.'[2]
Mrs H unites in kind regards to yourself & Mr S.C. – with

Yours very truly

Mrs Hall. Thos Hood

Devonshire Lodge / New Finchley Road / Tuesday 22d Oct. [*1844*]

MS editor
1/Unidentified
2/An echo of Crabbe's title *Tales of the Hall* (1819)

TO
MARY RUSSELL MITFORD

My dear Miss Mitford.
It is so long since we have corresponded, I almost want a re-introduction to you, myself, before presenting to you Mr Moore, who wishes to make to you a literary proposal. The proposal to set a good new example of novels in any number of

volumes, or a solitary one as may suit the author's time, inclination, or subject. Perhaps you will be tempted by this arrangement to write one for him.
Pray accept my earnest good wishes for your health & happiness, – from a sick man & a sufferer in various ways they have a peculiar sincerity.

I am
My dear Miss Mitford
Yours very truly

Thos Hood

Devonshire Lodge / New Finchley Road / St John's Wood / 23. October. [*1844*]

MS UCLA. Mary Russell Mitford (1787–1855), author of *Our Village* (1824–32), novelist and dramatist, had contributed to the *London Magazine.*

TO
EDWARD BULWER-LYTTON

Dear Sir
I cannot say how vexed I have been to find when too late that you had expressed a particular wish for a proof. The article only reached me in print on Thursday night, with a Memorandum on the M.S which led me to infer that you, being unwell, had confided the correction to myself or Mr Ward:[2] & having carefully compared the sheet with the M.S. I sent it to press, the holiday on Monday[2] urging me to forward the printing of the Magazine. I earnestly hope you will find no material error – and there was no addition needed to a Dramatic Sketch which must make the reading public in general feel more interest in the Greek Hamlet, than they commonly take in classical subjects.[3]
It is difficult to express how highly I estimate such a token of your great kindness & consideration; the more so remembering your state of health & probable disinclination to literary occupation with which my own experience made me sympathise so strongly that several times I have been on the point of writing to request you to dismiss the matter altogether from your mind till a fitter season, lest the mere heat of composition & the feverishness of an untimely task should *mull* the cold water cure.[4]
Pray accept my most heartfelt thanks for this, & the great interest you have elsewhere taken in my behalf.[5] I can accept kindness from literary men, as from

relations, which I could not take from others, not endeared to me by admiration, respect, community of pursuit, & that mental intimacy which far transcends a mere personal acquaintance, and makes a name, a household word.
If it be true, as I have understood that you have taken leave of authorship, I shall reckon it no light honour to have had your last words in my Magazine;[6] the final act of your pen being devoted to a kindly & consistent purpose. But I am not selfish enough to desire such a distinction at the expense of so wide a circle: as your readers. Yet I will not formally wish that you may write again for the world, knowing that you will not be able to help it, any more than the flow of the tide, should mental or moral impulse urge you to work out some beautiful fiction, illustrate some great principle, or advocate some good cause. But in any case you have richly earned that dignified leisure,[7] with all its delights, which no one wishes you more abundantly or fervently than

Dear Sir Your most obliged & grateful Servant

Thos Hood

I resumed the management of the Magazine last month, from which you will infer that I am better: as well, perhaps, as I can ever be with my complaints. It is not well for me to work so much: but besides the necessity for exertion, from long habit my mind refuses to be passive, & seems the more restless from my incapacity for bodily activity. I sleep little, & my head instead of a shady chamber is like a hall, with a lamp burning all night. And so it will be to the end. I must die in harness like a Hero – or a Horse.[8]

Sir E.L.B Lytton Bart

Devonshire Lodge / New Finchley Road / St John's Wood / 31 October [*1844*]

MS Lady Cobbold. Published in *Memorials* II 228–30. A version in the BM is generally the same, except that it begins with the sentence, 'By the same post which brings this you will receive a Copy of the Magazine,' and instead of 'Thursday night' has 'Friday evening.' Edward George Earle Lytton Bulwer-Lytton (1803–73), first Baron Lytton, novelist, editor of NMM (1831–3), MP (1831–41), assumed the surname of Lytton in December 1843.

1/The memorandum reads: 'Lead well out proof to Mr Ward & Mr Hood,' MS Bristol Central Library.

2/On the 28th the Queen opened the new Royal Exchange.

3/Bulwer-Lytton's contribution, 'The Death of Clytemnestra,' appeared in HM November.

4/Following a collapse about January 1844, Bulwer-Lytton benefited from a cold water cure, which he describes in NMM September 1845, 1–16.

5/On 15 October Egerton had made a further plea to Peel in the cause of Hood's pension.

6/In the Dedicatory Epistle to *The Last of the Barons*, dated January 1843, Bulwer-Lytton wrote:

'this fiction is probably the last with which I shall trespass upon the Public' (1853 ed.) xiii. However, his literary contributions after this date were voluminous.
7/Cicero *Pro Publio Sestio* sec. 45
8/Perhaps remembering *Macbeth* 5 v 51: 'Blow wind, come wrack / At least we'll die with harness on our back!'

TO
J.T.J. HEWLETT

Dear Peter,
What is become of you – ? I have heard nothing of you directly or indirectly for two months – since I have resumed the Mag. at any rate
I have been expecting daily to see you walk in or should have written you before.
I want to see you: for I think I can find a customer for your novel – quite as good as Colburn, & it will make you more independent of him. Let me know if you are coming to town, in which case you shall meet the party here – If not, I will put you in communication with him – I think it would be worth your coming up.

Yours very truly

T.H.

King regard from Mrs H. & all here.

Devonshire Lodge [St John's Wood] / Saturday./ 2 Novr [1844]

MS Texas. The customer Hood refers to would be J.C. Moore.

TO
MRS GEORGIANA ELLIOT

My dear Mrs. Elliot,
I feel so much pleasure in your pleasure, and therefore am so well pleased in pleasing you both, that I could not but be delighted with your kind note. If all who read the paper would but feel it as you do, my object would be gained.
It was written in very serious earnest, – the case having made the strong impression on me I have described. My hope is that the 'Times' will take up the subject; I have sent a copy, through a mutual friend, to the Editors,[1] also a copy to Sir J.

Graham, who has sent me a formal acknowledgment of the receipt.[2] I fear he will do no more; they say he is a cold, hard man, bigoted to the New Poor Law.
Your friendly inference as to my comparative vigour is correct. I am better than could have been expected from the fag of two months, and, this one, have done more than usual. And next number is to be a sort of 'Comic Annual' number, with cuts for Christmas. So that I have plenty of work cut out. I may come one day to Stratford, to dine with the H—'s,[3] if I get on well, in which case you will see us of course. In the meantime kiss dear May and Jeanie for me, and give my love to Dunnie, and tell him the monkey is very well, but rather chilly; and Tom is military mad, playing with soldiers. Fanny much better for her medicine, for which pray thank the Doctor, and don't 'wish him the same.'
Jane, and all, unite in love to you, wholesale and retail, with

Yours ever truly,

Thos. Hood.

Devonshire Lodge, [St John's Wood] Saturday [2] Nov. 1844.

From *Memorials* II 234–5, where it is published with the following letter.
1/'The Lay of the Labourer' was reprinted from HM November 1844, in *The Times* 27 November, 5. Hood was concerned over the sentencing to transportation for life of Gifford White, a young farm-labourer, for threatening arson.
2/Printed in *Works* IX 247. Sir James Robert George Graham (1792–1861), Home Secretary. He was unpopular, partly through his handling of the problem of the Scottish church and the opening of letters in the mails. These are both referred to incidentally in Hood's letters.
3/Hopkins's

TO
WILLIAM ELLIOT

Dear Doctor,
Many thanks for your congratulations. I know you would not say that you like the paper on the 'Labourers' as a mere compliment, which makes your opinion worth a hundred criticisms. I hope it will do good to all parties, – to me among the rest, to be very candid – for I am a Labourer too. I do not think that I have been so exhausted, as I expected to have been, in proportion to my work.
I had not seen Ward since our trip to Calais till we met at Renshaw's, on the day of the Queen's Procession to the City.[1] I concluded that he was very busy in his new

abode, as he has been, with bricklayers, &c., and did not therefore expect any help from him.

I am,
Dear Doctor,
Yours ever truly,

Thomas Hood.

[St John's Wood] November 3rd, 1844.

From *Memorials* II 233–4

1/On 28 October 1844 the Queen opened the Royal Exchange. Renshaw's office was at 356 Strand, along her route. He was the publisher of HM.

TO FREDERICK OLDFIELD WARD

private

Dear Ward.
Your note recd last night – The immediate purport of this is to tell you as early as possible of the result of the application to Peel – by a letter from Lord F. Egerton. He offers 100 a year – with the option of having it on the life of 'a very near female relative'.[1] I should have preferred a provision that would help me to prolong my own.
Seriously it seems to me the reverse of liberal – (*two* having lately fallen in)[2] – & assigns me a place so much beneath that which the public has bestowed on me, I feel exceedingly tempted to decline.
Besides any literary claim, the case laid before Peel was a strong one, & there are three instances at least, where I think I might compete in authorship. Banim who wrote 2 or 3 novels – Cary, translator of Dante – & Miss Mitford, chiefly known by her 'village sketches'. Cary had some church preferment. Banim had had his debts paid by a subscription – Miss Mitford ditto – & each had 150 pension.[3]
After all my best friends are the reading Public – which will include the people ere long – & not ministers. The 'Labourers' was well noticed in Examiner – Britannia – Weekly and Morning Chronicle – Spectator – taken out bodily by the Herald[4] –

& was quoted by the big man in Wellington Street[5] who sells Heavy Dry at 4^d^ a pot.

I hurry this off to save the post with the news.

Yours affectly

Thos Hood.

Do not speak of the subject of this except to the Dr till settled. I shall write to Bulwer to tell him the result.

F O Ward Esqre

[*St John's Wood*] *Wednesday.* [*6 November 1844*]

MS Columbia. This letter precedes that below to Peel which Hood himself dates 9 November.
1/Peel made this offer in a letter to Egerton of 4 November 1844. It is an offer of a pension either for the length of Hood's own life or that of his wife. Hood is disgruntled that his own early death should be so easily allowed for.
2/Hood is assuming that the deaths of pensioners increase the amount of the pension fund, but this does not seem to have been the case. One of the pensions which had 'lately fallen in,' worth £200, was that of Thomas Campbell who died 15 June 1844. The second pension, also worth £200, was that of H.F. Cary, died 14 August.
3/John Banim (1798–1842), Irish novelist, received a civil list pension of £150 in 1836, with a further pension of £40 on account of his daughter. Peel had supported the subscription on his behalf. Mary Russell Mitford benefited from a public subscription, and received a civil list pension of £100 in 1837.
4/These notices all appeared between 2 and 4 November.
5/A street running off the Strand

TO
WILLIAM ELLIOT

My dear Doctor ...
It is not a handsome one – but the reverse – so much so that I am exceedingly tempted to decline it. The case put to Peel was, apart from literature, a very strong one – his offer is of a pension *the lowest ever yet granted to an author or authoress.* One cannot forget that two pensions have just fallen in – Campbell's of 2 or 300 a year, & Cary's of 150.
Banim, author of two or three Novels, having had his debts 800 paid by a public subscription, had a pension of 150. Cary – only a translator tho' a fine one – 150. He had had a place in the British Museum & some Church preferment – And lastly

Miss Mitford, chiefly popular for some Village Sketches, having had a subscription to pay her debts – 150 or 200. In good health & never writes a word now. The position assigned to me, is not at all in accordance with the one granted to me by the public. The proposition, to grant the pension on some other life – a female relative appears considerate – but at the same time, it tacitly admits, one of the claims urged the very bad state of my health & great precariousness of my life – which a better provision by setting me more at ease, might have helped to prolong ...
On the whole I feel very little inclined to take it.
Perhaps my best plan will be to make these representations to Lord F. Egerton, & place myself in his hands.[1]
The 'Labourer' has made a hit. The Herald took it out entire – 2 columns. The Examiner quoted it – Weekly Chronicle – Morning Chronicle – Britannia – Spectator – all with high praise. Dilke put it in the Ath[n] for his own purpose, without any comment.[2] We have not had the country papers yet. So I think I had better trust to the public or the people rather – *& a change of Ministry ...*

[*St John's Wood, 6 November 1844*]

From Maggs Bros. *Autograph Letters* no. 346 (Whitsun 1916) 66–7. The letter precedes the following letter to Peel which Hood himself dates.

1/On 8 November 1844 Egerton wrote to Ward, being eager for a reply from Hood. The next day he wrote to Peel, apologizing for not having replied to Peel's letter.

2/*Athenaeum*, 2 November, 1005. In spite of the apparent rupture in the friendship between Hood and Dilke, *The Athenaeum* remained sympathetic. On 7 December, 1119, the journal hopes that Hood will receive a pension. On 10 May 1845, 461, it contained a generous obituary notice by H.F. Chorley.

TO
SIR ROBERT PEEL

Sir
In your comparative leisure at Brighton,[1] – if a Prime Minister have even comparative leisure, you may find time to accept & relish the sincere acknowledgments of one whom you have served from motives rarely attributed to such patrons. Complaints have been often made of the neglect of Literature & literary men by the State. I have joined in them myself; but with reference to Authors in general, & as little to myself, as I thought of receiving a pension from the hands of Sir Robert Peel when I saw him, many years ago, at the opening of the New Hall, Christ's

Hospital.[2] Indeed such complaints commonly pointed at official employments, which if I had any ambition that way, I should be physically unable to undertake. I am quite aware of my unfitness for any of those posts hinted at by Mr Smythe in his recent speech.[3] Almost too thin to represent myself, I should make but an indifferent Ambassador, or Consul even, – As a Home Secretary I should be quite abroad – and as a Foreign one any where but at home. You may rely therefore on my gratitude involving no such future favours.[4] It contemplates, solely, the benefits you have already conferred upon me.

As an Author, I cannot but think it of good omen that such a mark of your favour has fallen on a Writer so totally disconnected with party as myself, whose favourite Theory of government is – an Angel from heaven, & a Despotism. As a Man, a husband and a father, I am deeply sensible of a considerate kindness which has made this working-day world more park like to me, as well as to Manchester;[5] & will render the poor remnant of my life much happier & easier than it could be, with the prospect that was lately before me.

My humble name has sufficiently occupied your thoughts already: yet may it recur to you, with its pleasanter associations, as often as you meet with a discontented partisan, or political ingrate!

Lord Francis Egerton having kindly offered to convey my acceptance & choice to you, I have forwarded them accordingly; but could not resist this direct expression of my feelings, and the respectful sentiments with which I have the honour to be

Sir Your most obliged & grateful Servant

Thos Hood

The Right Honble
Sir R. Peel Bart
etc etc etc.

Devonshire Lodge / New Finchley Road / St John's Wood. / Saturday 9th Novr [1844]

MS BM. Printed in *Memorials* II 239-40. The letter shows Hood's sensible decision to accept the pension offered him, despite the urgings of wounded pride. Peel replied to the letter in a kindly manner on the following day.

1/Peel went down to Brighton on 1 November.

2/This took place on 29 May 1829.

3/George Augustus Frederick Percy Sydney Smythe, seventh Viscount Strangford, second Baron Penshurst (1818–57), MP (1841–52). In his speech to the Manchester Athenaeum, reported in *The Times* 5 October 1844, 6, Smythe had pointed to the neglect of authors in Britain and to the fact that several foreign ambassadors were men of letters.

4/An interesting passage, not included in the letter actually sent to Peel, is to be found in *Memorials*

II 240: 'Such impressions have occasionally received confirmation from unlucky oversights, such as I suppose to have caused the omission of "Literature" from the Queen's answer to the Civic address, in which it was inserted. An unlucky omission I presume to say; for whatever differences may obtain in society, that will be an unlucky one, which distinguishes a Sovereign from a reading public, rapidly becoming a reading people.'
5/Peel contributed £1000 towards setting up public parks in Manchester 'to provide for those who are doomed to almost incessant toil the means of healthful recreation': *The Times* 12 September 1844, 4.

TO
SIR EDWARD BULWER-LYTTON

Dear Sir.
Many thanks for your very kind letter – confirming me in an opinion at which you shake your head. Nevertheless my experience tells me that besides liberal appreciation as a writer, I have received more kindness from Authors than from others, including relations. Of course the poor pen and ink people have their common share of human envy hatred, malice & all uncharitableness – not more perhaps – Two tradesmen who can hardly spell, shall exhibit at a vestry meeting as much bad spirit & uncordial compounds as the worst of us –
But the immediate purpose of the present writing is to inform you of the result of your friendly interest & good exertions in my behalf – A letter from Lord F Egerton encloses the quotation, from one by Sir R. Peel, of which I enclose a copy.
The arrangement which gives me the option of another life is kind & considerate, & relieves me from a very painful anxiety. I have of course accepted it cheerfully & gratefully.
The flattering consideration of those who have helped to this result make me affluent in feeling – For your own share in the work, pray accept again the heartfelt thanks of Dear Sir Your very obliged and grateful servant

Thos Hood

Sir E.L.B Lytton Bart

Devonshire Lodge / New Finchley Road / St John's Wood / Saturday. [*9 November 1844*]

MS Lady Cobbold. Published by the Earl of Lytton *Life of Edward Bulwer* (1913) II 66–7. Probably written two days before the following dated letter. Bulwer-Lytton surely had Hood in mind when he wrote bitterly in the introduction to Laman Blanchard's posthumous *Sketches from Life* (1846) xxiii-xxiv: 'for the author there is nothing but his pen, till that and life are worn to the stump: and then, with good fortune, perhaps on his death-bed he receives a pension – and equals, it may be, for a few months, the income of a retired butler!'

TO
WILLIAM ELLIOT

Dear Doctor.
I send you copies of my letter to Sir R Peel, – & his *very kind* reply just come to hand.[1] It is very gratifying indeed.
I wrote to Lord Egerton – but think the Premier had not yet seen it, as thro our Post-irregularity, it would not get to Lord E. perhaps till today.
It is odd that it did not strike any of us that tho we got a longer life in Fanny's, – in case she married (say at 20) – it would be but 6 years – for then it would not be hers even. Perhaps this will be seen – as I only gave the names & ages of wife & daughter, not selecting either.[2]
Ward was to have dined with us yesterday but he had forgotten a previous engagement & did not come. But he was up here on Saturday night.
Now I have got the ear of the Premier what can I do for you? Should you like to be Physician to the Forces?
I am sorry that this cannot go tonight, as it is past 8 – for you will be pleased, and I wish it were sooner, after all my less agreable communications.

God bless you all. We join in loves to you
Yours ever truly

Thos Hood

We have sold 20 more copies of the Mag. this month. There was a capital notice in the League on Saturday which circulates 28000 – The effect of it, 'tis yet too soon to feel.[3]

Devonshire Lodge [St John's Wood] Monday Evening [11 November 1844]

MS Yale. Address: 'Dr Elliot.' The letter is dated in another hand the 12th, but Monday was the 11th. Published in part in *Memorials* II 242–3.

1/Printed in *Memorials* II 241–2
2/The pension was granted to Jane Hood.
3. *The League* 9 November 1844, 105–6

TO
J.T.J. HEWLETT

Dear P.P.
Do not *conclude* any thing with Colburn till I have seen you. It is not unlikely he may only offer *to share profits*, as he has proposed to Douglas – & of course there will be none to share, – any more than in my 'Whimsicalities'.
The party I allude to proposes to *purchase* novels – & you would be in good company – e.g. Gleig – Marryat – Mrs Norton etc. I have mentioned you, & that I believed you had a novel finishing or finished. All other matters when we meet

Yours very truly

Thos Hood

Devonshire Lodge [*St John's Wood*] / *Tuesday.* [*12 November 1844*]

MS Texas. Appears to follow that of 2 November to Hewlett, 660

TO
FREDERICK OLDFIELD WARD

Dear Ward
Peel's letter is very gratifying – and especially in the praise he bestows on my humourous writings, – but I should be very loth to publish it, or let it be published, with or without his leave, or so seem to make use of it for a puff or advertisement. It is highly flattering to have any man of cultivated mind & taste for a 'Constant Reader' & admirer – but the opinion even of a Premier has no *literarary* weight:[1] a letter from an eminent Critic or Author, like Lord Jeffrey, Coleridge, or Southey[2] would be a different matter & might appropriately be put forward as a testimonial from Judges in one's own Profession.
I feel sure Sir Robert intended a private communication & tho he might not refuse his assent a request could constrain him in future communications liable to be used as placards or posters.
Pray therefore do not let the copy go beyond yourself for whose private gratification it was intended. I am so anxious on this point that I write hastily to save the post.[3]

Yours affectly

Thos Hood.

[*St John's Wood, November 1844*]

MS Columbia. Ward suggested the publication of Peel's letter, referred to in Hood's last. On 16 November 1844 Peel wrote Hood a formal notification of the granting of the pension, and notified Egerton of this.

1/Perhaps Hood varies the spelling to emphasize the weight.

2/Robert Southey (1774–1843), poet laureate from 1813

3/That is, avoid missing

TO

WILLIAM ELLIOT

Dear Doctor,

Sir R. Peel came up from Burleigh on Tuesday night, and went down to Brighton on Saturday. If he had written by post I should not have had it till to-day. So he sent his servant with the following *on Saturday night*, another mark of considerate attention.

— wanted to write to Sir R. Peel for permission to publish his former letter, but I wrote and begged him not – it was obviously a private letter; and though Sir R. might not refuse, he would take care not to write to me again, if I merely used him as a puffing advertisement.

The 'Labourer' has made a great hit, and gone though most of the papers like the 'Song of the Shirt.' I think it will tell in the sale at the end of the year. I have been very unwell. One day, Jane says, I looked quite *green*. I don't wonder, there has been so much wet, and I observe all the compo ornamental part of the houses, finished here only in autumn, has turned green too. But my well is not dry. I have pumped out a sheet already of Christmas fun, am drawing some cuts, and shall write a sheet more of my novel.[1]

God bless you all.

Yours ever truly,

Thos. Hood.

Devonshire Lodge [St John's Wood], Monday Morning, Nov. [18], 1844.

From *Memorials* II 244, where the letter is dated 17th; however, Monday was the 18th. The Queen paid a visit to the Marquess of Exeter at Burghley House, Northamptonshire, adjoining Stamford in Lincolnshire (see 670), from 12 to 15 November. Peel was there during that time, so he must have come up on the Friday, not Tuesday as the Memorialists have it.

1/'Our Family,' serialized in HM, but not completed

TO
SIR ROBERT PEEL

Sir,

I have to acknowledge the receipt of your very gratifying communication, & the considerate kindness which provided for my receiving on Saturday evening so welcome a proof of your thoughts of me in Lincolnshire. It is well to be remembered by a Prime Minister: better still not to be forgotten by him in a Hurly: Burleigh. I am so inexperienced a Pensioner – unlike the father of a friend of mine, who was made in his infancy a superannuated Postman – as to be quite ignorant of the etiquette in such cases; but in the absence of knowledge, I feel that it would be but proper to thank the Queen for her gracious approval. May I request of your goodness to lay my humble, dutiful, & grateful acknowledgments at Her Majesty's feet, with the respectful assurance that an Author who has lived conscious of his good name being the better part of his children's inheritance will never disgrace her Royal favour?

Your letter of the 11th – which is deposited amongst my literary heir-looms – I hesitated to answer, partly because it gave rise to feelings which would keep without congealing; & partly from knowing, editorially, the oppression of too many 'communications from correspondents'. But I may say here how extremely flattered I am by your handsome judgment & liberal praise of my writings; nearly all of which you must have seen, if you have read the acknowledged ones. The Anonymous, comprise a very few trifles and reviews; and even against these, as a set off, my name has been affixed to pieces which I did not write – for instance, a Poem on the Sale of the Stud of King William the Fourth.[1]

As you have done me the high honour to seek beyond this impersonal acquaintance, I shall be most proud & happy to wait on you at your pleasure.[2]

I have the honour to be,
Sir
Your very obliged & grateful Servt

Thos Hood

The Right Honble
Sir R. Peel Bart
etc etc etc.

Devonshire Lodge / New Finchley Road / St John's Wood / 18th Novr 1844

MS BM. Published in *Memorials* II 245–6

1/See 331.

2/Hood and Peel did not meet.

TO

FREDERICK OLDFIELD WARD

My dear Ward.

I wish you had told me you had written to Bulwer on encreasing the pension. Pray let it be – I have written to Sir R. Peel today & closed the whole affair. My wish has been complied with as the arrangement stands: & I shall now be placed in a false position if you move in any such way & besides cannot & would not accept it. As to my writing only ½ a sheet a month, that is out of the question – injustice to the Magazine – who is to write instead of me – or have you engaged anyone to finish my novel for me?[1] –

Sir Robert will have my letter tomorrow morning which is *conclusive*. Do not force me to repudiate your application as I must, if you make it. In haste

Yours affectely

T. Hood.

I shall do nothing for the drains – which would be for the Landlord.[2]

It is but the other day that you wrote me a long note about Lady Bell[3] to persuade me that the pension was enough – at any rate as much as I could expect.

[*St John's Wood, 18 November 1844*]

MS Columbia. Written on the day of Hood's previous letter to Peel

1/Hood feels that Ward's assumption that he is so sick that he is unable to complete 'Our Family' is unwarranted, and an insult to his own desire to live and to lead an active life.

2/Perhaps Ward had suggested that the drains at Devonshire Lodge needed attention, and Hood is, in a typical mood of this unhappy stage of his life, rebuffing him.

3/Sir Charles Bell (1774–1842), discoverer of the distinct functions of the nerves. In 1843 his widow Marion was awarded a civil list pension of £100 in consideration of her husband's services to science.

TO
WILLIAM ELLIOT

Dear Doctor
Another Wardism – enclosed. On Sunday night I showed him Peel's note with the Queen's approval, so the thing is done & cannot be opened again, now at any rate. He never told me a word of writing to Bulwer tho we had a private tête à tête – and then yesterday comes the enclosed – the more inconsistent as he wrote to me about a week ago when I felt a little disappointed – about Lady Bell's 100 a year & that it was as much as I could expect. He will ruin me with Peel to whom I had written again expressing satisfaction. In fact the proposition which amounts to giving me 250 *more* would be insulting to Sir Robert. But there appears something more in the background.
I am to be pensionned off – & virtually give up the Magazine – for 8 pages a month would not allow even the carrying on the novel – which I presume Ward is then to assume. This may seem harsh, but his conceit is so insatiate & his conduct is so very strange that it is not reconcilable with any straight forward principle.
It worried me ill last night – for the thing was all settled & comfortable –

Yours ever truly

Thos Hood

Devonshire Lodge [*St John's Wood, 19 November 1844*]

MS Cameron. The letter is dated in another hand.

TO
FREDERICK OLDFIELD WARD

Dear Ward.
You certainly did *not* mention on Sunday night your correspondence with Bulwer about an increase of the pension, & the 'move' could not have my concurrence, as it must have occurred previously to Sunday, since you had his answer on *Monday*.
I could not concur in a proposition that would be almost an insult to Peel, – asking for £350, after his grant of 100, which I had accepted gratefully, in consideration of its being settled on another. You saw my letter, – & could not reconcile any such proceeding with the tone of it. I must beg therefore to know if you have written to him, as I shall be placed in that case in a false & apparently hypocritical position.

You saw too, Sir Robert's letter with the Queen's approval – which closed the matter at all events for the present. Any application for increase could only be made in future, & as in the case of my breaking down in health and giving up the Magazine. Certainly not now, when I am doing more than usual, & successfully – I am not a young hand at the work, – which is A.B.C to me as to the mechanical part, & as to the writing, if the spring flows what purpose would it answer to stop it? I have nearly got thro three months very well, – & have no *immediate* reason to fear sinking under it. If I can do a sheet – good – if I can do two – so much the better – for me and the Magazine. It is pleasanter to earn it than to have it by Pension.

Devonshire Lodge [*St John's Wood*] / *Wednesday.* [*20 November 1844*]

MS Columbia. The letter is placed here because it fits in with those given previously.

TO
WILLIAM ELLIOT

Dear Doctor
I send you another of Ward's notes, the last I shall trouble you with, as my mind is made up on the subject.
His first statement is simply an untruth. He did *not* mention the matter to me on Sunday – if so, why did he need to write to inform me of it on Monday? And I could not concur in a move on Sunday, – which he had *previously* made, for he had Bulwer's answer on Monday. And how could I join in any thing so outrageous, – & contrary to the tone & spirit of my own letter to Peel – which Ward saw, – & therefore, his proceeding was the worse.
Then he stated to me on Sunday that Phillips agreed with him as to the publication of Peel's letter, & concurred that it seemed written intentionally for publication. Phillips denies this, & says to me I ought to treat Peel as between one gentleman & another, not looking how in every way I can squeeze or turn him to account – Which is sense –
My own impression is that Ward is very anxious to inform the world that he has procured me a pension, & would like to publish my correspondence with Sir R. Peel along with one of his own.
As regards the Magazine, had his intentions been merely what he professed nothing could be more simple. To resign it to me, glad that I could resume it, holding

himself ready to afford future help if needed. But he surely did not consider *me* when he formed a scheme for turning the Mag. into a political one & told me in answer to my protest that he did not care for my prospectus. And it was part of his plan no doubt to make it the organ here, of Fourrierism, & his French Journalists, whom he corresponds with. All I got for my interference on my own behalf was the imputation of editorial jealousy.

After all that passed about the Polka paper, I was told, that there was a rise in the sale, & in consequence of that article, which actually did injury[1] – whereas it appears from Renshaw that *there was no rise whatever*. Now that there really is one he wants to step in again & divide the credit of it. The plea of helping me is a mere pretence. The very first month that I resumed the Magazine instead of the slightest help he deliberately hindered me – all the rest was done but his articles, & he would not even give up an additional delay to go home & hunt out mottoes for it – in spite of my remonstrance & the printer's, and a very severe rebuke from the head manager about night work & expense. And yet he warns me about disgusting Spottiswoode's on these very accounts – & taunts me with being almost too late last month – if it was so, not fault of mine but at the office, for my part was done – Yet, in the face of this, he himself wanted me to delay the Number still later to communicate with Bulwer, through his own omission, in not choosing to communicate to me Bulwer's letter about his article, & instructions. I may mention here that Ward *asks* to see my letters but keeps his own correspondence to himself – as regards the magazine – & has so much 'editorial jealousy' he has never asked me to meet any of the parties, nor even offered to introduce me to Winter, who has wished it. In fact with whatever better feelings he set out he has made the Mag. entirely subservient to his own views & vanity – not only putting his own name – unknown in literature, – before those of the other writers – & having his own papers separately printed for distribution, but paying himself at a higher rate than any one but myself. Most of the Contributors receive 10 and one receives 12 guineas a sheet – Ward charges 16, the same as I used to have from Colburn. The main spring of the whole is self conceit, which spoils every thing, & makes him alternate injury with benefit & kindness with insult. His very last proposition to help me, was by writing two articles ag^{t} which I objected. Another of his recent proposals was to have a number of French designs in the Magazine – to make it in short as little as possible Hood's or English. The result is I am so constantly worried & annoyed by ambiguous proceedings, that I have made up my mind *never to accept any service or help from him again.*[2]

I have been very unwell with short breath – it appeared to be consequent on some visceral obstruction from the hernia fever at the abdomen. And a slight influenza from so much wet – much rattling & wheezing in the chest, – a cough & expectoration, but merely loose phlegm & not a trace of blood. Meanwhile the spring runs fluently – my Mag is almost done – woodcuts & all. Mere *work*, whilst fluent, does not try me – I must sit or lie still, & must be employed – but agitation anxiety & worry knock me up. God bless you all

Yours ever truly

Thos Hood

[*St John's Wood, 21 November 1844*]

MS Cameron. The letter is dated in another hand.

1/Hood seems to have regarded the injury as moral rather than commercial.

2/It was evidently Ward who persuaded Landor to contribute to HM March and April 1845. Landor wrote to him on 13 February: 'Mr. Hood has a right to any services a literary man, great or small, can offer him': Emily Driscoll *Catalogue of Autograph Manuscripts* no 10 (1950) item 122.

TO

WILLIAM ELLIOT

Dear Doctor,

I took last night nearly a glass of wine in some gruel, which, with a good deal of sleep, has revived me. My head is clear (to begin with the author's index); the fever heat is gone – so are the musicals – the whistlings and wheezings; and I cough seldom. Heart quite quiet; this time it seems to have been blameless. On the whole, more comfortable than for some time while the attack was breeding.

I heard the other day the following fact – very creditable to the humbler class of readers. Holywell Street, Strand, is the head-quarters for cheap, blasphemous, and obscene publications, including the French. The chief man there is one —, but who has besides a more legitimate trade in distributing the periodicals among the minor dealers. To engage his services in this line, the proprietor of the 'N— T—,'[1] just starting, called on him, when — asked if it was to be respectable (*i.e.* not immoral), as otherwise he would have nothing to do with it: they had tried the other line, but it did not answer – it did not *take*.

Yours very truly,

Thos. Hood.

[*St John's Wood*] *November 23rd.* [*1844*]

From *Memorials* II 246–7
1/*Novel Times*

TO
MR and MRS D. KEAY

My dear Uncle & Aunt.
You will be glad to hear what follows, so I take the first opportunity of writing. One or two Pensions have lately fallen in to the Crown by the death of the parties. Out of these Sir Robert Peel with the Queen's approval has settled on me a Pension of One Hundred Pounds a year for my literary services, which as I am not a political writer is very flattering. I said settled on *me* – but I ought to have said, that my life being so precarious, it is considerately settled on my Wife's life instead, at my request.
In communicating this to me Sir Robert Peel wrote to me a most handsome letter, with high praise of my works, of which he is a reader, and expressing a wish for my personal acquaintance.
I have just had a rather serious attack of illness but am better. I hope you & my Uncle will get comfortably through the winter. Some of the weather: wise say we are to have a severe one.
We have not seen or heard any thing of Mr Nicholson – I suppose he has not come up yet – or has he built himself into London wall by mistake for a stone thereof? There is no news – or if there is I have not heard it. I have just written a song which like the Song of the Shirt has been in almost all the papers – called 'The Lay of the Labourer'. It will comfort me before I die to have done some service to my poor countrymen, & country women.
My Wife – Fanny – & Tom send their love to you both. Tom's little Marmoset, between a monkey & a squirrel, has survived the poor fellow who brought it for him from the Brazils – a young navy surgeon, by name Robert Douglas of Glasgow. I have not seen Betsey very lately but understand that Poor Jessy was expected lately to be let out, but it was found to be not safe. I fear it is now quite a hopeless case. She was so ill managed at first, which is the important time. Now her malady is confirmed.

God bless you both.
I am Dear Uncle & Aunt
Your affectionate Nephew

Thos Hood

Pray keep the 'Song of the Shirt' I shall be able in the beginning of the year to send you a Portrait that is being engraved from my Bust, & which is said to be a strong likeness.

Devonshire Lodge / New Finchley Road / St John's Wood / 30th Novr [*1844*]

MS Dundee. Published, with the reference to 'Poor Jessy' omitted, by Elliot 157–8

TO
J.T.J. HEWLETT

Dear P.P.
I hardly expected to see you again – so much as you must have to do in your short visits to town.
I am better – my cough and expectoration diminished– but am advised to keep in bed this severe weather, for fear of cold. It is bitter – & what a dull sky! However, I have kept up my spirits & done my drawings for next number. A propos – do not forget that it is Xmas month, & printers will make holiday – so pray let me have your paper early if it is to go in this number.
You mentioned as subjects Our Overseer, Our churchwarden – our guardian etc – *One* will do very well occasionally – but not as a regular series, as I am anxious for variety, and do not wish for a regular set at the Poor Laws à la Times – Do you understand?
I hope Colburn will come down handsome, for your Novel: – but he seems to be on the *vamping* lay[1] – to judge by that 'Comic Miscellany' by Poole,[2] which of course is of *old* matter – for Poole is past pen work.
We are going to have a hard winter I fear. Our water pipes are friz[3] – but the wine pipes isn't, which is a comfort.
I have seen nobody – so have no news to tell you.
Good shooting now in your parts I should think.

Yours ever truly

T. Hood.

Devonshire Lodge [*St John's Wood*] / *Saturday.* [*December 1844*]

MS Texas. Dated on the evidence of the second paragraph

1/Scheming to swindle. For 'vamp' Pierce Egan in *Grose's Classical Dictionary of the Vulgar Tongue* (1823) gives: 'to refit, new dress, or rub up old hats, shoes, or other wearing apparel: likewise, to put new feet to old boots. Applied more particularly to a quack bookseller.'

2/Advertised as now ready in *The Athenaeum* 21 December 1844, 1180
3/The earliest date given to this participle by Eric Partridge *Dictionary of Slang* (5th ed. 1961) is 1887.

TO
WILLIAM JERDAN

Dear Jerdan
Many thanks for your kind paragraph about the Pension.[1] I meant to send you an *authentic* report of it for the Gazette, but the intentions of sick men are far from performance. It was done most kindly & considerately by Sir R Peel from whom I had a very handsome letter. It is £100 a year – settled on Mrs Hood – at my request – for my life is not worth a year's purchase: my health & body are so shattered. In the Spring I had a desperate struggle – was at Death's door, & heard the hinges creak – but escaped. And it does not seem very consistent with my *appearance* in the Magazine – but I am writing this in bed where I have been for the last six weeks – under the care of two M.Ds from just beyond the Border. I seem adopted into the Elliot clan – for they have been to me such friends as relatives *ought to be*. Of course with a young Periodical to nurse I must work – one comfort is it keeps rising.

All good wishes to you & yours from
Dear Jerdan
Yours very truly

Thos Hood

W. Jerdan Esqre

Devonshire Lodge / New Finchley Road / St John's Wood / Dec. 30 [*1844*]

MS editor
1/In *Literary Gazette* 28 December 1844, 854

1845

TO

MR AND MRS D. KEAY

My dear Aunt & Uncle

Some time back I wrote to inform you of a piece of news that I thought would please you. That Sir Robert Peel had given me a Pension of £100 a year – which at my request was settled on my Wife – as likely to survive me. So that whatever may happen to me there is some provision so far for my family. As these Pensions are bestowed on men or women who have distinguished themselves in Science or Literature, it is honourable to me, & was rendered still more gratifying by a very handsome letter from Sir Robert, that he was a reader of my works of which he spoke in high terms – concluding with a wish for my personal acquaintance.

I have repeated this, fearing that my former letter may have miscarried. I hope you have not been ill. I am sorry to say that I have, – it is now six weeks that I have been in bed, but I hope to be up in a day or two.

I have no other news. We have not seen any thing yet of the Nicholsons.

I shall be able to send you next month a Portrait of me that is being engraved from the bust. They say it is a very good likeness.

Please to send me a line to say whether you got my former letter, – & that you have not been ill.

We all unite in love to you & Uncle. Fanny & Tom will write one of these days.

I am Dear Uncle & Aunt
Your affectionate Nephew

Thos Hood

Betsy was here yesterday – & poor Jessy continues in the same state. In fact the case is hopeless.

Devonshire Lodge / New Finchley Road. St John's Wood / Jany 4. [*1845*]

MS Dundee. Published, without the final reference to Jessy, by Elliot 159–60

TO
WILLIAM ELLIOT

Dear Doctor Elliot
It is my especial request that if any thing happens to me now, I may be opened, to see the cause of this extraordinary cough – seeming connected with the rupture. It is spasmodic between retching & coughing as if I wanted vainly to bring up part of my stomach or bowels.

God bless you all
here & hereafter

T. Hood

I feel sure you will find some unusual complaint.

[*St John's Wood, 7 January 1845*]

MS Yale. Address: 'Dr Elliot / Stratford Green / Stratford'; dated in another hand. According to *Memorials* II 270, the post-mortem examination which Hood here requests did take place.

TO
WILLIAM JOHN BRODERIP

My dear Sir.
I ought to have sooner acknowledged the receipt of your note with an explanation of the cause of the errors you alluded to. The *truth* is, tho it may seem very inconsistent with my doings in the Magazine for the last 2 months (say from the 15 Nov^r) I have been confined to my bed – & obliged to trust more than usual to the printers. You will easily however understand that with a young Periodical & the interest of another Proprietor at stake, there are efforts that I *must* make – even tho bedridden – & alas! that too many things must go undone.
I shall still hope some day to have the pleasure of making your personal acquaintance if I get taken up before you on purpose[1] & am My dear Sir Yours very truly

Thos Hood

W.J. Broderip Esqre.

Devonshire Lodge / New Finchley Road / S^t. John's Wood / Saturday. / in bed. /
[*January 1845*]

MS Bodleian. The letter is dated 1845 in another hand. Published in *Memorials* II 248–9, and in facsimile in *The Autographic Mirror* (1864) II 146. Hood indicates the month in the body of the letter.

1/Broderip was magistrate at the Thames police court.

TO

MARK LEMON

Dear Lemon.

I think it would be a funny design for Leech – A Scene in the Croix de Gardy? – Venus lamenting for Adonis (Lord Brougham) slain by the Wild Boar – Vide Shakespeare's Venus & Adonis – Also – Brougham playing at 'Follow my *Leader*'[1] I have not forgot Punch, ever, but I have had a sad time – at Death's door *& looked in* in Spring, a little better at Blackheath & then a relapse – I have now been the last two months *in bed*, & doubt if I shall walk again. All my animal spirits almost have been shaken out of me. Kind regards to B & E.[2]

In haste Yours very truly

Thos Hood

Devonshire Lodge [*St John's Wood*] / *Tuesday.* [*January 1845*]

MS editor. The reference to 'the last two months' suggests that the letter belongs to the time of that previously given.

1/Henry Peter Baron Brougham and Vaux (1778–1868), Lord Chancellor (1830–4). He returned from Paris on 2 February 1845, having been away since 26 October. I do not understand the meaning of Hood's allusion to him.

2/Bradbury and Evans

TO

N.N. HOLMES

There is money due for an article in my Magazine £9:7/–, unless he, (Mr Douglas), had drawn it thro' his Agent, which I will ascertain of my Publisher ... I have one or two little poems and some MS. of Douglas, which was not used, and will look it out and transmit it to his father.

[*St John's Wood, January 1845*]

MS Bristol Central Library. These sentences are quoted in a letter from N.N. Holmes to Jane Hood, asking for the money. The letter is dated 4 September 1845, but it bears the pencilled note, 'paid Febr 11–1845.'

TO
UNKNOWN CORRESPONDENT

As I have publicly acknowledged the authorship of the 'Song of the Shirt,' I can have no objection to satisfy you privately on the subject. My old friends Bradbury and Evans,[1] the proprietors of *Punch*, could show you the document conclusive on the subject. But I trust my authority will be sufficient, especially as it comes from *a man on his death-bed.*

[*St John's Wood, February 1845*]

From Jerrold, 368, who says the letter was written over a year after the publication of 'The Song of the Shirt.'

1/Indicative of this friendship are four letters from Jane Hood written in 1844 and 1845 to Bradbury and Evans which are in the *Punch* office.

TO
SIR ROBERT PEEL

Dear Sir.
We are not to meet in the flesh. Given over by my Physicians, & by myself, I am only kept alive by frequent instalments of mulled port wine. In this extremity, I feel a comfort for which I cannot refrain from again thanking you, with all the sincerity of a dying man – & at the same time bidding you a respectful farewell. Thank God my mind is composed, & my reason undisturbed – but my race as an Author is run. My physical debility finds no tonic virtue in a steel pen. Otherwise, I would fain have written one more paper – a forewarning one, against an evil, or the danger of it, arising from a literary movement in which I have had some share – a one-sided humanity, opposite to that catholic Shakespearian sympathy which felt with King as well as peasant:[1] & duly estimated the mortal temptations of both stations. Certain classes, at the poles of society are already too far asunder: it should be the duty of our writers to draw them nearer by kindly attraction, not to aggravate the existing repulsion, & place a wider moral gulf between Rich & Poor,

with Hate on one side, & Fear on the other. But I am too weak for this task, the last I had set myself. It is death that stops my pen, you see, – not a pension. God bless you, Sir – & prosper all your measures for the benefit of my beloved Country.

I have the honour to be
Sir
Your most grateful & obedient Servt

Thos Hood

The Right Honble
Sir R Peel
etc. etc, etc.

Devonshire Lodge / New Finchley Road / St John's Wood / Feby 17. 1845.

MS BM. Published in *Memorials* II 256–7, followed by Peel's reply.
1 / 2 *Henry IV* 3 i 1–31 and *Henry V* 4 i 226–80

TO
BRYAN WALLER PROCTER

Dear Procter, – I feel so *sure* that you do not know of my state, or you would come and see me, that I do not hesitate to ask it. I have been three months in bed, and am given over; but, as I have never been quite alive for some years, was quite prepared for such a verdict.
As one of my earliest literary friends, come and say good-bye to

Yours, ever truly,

Thomas Hood.

Devonshire Lodge, / New Finchley Road, / St. John's Wood [*February 1845*]

From Bryan Waller Procter *Autobiographical Fragment* (1877) 292

TO
MR and MRS D. KEAY

My dear Uncle & Aunt
With this you will receive a Magazine with the Portrait of me, which I promised. I little thought to have been alive at this date, – but some strong point in my constitution has made a desperate struggle to recover, though in vain. I am now helpless in bed, dreadfully swollen by dropsy from weakness & have suffered very much: – but only bodily – for my mind has been calm & resigned, as Mr Nicholson would inform you. I was glad he came, on that account, for I have been a good deal persecuted by Betsey, who you know has some peculiar religious notions of her own, & would very likely describe me to you, as dying a pagan, or infidel, because I do not conform to her views.
God bless you both – we shall soon meet I hope in a better world –
Let it comfort you to know that I die beloved & respected & have met with unexpected kindness & distinction from very many strangers as well as friends. These are probably the last lines I shall write.

Your Affectionate Nephew

Thos Hood.

24th Still alive – but cannot last long – God bless you & again a last Farewell – T.H.

Devonshire Lodge, / New Finchley Road, / St John's Wood / 12 March 1845.

MS Dundee. Published in facsimile by Elliot 161–3

TO
J.T.J. HEWLETT

Dear P.P.
Still alive – but enormously swollen with dropsy & cannot last long.
I fear you have been vexed at the omission of your paper – not more than I have been, – but the truth is Ward, under pretence of assisting, superseded all other arrangements for the purpose of getting in his own paper, at the last hour – & having reserved *first place* for it, overran the quantity, & you will perceive had to insert 4 extra pages, – numbered twice over with the same numbers.[1] He served

other contributors the same – & I do not feel disposed to bear the blame. Hence these few last lines for I know you did your *earliest* as I had requested.
God bless you, & goodbye – I have reserved for you a proof of the Portrait, *autographed* by

Yours ever truly

Thos Hood

Devonshire Lodge [St John's Wood] / Saturday [15 March 1845]

MS Texas. On the back is written: 'Hood's *last* March 15th 45.
1 /Ward's 'Phantoms and Realities of a Starlight Night,' the first article in HM March 1845

TO
G.B. WEBB

Sir
I have much pleasure in acceding to your wish, though I did not write the lines on Mr Bish,[1] having at the time to fry some other fish.
As I am about going I know not where, if you want another Autograph, you must apply to my Heir.

I am Sir
Yours most obeditly

Thos Hood

G.B. Webb Esqre

Devonshire Lodge / New Finchley Road / St John's Wood / 19 March / 1845.

MS John Clubbe. Published in facsimile by him facing 194.
1 /Lottery agent. Jerrold *Poetical Works* 422–3, attributes to Hood 'To Thomas Bish,' published in NMM, but I have not traced the poem there.

TO
DAVID MACBETH MOIR

Dear Moir,
God bless you and yours, and good-by! I drop these few lines, as in a bottle from a ship water-logged, and on the brink of foundering, being in the last stage of

dropsical debility; but though suffering in body, serene in mind. So without reversing my union-jack,[1] I await my last lurch. Till which, believe me, dear Moir,

Yours most truly,

Thomas Hood.

[*St John's Wood, March 1845*]

Published in *Memorials* II 255. On Monday 5 May 1845 Ward wrote to R.M. Milnes: 'Poor Hood has gone at last – released from sufferings the most protracted and terrible I ever witnessed. He died Saturday afternoon at 5.30': T.W. Reid *Life of Milnes* I 349.

1/Signal of distress

APPENDIX

TO
JAMES MONTGOMERY

Sir

I have the pleasure to be Editor & Partner in a Work called the Muses' Almanack to be published in November by my Friends Messrs Taylor and Hessey. It is intended to consist of poems by our most popular & esteemed Authors, and – to fulfil my wish – will be a kind of National Album. –

The following of my literary Friends have already favoured me with their kind promises – Mr Procter – Mr F H Cary – Mr C Lamb Mr A Cunningham – Mr John Hamilton[1] & John Clare – I reckon on many more to grace the Work, – but I must esteem the list ever incomplete if I may not add the name of Mr Montgomery. The favour of an early answer, whether I may or may not expect this honour, will oblige

Sir

Your mo obed S^{t}

Thos Hood

J Montgomery Esqre

Lower Street Islington. / 27th Septr 1823

MS with permission from the Carl and Lily Pforzheimer Foundation, Inc., on behalf of the Carl H. Pforzheimer Library. James Montgomery (1771–1854), poet and journalist, owned the *Sheffield Iris* from 1795. He published *The Wanderer of Switzerland* (1806) and *The World before the Flood* (1813). The *Almanack*, on behalf of which Hood is appealing, did not appear. The letter belongs on 42.

1/The pseudonym under which J.H. Reynolds published *The Garden of Florence* (1821).

TO
MARIANNE REYNOLDS

Hood has not left me any room to write in – let me hear from you by Green[1] –
– 'Ecrivez moi' &c –
Mrs Basilico[2] is dead [sketch of a skull and crossbones] [word illegible] sculpsit

My very dear Marianne

I have thought – before you went to Chelmsford – that there was a comfort for every evil, and I can think so still. You must give me credit for philosophy when I can indifferently bear your absence, – but I am not stone – I am not marble – and if it were for a longer period, – and not for your pleasure & good I might repine. – Do not curl your pretty under lip at this & cry cant! as you are wont, – tho I always like you the better when you do so, – but think, that as I have never written to you before, I must have a deal of love unexpressed towards you and I begin with that before I enter on levities. – It might seem that they should lie uppermost, – but it is only to write from my heart – like the Hebrews of old, – from the bottom first; – & there will be time enough for lighter words, when I have first put my affection on record. Besides it is more in the order of time to speak first for a feeling which dates from our earliest acquaintance, and I do not fear to grow graver on sudden against the close by recalling a period, which produced indeed much misery but was over-paid by such surpassing love and kindness. – There was – and is, but one Jane in the world and one Marianne. Methinks the first & best friend of love should not have been its late & last Correspondent. – but then I have silently indited more fond & grateful thoughts towards her, – than could ever have been passed thro a quill. – – There, I have written to you, some very earnest & disinterested kindliness – for it was penned at a time when I had not even a mock rose's chance of being in your thoughts and stood but an indifferent chance with a pearl comb: – Jane said that it was to have been written to you a post earlier & that I had promised – as if forsooth I would adventure my most mirthful thoughts and conceits against your liking when you had just subsided into the indolent languour and lassitude after a County Ball. – Why I can think of you, no otherwise, than as all curved and recumbent, and only casting, a faint shadow of a smile, from Green to Miss Longmore.[3] – a kind of retrospective glance, – full of music & lights & dance, – and thrilling feathers, – a retrospective review[4] of what had been, – *Here*, we sit & say, – Ah, – it's all over by this time, – or Ma' exclaims, that Jane Mackay / Sarah Huggins, (or some such old reminiscences of a name) has danced there where Marianne was a hundred times! – I envy the first fidler's left eye, – for that night, it was worth a Jew's, – & wonder what tunes you danced to and if your favorite Quad-rille was amongst them, – And who was your partner, – sometimes I fancy a young eldest son of the County Member – some times, a gallant unknown, attracting almost as much wonder & surmise as yourself – then I have given your hand to Green, – after he had gone down with Miss Longmore. – I thought I heard the first rustle of your flounce as you entered into the ballroom, – it sounded like a long crisp sigh, – & then came a singing in my ears, – which I took for the music. – Then I saw an elbow, – I saw no more, but I was sure it was Green's – and had a glimpse of Miss Longmore. – She was standing by a lustre but it looked a kitchen candlestick, – and her hands were glistening with rings. – Yet there was a touch of sadness in her face that, I attributed to the untimely fate of the rash Henry Lxxx[5] – poor fellow! – had she known or guessed his madness I believe she would have bid him hope & saved him; – but he despaired & died; –

Man born of Woman,[6] helpless Man
By Woman still is doomed to die
Lo! Adam's death in Eve began
And still the apple's in her eye! –

I do suppose that death raged like an epidemic at the Ball; – & dozens were murdered under the very eyebrow of Judge Park. –[7]

Long and *Wearey* was the night: –

Green will tell you how dangerous it is to be shot, thro woollen, – but what must it be, along with the ball, to have a sprigged gauze dress, & satin slip, flounces & all carried into the wound. - Pray send me a description of the dresses; – it will be a Godsend for my friend Baylis[8] and the Belle Assemblée – The only account that I could give here to my sister, of your own, was, that it was of silk cobweb. – (Pray turn over a new leaf)[9] – in a hoar frost, – covered with white leaves, – that in the sleeves were two, red roses sitting in a recess and that the border was as if of those skeleton globes that show the zones, – made of white satin ropes – You must own that I am good at drawing 'caparisons.'[10] – but I am wandering into, – as it were, a tinted avenue of John Bunyan's Vanity Fair; – What are silks and satins, – I hope as Lady Wade[11] said to her Mantua maker, – 'I hope you think of better things than these. – Lucy Drew[12] has been to *hear* Mr Irving,[13] & seems to have profited by what she has *seen.* – She liked him very much & threatens to relapse again to his Chapel. Jane asked if John[14] had taken her, there, – & she answered Y not? – do you think it would have *contaminated* him! – But John did not take her & so ran no risk of being bullied into heaven. – That reminds me of my own end, and I hope to make a good one, – so pray make my best respects to dear Miss Longmore, – & regards to Green, – who I hope is not booked a martyr to Beauty What is Beauty But a Bele. Ma' [word illegible] has kept her, – she was paid her wages yesterday, & Jane - but she will put in a word for herself.[15] – So in the pride, & love of my heart, I write myself down – now & for ever, – de [ar Marian]ne – Your most affectionate T. Hood –

Islington, 13 January 1824

MS with permission from the Carl and Lily Pforzheimer Foundation, Inc., on behalf of the Carl H. Pforzheimer Library. Address: 'Miss Reynolds / Mrs Longmore / Chelmsford / Essex.' PM: 'PAID/ 1824/13 JA 13.' The letter belongs on 54ff.

1/These two sentences written by Jane Hood
2/Unidentified
3/Probably Marianne Longmore, sister of George, who had married Eliza Reynolds
4/Perhaps a hint at the title of the magazine, begun 1820
5/Unidentified
6/The phrase from Job 14:1. Hood quotes the line, 'Man born of woman, must of woman die!' in his poem 'A Valentine,' in *Whims and Oddities* (1826).
7/Sir James Alan Park (1763–1838) conducted the celebrated trial of Thurtell, Probert, and Hunt for the murder of Mr Weare. The trial came to an end on 7 January. Park had officiated at the winter assizes at Chelmsford, 9–13 December.
8/Possibly Henry Baylis, later a member of the *Punch* circle. The British Museum Catalogue dates the *Belle Assemblée* 1806–10 and, New Series, 1824.
9/Written at the foot of the page
10/Mrs Malaprop's word in Sheridan's *The Rivals* (1775) 4 ii
11/Unidentified
12/Probably the sister of Joan Reynolds's wife Eliza
13/Edward Irving (1792–1834), divine, friend of Carlyle, from 1822 preached at the chapel connected with the Caledonian Asylum in Hatton Garden, Holborn, London.
14/Probably John Hamilton Reynolds
15/See the head of the letter.

TO

WILLIAM BLACKWOOD

Dear Sir.

I am ashamed to have two letters to answer, – especially when I am so much indebted in thanks. I have been so much engrossed by the trouble of getting rid of one house & finding another, that I have been obliged to defer matters of great moment.[1] This Excuse I hope will avail with you, but the Scotch word 'flitting' seems to say that your removals are mere fairy like operations.[2]

I was indeed very much flattered & gratified by the review in Maga: & to learn that it was from the pen of Mr Professor Wilson. Whatever he writes he makes worthy of reading for its own sake, – & the Whims & Oddities therefore could not fall into better hands. Pray make my best thanks to him, for a very great pleasure; and in the mean time write me down your own Contributor. It has happened only from the cause above-mentioned that I have not made up a packet to you. It shall be the work of my very first leisure.

The unexpected success of the Whims & Oddities the 1st Edition being sold in three weeks without advertizement, has made me alter my plan about the Tales & I have made arrangements for their publication immediately, with a few designs. The Second Series of Whims & Oddities is meantime in progress, – I have had several offers for it, but if it will be likely to suit you let me know, & I will await your proposition.[3]

I should like a print of the Progress of Cant to be presented in my name to Mr Wilson. I will order one therefore to be sent by the next parcel, & another for your own disposal. I am really much obliged by your kindness, – & hope that it will begin a connexion mutually pleasant & friendly. My future residence after the 9th of next month will be in town, I shall take care to send you the address, that when you come to London I may have the pleasure of seeing you. I am Dr Sir

Yours very truly

Thos Hood

Lower Street Islington [*23 January 1827*]

MS editor, acquired through the kind help of Professor Hans de Groot. Address: 'Mr Blackwood/ Publisher, / Edinburgh. NB.' PM: '23 JA 23/PAID 1827,' 'JAN 25 1827.' This letter precedes that to Blackwood on 75.

1/Hood was to move from Islington to 2 Robert St, Adelphi, on 9 February.

2/Compare Jane Welsh Carlyle writing a few months before: 'I wonder that among all the evils deprecated in the Liturgy no one thought of inserting *flitting*:' *Collected Letters of Thos and J.W.*

Carlyle, ed C.R. Sanders (Durham, N.C., 1970), IV 128.
3/*Whims and Oddities*, 2nd Series, was published by Chas Tilt in November 1827.

TO
WILLIAM SHOBERL?

Dear Sir.
Please to give the note sent herewith, – & which is *private* – to Mr Colburn. Having by calculation enough matter for the Mag. I did not open your M.S. but shall have great pleasure in reading it at my first leisure. On Monday I shall send down the rejected Commns & letters for Correspondants.
Please to send by Bearer 6 Comics for

Yours very truly

Thos Hood.

17 Elm Tree Road / Saturday. [*September 1842 ?*]

MS Princeton. Another business letter concerning NMM. This letter seems to follow that assigned to Shoberl on 493.

INDEX

The index which follows is of proper names, mainly those of persons, but also of places resided at or visited by Hood, works of literature referred to by him, and periodicals. In the listing, an italicized number indicates the page on which a letter to that person is to be found. An asterisk indicates the page on which the person's career is very briefly indicated, with, for example, dates, occupation, publications relation to Hood.

This book

was designed by

ELLEN HUTCHISON

under the direction of

ALLAN FLEMING

University of

Toronto

Press

www.ingramcontent.com/pod-product-compliance
Lightning Source LLC
Chambersburg PA
CBHW060606100726
47907CB00006B/1513

* 9 7 8 1 4 8 7 5 7 8 8 7 9 *